W9-BMG-872

Charles Babbage

Father of the Computer

Charles Babbage

Father of the Computer

Dan Halacy

CROWELL-COLLIER PRESS

Library of Congress Catalog Card Number: 79–119618

The Macmillan Company
866 Third Avenue
New York, New York 10022
Collier-Macmillan Canada Ltd., Toronto, Ontario
Printed in the United States of America

FIRST PRINTING

PICTURE CREDITS

Culver Pictures, Inc., 24, 122; U. *Eco and* G. B. *Zorzoli,* The Picture History
of Inventions, 88; *IBM,* 36, 41, 42, 44, 69, 87, 94, 115, 132, 155, 157,
162–63; *The Ministry of Public Buildings and Works, England, Crown Copy-*
right, 109; *The Science Museum, London,* ii–iii, vi, 25, 39, 46, 150, 153.

Contents

Charles Babbage,
photographed in 1860

 **Introduction**

When the British writer L. J. Comrie described the world's first practical automatic computer—the ASCC machine designed by Professor Howard Aiken of Harvard and constructed by IBM in 1944—he titled his article, "Babbage's Dream Comes True." For it was Charles Babbage who conceived, designed, and began building a calculating machine that could solve any mathematical problem given to it, automatically and without error.

Writing in the English magazine *Nature*, Comrie said,

> The black mark earned by the government of the day more than a hundred years ago for its failure to see Charles Babbage's difference engine brought to a successful conclusion has still to be wiped out. It is not too much to say that it cost Britain the leading place in the art of mechanical computing.

How could such scientific foot-dragging have come about? How could England, with the design for a computer that would have accomplished mathematical wonders, have failed to see its potential and exploit it? There are several answers.

Babbage was obviously far ahead of the technology of the day. He also had the unhappy gift of turning everyone from government leaders to organ grinders against him. One critical publication gleefully noted that "Babbage rhymes with cabbage!" Because he tried to silence them through court action, organ grinders came for miles to play their noisy instruments beneath Babbage's windows, and they were joined by other malicious individuals who tossed dead cats, smashed his windows, and blew bugles at him to increase his blood pressure.

This difficult "crank" was the same Babbage who, while still only thirty years old, built the forerunner of the modern automatic computer and convinced the English government to back the construction of a full-scale machine. Years later, after investing a small fortune in the project, the government got cold feet and withdrew its support. So discouraged was Babbage that he wrote:

> If, unwarned by my example, any man shall succeed in constructing an engine embodying in itself the whole of the executive department of analysis, I have no fear of leaving my reputation in his charge, for he alone will be able fully to appreciate the nature of my efforts, and the value of their results, but half a century will probably elapse before anyone will attempt so unpromising a task.

Babbage missed with his timetable. After his death, others suggested proceeding with his work, but a select committee recommended against it. It was not fifty years but *eighty* before Professor Aiken put together his computer in America. This was in many ways a more modest machine than that designed by Babbage, but it was electrical—an advantage not available to Babbage.

Before Babbage died he told a friend that he had never known a happy day in his life, and that he hated mankind in general and organ grinders and the English government most particularly! He died sure that he had failed, unable to know that a century later his dream would become one of the most potent forces in the science and society of that day. But for all his disappointments, Babbage enjoyed an exciting and stimulating life. He did more with his span on earth than six ordinary men.

As a child, Charles Babbage was sickly, and on at least two occasions near death. Mechanically minded, he pried toys open to see what made them work, and became particularly enamored of a beautiful silver lady automaton, operated by springs, gears, and levers inside. At a church school he created a furor by writing a parody of the minister's sermons; later he wrote an earnest treatise in which he reconciled his deep religious faith with science. He designed and built himself some "shoes" for walking on water and almost drowned when one of them failed to operate in the swift current of the river. In school he tried to conjure up the Devil, indulged in a binge on cognac and treacle (a sweet syrup), but also made it a practice to rise before dawn and sneak into the library to study mathematics.

He entered college knowing more calculus than his professors, and soon formed the Analytical Society in company with several other brilliant young men.

The first glimmerings of his mathematical engines came to Babbage as a student at college. His chin resting on a table, he pondered a table of logarithms so filled with mistakes as to be dangerous for navigators to use. "I wish to God these calculations had been executed by steam!" he protested, meaning that there should be engines to do mathematics just as they had begun to do physical work. The French government had produced mathematical tables by breaking the computations down to addition and subtraction and using unskilled help to do these simple tasks. If dull humans could produce complex results, could not a machine composed of gears and levers do an even better job? A machine would not get tired or make mistakes, Babbage reasoned correctly.

Demonstrating his brilliance and the soundness of his dreams, Babbage designed a simple Difference Engine, to construct accurate tables of squares, cubes, and so on. By 1822 he had completed a pilot model that performed so well that the government, prodded by the scientist Sir Humphrey Davy and others, began funding a more complicated engine. Had Babbage been a lesser man—or more realistic—he might have achieved success in his own time. A practical difference engine was an immense improvement over the laborious hand calculation of tables. But before he could perfect the Difference Engine, Babbage conceived a grander idea. It was his Analytical Engine, an amazing machine that would "move forward by biting its own tail," actually using the results of its computations to direct the next step in its operations. Here was a computer that would be programmed in advance, have a large memory of numbers to draw on, do all its work automatically, and print out the answers so there could be no possibility of mistake! Automatic typesetting machinery was unknown at that time.

In trying to make his engine bite its own tail, Babbage bit off more than the technology of his day could chew. But he gave the effort his best. In the process, even as he wrangled with his chief engineer to the point that the man quit him, he forced great improvements in the technology of the day, inventing machine tools to produce parts he needed. One of his mechanics would become famed, and later knighted, for his ability to work to microinches, or millionths of an inch. A manufacturer seeing Babbage's engines found in them mechanical contrivances that he adopted for his spinning machinery. Indeed, a government official pointed out that even if the Babbage engines were forgotten, England received full value for its expenditures simply from the tools he designed to produce them.

Work on the Analytical Engine began in 1834, when the

Difference Engine was abandoned by the government. Babbage produced 239 detailed engineering drawings, called by contemporaries the finest yet made. The engine was to have some fifty thousand parts, with hardly any of them standard shapes or sizes.

When he needed a mechanism to give instructions to his machine so it could perform the proper operations on numbers, he recalled the clever punched cards with which Joseph Marie Jacquard of France was "programming" his automatic looms. Jacquard had labor troubles because of the card-programmed looms. Babbage never did, fortunately. Perhaps accountants were less organized than weavers. His battles were with other scientists.

When government funds were cut off, and Babbage had exhausted most of his own money, he cast about for other ways to finance his engines. One plan was to build a game-playing machine to put on demonstrations and raise money. He was dissuaded by friends, as he was also from trying to write a long novel with which he hoped to earn several thousand pounds in a year's time.

Today it would be unthinkable for science to prosper without support from government. In Babbage's time, such was not the case, and science was mostly a gentleman's hobby or sport. He agitated loud and strong for government subsidy, pointing out the importance of science to society and arguing that it was thus the place of government to foster scientific progress. Dissatisfied with the goals and operation of England's scientific societies, he continually wrote many articles of protest, and delivered speeches pointing out the flaws in the system. Indeed, even while he was asking the Royal Society (of which he was a member) to help him with getting government backing for his engines, he was attacking that society in print and from speaking platforms. He was never one to be tactful.

In searching out tools and methods to build his fantastic Analytical Engine, Babbage originated the science of operations research, the formation of production methods to yield the highest efficiency and productivity. In a book called *On the Economy of Manufactures and Machinery*, Babbage ranged from the production of pins to the best locations for factories and methods of obtaining raw materials for them. His book was a spectacular success, going through several printings in England, being reprinted in America, and translated into several foreign languages. But instead of glorying in this best seller, the author immediately launched a battle against his publishers because they charged too much for the books and returned him too little profit. He actually made these complaints part of later printings. In addition to operations research, he also originated mechanical notation, a system of coding a mechanical drawing to indicate the function and movement of the parts described.

The translator of an Italian's paper on Babbage's engines was Countess Ada Augusta Lovelace, daughter of the poet Lord Byron. The lady had one of the keenest mathematical minds of the day, and she and Babbage became good friends. For Lord and Lady Lovelace, Babbage worked out a system on his computers for playing the horses. The Lovelaces were horse players and used his system until Lovelace ran short of funds, and Countess Lovelace actually had to pawn her jewels to pay off losses. Apparently horse racing was not an exact enough science to yield to computer analysis.

Babbage also became a consultant for railroad pioneers, managing to invent the cowcatcher in the process. He worked with Isambard Kingdom Brunel, the famous Little Giant who would later build the *Great Western*, a forerunner of the giant ocean liners. Babbage himself rode special railroad cars to gather the scientific data he needed, risking collisions with scheduled trains and often dodging onto sidings in the nick of time because of his keen hearing. On one occasion he "sailed" across a viaduct by using his cape as a sail, when an unpowered car unexpectedly ran out of momentum.

He discussed the elimination of wheels from trains and the substitution of "sledges" which would be lubricated to slide easily on a track. And he proposed continuously moving trains for short runs, with a method of taking on and discharging passengers without stopping.

Babbage proposed a mail delivery system consisting of wires strung on high towers, with cylindrical containers zipping along on a wheel rolling on the wire. And if this primitive monorail seems old-fashioned in light of subsequent advances in communication, consider that Babbage suggested that the wires themselves might be used "for a species of telegraphic communication yet more rapid." This was proposed in a book he published in 1832, six years before Morse patented his electrical telegraph. His observations on the postal service suggested to him that it would be better to charge a flat rate for postage, rather than try to base it on the distance a letter traveled. The result was that Postmaster Sir Rowland Hill created the famed Penny Post, with a letter going any distance in England for one fixed price. Here was an example of a practical application of Babbage's work in operations research.

Lighthouses were of interest to Babbage too, and he invented the system of flashing lights used for identification. He braved an oven at 265° F., explored live volcanoes, and wrote scientific treatises on dating archaeological finds by tree rings. In explaining his productivity he once pointed out that he devoted the hours from 2:00 A.M. to 6:00 A.M. to work on problems of particular interest to him. Babbage wrote the paper "Conjectures on the Physical State of the Surface of the Moon," and there is a crater on the moon named for him, not far from that named for his friend Herschel.

Babbage also invented a submarine, proposing to fuel it with liquid air. He designed an earthquake detector—consisting of a dish of molasses, or "treacle." He suggested the use of water meters in municipal areas. He wrote on his theories of glaciers and tree rings. He developed a colored light system for theaters and then choreographed a rainbow dance to demonstrate it. And he was especially proud of his ability to knock a round hole in a piece of glass without cracking it.

Babbage also found time to compile tables of logarithms, as well as insurance mortality tables that became a standard for that business and were used for many years. He became an expert on locks and lockpicking, as well as on codes and the science of deciphering. To aid him in his work with codes he compiled twenty-four special dictionaries. Babbage knew and moved among royalty, nobility, and government dignitaries, including Queen Victoria and Prince Albert, the king of Spain and the duke of Wellington.

In 1815 he looked through a telescope at the defeated Napoleon aboard the ship *Bellerophon* in the harbor not far from the Babbage family home at Teignmouth. Later he met many of the Buonaparte family in his travels in Europe.

His scientific friends included John Herschel (son of William Herschel, the astronomer), George Peacock, Humphrey Davy, Pierre Simon Laplace, François Marie Fourier, Baron Friedrich von Humboldt, Charles Darwin, Thomas Malthus, Siméon Poisson, and Jean Baptiste Biot among many others. He worked with engineers like Isambard Brunel of tunnel, bridge, and railroad fame; and George Stephenson, developer of the successful steam locomotive. A writer himself, he enjoyed his friendships with John Stuart Mill, Charles Dickens, Thomas Carlyle, Robert Browning, William Makepeace Thackeray, Lord Tennyson, Captain Frederick Marryat, and William Wadsworth Longfellow from America.

He was a sought-after dinner guest, and his own parties often hosted from two to three hundred people. On one occasion his home honored no less than seven bishops.

Throughout his career he of course had other duties to take care of, not all of them pleasant. He had married upon graduation from Cambridge. Of his eight children, five died at an early age. In a single year he lost his wife, two children, and his father. He ran for political office, and since he was not a tactful politician, was beaten badly.

When Babbage died in 1871, the Royal Society he had belonged to did not even print an obituary of its distinguished member. There was only one mourner besides the family group at his funeral. Despite the efforts of his son and others, the name of Babbage faded from the minds of even the educated, and no one remembered much about the Difference Engine and the even more marvelous Analytical Engine.

Some fifty years after Babbage had suggested that it would take that long before another picked up the work, Herman Hollerith was using a punched tape to run adding machines for the United States Census Bureau. But thirty more years would pass before the potential of the Analytical Engine was realized in Professor Aiken's ASCC. That machine labored around the clock in World War II, doing just what Babbage predicted it would. Far faster and far more accurate than a human computer, it solved complex problems for the American military effort that helped England remain free from domination by the Nazis.

In 1957 at the Festival of Britain, a high-speed computer called Nimrod amazed Britishers who visited the exhibition at the South Kensington Science Museum. Part of its startling repertoire was playing games and winning against all comers. Charles Babbage had once considered playing tick-tack-toe with his Difference Engine—but his engine was still hidden away elsewhere in the museum. Gathering dust in the darkness, the early ancestor of Nimrod remained a tribute to its builder, a man whose genius leaped far ahead of his time and whose dreams outpaced by a century the technology needed to make them come true. This was Charles Babbage's contribution to the automatic computer: he was in every sense its father. And his dream has indeed come true.

 **Young Babbage**

Charles Babbage was born at Totnes, Devonshire, England, the day after Christmas, 1792, to Mr. and Mrs. Benjamin Babbage. Mr. Babbage was a member of the banking firm of Praed, Mackworth, and Babbage, and he was well-to-do, with a home in London upstairs from the bank. Charles's father was known affectionately as Old Five Per Cent, since he had pioneered lending money at that low rate of interest.

Mrs. Babbage, the former Betty Plumleigh Teape, was of good family. Grandfather Ben Babbage had been mayor of Totnes.

Charles was one of several Babbage children, but life was more difficult for the young in those days, and except for one sister, who would outlive him, his brothers and sisters all died in infancy.

Charles thought he got what he called his "inveterate habit of contriving tools" from the race "who formed knives, and hammers, and arrowheads out of flint." He guessed that he might be descended from the biblical Tubal Cain, first worker with iron and brass, except that someone told him Cain had invented the organ—a version of which instrument Babbage was destined to hate.

There was much wealth in one branch of the Babbage family. Charles was fond of recollecting that his father had spent a considerable sum of money and much of his time in trying to locate, or establish the death of, one Richard Babbage, a young ne'er-do-well who had inherited a fortune from an uncle and gone off to America on a lark. Failure of the search resulted in Charles's not having the problem of great wealth, he dryly wrote. However, he was still quite well off because of his father's position in the bank.

A TIME TO BE BORN

In 1792 the United States of America was only sixteen years old, and George Washington had been in office three years. France had just abolished the old monarchy and proclaimed itself a republic. In England King George III still reigned, although there had been anxious moments in 1788 when for a brief period he seemed insane.

The English economist Adam Smith had published *The Wealth of Nations* in 1776, the year America declared its independence from England, and Smith's treatise was becoming the mainstay for economy and business in Babbage's time. James Hutton published his book *Theory of the Earth*, the foundation of modern geology, in 1785. Henry Cavendish had discovered hydrogen in 1766, which led to the development of the balloon in 1783. James Watt had improved the steam engine to the point where it was becoming a major force in industry.

It was a time of great political, economic, and scientific ferment. But in 1792 there were still no automobiles, no submarines, no telegraph, no steamboat, no locomotives, no gaslights, no bicycles, no electric motors, no typesetting machines, no cameras—not even an iron plow! The Industrial Revolution was beginning; but many people did not realize this, and it had not yet touched the scientific world.

In the Babbage bank, tellers figured accounts with pen and ink, just as they had done for centuries. The only calculating machines were fingers, or perhaps the ancient abacus which substituted sliding beads for fingers. The mechanical adding machine was unknown, except as an impractical curiosity developed by scientists.

Young Babbage grew up in a leisurely paced world. A world of horses and carriages, of Georgian architecture and manners. As a child he played in the streets with other children, rolling hoops and chasing dogs about. Weak and sickly as a youth, Babbage twice was struck down by fever, and only through diligent effort on the part of the family physician was his life spared. Babbage once slipped away from his nurse and his brother while the three of them strolled about in Montpelier Gardens in Walworth. Spying a bush of black berries which he thought were currants, Charles ate several handfuls of poisonous fruit, and only the timely dosage of castor oil at the hands of his worried father saved him from serious illness. These frightening experiences may have made Charles superstitious despite his Protestant upbringing by parents he described as highly moral and religious:

> My excellent mother taught me the usual forms of my daily and nightly prayer; and neither in my father nor my mother was there any mixture of bigotry and intolerance on the one hand, nor on the other of that unbecoming and familiar mode of addressing the Almighty which afterwards so much disgusted me in my youthful years.

Later, like other boys, Charles often tramped across London Bridge, gazing down at the many ships on the Thames River.

He retained an especially vivid recollection of crossing Tooley Street in London and having to wait carefully for the "traffic" until it was safe to cross. On this journey he became lost from his nurse, who panicked and sought out a town crier to whom she promised a reward for the safe return of her five-year-old charge. Meanwhile Charles told a shopkeeper who he was and calmly finished a dish of pears while listening to the crier shout that he was lost. He was reunited with his mother almost before she learned that he was missing.

THE SILVER LADY

As a baby Charles had been interested in toys. His main concern was not playing with them, however, but seeing how they were made. "Mamma," he was fond of saying, "what's inside of *this*?" And if his mother didn't have a satisfactory answer, Charles would find out by breaking the toy open. Later his mother catered to this interest by taking him to exhibits of machinery as often as she could.

One such show at Hanover Square featured a display by a robot master called Merlin after the great magician of English lore. Babbage was so interested that Merlin invited the boy to his workshop, where he was completing two little silver dolls that walked, bowed, danced, and peered through opera glasses. One carried a tiny mechanical bird on her wrist. The bird flapped its wings and opened its beak in lifelike fashion. Decades later Babbage bought one of the very robots that Merlin had showed him.

A second indication of the career ahead for Charles Babbage was his interest in mathematics. Perhaps his early awareness of numbers and the arithmetic they made possible stemmed in part from visits to his father's bank. But in the main the love of mathematics had been born in him.

OFF TO SCHOOL

At age ten, still weak from the second attack of fever, Babbage was put in the care of a church school in the town of Alphington, near Exeter. The minister was asked to concern himself mainly with the health of his young pupil, and he did this so diligently that Charles's formal education suffered. As a result he had more time on his hands than was good for an impressionable young mind, indoctrinated as it was with tales of ghosts, the Devil, and the like. One night Charles and another student succeeded in scaring the wits out of a third student simply by making menacing shadows on the walls of their bedroom. Observing the effect on his classmate, who did not fully recover from his fright for several days, Charles began to wonder if his elders were deluding him about ghosts and devils. He began his first scientific research—into the supernatural.

In secret conversations with a number of students he learned the various forms the Devil was supposed to take in his appearances on earth. These included the rabbit, owl, black cat, raven, and a man with a cloven foot. Another important factor was the writing in blood of a compact with the Devil. Young Babbage climbed into the attic of the school, intentionally cut his finger, and marked a circle in blood on the dusty floor. Then, to complete the preparations for a visit from the underworld, he shakily recited the Lord's Prayer backwards. With all these unholy rites performed, he sat down to wait—and wait—and wait. The Devil disappointed him completely by never putting in an appearance. And instead of fire and brimstone the only result of the attempted spell-making was that Charles could not say his prayers in the proper direction that night when he crept guiltily into bed. From this fruitless excursion into black magic Babbage determined that ghosts and devils were figments of the imagination and soon thereafter felt right again with the Lord.

Babbage engaged in another speculation into the supernatural when he was a little older. He made a pact with the young son of Admiral Richard Dacres that on the death of one of them, the departed should make every attempt to return as a spirit. His surviving friend would be alert for his return. Sadly, young Dacres was struck down with tuberculosis at the very beginning of a promising career at sea and died at eighteen. Although Babbage remained awake the entire night of Dacres' death, there was no evidence of the return of the young sailor's soul.

Another lesson came early. Once, as he rested in the garden to ease a severe headache while his classmates played in the yard, Babbage spied a gleaming coin beneath a tree. Thinking he had found a gold coin, he excitedly scooped up the treasure and sought out an expert opinion. Alas, the authority pointed out that the coin was only a brass weight from a doctor's set of scales. Babbage was no richer than before his discovery, but his headache was gone. He had learned that keeping his mind busy could chase away pain and other wasters of his time. Later he discovered an even simpler way to overcome pain—he read books like *Don Quixote* and *Robinson Crusoe* to get his mind off his hurts.

After some years at Alphington, Babbage was well and strong enough to be sent at last to a neighborhood school in Totnes. This was King Edward VI Grammar School, which his father had attended. At King Edward, Charles made his mark in typical fashion, carving it into the top of his desk. Years later he would proudly point out his handiwork to friends. Today the building is called Babbage House in his memory.

King Edward school was cold and drafty in winter; so bad, in fact, that the students sacrificed their copybooks to stop up the cracks about the windows in a vain effort to keep warm. Finally Charles was sent home ill, where he would remain for a year or so before recuperating sufficiently to return to school. In 1805 Benjamin Babbage retired from banking and moved his family to a fine house at 5 Devonshire Street in London. He had bought another home, too, at Teignmouth on the southern coast.

TWO DESTINED TO FAIL

When he was well again, Charles was sent for tutoring to the Reverend Stephen Freeman at Forty Hill, Enfield, Middlesex. He remained there for three years.

Each Sunday, Babbage and his classmates were required to write from memory the text of the sermon the pastor had preached. Babbage, with characteristic imagination and diligence, went somewhat further than his instructions. Wearying of simply writing down what the reverend said, he worked up a skeleton outline of what seemed a standard sermon the preacher gave. Then he filled in details to make a sermon of his own composition. As a text he took "Alexander, the coppersmith, hath done us much harm" and proceeded to use the minister's approach and deductions.

Proudly, the young writer showed his handiwork to some of the other students, who circulated copies. When these were discovered by the good reverend himself, Babbage was fortunate in that the work was taken as being original with his plagiarists, and thus the "awful explosion" he feared did not touch him directly.

Babbage's latent interest in mathematics had a chance to flower at Forty Hill. Although he managed to get into as much trouble as any other student, Babbage spent far more time in the library. Among his favorites was the book, *Ward's Young Mathematician's Guide*. So taken was he with it that soon he and another studious young man were arising at three o'clock in the morning (against the rules, of course), building a fire in the classroom stove, and studying until five-thirty, the normal time for getting up.

There was a Tom Sawyer sort of appeal about such a fantastic reversal of student behavior, and other boys demanded to be allowed to accompany the diligent pair. One of these was Frederick Marryat. Young Marryat was the son of a member of Parliament, and destined to be one of England's great novelists, famed for *Midshipman Easy* and many other popular books about seafaring. But in his school days Marryat had difficulty in getting up early and demanded that the dawn patrol awaken him. Babbage refused, afraid that too many bright and early scholars would lead to antics so wild that the schoolmaster would stop the whole project.

Now Marryat was more determined than ever to join the early risers and devised all sorts of schemes to be awakened by the others. First he put his bed in front of the door. This was handled easily by simply picking up bed, Marryat and all, and setting it out of the way. Next Marryat tied one end of a string to the door handle and the other end to his wrist. Babbage untied the string from the door, so Marryat used heavier and heavier string and finally rope, with tighter knots. Babbage was forced to use a penknife.

For all Babbage's determination, he had met his match in Marryat. The sleepyhead progressed to chain instead of rope, and finally put padlocks on the end of the chain. Babbage succeeded in tying a string to the chain and jiggling it so often that finally Marryat paid it no mind and slept through the door opening. But in the end the two added Marryat as the third predawn conspirator. Now what the original two had feared came to pass: several of Marryat's friends also joined the group, and the study period slowly became a play session. The end was a wild orgy of fireworks in the playground.

The young pupils were led astray again later. A Russian visitor with a bottle of cognac convinced Marryat he should try some and gave him a bottle. When Marryat invited his classmates to share the cognac, Babbage suggested that they should mix the drink with treacle. Treacle was found, and a flower pot was used as a mixing vat. Then the whole student body attacked the concoction with spoons, oyster shells, and whatever else they could find in the way of utensils. The next class session was something of a disappointment to the head-master with sick boys, dizzy boys, some boys asleep, and some talking more than ever before.

Years later, as one of England's most successful authors, Marryat proudly recalled that he and Babbage had been singled out at Forty Hill school as boys who were "not only bad, but who would never get on in the world."

YOUNG INVENTOR

Having conquered his illness to some extent, Babbage became an ardent outdoor enthusiast. A rugged swimmer, he was especially fond of the water. The Babbage country home at Teignmouth fronted on the sea, and the Christmas Day before he was sixteen Charles took his father's fowling piece and went to the beach for some target practice. He began to shoot at sea birds circling over the water and finally managed to hit one.

Somewhat surprised at having hit his target and feeling a bit guilty about killing a wild creature, Babbage decided to retrieve the bird and have it cooked to justify the deed. He had no dog to fetch the bird so he skinned out of his clothes, even though by now it was snowing, hid them in a cleft, swam out into the rough waves, and managed to find the bird. Back home, he gave it to the cook but found it too tough to eat. This ended his shooting of sea birds, but his experience by water had only begun.

Soon after the bird incident Babbage was swimming in the River Dart. The idea struck him that he could build shoes with which to walk on the water. Not on top of the water but at least enough to lift his upper body free of the river. He began his miraculous invention immediately.

Taking a pair of old boots, he attached the covers of two ancient and thick volumes to the soles of them. When he raised his foot the covers would fold together and offer little resistance to the water. But when he pushed down, the covers would open wide and give added thrust to his leg motions. He strode down to the river and confidently waded in. He found he was easily able to swim about with his crude water-walking shoes on his feet, and succeeded in keeping himself erect and high in the water with only a slight effort. His invention was successful, he thought, but a moment later he was not so sure.

As Babbage was drifting out with the tide, one "shoe" tipped him immediately to one side. Reverting to swimming, he headed for shore against the pull of the tide but found that he was still "lopsided" and could swim only in circles. By the time he finally managed to drag himself up on shore to safety, he was fully convinced that his water-walking days had ended the same day they began.

Finally, no longer a child, Charles Babbage survived his ill health. Despite the shortness of his education he had managed to learn a wealth of mathematics in addition to classical subjects. The time had come for him to begin college, and Cambridge was the chosen school.

 **Cambridge**

Banker Babbage, determined to do all he could to pave the way for Charles's success, invited a tutor from Cambridge to dine often with the Babbage family at Teignmouth. This bore little fruit, and the only specific advice Charles got from the learned professor was not to buy his wine at Cambridge.

With the memory of the cognac and treacle still in his mind, Charles was not keen on that sort of school spirits anyway, and he wondered why the tutor should assign such importance to so trivial a matter. The elder Babbage also seemed disappointed that all his hospitality had come to so little. Instead of using him, he selected an Oxford tutor. Charles studied with this teacher at Totnes for some months, concentrating on the classics. Charles was primarily interested in mathematics, of course, but this was not popular at Totnes. The most interesting project he could come up with was a universal language. With characteristic energy, he wrote a grammar and even worked up a dictionary. More correctly, he *started* the latter but was forced to abandon the project when he could find no logical way of arranging words or symbols so that they could be looked up when needed. His tutor either did not know, or failed to mention, an existing volume, *Bishop Wilkins on Universal Language.*

In his free time Babbage returned to his well-worn *Young Mathematician's Guide.* He added to his mathematical library such weighty texts as Madam Agnesi's *Analytical Institutions,* and the *Fluxions* (a branch of calculus) of Maclaurin and Simpson. Another work on fluxions, by Humphrey Ditton, he could not comprehend. But in Joseph Lagrange's *Théorie des fonctions* he learned the notation of the German mathematician Leibnitz and was impressed by his use of the letter d instead of the traditional dots of Newton's calculus. Although Babbage was not then aware of it, Leibnitz had done something else that would later endear him to the mechanical-toy-loving young mathematician: he had built a primitive calculating machine.

In 1811, Babbage headed for Cambridge at the rather advanced age of nineteen. Having heard of a new work by the French mathematician Silvestre François Lacroix, he stopped in London at a French bookseller to buy a copy. He had been told it was two guineas—about ten dollars—and he put that amount on the counter. Monsieur Dulau, the proprieter, mumbled his apology: the book was not two but *seven* guineas—nearly forty dollars! Babbage whistled and demanded to know how a book could be so expensive.

"The war, monsieur," Dulau explained, spreading his hands helplessly. "It is difficult to get books such as this. Perhaps— a cheaper work?"

"No," Babbage said at length, unable to put down the Lacroix book. With a groan he counted out the seven precious gold coins. What had the tutor said about not buying wine at Cambridge? Babbage would not have money to buy wine anywhere. With the new book under his arm, he reached Trinity College and checked in with his tutor, Dr. Hudson.

As soon as he was shown his rooms he slumped in a chair and began to flip through the pages of Lacroix's calculus text. It was almost daylight when he at last put down the ponderous book and climbed into bed. Trinity was acquiring a student she would soon wish had gone elsewhere.

THE YOUNG INFIDELS

In his first year at Trinity, Babbage devoured Lacroix and read widely in the works of Euler, Leibnitz, and other foreign mathematicians. He hit snags in the calculus and naturally he checked with Dr. Hudson for an explanation. To his surprise, Hudson said Babbage's worries were of no importance since that particular subject would not come up and he would not be quizzed on it.

"But I want to know," Babbage protested.

"Master Babbage," Hudson said in a superior tone, "you doubtless want to know *many* trivial things. It happens that I have more important matters at hand. Check with another instructor if you must have an answer."

Babbage checked. And got no answer. He checked with a third teacher, and at last reached the inescapable and startling conclusion: he knew more about calculus than did any of his instructors at Trinity College. What was worse, they would not admit it, but lied and evaded to cover their ignorance. If this was an example of English science, Babbage thought, the nation was in a bad way. The calculus of Leibnitz looked increasingly more attractive than that of Newton, and the stage was being set for a young student's attack on what he considered hidebound tradition in the schools.

Babbage entered his second year at Cambridge disillusioned but still possessing his sense of humor. A controversy had begun to rage in Cambridge over the plans of a group of scholars to publish a Bible with footnotes explaining certain points not clear in translation. This was sacrilege, protested traditionalists who considered the King James version as perfect as man could make it. Speeches were given nightly to fiercely partisan audiences, posters covered buildings and walls all over town, and children earned spending money delivering handbills praising one side or damning the other.

At first Babbage was only mildly interested, but as the battle continued he began to see the possibility for some fun. His parody of the preacher's sermons had led to trouble in his youth, but this time he planned to poke fun not at religion but the institution of Cambridge. The Bible controversy provided the plan for his attack. Quickly he composed a flier describing the formation of a militant group dedicated to the task of translating Lacroix's work on differential and integral calculus into English. The group would concern itself with propagating Leibnitz's d's and consigning to perdition all heretics who supported Newton's dots. It was a clever piece of work, and when Babbage gave it to his classmate Michael Slegg, the boy enjoyed it so much, he in turn showed it to the mathematician Edward Bromhead. Bromhead roared his appreciation and told Slegg and Babbage the idea was too good to let die. Why *not* set up a society for the cultivation of mathematics? he asked. In fact, he insisted that the group meet at his home to organize.

Delighted to have something challenging to do, Babbage got busy. At the first meeting, in addition to Babbage, Slegg, and Bromhead, were John Herschel, George Peacock, Edward Ryan, Frederick Maule, and others. All of these young men would one day be noted personages, from mathematicians to astronomers, ministers, judges, and members of Parliament. The group was duly constituted as the Analytical Society. A meeting room was hired and kept open daily. Regular meet-

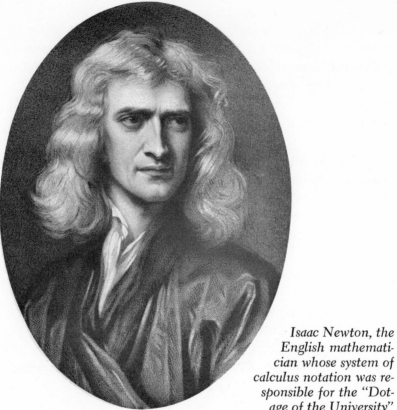

Isaac Newton, the English mathematician whose system of calculus notation was responsible for the "Dotage of the University"

ings were held, and mathematical papers were read and discussed.

While the shocked Cambridge dons protested strongly and hinted that the young infidels would come to no good, the society prospered. So many papers were written, mostly by Babbage and Herschel, that a volume of *Transactions* was published. For a title, Babbage came up with *The Principles of pure d-ism in opposition to the Dot-age of the University*. This scandalous pun did not endear the Analytical Society to Cambridge.

All was not humor, however. Of the group, John Herschel and George Peacock were as keenly interested in science as

Gottfried Wilhelm von Leibnitz's "d-ism" impressed Babbage

Babbage, and the trio formed an inner circle of the society. Babbage stated their goal briefly and to the point: "Let us leave the world a wiser one than we found."

THE LIFE AT CAMBRIDGE

Taunting the dot-age of the University did not command all of Babbage's time at Cambridge. He was instrumental in the formation of the Ghost Club, which investigated evidence of the supernatural. There was also the Extractors Club, whose tongue-in-cheek purpose was to make sure that "every effort, legal and illegal, shall be made to get [members] out of the madhouse." Hence the name Extractors.

Babbage was also an inveterate chess player who learned, when playing against an expert, to make an opening move so bad it had never been written in any book on the subject. Such tactics threw off the opponent so much he might not recover during the game. With other students, who would become famous for more serious pursuits in later years, he also played sixpenny whist regularly and until all hours.

Babbage had an allowance of £300 a year while he was at college, and generally drew on it from Praed, Mackworth, and Babbage at the rate of £30 at a time. With all his mathematical ability, he had difficulty with his checkbook, noting once in his accounts that a disagreement between him and Praed, Mackworth, and Babbage was most likely his error. Kind-hearted, he was an easy mark for borrowers, although he slowly learned that he was being taken advantage of and gradually became more cautious in lending.

Having lived much of his life near the water, Babbage was very fond of sailing and owned a "beautiful light London-built boat," in which he and friends often played hooky for trips of several days. This group was composed of a different sort of student from that in the Ghost Club, the Extractors, or the game-playing clubs. In fact, some of his sophisticated friends referred to these sailors as Babbage's Tom Fools since they indulged in tomfoolery and were selected mainly for their rowing strength on long trips against the wind or when the wind died.

Babbage had a servant whom he sent on such occasions to the druggist for a certificate of ill health called an *aegrostat*. Next, his man would go to the inn for meat pies, roast chicken, and wine. The *aegrostat* was filed with the college authorities as an absence excuse; the food and drink hampers were loaded into the sailboat and off the Tom Fools went for several days.

Besides mathematics, Babbage enjoyed chemistry and attended the lectures of Professor Smithson Tennant. Tennant had been interested in chemistry from boyhood, and this interest was fostered by his association with the noted chemists Joseph Black of England and Karl Wilhelm Scheele and Jons Jakob Berzelius of Sweden. Tennant was the first to prove a diamond was made up entirely of carbon, and he also discovered the elements iridium and osmium. Both Babbage and Herschel often assisted Tennant in preparing experiments, and Babbage finally set up a laboratory in a spare room he had. Herschel did the same, and the two young scientists began to vie with one another.

THE "BRAINPOWER" ENGINE

The Analytical Society continued its work, one part of which was checking celestial tables. These figures, published for astronomers, consisted of lists of thousands of numbers, each of which might be many digits long. Not only astronomers but mariners too depended on them, often for their lives and the safe and swift delivery of goods by ship. An example of the sad state of existing maritime tables is cited by England's Lord Bowden in the book *Faster than Thought*:

> During the uneasy peace which succeeded our interminable wars with Spain at the beginning of the last century, Captain Smyth, R.N., made a survey of the Mediterranean. He received a courtesy visit from a Spanish Captain, who gave him a silver salver as a souvenir of his visit. King's Regulations, which had been drawn up in detail by Mr. Pepys, made no provision for reciprocation in kind or for charging such gifts against petty cash, so Captain Smyth gave his visitor a handsome leather-bound set of the *Nautical Almanac*. This work had been compiled under the direction of that versatile genius, Thomas Young, whose real interest

lay in the development of the wave theory of light and the interpretation of the Rosetta Stone. It was notoriously un-reliable—it omitted 29th February altogether one leap year, and no Englishman ever dared to use it. The Spaniard, how-ever, who seemed to be unaware of its reputation, sailed away and was never heard from again, but Captain Smyth came safely home, using the Italian and French Navigational tables. "Peace hath her victories." This must rank among the most sophisticated operations ever undertaken by the Navy.

It was with such a set of tables that Babbage was working one evening in 1812. Here was a three that should have been an eight. Down on the next two lines numbers had been transposed, undoubtedly by a careless printer. Babbage mum-bled something under his breath, and Herschel called to him from across the table.

"Well, Babbage, what are *you* dreaming about?"

"I wish I were dreaming," Babbage retorted. "And I wish to God these tables had been produced by steam!"

There was a long silence, broken only by the scratching of Babbage's pen as he noted another error in the tables. Then finally Herschel answered him, his voice registering surprise.

"Do you know," he said, "I just think it might be done."

"What might be done?" Babbage demanded, marking his place with his finger.

"Producing those tables by machinery," Herschel answered.

"Indeed," Babbage said and sighed. "Isn't that what I said?"

HUSBAND AND FATHER

It was a beautiful dream; but it was only a dream, in spite of the deep frown of concentration on Herschel's face. To be sure, steam engines were substituting for the muscles of men

GCT (h m)	☉ SUN GHA	Dec.	♈ GHA	♀ VENUS-4.4 GHA	Dec.	♂ MARS 0.0 GHA	Dec.	♃ JUPITER-2.2 GHA	Dec.	☾ MOON GHA	Dec.
12 00	359 08	S23 02	280 30	319 34	S14 43	257 34	N10 26	208 27	N21 50	192 59	N18 30
10	1 38		283 01	322 04		260 05		210 58		195 24	30
20	4 08		285 31	324 34		262 35		213 28		197 49	30
30	6 38 ·	·	288 02	327 05	·	265 05	·	215 59 ·	·	200 15 ·	30
40	9 08		290 32	329 35		267 35		218 29		202 40	31
50	11 38		293 02	332 05		270 06		221 00		205 05	31
13 00	14 08	S23 02	295 33	334 36	S14 42	272 36	N10 27	223 30	N21 50	207 30	N18 31
10	16 38		298 03	337 06		275 06		226 01		209 55	31
20	19 08		300 34	339 36		277 36		228 31		212 20	31
30	21 38 ·		303 04	342 06 ·		280 07 ·		231 02 ·		214 45 ·	31
40	24 07		305 34	344 37		282 37		233 32		217 10	32
50	26 37		308 05	347 07		285 07		236 03		219 36	32
14 00	29 07	S23 02	310 35	349 37	S14 42	287 37	N10 27	238 33	N21 50	222 01	N18 32
10	31 37		313 06	352 07		290 08		241 03		224 26	32
20	34 07		315 36	354 38		292 38		243 34		226 51	32
30	36 37 ·		318 07	357 08 ·		295 08 ·		246 04 ·		229 16 ·	32
40	39 07		320 37	359 38		297 38		248 35		231 41	32
50	41 37		323 07	2 08		300 08		251 05		234 06	33
15 00	44 07	S23 01	325 38	4 39	S14 41	302 39	N10 27	253 36	N21 50	236 31	N18 33
10	46 37		328 08	7 09		305 09		256 06		238 57	33
20	49 07		330 39	9 39		307 39		258 37		241 22	33
30	51 37 ·		333 09	12 10 ·		310 09 ·		261 07 ·		243 47 ·	33
40	54 07		335 39	14 40		312 40		263 38		246 12	33
50	56 37		338 10	17 10		315 10		266 08		248 37	33
16 00	59 07	S23 01	340 40	19 40	S14 40	317 40	N10 28	268 38	N21 50	251 02	N18 34
10	61 37		343 11	22 11		320 10		271 09		253 27	34
20	64 07		345 41	24 41		322 41		273 39		255 52	34
30	66 37 ·		348 11	27 11 ·		325 11 ·		276 10 ·		258 18 ·	34
40	69 07		350 42	29 41		327 41		278 40		260 43	34
50	71 37		353 12	32 12		330 11		281 11		263 08	34
17 00	74 06	S23 01	355 43	34 42	S14 39	332 42	N10 28	283 41	N21 50	265 33	N18 34
10	76 36		358 13	37 12		335 12		286 12		267 58	34
20	79 06		0 43	39 43		337 42		288 42		270 23	34
30	81 36 ·		3 14	42 13 ·		340 12 ·		291 13 ·		272 48 ·	34
40	84 06		5 44	44 43		342 42		293 43		275 13	35
50	86 36		8 15	47 13		345 13		296 13		277 38	35
18 00	89 06	S23 01	10 45	49 44	S14 39	347 43	N10 29	298 44	N21 50	280 04	N18 35
10	91 36		13 16	52 14		350 13		301 14		282 29	35
20	94 06		15 46	54 44		352 43		303 45		284 54	35
30	96 36 ·		18 16	57 14 ·		355 14 ·		306 15 ·		287 19 ·	35
40	99 06		20 47	59 45		357 44		308 46		289 44	35
50	101 36		23 17	62 15		0 14		311 16		292 09	35
19 00	104 06	S23 01	25 48	64 45	S14 38	2 44	N10 29	313 47	N21 50	294 34	N18 35
10	106 36		28 18	67 16		5 15		316 17		296 59	35
20	109 06		30 48	69 46		7 45		318 48		299 25	35
30	111 36 ·		33 19	72 16 ·		10 15 ·		321 18 ·		301 50 ·	35
40	114 06		35 49	74 46		12 45		323 49		304 15	35
50	116 36		38 20	77 17		15 16		326 19		306 40	36
20 00	119 06	S23 00	40 50	79 47	S14 37	17 46	N10 30	328 49	N21 50	309 05	N18 36
10	121 36		43 20	82 17		20 16		331 20		311 30	36
20	124 06		45 51	84 47		22 46		333 50		313 55	36
30	126 35 ·		48 21	87 18 ·		25 16 ·		336 21 ·		316 20 ·	36
40	129 05		50 52	89 48		27 47		338 51		318 45	36
50	131 35		53 22	92 18		30 17		341 22		321 11	36
21 00	134 05	S23 00	55 53	94 49	S14 36	32 47	N10 30	343 52	N21 50	323 36	N18 36
10	136 35		58 23	97 19		35 17		346 23		326 01	36
20	139 05		60 53	99 49		37 48		348 53		328 26	36
30	141 35 ·		63 24	102 19 ·		40 18 ·		351 24 ·		330 51 ·	36
40	144 05		65 54	104 50		42 48		353 54		333 16	36
50	146 35		68 25	107 20		45 18		356 24		335 41	36
22 00	149 05	S23 00	70 55	109 50	S14 36	47 49	N10 31	358 55	N21 50	338 06	N18 36
10	151 35		73 25	112 20		50 19		1 25		340 31	36
20	154 05		75 56	114 51		52 49		3 56		342 57	36
30	156 35 ·		78 26	117 21 ·		55 19 ·		6 26 ·		345 22 ·	36
40	159 05		80 57	119 51		57 50		8 57		347 47	36
50	161 35		83 27	122 21		60 20		11 27		350 12	36
23 00	164 05	S23 00	85 57	124 52	S14 35	62 50	N10 31	13 58	N21 50	352 37	N18 36
10	166 35		88 28	127 22		65 20		16 28		355 02	36
20	169 05		90 58	129 52		67 50		18 59		357 27	36
30	171 35 ·		93 29	132 23 ·		70 21 ·		21 29 ·		359 52 ·	36
40	174 05		95 59	134 53		72 51		24 00		2 17	36
50	176 34		98 30	137 23		75 21		26 30		4 42	36
24 00	179 04	S23 00	101 00	139 53	S14 34	77 51	N10 32	29 00	N21 50	7 08	N18 36

Lat. N °	Sun-rise h m	Twil. m	Moon-rise h m	Diff. m
60	9 03	57	14 52	50
58	8 46	51	15 05	50
56	32	47	16	50
54	19	43	26	49
52	8 08	40	34	50
50	7 59	38	42	49
45	38	34	15 58	49
40	22	31	16 11	50
35	7 08	28	23	49
30	6 56	26	33	49
20	35	24	16 50	49
10	17	23	17 05	49
0	6 00	22	19	49
10	5 43	23	33	48
20	24	25	17 48	48
30	5 03	27	18 05	48
35	4 50	29	15	48
40	35	32	27	47
45	4 18	36	40	48
50	3 55	43	18 57	47
52	45	48	19 05	46
54	33	53	13	47
56	19	61	23	46
58	3 03	72	34	46
60 S	2 43	95	19 47	46

Lat. N °	Sun-set h m	Twil. m	Moon-set h m	Diff. m
60	15 04	57	7 19	50
58	21	51	7 06	50
56	36	47	6 56	49
54	48	43	46	50
52	15 59	40	38	49
50	16 08	38	30	50
45	28	34	14	49
40	45	31	6 00	50
35	16 59	28	5 49	49
30	17 11	26	39	49
20	32	24	22	49
10	17 50	22	5 08	48
0	18 07	22	4 54	48
10	25	23	40	48
20	18 43	25	25	48
30	19 05	27	4 08	48
35	18	29	3 58	48
40	32	32	47	47
45	19 50	37	34	47
50	20 12	44	18	46
52	22	49	10	47
54	34	54	3 02	46
56	20 48	61	2 52	46
58	21 04	73	41	46
60 S	21 24	96	2 29	45

A set of tables like these inspired Babbage to dream of producing them by machinery

and horses. James Watt in fact had measured the power of his great new engines in horsepower. But mental work involved brainpower, and how much brainpower did one horsepower contain? It was a fascinating idea, and it never left Babbage's mind from that day on. Indeed, it would seem that he thought of it always, awake or asleep. But it would be some time before Babbage produced the first rough engine that could be rated in brainpower.

After two years at Trinity, Babbage transferred from that college to Peterhouse. His reason was simple and typical: he knew that both Herschel and Peacock would probably beat him in the tripos or final honors examination to determine the senior wrangler or top scholar of the school. Babbage didn't want to be second to anyone, not even his closest friends. At Peterhouse he stood first in his class when he was graduated in 1814. And another, equally important event took place in 1814.

Babbage, as his portraits well show, was a handsome young man. Through his friend Edward Ryan he met charming Georgiana Whitmore, daughter of a fine family in Dudmaston, County Salop. Georgiana was a beautiful auburn-haired girl, a few months older than Charles. They were married in June of 1814. Ryan married Georgiana's sister and the two couples remained close friends.

The young husband had a new responsibility now. Although the couple had a home upstairs at 5 Devonshire plus a workshop for Charles above the stables, courtesy of his father, and no real financial worries, Babbage began to give some thought to a job.

He could have joined his father's bank as a junior partner, of course. There he would have been assured of financial rewards and social standing. Undoubtedly he would have been a successful banker, as his later papers on financial matters indicated. However, as a dedicated mathematician he looked with little favor on a career of handling pounds and shillings, a life bounded by the stability of sterling and the question of proper interest rates. Instead, Charles Babbage sought a post more in keeping with his scientific interests.

The Babbage's first child, named Benjamin Herschel, for Charles's father and his best friend, was born in 1815. That year, too, Napoleon, defeated finally in battle, sailed into the harbor at Torbay, not far from the Babbage home at Teignmouth. Charles, home for a visit, mounted a horse when he heard the news, and rode along the shore as close as he could get to the *Bellerophon*. With a pocket telescope he looked at the great military leader whom Wellington had defeated.

That same year, Professor Tennant was killed while riding his horse across a drawbridge at Boulogne. A bolt had been removed, and the bridge dropped him to his death. With his teacher's death, Babbage's interest in chemistry waned, giving him more time to devote to his real love—mathematics.

THE DOT-AGE OF THE UNIVERSITY

Babbage's first published paper had appeared in the *Memoirs of the Analytical Society* in 1813. In fact, he, together with Herschel and Peacock, wrote practically the entire first issue. However, he was soon publishing his papers in some of the older journals such as the *Philosophical Transactions* and the *Royal Institute Journal*. So well was he received that he was invited to become a member of the Royal Society in 1816, while still a graduate student at Cambridge. This was a high tribute to his ability in mathematics, since the members must have been painfully aware of his controversial views on much the society held dear.

The Analytical Society completed the translation of

Lacroix's work on calculus, which contained the "pure *d's*" of Leibnitz, in 1816. This was what the young infidels had promised—or threatened—and resistance from hidebound teachers was predictable. Even after several years, only two colleges had accepted the new and more effective notation in calculus. Newton had invented the calculus independently of Leibnitz, and there was great national pride in this English genius who had also formulated the law of gravity, the laws of motion, and many of the laws of optics. This pride held back the advance of mathematics and other sciences in England, while Europe moved ahead with newer methods.

Throughout his young life Babbage had persisted in doing things the way they could best be done. Now he saw a great wrong being done to English science because of its reliance on outmoded traditions, and he determined to do something about it. The Analytical Society had begun as a joke. But underlying it was the serious belief that a change must be made.

A case in point for the sad state of English science was the book *Principles of Fluxions* by Archdeacon William Dealtry, F.R.S. The *Edinburgh Review* pointed out that this book not only taught false notions, but it also did *not* teach many things known for a century or more. For example, a pupil might master Dealtry's book and still not be able to comprehend the first few pages of a current French text on celestial mechanics. Babbage knew the problem, and he thought he had the answer:

> It is always difficult to think and reason in a new language, and this difficulty discouraged all but men of energetic minds. I saw, however, that, by making it their interest to do so, the change might be accomplished. I therefore proposed to make a large collection of examples of the differential and integral calculus, consisting merely of the statement of each problem and its final solution. I foresaw that if such a publi-

cation existed, all those tutors who did not approve of the change of the Newtonian notation would yet, in order to save their own time and trouble, go to this collection of examples to find problems to set to their pupils. After a short time the use of the new signs would become familiar, and I anticipated their general adoption at Cambridge as a matter of course.

It was as "simple" as that. Babbage, aided by Herschel and Peacock, went on to publish the collection that would bring about the shift to the new notation.

UNEMPLOYED GENIUS

With two years of marriage behind him and his family growing, Charles Babbage stepped up his job-hunting, confident that his accomplishments would be all the credentials he needed. In 1816 he applied for a mathematics professorship at East India College in Haileybury. Although eminently capable, he was not hired because he did not have the right connections. This was a bitter pill, and he swallowed it with some complaint. But he continued his work at Cambridge. In 1817 he received the master's degree.

Adding this to his other credentials, he tried for the chair of mathematics at the University of Edinburgh—but failed to get it because he was not a Scot. These experiences embittered the young mathematician and strengthened his attack on the institutions of science and learning in his country. At the same time, however, unemployment gave Babbage time to pursue his first love—research in mathematics.

At the age of twenty-five Charles Babbage already had jolted the drowsy composure of British science and ousted Newtonian notation. He had formed the Analytical Society, and was toying with the idea of another Analytical something not yet ready to be born. In 1817 there were no attractive subsidies from the government to encourage a young genius to keep on with a project or dream. The universities were factories of learning—learning of a stodgy and stereotyped kind—with little encouragement and less money for the don who wanted to do research. The government did not yet realize the value of science to the point of lending financial help. So it was with his own money that Charles Babbage worked in his study at those things that fascinated him.

In 1817 Babbage published a paper in the *Philosophical Transactions* entitled "On Some New Methods of Investigating the Sums of several Classes of Infinite Series." This scholarly work did not express his feelings as enthusiastically as Babbage did in a letter to John William Whittaker, Fellow at St. John College at Cambridge:

> I send you a copy of a paper of mine on functions on which subject I am decidedly mad without the remotest possibility of a cure, seeing that it is so fertile in beautiful results that it might well occupy half a dozen lives without being near exhausted. I have received some excellent remarks on them from Bromhead, who is also a little touched.

The dream of an engine that could yield these "beautiful results," not in half a dozen lifetimes but in Babbage's own, prompted him to turn from mathematics to a powerful tool for its application, a tool that would make tables by steam.

CHAPTER FOUR

The Calculating Machine Comes of Age

Man began to count before he began to write. We know this from the crude paintings he made on cave walls to keep records—or perhaps even to boast—of how many bison or other animals he had slain. The notion of counting, the use of symbolic marks to represent animals, trees, or people, seems to have come some 25,000 years ago. Interestingly, the oldest surviving written documents are account books written in Sumerian, discovered in Erech, Mesopotamia. Charles Babbage could thus draw on a long history of counting, and even of a few rude mechanical counting machines.

Today, a child will almost automatically count on his fingers; it seems likely that our own digits were the first digital computers. It may be that the V standing for five in Roman numerals represented picture language for the whole hand, with thumb extended—five digits in all. The effectiveness of our ten fingers as a calculating device is barely appreciated. For example, used as a binary counter they can be used to tally up to 1023. But just as man substituted tools for his hands, he found tools to make the mental work of counting easier.

THE ABACUS

The first counting device we can honor with the name machine was undoubtedly the abacus. This is the familiar bead-and-rod device still used today by children learning their arithmetic, shopkeepers, and even some banks in many foreign countries. It was natural that early man used pebbles, sea-shells, and the like for counters when doing his sums. One theory is that he strung these on a string to make a handy

The first counting "machine" was undoubtedly the abacus

computer he could hang around his neck. From this it was a simple matter to make the further change to rigid rods arranged in rows. This was the abacus. The name is something of a misnomer, since it comes from the Greek *abax* or *abak*, which means slab. But then, early arithmetic was most likely done on a slab of rock or wood. (In fact the word "counter" in a store comes from the fact that the counter was actually that, with grooves cut in it for sliding beads or pebbles back and forth to tally an account.)

The abacus came into general use quickly after its introduction perhaps as early as 3000 B.C. It reigned supreme as a calculating device for thousands of years, and as late as 1947 a Japanese version called a *soroban* beat an electric calculator.

The wheel was invented even before the abacus, and it was inevitable that it would become involved in computing sooner or later. This seems to have been the case in the thirteenth century when the eccentric Spanish monk, Ramón Lull, constructed his "divine wheels" with which he claimed to solve all manner of problems by means of logic. Here was a crude attempt to simplify the process of reason, and it would be picked up by sophisticated logicians in later years.

LOGARITHMS ON A STICK

John Napier was a sixteenth-century Scottish mathematician whose neighbors feared he was a magician practicing the black arts. He was a believer in astrology and practiced divination. Fearful that Spain would invade the British Isles, he drew plans for all manner of strange defenses, from solar mirrors for burning ships at a distance to submarines and primitive tanks. However, his true fame rests on two great mathematical inventions: the decimal point and logarithms.

Today mathematicians take for granted these handy exponents of numbers that make it possible to multiply and divide by simple addition and subtraction. In Napier's day calculations were done laboriously in the old-fashioned way, and he fretted many hours over the time such arithmetic took. Finally, he wrote,

> Seeing that there is nothing that is so troublesome to mathematical practice, nor that doth more molest and hinder calculations, than the multiplications, divisions, square and cubical expansions of great numbers, which beside the tedious expense of time, are for the most part subject to many slippery errors, I began to consider in my mind by what certain and ready art I might remove these hindrances.

In 1594 the thought struck Napier that all numbers could be written in exponential form, or as powers of a certain base number. For instance, 4 is 2^2, and 8 is 2^3. This alone is not startling, but Napier saw beyond it to a simple way of multiplying 4 times 8 without really multiplying. 2^2 plus 2^3 equaled 2^5 in Napier's new arithmetic, and 2^5 equals 32, the same as the product of 4 times 8. The same principle applies to exponents of *all* numbers, although there was a fantastic amount of work involved in computing these exponents extensively. In fact, it was not until 1614, twenty years after his revelation of the basic idea, that Napier published his logarithm tables. The result was something like the introduction of the electronic computer in our time. Logarithms drastically reduced the amount of work involved in mathematics and relieved scientists, particularly astronomers, from a great burden of mental drudgery.

Not content with introducing a revolutionary mathematics system, Napier then marked the exponents on rods of ivory and used these "Napier's bones" to do logarithmic computations, much as the abacus handled digital numbers. Before

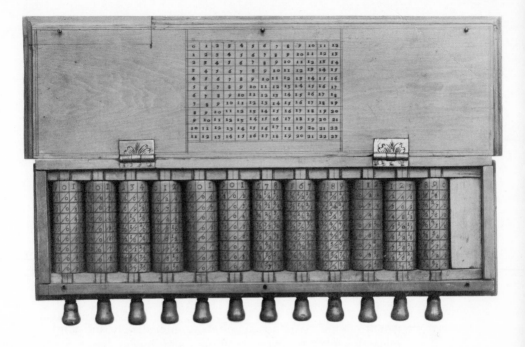

An eighteenth-century version of Napier's bones, arranged cylindrically as a mathematical calculator

long an English minister and amateur mathematician named William Oughtred invented the slide rule, perhaps inspired by Napier's ivory rods.

When Napier's bones were introduced, mathematicians must surely have thought they had gone to number heaven. Who could ask anything more? With calculations done in a fraction of the time, there would be no stopping mathematicians. But almost immediately they began to attack problems of much greater complexity or broadness of scope and ran into the same brick wall of time-consuming calculations. There was still drudgery, in spite of the new tools Napier had introduced. Calculating engines more sophisticated than the abacus and the slide rule were needed.

THE MECHANICAL CALCULATORS

It is difficult to track down the first of this new generation of mechanical calculating machines, but surely one of the earliest was that of Wilhelm Schickardt of Germany. Schickardt began his career as a professor of Biblical languages at Tubingen, but he later changed to mathematics and astronomy. Although he lived but forty-three years, he accomplished an enormous amount in his short career. In a letter written to his countryman, Johann Kepler, on September 20, 1623, Schickardt described his first calculating machine,

> which computes the given numbers immediately and automatically; adds, subtracts, multiplies and divides. Surely you will beam when you see how it accumulates carryovers of tens and hundreds by itself, or while subtracting takes something away from them.

This amazing calculator was quite simple in construction, with only eleven full gears and six partial ones. Unfortunately it was destroyed in a fire during the Thirty Years War. Drawings were found among Kepler's papers only recently by Dr. Franz Hammer of Stuttgart, editor of Kepler's literary remains. The calculator proved to be as good as Schickardt had claimed three hundred and fifty years ago.

Better known than the Schickardt machine is the work of the Frenchman Blaise Pascal, who constructed a computing machine of gears and shafts that would add a column of eight figures. He was still a teen-ager working in his father's tax office when he built the first model of this desk calculator.

Pascal was a prodigy. At sixteen he published a book on the geometry of conic sections, the first advance in that subject for almost one thousand nine hundred years. He pioneered the theory of probability while trying to help a gambler friend minimize his losses at the dice table. He set down Pascal's Principle, the basis for the hydraulic press which multiplies the force exerted on it. Like Babbage, he learned how to take his mind off physical problems, and shortly before his early death at thirty-nine he worked a complicated problem in geometry simply to forget an agonizing toothache.

In 1645, after five years' work and much difficulty, Pascal completed his computer, which was called Pascaline. A com-

One of the earliest mechanical calculators was devised by Wilhelm Schickardt of Germany in the early seventeenth century

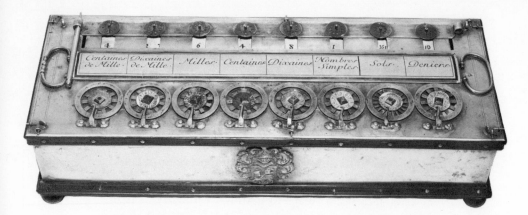

*"Brass and iron have been invested with the function of brain," said
Thomas Hobbes of the Pascal computer*

plex mechanism, it was 14 inches long, 5 inches wide, and 3½
inches high. His admiring sister said of it, with pardonable
exaggeration:

> He invented this arithmetical machine with which not only
> is it possible to perform calculations of every kind without
> pen or counters, but also to undertake such calculation with
> absolute accuracy, even without any knowledge of the rules
> of arithmetic. This instrument was judged to be a marvel,
> inasmuch as it reduces to mechanical terms a science residing
> wholly in the spirit, so that all operations can be performed
> with complete certainty, without the need for reasoning.

The English philosopher Thomas Hobbes hailed Pascal's
computer in these words:

> Brass and iron have been invested with the function of brain,
> and instructed to perform some of the most difficult opera-
> tions of mind. . . . In what manner so ever there is place
> for addition and subtraction, there also is place for reason,
> and where these have no place, there reason has nothing at
> all to do; for reason is nothing but reckoning of the conse-
> quences. . . . When a man reasoneth, he does nothing else
> but conceive a sum total from addition of the partials.

Despite these glowing tributes, the Pascaline computer was never a practical success, and some said that Pascal exhausted himself trying to perfect it.

Sir Samuel Moreland in England built a computing machine in 1666 that seems to have been similar to that of Pascal. In such devices the beads of the abacus were exchanged for the teeth of gears, and numbers were wrapped about wheels instead of being spread along rods. Like the abacus, the computing machine did not make mistakes. It "never dropped a sum," as Samuel Butler admiringly put it. However, it was slow in its operation and was costly since mechanical devices were handmade for the most part.

Gottfried Wilhelm Von Leibnitz was born in 1646, about the time Pascal had "perfected" his mechanical computer. In his seventy years Leibnitz demonstrated remarkable ability as a politician, philosopher, diplomat, and mathematician. Lieb-nitz was much impressed with Ramón Lull's logic wheels and also advanced the concept of binary, or two-valued logic. The numbers 1 and 0, he said, were of immense importance. He put wheels to another use as well and constructed a geared calculating machine that was an improvement over that of Pascal. This machine, built in 1671, could add and subtract. It could also laboriously multiply and divide by virtue of its cogged pinion gears, which allowed repeated additions and subtractions. Leibnitz's calculating machine resulted in his election to membership in the Royal Society in London. Eleven years later he published his calculus, a mathematical tool even greater in importance than logarithms.

Despite the tribute from the Royal Society, however, the machine was not widely used. Leibnitz himself said that. "It is not made for those who sell vegetables or little fishes, but for observatories, or the private rooms of calculators, or for others who can easily bear the expense, and need a good deal of calculation."

Even this was giving the machine too much credit. The calculating machines of Pascal and Leibnitz did not make mistakes within their gears and shafts. But they could be improperly used, and erroneously read, in spite of Pascal's doting sister's claim that one need know nothing of the rules of arithmetic. Besides this, they were available to only a few people, and even for them they offered little increase in speed. Mathematicians with calculators were like men going around the world on tricycles. What was needed was some faster means of reaching answers, and attempts were continually made by inventors.

In 1678 the Frenchman Grillet de Roven built a mechanical device designed to handle logarithms, with an automatic carryover when the scale was exceeded. An Italian marquis, Giovanni Poleni, built a calculating machine in 1709 which he claimed could be instructed what it was to do by setting various levers and then do it automatically and without error. The cranking mechanism was fitted with a speed governor to keep the mathematician from working too fast. Here was a first attempt at programming a computer, but there is no evidence that Poleni's machine was anything more than an impressive curiosity.

Leibnitz constructed a geared calculating machine that improved on Pascal's

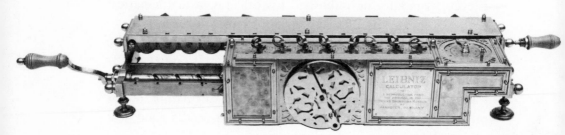

OLD WAYS ARE BEST

In Book Three of *Gulliver's Travels*, Jonathan Swift writes of a marvelous machine invented by the scientists of Laputa, whereby

> the most ignorant Person at a reasonable Charge, and with a little bodily Labour, may write books in Philosophy, Poetry, Politicks, Law, Mathematicks, and Theology, without the least Assistance from Genius or Study. He [the Laputan inventor] then led me to the Frame, about the Sides whereof all his Pupils stood in Ranks.
>
> It was a Twenty Foot Square, placed in the Middle of the Room. The Superfices was composed of several Bits of Wood, about the Bigness of a Dye, but some larger than others. They were all linked together by slender Wires. These Bits of Wood were covered on every Square with Papers pasted on them; and on these Papers were written all the Words of their Language in their several Moods, Tenses, and Declensions, but without any Order. The Professor then desired me to observe, for he was going to set his Engine to work. The Pupils at his Command took each the hold of an Iron Handle, whereof there were Forty fixed round the Edges of the Frame, and giving them a sudden Turn, the whole Disposition of the Words was entirely changed. He then commanded Six and Thirty of the Lads to read the several Lines softly as they appeared upon the Frame; and where they found three or four Words together that might make Part of a Sentence, they dictated to the four remaining Boys who were Scribes. This work was repeated three or four Times, and at every Turn the Engine was so contrived, that the Words shifted into new Places, as the square Bits of Wood moved upside down.
>
> Six hours a-Day the young Students were employed in this Labour; and the Professor showed me several Volumes in

large Folio already collected, of broken Sentences, which he intended to piece together, and out of those rich Materials to give the World a compleat Body of Art and Sciences; which however might be still improved, and much expedited, if the Publick would raise a large Fund for making and employing five Hundred such Frames in *Lagado*.

Published in 1726, sixty-six years before Babbage was born, this was a stinging satire of the notion that machines could do mental tasks. It seemed a fair appraisal too. Despite all the calculators and engines and machines, mathematics still consisted of the tedious, humanly computed additions and subtractions of columns of figures that consumed time and patience. Even the most skilful computers made mistakes. For instance, Nevil Maskelyne, the first astronomer royal, in 1766 completed the Nautical Almanac after years of careful work. Yet this laboriously prepared volume was later found

0 INCHES   3   6   9   12

to have more than one thousand errors, many of which must have resulted in the loss of British ships.

In 1769 Baron von Kempelen built a chess-playing robot and Johann Maelzel toured the world with it. The robot bested many noted figures, including Napoleon himself. But one day a suspicious onlooker cried "Fire!" and a midget hurtled out of the cramped innards.

Man was not yet ready—or able—to let machines take over the domain of mental work. Accounting in Babbage's time followed a system of recording the receipt of money by making notches on tally sticks, first introduced to the Exchequer by William the Conqueror. The tally system was abolished by Parliament in 1782, but it was not finally discontinued until the death of the last of the chamberlains in 1826. The tallies were stored in the Star Chamber, which was filled to overflowing. In 1834, when the room was needed for other purposes, they were ordered burned as "secret waste." One afternoon in October it was noticed that the House of Lords was warmer than usual. Soon the place burst into flames, and both houses of Parliament accidentally burned to the ground. With the tally sticks helping, the fire lasted nine hours, the biggest since the Great Fire of September, 1666. Not until World War II and the fire raids by German bombers would there be another such fire.

In that same year of 1834, Charles Babbage designed his *second* computer, the Analytical Engine that foreshadowed today's electronic brains.

Tally sticks, used in England until 1826 for recording the receipt of money

 The Difference Engine

Keenly interested in advancing the calculus as a potent branch of mathematics, Charles Babbage continued to write papers on his favorite subject. He had also begun work on a new branch of calculus, that of certain classes of infinite series. In 1817 he presented four papers detailing his investigations. But overriding his interest in analytical theory was a continuing desire to develop tools to better use that theory—a "mental engine."

Babbage began to collect early calculators, but none of them met his rigorous requirements. For example, not one was self-acting. One must ask, he said,

> whether, when the numbers on which [the machine] is to operate are placed in the instrument, it is capable of arriving at its result by the mere motion of a spring, a descending weight, or any other constant force? If the answer be in the affirmative, the machine is really automatic; if otherwise, it is not self-acting.

And Babbage would settle for nothing less than a self-acting engine. In 1819, established in his own well-equipped laboratory and shop, he began to squeeze into his busy schedule active work on two mechanical projects. One of these was a method of accurately marking the fine gradations on the scales of astronomical instruments.

It was of little use to have accurate tables if the astronomer could not aim his telescope at the proper angles of declination and right ascension. Babbage felt sure he had succeeded in devising a successful method of making the divisions on instruments, but to assure himself he asked Dr. William Wollaston, an eminent scientist, to consult with him on the new idea. Wollaston had been Professor Tennant's assistant, and it was he who actually completed the diamond-burning experiment that proved the gem was all carbon. Wollaston also developed a method for working the rare metal platinum and was paid a fortune for his secret. He also discovered palladium and rhodium, and did research in crystallography, electricity, magnetism, and optics.

Wollaston, who was secretary of the Royal Society, was a well-qualified consultant and almost immediately he pointed out that Babbage's idea was not original. The duke de Chaulnes had described it earlier in the *Memoirs of the French Academy of Sciences.*

Babbage was so embarrassed he hardly had the heart to mention his other "discovery." However, he finally gave Wollaston a sheaf of papers describing the Difference Engine.

Then for an agonizing half hour the elder man made no sound except for an occasional surprised grunt. Babbage sat on the edge of his chair, close to holding his breath. At length Wollaston pushed back the papers and told the young man that neither de Chaulnes nor anyone else had beaten him to this idea.

"You approve my idea, then?" Babbage asked hopefully.

"Approve it? Why should a scientist not approve—even applaud the most remarkable concept he has yet come across! Get to work, Babbage, for what you plan here may well require your efforts for a long time."

Had Babbage known that the long time predicted by Wollaston would stretch into the rest of his life and even then not result in success, he might have felt like bundling up his careful notes and pitching them into the grate. But the chances are better that he would have proceeded with his master plan. For the idea that obsessed him was like nothing else on earth. It was a first attempt to make an automatic computer—the initial effort in the revolution of mechanically augmenting man's brain.

TABLE OF DIFFERENCES

The theory of a difference engine is simple; so simple that many people think of it as soon as they see it. In describing the principle, Babbage used the example of a butcher selling meat by the pound. Rather than calculate each sale by multiplying the number of pounds by the price, he prepares a table or chart that tells him immediately and accurately the price of four pounds of mutton, for example. This is a table of differences, and can be worked by pen and paper with little difficulty, but always with the danger of human error somewhere along the line.

Meat in Babbage's day must have sold for 5 pence (5 d.) a pound (12 pence equals 1 shilling), for this is the sample table he used:

Pounds	Price	Difference
1	5d.	
		5d.
2	10d.	
		5d.
3	1s 3d.	
		5d.
4	1s 8d.	
		5d.
5	2s 1d.	

There are other, more complicated tables of differences. In mathematics a table of squares or other powers, or a table of logarithms is more involved than the simple example given above. A table of squares, for example, works this way:

Number	Square	Difference
1	1	
		3
2	4	
		5
3	9	
		7
4	16	
		9
5	25	

In the butcher's table the same quantity was added, 5 pence for each additional pound. But as the table of squares shows, there is a *different* difference for each succeeding square. However, if we make another table, a *second* difference table alongside the first, we arrive at a *constant* difference:

Number	Square	1st Difference	2nd Difference
1	1		
		3	
2	4		2
		5	
3	9		2
		7	
4	16		2
		9	
5	25		

This is still a very simple table of differences. Consider several piles of cannonballs, such as one sometimes sees in a park. This series begins with one cannonball. The next pyramid consists of three balls arranged in a triangle and one atop the three, making a total of four. In the next pile there will be six balls on the bottom, three atop that, and again one on the very top, for a total of ten. We have a table of pyramids that reads: 1, 4, 10, and so on. In this example it will be necessary to go to a third difference to arrive at a repeating number, in this case, 1:

Series Number	Total	1st Difference	2nd Difference	3rd Difference
1	1			
		3		
2	4		3	
		6		1
3	10		4	
		10		1
4	20		5	
		15		1
5	35		6	
		21		
6	56			

Other tables may require four, five, six, and more differences to reach a constant difference.

To put this principle of differences to work, Babbage used as an example the idea of several alarm clocks linked together. They were called repeating clocks in his day, for the user could pull a string at any time and have the clock strike the hour. If Clock A were set at one o'clock, it would ring once. Clock B, being set at three o'clock would ring three times, Clock C set for two, twice. By the same token, the clocks could be linked so each ring of C would advance B one hour, and each ring of B would advance A one hour. Babbage's difference engine would operate in much the same way as indicated by a table of clock movements.

To produce a table of squares Babbage would set a 1 on the wheel of the number column, a 3 on the first difference column, and a 2 on the second difference column. The first crank of the wheel would print a 1. The second crank would add 3 to the 1, yielding a 4, at the same time adding the difference 2 to 3 for 5 on the middle column. The next crank then would print 4 plus 5, or 9. And so on until the table was complete or the engine ran out of numbers.

A SELF-ACTING MACHINE

The above is a great simplification and does not do justice to Babbage's superb insight into the possibilities of such a computing machine. For example, Babbage wrote, "When we attempt to perform such additions by machinery we might follow exactly the usual process of the human mind." He was hinting at a mechanical brain one hundred fifty years ago. And our simplified description of the principle of difference engines does not touch on the difficulty of such details as the carrying of 10s, which the engine must do to be useful.

There was another problem, too, in the fact that Babbage insisted that his engine actually print out its results to avoid errors in copying.

The calculators of Pascal and Leibnitz, ingenious as they were, were still susceptible to human error, particularly in the misreading of a result. So Babbage wrote, "In order, however, to insure accuracy in the printed Tables, it was necessary that the machine which computed Tables should also set them up in type, or else supply a mould in which stereotype plates of those Tables could be cast." All very simple and straightforward for today's technology, but in Babbage's time there was not yet an automatic typesetting machine. He had to invent one.

Babbage began work on the first Difference Engine in his own workshop and quickly made a simple model whose few wheels proved the idea. He made the drawings and set to work machining parts on his own lathe. When he reached the limit of his mechanical abilities he farmed out his machine work to a wheel-cutter at Lambeth. For the printing portion of the engine he planned thirty thousand movable pieces of type, each cleverly locked so that mistakes could not occur in typesetting. He also tried printing from type permanently attached to the computing wheels. The actual printing was done on paper, copper plates, or plaster of Paris molds.

By 1822 Babbage had built two experimental difference engines. The first used ninety-six computing wheels mounted on twenty-four shafts, but he then shifted to a simpler version with eighteen wheels on three shafts. Thus he had an engine which could calculate only two orders of difference.

The three shafts were mounted vertically in the machine, and on each of them were six geared wheels, each marked with the numbers 0 through 9. The shaft to the right contained the second difference numbers, the center shaft the first difference numbers, and the shaft to the left the table of numbers itself. The bottom wheel on each shaft represented units, the next higher tens, the next hundreds, and so on. Each wheel could be set to any number desired.

If we were to set a 2 on the right-hand shaft, a 3 on the middle shaft, and a 1 on the left-hand shaft (see the table on page 52), we would have the Difference Engine ready to make a table of squares beginning with 1. Each crank of the handle would transfer numbers from the shafts to the shaft on its left by means of the gear teeth. There was a "carry" lever that actuated the wheel above when a total equaled or exceeded 10.

Babbage had proved the principle of his engine and now lacked only the financial backing to produce a full-scale model. He was still unemployed and dependent on his father for funds.

Along with all his other endeavors, Babbage had been instrumental in forming the new Astronomical Society in 1820. In June, 1822, he published in its *Memoirs* a "Note respecting the Application of Machinery to the Calculation of Mathematical Tables." However, the Royal Society continued as the most prestigious organization, and it was to the society Babbage had to go for help in promoting his Difference Engine.

While Babbage was trying to get help from the Royal Society, he was describing its Council as "a collection of men who elect each other to office, and then dine together at the expense of the Society to praise each other over wine, and to give each other medals." Nevertheless, on July 3, 1822, Babbage sat down and wrote a long letter to Sir Humphrey Davy, president of the Royal Society. In the second paragraph of this message he stated a great truth:

The intolerable labour and fatiguing monotony of a continued repetition of similar arithmetical calculations, first excited the desire, and afterwards suggested the idea, of a machine, which, by the aid of gravity or any other moving power, should become a substitute for one of the lowest operations of human intellect.

In the letter he retraced his inspiration for the Difference Engine. Adam Smith's book *The Wealth of Nations* had described the advantages of the division of labor, that is, the separation of manufacturing and other tasks so that each workman specialized. Monsieur G. F. Prony, commissioned by the French government to prepare extensive mathematical tables, chanced to read Smith's book and decided to put the concept of the division of labor to work. He organized his force of mathematicians into three echelons: at the top were the brilliant minds like his own, representing the executive branch of a business. These men, six in all, did the analytical work and determined what was to be computed and which formulas would be used to do so.

In the second echelon were eight skilled calculators able to do both analytical work and the actual computing of tables. This group of men, similar to foremen in a factory, set up the formulas and carried the work to where it became merely the repetitive addition or subtraction of numbers in the difference tables.

At this point, the calculators turned the boresome computing over to a large group of some seventy men who did only addition and subtraction, rapidly and fairly accurately. These were the laborers of the mental field.

In effect, the task of preparing mathematical tables of a complex nature was handled much like a metalworking job in the foundry, or the building of a house, with engineers, foremen, and journeyman workers who carried out simple tasks as ordered. In his letter to Davy, Babbage now proposed to take the next logical step. Why not let a machine do these "lowest operations of human intellect?" In his letter, Babbage also admitted: "I am aware that the statements contained in this letter may perhaps be viewed as something more than Utopian, and the philosophers of Laputa may be called up to dispute my claim to originality."

Here he was referring to Jonathan Swift's tale, perhaps thinking particularly of the words, "if the Publick would raise a large fund." For he ended his letter by getting to the main point—that of money:

> Whether I shall construct a larger engine of this kind, and bring to perfection the others I have described, will in a great measure depend on the nature of the encouragement I may receive.
>
> Induced, by a conviction of the great utility of such engines, to withdraw for some time my attention from a subject on which it has been engaged during several years, and which possess charms of a higher order [This refers to his work in developing the calculus of infinite series.], I have now arrived at a point where success is no longer doubtful. It must, however, be attained at a very considerable expense, which would not probably be replaced, by the works it might produce, for a long period of time, and which is an undertaking I should feel unwilling to commence, as altogether foreign to my habits and pursuits.

Davy was impressed by the Babbage proposal and reported glowingly on the Difference Engine to the Royal Society, with results that delighted Babbage.

GOLD AND SILVER

Babbage also wrote an article for *Brewster's Journal of Science*, but the original piece for the Astronomical Society resulted in the striking of that organization's first gold medal!

Mr. Henry Thomas Colebrooke, president of the Astronomical Society, stated on the occasion of presenting the medal to Babbage:

> In no department of science, or of the arts, does this discovery promise to be so eminently useful as in that of astronomy, and its kindred sciences, with the various arts dependent on them. In none are computations more operose than those which astronomy in particular requires;—in none are preparatory facilities more needful;—in none is error more detrimental. The practical astronomer is interrupted in his pursuit, and diverted from his task of observation by the irksome labours of computation, or his diligence in observing becomes ineffectual for want of yet greater industry of calculation. Let the aid which tables previously computed afford, be furnished to the utmost extent which mechanism has made attainable through Mr. Babbage's invention, and the most irksome portion of the astronomer's task is alleviated, and a fresh impulse is given to the astronomical research.

Babbage's cup of pride spilled over.

Davy and the Royal Society were so influential that by 1823 Babbage and the chancellor of the exchequer reached an unwritten agreement whereby England would provide funds for a Difference Engine. The first grant was £1,500, from the civil contingencies fund, toward a total cost which the two parties estimated at between £3,000 and £5,000 (something like a pound sterling per pound of engine weight since the complete engine would weigh about two tons). Babbage was to receive no compensation, donating all his efforts to the government.

It was specified that the project would be completed in about three years, but the rest of the bargain was vague. Problems would arise later partly because of this. But the next few years were perhaps the happiest of his life for Babbage. He had persuaded the government of the importance of his

Difference Engine, and he was now on his way to building a better engine that would calculate to six orders of difference and twenty places of accuracy. He knew it would be difficult:

> After examining all the resources of existing workshops, I came to the conclusion that, in order to succeed, it would become necessary to advance the art of construction itself. I trusted with some confidence that those studies which had enabled me to contrive mechanism for new wants, would be equally useful for the invention of new tools and of other methods of employing the old.

In 1823 Charles Babbage, thirty years old and a family man, mathematician, and inventor, set out to "advance the art of construction" so that he could complete his promising Difference Engine. He also continued to devote himself when he could to mathematics, "which possesses charms of a higher order." Babbage was interested in his calculating engines merely as a tool for mathematics, and in 1824 the *Transactions of the Cambridge Philosophical Society* published his paper entitled "On the Determination of the General Term of a new Class of Infinite Series."

A MAN OF VARIED INTERESTS

Also in 1824, with work on the Difference Engine progressing, there came the sudden prospect of a job. Babbage was still living on the top floor of his father's house in London and was dependent on him for his living. A group of businessmen interested in forming an insurance company asked Babbage to prepare tables and other information. Eagerly he studied the records of the Equitable Life Insurance Company, plus what little there was on actuarial statistics. The result was a short book entitled *A Comparative View of the Differ-*

ent Institutions for the Assurance of Life, and what were probably the first reliable life insurance tables.

Babbage could have been a good banker. He could also have been a good insurance man, so it is probably fortunate that the venture fell through and his job with it. German insurance men seized on the book and used the tables effectively, however, and Babbage was pleased with this foreign recognition even as he became convinced that truly a prophet was without honor in his own country.

While it was disappointing to have another dream shattered, he must have been secretly pleased. As a businessman he would not have been free for the wonderful research he carried on along with supervising the construction of the Difference Engine. His experiments with barometers, for example, were described in *Brewster's Edinburgh Journal of Science,* and the invention of "a new zenith micrometer" was reported in the *Memoirs* of the Astronomical Society. In 1825 he investigated electricity and magnetism with John Herschel, inventing the astatic or nonpolar needle in the process.

In 1826, one of his most productive years, Babbage, still interested in submarine craft, and remembering an 1818 undersea trip, wrote a prophetic article on the diving bell for an encyclopedia. Babbage also completed and published a new table of logarithms from 1 to 108,000, and found time to testify before a House of Commons committee on savings banks.

That same year the *Philosophical Transactions* published one of his most important contributions to mechanical drawing. Without a doubt, the Difference Engine was the most complex mechanical contrivance yet designed. So complex were its movements that Babbage had to invent what he called "mechanical notation," a way of lettering the drawings to indicate the function and movements of various parts.

But there were disappointments in 1826 as well. Babbage had received a Gold Medal from the Astronomical Society in 1823, but he longed for one from the Royal Society, whatever he might have thought and said about that scientific body. And so in 1826 he entered his paper on mechanical notation in the competition, only to see the prizes—advertised for work done within a year of the time of the award—go to projects dating back as far as twenty years!

There was another bitter disappointment for him in 1826. Long a productive member of the Royal Society, Babbage was at last in line for the secretaryship. He had, in fact, been promised that position, and he confidently told his friends and family. Instead, President Humphrey Davy appointed a friend as secretary.

Perhaps the finishing touch in 1826 was the appointment of George Biddell Airy to the Lucasian Chair of Mathematics at Cambridge. For Airy was becoming loud in his criticism of the Difference Engine. Worse yet, Airy was a younger man than Babbage and had had an even more brilliant record at Cambridge.

The chink in Babbage's armor was his pride. With these latest rebuffs he began to develop persecution feelings he could not rise above, and ever afterward his judgment and his actions would be marred by his thin-skinned reaction to wrongs, real or imagined.

THE SHADOWED DREAM

Perhaps the fantastic output in other fields by the inventor of the Difference Engine added fuel to the rumors beginning to circulate. The time tentatively set for the completion of the engine had arrived, and it was far from completion. Babbage, whispers went, was profiteering; he was using tax money to line his own pockets. After all, the man had no visible means of support. By 1827 Airy was saying of the Difference Engine, "The thing is a humbug!"

All these were vicious lies, of course. The £1,500 the government had advanced was nowhere near the total spent on the engine. In four years John Clement, the engineer supervising the construction, had received nearly that much as his salary alone. Babbage had spent perhaps twice what the government had and donated much of his time to the project. This added to his anger at the unfair charges by those opposed to the engine.

To some extent Babbage was to blame for the slow progress. With money from his father, Babbage enlarged his shops and hired more machinists to produce the intricate parts for the Difference Engine. But instead of proceeding according to the drawings he had finished, and which would have led to an entirely satisfactory engine, he was constantly improving as he went along.

For instance, when visitors were amazed to hear bells ringing as the engine performed its tasks, Babbage informed them that from these bells he could tell that the problem being solved involved finding the roots of a quadratic equation.

Commenting on the engine, Babbage wrote, "The mechanical means I employed to make these carriages bears some slight analogy to the operation of the faculty of memory." Later, "At last having exhausted, during the years of labour, the principle of successive carriages, it occurred to me that it might be possible to teach mechanism to accomplish another mental process, namely—to foresee."

Almost as fast as his machinists completed parts and assemblies, Babbage told them that the gear was obsolete and that he had designed a new and better mechanism. More than the three years of the agreement with the chancellor of the exchequer passed and still the engine was not completed. Work dragged along, with Babbage now funding it from his own pocket since the government was reluctant to advance more.

He was having other problems as well. Personal tragedies struck cruelly. Even as Charles's own brothers and sisters had died in childhood, his own youngsters perished from disease. In 1827 alone, two of them died as did his father, who had been sick for a long time. But the heaviest blow of all was the death of Charles's wife Georgiana. In thirteen years Georgiana had given birth to seven children. Most were doomed to a terribly short life. Babbage took Georgiana, pregnant with their eighth child, to stay with her family in August. In September, at the age of thirty-five she died giving birth to a son who survived only a short time. Babbage's world, sorely tried by the problems of the Difference Engine came crashing down around him.

There was a terrible irony for Babbage. According to the terms of his father's will, Babbage's mother received £21,000 plus family jewelry that was to be passed on to Charles at her death. The sum of £10,000 was set aside in trust for the surviving children when they reached maturity. With his father dead Babbage was suddenly a wealthy man, inheriting about half a million dollars. Georgiana would never know the wealth that was now his, never wear the fortune in jewels that would have been his through his mother. Crushed and bitter, Babbage erased Georgiana from his memory; never again would he write of her or even mention her name until he was on his own deathbed fifty-four years later.

Babbage had been subject to recurrent illness since his childhood, and now his health failed to the point that his mother, his friends, and his doctor insisted that he not only stop work but that he leave the country for a complete rest. How much of Babbage's sickness was due to domestic tragedy and troubles with his Difference Engine we cannot know. He would not have given up work simply because of adversity; in fact, he seemed to thrive on it. The year's hiatus was most likely caused by his physical breakdown and the insistence of his mother and his friends.

When he went to Europe in 1827, Babbage dutifully left sufficient drawings to keep Clement going on the engine, plus £1,000 in the bank for payments. He arranged to keep in touch with his engineer. The surviving children, Herschel, Georgiana, and young Dugald and Henry, were left with his mother, who later farmed them out to relatives.

CHAPTER SIX

The Thing Is a Humbug!

Just before leaving for the Continent, Babbage paid a visit to his friend, the engineer Isambard Kingdom Brunel. Brunel and his noted father were at that time building the Thames Tunnel, through which traffic would one day move beneath the river.

Babbage took his eldest son Herschel, who was then twelve, with him. The purpose of the visit was to get copies of a prospectus of the tunneling project, printed in both French and German, so that he could distribute them to acquaintances and interested parties in foreign countries. But there was an added thrill waiting for the two Babbages. As they stood on a rough wooden platform in the eerie lamplight and watched workmen boring away, there was a sudden spurt of muddy water from the "shield," a huge breastwork that held back the earth and the water above it. Babbage shouted for Brunel, and the engineer rushed forward to give orders for shoring up the leak that had sprung in the shield.

A week later the shield was breached again, and this time the result was not so fortunate. Six workmen drowned, and

Brunel himself escaped only because he was a strong swimmer and managed to fight his way to safety. But by then Babbage was in Europe, and only read of the tragedy from that distance.

Taking along Richard Wright, one of his workmen, Babbage sailed across the Channel to Holland. Then he went to Munich, where among other things he lent one of the newly invented stomach pumps to Dr. Weisbrod, the king's physician, so that he might make a copy of it. Babbage met a young Russian coach designer in Frankfort and received an invitation to visit Moscow. He turned down the offer but learned enough about coaches so that when he reached Italy he drew plans for a "strong light four-wheeled *calèche*," which served him for all his stay in that country. Babbage often cooked his breakfast in the carriage, which featured large, shallow drawers in which he kept his clothes, telescopes, drawings of his various inventions, and so on.

Money, Babbage said, was a traveler's fuel. He had plenty of money, but he carried other things that were even more valuable. Among these were small gold buttons, carefully packed in small sandalwood boxes as if they were rare treasures. In a way, they were, being stamped by a special steel die which Sir John Barton, comptroller of the Mint, had scribed with a diamond point in parallel lines 40,000 to the inch. The result was a "diffraction grating" that refracted light and made the ruled surface iridescent. Babbage always managed to convey the impression that he had only one of the wonderful buttons remaining, although he had a dozen packed away in his luggage. They opened many doors for him, as did the sample steel die Barton had given him.

Babbage kept learning how things were made. From Italian jewelers he learned their secret of making tiny chain. Elsewhere he watched casting and molding operations, the shearing and forming of metal, and the use of looms, spinning frames, tools such as lathes, and planing machines. He had done this in England for years, and so it was natural to go on investigating as he "rested" on the Continent.

Oddly, Babbage considered his ability to punch a hole in a sheet of glass without cracking it his greatest travel asset. He had learned this trick from a workman and needed only center punches, a hammer, an old file, and a vise.

Since Babbage was interested in a theory he had concerning the pulse rate and breathing rate of animals, he visited every menagerie and animal show he could and made measurements. He later wrote a paper, "Note on the Description of Mammalia," published after his return to England. At Adelsburg, Styria, Babbage visited some dark caverns and learned of tiny creatures called *porteus anguineus* that lived in them. These worms had eyes but did not open them since they lived in the dark. Babbage bought six and sent them to university laboratories in England, India, and the colonies. He was disappointed, however, that Richard Wright had let some die by putting them in well water instead of river water.

Babbage spent much of his year in Naples. At the invitation of the Royal Academy of Naples he visited the island of Ischia and investigated its hot springs. He arranged a more exciting investigation himself, a trip into the volcano Vesuvius. Conserving his strength by riding horseback and then in a chair carried by porters, he reached the summit of the active volcano. With another scientist he spent six minutes inside the cone between eruptions (which he had timed as lasting ten to fifteen minutes), equipped with instruments to measure heat, pressure, and so on. He survived a fall down a slippery slope, and when he later tried to take off his shoes, they came apart in his hands, literally burned to pieces.

HONOR FROM ENGLAND

While in Rome, Babbage came across an article with a Cambridge dateline in the newspaper printed by Calignani: "Yesterday the bells of St. Mary rang on the election of Mr. Babbage as Lucasian Professor of Mathematics."

Babbage was stunned. Here was high honor from the very school he had fought so hard, beginning with the Analytical Society and its attack on hidebound methods. The position he would take was the Chair of Newton, whose dots he had deplored in favor of the *d*'s of Leibnitz! Here was what he would later call the only honor his country ever afforded him, compared with the many that came from foreign lands. But there were two factors to consider: the amount of work still to be done on his Difference Engine, and Babbage's lingering bitterness at the failure of the government to see its importance.

Perhaps part of his reluctance stemmed from the knowledge that Professor Airy, who had been Lucasian professor, had been promoted to Plumian professor of astronomy and director of the Cambridge observatory. This was the man who had attacked the Difference Engine as a humbug. While Babbage lumped Airy with the ignorant Luddite weavers who smashed automatic looms, he was painfully aware that Airy's reputation overshadowed his own. Finally he decided to write to Cambridge thanking the university for the honor but declining the chair because of his other commitments, principally his Difference Engine.

Before he could mail the letter, two English friends, Reverend Lunn and Mr. Beilby Thompson, living near Babbage in Rome, stopped by to congratulate him on his Lucasian appointment. When he told them he proposed to decline,

Charles Babbage

Lucasian Professor of Mathematics
in the University of Cambridge.

Engraved by Roffe by permission from an original Family Painting.

Charles Babbage: *professor of* mathematics *at last!*

70 / Charles Babbage

they were shocked and argued with him to reconsider. Even if
it meant nothing to him, they reminded him, he should think
how much his mother would be pleased. To this Babbage
responded acidly that his mother already knew her son
deserved honors, since foreign countries had given them to
him.

When his friends reminded him that he would be doing an
injustice to those who proposed him for the chair, however,
Babbage finally tore up his letter of refusal and wrote another
accepting the professorship at Cambridge, surely enjoying at
least a twinge of vindictive glee when he considered the Chair
of Newton.

In January of 1829 Babbage was back in England to perform his first official duty as Lucasian professor. True to
form, he upset the applecart again, disagreeing with university officers on the winners of prizes for graduating students.
It was unfortunate for Cambridge—and Babbage as well—
that he spent so little of his time on the premises in the
eleven years he held the post, even though it paid him the
tiny sum of £80 a year.

Far more important to Babbage than the Lucasian chair
was his Difference Engine. His year away from it had renewed
his enthusiasm, and now he was ready to pick up where he
had left off.

TO PICK UP THE PIECES

Although his children remained at 5 Devonshire with their
grandmother, Babbage could not bring himself to return.
Claiming it was to "escape the din of the organ grinders," he
purchased the house at 1 Dorset Street, Manchester Square.
The place had been owned by Dr. Wollaston, first to encour-

age Babbage with his Difference Engine. Wollaston had died in December, 1828, just before Babbage's return.

Dorset Street was very quiet, and the house had large grounds surrounding it. Babbage converted the coachhouse into a forge and foundry for the metalwork the engine required and tried to begin work. It was difficult for a number of reasons.

Even before he had left Italy, Babbage had written Georgiana's brother, Wolryche Whitmore, to approach the former chancellor of the exchequer (now Lord Goderich) to arrange for more money. Unfortunately Goderich could not recall that any such additional appropriations had been discussed back in 1823. Furthermore, the vile rumors of Babbage pocketing government money were now being publicly printed in publications including the newspaper *The Record*.

Babbage's friends, led by John Herschel, had done what they could to set the record straight in *The Times*, but Babbake went to the duke of Wellington for more official backing. Wellington had often visited Babbage's home and was much impressed by the Difference Engine. On one such occasion he brought along the Countess Wilton, who also expressed great interest in the machine. As they stood watching the engine work, the countess asked Babbage what was the most difficult part in designing the machine.

"Ah, that is an easy question to answer, my Lady," said Babbage. "It is not so much the contriving of mechanisms to make each *individual* movement as it is of the almost innumerable *combinations* among all the contrivances." As he glanced at Wellington, the duke said, "I know that difficulty well," thinking no doubt of Waterloo and other military engagements.

Wellington asked the Royal Society to look into the matter and a committee was quickly formed. It backed Babbage to the hilt, as John Herschel's conclusion indicated:

Finally, taking into consideration all that has been already said, and relying not less on the talent and skill displayed as a mechanician, in the prosecution of this arduous undertaking, for what remains,—than on the matured and digested plan and admirable execution of what is accomplished—your Committee have no hesitation in giving it as their opinion, that in the present state of Mr. Babbage's engine, they do regard it as likely to fulfill the expectations entertained of it by its inventor.

J.F.W. HERSCHEL, Chairman

February, 1829

The committee estimated that another three years should see the completion of the Difference Engine, and the government therefore advanced another £1,500, making a total of £3,000 "the Publick" had put up. Babbage estimated that he had spent something more than twice that much himself.

The investigations took time, of course, and work on the engine was stopped on May 9, 1829, for a year. It became apparent to Babbage that even the new government grant would be only a drop in the bucket. Again with the help of friends, he prevailed on the chancellor of the exchequer, now Mr. Goulburn, to advance another £3,000. At this time, however, Goulburn told Babbage that the government would appreciate it if he could work on the calculating section and the printing section separately, so that in any event there would be some practical equipment resulting from all the work.

With continued strong backing from Wellington, Babbage received a further grant of £3,000, making a total of £9,000. The government also promised to build him a fireproof room on property adjoining his, for the safeguarding of his priceless blueprints. In the spring of 1830, then, work resumed on the Difference Engine.

There were still problems. For one thing, Babbage's health seemed about to break down again, and he told friends he must rest if he was ever to finish the engine. Work proceeded raggedly, and Clement was becoming a problem. Furthermore, there was no clearcut agreement as to who owned the engine, and so on.

In the midst of all his troubles with the engine, Babbage still found the time and energy to make more enemies. Shortly after the government had obligated itself rather heavily for development of his engine the lord chancellor, Henry, Lord Brougham, called Babbage to ask if he and John Herschel would accept knighthood. Instead of accepting with grace, Babbage bluntly told Brougham that knighthood was an honor fit for mayors and other persons but by no means sufficient for men of science. He made it plain that he would consider only a life peerage for himself. While John Herschel might accept the Order of the Bath, Babbage himself had no wish to join what he termed "the circle of the B-Knighted." Herschel did indeed accept the honor, and Harris Nicolas was knighted in Babbage's place. What queer sort of satisfaction Babbage got from such a perverse refusal we can only guess.

In the same year Babbage published his *Reflections on the Decline of Science in England and Some of its Causes.* He made it quite clear what—and particularly who—those causes were. While much of the book advanced good ideas, it was spoiled by Babbage's bias, vindictiveness, and personal attacks on men with whom he did not agree. It is a tribute to the patience and tolerance of the Royal Society that he was not expelled for the things he wrote about that organization.

There was much more that Babbage had to do on his return to England than merely catch up on work with the Difference Engine. First he had to prepare an account of the great Congress of Philosophers at Berlin in September of 1828, which he had attended on his way home. This appeared in the *Edinburgh Journal of Science,* as did his "Note on the Description of Mammalia."

With his wealth of information on machinery, Babbage

published the "Essay on the general Principles which regulate the Application of Machinery." This modest report was a hint of the monumental work to come from Babbage soon, and to which he devoted much of his time. In 1831 he printed *Specimen of Logarithmic Tables,* in twenty-one volumes. This was a set of tables like no other before it, as Babbage described it himself:

> The object of this Work, of which *one single copy only* was printed, is to ascertain by experiment the tints of the paper and colours of the inks least fatiguing to the eye.
>
> One-hundred and fifty-one variously coloured papers were chosen, and the same two plates of my stereotype Table of Logarithms were printed upon them in inks of the following colours; light blue, dark blue, light green, dark green, olive, yellow, light red, dark red, purple, and black.
>
> Each of these twenty volumes contains papers of the same colour, numbered in the same order, and there are two volumes printed with each kind of ink.
>
> The twenty-first volume contains metallic printing of the same specimen in gold, silver, and copper, upon vellum and on variously-coloured papers.
>
> For the same purpose, about thirty-five copies of the complete table of logarithms were printed on thick drawing paper of various tints.

Here was an example of the vast range of Babbage's curiosity and his logical, penetrating mind. Surely fatigue was a factor in the reading of long columns of figures, and this was an attempt to minimize that fatigue. Other publications included a letter in the *Correspondence Mathématique et Physique* "On the Proportion of Letters occurring in Various Languages," a "Sketch of the Philosophical Characters of Dr. Wollaston and Sir H. Davy," and a letter in the *Edinburgh Journal of Science,* "On the Proportion of Births of the two Sexes amongst Legitimate and Illegitimate Children."

OPERATIONS RESEARCH

The great work of Babbage in 1832—surely his finest book—was *Economy of Manufactures and Machinery*. A critic commented that "Yes, it is a very nice book—just the kind of book anybody could have written." Actually only Babbage could have done justice to the subject. In this one book he launched the concept of "operations research" that would not flower fully until World War II when such efficiency was needed to win a war. When the "efficiency expert" Frederick W. Taylor wrote his book in 1913, it was a distillation of much that Babbage had said about production eighty years earlier. Babbage's book went into many reprintings, was translated into four foreign languages, and was published in America. In 1963 it was reprinted in the United States as a classic and again went into several printings. In the words of one reviewer, the book was a "hymn to machinery." It was far more than that. Babbage was most proud of the fact that a workman who read it told the author: "That book made me think!" In the book, Babbage's own thoughts ranged far and wide:

> Political economists have been reproached with too small a use of facts, and too large an employment of theory . . . let it not be feared that erroneous deductions may be made from recorded facts; the errors which arise from the absence of facts are far more numerous and more durable than those which result from unsound reasoning respecting true data.

In discussing the division of labor, Adam Smith had pointed out three benefits: (1) the increase in dexterity of every particular workman, (2) saving in time formerly lost in passing parts from one form of work to another, (3) development of specialized machines letting one man do the work of many. Babbage added that it let one purchase only the skill needed for a particular job—one of his arguments in favor of calculating engines.

Babbage was also interested in the mail service, and even experimented with transmission systems using small cylinders running on wires to deliver messages within an office or from one building to another:

> Let us imagine a series of high pillars erected at frequent intervals, perhaps every hundred feet, and as nearly as possible in a straight line between two post towns. An iron or steel wire must be stretched over proper supports, fixed on each of these pillars, and terminating at the end of every three or five miles, as may be found expedient, in a very strong support, by which it may be stretched. A narrow cylindrical tin case, to contain the letters, might be suspended by two wheels rolling upon this wire; the cases being so constructed as to enable the wheels to pass unimpeded by the fixed supports of the wire.

Babbage's idea for a sort of mail-order monorail seems old-fashioned in the light of advances made in communication, but consider this incidental suggestion he made in connection with it: "Nor is it impossible that the stretched wire might itself be available for a species of telegraphic communication yet more rapid."

This was written in 1832, six years before Morse patented his telegraph. Babbage suggested that the government go into the business of carrying books and parcels in addition to just letters since they already had the organization. He had another idea that was simple but perceptive and brilliant.

When Babbage and Georgiana first set up housekeeping in 1814 on Devonshire Street, a relative supplied them with game free. However, Babbage found that the cost of sending the meat was as much as if he had bought it. He later applied this idea to the mail service which at that time charged for letters depending on how far they were sent. Babbage's argument was that the actual transport of the mail was slight in cost compared with the collection and delivery costs. Why not charge a fixed price, regardless of how far the mail was sent? Today we accept this as common practice, but in Babbage's time the idea was revolutionary, and it was some time before Sir Rowland Hill of the postal department did adopt it. To Babbage must go the credit for the original "Penny Post," eventually used around the world.

There were many other projects, as varied as his far-ranging imagination could conceive. For instance, he made an "air-shot gun" by stretching parchment over the mouth of a large funnel and put out the flame of a candle several feet distant. The gun also reproduced the coronet of smoke he had seen at Vesuvius.

THE POLITICIAN

With all his other interests, Babbage found time to involve himself in politics. At first this consisted only of aiding the campaigns of others, including his brother-in-law, Wolryche Whitmore at Bridgnorth, and Henry Cavendish, candidate from Cambridge. But after the passing of the Reform Bill in 1832 and the dissolution of Parliament, he himself became a candidate for Commons from the borough of Finsbury. He ran on the Whig, or Liberal ticket, and one of his goals was freedom for slaves.

It is strange that he should have taken the chance of becoming a member of Parliament since this would have forced him to neglect the Difference Engine. It did not matter, for he was beaten badly, coming out last on a slate of four. He wrote a play, entitled *Politics and Poetry, or the Decline of Science*, heavily laden with his bitterness over favoritism and unfair treatment. The concluding speech aptly described his own position: "I am fairly beaten—thrown overboard, with not a leg to stand upon; and all I have to do is go to bed now, to sleep off this fever; and tomorrow, take leave of politics, and try to be myself once more."

There were serious and growing troubles with the Difference Engine. In later years his son would claim that a few hundred more pounds would have completed the engine, but Babbage's friend Isambard Brunel was not so optimistic: In 1831 Brunel estimated another £12,000 was required to finish the engine, plus a cost of £2,000 to £2,500 a year for keeping up the shops and buildings.

By now the Difference Engine had grown in size to about that of a large barrel, and its potential grew accordingly. If at this point his other projects could have kept Babbage from improving his original designs, the engine might have been successfully achieved. But such was not to be the case. As before, he changed the plans faster than his workmen could complete the mechanical parts. These changes cost money, and there were delays in getting payment to Clement and his crew.

The engine was still housed in Clement's machine shop, where it represented perhaps a third of his total work. But as the years passed with little progress toward a practical engine, relations between inventor, government, and engineer grew increasingly strained. Crisis came again in 1833, when Babbage ordered Clement to transfer the engine to the now completed workshop at his home. Claiming he was owed money, Clement refused, holding the engine, the drawings, and the tools built to make the engine as insurance against the debt. On April 10 Clement discharged the men working on the Difference Engine.

THE ENGINE STOPS

Alarmed at these developments, and disappointed at the small return on the £17,000 it had spent, the government again stopped its payments. In the ensuing legal argument over who owed whom and owned what, it was agreed that Babbage could have some of the completed parts of his engine and his drawings. Clement insisted on keeping the complicated tools that had eaten up most of the money. Worse, he told Babbage that should there be a fire or other catastrophe in his shops, he would not be responsible for what became of the engine. It must have been enough to make Babbage ill again—surveying the result of more than ten years of his life in the small assemblage of gears and shafts, rods and levers that sat forlornly in the empty workshop amid the hundreds of square feet of drawings that had poured from Babbage's fertile brain.

AN EVEN GRANDER DREAM

Charles Babbage was forty-one years old, a widower with three children, a fine home, and a fair amount of money. He was a respected member of a number of societies. His ability as a mathematician was unquestioned. Even without his Difference Engine he would have been acclaimed as scientist and engineer. Surely he would have been a happier man. But without question he had become obsessed with the idea of a mechanical computer and dedicated his life to its perfection.

Describing his predicament and how he had profited so much less than his workers, Babbage wrote:

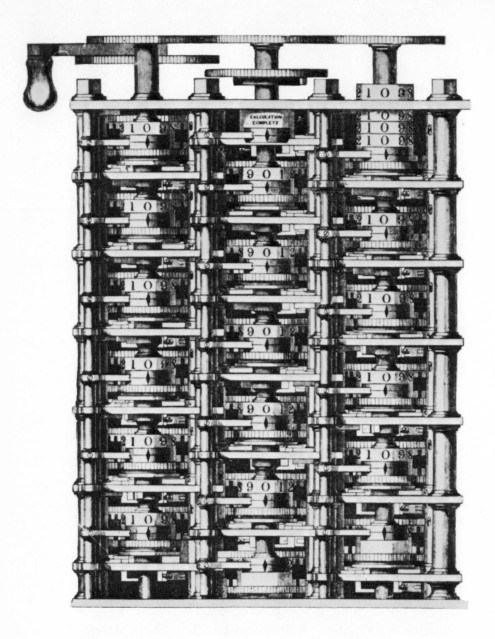

A small portion of the Difference Engine that Babbage assembled
in 1833

> When I first employed Clement he possessed one lathe (a
> very good one) and his workshop was in a small front
> kitchen. When I ceased to employ him, he valued his
> tools at several thousand pounds, and he had converted a
> large chapel into a workshop. Whitworth has made a fortune
> of which he spends with great liberality.

This was true, for Joseph Whitworth became the greatest
toolmaker in England, working to a precision of millionths of
an inch, and developing screw threads that served as British
standards until the 1940s. He was knighted for his work.

Dr. Dionysus Lardner, an expert on technical matters,
pointed out angrily that Watt and his backers had spent
£50,000 merely *improving* the steam engine before they
made a penny from it, a sum several times that spent by the
government on the Difference Engine: "A proposition to
reduce arithmetic to the dominion of a mechanism—to substitute an automaton for a compositor—to throw the powers
of thought into wheelwork could not fail to awaken the
attention of the world."

The world had been awakened, but barely, and now it
seemed about to go back to sleep. Lord Rosse would admit
that "if the Calculating Engine itself had entirely failed, the
money expended by Government in the attempt to make it
would be well repaid by the advancement it caused in the art
of mechanical construction." And the engine had not
"entirely failed." In 1833 Babbage desperately ordered a small
section of it put together. This section, consisting of part of
the calculating portion, functioned perfectly and remains
today in the Science Museum at South Kensington, a tribute
to Babbage's vision.

Had Babbage settled for a simpler Difference Engine he
might have completed it and made good his bargain with the
government. However, perhaps science was the winner after
all, for Babbage might have become so wrapped up in the

modest but successful engine he would not have had time for the far greater invention now bursting from his busy brain— a machine to make the Difference Engine seem a child's toy, like the silver dancing lady of the robot-maker Merlin.

Merlin had never disposed of that little silver dancer. After he died it was sold to Weekes Museum on Cockspur Street. When that firm went out of business, the toy was sold at auction. Walking through London one day, Babbage was pleasantly surprised to see the familiar little figure—completed at last—in a shop window. He lost no time in buying the marvelously made automaton, remembering his youthful fascination with the toy.

He kept the dancing lady in one glass case in his drawing room and a small working model of the Difference Engine in another. When he had guests he would often set both "engines" to going at once, the lady dancing gaily and the engine diligently computing tables. Sadly, but with little surprise, Babbage noted that the dancing doll always drew more attention, and on one occasion all but an American and a man from Holland were grouped happily about the silver lady. He sadly said to a friend, "Look, in that further room— England. Look again at this—two foreigners!"

A lesser man than Babbage would have been defeated after the setbacks he had suffered. But with the Difference Engine a shambles of failure, he rose from its wreckage with an idea for another engine. Charles Babbage would build an Analytical Engine—a machine that would not merely follow a set pattern to produce tables, it would solve *any* problem put to it!

 The Analytical Engine

In the last grim days of his Difference Engine, Babbage put together a small part of that machine in the hope of demonstrating its worth to the government. The engine had powers far beyond what he had originally promised. For example, by adding a few more connecting gears, the result produced in the last column of wheels could be fed back to other parts of the machine. This gave Babbage the idea of arranging the engine not in a line, as originally designed, but with its axes around a central shaft. The result column was then near the input column and easily useful. This operation, which Babbage described as "the engine biting its own tail," meant the machine controlled itself. A result produced from the engine could be used to call up further information from the engine's memory store. By feeding this information to its mill, more complete answers would be produced. Here was the germ of today's computer program that makes such machines automatic. Babbage foresaw his engine working out a multiplication problem, extracting the square root of that product, then finding the logarithm of the root so that further mathematical operations could be done.

Babbage described the birth of the idea for his Analytical Engine in these words:

> At last having exhausted, during years of labour, the principle of successive carriages, it occurred to me that it might be possible to teach mechanism to accomplish another mental process, namely—to foresee. This idea occurred to me in October, 1834. It cost me much thought, but the principle was arrived at in a short time. As soon as that was attained, the next step was to teach the mechanism which could foresee to act upon that foresight. This was not so difficult; certain mechanical means were soon devised which, although

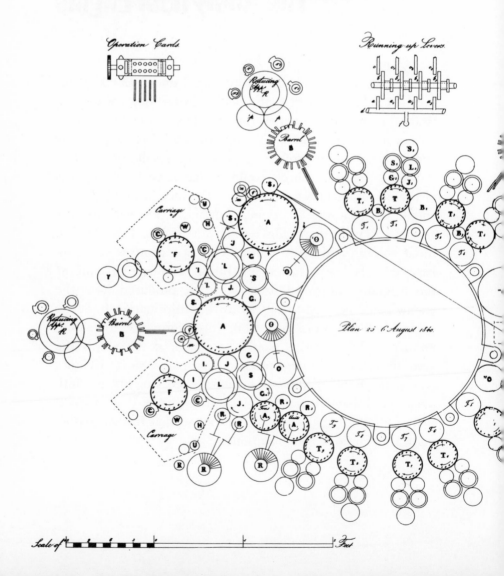

far from simple, were yet sufficient to demonstrate the possibility of constructing such machinery.

The circular arrangement of the axes of the Difference Engine round large central wheels led to the most extended prospects. The whole of arithmetic now appeared within the grasp of mechanisms. A vague glimpse even of an Analytical Engine at length opened out, and I pursued with enthusiasm the shadowy vision. The drawings and the experiments were of the most costly kind. Draftsmen of the highest order were necessary to economize the labour of my own head; whilst skilled workmen were required to execute the experimental machinery to which I was obliged constantly to have recourse.

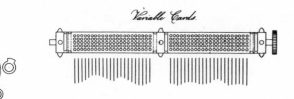

The general plan of Babbage's new calculator

The unfinished Difference Engine had proved fantastically expensive; the government and Babbage had spent the equivalent of about $180,000—equal to several millions of dollars today. It was obvious that the Analytical Engine would be even more expensive.

The Difference Engine was designed to do the most menial mental labor in the field of mathematics, that of simple and repeated additions to a set rule. The Analytical Engine, on the other hand, would tackle the most difficult mental tasks. There were to be two major parts to the engine: a store where numbers and tables would be kept, and an operating part called the mill. The mathematics would be performed in the mill on numbers taken from the store section. (In the United States the words "memory" and "arithmetic unit" have replaced Babbage's terms, but British computer people still say store and mill.) In addition there would be an input and an output, the latter printing out the results of the engine's computations.

A LOOM FOR WEAVING NUMBERS

The earlier Difference Engine was set by hand and then cranked to produce its tables. The vastly more complex Analytical Engine, capable of working any kind of problem in mathematics, required a much more sophisticated input or program. Babbage planned to program the engine with punched cards, much like the IBM cards in use today. This clever idea exploded in his brain one day as he admired a portrait of the Frenchman Joseph Marie Jacquard woven with silk thread. Jacquard's loom had produced the picture automatically, controlled by some 24,000 cards, each punched with 1,050 holes into which the needles fitted as required to weave the patterns.

J.M. JACQUARD.

Né a Lyon le 7 Juillet 1752
Mort le 7 Août 1834

Jacquard's portrait woven with colored thread gave Babbage the idea of using punched cards in his Analytical Engine

The weaving of pictures with colored threads probably began in China, and by 1000 B.C. it was a well-developed art. At first these artisans in silk wove patterns manually and most likely freehand. Later it was found that a pattern drawn on paper was an aid to the weavers as they moved the shuttle and its thread through the warp threads. Gradually the pattern came to be made on a paper ruled in squares that simulated the crossing of warp and weft or woof threads.

Even the early Chinese patterns required hundreds, or thousands of liftings of the warp threads. To save time it became the custom simply to punch holes in the squared paper to mark the proper pattern. Finally, in 1725, the weaver Basile Bouchon of Lyons, France, thought of a clever improvement: instead of lifting threads by hand, Bouchon did the job automatically. He set the ends of the loom's needles against a roll of paper on which a pattern was punched. This moved the proper needles more accurately and quickly than a human assistant could and mechanized the weaving of patterns in cloth.

A French engineer named Falcon improved the idea in 1728 by using punched cards instead of a roll of paper, and by 1801 Jacquard had developed an automatic loom that one

A *Jacquard loom: "The analogy of the Analytical Engine with this well-known process is nearly perfect,"* stated Babbage

man could run. As a demonstration of what his looms could do with their punched card instructions, Jacquard had them weave a number of portraits of himself. These were some thirty inches square, precise as a line engraving but in beautiful colors. His looms were so successful they sold by the tens of thousands.

In England, the Luddites, led by half-witted Ned Ludd, had earlier smashed machinery for weaving stockings. And in France the weavers rose up against Jacquard's new loom because they thought it threatened their livelihood. On one occasion Jacquard barely escaped a mob intent on killing him. Jacquard received the Legion of Honor and a pension from Napoleon. He died in August, 1834, just two months before Babbage conceived the idea of the Analytical Engine. Gratefully the Englishman adopted the punched-card idea from France:

> It is known as a fact that the Jacquard loom is capable of weaving any design which the imagination of man may conceive. It is also the constant practice for skilled artists to be employed by manufacturers in designing patterns. These patterns are then sent to a peculiar artist, who, by means of a certain machine, punches holes in a set of pasteboard cards in such a manner that when those cards are placed in a Jacquard loom, it will then weave upon its produce the exact pattern designed by the artist.
>
> Now the manufacturer may use, for the warp and wefts of his work, threads which are all of the same colour; let us suppose them to be unbleached or white threads. In this case the cloth will be woven all of one colour but there will be a damask pattern upon it such as the artist designed.
>
> But the manufacturer might use the same cards, and put into the warp threads of any other colour. Every thread might even be of a different colour, or of a different shade of colour; but in all these cases the *form* of the pattern will be precisely the same—the colours only will differ.
>
> The analogy of the Analytical Engine with this well-known process is nearly perfect.

THE ENGINE'S INPUT

Babbage's son, Henry, was once asked "How do you set the question? Do you write it on paper and put it into the machine?" The questioner was no doubt surprised when Babbage described how close he was to the answer:

> given the problem, the mathematician must first of all settle the operations and the particular quantities each is to be performed on and the time for each operation.
>
> Then the superintendent of the engine must make a "Number Card" for each "given number," and settle the particular column in the machine on to which each "given number" is to be first received and assign columns for every intermediate result expected to arise in the course of the calculation.
>
> He will then prepare "Directive Cards" accordingly, and these, together with the necessary "Operation Cards" being placed in the engine, the question will have been set; not exactly as my friend suggested, written on paper, but in cardboard, and motion being supplied the engine will give the answer.

THE STORE OR MEMORY

The store was similar to present-day computer memories, where information the computer will need to solve problems is kept.

> I propose in the Engine I am constructing to have places for only a thousand constants, because I think it will be more than sufficient. But if it were required to have ten, or even a hundred times that number, it would be quite possible to make it, such is the simplicity of that portion of the Engine.

This led Babbage to two remarkable concepts: the general purpose computer and the program, which is used to instruct the machine.

> The Analytical Engine is therefore a machine of the most general nature. Whatever formula it is required to develop, the law of its development must be communicated to it by two sets of cards. When these have been placed, the engine is special for that particular formula. The numerical value of its constants must then be put on the columns of wheels below them, and on setting the Engine in motion it will calculate and print the numerical results of that formula.
>
> Every set of cards made for any formula will at any future time recalculate that formula with whatever constants may be required. Thus the Analytical Engine will possess a library of its own. Every set of cards once made will at any future time reproduce the calculations for which it was first arranged. . . .

Echoing his father, Henry Babbage also accurately predicted what computer people today call "software." He said:

> the cards, once made for any given problem, can be used for the same problem, with any other "given numbers," and it would not be necessary to prepare them a second time— they could be carefully kept for future use. Each formula would require its own set of cards, and by degrees the engine would have a library of its own.
>
> Thus the values for any number of Life Insurance Policies might be calculated one after the other by merely supplying fresh cards for the age, amount, rate of interest, etc., for each individual case.

The insurance industry was among the first to make use of the electronic computer when it became available a century later.

A set of three "operation cards" for the Analytical Engine is reproduced here.

Directive Card	Operation Card	
1st	..	Places a on column 1 of Store
2nd	..	" b " 2 "
3rd	..	" c " 3 "
4th	..	" d " 4 "
5th	..	Brings a from Store to Mill
6th	..	" b " " "
..	1	Multiplies a and $b = p$
7th	..	Takes p to column 5 of Store where it is kept for use and record
8th	..	Brings p into Mill
9th	..	Brings c into Mill
..	2	Adds p and $c = q$
10th	..	Takes q to column 6 of Store
11th	..	Brings d into Mill
12th	..	" q "
..	3	Multiplies $d \times q = p_2$
13th	..	Takes p_2 to column 7 of Store
14th	..	Takes p_2 to printing or stereo-moulding apparatus

It is remarkable to compare it with the following sample taken from a text on computer programming:

Symbol	Operation Code	Meaning
S	0	Stop.
R	1	Read data from input device and place in proper "address."
W	2	Write data located in specified address on input-output device.
B	3	Branch if number has negative sign.
A	4	Add data in specified address to major accumulator.
S	5	Subtract data from major accumulator.
SH	6	Shift accumulator contents (right or left as specified).
ST	7	Store contents in accumulator in specified address.
SP	8	Perform special operation.

If any special tables were required, the Analytical Engine could calculate them.

> Thus the Analytical Engine first computes and punches on cards its own tabular numbers. These are brought to it by its attendant when demanded. But the Engine itself takes care that the *right* card is brought to it by verifying the *number* of that card by the number of the card which it demanded. The Engine will always reject a wrong card by continually ringing a loud bell and stopping itself until supplied with the precise intellectual food it demands.

THE MILL OR ARITHMETIC UNIT

The mill was an impressive piece of machinery that performed the actual calculations.

> The Analytical Engine I propose will have the power of expressing every number it uses to fifty places of figures. It will multiply any two such numbers together, and then, if required, will divide the product of one hundred figures by numbers of fifty places of figures.
> Supposing the velocity of the moving parts of the Engine to be not greater than forty feet per minute, I have no doubt that
> > Sixty additions or subtractions may be completed in one minute
> > One multiplication of two numbers, each of fifty figures, in one minute
> > One division of a number having 100 places of figures by another of 50 in one minute.

THE OUTPUT

Like the Difference Engine, the Analytical Engine would print out its answers automatically. However, this output portion would be more sophisticated. The printing section would provide one or two copies of the results, as desired. It would also produce a stereotype mold for printing a quantity of copies of the results. Printing could even be done on metal plates if necessary. In addition to this automatic printout of

A drawing of the mill or arithmetic unit: Figure 1 is a gear system for carrying tens. Figure 2 shows a toothed wheel for adding digits to numbers already in the mill. Figure 3 shows racks and spur gears for adding series of numbers

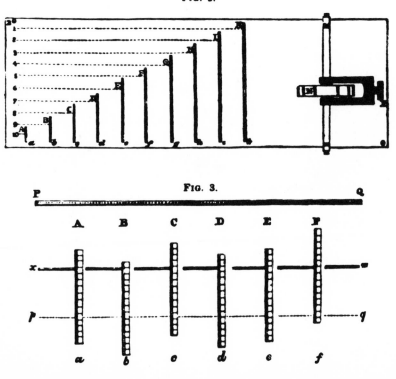

Fɪɢ. 1.

Fɪɢ. 2.

Fɪɢ. 3.

results, the Analytical Engine would also include a device for punching the required holes in cards, a forerunner of the keypunch machine. Babbage's punched cards contained eleven rows, with places for nine holes in each row for a total of ninety-nine holes per card.

Babbage had earlier devised a method of locking together the metal number plates selected by the engine for printing an answer. To test how well the locking mechanism held, he gave the linked plates to his children to play with. They survived several years of "rather rough" use, he reported.

PROBLEM-SOLVING MACHINE

When Babbage described the four most difficult parts of the Analytical Engine, the first was the matter of "carrying tens." He successfully worked out a mechanism for making additions simultaneously in the Engine. Today this is called parallel processing and greatly increases the speed of a computer.

The second problem was building an engine that could operate with an infinite number of terms. Here, Babbage substituted time for space, and proposed to replenish the 1,000-term store with different information as often as necessary over the required time.

The third difficulty lay in making the engine capable of using logarithms, sines, and so on. This snag was handily solved by having the engine ring a bell as a signal for such information.

The fourth hurdle was to make the engine entirely foolproof and accurate in spite of errors or even deliberate attempts by operators to throw it off. Babbage designed protective mechanisms which would guard against such happenings. Visitors frequently asked Babbage, "Can the engine produce the right answers if it gets the wrong information?" The computer engineer of today answers this with an expression called GIGO. This stands for "Garbage In, Garbage

Out." In other words, the computer's answer is only as good as the information put into the machine.

"As soon as the Analytical Engine exists, it will necessarily guide the future course of science. . . ," Babbage wrote prophetically. More specifically, he said:

> The whole branch of chemistry, and with it crystallography, would become a branch of mathematical analysis, which like astronomy, taking its constants from observation, would enable us to predict the character of any new compound, and possibly indicate the source from which its formation might be accepted.

His accuracy was borne out in a 1953 article detailing the development of computers at Cambridge and listing some scientific applications, with the following at the head of that list:

Theoretical Chemistry

Crystallography

In the 1830s there was not the benefit of this century and more of hindsight, and Charles Babbage fought a losing fight for his wonderful engine.

THE GOVERNMENT GIVES UP

In spite of Babbage's mechanical successes, the government decided to stop its aid no matter what sort of engine Babbage wanted to build—even the amazing Analytical Engine with a memory, able to foretell!

Babbage had a decision to make, a financial one crucial to his career. His draftsman was demanding more money. Needing advice, Babbage wrote to his mother, outlining the problem. She answered immediately: "My dear son, you have advanced far in the accomplishment of a great object, which is worthy of your ambition. You are capable of completing it. My advice is—pursue it, even if it should oblige you to live on bread and cheese."

Reinforced, Babbage made his decision: "I at length laid down a principle—that, except in rare cases, I would never do anything myself if I could afford to hire another person who could do it for me." On this costly basis he continued as best he could the work on the Analytical Engine. As always, Babbage's fertile mind was involved in many other ways as he wrestled with the technical and financial problems of developing his great Analytical Engine.

In 1834 tragedy struck him again. His second Georgiana died—his daughter in her teens. He was desolate. Only three of his eight children remained: Herschel, Dugald, and Henry. He threw himself deeper into his work.

That year, he read a paper called "Geological Theory of the Isothermal Surfaces of the Earth," based on observations he had made at the Temple of Serapis, Possuoli, Italy. In 1835 and 1836 Babbage did some work for the Bank of England on improving printing and eliminating the dangers of forgery. As a member of a committee, Babbage turned up the solution in a method of printing banknotes used in Scotland. He was rewarded with only a vote of thanks and bitterly noted that this "tribute" usually was reserved for warriors and statesmen. Another rebuff had come in 1835: he wanted the post of registrar-general of births, deaths, and marriages, but a brother-in-law of someone got it.

A MAN FOR ALL SCIENCE

In 1837 he published *The Ninth Bridgewater Treatise, A Fragment,* a statement of his views on how science and religion could be reconciled. The Bridgewater Treatises had originally been published with a grant calling for evidence favoring natural religion, but Babbage published the Ninth at his own expense. In it he argued against the implications in the original series that science, and mathematics in particular, was incompatible with religion. In commenting on religious miracles, Babbage drew a parallel with his calculating engines. As one writer later put it, Babbage thought of God as a supernatural "programmer."

He published his paper "On Some Impressions in Sandstone" in the *Proceedings of the Geological Society*. And at an 1838 meeting of the British Association at Newcastle he read a paper entitled "Short account of a method by which Engraving on Wood may be rendered more useful for the Illustration and Description of Machinery."

Babbage resigned from his Lucasian professorship in 1839, "to devote himself more fully to completion of his engines," although it would not seem that the professorship was a great responsibility. In the eleven years he held the chair, he had never lived or even lectured at Cambridge.

THE RAILROAD YEARS

Brunel, who was now building railroads, retained Babbage on a consulting basis. Babbage brought his usual thoroughness to this assignment and spent many hours in a railroad car, recording its motion on a long graph. His careful "dynamometer" analyses—at his own expense—resulted in the adoption of the wide gauge track for British railroads. He recommended many safety features such as speed indicators for all locomotives. He suggested a primitive recorder of the speed and motions of a train. And he even invented the cowcatcher, which soon became standard.

Among his safety suggestions was one for separating a

derailed engine from the rest of the train. He also described a semaphore signal for railroads that would not only warn an engineer of a train ahead, but tell him how long since it had passed the signal. This was done by the locomotive actuating the signal to a vertical position when it passed. Then the semaphore arm slowly moved back down to the horizontal in a certain length of time. The following engineer could tell the time interval by noting the angle of the semaphore.

Once, making scientific tests of how far an unpowered car would roll when released at a given speed, Babbage and his son Herschel were stranded in the car on a bridge. Spreading his cape for a sail, Babbage let the wind blow the car to the other side of the bridge and safety.

The time was one of exciting ideas. Sir George Cayley had Babbage inspect a new kind of engine for him. Unlike Watt's steam engines, this was a gas engine, and Cayley had in mind to use it—of all things—for a flying machine! Babbage made no comment.

But it was also a conservative time. It can be imagined how Babbage felt at a luncheon to have a banker oppose railroad development on the grounds that it would permit a teller to rob him and escape "at 20 miles an hour." Particularly when Babbage had recorded a speed of 78 miles an hour on one of his test runs.

MISSING MILESTONE

The two men with whom Babbage had in 1812 formed the Analytical Society had become successful and well known. John Herschel, after a short try at being a lawyer, had gone into astronomy and picked up his father's work. Knighted in 1830 (when Babbage had declined that "dubious honour"), he spent a very successful four years at Cape Colony in South

Africa cataloging the stars in the southern hemisphere as his father William had done in the northern hemisphere. Returning, he was made a baronet by Queen Victoria at her coronation in 1838. Later he became president of the Royal Astronomical Society and then master of the Mint. George Peacock had achieved a reputation as an astronomer and mathematician but then went into the ministry. He took his doctor of divinity degree in 1839 and soon was named dean of Ely College, in which position he served well.

Two of the brash, brilliant young trio of Cambridge rebels had achieved solid fame. But for Charles Babbage there was growing bitterness as his bright dreams began to fade.

 **Lady Lovelace**

In his paper on the Difference Engine in 1834, Dr. Dionysus Lardner had said that the world could not ignore an engine that put thought into wheelwork. Yet the world, or at least the English world, *did* ignore it. They paid no heed to the Analytical Engine either, perhaps because of the apparent failure of the earlier engine. Babbage's decision to work on his engines rather than write about them contributed to this neglect. The theory of the Analytical Engine was never described simply and briefly. Aside from a handful of friends, no one knew much about the new machine, and no one seemed to care. The first real recognition came from Italy.

Babbage's Italian friend, Baron Plana, learned enough through correspondence to be impressed with the engine and wrote to Babbage that it would give mathematical analysis a powerful tool for executing even difficult formulas and equations. Babbage received an invitation through Plana to attend a scientific meeting in Turin and describe his new engine. Delighted, Babbage made the trip in 1840. There were, in fact, a number of Babbages who went to Italy that year.

Herschel had married a girl named Laura Jones, and in 1840 the couple set off for Italy, where he would assist Brunel who was making surveys for the Genoa-Turin Railway. Dugald and Henry had each spent two years at University College and had some training at Babbage's workshops at 1 Dorset Street where they were taught drafting and some mechanical work. Shortly after Herschel left, Dugald too journeyed to Italy to serve as an apprentice engineer with him.

Charles Babbage had been welcomed and well treated in Italy in 1827; he looked forward to this return visit. Gathering up his papers, drawings, and a few models, he set out for Turin. Not only was his presentation hailed loudly by Plana and other scientists, but he was treated to three audiences with the king. They discussed scientific subjects—including the new electric telegraph—and visited a winery. Babbage was even permitted to present a gift to the queen, one of Jacquard's woven portraits. When Babbage took final leave of the king, he was presented with a medal.

DEFEAT AT HOME

Returning from Italy confident and with renewed enthusiasm for the Analytical Engine, Babbage again approached the government. He met on several occasions with Prime Minister Sir Robert Peel and argued eloquently for the continuation of *any* program—Difference Engine Number 1, Analytical Engine, or Difference Engine Number 2. Circumstances were against him.

Most confusing was Babbage's introduction of the new Analytical Engine, Peel told him. Perhaps if he had kept quiet about it. . . . Was the prime minister suggesting that Babbage should suppress the monumental idea of the new computer? No, but surely Babbage must realize the government's awkward position. It had spent £17,000 on a calculating engine only to have the inventor tell them he had a far better idea. What would that require and how explain it to the taxpayers?

Behind the scenes, Sir George Airy, now astronomer royal, continued to tell Peel that the engine was a humbug, no matter what Babbage called it. But it was not Airy alone who killed Babbage's chances. Peel did have a serious problem with Parliament which he expressed in this way to a friend: "I should like a little previous consideration before I move in a thin house of country gentlemen a large vote for the creation of a wooden man to calculate tables from the formula $X^2 + X + 41$."

It was the age-old battle of ignorance versus science, and in the House of Commons Peel scathingly suggested that Babbage's engine be set to calculate the year when it would be of use. Mr. Hawes of Lambeth was the only "Aye" for the engine when Peel had finished.

The Difference Engine and its successor toppled again amid the rubble of government blunders and the dust of indifference. But even as Babbage's future looked bleakest, things were happening again in Italy that would give his engines another push toward life.

THE COUNTESS ADA

At Turin there had been a mathematical engineer named L. F. Menebrea, and like Baron Plana he was impressed with what he heard. He went further than Plana, however, and in October, 1842, he published an article called "A Sketch of the Analytical Engine Invented by Charles Babbage" in *Bibliothèque Universelle de Genève*. Menebrea fully understood Babbage's new machine, producing as good a description of it as Lardner had done in 1834 for the Difference Engine.

In summarizing, Menebrea pointed out that the Analytical Engine would offer "rigid accuracy . . . economy of time," and most important, "economy of intelligence."

> Now the engine, from its capability of performing by itself all purely material operations, spares intellectual labour, which may be more profitably employed. Thus the engine may be considered as a real manufactory of figures, which will lend its aid to those many useful sciences and arts that depend on numbers. Again, who can foresee the consequences of such an invention? In truth, how many precious observations remain practically barren for the progress of the sciences, because there are not powers sufficient for computing the results! And what discouragement does the perspective of a long and arid computation cast into the mind of a man of genius, who demands time exclusively for meditation, and who beholds it snatched from him by the material routine of operations. Yet it is by the laborious route of analysis that he must reach truth; but he cannot pursue this unless guided by numbers; for without numbers it is not given to us to raise the veil which envelops the mysteries of nature. Thus the idea of constructing an apparatus capable of aiding human weakness in such researches, is a conception which, being realized, would mark a glorious epoch in the history of the sciences.

All this was quite true, Babbage agreed, and how wonderful to hear someone else say it. Here was high praise again from a foreign land. Then, almost before the pleasant shock of Menebrea's article passed, Babbage learned that his case was also being taken up in England. A countrywoman translated the sketch into English. This talented translator was none other than Countess Lovelace, the beautiful Ada Augusta to whom Babbage had shown his Difference Engine a few years earlier and whose brilliant understanding of it had impressed him.

Lady Lovelace was the only legitimate child of Lord Byron, the adventurous poet of the early nineteenth century. He was born shortly before Charles Babbage and each married about the same time, Byron in 1815. He married Anne Isabelle Milbanke, a well-born young heiress, and had one child, Ada Augusta. In 1816 Anne Isabella left him because of his infidelities. He never saw his daughter again and died bemoaning that fact.

Ada, reared and educated by her mother, developed into a charming and brilliant woman. An excellent musician, she was also greatly interested in mathematics. Seeing Ada's ability, her mother had her tutored by mathematicians and encouraged her to develop this interest. Her teacher, Augustus De Morgan, compared her with a brilliant woman mathematician, Maria Agnesi. He said if she had been a man her aptitude for grasping the strong points and the real difficulties of first principles would have made her an original mathematical investigator, perhaps of first-rate eminence. De Morgan's wife accompanied Ada on a visit to see Babbage's work and described her reaction.

> While the rest of the party gazed at this beautiful instrument with the same sort of expression and feeling that some savages are said to have shown on first seeing a looking glass or hearing a gun, Miss Byron, young as she was, understood its working and saw the great beauty of the invention.

Babbage, on his part, was completely taken by the brilliant and beautiful Miss Byron, who was the exact age of his late daughter Georgiana.

In 1835, Ada married William, eighth Lord King, who would subsequently become first earl of Lovelace. Although the couple moved in the highest social circles, Lovelace encouraged his wife to continue her mathematical interests. When Menebrea published his sketch of the Analytical Engine, Lady Lovelace decided to translate it, despite its complex nature. She succeeded so well that it has been said she understood Babbage's concept of the computer better than anyone else would for one hundred years.

After she had completed the translation, Lady Lovelace showed it to Babbage. Highly flattered, he was nevertheless surprised that she had not instead written an original article on the engine. Thus far such a piece had not been produced in English. Babbage himself was still so busy with his many projects he had no time for writing. It seemed that no one else cared about the Analytical Engine, or that no one had the competence to write on the subject. Finally, Babbage suggested that Lady Lovelace at least add some explanatory notes of her own, which she did. So extensive were these notes that they were several times as long as Menebrea's original sketch.

Lady Lovelace found serious errors in work Babbage had done on some theorems by the Swiss mathematician Bernouilli that were to be included in the notes. She corrected them herself and pointed out the flaws to the embarrassed Babbage.

PERCEPTIVE LADY

Lady Lovelace quickly saw that the Analytical Engine *"weaves algebraical patterns* just as the Jacquard-loom weaves flowers and leaves." She went on to point out something that probably never occurred to Babbage, whose hatred of organ grinders must have killed any musical interests he had:

> If the fundamental relations of sounds in the science of harmony and musical composition were susceptible of adaption to the notation and mechanism of the Engine, it might compose elaborate and scientific pieces of music of any degree of complexity and extent.

Of course, such music is composed today, just as she suggested it might be. She also made much of the engine's ability to perform what are now called "subroutines," or loops, by using a card or cards over and over again:

> A method was devised of what was technically designated *backing* the cards in certain groups according to certain laws. The object of this extension is to secure the possibility of bringing any particular card or set of cards into use *any number of times successively* in the solution of one problem.

This is the subroutine idea. And she noted one of the most intriguing abilities of the machine: "The engine is capable, under certain circumstances, of feeling about to discover which of two or more possible contingencies has occurred, and of shaping its future course of action accordingly."

At the same time she avoided crediting the engine with too much humanlike power: "The Analytical Engine has no pretensions whatever to *originate* anything. It can do whatever we *know how to order it* to perform. It can *follow* analysis; but it has no power of *anticipating* any analytical relations or truths. . . ."

Today some computer people would argue with this view, but it is difficult to argue with another observation the young countess made:

> It is desirable to guard against the possibility of exaggerated ideas that might arise as to the powers of the Analytical Engine. In considering any new subject, there is frequently a tendency, first, to *overrate* what we find to be already interesting or remarkable; and secondly, by a sort of natural reaction, to *undervalue* the true state of the case, when we do discover that our notions have surpassed those that were really tenable.

The Analytical Engine would be "undervalued" for a long

time. Because it was 1843, and not 1943, Countess Lovelace was forced to publish her translation and notes anonymously, signing them simply A.A.L. It was not thought dignified for a noblewoman to involve herself in such affairs. However, it was common knowledge among her friends that A.A.L. was none other than the lovely Ada Augusta Lovelace.

Even as he literally picked up the pieces of his Difference Engine by purchasing them from the government after it ended its arrangement with him, Babbage clung to his eternal hope. Ada's translation, published in *Taylor's Scientific Memoirs*, could yet win the help he needed. With this thought he entertained Prince Albert in the fireproof room that still held some of the detailed drawings of the great engine. Albert had demonstrated his keen perception when he noted that the Jacquard portrait was not an engraving—as even Wellington had thought—but the product of a loom. With Lady Lovelace, Babbage plotted and planned to get royal backing that even Sir Robert Peel could not put down. But in the end Ada convinced him that he was being unrealistic.

A FEMININE FRIEND

Eagerly Babbage waited for some good development from Lady Lovelace's work. She moved in high circles and the Lovelaces were respected by London Society. Surely now there would be revived interest on the part of government and money would be available for building the Analytical Engine. Babbage was in his fifties; he would not live forever. All the long years he had devoted to his engines had not yet brought him close to the completion of his great dreams. Disappointingly, the Lovelace paper, brilliant and provocative though it was, produced polite yawns from the men with the purse strings in English government.

Lady Lovelace, Babbage's friend and collaborator

Lady Lovelace's work brought Babbage into the company of the Lovelaces a great deal. Next to his mother, Lady Lovelace surely became Babbage's best friend, combining her charming femininity with brilliant intellect and bubbling personality. They exchanged letters for many years. Writing to her once to explain his apparent negligence of them, he revealed a poignant truth about his life.

> It is an odd fatality but I seem always to neglect most those friends I most highly value. You have I think half found this out. It is certainly no small sacrifice I make for the sake of the calculating that I often forego the enjoyment of the society I most delight in.
> With best regards to Lord Lovelace,
> Believe me, Ever sincerely yours,
> C. BABBAGE.

He went often to the theater with the Lovelaces, for she was a talented musician and enamored of concerts. This was a major concession on Babbage's part, for as he put it, "My love of music is not great." Apparently he stated the case fairly, for Lady Lovelace once added a postscript to her letter: "The nightingales say you must write them but (as you can't sing and hate music) I wonder how you will manage to send them any intelligible song."

Babbage, however, did not let this failing embarrass him at musical performances. He could, simply by discreetly watching someone more schooled in the subject than he, tell when and how loud to applaud. At a performance of the opera *Don Juan*, Babbage became so bored that he took himself backstage—and even under the stage, where he had an exciting time with two of the devils and a trapdoor.

THE RACETRACK SCHEME

The Lovelaces were ardent racing fans and Babbage attended the races with them. This gave Babbage a desperate idea: he would devise a mathematical scheme for predicting the winners of the races, and he and the Lovelaces would share the profits. With his share he would again begin work on the Analytical Engine, too long delayed.

Eagerly he plunged into the business of working out his system that would pick winners at the tracks near London. At last it was finished, and the three conspirators placed their bets. At first they won, and Babbage and the Lovelaces were elated. Then they lost—and lost—and lost. Flaws were found in the system, and Babbage and the countess tried to correct them with more tables. They bet again. Results were mixed, and they consoled themselves that their chances were based on statistics that would average out over a long period of time until they finally would come out ahead. But a year passed and they were still losing money—heavily. Babbage dropped out when his funds were exhausted. The earl stopped using the system, which had proved a failure like the many contrived before then.

Countess Ada, apparently obsessed with the plan she had helped devise, and in debt to unscrupulous bookmakers, continued to bet heavily on its recommendations. Only after she had lost so much money that it was necessary to pawn her jewels was she able to stop gambling. Lady Byron twice redeemed the jewels after the countess had been harassed by her creditors. In poor health for some time, Lady Lovelace now became very ill and was never to recover fully, much to Babbage's distress.

THE GAME-PLAYING MACHINE

The failure of the great horse race scheme was a bitter disappointment to Babbage, but he was not yet beaten. There must still be a way to succeed in publicizing his great engine so that funds would be available from the government. If he could demonstrate that his engine could *think*, would not that convince any doubting Thomas?

Babbage next conducted a survey of "the opinions of persons in every class of life and of all ages, whether they thought it required human reason to play games of skill." Not surprisingly, Babbage found that nearly everyone responded that indeed it required human reason to play a game of skill. In fact, some added with no prompting that if this was not true, then a *machine* could play such games!

This was exactly the reaction Babbage had hoped for, and now he set out to see if his engines could be taught to play a game of skill. Some of his scientific friends, while agreeing that in theory a machine might be able to play a game, claimed that in practice there were such a vast number of different combinations in a game that a machine just could not be built to handle all possible contingencies. Babbage was convinced they were wrong. He satisfied himself that his Analytical Engine would have sufficient memory storage and operational capability to play even so complicated a game as chess. He set down a list of questions that the engine called Automaton would have to ask itself as it played:

1. Is the position of the men, as placed before him on the board, a possible position. That is, one which is consistent with the rules of the game?
2. If so, has Automaton himself already lost the game?

3. If not, then has Automaton won the game?
4. If not, can he win it at the next move? If so, make that move.
5. If not, could his adversary, if he had the move, win the game?
6. If so, Automaton must prevent him if possible.
7. If his adversary cannot win the game at his next move, Automaton must examine whether he can make such a move that, if he were allowed to have two moves in succession, he could at the second move have *two* different ways of winning the game; and each of these cases failing, Automaton must look forward to three or more successive moves.

Babbage also wrote: "I have already stated that in the Analytical Engine, I had devised mechanical means equivalent to memory, also that I had provided other means equivalent to foresight, and that the Engine itself could act on this foresight."

Even though he felt the Analytical Engine could play chess, Babbage wisely decided on tick-tack-toe instead. This game was the simplest he could think of. "Usually played by children," it calls for a board divided into only nine squares, and ten counters, five for each player, of which only nine will ever be used in a single game. Babbage found the number of combinations required for all the possible moves (362,880) to be "relatively insignificant," an understandable judgment for a man who had designed an engine which could store one thousand fifty-digit numbers in its head.

It is quite probable that Babbage could have built a machine to play an unbeatable game of tick-tack-toe. But again Babbage ran true to form and embroidered his basic idea so much that the game-player became completely impractical.

Babbage planned to put two small figures of children on top of the machine. The one on the winner's side would clap its hands while the other would wring its hands in despair. There would also be a rooster that would crow for victory and a lamb that would bleat when beaten. Babbage was again the little boy in love with the silver doll which pirouetted so gracefully.

If there were two winning choices of play open to the machine, the engine would choose according to whether it had won an odd or even number of games previously. This would not only solve the problem of choice but also make the engine play the game in different ways instead of always making the same move. Otherwise it might behave like a donkey with two bales of hay at equal distances from it, unable to make up its mind which to eat.

Game-playing is one test of intelligence, but Babbage greatly underrated the complexity of chess. Although a Spaniard named L. Torres y Quevedo built a simple "end-game" chessplayer in 1890, it was not until 1951 that an electronic computer—at Manchester University in England—was actually able to solve chess problems.

Seeing no government interest in his idea, Babbage proposed to build six game-playing engines operated by commercial exhibitors in three different locations at once so that each exhibitor could have one spare engine as a reserve. He soon learned that he was wasting his time. Babbage consulted in London with exhibitors and learned his engine was doomed. Previously someone had built a machine that composed poems in Latin, and even one that spoke in German, and each had been a dismal financial failure. The experts advised Babbage to leave the entertaining to *human* freaks, since the most successful of all the recent shows was P. T. Barnum's midget, General Tom Thumb.

Disappointed, Babbage departed. Maybe a chess-playing

Two ways of playing chess by machine: an automaton operated by a
concealed midget and a modern computer

automaton operated by a concealed midget was the smartest way to do the job after all, but he was above such trickery. So the great plan for raising money to build the Analytical Engine was dropped.

BABBAGE THE NOVELIST

Babbage had still another plan up his sleeve. He had written a fair amount, including the book, *Economy of Manufactures*, that had been well received and made some money. He thought now to write a book expressly for making money, and he devoted himself to outlining a huge, three-volume, illustrated fictional work. In typical fashion, Babbage had worked out two methods for writing. In the first he simply wrote things down roughly as they occurred to him, and later polished them. In the second method he polished as he went along.

When he had the plan complete, he confided his plans to his friend, the poet Samuel Rogers. Babbage was horrified to learn that Rogers often wrote no more than four to six lines in a whole day; this surely was no way to write in the quantity Babbage had in mind. Nowhere is there an outline or any evidence of the story he had in mind, since Rogers' advice was to forget the project. When Babbage told the poet that he wanted to be sure of making £5,000 (about $25,000) on the book, Rogers told him that he himself spent the sum of £15,000 on one of his books of poetry before it started to return him any money. Writing was apparently as expensive as building calculating engines! Perhaps it is as well for literature that Babbage gave up. He had made it his life work to find and point out errors in scientific treatises and mathematical tables. But whether such a rigorous adherence to fact should be applied to poetry is another question. In Lord Tennyson's poem, "The Vision of Sin," two lines read as follows:

> Every minute dies a man,
> Every minute one is born.

Babbage took exception to this and wrote Tennyson about its inaccuracy:

> I need hardly point out to you that this calculation would tend to keep the sum total of the world's population in a state of perpetual equipoise, whereas it is a well-known fact that the said sum total is constantly on the increase. I would therefore take the liberty of suggesting that in the next edition of your excellent poem the erroneous calculation to which I refer be corrected as follows:
>
> > Every moment dies a man,
> > And one and a sixteenth is born.
>
> I may add that the exact figures are 1.067, but something must of course be conceded to the laws of metre.

No one knows whether Tennyson thought Babbage was sincere or only joking. However, editions of the poem after 1850 were changed to read:

> Every moment dies a man,
> Every moment one is born.

This was at least token consideration of Babbage's technical objection.

COUP DE GRÂCE

Not slighting the learned journals, Babbage published a "Note on the Boracic Acid Works in Tuscany" in 1843; "On the Principles of Tools for Turning and Planing Metals," in 1846; "On the Planet Neptune," in 1847; and "Thoughts on the Principles of Taxation, with Reference to a Property Tax and its Exceptions," in 1848.

Later, Babbage would all but invent the coronagraph. In 1847 he did invent the ophthalmoscope, a device for examining the eye. Busy as he was, he turned the invention over to a doctor friend for testing, but the doctor put it aside and forgot about it. So did Babbage, and it was the German Hermann Ludwig von Helmholtz who is remembered for the invention—in 1851, some four years after Babbage.

Babbage must have suspected that his Analytical Engine would never be completed in his time. In 1848, despairing of his monumental task, he abandoned what little work he was doing on it and returned to the dust-covered Difference Engine. He had an idea far different from Difference Engine Number 1, however, and he titled it Difference Engine Number 2. It embodied many of the features he had worked out for his Analytical Engine. With a complete set of drawings for the third computer he had designed, he again went hat in hand to the government and offered them everything, with no compensation, if they would simply build the engine.

The great Benjamin Disraeli, now chancellor of the exchequer in his climb to power, spoke pointedly against the engine, quoting Professor Airy and reminding one and all that none had ever been built. Unfortunately Babbage lost his temper and wrote a scorching attack on Disraeli, sarcastically suggesting that he was not competent to make judgments requiring some mental ability. "The machine upon which everyone could calculate had little chance of fair play from the man on whom nobody could calculate," Babbage wrote, perhaps spurred by jealousy at Disraeli's success as a novelist and politician, in both of which fields Babbage had failed. But a man who could successfully outmaneuver the shrewdest heads of state wasted no time on poor Charles Babbage. In despair, Babbage gave up on the government for the last time, with this parting shot at the chancellor of the exchequer: "The Herostratus of Science, if he escapes oblivion, will be linked with the destroyer of the Ephesian Temple!" As usual, it was an aptly cutting remark, especially since the Temple at Ephesus had been pulled down twice. But it would be Babbage, and not Disraeli, who would not escape oblivion.

By now Babbage was fifty-six, an embittered old man who had carried his hatred of organ grinders and other street musicians to the ridiculous point of writing tracts against them and prosecuting them in court.

LONELY INVENTOR

Despite Babbage's attempts to make a mathematician, an engineer, or an inventor of Henry, the boy set his heart on military service. In 1842, then, Babbage asked around among his friends and arranged for a cadetship. In February of 1843 Henry left for India, in the service of the East India Company.

During that month, he wrote, his father never seemed to have fewer than thirteen invitations a day for every day of the month. Babbage did turn some down to spend a little time with his son before he left the country, but when it was time to leave, he said good-by in his library, not accompanying Henry even as far as the cab. Later, at the pier, Henry was asked to look out for a youngster being sent on the ship alone and wished for such concern on the part of his own father.

All Babbage's children were gone away now. In 1844, his mother died, a terrible loss because he had leaned on her strength in many of his crises.

Casting about for something to fill the gap, he sought the

post of railroad safety commissioner, which he could have filled admirably. As usual this position went to someone with "better connections." In 1846 there was an even juicier plum, seemingly easily within reach. The mastership of the Mint became vacant, and Babbage tried hard for it, seeing in the £2,000 a year salary a chance to pile up enough—£20,000 in ten years—to complete his Analytical Engine! This too was a vain hope, and a political favorite was appointed. His bitterness was added to some years later when his friend John Herschel got the job.

 # House of Glass

The great Crystal Palace was built in London for the Exhibition of 1851. A unique structure, it featured more glass than had ever been used in a building before and was praised by most. But the astronomer royal, Sir George Airy, warned that the artillery salutes fired to welcome the queen would knock the palace down! The salutes were fired as scheduled, and the palace stood firm. Airy's lack of scientific knowledge was not news to Babbage.

Once, requesting some Greenwich computations for his work, Babbage was told none were available. He later found the tables, some five tons of them, in a scrap paper manufacturer's plant. Surely the astronomer royal knew best what to do with his own publications, Babbage commented acidly. But he objected to the establishment of an astronomical observatory whose sole purpose was to produce wastepaper! The final straw was the discovery that Airy had the "waste paper concession" as a profitable sideline. Perhaps Airy also saw to it that Babbage was not an exhibitor at the Exhibition.

Airy seems to have been among those who decreed that

although Babbage was an outstanding authority on industry, he was not to be invited to assist in planning the Exhibition. Some 15 years later Lord Lyon Playfair of Edinburgh University, the man who did become Exhibition commissioner, told Babbage that he had suggested him for chief industrial commissioner, and Prince Albert had seconded the idea. However, they were told that Babbage was so "hostile" to the government—because of his Difference Engine—that he would not be asked. This ban extended not just to Babbage but to his Difference Engine as well, an engine which seemed to have vanished from sight.

Babbage had wanted the government to place the Difference Engine—what there was of it—in the British Museum so that it might be seen by many people. However the government instead sent it to Somerset House, King's College. As

The great Crystal Palace featured more glass than had ever been used in a building

far as Babbage was concerned, the engine had been buried. It was asked for at the Dublin Exhibition in 1847 but permission was refused, as it was when New York exhibitors asked to show the engine. Apparently the government was still embarrassed over its £17,000 failure, and it was nowhere in sight in the Crystal Palace.

All Babbage could show at the Exhibition was a privately printed paper, distributed gratis, entitled *Laws of Mechanical Notation*. This was a refinement of the work he had done a quarter of a century ago. Almost wistfully, the author added a note to the end of the paper: "Mr. Babbage will feel obliged by any criticism, or additions to these rules of Drawing and to the Mechanical Alphabet, and requests they may be addressed to him by post, at No. 1 Dorset Street, Manchester Square. July, 1851."

With mixed feelings Babbage walked among the machine-tool exhibits of Joseph Whitworth—the same machinist who had once worked on the Difference Engine—now England's leading toolmaker with twenty-three exhibits; no other firm showed more than three.

OF ECLIPSES AND LIGHTHOUSES

Babbage kept up his running battle with the institutions of science in England, and with his mortal enemies, the organ grinders and other street musicians. There was still enough ambition and energy in the aging scientist to keep him active on many projects in addition to his work on the Analytical Engine and Difference Engine Number 2.

Lady Lovelace had once written Babbage for directions on observing an eclipse—she supposed smoked glass would do. Babbage had a much better idea. In 1851, there was a total eclipse of the sun. During such phenomena, the solar prominences, those awesome offshoots of flame that reach thousands of miles above its surface, can be observed. Millions of men before Babbage, many of them of scientific mind, had witnessed eclipses. But he seems to have been the first to realize that if the moon could block out the sun during these rare natural events, man could devise a telescope instrument for blocking it out artificially whenever he wanted to. This was the concept of the coronagraph, which Bernard Lyot of France would perfect in 1930. Babbage published his idea in the *Proceedings of the Astronomical Society* as "Note respecting the pink projections from the Sun's disc observed during the total solar eclipse in 1851."

Babbage also became interested in lighthouses and methods of using their lights as signals. This was an example of serendipity, or accidental discovery—one of those turnings to advantage of a chance, useless discovery. Babbage had devoted much of his time and investigations to learning how man is led to scientific discoveries. Babbage described one of the principles he discovered:

> Whenever we meet with any defect in the means we are contriving for the accomplishing of a given object, that defect should be noted and reserved for future consideration, and inquiry should be made—

> *Whether that which is a defect as regards the object in view may not become a source of advantage in some totally different subject.*

Interested in the experimental work being started with electricity as a light source, Babbage attended an exhibition of "voltaic light," an exhibition marred by the frequent breaking of the circuit and the intermittent flashing of the light as a result. This was definitely a "defect as regards the object in view," but Babbage wondered if such an interruption of the electric light done purposely and at regular intervals might produce a signaling device.

Babbage proceeded from the idea of electrical switching for signals to a mechanical signaling system for gaslight, an idea that had not been developed. Using a clockwork, he produced a sliding-sleeve shutter arrangement that could be made to signal any number. Testing the light, he walked some two hundred fifty yards away from it and was pleased to see that the coded number was easily readable. There was a slight problem, but he was sure he could eliminate the slight blinking it produced. Walking on another two hundred fifty yards he was still able to see the signaled number—but no blink.

Most engineers would have simply eliminated the blink and forgotten it. But Babbage saw a method of signaling not only a coded message but also the distance the observer was from the light. Since this would be particularly advantageous for a lighthouse, he developed a complete lighthouse signaling method and exhibited it in 1851—not at the Crystal Palace, but at home. Whether it was, as he said, because the

A sketch illustrating Babbage's lighthouse signaling method

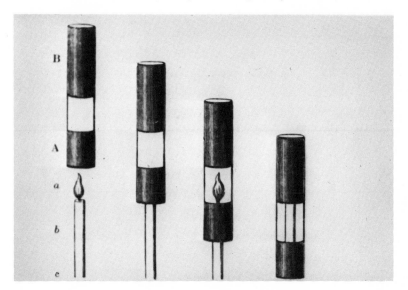

government withdrew a £5,000 prize originally offered for novel ideas (a way to finance more work on the Analytical Engine!) or because of his bitterness over the Difference Engine not being exhibited, he chose not to favor the Exhibition with his "occulting" light system but mounted it atop his home at 1 Dorset Street.

Shortly after the Exhibition, Babbage received a letter from a friend in the United States expressing interest in the clever occulting light. Babbage sent him a full description and also thought to do the same for the maritime authorities of eleven other countries. From America came serious interest in the lighthouse signals. Congress had approved a grant of $5,000 for a series of experiments, and Babbage was asked to come to the United States to assist in setting up the signal lights. He was to be given passage on the *Arctic*, the "finest vessel in the mercantile navy," in October, the best month for the Atlantic crossing. Although eager to go to America, Babbage turned down the invitation since he felt it would be wrong to go and stay for less than a year. And at the moment he just couldn't afford to be away from England that long because of his many commitments. The *Arctic* sailed without Babbage, fortunately for him. It was rammed by a smaller vessel while approaching Newfoundland and sank quickly, with great loss of life.

The Russians also were interested in Babbage's signal lights. Babbage allowed the Russian representative to copy the description of the system, and several years later the Russians used Babbage's occulting light signals against the British at the siege of Sebastopol during the Crimean War.

An outgrowth of the lighthouse signals was "an occulting hand-lantern," with a shade for occulting by the pressure of the thumb, and with two other shades of red and green glass. Babbage suggested that this might be made available for military purposes or for the police. Surely he must have thought of railways, for one day they would adopt such signal lanterns. It is ironic that a Royal Navy officer in 1862 patented the occulting light and got what money and credit there was to be had.

TO BREAK THE CODE

With his mathematical mind and work on signal lights it is not surprising that Babbage would become interested in codes and deciphering. He would produce an uncipherable code and then proceed to cipher it. In his work with ciphers he made up special dictionaries with words of various letters, words containing triplets and double letters, words that could be rewritten as other words. For mental exercise he solved word puzzles like: From the sentence "I tore ten Persian mss," make a single word. Here is how Babbage solved this one.

The first process is to put opposite each letter the number of times it occurs, thus:—

i	2		
t	2		
o	1		
r	2	It contains—
e	3	2 triplets
n	2	4 pairs
p	1	4 single letters
s	3	
a	1	
m	1	
	18	

Now, on examining the dictionary of all words of eighteen letters, it will be observed that they amount to twenty-seven, and that they may be arranged in six classes:—

7 having five letters of the same kind.
5   ,,   four   ,, ,, ,, ,,   ,,
3   ,,   three triplets.
7   ,,   two triplets.
3   ,,   one triplet.
2   ,,   seven pairs.
$\overline{27}$

Hence it appears that the word sought must be one of those seven having two triplets, and also that it must have four pairs; this reduces the question to the two words—

misinterpretations,
misrepresentations.

The latter is the one sought, because its triplets are e and s, whilst those of the former are i and t.

Babbage suggested that the interested reader might want to find a word of eighteen letters formed by the sentence, "Art is not in, but Satan." The task will be easier if you own a dictionary like Babbage's.

Another of Babbage's unusual interests was lockpicking. He wrote a paper entitled "On the Art of Opening all Locks," then went on to design an unpickable lock. At the 1851 Exhibition he spent hours with a Mr. Hobbs, a famed lockmaker, and even invited the duke of Wellington to join them in the discussion and demonstrations of picking locks. Hobbs had designed the unpickable lock, and planned to patent it. Babbage happily pointed out to Hobbs that his system was precisely the one that Babbage had in mind.

THE SCIENTIFIC GADFLY

Despite his disappointments in connection with the Exhibition at the Crystal Palace, 1851 was a notable year for Charles Babbage. The proud and confident English were pleased that the English exhibits took nearly every prize, even though the judging was done by international committees. Babbage, however, was concerned about English science and technology and warned that something must be done if England were to maintain its position of leadership. He wrote a book about it, *The Exposition of 1851; or Views of the Industry, the Science and the Government of England.* However, while taking the scientific fraternity to task again as he had done in *Decline of Science,* he hailed the Crystal Palace and its contents as evidence of man's progress.

> It is not a bad definition of *man* to describe him as a *tool-making animal.* His earliest contrivances to support uncivilized life were tools of the simplest and rudest construction. His latest achievements in the substitution of machinery, not merely for the skill of the human hand, but for the relief of the human intellect, are founded on the use of tools of a still higher order.
>
> The Crystal Palace, and all it splendid contents, owe their existence to *tools* as the physical means—to intellect as the guiding power, developed equally on works of industry or on objects of taste.
>
> The contrivance and the construction of tools, must therefore ever stand at the head of the industrial arts.
>
> The next stage in the advancement of those arts is equally necessary to the progress of each. It is the art of drawing. . . . The resources of mechanical drawing have not yet been sufficiently explored: with the great advance now taking place in machinery, it will become necessary to assist its powers by practical yet philosophical rules for expressing still more clearly by signs and by the letters themselves the mutual relations of the parts of a machine.

With pardonable pride he mentioned his own contribution:

> As we advance towards machinery for more complicated objects, other demands arise, without satisfying which our fur-

ther course is absolutely stopped. It becomes necessary to see at a glance, not only every *successive* movement of each amongst thousands of different parts, but also to scrutinize all contemporaneous actions. This gave rise to the Mechanical Notation, a language of signs, which, although invented for one subject, is of so comprehensive a nature as to be applicable to many. If the whole of the facts relating to a naval or military battle were known, the mechanical notation would assist the description of it quite as much as it would of any complicated engine.

Babbage was foretelling the future. Operations research did just that in World War II when British strategists adapted such scientific methods of battle planning. A brochure published recently by a research and development organization describes a project called OMEGA, for Operations Model Evaluation Group—Air Force. This is "an air battle model which simulates in detail possible strategic warfare." Also mentioned is the fact that "scientists are developing for the United States Navy techniques and computer equipment requirements to process and display in real time the data required to control a wide variety of operations."

TRAGEDY AND TRIUMPH

In 1852 Lady Lovelace, who had been ailing for many years, died of cancer. She was in such terrible agony at the last that her room had to be padded to prevent her from injuring herself. Babbage felt responsible in part for her suffering. The ill-fated horse-racing venture had been his doing, and harassment by her creditors for gambling debts had come close to disgracing her before she died. In fact, Babbage and Ada's mother had to hire attorneys to ensure that there would be no scandal. His "lovely interpretress" was only thirty-six when she died.

Babbage's workshops were still littered with parts of his engines, and the walls and tables were covered with drawings of his great dreams. But no progress was being made by the inventor.

Henry Babbage was home on leave from India with his wife, Minnie, and Babbage's third Georgiana, their two-year-old daughter. He welcomed the little family, even insisting that they stay with him. Henry had inherited his share of the £10,000 his grandmother had held in trust for him and was financially independent of his father. While they were visiting at 1 Dorset Street, Minnie had her second child, a son. With all their domestic demands, Henry and his father found time to promote the Scheutz Difference Engine, a calculating machine that really worked and was commercially available.

Two of the men who read Dr. Lardner's account of the Difference Engine in the *Edinburgh Review* in 1834 had done something about it. One of them was George Scheutz, a printer in Sweden. He was interested in what amounted to an automatic typesetting machine that could also prepare mathematical tables, and so he set out to build a difference engine of his own, using Babbage's design as a model.

Scheutz was a lesser craftman than Babbage, and he had a difficult time building the engine. However, with the help of his son and a little financial assistance from the Swedish government and the Swedish Academy, he eventually produced a successful machine.

Sweden gave Scheutz a grant of 5,000 rix-dollars, some £280, with the understanding that if the engine did not work he would repay that sum. When it did work they gave him another £280 pounds as a prize. So Sweden spent only £560 for a successful engine, compared with the £17,000 England gave. Scheutz triumphantly brought his engine to England in 1854.

Scheutz's difference engine was more ambitious than Babbage's demonstration model of 1822 but not so grand as that commissioned by the English government. It computed four orders of differences and printed the results automatically to fourteen places. Babbage praised Scheutz highly, personally assisted him with refinements, and took to the rostrum of the British Royal Society to recommend that Scheutz and his son be given a medal for their work. Babbage spoke quite bluntly on one aspect, echoing his earlier warnings to England:

> Sweden has thus secured for herself the glory of having been the first nation, practically to produce a machine for Calculating Mathematics Tables by Differences and printing the results. Wealthier and more powerful nations will regret that the country of Berzelius should thus have anticipated them.

A detail of the Scheutz calculator showing the printing mechanism

Babbage and Henry made up drawings and mechanical notation to explain the operation of Scheutz's machine, which added to its honors by taking a gold medal in the 1855 Exhibition in Paris. Babbage's engine was not even displayed.

In 1856 the Scheutz machine was purchased (for the bargain price of $5,000!) for use in the Dudley Observatory at Albany, New York, marking the first operation of an automatic computer in the United States. At Dudley it was used in printing *Ephemerides*, or astronomical tables, and led to the development of similar machines to record and print out barometric pressure changes. An exact copy of the Scheutz machine was later made by Donkin and Co. for the British government, which used it to compute "English Tables of Lifetimes, Annuities, and Premiums." In 1870 these finally superseded the tables Babbage had compiled in 1826.

A difference engine was also built by a fellow Britisher, a Mr. Deacon of Beaufort House, Strand. Deacon, an accomplished machinist and mechanic, built only the mathematical part of the engine, omitting the automatic printing portion. Babbage did not see the Deacon engine until after the Scheutz machine had been exhibited in London, although Deacon had built it long before.

DISCORDANT NOTE

According to one writer of the times, the successful Scheutz engine could be cranked "with about the force required to operate a small barrel organ." This was surely an attempt to irritate Babbage, who by now had carried his battle with organ grinders to the status of a major crusade. He did manage to keep some semblance of his earlier sense of humor, however, and when someone asked him point-blank if he really believed a man's brain could be injured by listening to a hand organ, Babbage said no, "because no man having a brain ever listens to street musicians!"

Thomas Carlyle escaped the street musicians in a sound-proof room, but not Babbage who prosecuted them. Jeering children followed him through the streets. Fife and drum bands went out of their way to serenade him. Drunks blew bugles under his windows night and day, and those windows were sometimes smashed by bricks! In fact, *Mechanics Magazine* for January 24, 1857, published a rather unusual article by Babbage. It was entitled "Table of the Relative Frequency of Occurrence of the Causes of Breaking Plate Glass Windows."

His preoccupation with hecklers did not stop his scientific work, although for a time there was a warlike tone to many of the papers he published. For example, *The Times* printed one entitled "On a Method of Laying Guns in a Battery without exposing the men to the shot of the enemy." He also suggested a rocket launcher for projectiles and studied the shapes of such missiles. "On Submarine Navigation" appeared in *Illustrated News* for June 23, 1855, detailing a four-man screw-propelled submarine capable of entering harbors unobserved and destroying even iron-hulled ships.

The November, 1856, issue of *Quarterly Journal of the Geological Society* contained an article by Babbage "On the Action of Ocean Currents in the Formation of the Strata of the Earth." In a note to *The Ninth Bridgewater Treatise* Babbage had reasoned that the rings in trees could be used to find the archaeological conditions back through the ages. This idea was taken up in 1904 by Professor Andrew Ellicott Douglass at the University of Arizona to date the timbers in dwellings several thousand years old. On a similar subject Babbage wrote his last original paper, "On Remains of Human Art, mixed with the Bones of Extinct Races of Animals." This appeared in the *Proceedings of the Royal Society*, May 26, 1859.

In 1856 Babbage again bid his soldier son a farewell as Henry left for duty in India. This time, however, he did not say a routine good-by in the library but accompanied the family to the station and watched and waved until the train was out of sight. He was lonely for the son he had at last come to admire for what he was, and also for Herschel, now a confirmed resident of Australia where he was helping open this new land. Henry would prove his valor in the Indian Mutiny a year later, to his father's great pride, and he would be a major-general when he returned.

Charles Babbage ventured out much less now than in earlier days when Lady Lovelace had been alive and well. But on one rare occasion when he did, his imagination again showed its range. Watching the play of moonlight on an outdoor opera gave Babbage the idea of using colored lights to add to the effect of stage plays—then a new concept. He developed such lights, and to exploit them he wrote an ambitious ballet entitled *Alethes and Iris*. With two fire engines standing by, he failed to sell the idea to theatermen since they feared the fire hazard of the lights, which were open flame and not electric. In fairness, Babbage agreed, pointing out that while the showmen could insure their theaters they could not insure audiences.

 **The Last Years**

At the Exhibition of 1862 the government finally displayed Babbage's Difference Engine at the insistence of his friend William Gravatt. Babbage was at first delighted with this belated recognition. Enthusiastically he proposed that the copy of the Scheutz engine be borrowed from its work and set alongside the Babbage engine, both of them operated slowly and continuously "by the same catgut" so that visitors could understand what the machines did.

The government protested that the Scheutz engine was much too busy computing insurance tables, and declined to make the Babbage engine a working exhibit. As an alternative Babbage suggested displaying the drawings of his engine, complete with the Mechanical Notation that son Herschel had done. There was sufficient empty wall space near the four-by-five-foot cubbyhole the engine had been assigned when he made his request, but this was soon filled with oil-cloth samples and rugs. Angrily Babbage offered this as proof that the authorities were "better able to appreciate furnishings for the feet than for the head!"

Babbage also offered to exhibit his collection of calculating engines, ancient and modern:

> 2 Morland calculators
> 1 original set of Napier's bones
> 1 Stanhope calculator
> 2 Mahon calculators
> 1 Deacon Difference Engine (patterned
> on Babbage's)

But the management was uninterested. He found a man conversant with the principle of the Difference Engine and willing to act as lecturer at the Exhibition for only six shillings a day. But the powers-that-were said such money was not available. So the proud inventor, now seventy years old, was on hand every day to try to explain the workings of his complicated device. Told by one visitor that the Chinese were interested in the engine and wanted to know if it was something that would fit in the pocket, Babbage mustered a wry smile and admitted that his was an "out-of-pocket" computer.

He noted too that there were prizes for children's toys but none for calculating engines. More alarming was the decline in the number of prizes English exhibitors won at the international competition—the very thing that he had prophesied in 1855. A younger Babbage would have sat himself down and delivered himself of another book on his favorite topic, the decline of science in England. But most of the old fire was gone now, and the book to write was his autobiography. Meanwhile, the Difference Engine was treated to the humiliation of being temporarily homeless when King's College refused to take it back after the Exhibition. Finally it was sent to the South Kensington Museum, where it has remained.

A PHILOSOPHER'S LIFE

In 1864 Babbage published his autobiography, entitled *Passages from the Life of a Philosopher*. It was dedicated not to Queen Victoria of England, but to Victor Emmanuel II, king of Italy, because of the respectful recognition that Italy's scientists had given him in inviting him to speak on his engines at Turin in 1840. He expressed his deep sense of obligation to the sovereign of united Italy, the country of Archimedes and of Galileo. Perhaps he forgot the cruel treatment Galileo himself had received at the hands of his country (and that most organ grinders came from Italy!), remembering only that England had done little to honor Charles Babbage during his long years of work with the engines. The Preface to the volume is interesting and reflects from deep within Babbage's heart and soul:

> Some men write their lives to save themselves from *ennui*, careless of the amount they inflict on their readers.
>
> Others write their personal history, lest some kind friend should survive them, and, in showing off his own talent, unwittingly show them up.
>
> Others, again, write their own life from a different motive, from fear that the vampires of literature might make it their prey.
>
> I have frequently had applications to write my life, both from my countrymen, and from foreigners. Some caterers for the public offered to pay me for it. Others required that I should pay them for its insertion; others offered to insert it without charge. One proposed to give me a quarter of a column gratis, and as many additional lines of elege as I chose to write and pay for at ten-pence per line. To many of these I sent a list of my works with the remark that they formed the best life of an author; but nobody cared to insert them.

I have no desire to write my own biography, as long as I have strength and means to do better work.

The remarkable circumstances attending those Calculating Machines on which I have spent so large a portion of my life, make me wish to place on record some account of their past history. As, however, such a work would be utterly uninteresting to the greater part of my countrymen, I thought it might be rendered less unpalatable by relating some of my experiences amongst various classes of society, widely differing from each other, in which I have occasionally mixed.

This volume does not aspire to the name of an autobiography. It relates a variety of isolated circumstances in which I have taken part—some of them arranged in order of time, and others grouped together in separate chapters, from similarity of subject.

The selection has been made in some cases from the importance of the matter. In others, from the celebrity of the persons concerned; whilst several of them furnish interesting illustrations of human character.

The most interesting illustration of human character, of course, is that of Babbage himself. After his byline on the title page there are some two dozen honors and societies, including his Italian order in very large type. The frontispiece, most appropriately, was a woodcut of the first Difference Engine. A wheel at the top center reads proudly, "Calculation Complete," yet every one of the nineteen dials shows a zero above the pointer, an ironic commentary on Babbage's lifetime of work, summing up to nothing when the calculations were complete.

The book was a long one, taking the reader through thirty-six chapters and an appendix of his eighty published works. The first chapter touched on his ancestors, suggesting that he might be descended from Tubal Cain, since they both worked in iron (on the other hand Tubal Cain was supposed to have invented organs!). His childhood and boyhood were covered, and then the years at Cambridge. Next the Calculating Engines were described in great detail.

PASSAGES

FROM

THE LIFE OF A PHILOSOPHER.

BY

CHARLES BABBAGE, ESQ., M.A.,

F.R.S., F.R.S.E., F.R.A.S., F. STAT. S., HON. M.R.I.A., M.C.P.S.,

COMMANDER OF THE ITALIAN ORDER OF ST. MAURICE AND ST. LAZARUS,

INST. IMP. (ACAD. MORAL.) PARIS CORR., ACAD. AMER. ART. ET SC. BOSTON, REG. ŒCON. BORUSS.,
PHYS. HIST. NAT. GENEV., ACAD. REG. MONAC., HAFN., MASSIL., ET DIVION., SOCIUS.
ACAD. IMP. ET REG. PETROP., NEAP., BRUX., PATAV., GEORG. FLOREN, LYNCEI ROM., MUT., PHILOMATH.
PARIS, SOC. CORR., ETC.

"I'm a philosopher. Confound them all—
Birds, beasts, and men; but no, not womankind."—*Don Juan.*

" I now gave my mind to philosophy: the great object of my ambition was to make out a complete system of the universe, including and comprehending the origin, causes, consequences, and termination of all things. Instead of countenance, encouragement, and applause, which I should have received from every one who has the true dignity of an oyster at heart, I was exposed to calumny and misrepresentation. While engaged in my great work on the universe, some even went so far as to accuse me of infidelity;—such is the malignity of oysters."—"*Autobiography of an Oyster*" *deciphered by the aid of photography in the shell of a philosopher of that race,—recently scolloped.*

LONDON:

LONGMAN, GREEN, LONGMAN, ROBERTS, & GREEN.

1864.

In other chapters Babbage recounted his experiences with the greats of England and Europe, his "Experience by water," and "Experience by fire." Lockpicking and deciphering were treated, as well as his electioneering, his visits with workmen and beggars, his running battle with street musicians, his railway work, hints for travelers, miracles, religion, and on and on. The last chapter was wistfully entitled "Agreeable Recollections," a summary that does not square with Babbage's pronouncement to the Honorable Lionel Tollemache shortly before his death that he had not experienced one happy day in his life and that he despised everything and everyone—in particular the English government and organ grinders. In this chapter he told of the joy of being made a member of the French Academy of Moral Sciences. And that a Swedish sea captain named Orling was kind to Herschel in Australia because of Babbage's help to Scheutz. In his chapter "Contributions to Human Knowledge," Babbage himself wrote his best epitaph:

> If I survive some few years longer, the Analytical Engine will exist, and its works will afterwards be spread over the world. If it is the will of the Being, who gave me the endowments which led to that discovery, that I should not survive to complete my work, I bow to that decision with intense gratitude for those gifts; conscious that through life I have never hesitated to make the severest sacrifices of fortune, and even of feelings, in order to accomplish my imagined mission.
>
> The great principles on which the Analytical Engine rests have been examined, admitted, recorded, and demonstrated. The mechanism itself has now been reduced to unexpected simplicity. Half a century may probably elapse before any one without those aids which I leave behind me, will attempt so unpromising a task. If, unwarned by my example, any man shall undertake and shall succeed in really constructing an engine embodying in itself the whole of the executive department of mathematical analysis upon different principles or by simpler mechanical means, I have no fear of leav-

ing my reputation in his charge, for he alone will be fully able to appreciate the nature of my efforts and the value of their results.

There were two human characters glaringly omitted from the book. Lady Lovelace is mentioned only briefly in connection with her translation of the Menebrea paper; his wife, Georgiana, is not mentioned at all! It is as though Babbage forced these two from his memories as a defense against the grief they would recall.

He analyzed the subject of wit in his book and pronounced that puns were detestable, forgetting perhaps his own terrible pun on the "dot-age" of Cambridge in his youth. He described how his enjoyment of the theater was severely limited. Babbage did not care for tragedy, he said, perhaps because there was so much of it in his real life. And comedy, he said, "frequently excited my feelings more than the dignity of the philosophic character sanctioned." A strange predicament indeed for a man who never knew a happy day.

THE END DRAWS ON

Babbage also continued to detest the estimated one thousand organ grinders in London and thought of hooking a steam engine to "a collection of shrill organ pipes" to give them a taste of their own medicine. Nor was it just organs he deplored. He listed the "Instruments of torture permitted by the Government in the streets of London":

> Organs
> Brass Bands
> Fiddles
> Harps

Harpsichords
Hurdy Gurdies
Flageolets
Drums
Bagpipes
Accordions
Halfpenny whistles
Tom-toms
Trumpets
The Human voice, used by
venders, in religious
chanting, and psalm-
singing

Because of this continual din, he claimed one-fourth of his working power was destroyed, a tax he could not afford to pay. Furthermore, he calculated that at any given time 4.72 per cent of the population was ill. With fifty-six houses on his street and about 10 people in each house, he estimated that there were twenty-six sick people always suffering from noise. There were other dangers, he pointed out, quoting a newspaper story about horses bolting at the sound of street musicians and "mutilating six young children!"

It was common now for him to be followed wherever he went by bands of hecklers, sometimes as many as one hundred at a time, shouting threats to burn his house or turn over the cab he rode in. In a single year he spent £104 on court costs against such nuisances but was unable to curb them. Shakespeare has Timon of Athens say:

I am sick of this false world and will love naught
But even the mere necessities of it.

Charles Babbage was surely a Timon of the scientific world,

as he was called. Yet there remained a tender streak through him, and he was solicitous of beggars—until he spent many hours of investigations that proved their woeful tales to be falsehoods.

In the course of his investigations on just about every subject imaginable, Babbage had once calculated that the chance of a man coming back from the dead was about one in a trillion. This was a safe guess, since this many men haven't yet been born. But he also speculated that as long as the memory could be preserved, then such a reincarnation was possible. Now, as he grew old, he said he would gladly give up the remainder of his time on earth if he could come back for just three days, five hundred years in the future, and have a guide explain the scientific discoveries made since his death.

MATHEMATICIAN'S FUNERAL

Henry Babbage returned from India on furlough in March of 1871. By then his father was no longer capable of taking care of himself or his affairs, and Henry arranged for Sir Edward Ryan, his uncle, to look after things. Henry was staying in Bromley with his family, but when word came from Ryan that the end was near, he and Minnie came to London to stay with the old man. Ryan helped Charles Babbage write his last will and testament on October 13. He left something less than £40,000 to be divided equally among his three sons. However, Herschel was to have an additional £1,000 and Henry all the remains of the calculating engines. There was also a bequest of £3 per month to Mary Wilson, who had been his servant during his friendship with Lady Lovelace and was involved in the undercover dealings with the bookmakers who ruined Ada.

Henry Babbage

The end came at last on the night of October 18, some two months short of his eightieth birthday. When he was dying, Henry and his wife Minnie, of whom Babbage was fond, were at his bedside. "What a tableau," Babbage whispered once, looking up at the anxious figures keeping their vigil above him. At about eleven o'clock he asked "What o'clock is it, Henry?" and at 11:35 he died. Kidney trouble and complications were the cause of death.

When Babbage died, *The Times* cruelly commented that he had lived to be almost eighty despite "organ-grinding persecutions." Another writer spoke bleakly of the "wreckage of a brilliant and strenuous career" and predicted Babbage had designed a "machine which will probably remain forever a theoretical possibility."

Except for the family, undertakers, and others required to be there, there was only one mourner, the duchess of Somerset. Babbage had outlived his friends as well as his enemies.

A book popular at the time of Babbage's death was Samuel Butler's novel, *Erewhon*, a satirical prediction of the future.

It is evident that the author was taking into account the calculating engines of Babbage when he wrote the prophetic lines:

> There is no security against the ultimate development of mechanical consciousness in the fact of machines possessing little consciousness now. Reflect upon the extraordinary advance which machines have made during the last few hundred years, and note how slowly the animal and vegetable kingdoms are advancing. The more highly organized machines are creatures not so much of yesterday, as of the last five minutes, so to speak, in comparison with past time.
>
> Do not let me be misunderstood as living in fear of any actually existing machine; there is probably no known machine which is more than a prototype of future mechanical life. The present machines are to the future as the early Saurians to man. . . . What I fear is the extraordinary rapidity with which they are becoming something very different to what they are at present. . . .
>
> Our sum-engines never drop a figure [we can almost hear Babbage applaud!], nor our looms a stitch; the machine is brisk and active, when the man is weary, it is clearheaded and collected, when the man is stupid and dull, it needs no slumber. . . .

ECHOES FROM THE GRAVE

The fate of calculating engines in England hardly seemed brighter. In the year Babbage died, the government appointed a committee from the British Association to investigate the prospects of the Analytical Engine. In 1878, six years later, the Cayley committee tendered its official report. Back in 1823 Babbage had told the government he would *build* the Difference Engine in half that time!

The committee was headed by Arthur Cayley, one of the leading mathematicians of the day. The Cayley committee was charged with the sticky problem of what to do with what some called "the wreckage of Babbage's life," strewn about in his and Clement's shop. Their formal conclusions were summarized as follows:

> Having regard to all these considerations, we have come, not without reluctance, to the conclusion, that we cannot advise the British Association to take any steps, either by way of recommendation or otherwise, to procure the construction of Mr. Babbage's Analytical Engine and the printing of tables by its means.

There was a final suggestion, added very cautiously so it would be clear there was no commitment on their part:

> We think it, however, a question for future consideration whether some specialized modification of the engine might not be worth construction, to serve as a simple multiplying machine, and another modification of it arranged for the calculation of determinants, so as to serve for the solution of simultaneous equations. This, however, inasmuch as it involves a departure from the general idea of the inventor, we regard as lying outside the terms of reference, and therefore perhaps rather for the consideration of Mr. Babbage's representatives than ours. We accordingly confine ourselves to the mere mention of it by way of suggestion.

"Mr. Babbage's representatives" had already begun work along much the same lines the committee had hesitantly suggested.

THE ANALYTICAL ENGINE WORKS!

Henry Babbage was home from India on furlough in 1871. His father's will had left him all that existed of the Analytical

Engine, its drawings and notation, as well as his workshop and tools. Still filled with admiration for his father and faith in his ideas, Henry began to complete the work on the Analytical Engine, "as far as instructions in the hands of the workmen admitted," using the few finished parts his father had left. He had to return to duty in India, but in 1874 he retired from the service and came home.

For the next five years Henry worked at completing the Difference Engine, untouched since 1834 when the government had stopped work on it. As best as he could, Henry made new frame pieces and even a driving gear that worked perfectly. Because so many parts were missing, he was forced to spend large sums of money replacing them.

The cost of machine work was so high that Henry regretfully brought his work to a close. Saving a few of the finished smaller parts, he melted up the larger frame pieces for the brass in them and wrote an end to Charles Babbage's dreams of the Difference Engine. Then, just after he had done this, he learned that a Mr. Wilkinson, a nephew and successor to Clement, had also just dumped into his melting pots all the parts Clement had retained in the legal battles over the engine. Sick at heart, Henry estimated that with those parts he could have completed the Difference Engine for something like £500.

While he worked on the Difference Engine, Henry had also been thinking about the more ambitious Analytical Engine. The ironic misfortune of the Difference Engine made him decide in 1879 to go ahead with that project, concentrating on the mill and the printing section rather than attempting to complete the whole engine. In 1880 he had the large iron top and bottom frames cast in a foundry. As fast as he could, he continued the work, using the parts his father had made and having others made at his own expense, until finally, on January 21, 1888, he turned the crank of the mill. He smiled to see the printing machine produce a table of the multiples of pi to twenty-nine places. The engine performed flawlessly through thirty-one multiples, but on the thirty-second the carriage failed, and a wrong number was printed.

In September, 1888, Major-General Babbage read a paper at a meeting of the British Association on the Analytical Engine, noting that it had been ten years since the committee had reported unfavorably on it. He began on an optimistic note:

I am well assured that a time will come when such an engine will be completed and be a powerful means of enlarging not only pure mathematical science, but other branches of knowledge, and I wish, as far as in me lies, to hasten that time, and to help towards the general appreciation of the labours of my father, so little known or understood by the multitude even of the educated.

He went on to describe the engine, explaining how a problem was set in. The placing of the "number" cards, "directive" cards, and "operative" cards in the engine sounds like the programming of a modern computer with IBM cards. He told how the various parts of the engine were linked to work in unison by a "chain" mechanism that insured synchronization. In modern electronic computers this is called a "clock pulse" and is electrical.

Henry referred to the more than two hundred detailed drawings made to full scale that his father had produced. He felt confident that the engine could be built, much as Babbage had designed it long ago. But his closing paragraph was not in the same confident tone of the beginning of the paper:

I see no hope of any Analytical Engine, however useful it may be, bringing any profit to its constructor, and beyond the preparation of this Paper, and the publication of the

The mill and printing parts of the Analytical Engine along with the multiples of pi it calculated to twenty-nine places

MULTIPLES OF π.

00001	03141592653589783238462643383
00002	06283185307179566476925286766
00003	09424777960769349715387930149
00004	12566370614359132953850573532
00005	15707963267948916192313216915
00006	18849555921538699430775860298
00007	21991148575128482669238503681
00008	25133741228718265907701147064
00009	28275333882308049146163790447
00010	31415926535897832384626433830
00011	34557518818348761562308907721 3
00012	37699111843077398861551720596
00013	40840704496667182100014363979
00014	43982297150256965338477007362
00015	47123889803846748576939650745
00016	50265482457436531815402294128
00017	53407075111026315053864937511
00018	56548667764616098292327580894
00019	59690260418205881530790224277
00020	62831853071795664769252867660
00021	65973445725385448007715511043
00022	69115038378975231246178154426
00023	72256631032565014484640797809

volume I have mentioned as shortly to follow, there is little or no temptation to do more. Those who wish for such an engine, would, I think, give it a helping hand if they could show what pecuniary benefit it would bring. The History of Babbage's Calculating Machines is sufficient to damp the ardour of a dozen enthusiasts.

Henry turned to other, "less expensive pursuits" and offered the Analytical Engine to the South Kensington Museum, which accepted and displayed it.

In 1906, other work accidentally attracted Henry again to the Analytical Engine, and he solved the problem of the faulty carriage. The engine was sent to the shops of R. W. Munro at Tottenham and, under Henry's supervision, was modified to the extent that it printed out tables perfectly.

TO CIPHER THE UNCIPHERABLE

In 1907, the year after Babbage's mechanical brain was made to perform at last, his real brain was carefully examined by the eminent specialist, Sir Victor Horsley. The brain had been preserved in alcohol for thirty-six years and had shrunk in size by one-third. Horsley estimated that its original weight had been somewhat more than average. He summarized his findings in these words:

> The brain of Mr. Babbage is worthy of record as presenting evidence on:—
> (1) The neurological value of symmetry as a feature of cerebral growth in an individual of high intellectual ability.
> (2) The relative development of the areas of representation of locutory and graphic function in contrast to sensorial representation.

The rear of the Analytical Engine

But the skill of the scientist had not yet reached the point at which the human intellect could be weighed and measured, any more than it can now. Man, fortunately, can build a computer crudely modeled on his own brain without fully understanding that "wondrous raveled knot," as Sir Charles Sherrington, Nobel Prize-winning physiologist, called it.

CHAPTER ELEVEN

Babbage's Dream Comes True

Charles Babbage died bitterly disappointed over the vacuum that seemed to have swallowed up his calculating engines. His son Henry had much the same feeling when he said there was little incentive to do more. It was not all that hopeless, however. In fact, progress *was* being made, not just on the digital computer that Babbage had pioneered, but on other types as well. It would be some seventy years before the work of Babbage, and efforts from two other directions, would fuse and result in the modern computer. But work was going ahead, invisible though it might have been to most of the scientific world. Men were developing "logic" machines and putting punched cards to use.

In 1869, William S. Jevons, an economist and logician, built a "logical piano." On this machine one played not tunes but solutions to logic problems. This was two years before Babbage died, and he was aware of Jevons' work.

In 1881 an American named Allan Marquand also built a machine which could handle propositional logic problems. Another logician was Charles L. Dodgson, better known as

Lewis Carroll, author of *Alice in Wonderland*. In 1886, fifteen years after Babbage died, Dodgson devised a logic machine consisting simply of a ruled board and small counters to be placed in appropriate squares to solve mathematical and logical problems.

HOLLERITH'S GIANT STEPS

Another giant step was made in 1886. This was the practical application of punched cards, as Babbage had proposed, and the use of electrical circuits instead of mechanical linkages in a calculating machine.

William S. Jevons's "logical piano" played solutions to logic problems

Dr. Herman Hollerith contracted with the United States Government to compile the census of 1890. The 1880 census was still being tabulated in 1886, and it was obvious to everyone concerned that it would soon be impossible to complete a census every ten years using old-fashioned manual methods on the great mass of calculations. Dr. Hollerith devised a way to handle the millions of numbers more rapidly.

How much he knew of Babbage's work with punched cards is a question, but Hollerith knew about Jacquard. He made punched cards that could communicate directly with the adding machines he used. As Babbage had accurately foreseen, this had many benefits. Numbers could be code-punched into cards, stacks of which could then be fed to the machine that would "read" them and perform the necessary arithmetic. Instead of Babbage's gears and cogs, Hollerith substituted electricity. As the cards moved above a pool of mercury, pins brushed over them. These pins contacted the mercury through the punched holes and completed appropriate electrical circuits which then accomplished the arithmetical operations. Hollerith had created a new kind of adding machine, fed by punched cards and rapidly operated by electricity.

By 1890 the population of the United States had grown to sixty-two million. The 1880 census had taken seven years to tabulate. Hollerith counted 25 per cent more people, yet took only three years, remarkable evidence of the speed of his new machines. Hollerith's firm merged with others to form the Computing-Tabulating-Recording Company, later the International Business Machine Corporation. This new firm would one day make computer history, but there were intermediate steps to be accomplished.

The Ford Instrument Company in 1915 produced a device called Range Keeper Mark I. Used in military applications,

The Hollerith machine was operated by electricity and used punched cards

this was perhaps the first electrical "analog" computer, a *measuring* computer that dealt in quantities rather than discrete numbers. The gasoline gauge in an automobile is a simple analog computer; so is a slide rule. Babbage's engines, like the ancient abacus and the modern digital computer, count numbers. Five years later General Electric also built an electrical analog machine for testing circuits. When it was found that it had uses as a computing device, mathematicians began to make use of it.

In 1929, Vannevar Bush, an American scientist at Massachusetts Institute of Technology, picked up Lord Kelvin's idea of a mechanical difference analyzer for doing calculus problems. By 1930 he had a working model, and in 1935 he followed this success with a design for one which used electricity. Completed in 1942, it was used secretly in war work. None of these were automatic digital computers of the kind Babbage had designed, however. Hollerith's machines were adding machines, and the electrical computers being produced were analog devices, not true counting devices.

In 1928, L. J. Comrie linked Hollerith cards to his Babbage-inspired difference engine to produce accurate *Nautical Almanac* moon tables for 1935 to 2000. Professor E. W. Brown had hand-computed the original *Tables of the Moon,* and he watched with "ecstasies of rapture" as the Comrie machine processed his laborious computations at twenty to thirty per second. The first Babbage Difference Engine worked to five places and two orders of difference. His full-scale design was to do twenty places and six orders. The Burroughs accounting machine, the first in England, worked in 1913 to fifteen places but only one difference. Comrie's machine, in use until 1954, did thirteen places and six orders of difference. A century after Babbage's Difference Engine no one had improved much on his ideas.

LOGIC TO THE RESCUE

Now it was time for help from the logicians. In 1939 Dr. George Stibitz of Bell Telephone Laboratories decided that he could wire together some telephone relays and other circuitry and make a digital computer to save a great deal of time in his work. This involved complex numbers such as the square root of minus one, an "imaginary" number that is useful in electrical engineering, among other applications.

With the use of relays Stibitz converted decimal numbers to "binary" or two-valued numbers which could be represented by a switch being on or off.

We generally use the decimal, or ten-valued number system in our everyday mathematics. Using nine numbers and zero we arrange them to represent units, tens, hundreds, and so on. The binary system uses only 1 and 0, but they too are arranged so that their place denotes powers of two (instead of powers of ten as in the decimal system). Here are place values for the binary system, with sample binary numbers:

Binary				*Decimal*
8	*4*	*2*	*1*	
0	0	0	1	1
0	0	1	0	2
0	0	1	1	3
0	1	0	0	4
0	1	0	1	5
0	1	1	0	6
0	1	1	1	7
1	0	0	0	8
1	0	0	1	9
1	0	1	0	10

Using the method of mathematical logicians, Stibitz was able to multiply and divide his complex numbers electromechanically. The power and speed of the binary system was added to Babbage's concept of machine calculation. Stibitz's "Complex Computer" was used for several years, and even proved it could solve problems via telephone line for engineers hundreds of miles away by sending binary-coded electrical inpulses through the wires.

By now America was at war with the Axis powers. Military demands on mathematicians pressed them to develop faster methods of computation. IBM was producing a variety of punched-card calculating machines. At Harvard University, Professor Howard H. Aiken had some ideas for extending Stibitz's relay idea to make a large-scale calculating machine. Backed by the military, he and IBM worked together on this.

Aware of Babbage's pioneering work, Aiken thought it was now feasible to construct an Analytical Engine. Using hundreds of electromechanical relays, Aiken built the Mark I Automatic Sequence-Controlled Calculator, or ASCC. It was completed in April of 1944, and immediately was recruited for war work on a twenty-four-hour basis.

BABBAGE'S DREAM COME TRUE

Babbage had designed a memory store of one thousand fifty-digit numbers. The ASCC had seventy-two twenty-three-digit numbers. The Babbage engine was to add numbers in one second; the ASCC was three times that fast, using electricity instead of gears and shafts. Babbage's engine was to do one multiplication (of fifty-digit numbers) in one minute, the ASCC could do ten a minute. The IBM computer was eight feet high and more than fifty feet long, truly a "giant brain."

Babbage had designed his machine with three sets of punched cards. The Mark I used Hollerith cards for part of its operations, but was controlled by a punched *tape* which contained all the necessary instructions for the various steps in a problem. As Babbage had suggested, the machine was capable of using cards punched with information, or forming its own tables. Also, as he had predicted, many programs, once prepared, could be stored for use when needed.

Babbage had always stressed the need for printing out results so that errors would not be made in transcribing. Interestingly, the ASCC typed out answers on an electric typewriter, and photo copies were made to guarantee against anything being changed accidentally. Professor Aiken proudly estimated that the ASCC, in just one day's time, did the work a manual computer could turn out in six months. This was the key point Babbage had stressed, and the computer played a vital role in aiding the national interest.

When L. J. Comrie published in *Nature* his article titled "Babbage's Dream Comes True," it sounded like an echo of Charles Babbage himself. Comrie charged that the black mark the government of England had earned a century ago in not building the Analytical Engine still had to be wiped out. Noting that IBM donated the ASCC to Harvard when it was completed, Comrie said, "Would that this example were followed by their opposite numbers in Great Britain!"

The ASCC was far from the final answer. One authority described the situation:

> Harvard Mark I cannot fully exploit the power of automatic judgment which Babbage proposed to incorporate in his analytical engine. When first it was built, the only alternatives between which the machine could choose were to "continue with the next instruction on the tape" or "stop" and it decided between these two according to whether the number it had computed was greater or less than the amount specified by the programmer. The flexibility of control has since been improved, but for the first part of its life it could not compute its own programme in the manner in which Lady Lovelace suggested.

IBM's Selective-Sequence Electronic Calculator (SSEC) was probably the first to have a "conditional transfer" system of control instruction in the sense that Babbage and Lady Lovelace recommended. It was used from 1948 to 1952 and did a job for the Atomic Energy Commission in six months that would have taken one hundred years of human computation.

Great improvement that it was, the ASCC was but a

DEWEY
Decimal Classification®

DEWEY

Decimal Classification
and
Relative Index

Devised by

MELVIL DEWEY

Edition 19

Edited under the direction of
BENJAMIN A. CUSTER

Volume 1

Introduction
Tables

FOREST PRESS
A Division of
Lake Placid Education Foundation

ALBANY, N.Y. 12206 U.S.A.
1979

Library of Congress Cataloging in Publication Data

Dewey, Melvil, 1851–1931.
 Dewey decimal classification and relative index.
 First published anonymously in 1876 under title: A classification and subject index. 2d ed. published under title: Decimal classification and relativ index.

 CONTENTS: v. 1. Introduction. Tables.—v. 2. Schedules.—v. 3. Relative index.

 1. Classification, Dewey decimal. I. Custer, Benjamin Allen, 1912– . II. Title.
Z696.D519 1979   025.4′3   77–27967
ISBN 0–910608–19–9 (v. 1)

Vol. 1: ISBN 0–910608–19–9
3-vol. set: ISBN 0–910608–23–7

This Edition of the

Dewey Decimal Classification

is

Respectfully Dedicated

to the

Memory

of

Godfrey Dewey

1887–1977

One Time Editor

and

Long Time Supporter of the Classification

Contents

Volume 1

Contents

Volume 2

Volume 3

Publisher's Foreword

The Dewey Decimal Classification observed its centennial as this, the nineteenth edition, neared completion. When one compares the first and the nineteenth editions of the Classification and reviews the phenomena that have contributed to its development, the one-hundred year retrospect comprises an impressive vista.

The Classification has grown from an anonymous 44-page pamphlet to a three-volume work of some 3,000 pages. Concurrent with this growth and indeed a major reason for it have been the dramatic increase in knowledge and information and the ensuing increase in the production of books and other communications media. In addition, continuing Melvil Dewey's commitment to provide libraries with a subject approach for arranging their collections, the schedules have been expanded and number-building devices have been developed to permit further specification by language, geography, literature, and persons, as well as by standard subdivisions.

The first edition of the Dewey Decimal Classification was tested by applying it to the collection of books in the Amherst College Library. It was immediately and enthusiastically received by libraries in the United States. Since that time, and especially in recent years, the Classification has spread to more than 130 countries throughout the world, a testimonial to its international, as well as its domestic, utility. Today, the Dewey Decimal Classification is the most widely used of any classification of books.

Along with its growth in size and use, the Classification has become increasingly complex to produce. Many individuals join in a cooperative effort to bring out each edition; the contributions of each and the interrelationships among them deserve mention here.

Forest Press, the publisher of the Classification, is a division of the Lake Placid Education Foundation, which was chartered in 1922 at the request of Melvil Dewey by the Board of Regents of the University of the State of New York. The Forest Press Committee, which is responsible for developing and formulating policy with respect to editing and producing the Classification, is appointed by the Trustees of the Foundation. The Committee includes, in addition to members representing the Foundation's Board of Trustees, the following members representing library concerns: Walter W. Curley, Chairman, President of Gaylord Bros., Inc.; John A. Humphry, former Chairman, continuing Committee member, and Executive Director of Forest Press; Robert L. Talmadge, Director of Technical Departments of the University of Illinois Library; Richard W. Gardner, Professor of Library and Information Science, University of California at Los Angeles; and J. Michael O'Brien, Head Librarian, Oaklawn Public Library, Illinois.

Forest Press and the Forest Press Committee are assisted in their editorial responsibilities by an advisory group known as the Decimal Classification Editorial Policy Committee. The Editorial Policy Committee represents the libraries that use Dewey, and usually meets twice a year on matters relating to the development of the Classification. The Committee is made up of professionals who have experience in a wide variety of libraries, here and abroad, and who are well versed in the theory and application of the Classification. The members of the Committee who served during the preparation of Edition 19 are listed in the Preface.

For the actual editing of the Schedules, Tables, and Index, Forest Press contracts with the Library of Congress, whose table of organization includes a Decimal Classification Division within its Processing Department. The Chief of the Decimal Classification Division, which oversees the application of Dewey numbers to Library of Congress catalog cards, is also the Editor of the Classification. In this way classification theory and practice are combined, allowing for continuous and thorough editorial review. The past four editions, 16 through 19, have been edited under the expert direction of Benjamin A. Custer.

A major innovation for Edition 19 should be brought to the attention of users of the Dewey Decimal Classification. The Forest Press Committee and the Executive Director have been working for several years with consultants at Arthur D. Little, Inc., studying and analyzing the potential benefits that might accrue to the development of the Classification through the application of computer technology. Feasibility studies indicated such sufficiently positive results that this edition of the Dewey Decimal Classification was produced by computerized photocomposition. It is expected that the success of this edition will dictate continuation of the process. In addition, computer technology will have a positive impact on the editorial process.

The international acceptance of the Dewey Decimal Classification continues to grow. The British National Bibliography adopted Edition 18 in 1971, permitting British libraries and many others throughout the English-speaking world to apply Dewey numbers to their collections. The Canadian, Indian, South African, and Australian National Bibliographies also use Dewey numbers in their bibliographic publications. It is expected that other national bibliographies will adopt Edition 19, thus enhancing the Classification and its application, and benefiting the users of libraries everywhere by helping to standardize the subject approach to library materials. The value of working with the directors of national bibliographies around the world is therefore inestimable.

In July 1977, a change of administration at Forest Press took place, at which time the undersigned succeeded Richard B. Sealock as Executive Director. During Richard Sealock's nine-year tenure as Executive Director, the Press and all its publications enjoyed wide acclaim from the library community throughout the world, a tribute to Mr. Sealock's professional competence and ability.

John A. Humphry
EXECUTIVE DIRECTOR
Forest Press Division
Lake Placid Education Foundation

31 October 1977

DEWEY DECIMAL CLASSIFICATION ADDITIONS, NOTES, AND DECISIONS

To keep users of Dewey Decimal Classification Edition 19 up to date on developments regarding the Classification, *Dewey Decimal Classification Additions, Notes, and Decisions*, popularly known as *DC&*, is published at occasional intervals. All purchasers of Edition 19 are entitled to a free copy of *DC&* and may be placed on the mailing list for this publication by either returning the enclosed card or by writing to Forest Press, 85 Watervliet Avenue, Albany, New York 12206, U.S.A.

Preface by the Decimal Classification Editorial Policy Committee

The Decimal Classification Editorial Policy Committee, which had its origins in 1937, plays an important advisory role in determining the general direction of the Dewey Decimal Classification. Its constituency consists of libraries, the users of the Classification, and it is their needs that primarily concern the Committee. The membership of the Editorial Policy Committee therefore represents as wide and divergent a group of library interests as possible, and now includes a representative of the (British) Library Association, in recognition of the growing international application of the Classification. In addition, a Canadian librarian, a member of the American Library Association, also serves on the Committee. With its users in mind, the Committee advises the publisher of the DDC, Forest Press, and also works with the Editor of the DDC, carefully overseeing changes and innovations in the Classification.

Each edition of the DDC is greeted with mixed feelings, for it is composed of the cherished old and the unknown new. Edition 19, in the Committee's estimation, has been faithful to stability where stability is more useful than change, and it has been changed where a new vision serves us better than the old. There are only three phoenix sections in Edition 19: (1) the badly crowded 301 section has been replaced by Phoenix 301–307 Sociology; (2) political parties, regardless of their locale, have been provided for by Phoenix 324 The political process; and (3) extensive changes in the local subdivisions of England, Northern Ireland, Scotland, and Wales have been provided for by phoenix treatment of area notations 41–42. A detailed review of the changes in Edition 19 is presented by the Editor in sections 1–3 of his introduction.

Though the problems and special needs of libraries using the DDC in countries throughout the world continued to receive careful consideration in the preparation of Edition 19, a special attempt was made during this time to gather data regarding the use of the DDC in the United States and Canada. This user survey, sponsored by Forest Press and conducted in 1975, was an attempt to determine the problems of DDC users in the United States and Canada and to seek the opinion of librarians in these two countries regarding the development of the DDC. Some of what was learned in the survey has been applied to the schedules of Edition 19—for instance, the relocation of political history from 320.9 to the 900s—and also will have an impact on the schedules of Edition 20.

The survey also revealed problems regarding the correct application and use of the DDC. In order to expedite and improve this situation, the Editor's Introduction has been reorganized, notes are more plentiful, the index has been rendered more responsive, seminars for classifiers and teachers have been planned, and a manual for application of Edition 19 will appear shortly after publication of the edition. Confirming our faith in the Editor's wisdom, many of the modifications of the DDC that the survey found to be desirable had been anticipated by him for Edition 19.

The members of the Editorial Policy Committee recommend change and revision only after careful thought and much discussion, always keeping uppermost in their minds the needs and desires of the worldwide library community they serve. As a listing of their names and positions indicates, they represent, as much as is possible, the varied interests and needs of libraries. Serving on the Committee during the preparation of Edition 19 were: Lois M. Chan, Associate Professor, College of Library Science, University of Kentucky; Margaret E. Cockshutt, Associate Professor, Faculty of Library Science, University of Toronto; John P. Comaromi, formerly Associate Professor, Western Michigan University, Kalamazoo, Michigan, now Associate Professor, Graduate School of Library and Information Science, University of California at Los Angeles; Betty M. E. Croft, Catalog Librarian, University of Illinois Library; Joel C. Downing, Director of Copyright and English Language Services of the Bibliographic Services Division of The British Library; Doralyn J. Hickey, formerly Associate Professor, School of Library Science, University of North Carolina, then Director, School of Library Science, University of Wisconsin at Milwaukee; Frances Hinton, Chief of the Processing Division of the Free Library of Philadelphia; Joseph H. Howard, Director of the Processing Department of the Library of Congress, and representative of the Library of Congress; John A. Humphry, Assistant Commissioner for Libraries in the New York State Education Department, and representative of Forest Press; Mary Louise Mann, Coordinator of Secondary School Libraries of the Metropolitan School District, Washington Township, Indiana, and representative of the American Library Association; Clare E. Ryan, Head of Technical Processing of the New Hampshire State Library, and representative of the American Library Association; Marietta D. Shepard, Chief of the Library Development Program of the Organization of American States; and William J. Welsh, Director of the Processing Department of the Library of Congress, now Deputy Librarian of Congress.

The Editorial Policy Committee recommends Edition 19 to you with mixed feelings of pride and humility. We believe it continues the high standards set by the recent editions of the Classification. At the same time, we are well aware of its imperfections, perhaps inherent in the very nature of classification systems, and again urge you, the users of the DDC, to continue to provide us with your ever-welcome advice and suggestions.

> John P. Comaromi
> CHAIRMAN
> Decimal Classification Editorial
> Policy Committee

Graduate School of Library and Information Science
University of California
Los Angeles, California 90024
30 September 1977

Acknowledgments

For the fourth, and no doubt the last time, I have the pleasure of expressing publicly my appreciation to those many colleagues and others whose labor and support have assisted and sustained me throughout the compilation and publication of Editions 16, 17, 18, and now 19.

Specifically as to the present edition, I should like first of all to offer my heartfelt thanks to the users and critics of the Classification. An international group coming from many of the over one hundred lands in which the system is known to be used, they have read, studied, commented upon, queried, condemned, and praised each edition, transmitting their comments to me in a most helpful manner.

Formal groups connected with library associations have provided me with invaluable advice and guidance. Among these are the Subject Analysis Committee and the Policy and Research Committee of the Cataloging and Classification Section of the Resources and Technical Services Division of the American Library Association, the Dewey Decimal Classification Sub-Committee of The (United Kingdom) Library Association, the Dewey Decimal Classification Liaison Committee of the Library Association of Australia, and a group from the South African Library Association.

I should like also to extend my deep appreciation to those libraries with which the Decimal Classification Division corresponds regularly on interpretation of particular numbers and their centralized application to specific titles, that is, The British Library (especially Joel C. Downing and Robert R. Trotter), and the national libraries of Canada (Cynthia Durance, Clarisse Cardin, Blair Cowan), Australia (Janet Braithwaite, Judith Baskin, Peter Haddad), and South Africa (Mrs. E. Nel). Expansions and improvements in the area table for the British Isles, Canada, Australia, South Africa, Latin America, and France have been made through cooperative efforts with libraries or librarians in the countries concerned.

I have received unstinting support and cooperation from those individuals who are associated officially or formally with the Dewey Decimal Classification. These include the members of the Forest Press Committee, whose names are listed in the Publisher's Foreword; and those of the Decimal Classification Editorial Policy Committee, whose names are listed in the Preface; the former

Executive Director of Forest Press, Richard B. Sealock, and the late Assistant Executive Director, Pauline A. Seely; the former Chairman of the Forest Press Committee, John A. Humphry, currently Executive Director of Forest Press; and my superiors at the Library of Congress, with special bows to William J. Welsh and Joseph H. Howard.

To the staff members of the Decimal Classification Division, who have suffered me, assisted me, badgered me, and sustained me even as they have contributed to the edition, I offer my everlasting gratitude. Former members of the Division during the production of Edition 19 are Charles H. Brackett, Joyce Elaine Butcher, Elaine H. Canlas, Emiko Hara Custer, Idalia V. Fuentes, Lydia C. Hsieh, Ronald W. Johnson, Geraldine O. Matthews, Marilyn Nasatir, and Helen L. Pritchett; present members are Melba Davis Adams, Rosalee Connor, Eve M. Dickey, William S. Hwang, Letitia Jew, Virginia A. Schoepf, Emily K. Spears, Cosmo D. Tassone, and Edna E. Van Syoc. Most of the direct work on this edition has been performed by Levon Avdoyan, Frances Ann Bold, Constance M. Bradshaw, Judy C. McDermott, Allene M. McDuffie, Gregory R. New, Marisa C. Vandenbosch, Steven C. Wilkshire, and especially by Winton E. Matthews, Jr., and by Margaret J. Warren, a diligent and creative assistant editor.

Finally, I wish to express my most profound appreciation to the late Arline Kern Custer, who at all times through three and one half editions, drove me, led me, cajoled me, supported me, and inspired me. In the best sense of the phrase, she was the editor's "better half."

Benjamin A. Custer
EDITOR

Decimal Classification Division
Processing Department
The Library of Congress
Washington, D.C. 20540
31 August 1977

Editor's Introduction

I. Characteristics of Edition 19

1 Consolidation of gains. Edition 19 represents a consolidation of the generally accepted and well-received revisions and additions included in Editions 17 and 18.

1.1 EXPANSION. There are more entries, provisions for more topics, and therefore more opportunities to build numbers. This is a result not only of the greater breadth and depth of knowledge, but also of the growing use of the Classification as an efficient method of organizing materials by subject and of retrieving information from machine-readable storage. However, the determination of how far to expand a given section continues to be based on a calculation of how many titles there are in that field or how many may be expected, i.e., on literary warrant.

A comparative table of the number of schedule and table entries in Editions 18 and 19 follows. This does not include centered entries, which are duplicated by the separate entries that follow and are encompassed by them. Neither does it include entries for which the numbers are printed in square brackets. "Entries that may be expanded" are those entries included in the total that can be developed into many entries by the application of instructions that appear in the schedules and tables. When one considers that every number can also be expanded by application of Tables 1, 2, 5, and 7, it is obvious that the DDC's potential for detailed classification is many times greater than the existence of 21,504 entries in the schedules might suggest.

1.2 FACETING. There is more recognition of the possibilities of subdividing various subjects according to more than one characteristic, and there are more notes establishing the order in which the classifier is to consider or combine those characteristics.

1.3 NOTES. There are more notes of explanation and instruction. In a by-now almost total reversal of Edition 17's policy of strict frugality of notes, directions appear at hundreds of places where there is evidence to indicate that busy classifiers tend to become confused. In particular, very detailed step-by-step instructions for building numbers in the 800s have been introduced both into that schedule and into Table 3, "Subdivisions of Individual Litera-

Class	Edition 19		Edition 18		Increase	
	Total entries	Entries that may be expanded	Total entries	Entries that may be expanded	Total entries	Entries that may be expanded
0	511	100	443	69	68	31
1	670	14	643	22	27	−8
2	1,411	296	1,291	286	120	10
3	4,321	1,080	3,430	398	891	682
4	268	133	280	114	−12	19
5	3,144	897	2,830	698	314	199
6	6,089	1,021	5,694	921	395	100
7	2,222	484	1,912	270	310	214
8	327	187	425	149	−98	38
9	2,541	400	2,032	391	509	9
Total schedules	21,504	4,612	18,980	3,318	2,524	1,294
Table 1	116	20	112	17	4	3
2	6,933	6	5,939	12	994	−6
3	75	57	235	31	−160	26
4	29	5	28	5	1	0
5	192	191	182	181	10	10
6	239	0	234	0	5	0
7	440	1	431	1	9	0
Total tables	8,024	280	7,161	247	863	33
Grand total	29,528	4,892	26,141	3,565	3,387	1,327

tures," and Table 3 has been augmented by supplementary Table 3–A, which replaces numerous repetitions of a long array of concepts.

In addition to various new provisions in Table 1, "Standard Subdivisions," there are more directives leading from unused standard subdivisions at particular places in the schedules to those numbers where, for historical reasons, the standard subdivision concepts have been placed, e.g., from 530.0151.

1.4 INDEX. While the index retains the same pattern as in Edition 18, it has been refined and made into a more efficient tool. Many cross references have been deleted and replaced by numbers; more synonyms have been added; some of the less-used aspects of various subjects, e.g., production economics, have been largely removed. Topics and numbers that can be subdivided are no longer printed in bold-face type.

1.5 INTRODUCTORY MATTER. The introduction has been reorganized and partly rewritten. Melvil Dewey's mostly obsolete introduction has been dropped, but those parts of it still valuable for the practitioner and student have been incorporated into other preliminary sections. Those who wish to consult Dewey's text for historical purposes may find it in Editions 12–14 and 16–18.

1.6 INTERNATIONAL UTILITY. Permeating the entire edition is a continually increasing commitment to the international use and value of the DDC, which is reflected in more hospitality to needs of other cultures both through expansions generally, e.g., at area notations 41–42 and 8, and through introduction of more options to emphasize favored languages, religions, and the like; also in a return to conventional American spelling from the residual simpler spellings of Editions 16–18, e.g., divorst, publisht, which greatly frustrated those whose native tongue is not English. The Decimal Classification Editorial Policy Committee and the Forest Press have adopted the following editorial rule to govern the objective of making Edition 19 internationally useful:

> In preparing an edition it is desirable to allow positively for the needs, both in detail and in order, of countries outside the U.S. Where there is a conflict between these needs and those of the U.S. the Editor should give his preference to the needs of the U.S., but must make provision for an alternative use by libraries outside the U.S. in a manner appropriate to the particular problem.

2 Other general characteristics.

2.1 OPTIONS. While optional provisions to meet the needs of countries outside the United States have grown in number and in detail, some of the other options that have been authorized during the years to satisfy the needs of particular libraries, but that do not promote correct classification, have been discontinued. Libraries following such options will continue to sacrifice the benefits to be derived from numbers assigned by centralized classification services.

2.2 PHOENIX SCHEDULES AND TABLES. Completely remodeled provisions have been prepared for the following:

301–307 Sociology has been recast from the former 301, making use in addition of 302–307, numbers that have been unused since Edition 16, when they were the standard subdivisions of the social sciences.

324 The political process has been recast from the former 324 and 329, and does away with the previous notational bias that favored United States political parties.

Area notations 41–42 have been revised to conform to the reorganized local administrative pattern of the United Kingdom.

Phoenix schedules and tables are approved by the Editorial Policy and Forest Press Committees only when the provisions of earlier editions are deemed entirely inadequate for classification of modern concepts. A phoenix schedule was announced also for 560–590 Life sciences, but has been withheld from this edition because it required more time for careful study and consultation than was available, and also because there appeared to be more pressing need for the revisions named above.

As usual, lists are printed of significant topics whose numbers have been changed. These lists were formerly known as "tables of concordance" and they appeared after the index in volume 3. In this edition they are called "lists of changed numbers" and they are to be found near the close of volume 1. It is a new policy with Edition 19 not to reprint for one final time the superseded schedules.

2.3 RELOCATIONS. In addition to the relocations in the phoenix schedules, there are 340 other relocations; this figure may be compared with approximately 1600 in Edition 16, 800 in Edition 17, and 400 in Edition 18. The count and distribution by main class and table are as follows:

Class	Number of relocations
0	24
1	15
2	43
3	91
4	1
5	32
6	68
7	17
8	1
9	13
Table 1	9
2	21
3	2
4	1
5	0
6	2
7	0

They are all listed in this volume following Tables 1–7.

2.4 REUSE OF NUMBERS. The long-standing rule limiting the reuse of old numbers with new meanings (except in phoenix schedules) has been somewhat relaxed, so that the editors may have a freer hand to make logical and useful developments. The new rule permits a number previously used to be freely reused if it has been vacated for at least two consecutive editions (instead of for 25 years). This means that this edition reuses routinely numbers that had a meaning in Edition 16 (1958) but that were without meaning in Editions 17 (1965) and 18 (1971), e.g., 302–307. Numbers are occasionally reused more speedily, but only by express permission of the Decimal Classification Editorial Policy Committee and the Forest Press, and in such cases are printed in italics; in this edition the following eleven numbers have been reused by such permission: 025.49, 351.007, 351.4, 567.9, 597.9, 614.1, 879.9, 901.9, 910.8, 941.081, *area*–719. Another number offered only as an option would, if so used, be re-used: 940.11.

3 Other notable specific additions. To name some expansions and explanations as notable courts the danger of omitting mention of others that users and critics may consider more significant. Yet it is doubtful that anyone will consider any of the following to be insignificant:

In Table 1, "Standard Subdivisions," there is a table of precedence, and 088-089 will be welcomed by many as a device for arranging any subject by ethnic groups or classes of persons, while standard subdivision 068 replaces class 658.9 as the preferred treatment for management of enterprises engaged in specific kinds of activities. The use of 08 for collections has been discontinued except in the field of belles-lettres.

In 340 optional provision is made to arrange law by jurisdiction and also to class law of a favored jurisdiction in a shorter number.

In 900 there are substantial expansions in the history periods.

II. Basic Plan

4 The purpose of classification. A major objective of libraries is to see that optimum use is made of their collections by leading each reader or student as directly as possible to the material that he needs. As an aid to the achievement of this purpose, nearly all libraries find it helpful, indeed necessary, to apply subject control to their books and other materials.

One such form is classification, or systematic arrangement by subject. To classify a collection of objects is to place together in classes those objects which have certain characteristics in common and to separate from them the objects which do not have those characteristics. For instance, textile fabrics can be classified (1) according to the process by which they are made, each of which may then be considered a separate class, e.g., knitted material, braided material, crocheted lace, woven cloth. Fabrics can also be classified according to any one of several other principles, such as: (2) according to the material from which they are made, e.g., silk, linen, cotton, wool; (3) according to function, e.g., clothing, napery, hangings, carpets; (4) according to color, e.g., red, blue, black, white. If primary division is by process, each process can then be divided (or classified) by materials, e.g., woven cloth of silk, linen, cotton, wool, the result of which may be considered an array of subclasses; and each subclass may be further divided into subsubclasses according to function, e.g., woven cotton shirts, tablecloths, towels.

Similarly, persons may be classified, among other ways, according to (1) occupations, (2) physical and mental characteristics, e.g., healthy, blind, mentally retarded, (3) social status, e.g., criminals, unemployed, retired, (4) marriage status, (5) level of cultural development, (6) social and/or economic level, e.g., slaves, middle class, royalty, (7) age, (8) sex, (9) racial, ethnic, national backgrounds.

Classification may be applied not only to tangible objects and beings, but also to processes, to actions, to relationships, to mental concepts, in fact to any kind of subject or group of subjects the members of which show likenesses as well as differences.

A system of notation, though not an essential part of a classification system, is a major convenience, (1) in designating briefly the different classes and subclasses, especially if there are a great many of them in a complex pattern of relationships, (2) in identifying the objects or concepts that belong to the various classes, and (3) in determining, for physical objects, their actual distribution and arrangement according to a desired and systematic sequence.

Librarians classify their works (books, periodicals, pamphlets, sound recordings, films, slides, pictures, prints, maps, microforms, and other media of information and communication) according to various kinds of characteristics. For example, because of differing problems of shelving, handling, and giving service, they usually separate recordings, films, atlases, newspapers, and the like, from bound volumes of more or less conventional size: in this case the characteristic of division is physical form. In libraries of rare books the works are often classified according to date and place of publication. Another common characteristic upon which division is based is specific kind of use, so that reference books, children's books, books in particular languages, books for popular reading collections, or books of current interest may be set aside in separate groups. But most commonly, either overall or within such categories as those named above, librarians classify works according to subject content. For example, they bring together the history books and separate them from the engineering books, within the history section they bring together the books on United States history and separate them from the books on European history, and within the U.S. history group they bring together works on Abraham Lincoln and the Civil War and separate them from works on Franklin D. Roosevelt and the New Deal. Such an arrangement is most useful for effective retrieval of the kind of information wanted by the majority of patrons and the librarians serving them.

In addition to organizing materials by subject arrangement on shelves, libraries also develop catalogs, bibliographies, and indexes in which they list books, parts of books, reports, articles, tapes, pictures, and the like in a systematically subject-classified order. These may be made manually or printed out by computer, and are capable of showing very detailed and subtle subject distinctions and relationships for the convenience of users in identifying appropriate works.

The individual librarian may develop his own system of subject classification for the collection for which he is responsible, catering to the special needs of its users. In the past many librarians did this, and some, mainly in special libraries, still do. Some public libraries organize their collections of works of current popular interest in somewhat heterogeneous groups according to a reader-interest arrangement, e.g., works of interest to homemakers, regrouping titles and developing new categories as interests of patrons shift.

However, the development of an integrated plan that will provide systematically for the hundreds of thousands of subjects with which works may deal in this age of rapidly increasing knowledge has become highly complex. It requires the intense efforts of specialists in librarianship, in subject classification, and in the many disciplines which comprise the world of information and learning, from religion to mathematics to sculpture to public administration to aeronautical engineering to football. For this reason, librarians have generally found it advantageous to follow one of the already existing book classification systems, the best known of which are the Decimal Classification of Dewey, the Bibliographic Classification of Bliss, the Colon Classification of Ranganathan, the Library of Congress Classification, and the Universal Decimal Classification.

Use of one of the recognized systems has the further advantages (1) that the arrangement and notation of each are widely known and comprehended by other librarians and also by laymen, and (2) that in the case of some of the systems, notably Dewey, Library of Congress, and Universal Decimal, individual works are centrally classed by one or more bibliographic services whose decisions may be utilized by subscribing institutions.

Of these commonly used systems, Dewey's Decimal Classification is the oldest and most widely used. In the United States it is the system followed by a substantial majority of all libraries, including nearly all public libraries and school libraries; in other English-speaking countries it has been adopted by a majority of libraries; elsewhere it has users in almost every nation on the globe. It has been translated, with or without abridgment, expansion, or adaptation, into scores of languages from Spanish, Norwegian, Turkish, and French to Japanese, Sinhalese, Portuguese, and Thai. The Dewey system is now used, in one form or another, by such varied services as the Library of Congress's catalog cards and book catalogs; the American Library Association's *Booklist;* the H. W. Wilson Company's *Standard Catalog Series* and *Book Review Digest;* the R. R. Bowker Company's *Publishers' Weekly* and *American Book Publishing Record;* the British and a number of other national bibliographies. Titles in many reading lists, book guides, and bibliographies have been arranged or their subjects have been identified by the Dewey Decimal Classification. Recently DDC numbers have been recorded on the MARC (MAchine Readable Cataloging) magnetic tapes of the Library of Congress, The British Library, and other national systems; they have been printed in publications themselves wherever a cataloging-in-publication program is in operation.

In 1895 the forerunner of what is now the International Federation for Documentation (FID), by agreement with Melvil Dewey as to concordance and bibliographic use, adopted the Decimal Classification as the basis for its international subject index. This grew into the Classification Décimale, otherwise known as the Brussels Classification or, now, as the Universal Decimal Classification (UDC), which has itself been translated into many languages. While many differences between DDC and UDC have appeared in the intervening years, the foundations of the two remain recognizably the same.

5 Dewey Decimal Classification.

5.1 STRUCTURE.

5.11 *Basic plan.* The Dewey Decimal Classification is a hierarchical system using the decimal principle for the subdivision of knowledge, as represented in publications; that is, each group in the successive division of knowledge, from the broadest to the most minute, is divided on a base of ten.

The first division is into ten main classes, 0–9, which embrace the whole of human knowledge and intellectual endeavor. Main class 0 is used for general works on many subjects from many points of view, such as general newspapers and encyclopedias, and also for certain specialized disciplines that deal with knowledge generally, such as information and communication, library science, and journalism. Main classes 1–9 consist each of a major discipline or group of related disciplines. Following are the ten main classes with their assigned meanings:

0	Generalities	5	Pure sciences
1	Philosophy and related	6	Technology (Applied sciences)
	disciplines	7	The arts
2	Religion	8	Literature (Belles-lettres)
3	Social sciences	9	General geography and history
4	Language		and their auxiliaries

So that the structure may be more readily understood, in the following explanation we use one or two digits, although in practice the notation always consists of at least three digits, with zero being given its normal arithmetical value where required to fill out a number to three digits. Thus the full DDC notation for main class 6 is 6̲0̲0̲. The notation used to designate the complete span of each main class consists of one hundred three-digit numbers, e.g., 0̲0̲0̲–0̲9̲9̲ for generalities, 3̲0̲0̲–3̲9̲9̲ for social sciences, 6̲0̲0̲–6̲9̲9̲ for applied sciences.

Each main class consists of ten divisions, likewise numbered 0–9. These division numbers occupy the second position in the notation. Division 0 is used for general works on the entire main class, 1–9 for subclasses of the main class. Thus, 6̲0̲ is devoted to general works on the applied sciences, 6̲1̲ to medical sciences, 6<u>2</u> to engineering and allied operations, 6<u>3</u> to agriculture and related technologies, etc. The full DDC notations for these divisions, each filled out by the addition of a zero, are 6<u>00</u> for general works on main class 6, 6<u>1</u>0 for medical sciences, 6<u>2</u>0 for engineering, 6<u>3</u>0 for agriculture.

Again, each division has, or at least is capable of having, ten sections, also numbered 0–9. The section numbers occupy the third position in the notation. Thus, the full span of section numbers for each division listed above is 600–60<u>9</u>, 61<u>0</u>–61<u>9</u>, 62<u>0</u>–62<u>9</u>, 63<u>0</u>–63<u>9</u>. In the sections, the 0 in the third position in the number is applied to general works on the entire division, and 1–9 are used for subsubclasses. Thus, 63<u>0</u> is assigned to agriculture and related technologies in general, 63<u>1</u> to crops and their production, 63<u>2</u> to plant injuries, diseases, pests, 63<u>3</u> to field crops, 63<u>6</u> to animal husbandry. The system permits further subdivision to any degree desired, with a continued decimal notation, which consists of the addition, following any set of three digits from 000 to 999, of a decimal point and as many more digits as may be required. Thus, 636 animal husbandry is divided into 636.<u>1</u> horses and other equines, 636.<u>2</u> cattle and other bovines, 636.<u>3</u> sheep and other small ruminants, 636.<u>4</u> swine, 636.<u>5</u> poultry, 636.<u>6</u> other birds, 636.<u>7</u> dogs, 636.<u>8</u> cats, 636.<u>9</u> other warm-blooded animals; 636.1 is further divided into 636.1<u>1</u> Oriental horses, 636.1<u>2</u> racehorses and trotters, 636.1<u>6</u> ponies, 636.1<u>8</u> other equines such as mules, and others.

Individual numbers in Dewey are not necessarily limited each to a specific or single subject. Although many subjects have their own numbers, e.g., husbandry of Arabian horses 636.11<u>2</u>, many other specific subjects are grouped together in a single notation, e.g., husbandry of asses, mules, and zebras all 636.18.

At the end of this volume are three summaries, showing in full notation the ten main classes, the almost one hundred divisions, and the almost one thousand sections.

5.12 *Application of the Classification to specific works.* Each work acquired by a library may be assigned to one of the main classes, divisions, sections, or subsections to the degree of specificity provided by the schedules of the DDC, or to any lesser degree of specificity appropriate to the situation (see section 5.3), and it may be identified as belonging to its specific class by use of the appropriate notation. (The word "class" is used to refer to a main class or a subdivision of any degree, be it 300 or 330 or 338 or 338.47669.) The notation, or number, designates the work's class; when written on the work and on the records that describe the work, it provides a shorthand identification of the work's subject and determines its relative position within the library's entire collection and within the appropriate discipline.

Similarly, each subject, simple or complex, entered in a subject catalog, bibliography, or index may be assigned to a DDC class and arranged in classified order. Classified—or "classed"—catalogs are not well known in North America, though widely used elsewhere. In them each work is entered under one or several classification symbols (together with the natural-language concept that each stands for), all arranged in systematic classified order. For example, if the DDC is used, this brings together under 669 general works on metallurgy and works on the metallurgy of copper, lead, zinc, tin, and aluminum, which, in an alphabetic subject catalog, would be scattered from A through M to Z. At the same time it separates works on copper industry (338), copper mining (622), copper metallurgy (669), and copper art work (739), which, in an alphabetic subject catalog, would be fairly close together under the letters C-o-p-p-e-r.

5.121 *Book numbers.* In large collections even highly specific, or close, classification leaves several works in a single class. To distinguish further the works in a class and to expedite identification, shelving, and physical retrieval many libraries add to the class number a book number; these together constitute the call number. The book number is usually based on authorship, but may, as in biography, be based on alphabetical subarrangement of individual subjects within the class notation. For the use and construction of book numbers the reader should consult Bertha R. Barden's *Book Numbers* (Chicago, American Library Association, 1937). Many libraries select author numbers from the Cutter or Cutter-Sanborn *Author Tables* (Chicopee, Mass., H. R. Huntting Co.), or follow the system of *Author Numbers* used by the Library of Congress (Washington, D.C.). Lists of author numbers have also been devised for libraries in which the names have different letter frequencies than are normally to be found in North American libraries, e.g., for libraries with mainly Hispanic authors. A special book number arrangement for works by and about William Shakespeare, which may be adapted for use with any other specific author, appears in the DDC schedules under class 822.33.

Among the other systems used for separation of works within classes are arrangement by authors' surnames spelled out, by initials of authors' surnames, and by dates of publication.

5.13 *Discipline.* The concept of discipline, that is, branch of knowledge or learning, is fundamental to an understanding of Dewey's system. The primary basis for DDC arrangement and development is by discipline, as defined by the main and subordinate classes, while, strictly speaking, subjects, that is, concrete objects, abstract concepts, activities, or processes not necessarily limited to one field of study, are secondary. There is no one place for any subject in itself; a subject may appear in any or all of the disciplines. No class can be said to cover the scope of marriage, or of water, or of copper, or of Brazil; in other words, there is no single number for any of these concepts or subjects. A work on marriage belongs in 306 if it treats the subject from the point of view of sociology, in 155 if from the point of view of psychology, in 173 if from the point of view of ethics, in 392 if from the point of view of customs, in 613 if from the point of view of hygiene. Similarly, a work on water may be classed with many disciplines, such as metaphysics, religion, economics, commerce, physics, chemistry, geology, oceanography, meteorology, and history.

No other feature of the DDC is more basic than this: that it scatters subjects by discipline. The index, which appears in volume 3, illustrates this quite clearly. There, under each subject, will be found the numbers in which it may be classed according to the disciplines under which it may fall. Here are two modified examples:

Aerodynamics	
aeronautical engineering	629.132 3
astronautical engineering	629.415 1
mechanics	533.62
meteorology	551.515 3
Copper	
arts	739.511
chemistry	
inorganic	546.652
organic	547.056 52
technology	661.065 2
construction	
architecture	721.044 73
building	693.73
materials	
building	691.83
engineering	620.182
foundations	624.153 82
shipbuilding	623.820 7
metallography	669.953
metallurgy	669.3
mineral aspects	
economic geology	553.43
mineralogy	549.23
mining	622.343
prospecting	622.184 3
pharmacology	615.265 2
products	673.3
toxicology	615.925 652

5.14 *Hierarchy.* The DDC is basically hierarchical in its notation and in its structure.

5.141 *In notation.* Hierarchy in notation means that at each level there is an array of concepts, called classes, which are mutually exclusive, and which stand in a coordinate relationship to each other. With each new level the specificity of the subject's subdivision increases; that is, the classes get progressively more specific, more minute. The classes at any given level stand in a subordinate relationship to a class at the next higher level. Any specific class, then, has two or three sets of relationships: coordinate, subordinate, and sometimes superordinate. A given class can be (and usually is) coordinate with one or more other classes at the same level; and it is immediately subordinate to only one class at the next higher level; and it may be superordinate to one or more classes at the next lower level. The increasing specificity of subjects is usually indicated by the addition of one new digit at each new level of division.

An example of a hierarchical chain follows. For convenience in printing, indention is not used to show the subordination of a division (level 2) to its main class (level 1).

600	Technology (Applied sciences)	[Significant notation is 6]
630	Agriculture and related technologies	[Significant notation is 63]
636	Animal husbandry	
636.1	Horses	
636.12	Racehorses	

The diagram that follows shows how the DDC hierarchical classification proceeds from the general to the specific. The unique feature of the DDC notation is that these progressive steps are indicated by the addition of one new digit at each level of division.

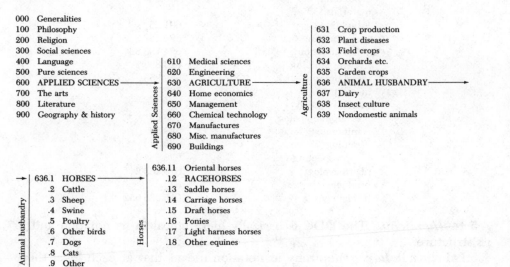

Here is another, longer, hierarchical chain:

600   Technology (Applied sciences)
620   Engineering and allied operations
621   Applied physics
621.3   Electromagnetic and related branches of engineering
621.38   Electronic and communication engineering
621.384   Radio and radar engineering
621.384 1   Radio
621.384 13   Components and apparatus
621.384 136   Receiving sets
621.384 136 6   Types of sets

The spaces between the sixth and seventh digits of the last four numbers and between the ninth and tenth digits of the last number are not a basic part of the notation, but, for ease in reading and copying are left after each successive set of three digits beyond the decimal point in all numbers enumerated in the classification schedules and index.

Even though these principles of hierarchy are employed often enough to make them a useful basis for examining the system, there are exceptions, four of which are described below.

(1) Sometimes there are steps in the successive divisions of the discipline or subject for which positions in the lengthening notation are not available. Such steps are shown in the schedules by spans of numbers called centered entries, because they appear with numbers, headings, and notes centered on the page instead of with numbers in the usual number column. Centered entries show the spread of a sequence of numbers which is spelled out in detail immediately following, and help to show the organization of material by substituting for a broad comprehensive number that does not exist and cannot be inserted. For example, under 380 trade is covered in 381–382, communication in 383–384, transportation in 385–388. There are no digits available to express any of these major subdivisions of 380, and each is shown in the schedules, therefore, by a centered entry, e.g.,

▶   385–388 Specific kinds of transportation

385   Railroad transportation

Another example is 540 "Chemistry and allied sciences," which includes chemistry in 541–547, crystallography in 548, and mineralogy in 549; the span of chemistry is reflected in the centered entry 541–547.

(2) In a few instances the notation is not hierarchically expressive. In these cases the indentions are irregular, since they do not correspond to the length

of the notation. For example, 929.7999 is printed as coordinate with 929.73–.79, because royalty and peerage of countries outside Europe is a concept coordinate with, not subordinate to, the concept of royalty and peerage of countries of Europe.

(3) The subdivisions of a discipline or topic are not always to be found in notations subordinate to, and therefore longer than, the notation for the discipline or topic itself; these situations reflect the desire of Melvil Dewey and his successors to keep the notation as short as possible. For example, although biology is denoted by 574, its branches the botanical and zoological sciences are classed in 580 and 590 respectively, rather than in 574+. Another example is analytical chemistry in 543, with its branches qualitative chemistry in 544 and quantitative chemistry in 545 instead of in 543.1 and 543.2 respectively. This second example shows that within an array concepts are not always mutually exclusive.

(4) The digit 0 when not in a terminal position distorts the hierarchy but provides a device for extending numbers. It is generally used to indicate a different basis for division of the discipline or subject represented by the digits preceding the 0. In the following sequence 599.01–.09 are used for general treatment of mammals as a group, whereas 599.1–.9 are used for works on specific kinds of mammals, e.g., on kangaroos, on whales, on monkeys.

500	Pure sciences
590	Zoological sciences
599	Mammalia (Mammals)
599.01	Physiology of mammals
599.02	Pathology of mammals
599.05	Ecology of mammals
599.2	Marsupialia
599.5	Cetacea and Sirenia
599.8	Primates

5.142 *In structure.* Hierarchy in structure means that every concept in a notation more specific than that of a main class is subordinate to all the broader concepts of which it is a part, and whatever is true of each whole is true of all its parts. For example, whatever is stated to be true of 600 is likewise true of all its subdivisions, what is true of 630 is true of all *its* subdivisions, what is true of 631 is true of all its subdivisions, and so on down to the finest subdivision. Hence the note under 631.2 Agricultural structures, "Description, use, place in agriculture," applies to each subdivision: to 631.21 Farmhouses, to 631.23 Granaries, silos, grain elevators, to 631.27 Fences, walls, hedges, and to all the others. Similarly, the instruction under 631 Crops and their production, "Class production of specific crops [and] products . . . in 633–638" applies to every part of 631; consequently, harvesting corn should be placed not in 631.55 Harvesting but in 633.15 Corn.

5.2 AUXILIARY TABLES AND OTHER MEMORY AIDS. The DDC notation lends itself readily to subject synthesis, or number building, with the benefit of numerous memory aids, or, as Melvil Dewey called them, mnemonics. The auxiliary tables in this volume form the basis for much of the number building that results in uniform meanings of numbers in various contexts.

5.21 *Areas.* The most notable memory aid is the constant repetition of a standard pattern of area arrangement. In nearly all area developments, the digits 44, for instance, stand for France, 45 for Italy, 46 for Spain, 52 for Japan, 73 for United States. Consequently, since 9 is the significant notation for general history, 944 denotes history of France, 945 of Italy, 946 of Spain, 952 of Japan, 973 of United States. Likewise, since 91 is the significant notation for general geography, 914.4 designates geography of France, 914.5 of Italy, 917.3 of United States (in each case with a decimal point following the third digit). Table 2, "Areas," which specifies these area numbers, constitutes the largest part of this volume.

5.22 *Languages.* Another common repetition is that of the numbers for languages. In this pattern 2 or 21 is used for the English language, 3 or 31 for German, 4 or 41 for French, etc. In most cases the numbers for the various languages in main class 400 and the various literatures in main class 800 are the same, e.g., 420 English language, 820 English literature, 430 German language, 830 German literature. In other subjects where the basis of subdivision is linguistic, the language sequence is closely parallel to that of 400 and 800. Under 030 Encyclopedias, for example, 031 is used for United States and Canadian English-language encyclopedias, 032 for other English-language encyclopedias, 033 for those in the Germanic languages, etc. The numbers in Table 6 Languages, which is used as the basis of subdivision under many subjects throughout the classification, in most respects have the same meanings as the language numbers in 400.

5.23 *Other.* Many other patterns appear as a result of parallel subject developments, a full development at one place being repeated by analogy at other places. For example, in 372.11–.18 and 373.11–.18 the organization and administration of elementary and secondary education are each given the same development as education as a whole (by means of the instruction "add . . . the numbers following 371"); in 420–490 each language is given the same development ("add 'Subdivisions of Individual Languages' notation . . . from Table 4"); in 633–635 each agricultural crop is developed according to the general principles in 631–632. In fact some classes of material, among them bibliographies and catalogs of specific disciplines and subjects (in 016) and libraries devoted to specific disciplines and subjects (in 026), are given the same development as the whole classification, e.g., bibliography of the applied sciences 016.6, of agriculture and related technologies 016.63, of racehorses 016.63612. (A number never ends in a 0 to the right of the decimal point, since such a 0 is meaningless; hence, 016.6 instead of 016.600.)

5.24 *Standard subdivisions.* A special kind of patterned repetition is that of the standard subdivisions, listed in Table 1. Virtually any subject or discipline may be presented in various forms: in a synopsis or outline, in a periodical, in tables, in illustrations. Similarly, most subjects may have certain modes of treatment in common: theory, technique, study and teaching, history. These common forms and modes are designated collectively as standard subdivisions, and they may be applied wherever they are appropriate. Their notation consists of two or more digits, of which the first is 0, e.g., 05 Serial publications. These digits may be added to any significant notation taken or derived from the schedules, e.g., serials on the applied sciences 605 (main class 6 plus standard subdivision 05), serials on agriculture and related technologies 630.5 (division 63 plus 05, with a decimal point following the third digit), serials on animal husbandry 636.05, on racehorses 636.1205.

5.3 VERSATILITY AND FLEXIBILITY. A valuable feature of Dewey, not shared by some of the other commonly used classification systems, is the adaptability of its notation to the needs of libraries of different sizes and natures. The DDC can be used equally as well for broad classification as for close. For example, a small library, or a large one with only a few titles on the subject, can class the production of any and all field crops in 633, without subdivision. A somewhat larger library can class general works in 633, works on production of cereal crops in 633.1, of forage crops in 633.2 and so on. A library with a still larger collection can divide its books into such detail as it requires. As any library's collection increases in size, its books can be differentiated to a finer and finer degree of specificity simply by the addition of further digits to the notation. A work on crystal radio sets can be placed in 621, 621.3, 621.38, 621.384, 621.3841, 621.38413, 621.384136, 621.3841366, depending on the degree of closeness in classification required. The full edition of the DDC may be used by general libraries of any size, from the largest, which may follow it in full detail for most subjects, to the smallest, which may reduce any or all schedules to the degree considered desirable. The abridged edition supplies reduction on a ready-made basis and is convenient for small libraries to use on that account. Except at and below its own level, the abridged version does not uniformly provide help in making judicious decisions about what schedules to reduce and how far to reduce them to meet specific local needs; this the classifier must decide on the basis of the recognized demands of the local situation and expected patterns of growth.

III. A Practical Guide to the Use of the Classification

Note: *In this guide an extensive repetition of pronouns to denote the classifier is unavoidable. While realizing that some readers will find distasteful the constant use of "he," "his," and "him," to refer generically to classifiers of both sexes, the editors and the Decimal Classification Editorial Policy Committee find any other device or circumlocution either awkward or artificial, or an intrusion upon the sense of the exposition, and they have agreed to use the traditional masculine forms in their generic sense.*

6 Preliminaries. Before the classifier tries to use the Dewey Decimal Classification, he should acquaint himself with the system as a whole. In particular, he should study the three main summaries at the end of this volume and learn the first summary of the ten main classes; he should then leaf through the schedules in volume 2, observing the many summaries of specific portions of them. Knowledge of the pattern will come rapidly with use, and especially so if, in classifying, he consults the schedules first and only verifies his decisions with the index. He should notice the effect of the principle of hierarchy: each entry is a part of and governed by every entry superior to it. To understand the full meaning and force of 621.3841366, he must view it as a part of 621.384136, which, in turn, is a part of 621.38413, which is a part of 621.3841, which is a part of 621.384, which is a part of 621.38, which is a part of 621.3, which is a part of 621, which is a part of 620, which is a part of 600.

He should not fail to look through the seven auxiliary tables in this volume.

He should also observe carefully the special nature of main classes 8 and 0. In class 8, subject is disregarded for works of literature (belles-lettres), e.g., a play about Julius Caesar and Roman history is a piece of imaginative literature, and belongs in the appropriate part of 800 instead of under history or biography. Arrangement of individual works of belles-lettres is first by the discipline literature, then by original language, then by literary form, then by period of composition. Detailed instructions appear under centered entry 810–890.

In main class 0, general encyclopedic works (030), general serial publications (050), general newspapers (071–079), general collections (080), and general publications of general organizations (061–068) have no specific subject, and are part of no one discipline; the most significant thing about them, after their generality, is their form. Arrangement of such generalities is first by form, then by language or place as the schedules provide.

In all other classes (000–029, 069, 070.1–.9, 090, 100–700, 900), unless a different sequence is prescribed, arrangement is first by most specific discipline and most specific subject under it, then by area specification, then by time specification if the schedules permit, then by form of presentation. For example, a work on the native snakes of Texas is classed as follows:

Discipline:	Science	5			
	Zoology	9			
Subject:	Cold-blooded vertebrates	7			
	Reptiles	9			
	Snakes	6			
Area:	[Sign of geographic concept to follow]	09			
	North America	7			
	South central United States	6			
	Texas	4			

Thus, 597.9609764.

If the work were about the *culture* of snakes in Texas, the chain would be:

Discipline:	Technology	6			
	Agriculture and related	3			
Subject:	Nondomesticated animals	9			
	Culture of cold-blooded vertebrates	3			
	Reptiles	9			
	Snakes	6			
Area (as above):		09764			

Thus, 639.39609764.

In history and law, however, the place is identified as a major characteristic of the subject. For example, a periodical on the history of the New Deal gives this chain:

Discipline:	History	9			
Subject:	North America	7			
	United States	3			
Time:	Twentieth century	9			
	Early, 1901–1953	1			
	Franklin D. Roosevelt	7			
Form:	[Number indicating special form]	0			
	Periodical	5			

Thus, 973.91705.

A periodical on the Texas law of commercial leases gives the following:

Discipline:	Social sciences	3		
	Law	4		
	Private law	6		
Subject:	Jurisdiction of Texas (as above)	764		
	Property		04	
	Real property		3	
	Tenancy		4	
	Leases		6	
	Commercial		2	
Form (as above):				05

Thus, 346.76404346205.

7 Analysis of a work. Before he can fit a work into the system, or class it, the classifier must know exactly what its subject is, and from what point of view and in what form that subject is treated. To discover this is not always easy:

(1) Sometimes the *title* indicates what the work is about; however, this is often misleading, and some further investigation should always be made as a check.

(2) For a book, the *table of contents* is usually an excellent guide to the subject matter.

(3) If there is no table of contents, *chapter headings* and *marginal notes* are likely to give a good indication of the contents. Clues may also be provided by *bibliographies* and *lists of sources* used by the author.

(4) It is always wise to scan the *preface* for the author's point of view, and the *blurb* for a general description of the work, though the latter may be misleading.

(5) If such sources prove unsatisfactory, a careful examination of the *text* may be necessary.

(6) If the subject is complex or unfamiliar to the classifier, he may have to go to external sources. Information regarding the subject of the work may often be obtained from bibliographies, catalogs, biographical dictionaries, histories of literature, encyclopedias, reviews, and other *reference works.*

(7) Subject *experts* should be consulted when all other methods fail, and sometimes for verification of a tentative decision.

The classifier should note that many works cover two or three or many subjects, considered separately or in their interrelationships. Also, many works deal with two or more aspects of one or more subjects, that is, with a subject or subjects within two or several disciplines; examples are works treating of both the economics and the technology of the textile manufacturing industry; of both nuclear physics and nuclear engineering; of both architectural design and construction principles of dwelling houses; and of the sociological, ethical, eligious aspects of divorce. The classifier should note, too, the current tre..1 toward interdisciplinary studies in depth, particularly in the social sciences. To become a good practitioner of classification, it is most important that he analyze each work carefully, not only to ascertain its subject or subjects but also to determine to what extent it crosses traditional disciplinary lines of study.

8 Basic rules for selection of class number. Before considering the problems involved in the application of the schedules to such compound and complex subjects as those just mentioned, it is desirable to delineate the procedures for classing a work on one subject in one discipline.

8.1 APPROACH. Having determined the subject of the work, and the discipline within which that subject is treated, the classifier is ready to class it, or place it within the system. There are two basic approaches to the Classification: direct, through the schedules, and indirect, through the index. Beginners will usually find the latter approach speedier, but it is not recommended because it delays the process of becoming fully acquainted with the system. In fact, the classifier should note that, whether he is a beginner or an expert, he should *never* class solely from the index. The index provides leads to the schedules but is not exhaustive and can never reproduce the wealth of information available in them. On the other hand, the index can be used profitably to verify the correctness of a number chosen from the schedules.

If his approach is direct, the classifier will first determine into which of the ten main classes the work falls. If the subject is copper, he must decide whether it relates to the science of copper (class 5, i.e., 500–599), the technology of copper (class 6), the economics of the copper industry (class 3), artistic work in copper (class 7), or even copper in the Koran (class 2). Having chosen the proper main class, then, excluding all other main classes from his mind, he determines into which of its divisions the book falls. If the subject is copper technology, it may be copper as an engineering material (division 62, i.e., 620–629), fabrication of articles in copper (67), copper in hardware (68), in building (69). Then in the same way he determines the proper section, subsection, and subsubsection, until he has come to the most specific number, used by or appropriate to the library, that will encompass the subject of the work. (See also section 10 on reduction.) Even if that number is less specific than the subject of the work in hand, he has found the right place. Possibly a future expansion will give an even more detailed number. For example, a work on the infinitive in the English language belongs under 425, even though 425 encompasses all of English grammar.

At each step on the way the classifier should look carefully at the notes and directions, making certain that he has not followed a false trail, perhaps even chosen the wrong main class. He should not depend solely on the three main summaries or on any of the special summaries; they exist only to speed

him to tentative decisions and lack the close distinctions that must be considered before any decision is final.

If he knows the schedules well, the classifier may start at once with a specific number. In that case it is most important that he go up the hierarchical ladder, testing at each level to see if the particular subject of his book belongs within the concept named and described. Whether he goes up or down he should analyze every step, not overlooking centered entries (which are readily identified by the inch-long lines preceding them and the indicators adjacent to them). He should read carefully every heading and note.

If the classifier's approach in a given situation is through the index, he should first locate the entry for the subject, then examine the subheads under it for the proper aspect. If, for example, his work is on copper, he will find under "Copper" various aspects, subaspects, and subsubaspects. Finding the most specific one that characterizes his work, he can then turn to the correct part of the schedules and analyze the specific number that appears to fit. The more reliable approach, however, is to go directly to the schedules, using the index if necessary to locate the proper discipline; only when he is uncertain about the relevance of a particular part of the schedules is it recommended that the classifier turn to the index. For more detailed information on use of the index, see section 11.

A full description of the important features of the headings and notes follows in sections 8.2–8.6.

8.2 HEADINGS. Each heading consists of a word or phrase so inclusive that it covers all subordinate topics and entries. The actual wording may be incomplete, because, from the principle of hierarchy, the heading must be read as part of the larger group that includes it, e.g., at 469 "Portuguese" means the Portuguese language, but at 869 the same heading means Portuguese literature.

Two terms in a heading separated by "and," and similarly three or more terms separated by commas, are coordinate and mutually exclusive, e.g., in Table 2, "Areas" notation 62 Egypt and Sudan, —75563 Prince Edward, Amelia, Nottoway Counties. If two terms in a heading are separated by a space, the first includes but is broader than the second, e.g., in the same table, —72 Middle America Mexico, where all of —721–729 comprises Middle America, but only —721–727 comprises Mexico. A term in parentheses is synonymous or nearly so with the term preceding it, e.g., —691 Madagascar (Malagasy Republic).

A heading includes the total concept expressed by it, even if some parts of that total concept are explicitly provided for in numbers that are not subdivisions of the number assigned to the heading. Cross references (section 8.58) lead the classifier to component parts of the concept which, when dealt with separately, are classed in numbers that are not notationally subordinate to the general number, and the presence of a cross reference is a clear sign that a part of the main subject is dispersed in this way. For example, 820 Literatures of English . . . language is followed by a cross reference, *"For American literature in English, see 810."* This combination constitutes a clear directive to the classifier: class a work on English-language literature of Britain here in 820 and its subdivisions, class a work on English-language literature of Britain *and* America here in 820, but class a work on English-language literature of America in 810. In like fashion "574 Biology; *For evolution, see 575; . . . zoological sciences, 590"* says: class general works on biology in 574 and its subdivisions, but works dealing only with evolution in 575, works dealing only with zoological sciences in the 590s. (See also section 8.511 on comprehensive works.)

8.21 *The word "specific."* When the word "specific" appears in a heading—or, for that matter, in a note—it usually means that here are classed works on individual instances of the subject named; works dealing collectively with a number of instances of the subject are in such cases classed in some other notation earlier in the schedule or higher in the hierarchy. For example, 693.8 "Construction for specific purposes" is a number with subdivisions but not in itself to be used, inasmuch as a work on construction for several specific purposes, with a chapter devoted to each, would be classed in 690. On the other hand, when the text says "various specific," works dealing collectively with a number of instances of the subject are to be classed in the number at hand. For example, 693 "Construction in various specific materials" has subdivisions and is itself to be used for a work on construction in several different materials, e.g., in masonry, in wood, in tiles, in metals, with a chapter devoted to each.

8.3 DEFINITIONS, SCOPE NOTES, EXAMPLE NOTES. In some instances a heading requires, for complete understanding, the limitations stated in the note following it, e.g., 790.068 Recreation centers: "Indoor and outdoor." Others are followed by definitions, e.g., 330 Economics: "The science of human behavior as it relates to utilization of scarce means for satisfaction of needs and desires through production, distribution, consumption." When no definition is given, the term is understood to be used as delimited by its subdivisions, or as defined in *Webster's Third New International Dictionary of the English Language,* or in other general unabridged dictionaries.

Other headings are followed by scope notes enumerating specific qualifications applicable to the subject and its subdivisions, e.g., 631.2 Agricultural structures: "Description, use, place in agriculture" of farmhouses (631.21), of barns (631.22), and of other structures. These aspects of agricultural buildings are thus differentiated from the architectural aspects; classification of farmhouses in 728.67 and of barns in 728.922 when considered architecturally is governed by part of the scope note under 725–728: "interdisciplinary works on design and construction."

Still other headings are followed by notes giving examples that explain the heading by indicating the kinds of entities that the heading names or describes, e.g., 025.313 Form [of the catalog]: "Examples: card, book, microform, online"; 025.315 Structure [of the catalog]: "Examples: divided, unified, classified."

When the heading bears little resemblance to the heading used for the same concept in the previous edition of the Classification, a note appears indicating the former heading, e.g., 331.128 Placement: "Former heading: Obtaining employment."

All such notes have hierarchical force; that is, they must be taken into consideration in analyzing subordinate entries.

8.4 INCLUSION NOTES. Notes beginning "Including" do not have hierarchical force. They are enumerations of subordinate topics, not obviously part of the heading, on which there is as yet insufficient literature to justify separate provision. For example, 351.778 [Government] control of product hazards is a topic that has separate subdivisions for food, medicines, cosmetics, but includes also textiles, toys, household appliances. These latter topics are for the present given "standing room" in the general number awaiting the time when there is literary warrant for giving each its own number.

8.5 INSTRUCTION NOTES. Notes of instruction are of various kinds, as enumerated below.

8.51 *Class here notes.* An instruction to class a certain topic or concept "here" has hierarchical force; it means, class the specified topic or concept in "this" number and/or appropriate subdivisions of this number.

The note is used to indicate subordinate concepts, not obviously part of the heading, that are of a general nature and have applicability to the subject and its subdivisions; for example, 725–728 [Architecture of] specific types of structures: "Class here specific structures," which means class architecture of specific buildings in any appropriate subdivision, e.g., of a specific parliamentary building in 725.11, of a specific department store in 725.21, of a specific synagogue in 726.3, of a specific castle in 728.81.

The class here note is used also to make provision for concepts that overlap the heading, e.g., "Areas" notation 78 Western United States: "Class here . . . Rocky Mountains." Rocky Mountains and Western United States overlap like two intersecting circles, because the concept Rocky Mountains is both narrower and broader than the heading to which it is assigned, being located in only four of the eight states enumerated under —78 but also in other areas outside —78, such as Arizona and Alberta.

8.511 *Comprehensive and interdisciplinary works.* One kind of concept that overlaps the heading is that of comprehensive works, e.g., 260: "Class here comprehensive works on Christian church"; 612: "Class here comprehensive works on anatomy and physiology." By its nature, such a note is always followed by a class elsewhere note or a cross reference (sections 8.57 and

8.58) leading to those component parts of the topic treated comprehensively at this point that will be found in other numbers.

A special kind of comprehensive work is the interdisciplinary work, which deals with the topic from the point of view of more than one discipline, e.g., 669: "Class here interdisciplinary works on metals," which is to say, class here and in appropriate subdivisions works dealing with metals, or a specific metal, from such diverse aspects as prospecting, mining, physics, chemistry, geology, metallurgy, industrial fabricating, art work, economics. For more detail, see section 9.2.

8.52 *Optional provision.* Because there are sometimes legitimate reasons for placing works in numbers other than those provided in the schedules, some alternatives are provided, with the editors' preference clearly shown. For example, 936.2 Southern Britain to [the year] 410: "If preferred [i.e., if the classifier prefers], class in 942.012." At 942.012 "(Use of this number is optional; [the editors] prefer 936.2)." The preferred number will be used on Library of Congress cataloging records, and usually in the *British National Bibliography* and similar services. More detail on options is given in section 13.21.

8.53 *Use of more than one 0 in standard subdivisions.* Standard subdivisions, which are enumerated in Table 1, generally consist of two or more digits of which the first is 0, and may be used with any number at any level whenever they are appropriate. (See section 8.7 for application of standard subdivisions.) But in some classes, for various reasons, notation beginning with 0 is or has previously been used for another purpose, in which case the classifier is instructed to use two 0s, e.g., "Use 335.001–335.009 for standard subdivisions." On occasion he is instructed to use for this purpose three or even four 0s. This instruction does not have hierarchical force, but applies only exactly as stated, *except under the circumstances described below in the second example in section 8.545.*

Sometimes the use of a 0 for another purpose appears inconspicuously in an add note (see section 8.54). For example, at 327.3–.9, 0 is added to 327.41 foreign policies and relations of the United Kingdom before the addition of another area number for France 327.41044, or the United States 327.41073, or the Far East 327.4105. It follows that standard subdivisions on United Kingdom foreign policy must be classed in 327.41001–327.41009. Otherwise 327.4105 would be doing double duty, for general works on foreign relations between the United Kingdom and the Far East and also for serial publications on foreign policies and relations in general of the United Kingdom. The classifier is reminded of this requirement by an asterisk and footnote, "Use extra 0s for standard subdivisions; see instructions at beginning of Table 1."

8.54 *Synthesis of notation (number building).* Frequently a note offers the opportunity to expand a given number or series of numbers even though the subdivisions are not specifically enumerated in the schedules. The procedures to be observed are as follows:

8.541 *Add from tables.* Tables 2–7 supply digits which the classifier may add to certain numbers in the schedules to make them more specific. The numbers in these auxiliary tables are not class numbers and the classifier should never use them by themselves. Each instruction indicates exactly what may be added, from which table to what base. For example, under 331.291–.299 Geographical treatment [of wages], there appears the instruction, "Add 'Areas' notation 1–9 from Table 2 to base number 331.29." This means that for a work on wages in Japan, for example, the number 52 for Japan from Table 2 is to be placed following 331.29, which results in the full class number 331.2952. Again, under 155.84 [Psychology of] specific racial and ethnic groups, is the instruction, "Add 'Racial, Ethnic, National Groups' notation 01–99 from Table 5 to base number 155.84," whereby, when the appropriate number from the table is added to 155.84, the number for ethnopsychology of Nordics is 155.843, of Bretons 155.849168, of Afro-Americans 155.8496073.

Sometimes combinations for adding twice in succession appear, as at 323.11 [Relation of state to] racial, ethnic, national groups: "Add 'Racial, Ethnic, National Groups' notation 2–9 from Table 5 to base number 323.11, e.g., relation of state to Jews 323.11924 . . . then, unless it is redundant, add 0 and to the result add 'Areas' notation 1–9 from Table 2, e.g., relation of state to Jews in Germany 323.11924043."

It will be seen that the base number, to which digits from the table are added (e.g., 331.29), is not necessarily exactly the same as the number appearing in the number column for the heading (331.291–.299); however, the base number is always explicitly stated in the accompanying note.

Occasionally the base number is less than three digits. In this case, if the combined number consists of four or more digits a decimal point must be inserted after the third digit. For example, to obtain numbers for geography of a specific location, area notations are added to 91. The number for geography of Japan will be 915.2, that is 91 (geography) followed by 52 (Japan) with a decimal point inserted after the third digit. Or, history (9) of Ohio (771): 977.1.

8.542 *Add from schedules.* Similarly, the base number is always stated in the instruction to create a sequence by adding digits from another sequence in the schedules. For example, under 581.19 Biophysics and biochemistry [of plants]: "Add to base number 581.19 the numbers following 574.19 in 574.191–574.192, e.g., enzymes 581.1925." The procedure to be followed here is: (1) in the sequence 574.191–.192 (biophysics and biochemistry in general) the number for enzymes is 574.1925; (2) in this notation the numbers following 574.19 are 25; (3) the classifier adds the digits 25 to the base number 581.19 to obtain 581.1925.

The base numbers in the two sequences are not necessarily of the same length, e.g., 636.089 Veterinary sciences: "Add to base number 636.089 the numbers following 61 in 610–619, e.g., veterinary viral diseases 636.0896925." Here the number for viral diseases in the sequence 610–619 is 616.925; ignoring the decimal point, the classifier adds the 6925 that follows 61 to 636.089 and obtains 636.0896925.

Sometimes a complete class number is added to another class number, e.g., under 338.47 [Production of secondary] goods and services: "Add 001–999 to base number 338.47, e.g., textile manufacture 338.47677" (677 being the complete number for the technology of textile manufacture).

Sometimes one "add" must be derived from another "add." For example, 636.59201–.59208 General principles [of turkey husbandry]: "Add to base number 636.5920 the numbers following 636.0 in 636.01–636.08." The classifier who has a work on erysipelas in turkeys (1) writes down 636.5920; (2) adds 89 from 636.089 to obtain 636.592089; (3) then, in accordance with the instruction under 636.089 to add to that number the numbers following 61 in 610–619, he adds 6942 from 616.942 and obtains the result 636.5920896942.

8.543 *Add from both tables and schedules.* Sometimes numbers are derived by adding first from a table and then from another schedule, or, in the reverse order, first from another schedule and then from a table, e.g., 271 Religious congregations and orders in church history: "Add to base number 271 the numbers following 255 in 255.01–255.98, e.g., Franciscans in church history 271.3; then add 0 . . . and to the result add 'Areas' notation 1–9 from Table 2, e.g., Franciscans in United Kingdom 271.3041."

8.544 *General suggestions.* The classifier should add only to the extent that is appropriate to the sequence that is to be developed. Occasionally some numbers in a sequence from which numbers are to be added should be omitted because the topics in those numbers are otherwise provided for. For example, at 614.59 "[Incidence, distribution, control of] other diseases" means diseases other than those already provided for in 614.51–.57; consequently, the classifier must exclude from the add note under 614.591–.598 diseases in those numbers, and it follows that the correct number for control of influenzas, which from the add note might be expected to be 614.59203 (from 616.203), is instead 614.518. Another example occurs at 551.464, to which the classifier is instructed to add the numbers following 163 in "Areas" notation 1636–1637. Application of this instruction produces the number 551.46465 for oceanography of the Caribbean Sea, but this number should not be used because Caribbean Sea is an exception to the basic instruction, as is shown by the exception to the add note: "however, class Caribbean Sea . . . in 551.463," where, after applying another add note, the classifier obtains the correct number 551.4635.

The classifier is more likely to construct correct numbers if he ignores the decimal point until the final sequence of digits is obtained, after which he

684.13 Chairs and tables, not in 684.105 Metallic furniture; class doctrines of Jehovah's Witnesses on salvation in 234 Salvation, not in 230.992 doctrines of Jehovah's Witnesses, and even less so in 230.044 Protestant theology.

In the rare instances where this general rule for 0s is not to be applied there is a specific instruction in the schedules. For example, in accordance with the instruction at centered entry 262.3–262.4, class government and organization of United Methodist Church in 262.076, not 262.3.

(3) If there are neither stated instructions nor a difference in the number of 0s (two or more characteristics of division are sometimes provided for in notation with the same number of 0s as well as in notation with no 0s) cite by most specific discipline and subject, then by geographic specification, i.e., place, then by temporal specification, i.e., time, then by form. Example: Class earthquakes in Japan in 551.220952 (551.22 Earthquakes, 0952 Japan), not in 555.2 (Geology of Japan).

It may be observed that, since place and time specifications are mostly shown by standard subdivisions 091–099 and 0901–0905 respectively, and since standard subdivisions may be used with any subject (see section 8.7)—though not place and time subdivisions together except where specifically provided for as at 330.9—it is usually feasible in the notation to show a place or time characteristic in addition to any other characteristics.

(4) Lacking any of the foregoing principles, apply the following citation order formula, which will generally prove to be reasonable and helpful: class by things; kinds of things; parts of things; materials from which the things, kinds, or parts are made; properties of the things, kinds, parts, or materials; processes within the things, kinds, parts, or materials; operations upon the things, kinds, parts, or materials; agents performing such operations. Example: Class harvesting of club wheat in 633.117 (Varieties of wheat, including club wheat), not in 633.115 (Harvesting of wheat), club wheat being a kind of thing and harvesting an operation.

(5) Sometimes the classifier's life will be made more difficult by his realization that none of the foregoing rules reflects the author's intention and emphasis, and he will be faced with the temptation to flout the rules. Given adequate reason, he should do so. For example, a work on quiltmaking should, according to both section (1a) above—"Other textile products" in 746.9 before "Needle- and handwork" in 746.4—and section (4)—things before operations—be classed in 746.97 with bedspreads rather than in 746.46 with quilting; but it is obvious that the author's intention is to emphasize the process quilting rather than the product quilted bedspreads, and 746.46 is, indeed, the better number. (Compare sections 9.1 and 9.2 on emphasis.)

8.551 *Special topics of general applicability.* Related to citation order is the principle of special topics of general applicability, i.e., subdivision of a subject according to a characteristic which has general applicability to other subdivisions of the subject which are based on different characteristics. For example, breeding (636.7082), housing (636.70831), feeding (636.7084) are all special topics in the general subject of dog husbandry (636.7), but they are also applicable to the husbandry of any specific kind of dog, e.g., breeding terriers (636.755), feeding terriers (636.753). Often the notation provides for the special concept not only at the general level, as with dog breeding and feeding, but also at specific levels, using the add device to derive the notation, e.g., 616.075 diagnosis of diseases, 616.3999 gout, 616.3999075 diagnosis of gout. For the use of standard subdivision notation 04 for special topics of general applicability, see section 8.76.

8.56 *Relocations.* A relocation is an adjustment in the schedules resulting in the shifting of a topic between successive editions from one number to another that differs in respects other than length, e.g., the shift of mosaic painting from 751.48 in Edition 18 to 738.5 in Edition 19. Similarly the shift from 940.11 to 940.12 of the period 500–799 in European history is a relocation, but the extension of 759.06 to 759.0663 for surrealism in painting is not.

If the relocation is total, i.e., if the entire number formerly used is to be vacated, the number is enclosed in square brackets, and there is an instruction showing where the subject formerly in that number is now placed, e.g., [751.48] Mosaic painting: "Class in 738.5."

If the relocation is only partial, it is indicated in an instruction note, e.g., 704.947 Mythology and legend: "Class religious mythology [*formerly* 704.947] in 704.948."

Total relocations are not to be confused with other, similar types of entries in square brackets and their instructions. One type, described more fully in section 8.73, is entries showing that concepts normally belonging in standard subdivision notations are to be placed instead in other numbers, e.g., [720.93] [Architecture] in the ancient world: "Do not use; class in 722." Another is entries and instructions showing schedule reduction, e.g., [355.229] Woman-power: "Number discontinued; class in 355.22"; this is not a relocation, but a mere shortening of the number that was assigned to this topic in the previous edition. (However, the effect of all these, like that of the class elsewhere notes described in section 8.57, is the same: the classifier is instructed to class else-where a topic that he may have reason to think he should class at the point of instruction.)

Relocation notes are hierarchical in force at the point of instruction, and usually also at the point led to. For example, the note under 614.3, "Class [product hazards] in 363.19," tells the classifier that, while the subject was formerly in 614.3 and appropriate subdivisions, it is now to be classed in 363.19, and in appropriate subdivisions of 363.19 if its treatment at that number war-

l

rants it. Since at 363.19 the topic is shown in the heading, it may be classed also in the subdivisions of 363.19; if it had been shown in an inclusion note (see section 8.4), the topic would have been classed in 363.19 only and not in its subdivisions.

8.57 *Class elsewhere notes.* Class elsewhere notes are used for a variety of purposes, but in effect all of them instruct the classifier to class in a different number topics in some way related to one or more of the topics covered by the entry in which the note appears. The chief purposes are the following:

(1) To avoid inconsistent classification by specifying citation order, as described in section 8.55 (1) (c), e.g., 331.2 Conditions of employment: "Class . . . conditions of employment of workers with specific personal characteristics in 331.3–331.6."

(2) To show in which single number to class comprehensive works on a concept covered by a centered entry (compare section 9.3), e.g., 532.52–532.56 Flow variations: "Class comprehensive works in 532.51."

(3) To scatter the subdivisions of a subject, e.g., 778.3 Special kinds of photography: "Class a specific application with the subject, e.g., use of photography in astronomy 522.63."

(4) To indicate related numbers when potential confusion exists, e.g., 371.62 [School] buildings: "Class architecture of buildings for educational purposes in 727." Except when needed to clear up persistent misconceptions, the schedules make no effort to lead from the subject in one discipline or aspect to the same subject in other disciplines; this is the function of the index (see section 11). See also section 8.58.

All class elsewhere notes have hierarchical force.

8.58 *Cross references.* Not all subdivisions of a concept are necessarily to be found in notations subordinate to that used for the concept as a whole. (Compare section 8.2.) Cross references are a special kind of instruction note leading the classifier from the stated or implied totality of a given subject to component parts of that subject that are provided for elsewhere than in the number referred from or numbers directly subordinate to it, e.g., 574 Biology: *"For botanical sciences, [see] 580; zoological sciences, 590";* 351 Central governments: *"For specific central governments, see 353–354. "* The totality from which component parts are separated need not appear in a heading, but may be in a note, e.g., 382.7 Tariff policy, Class here comprehensive works on trade barriers and restrictions: *"For nontariff barriers to trade, see 382.5."* Like class elsewhere notes, cross references are not used to lead from one aspect of a subject to another aspect that belongs in a different discipline; they lead only from the whole subject to parts of the subject located elsewhere. Only the index shows dispersion of a subject by disciplines.

Some cross references have also the force of cross classification notes; for example, the cross reference at 591 Zoology, *"For specific animals and groups of animals, see 592–599,"* is interpreted to mean that *everything* about a specific animal or group of animals is to be classed in the appropriate subdivision of 592–599, e.g., migrations of mammals 599.0525, not 591.525. Compare section 8.55 (1) (c).

Cross references have hierarchical force. For example, the cross reference from 500, in which are classed comprehensive works on pure and applied sciences, to 600, means that any subdivision of 500, in its applied aspect, belongs in 600, e.g., applied physics in 621, applied chemistry in 660.

8.6 SUMMARY OF HIERARCHICAL FORCE OF ENTRIES. By the principle of hierarchy the heading and notes applying to a given class should apply also to all its subdivisions, but analysis of the different types of notes in sections 8.3–8.5 has shown that there are certain exceptions. These exceptions are here summarized. The following parts of an entry *do not have hierarchical force:* (1) Inclusion notes (section 8.4); these mention topics not yet requiring their own numbers and hence given "standing room" in the main number. (2) Instruction notes about (a) the use of more than one 0 for standard subdivisions (section 8.53), and (b) number building (section 8.54); such instructions have hierarchical force only when specifically so designated, in which case the subdivisions to which they are applicable are identified by asterisks and repeated instructions in footnotes.

All other parts of an entry have hierarchical force.

8.7 STANDARD SUBDIVISIONS. Having analyzed the number chosen for the work in hand through all the steps of its hierarchical ladder, and having decided that it is the best and most specific number, the classifier is ready to consider what further specification is desirable, i.e., whether any of the standard subdivisions are applicable. If, for example, the work deals with the subject in the United States only, or in Norway or in Fiji, he may add 0973 or 09481 or 099611, as the case may be. The complete list of standard subdivisions appears in Table 1 in this volume.

8.71 *Restrictions.* The classifier should observe several important restrictions on the use of standard subdivisions.

8.711 *Nonspecific numbers.* The first is that, unless there are instructions permitting their use, he should be cautious about adding standard subdivisions to a number chosen for a work that deals with a subject more specific than the content of the number, i.e., if the subject of the work does not have its own specific number. For example, he should class a serial publication on architecture of office buildings in 725.2305, but a serial on architecture of medical office buildings in 725.23. The reason is that there is the chance that in a later edition the subject will be subdivided and he will then face complications in adjustment. For example, perhaps in Edition 20 medical office buildings will be provided for specifically in some new number such as 725.237, and he can then use 725.23705 for a serial on the architecture of medical office buildings.

This restriction generally need not be applied to standard subdivision 0924 Individual [persons], e.g., Rodin 730.924; even though Rodin does not approximate the whole of sculpture, it is unlikely that a separate class number will ever be assigned to him.

Neither need this restriction apply to any number which, because of the nature of its subject content, appears unlikely to be given future subdivision, e.g., it is permissible to use standard subdivisions with 929.3 for registers alone as well as for various kinds of genealogical sources. (See also section 9.1, parts (3)–(4).)

Neither should this restriction apply if the subject of the work, even though less than the whole number, constitutes the greater part of the number ("approximates the whole"), or constitutes several subdivisions of it. Nor should the restriction apply if the subject of the work overlaps or is broader than the heading, as, for example, at 725.33, which is basically the number for railroad accessory buildings but is also used for comprehensive works on railroad buildings; standard subdivisions on either concept may be classed in 725.3301–.3309.

Contrary or special instructions are to be followed when given, e.g., at 760, where 760.01–.09 are to be used for standard subdivisions of the broader concept in the heading, graphic arts, and 760.1–.9 for standard subdivisions of the narrower concept, printmaking and prints.

8.712 *Redundancy.* A second restriction is that the classifier should not add standard subdivisions when they are redundant, e.g., if the number already means technique, it is unnecessary for him to add standard subdivision 028 Techniques, procedures, apparatus, equipment, materials; if it already means carpentry, as at 694, it is unnecessary to add 024694 for works for carpenters.

8.713 *Two or more.* The editors recommend that the classifier not add one standard subdivision to another standard subdivision unless there are specific instructions to do so. If the classifier finds that two or more standard subdivisions are applicable to a particular work, he should use the table of precedence at the beginning of Table 1 to determine which one he should use. And if for some reason he feels he *must* use more than one, that table indicates the order in which to use them.

Even if standard subdivisions in their strictest sense are not involved in any of the situations described above, the editors recommend that the classifier not add notation for place twice, except when the work deals with a topic *of* one place (which is really a subject qualification) *in* another place (which is truly a geographic specification), e.g., an exhibit of French paintings in New York City 759.407401471. Needless to say, this recommendation is not in effect where specific instructions authorize the double use of area notation, e.g., 327.41073 for foreign relations between United Kingdom and United States.

8.72 *Extended meanings.* Although it is their standard meanings that make these subdivisions "standard," sometimes a particular standard subdivision when applied to a given subject may logically be assigned one or more meanings that are extensions of and compatible with the basic meaning, and the classifier will then find in the schedules an entry or group of entries specifying the extension. For example, in 669.0282–.0284 a special expansion of standard subdivision 028 is provided for techniques, procedures, apparatus, equipment applicable to metallurgy, it being specified by note that the usual "materials" of —028 are classed elsewhere. Other examples are the substantial extensions in 701–709.

8.73 *Irregular notation.* Sometimes a concept ordinarily placed in a standard subdivision number is found instead with an irregular notation; most such instances date from earlier editions of the DDC, prepared before the table of standard subdivisions became as detailed as it now is. These instances are noted under the numbers where the classifier would normally expect to find them. Examples:

[747.09]   Historical and geographical treatment
          Do not use; class in 747.2
373.09   Historical and geographical treatment
          Class treatment by specific continents, countries, localities in
          373.3–373.9 (*not* 373.093–373.099)

See also section 8.56.

The warning in section 8.711 to be cautious in using standard subdivisions for a work that deals with less than the whole subject covered by the number applies equally to those situations where standard subdivision concepts, including area and time specification, appear in irregular notation.

It is obvious that the classifier should not use a standard subdivision until he has made sure from the schedules that it has not been assigned an irregular notation or meaning.

8.74 *Use of more than one 0.* See section 8.53.

8.75 *Subdivision.* When a standard subdivision or span of standard subdivisions is specifically named in the schedules, it is understood that, unless there are contrary instructions, the usual subdivisions to the standard subdivision may be used, e.g., 332.67309 Historical and geographical treatment is to have temporal divisions 01–05 from 0901–0905 in Table 1, and "Areas" notation 1–9 from Table 2, added to it the same as any standard subdivision 09: international investment in the 1970s 332.67309047, international investment in India

332.6730954. In similar manner 510.1 is to be broken down into 510.12, 510.13, 510.14, 510.148, and so on exactly like standard subdivision 01.

8.76 *Special topics of general applicability.* One standard subdivision requires special mention, 04 Special topics of general applicability. As the note in Table 1 points out: "Use this subdivision only when it is specifically set forth in the schedules. [Contrary to section 8.713] add other standard subdivisions—01–09 to it and its subdivisions as required." This device is introduced at those places where no other kind of notation is feasible for this kind of topic, and it follows the rules for citation order in section 8.55.

8.8 SUBJECT NOT PROVIDED FOR. The fields of knowledge grow so fast that any edition of the DDC is outdated before it appears. There is little doubt that the classifier will have works on subjects for which the schedules and index have provided no place either explicitly or implicitly. He should *not* make up his own number for such a subject: the next edition could easily place the subject in a different number and use the number he devised for something else. The classifier's guiding principle is to follow exactly the procedure outlined in section 8.1: to determine first the correct main class, then the correct division, then the correct section, continuing until he has arrived at the most specific entry that will contain the subject of his work. If he does this carefully, he will rarely be proved wrong. He should always use the most specific number possible in the schedules, even if it is only a three-digit number. Then, if the editors supply a more detailed number later, he may use it by simply adding digits to the number originally chosen. Two examples from the past may be illustrative. Edition 16 provided for astronautical engineering in 629.1388 (later relocated to 629.4) but for no other aspect of humankind in space. A classifier with a work on bioastronautics (the physiology of humankind in space) might have been tempted to class it in 629.1388, but he should have used 612.01 or even just 612, which was later expanded to 612.0145 for the precise subject. Edition 17 provided no place for DNA and RNA, but a classifier following the principles outlined here would have used 574.873, or more likely 574.87, and found his decision confirmed by the appearance of both as "included" topics under 574.8732 in Edition 18 and by the specific provision of 574.873282–.873283 in the present edition.

A third example is a classic illustration of what not to do. In the 14th and prior editions 323.1, the relation of the state to races within it, was not developed in as much detail as it would be later, and 301 Sociology was hardly developed at all. As a consequence many classifiers placed works on the sociology and political relations of Jews not in "standing room" in the broad numbers 301 and 323.1 respectively but in 296, which by the principle of hierarchy should have been reserved for the religion of the Jews.

8.9 THE VALUE OF POSITION. The importance to the classifier of an awareness of the meaning of schedule structure cannot be overstated, and the principles are here restated for emphasis. Regular structure speaks its own clear and distinct language, reducing the need for complex definitions and instructions. The position of a notation, whether for a *direct* or a *general* subdivision of a topic, imparts a meaning to the provision attached to that notation. (See section 8.551, Special topics of general applicability.)

Direct subdivisions follow superordinate entries without the interposition of 0s in the notation. The length of the notation is generally a reliable indication of the degree of specificity of the entry in relation to its basic discipline. The specific entry regardless of length is described by the preceding superordinate entries (those with shorter notation) all the way up to the main class. A topic subordinate to a broader concept must have all the properties of that broader concept, except that it is more specific. The fact that coordination and subordination are meaningful is based on the simple premise that in a hierarchical system what is true of the whole must be true of each of its parts.

General subdivisions are usually developed from superordinate entries through the introduction into the notation of one or more 0s. Standard subdivisions are of this category. General subdivisions always precede direct subdivisions of the entry to which they are subordinate. However, general (0) concepts that apply to direct (non-0) subdivisions of that entry must be classed with those subdivisions. For example, periodicals on agriculture *in general* are classed in 630.5, while periodicals on crop production are classed in 631.05.

A very few concepts in 0 notation are not general, e.g., 616.201–.208 for certain respiratory diseases and 546.401–.403 for two chemical elements.

9 Complexities in selection of class number. The foregoing rules and principles provide a basis for classing a work on one subject in one discipline. However, as noted in section 7, analysis of a work may show that it deals with two or three or many subjects, considered separately or in their interrelationships; or with two or more aspects of one or more subjects. If the DDC is being used as a shelf classification, obviously the classifier must choose one place and class the work there. Since most libraries employ other types of subject control in addition to shelf classification, such as a subject catalog, either alphabetical or classified, it is likely that other leads will be provided through such tools. Specific instructions for classing a whole variety of compound and complex subjects are provided in such sources as W. S. Merrill's *Code for Classifiers,* 2d edition (Chicago, American Library Association, 1939) and *Guide to Use of* [*16th edition of*] *Dewey Decimal Classification, Based on the Practice of the Decimal Classification Office at the Library of Congress* (Lake Placid Club, N.Y., Forest Press, 1962). Because it is impossible to anticipate all combinations, or even a considerable percentage of them, a few basic principles, from which all the specific rules stem, are here set forth for guidance.

9.1 MORE THAN ONE SUBJECT.

(1) The classifier should class a work dealing with two or more interrelated subjects with the one that receives the chief emphasis. This emphasis may be a reflection of the relative amount of space devoted to each subject, or of the author's purpose, or of both. For example, as a general rule the classifier should class with Keats an analytical work dealing with Shakespeare's influence on Keats. The author's purpose in such a work may be said to be an exposition of Keats's work. Even though the treatment of Shakespeare may actually occupy more space, if the author's purpose is pervasive throughout then greater weight should be given to purpose, which would place the work with other works on Keats. But if the treatment of Keats occupies only a small portion of the work, say less than a third, and does not permeate the portion that deals specifically with Shakespeare, then the preponderance of space devoted to Shakespeare should carry more weight than the author's purpose of explaining Keats, and the work should be placed with other works on Shakespeare. Such decisions are sometimes very difficult to make.

(2) The classifier should class a work dealing with two or more subjects that are not particularly interrelated, e.g., a description of the beliefs and practices of Judaism, Christianity, and Islam, with the one that preponderates.

(3) If no emphasis or preponderance is readily apparent, he should class a work on *three or more* subjects that are all subdivisions of a broader subject with the broader one, e.g., a work dealing approximately equally with Hinduism (294.5), Judaism (296), and Islam (297) in 290. If the three or more constitute the major part of the broader subject, he may use standard subdivisions as if his work approximated the whole broader subject (see section 8.711). If the three or more are not part of a single broader subject or discipline, he should class the work in the 000s, e.g., in 001 or 030 or 050 or 080.

(4) If no emphasis or preponderance is readily apparent and there are no contrary instructions, he should class a work on *two* subjects with the one coming first in the schedules, e.g., a work dealing equally with Judaism and Islam in 296; however, if those two subjects are both subdivisions of a broader subject and together constitute the major portion of the broader subject, he should class the work with that broader subject (and use applicable standard subdivisions as if his work approximated the whole broader subject), e.g., a work dealing with lizards and snakes but not with the relatively unimportant tuataras should be classed in 597.94 with the encompassing Lepidosauria rather than in 597.95 lizards. Some classifiers prefer to class any work on two subjects that are both part of a broader one with the broader, and some prefer to class such a work with the one treated first in the work, but these procedures are not recommended.

9.11 *Historical periods* constitute a recurring problem. Assuming there is no preponderance or emphasis, and using 941.06–.08 as an example:

Class work on	In	Because	By rule from preceding paragraph
1702–1727	941.069	first of two	(4)
1702–1760	941.069	the three periods covered fall into two broader periods, with only 1702–1714 being in the first; hence, first of two	(4)
1689–1727	941.068	first of two periods within the first of two broader periods	(4) applied twice
1689–1760	941.068	same reason	(4)
1689–1820	941.068	same reason	(4)
1685–1820	941.06	three periods within the first of two broader periods	(4) then (3)
1685–1901	941	three broad periods	(3)
1685–1910	941	same reason	(3)

9.12 *One part approximates the whole.* In certain subjects, one subtopic may be so large, or so often written about, or so emphasized in library materials, that it can usually be said to approximate the whole subject. Works on such subjects should be classed with the whole except where the work itself emphasizes that it deals with the part. Examples: (1) Many works on "natural history" deal briefly with rocks and minerals, but 90% with plants and animals; many others deal with plants and animals only. Class in 500 unless the work makes a point of being about living organisms, in which case class in 574. (2) Most works on "prison economy" deal with prisons for male adults as the norm. Class in 365.6 unless emphasis is laid on the fact that the work is about prisons for adult *male* offenders (365.44). (3) In the years before 1803 the United States was limited to the area east of the Mississippi River, for which the area number is —74. Class general U.S. histories of the period in 973.2–.4, using 974+ and 975+ only for works frankly avowing that they are state (or colony) histories. Note use of 973.21–.22 for founding of colonies as part of U.S. history.

9.2 MORE THAN ONE ASPECT.

(1) The classifier should place an interdisciplinary work, dealing with a subject within two or more disciplines, i.e., from two or more points of view or aspects, with the aspect that receives the most emphasis. For example, a work dealing with both the scientific and the engineering principles of electrodynamics is classed in 537.6 if the engineering aspects are introduced primarily for illustrative purposes, but in 621.31 if the basic scientific theories are intro-

duced primarily as a preliminary to the author's development of an exposition of engineering principles and practices. (See also section 9.4.)

(2) He should class a work dealing with a subject from two or more aspects, but having no apparent emphasis, with the aspect that preponderates.

(3) He should class a work dealing with a subject from two or more aspects, but having no apparent emphasis or preponderance, in accordance with instructions on treatment of interdisciplinary works given in the schedules, when such notes occur (compare section 8.511), e.g., interdisciplinary works on abrasive materials in 553.65, as specified at 553. (However, such an instruction is not valid and should not be followed unless one of the aspects treated in the work is the one properly classed in the number designated for interdisciplinary use, e.g., 553.65 is not a valid number for an interdisciplinary work on abrasive materials unless economic geology is one of the aspects considered in the work.)

(4) Lacking apparent emphasis or preponderance, and lacking specific valid instructions on treatment of interdisciplinary works—and relatively few such notes appear—the classifier should class a work dealing with a subject from two or more aspects with the underlying, broader, or purposive discipline, e.g., science underlies technology, art is broader than belles-lettres, utilization is the purpose of fabrication, hence, prefer 500s to 600s, 700s to 800s, 330 to 600s, 794.1 to 688.741.

(5) Lacking any other principle, he should class in the discipline that comes first in the schedules.

To class a work on two or more interrelated subjects considered from two or more aspects, the classifier may have to apply a combination of the foregoing rules, and he should not overlook the possibilities of main class 0.

9.3 COMPREHENSIVE WORKS ON CONCEPTS IN CENTERED ENTRIES. Sometimes there are steps in the successive divisions of a discipline or subject for which positions in the lengthening notation are not available. These are represented by spans of numbers in centered entries. (Compare section 5.141.) Since in a shelf classification a given book can have but one class number, every centered entry is followed by a note stating what single number the classifier should use for comprehensive works on the concept expressed in the entry. (See also section 8.57 (2).) The basis for the editors' choice of number varies, since each case is dependent on the schedule structure for the particular subject. The classifier will observe that the comprehensive number specified may be (1) the next higher number in the hierarchy, e.g., diseases of urinary system (616.61–.64) in 616.6, England ("Areas" notation 421–428) in notation 42; (2) a general, or 0, subdivision of the next higher number, e.g., woodwind instruments (788.5–.9) in 788.05; (3) a preceding specific number, e.g., flow variations (532.52–532.56) in 532.51; (4) the first or one of the other numbers subordinate to the centered entry, e.g., libraries for educational institutions (027.7–027.8) in 027.7.

9.4 APPLICATIONS. The classifier should class the application of a principle, concept, science, procedure, or technique with the principle, concept, science, procedure, or technique to which it is applied. For example, general principles of radio communication engineering are classed in 621.3841, and special developments of radio engineering, such as the circuitry and instruments used in space communication, in 621.384197; but the application of space communication to (i.e., its use in) astronautics is classed in 629.437 and 629.457, and the application of astronautics to weather forecasting in 551.6354.

9.5 WORKS RELATED TO OTHER WORKS. The classifier should ordinarily place with the original work translations, abridgments, criticisms, and reviews of it, commentaries on it, indexes and concordances to it. However, works about manuscripts and book rarities should be classed in 090, and works about the art in a book with the appropriate art. Since an adaptation modifies the original work in form, scope, presentation, and possibly language, it may or may not be classed with it, depending upon the amount and kind of modification. It is normally the function of the book number to distinguish among such related works.

10 Reduction. It has been noted that one of the valuable features of the DDC notation is its adaptability to both close and broad classification. How close or how broad the classification of a specific library should be is a matter of administrative determination. While bibliographies and classed catalogs should generally be highly detailed, it is unlikely that any library, no matter how large or specialized, will in its shelf classification follow the present edition to its fullest expanded detail in every section. Most libraries using these schedules for shelving purposes will probably reduce their expansions in some or many parts. The detail supplied herein is intended to be more rather than less than what most libraries will require, because it is relatively easy to cut back, either from the schedules themselves or from the numbers recommended by central classification services for specific titles, but it is not easy, or advisable, to expand beyond what is officially provided. (See also section 13.34.) According to the printed schedules, a work on the fresh-water plants of Lake Okeechobee would be classed in 581.92975939, a number of substantial usefulness in a classed catalog, but for shelving purposes likely to be required only for a botanical library or a general library with a very large collection in botany; most libraries will be adequately served by 581.929 or even 581.92.

10.1 HOW TO REDUCE NOTATION. The classifier should never reduce the notation to less than the most specific three-digit number, no matter how small his collection may be.

The classifier should cut at a point that will bring about a useful grouping. This requires special care when applied to synthesized numbers. For example, if the library has a large collection on the subject of wages, the classifier may find it desirable to place a work on wages in the cotton textile industry in 331.287721, while in smaller collections he may find 331.2877 (wages in the textile industry) or 331.287 (wages in manufacturing) or 331.28 (wages by occupation) to be useful groupings. However, it is doubtful if 331.28772 (wages in textile industries using seed-hair fibers) would prove very useful.

Many librarians consider geographic breakdown beyond the level of country unnecessarily detailed except in 930–990 for general history and 913–919 for geography. Indeed, with a quite small collection the classifier may consider 330.94 satisfactory for works on economic conditions in all or any part of Europe.

A number should never be reduced so that it ends in a 0 anywhere to the right of the decimal point, since such a 0 is meaningless.

The classifier should be sure that when he cuts he does just that; he should not change digits. For example, if his collection of works on history of Norway is so small that he does not wish to take advantage of the differentiation provided by 948.2, 948.3, 948.4, he should not use 948.1 as a general gathering place for all works on the subject, even though it is headed "Norway"; instead he should cut right down to 948. If he uses 948.1, he will be obliged, if future growth requires that his works on Norway be divided, to remove the "1" and substitute "2", "3", or "4".

The classifier should record in the schedules all decisions for reduction. This may be done by drawing a line through the numbers in the number column to cut off the digits that are not to be used, or by canceling add notes. The classifier should not try to record decisions of this nature in the index.

10.2 SEGMENTATION IN CENTRALIZED SERVICES. To assist classifiers who have neither the time nor the inclination to make cuts, Dewey Decimal numbers recorded since 1967 on Library of Congress catalog cards, printed catalogs, and MARC tapes, and since 1971 in the *British National Bibliography* (see section 12) have been presented in from one to three segments. This service enables those libraries that find some DDC notations excessively long for their purposes to cut the numbers meaningfully. Places are designated in the notation at which libraries of various sizes may find it desirable to terminate the number.

(1) Many numbers are printed in one segment; it is recommended that libraries of all sizes consider using such numbers without reduction. (2) Other numbers are printed in two segments; it is recommended that small libraries, or libraries with small collections in the specific subject, consider using only the first segment of such numbers, and all other libraries the whole number. (3) Still other numbers are printed in three segments; it is recommended that small libraries, or libraries with small collections in the specific subject, consider using the first segment of such numbers, that medium-sized libraries,

or libraries with moderate-sized collections in the specific subject, consider using the number made up of the first two segments, and that large libraries, or libraries with large collections in the subject, either use the whole number, or, in very long numbers, if they wish, omit one or more complete synthetic elements from the last segment (see second following paragraph).

Segmenting is shown by prime marks; it must be emphasized that these marks are not part of the notation. For example, with 305.8'951'073, libraries making cuts at the recommended places in the notation will mark their cards and books 305.8 or 305.8951; while 305.8951073 will be used if no reduction is desired.

Segments on LC cards, with many exceptions, consist of the base number appearing in the abridged edition, the base number in the full edition and the various synthetic elements that together make up a complete DDC number, e.g., 331.88, 331.88'12, 331.88'0973, 331.88'12'92. Since there are never more than three segments, the final one may consist of more than one synthetic element, as in 331.88'12'920973.

This basis for segmentation is followed on the assumption that small libraries generally consider 5-digit numbers to be of maximum desirable length, and that medium-sized libraries generally consider 7-digit numbers to be of maximum desirable length. Some recommendations provide numbers longer than this, but they occur relatively infrequently.

11 Index. In order to make best utilization of the index, which will be found in volume 3, the classifier should know what he may expect to find in it, how it is organized, and how to use it. The index is highly structured but will furnish much assistance to the classifier who understands it.

11.1 BASIC CONTENT. The index contains an entry for every significant term named in the schedules and tables, with leads, sometimes through several successive referrals, to many aspects that are named or implied by add notes. Class numbers are given for most subjects that have their own numbers in the schedules and for many subjects whose numbers are obtained through number building. However, it is not feasible to include in the index *every possible* aspect even for those topics that are included, and still keep it within a reasonable size. The index does *not* include all names of persons, cities, organizations, minerals, plants, animals, chemical compounds, drugs, manufactured articles, and similar enumerations.

11.2 RELATIVITY. The index is considered relative (and is traditionally known as the "relative index") because of its inverse relationship to the schedules. Whereas in the schedules the different aspects of a subject are scattered according to discipline, in the index they are brought together under the name of the subject, with their various locations in the schedules indicated. For example, if the classifier has a work on copper and looks under that term, he will find many aspects and subaspects, including arts, chemistry, materials, metallurgy, mining, and products, each leading to one or more specific precise numbers in the schedules.

11.3 Cross references. In order to conserve space but still provide a maximum amount of information, the index utilizes many cross references, both direct and generalized.

Direct references are of two kinds, those that refer to a different term of the same level, and those that refer up to a term on a broader level. Those in the first category usually refer to a synonym or a variant spelling, e.g., Hansen's disease *see* Leprosy, Keramic *see* Ceramic, Underground *s[ee] a[lso]* Subterranean. Refer up references are supplied to help the classifier find the proper location for specific topics that do not have their own numbers in the schedules and to alert him to additional aspects which because of space limitations cannot be repeated in the index under countless specific headings. In some cases references continue upward in two or more successive steps. This type of reference is possible in the index because of the hierarchical principle on which the schedules are based, whatever is true of a whole being true also of its parts.

Generalized (or scatter) references are used freely to lead to applications, kinds, uses, occurrences of the topic.

Examples of cross references follow:

Under "Copper compounds plant nutrition" is a direct reference to see "Trace elements plant nutrition." While the two terms are not synonymous, there is no number uniquely assigned to copper compounds in this context, and they, along with manganese, zinc, boron and certain other compounds, are always classed in the numbers assigned to the broader concept Trace elements. The classifier turning to "Trace elements plant nutrition" will find two numbers in 581, one for plant physiology and the other for plant pathology, and a further reference to see also specific plants. This reference reflects the cross reference in the schedules at 581 that instructs the classifier to class all the general principles of botany (including plant nutrition) as they apply to specific plants and groups of plants in the appropriate numbers under 582–589. See section 8.58. (*"S.a. spec. plants"* is a short way of saying "see also specific plants and groups of plants.") Thus the classifier seeking in the index numbers to use for copper compounds in plant nutrition has been given the two numbers 581.213356 for pathology and 581.13356 for physiology of plants in general, and has been told that copper compounds in nutrition of any specific plant or group of plants is to be classed with works on that plant or group (many of which will be found in the index under their own names).

Often a subject has its own number(s) for one or more aspects, but in other aspects shares a number or numbers with a broader concept (unlike the concept Copper elements, which in *all* plant nutrition aspects shares the numbers used for the broader concept Trace elements). In such a case, the specific numbers that apply are given under the name of the subject. The other aspects are covered by generalized references, which tell the classifier: for *"other aspects see,"* or for *"miscellaneous aspects see"* the term for the broader concept. Turning to the broader concept the classifier will usually find some numbers that he can ignore, because they are shorter and broader versions of the same numbers he has already found under the narrow concept; but he will also find new numbers.

For example, under Apples the classifier will find 634.11 for culture, 641.3411 for food in general, 641.6411 for domestic preparation, 664.80411 for commercial preparation, and the reference *"other aspects see* Rosaceae; *also* Fruits." Under Fruits he will find 634, 641.34, 641.64, and 664.8, all of which are repetitions at a broader level of numbers already found under Apples. He will also find several new numbers, such as 634.987 for fruits as forest products, 636.0874 for fruits as animal feeds, and 641.41–.47 for domestic preservation of fruits, all of which, of course, include apples. Under Rosaceae he will find no repeated numbers, but several new ones, such as 583.372 for botany, and the reference *"other aspects see* Plants." Under Plants he will find three numbers for art representation, one for conservation techniques, one for landscape design, and several for literary treatment; all of these numbers may be used for plants, for specific families of plants such as Rosaceae, and for specific Rosaceae such as apples. Under literary treatment the classifier is led still further to Natural phenomena.

Another example that the classifier may wish to trace through the index is Beavers, which will lead him to Sciuromorpha, thence to Rodentia, thence to Animals. At all levels except Beavers new numbers are brought in for consideration, and at both Rodentia and Animals old numbers are also repeated at shorter length on broader levels.

In many cases when only one aspect of a subject is entered in the index, a generalized reference suggests the possibility of other aspects, e.g., "Abbreviated longhand writing systems 653.2; *see also specific applications e.g.* Practical pharmacy"; "Accelerometers aircraft engineering 629.1352; *see also other specific uses."* But in the case of "Aladdin ovens cookery 641.588," the printing of "cookery" on a separate line is expected to remind the classifier that other aspects, such as manufacture, are possible, even though not mentioned.

Some of the numbers in the example under Apples are illustrative of synthesized, or built, numbers, e.g., 641.3411. Synthesized numbers are included in the index for many concepts that may be commonly sought. However, it is not feasible to include in the index all of the possible specific numbers that may be derived, especially in the case of subjects whose numbers may be extended by the addition of notations for very many specific topics. There will still be plenty of cases where the classifier must use the information at hand to build the number himself. For example, under the index entry Economics there appear Biblical treatment 220.833, curriculums 375.33, journalism 070.44933, libraries 026.33 (all of the 33s coming from the addition of the basic number for economics 330), and the instruction for other aspects to see Social sciences. Under the latter term are found most of the same numbers (ending in 3 instead of 33), and also library classification 025.463, museology 069.93, subject headings 025.493. To derive the number for library classification of economics, it is necessary to extend 025.46 by adding 33[0], the full number for economics.

In section 8.1 the classifier was advised that he should not class solely from the index, because he might miss helpful guidance that appears only in the schedules. One example of this may be seen when a schedule entry directly indicated by an index entry incorporates a cross reference or a class elsewhere note. For such a situation the index does not undertake to show the numbers for the detached or related parts of the subject; it assumes that the classifier will look in the schedules at the number named and there acquire further necessary information. For example, the index entry for "Water transportation commerce 387" does not point out that inland waterway and ferry transportation are in 386. This information is obtained by the classifier only when he turns to 387 in the schedule.

However, if the cross reference or class elsewhere note is not immediately at the entry designated by the index, the additional information *is* given in the index. For example, under "Matriculation schools 371.21" there is a reference *"see also specific levels of education."* In the schedule, the fact that all topics in subdivisions of 371 are to be classed with the specific level when limited to that level is stated at 371, but not at 371.21 or any other of its many subdivisions.

In order that full utilization may be made of cross references to keep the index within a reasonable length, they will be found on occasion to lead to an arbitrary term which, even though of itself no one would look under it, has been chosen by the editors as a group designation under which to gather all the appropriate information. For example, under "Minor metals" the classifier will find consolidated numerous aspects applying to niobium, hafnium, germanium, and eighteen other elements, from all of which reference is made to "Minor metals" in lieu of repetition of the various aspects under each.

11.4 COORDINATION WITH SCHEDULES. It is obvious that the index entries, because they are closely coordinated with each other and with the schedules, must be used with care and thought; and further that it is not advisable to use a number printed at the topic sought without first following up the pertinent cross references. It is equally not advisable to classify from the index alone without referring to the schedule, which is the only place where, on the various steps of the hierarchical ladder, may be found all the information about coverage and correct use of the numbers. To quote Melvil Dewey, in his introduction to Edition 12: "Assyn numbers by uzing Tables [i.e., schedules] alone, and then always verify yur result by the Index. . . . As a chek against error, even tho familiar with the skeme, uze Index freely."

11.5 ARRANGEMENT AND OTHER GENERAL INFORMATION. Except where sense or syntax requires otherwise, nouns are entered in the index in plural form.

If the subject that a classifier wants is not found in the index, he should look for it under a synonym, under another word of the same root, under a related term (for example, if what is wanted is not found under "heart," he should try "cardi-"), or under a broader subject.

Unless relativity requires inversion, adjective + noun phrases are entered in direct form only, e.g., Mechanical engineering, not Engineering mechanical. However, if the classifier cannot find such a phrase under the adjective he should look under the noun alone, e.g., not finding Anglican bishops or apple pies he should look under Bishops and Pies respectively.

Index entries are arranged alphabetically word by word. Terms indented below the main headings are alphabeted in one group even though they may be a mixture of topical subheadings and words that, when combined with the main heading, form phrases or inverted subjects. Indention in the index has the same hierarchical force that it has in the schedules. Terms followed by explanatory words in parentheses are alphabeted separately. Hyphenated words are considered to be single words. Hyphens are often used to make syntactical distinctions, e.g., Grinding cereal grains, Grinding-tools, and the classifier should check all such possibilities. Abbreviations are filed as if spelled in full. A list of abbreviations used precedes the index. Initials such as UHF and USSR are filed as if each letter were a separate word. Names beginning with Mc and M' are arranged as if spelled Mac. Modified vowels, such as ä, ö, ü, are arranged as a, o, u.

Numbers preceded by a dash and a term in italics will be found in the auxiliary tables. For example, numbers preceded by *"s.s.–"* are in Table 1 Standard Subdivisions, *"area–"* refers to Table 2 Areas, *"lang.–"* to Table 6 Languages. Numbers supplied by the tables are never used alone, but are added as appropriate to numbers from the schedule. Numbers preceded by *"law s.s.–"* are to be found in the specially extended standard subdivisions for law that are enumerated under centered heading 342–347 and may be added to class numbers from that span as appropriate.

Digits to the right of the decimal point, and digits in numbers from the tables, are printed in groups of three. This device is purely for ease in reading and copying. The spaces are not part of the numbers, and the groups are not related to those shown in DDC numbers on Library of Congress and other centralized cataloging records, for which see section 10.2.

12 General suggestions. The classifier may be repaid by checking to determine whether one of the centralized classification services has already assigned a number. Even if an individual library does not follow the same edition of DDC or the same policies as the central service, or has made local adaptations of its own, the decisions of experts are helpful. Among the more important sources for Dewey numbers from the latest unabridged edition are Library of Congress catalog cards, book catalogs, and tapes; the ALA *Booklist, Publishers' Weekly,* and *American Book Publishing Record.* Numbers from the latest abridged edition appear in *Book Review Digest* and the various parts of the *Standard Catalog Series.* Since 1969 the *British National Bibliography* has followed the latest edition mostly without change, and more recently *Canadiana* and the *Australian National Bibliography* have done likewise.

It has sometimes been proposed that Library of Congress catalog cards should include a book number along with each Dewey Decimal Classification number, but this has not been considered feasible, because (1) different existing libraries use different book numbering systems; (2) even newly established libraries, which might be expected to find this service most useful, class and number works not covered by printed cards, and in so doing may be expected, in a given class, to preempt book numbers that would later appear on printed cards for other titles in the same class.

To promote consistency and future efficiency, the classifier should make a local record of all decisions. Most libraries maintain a shelflist or similar record which lists all works in classified order, thus showing the application of the different class numbers to specific works. Decisions on specific problems may be written at the pertinent point in the classification schedules or recorded in the shelflist or kept in a separate file, or a combination of methods may be employed.

13 Variations from recommended practice.

13.1 PRINCIPLE OF USEFULNESS. Although an important feature of the DDC is that its notation provides a universal language that can be understood in all libraries and in all countries, nevertheless, in serving the special needs of a library's clientele, a classifier may sometimes find it desirable to modify specific printed provisions in ways other than reduction (for which see section 10). This is permissible if there is a *real* and *permanent* local need. By "real" is meant that each variation should have a demonstrable reason that can be recorded and defended. By "permanent" is meant that a specific need of a temporary or short-term nature should not be met by adjustment of class numbers. In any event variations should be adopted only with caution; see section 13.4.

The classifier should record in the schedules every decision for variation. As with reductions, he should not, however, try to record such decisions in the index.

13.2 OFFICIALLY RECOGNIZED VARIATIONS. A number of important variations appear in the printed schedules or are otherwise officially recognized. They are available and recommended for use by libraries whose needs they will serve, but are not reflected in the practices of the Decimal Classification Division as recorded on Library of Congress cataloging records.

13.21 *Optional provision.* Certain topics are given two (or more) specific placements. One of these is always preferred by the editors, and in each case an instructional note appears under both the preferred and the optional numbers (see section 8.52). Several examples follow.

Instead of the traditional DDC arrangement of belles-lettres by form, which separates the works of an author who writes in different forms, e.g., poetry and drama, some libraries, especially those in colleges and universities, prefer to have all of the literary works of an author classed together. Under each language they may then arrange all of the works written in that language in one alphabetical author sequence or in groups by chronological periods, regardless of the literary form of the works. The DDC recognizes this method of arranging literary works by a note in Table 3 Subdivisions of Individual Literatures, under centered heading —1–8 Specific forms: "Class description, critical appraisal, biography, collected works of an individual author with the form with which he is chiefly identified; or, if preferred, class description, critical appraisal, biography, single and collected works of all individual authors regardless of form in —8." (In the preferred arrangement, even when description, criticism, collected works, etc. of an author are classed with the form with which he is chiefly identified, single works should still be classed by form, e.g., John Galsworthy as a whole, and his novels, in 823, but his plays in 822.) Under —8 the classifier will find: "(It is optional to class here description, critical appraisal, biography, single and collected works of all individual authors regardless of form; prefer —1–8)."

Treatment of biography varies greatly from one library to another. Many academic libraries prefer it arranged with pertinent subjects, e.g., biography of engineers with engineering, of statesmen with general history of appropriate countries, of artists with art. On the other hand, most popular libraries prefer all or most biography together, either subarranged by subject or (for individual biography) in one alphabet by biographee. Accordingly, while use of standard subdivision 092 with each subject is the editors' recommended treatment of biography, a note appears in Table 1 under 092, "If preferred, class biography in 920.1–928.9," and under 0924 Individual, "If preferred, class individual biography in 92 or B [these being traditional notations used widely for individual biography kept together in one alphabetical span]; or, if preferred, class individual biography of men in 920.71, of women in 920.72."

Traditionally, Dewey has placed the various branches of geography under the specific topics that are considered by area, e.g., economic geography 330.91–.99, phytogeography 581.9, medical geography 614.423–.429. However, with a growing academic and research interest in geography, in recent years numerous libraries have come to prefer an arrangement that brings all geography together. Such an arrangement is supplied optionally at 910.1 Topical geography, which is subdivided by subject, e.g., economic geography 910.133, phytogeography 910.158, medical geography 910.1614.

Ancient history of various places is classed by editors' preference in the 930s, but, optionally, may be classed in 940–960 immediately preceding later periods in the history of the places concerned, e.g., ancient Egypt preferred in 932 but optional in 962.01.

13.22 *Devices for giving more emphasis to favored subjects.* The decimal notation being limited to nine significant digits, Melvil Dewey usually assigned 1–8 to those places, races, languages, cultures, religions that were most significant to American libraries of 1876, grouping others in 9. As a result, there are places, races, languages, cultures, religions on which there is now a mass of literature that have been assigned notations with long base numbers, e.g., Urdu language 491.439 (while English is 42), Hinduism, 294.5 (while Christianity is 23–28). Consequently, libraries serving Eastern and other cultures are likely to find the bulk of their collections classed near the end of long sequences and denoted by long numbers.

13.221 *Artificial digits.* As one means of correcting this situation, the schedules and tables frequently suggest as an option that a letter or other symbol be used as an artificial digit to bring into prominence and give a shorter number to any desired linguistic, ethnic, or cultural approach. For example, a note at 081–089 provides that general Urdu anthologies may be placed in 08U (or 08* or 08†), instead of 089.91439, and shelved before 081; a note at 292–299 provides that Hinduism may be placed in 2H0 (or 2*0 or 2†0), instead of 294.5, and shelved before 220, or, as another option, 29H may be used preceding 291 or 292.

13.222 *Use of established numbers with unofficial meanings.* Another method for featuring and giving shorter notation to a specific race, language, or culture is to use for the favored subject the notation that has been assigned to the subject given prominence by the official schedules or tables. An example may be found under 810: "(If it is desired to give local emphasis and a shorter number to a specific literature other than American literature in English, e.g., Afrikaans literature, it is optional to class it here; in that case class American literature in English in 820)." Another example under 230–280 reads: "(If it is desired to give local emphasis and more and shorter numbers to a specific religion other than Christianity, e.g., Buddhism, it is optional to class it in these numbers, its sources in 220, comprehensive works in 200; in that case class Bible and Christianity in 298)." The classifier will observe that the note always tells where to class the subject displaced by the subject to which he wishes to give prominence.

13.23 *Types of works not classified.* Many popular libraries follow the policy of not classifying certain categories of works, but, instead, of arranging them alphabetically. Most frequently this kind of treatment is given to individual works of fiction in the language commonly read by the library's patrons. For example, in the United States, fiction published in English language, no matter what the country of origin or language of composition, is arranged by author, e.g., Dickens, Hemingway, Proust, Zweig. In a similar manner, some libraries arrange all their bound periodical sets, no matter what the subject, in a single sequence by title.

13.3 UNOFFICIAL VARIATIONS. Other variations may prove to be useful in specific situations even though not officially recognized.

13.31 *Alphabetical arrangement.* As an alternative to systematic arrangement, or as a means for homemade expansion (see also section 13.34), alphabetical arrangement using the Cutter, Cutter-Sanborn, or Library of Congress author tables (see section 5.121) may serve specific local purposes. It is most useful when there are large numbers of specific coordinate subdivisions with accepted names and when the full DDC numbers would be very long. Examples of numbers with many subtopics that the classifier may wish to consider for alphabetical subarrangement are families of dicotyledonous plants in 583, counties of United States in "Areas" notation 74–79 from Table 2, occupations in 331.28, goods in 338.47. Care must always be exercised to avoid duplicate listing of the same concept under different terms. For example, in lists of occupations, works on welding should not appear under both "welding" and "metalworking."

Sometimes the editors are asked why a particular subject should not have an alphabetical rather than a classified geographical arrangement, e.g., U.S. states arranged alphabetically instead of by the area notation. It is true that the sequence Alabama, Alaska, Arizona, Arkansas, California . . . Wyoming is quite familiar and easy to understand. It is true also that under many subjects, e.g., statistics, such an arrangement is entirely satisfactory. But under others, e.g., fauna and flora, it is more satisfactory to find Virginia and West Virginia side by side rather than separated by Washington state. A separate alphabetical arrangement for cities, distinct from that for states, will bring close together treatment of churches (or any other appropriate subject) in Springfield, Illinois, and Springfield, Massachusetts, but only separate churches in the latter city from those in Quincy, Newton, and Lynn, Massachusetts.

13.32 *Omitting digits.* Occasionally, in order to shorten a number, it is possible to omit a digit from within the number. This may be done relatively safely in certain circumstances, e.g., when a relocation between editions has forced the editors to use an additional 0 in the new edition in order to avoid a reuse of an old number or numbers with a new meaning or meanings, but the individual library has not used the number(s) with the earlier meaning(s). For instance, in Table 3 Subdivisions of Individual Literatures it is possible to omit a 0 from certain numbers. Since the publication of Edition 17, in main class 8 each literature has had its own period divisions, which are different from those in the 16th and earlier editions, because those were based on the period numbers in standard subdivisions 0901–0904. For example, the numbers for period divisions of history and criticism of United States literature are now 810.9001–.9005 rather than 810.903–.904 as in the 16th and earlier editions. Any library that has not previously used 810.903–.904 may omit one of the 0s from 810.9001–.9005 and class periods of U.S. literature in 810.901–.905. However, any such variations should be made with caution, because of the possibility of changes in future editions.

13.33 *Attraction.* Because of special local interest or special collections of books, it may on occasion appear desirable to bring together all works on a given subject in only one of the several possible disciplines, e.g., *all* works on Jews in 296, *all* works on automobiles in 629.2.

An extension of this practice is the complete reversal of DDC order. For example, a library devoted to travel and area study, or to maps, might make an administrative decision to arrange its collections entirely by place. To achieve this arrangement it could use the "Areas" notations for the basic classes, followed, when appropriate, by 0 and the DDC subject numbers. Then everything on Japan would be placed in class 52; religion in 5202, economic situation in 52033, art in 5207. In such a system works not limited by area could be placed in notation 0 followed by the regular DDC notation, e.g., economic conditions of the whole world 033. Needless to say, this kind of use of DDC would be purely local, and would receive no support from central classification services.

13.34 *Expansion.* The demands of an extraordinarily large collection in a given subject may appear to encourage the development of a homemade expansion. Such a step is strongly discouraged. An institution needing an expansion should consult with the Decimal Classification Division of the Library of Congress, which, if the need appears to be general, will undertake to prepare it. In the meantime the broader classification should be made to serve until the official expansion is available. A good expansion requires time for study, research, interviewing, and correspondence, and necessitates a broad and dispassionate overall approach. The librarian who makes his own changes or expansions should remember that, once a change is made, the library, because of the expense of reclassifying, in all probability will be forced to abide by it indefinitely, unable to make use of official expansions and improvements in subsequent editions. This warning applies also to unauthorized number building, including successive division by more than one principle. It is best, if local additions must be made and cannot await editorial action, that letters or other artificial digits be used.

13.35 *Standard subdivisions.* Some libraries will prefer to keep their employment of standard subdivisions consistent, always using regular notations instead of the irregular notations described in section 8.73. This is not likely to create future difficulty, and may be effected by canceling the special instructions to use irregular notation under specific subjects.

13.36 *Showing language in notation.* Libraries wishing to establish separate collections for their works in different languages can do so by prefixing to each class number appropriate numbers from the languages notation of Table 6, e.g., (21)536.2 and (21)709.54 for works in English on heat transfer and Indian art respectively, (9144)536.2 and (9144)709.54 for works in Bengali on the same subjects. Libraries wishing to class conventionally by discipline and subject, and then differentiate by language, can follow the reverse procedure, e.g., 536.2(21), 536.2(9144), 709.54(21), 709.54(9144). The parentheses are only for illustrative purposes; any other device, provided its use and meaning are clearly understood, can serve the same purpose.

13.4 CAUTION. Although it is possible to adopt variations from recommended practice when they will prove useful, many such adoptions are shortsighted, and variations should be held to the barest minimum. Raynard C. Swank has summed this up as follows: "Every modification of an established classification schedule means additional work for the catalogers in the future, since these modifications prevent the department from taking full advantage of centralized cataloging at the Library of Congress. . . . As the library grows, simplifications adopted now might have to be undone and the books redistributed among the original or other similar schedules. By and large, I doubt that any tampering with the Dewey schedule is worthwhile. I have never worked in a library that has not regretted, sooner or later, departures from the standard schedules of classification." (Quoted in Schultheiss, Culbertson, Heiliger, *Advanced Data Processing in the University Library.* New York, Scarecrow Press, 1962, p. 7.)

14 Special problems.

14.1 LONG NUMBERS. The DDC has been criticized for the length of its notation in certain classes, especially those that have grown rapidly since Melvil Dewey's original apportionment of numbers. Without doubt, the distribution is poor in the light of present knowledge (e.g., the schedule for section 621 alone is longer than those for the entire main classes 000–099 or 400–499), and repair is virtually impossible in view of the traditional policy of integrity of numbers, a policy which permits only the most sparing reuse of numbers with new meanings (see section 14.23). To reapportion the notation so that it would be equally hospitable to all disciplines and subjects represented in libraries today would require the development of a wholly new system and would only establish a base for other inequities in a future that today cannot be imagined, just as much of the knowledge of the 1970s and '80s could not be foreseen by Dewey in the 1870s. So long as the DDC continues to expand in order to keep pace with knowledge, its users will encounter "long" numbers, but they need not necessarily accept them. A classification scheme may be used for two distinct purposes: (1) for storage and retrieval of precise and detailed information, and (2) for arranging works on shelves in subject groupings. For the first purpose long numbers are inevitable. For the second, most users feel that shorter numbers are adequate, and suggestions have been given for reducing numbers in section 10. Some few libraries shelve by numbers of limited length, but on catalog and shelflist cards and inside each book give a complete number based on the full DDC schedules, with the shelving digits in black and the nonshelving digits in red. Another possible method for shortening numbers is the substitution of arbitrary signs for the basic part of heavily used long numbers. For example, an engineering library can substitute letters of the alphabet for some of the larger engineering subdisciplines with long notations, such as E (for electrical) in lieu of 621.3, AE (for aeronautical) in lieu of 629.1, AU (for automotive) in lieu of 629.2, AS (for astronautical) in lieu of 629.4. If it is not feasible to shorten numbers, transcription and reading of many digits may be made easier by writing long numbers on several lines, e.g., 581 instead of 581.92975939.

.929

759

39

14.2 CHANGES BETWEEN EDITIONS. Several kinds of changes occur between editions that require special methods for adjustment within established library collections: (1) expansions and reductions, which result in topics being assigned longer or shorter numbers than in earlier editions; (2) relocations (see section 8.56); (3) reused numbers; and (4) phoenix schedules, which are totally new developments on established bases.

Ideally, for maximum utilization of the Classification, all such changes should be adopted promptly, not only for materials currently received but also for materials classed earlier. However, this is not usually practical, and the following compromises may be considered:

14.21 *Expansions and reductions.* Most libraries adopt each new expansion that is expected to serve a special need, and assign the lengthened number to works received after the date of adoption. Not often, however, do they reclassify older materials into a more specific number. There is no great loss in this omission, because the older works in the shorter number will remain either adjacent to or near the new works in the longer number and will be grouped with works on the broader subject of which their specific topics form a part.

Libraries are somewhat less likely to adopt a new reduction, though in cases where there are no numbers intervening between the longer and shorter numbers, there is little reason for not doing so. It should be kept in mind that an editorial reduction does not necessarily reflect merely a lessening amount of publication on the subject, but may be introduced in anticipation of future development of a new and better expansion.

14.22 *Relocations.* It is a good policy for a library to adopt each relocation as soon as it can, and in any event to use the new number for classification of new materials. Failure to adopt the relocation for future use means loss of the benefits of centralized classification service and the courting of future conflict. Failure to reclassify older materials means separation of works on a given subject. However, local circumstances, such as an active weeding program and the shelving of older material in closed stacks, may make this tolerable. Suggested methods of alleviating the inconveniences are to place cross references in the shelflist and appropriate labels or wooden-block dummies on the shelves. A list of relocations in this edition appears in this volume following Tables 1–7.

14.23 *Reused numbers.* Assignment of new topics to recently vacated numbers is held by the editors to an absolute minimum (except for phoenix schedules, for which see section 14.24), because such reuse is a potential source of very great confusion. Unlike relocations, which may separate like materials, reuse of numbers results in unlike materials sharing the same number. For example, the 14th and earlier editions used 621.46 for animal motors and treadmills, the 15th–17th editions did not use it at all, and the 18th and present editions use it for Electric propulsion technology. In this edition there are eleven reused numbers, exclusive of those in phoenix schedules; they are identified by italics, and they are listed in section 2.4. It is strongly recommended that old material be removed from them and placed in appropriate new locations when each number is first used with its new meaning.

14.24 *Phoenix schedules.* Each recent edition has provided a completely new development of the schedule for one or more disciplines for which the older development was totally inadequate to meet the requirements of modern literature: inorganic and organic chemistry in Edition 16, psychology in Edition 17, law and mathematics in Edition 18. In this edition there are phoenix developments for sociology, the political process, and British local administrative units. For important topics in each of these fields there appears in volume 1, preceding the summaries, a list of changed numbers. The editors realize that introduction into an existing book collection of the provisions of these new schedules is difficult and expensive, but recommend nevertheless that they be adopted. Failure to do so will mean continued use of schedules incapable of dealing with publications of the 1970s and '80s. In order to avoid chaos in the collections, reclassification, with the aid of the lists of changed numbers, of works previously classed according to the older schedules should proceed as rapidly as possible.

15 How an edition of the Dewey Decimal Classification is prepared. Each new edition is based on its immediate predecessor. First, editorial rules are revised to improve clarity in textual presentation. Then, taking into consideration the response of users (including those in the Library of Congress's Decimal Classification Division) to the immediately preceding as well as earlier editions, the editors in consultation with the Decimal Classification Editorial Policy Committee and the Forest Press Committee determine which schedules require what degree of revision and review, from full phoenix treatment, which provides a totally new development on the old base number, to routine review, which may be little more than modification of the text to conform to changes in the editorial rules.

Major revisions are prepared with the advice of subject experts. All revision includes at least a routine review of LC's Dewey-classed file to see if the textual provisions of the previous edition have been adequate for the literature and clearly understood by the user. The actual mechanics of setting forth revised text and cross checking every detail constitute a time-consuming and detailed effort.

At all times the editors must keep in mind the needs of diverse users, including practitioners in small and large, popular and research libraries, as well as teachers and students. They must also provide guidance for international usage. They must balance innovation against stability, required degree of detail against length of notation.

Glossary

References to further information on the terms defined may be found in the Index to Editor's Introduction and Glossary, which follows.

Add note. An instruction directing the addition to a designated base number of digits derived either from a number sequence in the schedules or from a table. Replaces the former instruction to "divide like." *See also* **Number building.**

Application. A principle, concept, procedure, or technique basic to a specific discipline, used in another discipline. Example: application of psychology to management.

"Areas". Table 2. A table of notations designating geographical areas. Applied to other notations in the schedules and tables through use of add notes.

Artificial digit. A letter or other symbol used in certain cases as a substitute for digits 0–9 to provide a more prominent location or shorter notation for various languages, literatures, religions, cultures, ethnic groups.

Aspect. That part of a single subject which belongs to a specific discipline. Examples: the technical and economic aspects of automobile manufacture.

Attraction. Classification of a specific aspect of a subject in the wrong discipline, usually because the correct discipline contains no named provision for the subject in question. Examples: classification of space medicine with astronautical engineering instead of with medicine; classification of Jewish sociology with Judaism instead of with sociology.

Author number. A combination of letters and/or figures representing the name of an author.

Auxiliary table. *See* **Table.**

Base number. (1) In a sequence of numbers, that portion which does not vary but remains the same in each member of the sequence. To this number digits from the tables or from another sequence in the schedules may be added as instructed. (2) The unvarying portion of a sequence from which digits are taken to form another sequence may also be referred to as a base number.

Bibliographic classification. *See* **Close classification.**

Book number. That portion of a call number which designates a specific individual work within its class. May consist of author number and/or other elements, e.g., subject of a biography.

Broad classification. (1) Use of only the more inclusive classes of a classification scheme, omitting detailed subdivision. Also called reduction of numbers. (2) A classification scheme which does not provide for minute subdivison of topics. *See also* **Reduction of numbers.**

Call number. A set of letters, numerals, and/or other symbols providing complete identification of an individual work and its relative location, consisting of class and book number and sometimes of such other data as date, volume number, copy number, location symbol.

Centered entry. An entry representing a concept for which there is no specific number in the hierarchy of notation, and which, therefore, covers a span of numbers.

Characteristic of division. Any of the various ways in which a given subject may be divided. Example: division of textiles by material, process used in manufacture, color, destined usage, etc.

Citation order. The order in which the classifier should take account of the subdivisions of a subject that is divided by more than one characteristic. Example: weaving cotton textiles is classed first by material (cotton), then by process (weaving). May be specified by a **Class elsewhere note, an Order of precedence note,** or a **Table of precedence** *(q.v.).*

Class. *(noun)* (1) A group of objects exhibiting one or more common characteristics, usually identified by a specific notation. (2) One of the ten major groups numbered 0–9 of the DDC. Also known as **Main class.** (3) A subdivision of the DDC of any degree of specificity. *(verb)* To assign a class number to an individual work. *See also* **Classify.**

Class elsewhere note. An instruction under a heading directing that certain specific portions of the topic, or related topics, be classed in another number.

Class here note. An instruction under a heading directing that topics broader than the heading, or otherwise not obviously part of the heading, be classed in the given number *and,* by implication, *its subdivisions.*

Class number. That portion of a call number which designates the class of a given work.

Classification. (1) An arrangement in some logical order of the whole field of knowledge, or of some specified portion thereof. (2) The art of arranging books or other objects in conformity with such a scheme.

Classified catalog. A catalog arranged according to the order of a classification scheme rather than alphabetically.

Classify. To arrange a collection of works according to the provisions of a classification scheme. *See also* **Class** *(verb).*

Close classification. (1) A classification providing for minute subdivision of topics. Also called bibliographic classification. (2) Arrangement of works in conformity with the provisions of such a scheme.

Comprehensive work. A work on a given subject *within one discipline* covering all, or most, of the subdivisions of the subject. *See also* **Interdisciplinary work.**

Cross classification. A situation in which a given work deals with two or more subdivisions of a subject, with each subdivision representing a different characteristic of division. Such a situation creates the possibility of inconsistent classification. Example:

a work on weaving cotton cloth deals with two subdivisions of textile technology, cotton (material) and weaving (process), and may be classed with either. *See also* **Citation order.**

Cross reference. An instruction note leading from the point at which comprehensive works on a subject are classed (whether stated or implied) to subdivisions of the topic located in numbers other than those subordinate to the number used for comprehensive works.

DDC. Dewey Decimal Classification.

Discipline. An organized field of study or branch of learning dealing with specific kinds of subjects and/or subjects considered from specific points of view.

Discontinued number. A number from the immediately preceding edition vacated because its content has been moved back to a more general number.

Divide-like. *(Obsolete)* An instruction to develop a span of numbers like another sequence by using the same pattern of terminal digits. Superseded by **Add note** *(q.v.)*.

Division of DDC. The second degree of subdivision in the Classification (the first degree of subdivision of one of the ten main classes), represented by the second digit in the notation, e.g., the 2 in 620. There are approximately 100 divisions.

Entry. (1) In schedules and tables a self-contained unit of the text consisting of a number or span of numbers, a heading, and often one or more notes. (2) In index a term or phrase followed by information in the form either of a number or of a reference to another term or phrase.

Expansion. The development of a concept or series of concepts in the schedules or tables to provide for more minute subdivision.

Faceting. The division of a subject by more than one characteristic. *See also* **Characteristic of division.**

General special concept. *See* **Special topic of general applicability.**

Heading. A word or phrase used as the title or rubric of a given class.

Hierarchical force. The property by which headings and certain notes apply to all subdivisions of the topic described and defined.

Hierarchy. The arrangement of disciplines and subjects in an order ranging from the most general to the most specific. In DDC degree of specificity is usually indicated by length of notation and always by depth of indention.

Inclusion note. An enumeration of subordinate topics under a heading, not obviously part of it, that have not yet been given separate provision. Such notes do *not* apply to subdivisions of the topic.

Instruction note. A note directing the user to take some specific step which is not obvious from the heading and its context or from the general notes.

Interdisciplinary work. A work dealing with a specific subject from the point of view of more than one discipline.

"Languages". Table 6. A table of notations designating specific languages. Applied to other notations in the schedules and tables through use of add notes. Used where topics were formerly divided like 420–490 to indicate language.

Literary warrant. Justification for the various provisions of a library classification system based not on theory but on the existence of actual works and their probable acquisition by libraries.

Main class of DDC. One of the ten major subdivisions of the Classification, represented by the first digit in the notation, e.g., the 6 in 600.

Memory aid. Any of various methods of using the same combination of numbers to represent the same topic in various contexts.

Notation. Numerals, letters, and/or other symbols used to represent the main and subordinate divisions of a classification scheme.

Number building. The process of making a number more specific through addition of segments taken from other parts of the classification. *See also* **Add note.**

Number column. The column of numbers printed at the left side of the entries in the schedules and tables, and at the right side of those in the index.

Optional provision. A variation from the preferred provision, offered to users in the printed schedules and tables of the DDC, but not used in centralized classification as supplied by the Library of Congress and rarely used by other centralized services of national libraries.

Order of precedence note. A note stating the correct citation order under a subject that the schedules subdivide according to more than one characteristic. *See also* **Citation order.**

"Persons". Table 7. A table of notations designating persons by specific occupational and other classes. Applied to other notations in the schedules and tables through use of add notes.

Phoenix schedule. A completely new development of the schedule for a specific discipline. Only the basic number for the discipline is certain to remain the same as in previous editions, all other numbers being freely reused to the extent required.

Precedence order note. *See* **Order of precedence note.**

Precedence table. *See* **Table of precedence.**

"Racial, Ethnic, National Groups". Table 5. A table of notations designating specific racial, ethnic, or national groups. Applied to other notations in the schedules through use of add notes.

Reduction of numbers. Dropping by the classifier of one or more digits at the end of a number given in the schedules or tables. Results in a shorter number with a more inclusive meaning, thus in broader classification. *See* **Broad classification** (1).

Reduction of schedules. Dropping by the editors of some or all of the previous subdivisions of a number with resultant classification of these concepts in a higher number. This results in a notation for the topic that is one or more digits shorter than it was in the immediately preceding edition. *See* **Discontinued number.**

Relativity. That property of the index which reverses the subordination of subject to discipline, thus bringing together from all disciplines the various aspects of individual subjects.

Relocation. An adjustment in the schedules resulting in the shifting of a topic between successive editions from one number to another that differs in respects other than length.

Reuse of numbers. A total change in the meaning of a given number from one edition to another. Rarely occurs in DDC unless the reused number has been vacant for two consecutive editions.

Scatter note. A class elsewhere note that does not lead to a specific location, but indicates that the topic will be classed in a wide variety of applicable locations.

Scatter reference. A cross reference in the index not referring to a specific term but suggesting a variety of possibilities.

Schedules. The series of numbers constituting the notation for the ten main DDC classes and all their subdivisions. Formerly called general tables or tables.

Scope note. A note enumerating special qualifications generally applicable to a subject and its subdivisions but not given a separate development.

Section of DDC. The third degree of subdivision in the Classification (the second degree of subdivision of one of the ten main classes, and the first degree of subdivision of one of the 100 divisions), represented by the third digit in the notation, e.g., the 9 in 629. There are approximately 1000 sections.

Shelf classification. A classification designated for use in arranging books on shelves rather than for minute precision in designating subject areas and relationships.

Special topic of general applicability. A kind of subdivision of a subject or discipline which is also a part of a different kind of subdivision of that subject or discipline. Example: textile technology is subdivided by the characteristic of process into weaving and knitting (among others); by the characteristic of material textile technology is also subdivided into cotton and wool (among others), and each of these material subdivisions may then be further subdivided by the process subdivisions, e.g., weaving cotton, knitting wool. *See also* **Characteristic of division.**

"Standard Subdivisions". Table 1. A table of notations designating certain frequently recurring forms or methods of treatment applicable to any subject or discipline. May be added, as required, to any number in the schedules.

"Subdivisions of Individual Languages". Table 4. A table of notations designating regularly recurring topics applicable to any language. May be added, as directed, to individual languages in 420–490.

"Subdivisions of Individual Literatures". Table 3. A table of notations designating regularly recurring topics applicable to any literature. May be added, as directed, to individual literatures in 810–890.

Subject. A specific unit or object of study. May be a person, group of people, thing, place, process, activity, abstract concept. Usually exhibits aspects belonging to more than one discipline.

Summary. A listing of the chief subdivisions of a number (i.e., those one digit longer) set forth at the head of the full development of the topic. The first three summaries (of main classes, divisions, sections respectively) stand at the head of the whole classification.

Synthesis of notation. *See* **Number building.**

Table. A sequence of dependent notations indicating various special concepts used repeatedly with a variety of subjects and disciplines. Used in number building but never by itself. Also called auxiliary table. Formerly called supplementary tables. The term **Tables** was formerly used also for what are now called **Schedules** *(q.v.)*.

Table of precedence. A table stating the correct citation order under a subject that the schedules subdivide according to more than one characteristic. *See also* **Citation order.**

Work. A unit or series of units of information having physical form and lending itself to bibliographic description. Examples: books, periodicals, phonorecords, films, microforms.

Index to Editor's Introduction and Glossary

References to the Editor's Introduction are identified by section numbers. References to G indicate that a definition may be found in the alphabetically arranged Glossary. Section numbers printed in boldface type are those where the most important information is supplied, e.g., under Add notes, **8.54–8.545.**

Tables

Use of the Tables

These are auxiliary tables, and are used only in conjunction with the classification schedules. In some instances, the numbers from one table may be added to those of another table, but in all cases the numbers from one or a combination of tables are to be used only with appropriate numbers from the schedules.

The dash preceding each number merely shows that the number never stands alone. The dash is omitted when the table number is added to a schedule number to make a complete class number.

Full instructions may be found in the Editor's Introduction, those for the use of Table 1 in section 8.7, and those for Tables 2–7 in sections 8.541 and 8.543–8.545.

Coordination and subordination of subjects are shown by indention and length of number, and are shown also in part by the prominence of the type face.

A number in square brackets [ ] is not in use, or is not recommended for use, or is no longer in use with the meaning indicated.

A number in *italics* is a reused number, i.e., it has a different meaning from that which it had in one or both of the earlier Editions 17 (1965) and 18 (1971).

Specific directions as to applicability precede each table.

Table 1. Standard Subdivisions

The following notations are never used alone, but may be used as required with any number from the schedules, e.g., classification (—012 in this table) of modern Indic languages (491.4): 491.4012. When adding to a number from the schedules, always insert a decimal point between the third and fourth digits of the complete number.

If at any given number there are subdivisions having a notation beginning with 0 for a special purpose, use 001–009 for standard subdivisions; if notations beginning with 0 and 00 both have special purposes, use 0001–0009 for standard subdivisions.

Unless other instructions are given, class works to which two or more standard subdivisions are applicable according to the following table of precedence, e.g., illustrations of the technique of the subject —028 (*not* —022):

Special topics of general applicability	—04
Persons associated with the subject	—092
Techniques, procedures, apparatus, equipment, materials	—028
Study and teaching	—07
(*except* —074, —076, —077)	
Management	—068
Philosophy and theory	—01
(*except* —014, —016)	
The subject as a profession, occupation, hobby	—023
Patents and identification marks	—027
Commercial miscellany	—029
Treatment by specific continents, countries, localities; extraterrestrial worlds	—093–099
Treatment by areas, regions, places in general	—091
Treatment among groups of persons	—08
Historical periods	—0901–0905
Works for specific types of users	—024
Museums, collections, exhibits	—074
Review and exercise	—076
Programmed texts	—077
Miscellany	—02
(*except* —023, —024, —027, —028, —029)	
Organizations	—06
Languages (Terminology) and communication	—014
Dictionaries, encyclopedias, concordances	—03
Serial publications	—05
Indexes	—016

SUMMARY

—01 Philosophy and theory
—02 Miscellany
—03 Dictionaries, encyclopedias, concordances
—04 Special topics of general applicability
—05 Serial publications
—06 Organizations and management
—07 Study and teaching
—08 History and description of the subject among groups of persons
—09 Historical and geographical treatment

—01 Philosophy and theory

—012 Classification

Divisions of the discipline or subject and their interrelations

—013 Value

—014 Languages (Terminology) and communication

Class subject headings and thesauruses in information retrieval in 025.49001–025.49999

For dictionaries, see —03

—014 1 Communication

For nonlinguistic communication, see —0147

—014 2 Etymology

—014 7 Nonlinguistic communication

Pantomine, smoke signals, drumbeats, flags, lights, other devices representing total concepts

—014 8 Abbreviations and symbols

—015 Scientific principles

Use of pure science to analyze and describe the subject, to support or attack its validity, to carry out operations in the subject

Add to base number —015 the numbers following 5 in 510–590, e.g., mathematical principles —0151

Class scientific and statistical method in —072

For psychological principles, see —019

—016 Indexes

(It is optional to class here subject bibliographies and catalogs; prefer 016)

Table 1. Standard Subdivisions

—018	**Methodology**

The study of methods, rules, postulates employed by a discipline

—[018 2]	Statistical method

Class use in techniques and procedures employed in the subject in —028, in research in —072

—[018 3]	Data processing

Class use in techniques and procedures employed in the subject in —0285, in research in —072

—[018 4]	Operations research

Class in —072

—019	**Psychological principles**
—02	**Miscellany**
—020 2	Synopses, outlines, manuals
—020 7	Humorous treatment
—020 8	Audiovisual treatment
—021	**Tabulated and related materials**
—021 2	Tables, formulas, specifications, statistics
—021 6	Lists, inventories, catalogs of articles

Class catalogs and lists offering articles for sale in —0294, catalogs of collections and exhibits in —074

—021 8	Standards

For specifications, see —0212

—022	**Illustrations and models**

Class humorous cartoons in —0207; atlases, maps, charts, plans depicting specific subjects on surface of earth or of extraterrestrial worlds in 912.1001–912.1899

—022 1	Drafting illustrations [*formerly* 604.26]
—022 2	Pictures, charts, designs
—022 3	Plans and diagrams
—022 8	Scale models

Class mathematical and analogue models in —072

—023   **The subject as a profession, occupation, hobby**

> Add "Areas" notation 1–9 from Table 2 to base number —023, e.g., the subject as a profession in England —02342

—024   **Works for specific types of users**

> Add "Persons" notation 03–99 from Table 7 to base number —024, e.g., works for engineers —02462

—025   **Directories of persons and organizations**

> Add "Areas" notation 1–9 from Table 2 to base number —025, e.g., directories of Ohio —025771
>
> Class directories of products and services offered for sale in —0294

—[026]   **Law**

> (Use of this number is optional; prefer 340)
>
> Add "Areas" notation 1–9 from Table 2 to base number —026, e.g., law of Australia —02694

—027   **Patents and identification marks**

—027 2   Patents

▶   **—027 5–027 8 Identification marks**

> Class comprehensive works in —027

—027 5   Trademarks and service marks

—027 7   Ownership marks

—027 8   Artists' and craftmen's marks

—028   **Techniques, procedures, apparatus, equipment, materials**

> Ways in which the objectives of an art or skill are obtained ("how-to-do-it"); use of necessary tools and materials
>
> Class here statistical method [*formerly* —0182], laboratory manuals
>
> Class laboratory manuals for study and teaching in —076
>
> *For drafting illustrations, see —0221*

Table 1. Standard Subdivisions

—028 5   Data processing [*formerly also* —0183]

> Class here comprehensive works on data processing as applied to the subject

> Add to base number —0285 the numbers following 001.6 in 001.61–001.64, e.g., programming —028542

> Class data processing in research in —072

▶   —028 7–028 9 Auxiliary procedures

Class comprehensive works in —028

—028 7   Testing and measurement

—028 8   Maintenance and repair

> Use this subdivision only with numbers denoting fabrication, manufacture, construction, installation, not with numbers denoting operation, application, use when these are different, e.g., maintenance and repair of textile manufacturing machinery 681.76770288 (not 677.02850288), but of tools 621.900288

—028 9   Safety measures

—029   **Commercial miscellany**

> Including house organs, prospectuses

—029 4   Price lists and trade catalogs

> Publications listing or describing products and services offered for sale with or without prices

> Add "Areas" notation 4–9 from Table 2 to base number —0294

> Class catalogs of collections and exhibits in —074, price trends for collectors in —075

—03   **Dictionaries, encyclopedias, concordances**

—032–039   **By language**

> Add "Languages" notation 2–9 from Table 6 to base number —03, e.g., German —0331

—04   **Special topics of general applicability**

> Use this subdivision only when it is specifically set forth in the schedules. Add other standard subdivisions —01–09 to it and its subdivisions as required, e.g., incidence of crime in France 364.0420944

—05 Serial publications

Class administrative reports and proceedings of organizations in —06, directories in serial form in —025

—06 Organizations and management

Class government organizations [*formerly* —06] in 350

▶   —060 1–060 9 Organizations

History, charters, regulations, membership lists, administrative reports and proceedings of permanent [*formerly* —062] and temporary [*formerly* —063] organizations

Class comprehensive works in —06

—060 1 International organizations

—060 3–9 National, state, provincial, local organizations

Add "Areas" notation 3–9 from Table 2 to base number —060, e.g., national organizations in France —06044

—[062] Permanent organizations

Class in —0601–0609

—[063] Temporary organizations

Class in —0601–0609

—[065] Business organizations

Class in 338.7–338.8

—068 Management of enterprises engaged in specific fields of activity, of specific kinds of enterprises [*both formerly* 658]

If preferred, class in 658.9

—068 1 Financial management

Securing funds, investment, management of income and expense, disbursements, budgeting, reporting

Class procurement of equipment and facilities in —0682, wage and salary administration in —0683

—068 2 Plant management

Selection, location, specifications, layout, maintenance

Including equipment and facilities

—068 3 Personnel management

Class labor relations in 331.88

Table 1. Standard Subdivisions

—068 4   Internal organization

> Line, line and staff, functional, by departments

—068 5   Organization of production

> Scheduling, routing, sequencing, work loads, time and motion study, quality control
>
> Class production management in manufacturing and construction enterprises in 658.5

—068 7   Management of materials

> Procurement, receiving, storage, inventory (stock) control, physical distribution

—068 8   Management of marketing

> Class here comprehensive works on distribution
>
> *For physical distribution, see —0687*

—07   Study and teaching

> Class here resources
>
> Class textbooks on a subject as treatises; do not use —07
>
> Class education and training on the job in 351.5, 658.3124

—070 1–9   Geographical treatment

> Add "Areas" notation 1–9 from Table 2 to base number —070, e.g., study and teaching in France —07044; however, class persons engaged in study and teaching in —092

—071   **Schools and courses**

—071 01–09   Geographical treatment

> Add "Areas" notation 1–9 from Table 2 to base number —0710, e.g., schools and courses in Brazil —071081; however, class persons in —092

▶   —071 1–071 5 Specific levels

> Class comprehensive works in —071, specific activities at any level in —072–079, the subject at elementary level in 372.3–372.8

—071 1   Colleges and universities

> Add "Areas" notation 1–9 from Table 2 to base number —0711, e.g., university courses in Japan —071152; however, class persons in —092

—071 2   Secondary schools

Add "Areas" notation 1–9 from Table 2 to base number —0712, e.g., secondary schools in regions of low economic development —07121724; however, class persons in —092

—071 5   Agencies for adult education

Class here continuing education

—071 52   Institutes and workshops

—071 53   Radio and television classes

—071 54   Correspondence courses

—072   **Research**

Activities and facilities for conducting inquiry or investigation into a subject in order to discover or revise facts, theories, applications

Class here statistical method [*formerly* —0182], data processing in research [*formerly also* —0183], operations research [*formerly* —0184]

—072 01–09   Geographical treatment

Add "Areas" notation 1–9 from Table 2 to base number —0720, e.g., research in England —072042; however, class persons in —092

—072 2   Historical research

Including case studies

—072 3   Descriptive research

Including surveys and appraisals

Class collecting of objects in —075

—072 4   Experimental research

Including models (simulation)

—073   **Students, learners, apprentices, novices**

—074   **Museums, collections, exhibits**

Guidebooks, catalogs, lists regardless of whether or not articles are offered for sale

Table 1. Standard Subdivisions

—074 01–09   Geographical treatment

> Class here specific galleries, museums, exhibits
>
> Add to base number —0740 the numbers following 708 in 708.1–708.9, e.g., museums and exhibits in Pennsylvania —0740148; but, if it is desired to give local emphasis and a shorter number to museums and exhibits of a specific country, place them first by use of a letter or other symbol, e.g., museums and exhibits in Japan —0740J (preceding —07401)

—075   **Collecting objects**

> Class here price trends for collectors
>
> Class museums, collections, exhibits in —074

—075 09   Historical and geographical treatment

> Add to base number —07509 the numbers following —09 in —0901–099, e.g., biography of collectors —075092

—076   **Review and exercise**

> Workbooks with problems, questions, answers; tests, testing, test construction and evaluation
>
> Including civil service examinations
>
> Class review and exercise involving use of apparatus and physical equipment in —078

—077   **Programmed texts**

> Class programming of texts and their use in —07

—078   **Use of apparatus and equipment in study and teaching**

—079   **Competitions and awards**

> Prizes, scholarships, fellowships, honorary titles

—08   **History and description of the subject among groups of persons**

> Use of this number for collections discontinued; class in main number
>
> Class persons associated with a specific subject in —092

—088 **Treatment among groups of specific kinds of persons**

Other than racial, ethnic, national

Add "Persons" notation 04–99 from Table 7 to base number —088, e.g., the subject among adolescents —088055, among lawyers —088344

Do not use if redundant, e.g., medicine among physicians, Lutheran doctrine among Lutherans

—089 **Treatment among specific racial, ethnic, national groups**

Add "Racial, Ethnic, National Groups" notation 01–99 from Table 5 to base number —089, e.g., the subject among North American native races —08997, among South American native races —08998, among Chinese —089951, among Chinese in United States —089951073

If preferred, class treatment among North American native races in North America in "Areas" notation 701 from Table 2, among South American native races in South America in "Areas" notation 801 from Table 2

Class treatment among specific racial, ethnic, national groups in places where they predominate in —091, —093–099; treatment among groups of specific kinds of persons of a specific racial, ethnic, national group in —088

—09 **Historical and geographical treatment**

Of subject and discipline

Class directories of persons and organizations regardless of time or place in —025; price lists and trade catalogs regardless of time or place in —0294; historical and geographical treatment of organizations in —06, of museums, collections, exhibits in —074

▶ **—090 1–090 5 Historical periods**

Not limited geographically

Class comprehensive works in —09

SUMMARY

—090 1	To 499 A.D.
—090 2	500–1499
—090 3	Modern period, 1500–
—090 4	20th century, 1900–1999
—090 5	21st century, 2000–2099

—090 1 To 499 A.D.

—090 12 To 4000 B.C.

Table 1. Standard Subdivisions

—090 13	3999–1000 B.C.
—090 14	999–1 B.C.
—090 15	1–499
—090 2	500–1499
—090 21	500–1199
—090 22	13th century, 1200–1299
—090 23	14th century, 1300–1399
—090 24	15th century, 1400–1499
—090 3	Modern period, 1500–

For 20th century, 1900–1999, see —0904; 21st century, 2000–2099, —0905

—090 31	16th century, 1500–1599
—090 32	17th century, 1600–1699
—090 33	18th century, 1700–1799
—090 34	19th century, 1800–1899
—090 4	20th century, 1900–1999
—090 41	1900–1919
—090 42	1920–1929
—090 43	1930–1939
—090 44	1940–1949
—090 45	1950–1959
—090 46	1960–1969
—090 47	1970–1979
—090 48	1980–1989
—090 49	1990–1999
—090 5	21st century, 2000–2099

—091   **Treatment by areas, regions, places in general**

History and description

Add "Areas" notation 1 from Table 2 to base number —09, e.g., the subject in Torrid Zone —0913

Class persons associated with the subject regardless of area, region, place in —092; treatment by specific continents, countries, localities in —093–099; history and description of the subject among groups of specific kinds of persons in —088, among specific racial, ethnic, national groups nondominant in their places in —089

—092   **Persons associated with the subject**

Description and critical appraisal of work, biography, autobiography, diaries, reminiscences, correspondence of persons regardless of area, region, place who are part of the subject or who study the subject, e.g., criminals, victims of crime, criminologists

If preferred, class biography in 920.1–928.9

Class biography not clearly related to any specific subject in 920, belletristic diaries, reminiscences, correspondence in 800, treatment of the subject among groups of persons in —08

Observe exceptions to use of —092 under 180–190, 232.9, 739.22, 739.23, 739.3, 739.4, 741.5, 745.4, 746.3, 746.7, 747.2, 748.2, 748.5, 749.2, 750, 809, 810–890 (as directed in "Subdivisions of Individual Literatures" notation 09 from Table 3)

—092 2   **Collected**

If preferred, class collected biography in 92, or 920 without subdivision

—092 4   **Individual**

If preferred, class individual biography in 92 or B; or, if preferred, class individual biography of men in 920.71, of women in 920.72

—092 6   **Case histories**

Table 1. Standard Subdivisions

—093–099   **Treatment by specific continents, countries, localities; extraterrestrial worlds**

History and description by place, by specific instance of the subject

Add "Areas" notation 3–9 from Table 2 to base number —09, e.g., the subject in United States —0973, in Brazil —0981, in North America —097

Class persons associated with the subject regardless of area, region, place in —092; treatment by areas, regions, places not limited by continent, country, locality in —091; history and description of the subject among groups of specific kinds of persons in —088, among specific racial, ethnic, national groups nondominant in their continents, countries, localities in —089

Table 2. Areas

The following notations are never used alone, but may be used as required (either directly when so noted or through the interposition of "Standard Subdivisions" notation 09 from Table 1) with any number from the schedules, e.g., wages (331.29) in Japan (—52 in this table): 331.2952; railroad transportation (385) in Brazil (—81 in this table): 385.0981. They may also be used when so noted with numbers from other tables, e.g., "Standard Subdivisions" notation 025 from Table 1. When adding to a number from the schedules, always insert a decimal point between the third and fourth digits of the complete number.

SUMMARY

—1	Areas, regions, places in general
—2	Persons regardless of area, region, place
—3	The ancient world
—4	Europe Western Europe
—5	Asia Orient Far East
—6	Africa
—7	North America
—8	South America
—9	Other parts of world and extraterrestrial worlds Pacific Ocean islands (Oceania)

—1   Areas, regions, places in general

Not limited by continent, country, locality

If desired, add to each number as follows:
03–09   Treatment by continent, country, locality
Add 0 to base number and then add "Areas" notation 3–9 from this table, e.g., Torrid Zone of Asia —1305, rivers of England —1693042, Italian-speaking regions of Switzerland —175510494, cities of ancient Greece —1732038
(An alternative treatment is shown under —3–9)

Unless other instructions are given, class complexly defined areas with aspects in two or more subdivisions of this table in the number coming last in the table, e.g., forested plateaus in North Temperate Zone —152 (*not* —123 or —143)

Class persons regardless of area, region, place in —2; specific continents, countries, localities in —3–9

Table 2. Areas

SUMMARY

—11 Frigid Zones
—12 Temperate Zones (Middle Latitude Zones)
—13 Torrid Zone (Tropics)
—14 Land and land forms
—15 Regions by type of vegetation
—16 Air and water
—17 Socioeconomic regions
—18 Other kinds of terrestrial regions
—19 Space

—11 **Frigid Zones**

—113 North

—116 South

—12 **Temperate Zones (Middle Latitude Zones)**

—123 North

—126 South

—13 **Torrid Zone (Tropics)**

—14 **Land and land forms**

—141 Continents

Including continental shelves

—142 Islands

Including atolls, other coral reefs

—143 Elevations

Mountains, plateaus, hills, slopes

—144 Depressions and openings

Valleys, canyons, gulches, chasms, gorges, ravines, caves, karsts

—145 Plane regions

Prairies, steppes, plains, tundras, pampas

—146 Coastal regions and shorelines

Including beaches, deltas

—148 Soil

—15	**Regions by type of vegetation**
—152	Forests
—153	Grasslands
—154	Deserts
—16	**Air and water**

SUMMARY

—161	Atmosphere
—162	Oceans and seas
—163	Atlantic Ocean
—164	Pacific Ocean
—165	Indian Ocean
—167	Antarctic waters
—168	Special oceanographic forms
—169	Fresh and brackish waters

—161	Atmosphere
—161 2	Troposphere
—161 3	Stratosphere
—161 4	Ionosphere
—162	Oceans and seas

Class ocean and sea basins in —182

For Atlantic Ocean, see —163; Pacific Ocean, —164; Indian Ocean, —165; special oceanographic forms, —168

—163	Atlantic Ocean

SUMMARY

—163 1	North Atlantic
—163 2	North Polar Sea (Arctic Ocean)
—163 3	Northeast Atlantic
—163 4	Northwest Atlantic
—163 5	South Atlantic
—163 6	Southwest Atlantic
—163 7	Southeast Atlantic
—163 8	Mediterranean Sea

—163 1	North Atlantic

For North Polar Sea, see —1632; northeast Atlantic, —1633; northwest Atlantic, —1634

Table 2. Areas

—163 2	**North Polar Sea (Arctic Ocean)**
—163 24	European sector
	Including Denmark Strait; Greenland, Norwegian, Barents, White Seas
—163 25	Asian sector
	Including Kara, Laptev, East Siberian, Chukchi Seas
	For Bering Strait, see —16451
—163 27	American sector
	Including Beaufort and Lincoln Seas, seas of Canadian Arctic Archipelago, Hudson and Baffin Bays
	For Bering Strait, see —16451
—163 3	**Northeast Atlantic**
—163 34	Baltic Sea
	Including Gulfs of Bothnia, Finland, Riga; Great and Little Belts; Oresund, Kattegat
—163 36	North Sea and English Channel
	Including Skagerrak, Strait of Dover, Firth of Forth
—163 37	Western waters of British Isles
	Including Irish Sea, North and Saint George's Channels, Firth of Clyde, Solway Firth
—163 38	French and Spanish coastal waters to Strait of Gibraltar
	Including Bay of Biscay
	For Strait of Gibraltar, see —16381
—163 4	**Northwest Atlantic**
—163 42	Davis Strait
—163 43	Labrador Sea
—163 44	Gulf of Saint Lawrence
—163 45	North American coastal waters from Bay of Fundy to Massachusetts Bay
	Including Cape Cod Bay

—163 46	United States coastal waters from Cape Cod to Cape Charles
	Including Nantucket, Rhode Island, Long Island Sounds; Buzzards, Narragansett, New York, Delaware Bays
—163 47	Chesapeake Bay
—163 48	United States coastal waters from Cape Henry to Straits of Florida
	Including Albemarle, Pamlico Sounds; Raleigh, Biscayne Bays
	For Straits of Florida, see —16363
—163 5	South Atlantic
	For southwest Atlantic, see —1636; southeast Atlantic, —1637; Atlantic sector of Antarctic waters, —1673
—163 6	Southwest Atlantic
	Class here west Atlantic
	For northwest Atlantic, see —1634
—163 62	Sargasso Sea
—163 63	Bahama waters
	Including Straits of Florida
—163 64	Gulf of Mexico
	Including Yucatan Channel
	For Straits of Florida, see —16363
—163 65	Caribbean Sea
	Including Gulfs of Honduras, Darien, Venezuela
	For Yucatan Channel, see —16364; Panama Canal, —1641
—163 66	South American coastal waters from Gulf of Paria to Cape São Roque
—163 67	Brazilian coastal waters southward from Cape São Roque
—163 68	Uruguayan and Argentinian coastal waters
	Including La Plata estuary, Bahia Blanca, Bahia Grande, Gulfs of San Matias and San Jorge

Table 2. Areas

—163 7	**Southeast Atlantic**
	Class here east Atlantic
	For northeast Atlantic, see —1633; Mediterranean Sea, —1638
—163 72	African coastal waters from Cape of Good Hope to Zaïre River
—163 73	Gulf of Guinea
	African coastal waters from Zaïre River to Cape Palmas
—163 75	West African coastal waters from Cape Palmas to Strait of Gibraltar
	For Strait of Gibraltar, see —16381
—163 8	**Mediterranean Sea**
—163 81	Western Mediterranean
	Strait of Gibraltar to Strait of Sicily
	Including Alboran Sea
	For waters between Spain and Sardinia-Corsica, see —16382; Tyrrhenian Sea, —16383
—163 82	Waters between Spain and Sardinia-Corsica
	Including Balearic and Ligurian Seas, Gulf of Lion
—163 83	Tyrrhenian Sea
	For Strait of Messina, see —16386
—163 84	Eastern Mediterranean
	East of Strait of Sicily
	For Adriatic Sea, see —16385; Ionian Sea, —16386; Mediterranean east of Crete, —16387; Sea of Crete and Aegean Sea, —16388; Black Sea, —16389
—163 85	Adriatic Sea
	Including Gulf of Venice, Strait of Otranto
—163 86	Ionian Sea
	Including Strait of Messina, Gulfs of Taranto and Corinth
	For Strait of Otranto, see —16385
—163 87	Mediterranean east of Crete
	For Suez Canal, see —16533

—163 88   Sea of Crete and Aegean Sea

> *For Dardanelles, see —16389*

—163 89   Black Sea

> Including Dardanelles, Bosporus, Seas of Marmara and Azov

—164   Pacific Ocean

SUMMARY

—164 1	Southeast Pacific
—164 2	East Pacific
—164 3	Northeast Pacific
—164 4	North Pacific
—164 5	Northwest Pacific
—164 6	West Pacific
—164 7	Southwest Pacific
—164 8	South Pacific
—164 9	Central Pacific

—164 1   Southeast Pacific

> American coastal waters from Strait of Magellan to Mexico-United States boundary
>
> Including Gulfs of Guayaquil, Panama, Tehuantepec, California; Panama Canal
>
> *For Strait of Magellan, see —1674*

—164 2   East Pacific

> *For southeast Pacific, see —1641; northeast Pacific, —1643*

—164 3   Northeast Pacific

> North American coastal waters from California to tip of Alaska

—164 32   United States waters

> Including Monterey and San Francisco Bays, Strait of Juan de Fuca, Puget Sound
>
> *For Alaskan waters, see —16434*

—164 33   Canadian waters

> Including Strait of Georgia, Queen Charlotte and Hecate Straits, Queen Charlotte Sound, Dixon Entrance
>
> *For Strait of Juan de Fuca, see —16432*

—164 34   Alaskan waters

> Including Gulf of Alaska, Cook Inlet, Shelikof Strait
>
> *For Dixon Entrance, see —16433*

Table 2. Areas

—164 4	**North Pacific**
	For northeast Pacific, see —1643; northwest Pacific, —1645
—164 5	**Northwest Pacific**
—164 51	Bering Sea
	Including Bering Strait
—164 52	Coastal waters of southeast Kamchatka
—164 53	Sea of Okhotsk
	Including La Pérouse Strait
—164 54	Sea of Japan
	Including Tatar, Tsugaru, Korea Straits
	For La Pérouse Strait, see —16453
—164 55	Eastern coastal waters and inner seas of Japan
—164 56	Yellow Sea
—164 57	East China Sea
	Including Formosa Strait
	For Korea Strait, see —16454
—164 58	Philippine Sea
	Including Luzon Strait
—164 6	**West Pacific**
	For northwest Pacific, see —1645; southwest Pacific, —1647
—164 7	**Southwest Pacific**
—164 71	Inner seas of Philippines
	For Sulu Sea, see —16473
—164 72	South China Sea
	Including Gulfs of Tonkin and Siam, Singapore and Karimata Straits
	For Formosa Strait, see —16457; Luzon Strait, —16458
—164 73	Inner seas of Malay Archipelago
	Including Sulu, Celebes, Molucca, Ceram Seas; Makassar Strait
	For seas adjoining southern Sunda Islands, see —16474

—164 74	Seas adjoining southern Sunda Islands
	Including Java, Bali, Flores, Savu, Banda Seas
	For Karimata Strait, see —16472
—164 75	Arafura Sea
	Including Gulf of Carpentaria
	For Torres Strait, see —16476
—164 76	Coral Sea and seas adjoining Melanesia
	Including Bismarck and Solomon Seas, Gulf of Papua, Torres Strait; eastern Queensland coastal waters
—164 77	Fiji Sea
—164 78	Tasman Sea
	Including New South Wales coastal waters, Cook Strait
	For Tasmanian coastal waters, see —16576
—164 79	Eastern coastal waters of New Zealand
—164 8	South Pacific
	For southeast Pacific, see —1641; southwest Pacific, —1647; Pacific sector of Antarctic waters, —1674
—164 9	Central Pacific
—165	Indian Ocean
	For Indian Ocean sector of Antarctic waters, see —1675
—165 2	Southwest Indian Ocean
	Class here west Indian Ocean
	For northwest Indian Ocean, see —1653
—165 23	Eastern coastal waters of Madagascar
—165 24	Coastal waters of south and southeast Africa
	From Cape of Good Hope to and including Delagoa Bay
—165 25	Mozambique Channel
—165 26	Coastal waters of east Africa
	From Cape Delgado to Cape Guardafui (tip of the "Horn")

Table 2. Areas

—165 3   Northwest Indian Ocean

—165 32   Gulf of Aden

                    Including Bab el Mandeb

—165 33   Red Sea

                    Including Gulfs of Aqaba and Suez, Suez Canal

                    For Bab el Mandeb, see —16532

—165 35   Persian Gulf

                    Including Strait of Hormuz

—165 36   Gulf of Oman

                    For Strait of Hormuz, see —16535

—165 37   Arabian Sea

                    Including Laccadive Sea, Gulf of Mannar

—165 6   Northeast Indian Ocean

—165 64   Bay of Bengal

—165 65   Andaman Sea

                    Including Gulf of Martaban, Strait of Malacca

                    For Singapore Strait, see —16472

—165 67   Coastal waters of southern Sumatra, Java, Lesser Sunda Islands

                    For Timor Sea, see —16574

—165 7   Southeast Indian Ocean

                    Class here east Indian Ocean

                    For northeast Indian Ocean, see —1656; Arafura Sea, —16475

—165 74   Northwest Australian coastal waters

                    From Melville Island to Northwest Cape

                    Including Timor Sea

—165 75   West Australian coastal waters

                    From Northwest Cape to Cape Leeuwin

—165 76   South Australian coastal waters

                    From Cape Leeuwin to Cape Howe

                    Including Great Australian Bight, Bass Strait, Tasmanian coastal waters

—167	Antarctic waters
—167 3	Atlantic sector

               Including Drake Passage, Scotia and Weddell Seas

               For Strait of Magellan, see —1674

—167 4	Pacific sector

               Including Strait of Magellan; Bellingshausen, Amundsen, Ross Seas

—167 5	Indian Ocean sector
—168	Special oceanographic forms

               Salt-water lagoons, inland seas, coastal pools

—169	Fresh and brackish waters

▶   **—169 2–169 4 Surface waters**

               Class comprehensive works in —169

—169 2	Lakes, ponds, fresh-water lagoons
—169 3	Rivers and other streams
—169 4	Waterfalls
—169 8	Ground waters (Subsurface waters)
—17	**Socioeconomic regions**

SUMMARY

—171	By political orientation
—172	By degree of economic development
—173	By concentration of population
—174	Regions where specific racial, ethnic, national groups predominate
—175	Regions where specific languages predominate
—176	Regions where specific religions predominate
—177	Nations belonging to specific international organizations

—171	By political orientation
—171 2	Noncontiguous empires and political unions

               Add "Areas" notation 3–9 for "mother country" to base number —1712, e.g., French Community —171244

               Class Roman Empire in —37

—171 3	Western bloc

Table 2. Areas

—171 6	Unaligned blocs
—171 65	Afro-Asian bloc
—171 7	Communist bloc
—171 8	Wartime groupings
—171 82	Belligerents
—171 83	Nonbelligerents and neutrals
—171 9	Nonself-governing territories
—172	By degree of economic development
—172 2	High
—172 3	Medium
—172 4	Low
—173	By concentration of population
—173 2	Urban regions
—173 3	Suburban regions
—173 4	Rural regions
	Including rural villages
—174	Regions where specific racial, ethnic, national groups predominate
	Add "Racial, Ethnic, National Groups" notation 01–99 from Table 5 to base number —174, e.g., regions where Arabs predominate —174927
—175	Regions where specific languages predominate
	Add "Languages" notation 1–9 from Table 6 to base number —175, e.g., regions where Spanish language predominates —17561
—176	Regions where specific religions predominate
—176 1	Christianity
—176 12	Catholicism
—176 14	Protestantism

—176 2–176 9   Other religions

> Add to base number —176 the numbers following 29 in "Persons" notation 292–299 from Table 7, e.g., regions where Islam predominates —17671

—177   Nations belonging to specific international organizations

> Examples: United Nations, World Health Organization, North Atlantic Treaty Organization, Organization for Economic Cooperation and Development
>
> Arrange alphabetically by name of organization, e.g., nations belonging to Council of Europe —177 C7

—18   **Other kinds of terrestrial regions**

—181   Hemispheres

> Class zonal, physiographic, socioeconomic regions in a specific hemisphere in —11–17

—181 1   Eastern

—181 2   Western

—181 3   Northern

—181 4   Southern

—182   Ocean and sea basins

> The totality of continents facing and islands in specific major bodies of water
>
> Class ocean and sea waters in —162; zonal, physiographic, socioeconomic regions in a specific ocean or sea basin in —11–17

—182 1   Atlantic region   Occident

—182 2   Mediterranean region

—182 3   Pacific region

—182 4   Indian Ocean region

—19   **Space**

> Class extraterrestrial worlds in —99

Table 2. Areas

—2 **Persons regardless of area, region, place**

> When instructed to add "Areas" notation 1–9 directly from Table 2 instead of adding "Standard Subdivisions" notation 091–099 from Table 1, class here description and critical appraisal of work, biography, autobiography, diaries, reminiscences, correspondence of persons associated with the subject, e.g., elementary educators 372.92

—22 **Collected**

—24 **Individual**

—26 **Case histories**

▶ **—3–9 Specific continents, countries, localities; extraterrestrial worlds**

> Class here specific instances of the subject
>
> If desired, add to each number as follows:
> 009   Regional treatment
>   Add to 009 the numbers following —1 in —11–19, e.g., Torrid Zone of Asia —50093, rivers of England —42009693, Italian-speaking regions of Switzerland —4940097551, cities of ancient Greece —38009732 (An alternative treatment is shown under —1)
>
> Class an area in its present number even if it had a different affiliation at the time under consideration, e.g., Arizona under Mexican sovereignty —791 (*not* —72)
>
> Class areas, regions, places not limited by continent, country, locality in —1; persons regardless of area, region, place in —2

—3 **The ancient world**

> Class a specific part of ancient world not provided for here in —4–9
>
> If preferred, class specific parts in —4–9 as detailed below

SUMMARY

—31	China
—32	Egypt
—33	Palestine
—34	India
—35	Mesopotamia and Iranian Plateau
—36	Europe north and west of Italian peninsula
—37	Italian peninsula and adjacent territories
—38	Greece
—39	Other parts of ancient world

—31 **China**

If preferred, class in —51

—32 **Egypt**

If preferred, class in —62

—33 **Palestine**

Including Judea

If preferred, class in —5694

—34 **India**

If preferred, class in —54

—35 **Mesopotamia and Iranian Plateau**

If preferred, class Mesopotamia in —5674, Iranian Plateau in —55

Class central Asia in —396

—36 **Europe north and west of Italian peninsula**

Class here comprehensive works on Europe

If preferred, class in —4

Class a specific part of Europe not provided for here with the subject, e.g., Greece —38

—361 **British Isles [*formerly* —362] Northern Britain and Ireland**

If preferred, class in —41

Add to base number —361 the numbers following —41 in —411–419, e.g., ancient Border Country —36137

For southern Britain, see —362

—362 **Southern Britain England**

If preferred, class in —42

Add to base number —362 the numbers following —42 in —421–429, e.g., ancient Chester —362714

Class comprehensive works on British Isles [*formerly* —362] in —361

—363 **Germanic regions**

If preferred, class in —43

For British Isles, see —361

Table 2. Areas

—364	Celtic regions

Including Gaul

If preferred, class in —44

For British Isles, see —361

—366	Iberian Peninsula and adjacent islands

If preferred, class in —46

—37	**Italian peninsula and adjacent territories**

Class here Roman Empire

If preferred, class in —45

Class a specific part of Roman Empire not provided for here with the subject, e.g., Britain —361

—371	Liguria

If preferred, class in —4518

—372	Gallia Cisalpina

If preferred, class in —451

—373	Venetia and Istria

If preferred, class Venetia in —453, Istria in —4972

—374	Region northeast of Rome

Including Umbria, Picenum

If preferred, class Umbria in —4565, Picenum in —4567

—375	Etruria

If preferred, class in —455

—376	Latium

Including city of Rome

If preferred, class in —4562

—377	Southern Italy

Campania, Samnium, Apulia, Calabria, Lucania, Bruttium

If preferred, class southern Italy in —457, Campania in —4572, Samnium in —4571, Apulia, Calabria in —4575, Lucania in —4577, Bruttium in —4578

—378	Sicily and Malta

If preferred, class Sicily in —458, Malta in —4585

—379   **Sardinia and Corsica**

> If preferred, class Sardinia in —459, Corsica in —44945

—38   **Greece**

> Class here comprehensive works on Greece and Rome
>
> If preferred, class in —495
>
> Class Rome in —37; a specific part of Greece not provided for here with the subject, e.g., Ionia —3923, Aegean Sea islands —391

—381   **Macedonia**

> If preferred, class in —4956

—382   **Thessaly, Epirus, adjacent Ionian islands**

> If preferred, class Thessaly in —4954, Epirus in —4953, Ionian islands in —4955

—383   **Acarnania, Aetolia, Locris, Doris, Phocis, Ithaca**

> If preferred, class Acarnania, Aetolia, Locris, Doris, Phocis, in —4951, Ithaca in —4955

—384   **Boeotia, Megaris, Euboea**

> If preferred, class Boeotia, Euboea in —4951, Megaris in —4952

—385   **Attica**

> If preferred, class in —4951

—386   **Peloponnesus and adjacent Ionian islands**

> If preferred, class Peloponnesus in —4952, Ionian islands in —4955
>
> *For divisions of Peloponnesus, see —387–389*

▶   **—387–389 Divisions of Peloponnesus**

Class comprehensive works in —386

—387   **Corinthia and Achaea**

—388   **Elis, Arcadia, Argolis**

—389   **Messenia, Laconia, Sparta**

Table 2. Areas

—39 **Other parts of ancient world**

SUMMARY

—391   Aegean Sea islands
—392   Western Asia Minor
—393   Eastern Asia Minor and Cyprus
—394   Syria and Arabia
—395   Black Sea and Caucasus regions
—396   Central Asia
—397   North Africa
—398   Southeastern Europe

—391   Aegean Sea islands

If preferred, class in —499

—391 1   Northern islands

Northern Sporades, Thasos, Samothrace, Imbros, Tenedos, Lemnos

—391 2   Lesbos

—391 3   Chios

—391 4   Samos

—391 5   Southwestern islands

Including Cyclades

—391 6   Rhodes and Southern Sporades

If preferred, class in —4996

—391 7   Karpathos

If preferred, class in —4996

—391 8   Crete

If preferred, class in —4998

—392   Western Asia Minor

Class here comprehensive works on Asia Minor

If preferred, class in —561

For eastern Asia Minor, see —393

—392 1   Mysia and Troas

Including Troy

If preferred, class in —562

—392 2   Lydia

If preferred, class in —562

—392 3   Ionia

             If preferred, class in —562

             For Aegean Sea islands, see —391

—392 4   Caria

             If preferred, class in —562

—392 5   Bithynia

             If preferred, class in —563

—392 6   Phrygia

             If preferred, class in —562

—392 7   Pisidia

             If preferred, class in —564

—392 8   Lycia

             If preferred, class in —564

—392 9   Pamphylia

             If preferred, class in —564

—393   Eastern Asia Minor and Cyprus

             If preferred, class eastern Asia Minor in —561

▶   —393 1–393 6 Eastern Asia Minor

          Class comprehensive works in —393

—393 1   Paphlagonia

             If preferred, class in —563

—393 2   Galatia

             If preferred, class in —563

—393 3   Pontus

             If preferred, class in —565

—393 4   Cappadocia

             If preferred, class in —564

—393 5   Cilicia

             If preferred, class in —564

—393 6   Commagene

             If preferred, class in —564

Table 2. Areas

—393 7	Cyprus
	If preferred, class in —5645
—394	Syria and Arabia
	Including Palmyra
	Class here Middle East
	If preferred, class Syria in —5691, Arabia in —53, Middle East in —56
	Class a specific part of Middle East not provided for here with the part, e.g., Egypt —32
	For Palestine, see —33; Commagene, —3936
—394 4	Phoenicia
	If preferred, class in —5692
—394 6	Edom and Moab
	If preferred, class Edom in —56949, Moab in —56956
—394 7	Arabia Deserta
	If preferred, class in —5673
—394 8	Arabia Petraea
	Including Sinai Peninsula
	If preferred, class Arabia Petraea in —53, Sinai Peninsula in —531
—395	Black Sea and Caucasus regions
	Including Sarmatia, Colchis, Iberia, Albania
	If preferred, class Black Sea region in —477; Caucasus in —479; Sarmatia in —4771; Colchis, Iberia in —4795; Albania in —4791
—395 1	Scythia
	If preferred, class in —4983
—395 5	Armenia
	If preferred, class in —5662

—396   Central Asia

                 Including Sogdiana, Hyrcania, Margiana, Bactria, Ariana

                 If preferred, class Central Asia in —58, Sogdiana in —587, Hyrcania in —5523, Margiana in —585; Bactria, Ariana in —581

—397   North Africa

                 If preferred, class in —61

                 For Egypt, see —32

—397 1   Mauretania

                 If preferred, class in —64

—397 2   Numidia

                 If preferred, class in —655

—397 3   Carthage

                 If preferred, class in —611

—397 4   Tripolis

                 If preferred, class in —612

—397 5   Cyrenaica

                 If preferred, class in —612

—397 6   Marmarica

                 If preferred, class in —612

—397 7   Gaetulia

                 If preferred, class in —657

—397 8   Ethiopia

                 Class here Nubia, Cush

                 If preferred, class in —625

—398   Southeastern Europe

                 Including Dacia, Pannonia, Illyria, Moesia, Thracia

                 If preferred, class southeastern Europe in —496, Dacia in —498, Pannonia in —439, Illyria in —497, Moesia in —4977, Thracia in —4957

                 For Greece, see —38; Black Sea region, —395

Table 2. Areas

▶ **—4–9 The modern world; extraterrestrial worlds**

(It is optional to class here specific parts of the ancient world; prefer —3)

Class comprehensive works on specific physiographic regions or features extending over more than one country, state, county, or other unit and identified by * with the unit where noted in this table, e.g., Lake Huron —774, Appalachian Mountains —74. Class works on a part of such a region or feature with the specific unit where the part is located, e.g., Lake Huron waters and shores in Ontario —7132, Cumberland Mountains —7691, Cumberland Mountains in Bell County, Kentucky —769123. If desired, add —0094–0096 to the appropriate number as suggested under —3–9

Arrange as below; but, if it is desired to give local emphasis and a shorter number to a specific country, place it first under its own continent or major region by use of a letter or other symbol, e.g., Pakistan —5P (preceding —51); then subarrange each such number like the corresponding number in this table, e.g., Peshawar —5P23. Apply like any other area notation, e.g., geology of Peshawar 555.P23, history of Pakistan since 1971 95P.05, history of medical sciences in Pakistan 610.95P

—4 Europe   Western Europe

(It is optional to class here ancient Europe; prefer —36)

Class Eurasia in —5

—400 9   Regional treatment

Add to base number —4009 the numbers following —1 in —11–18 of this table, e.g., parts of Europe with high economic development —4009722

SUMMARY

—41	**British Isles**
—42	**England and Wales**
—43	**Central Europe Germany**
—44	**France and Monaco**
—45	**Italy**
—46	**Iberian Peninsula and adjacent islands Spain**
—47	**Union of Soviet Socialist Republics (Soviet Union)**
—48	**Scandinavia**
—49	**Other parts of Europe**

▶ ## —41–42 British Isles

This table is extensively revised, —411–416, —425, and —428–429 in particular having been prepared with little reference to earlier editions. All italicized numbers have been given new meanings

For the convenience of those wishing to compare the present table with the one it replaces, there will be found near the end of volume 1 a list of numbers changed between Editions 18 and 19 for a considerable group of names

Class comprehensive works in —41

—41 British Isles

Class here Great Britain, United Kingdom

(It is optional to class here ancient British Isles, northern Britain, Ireland; prefer —361)

For England and Wales, see —42

SUMMARY

—411	Scotland	
—412	Northeastern Scotland	
—413	Southeastern Scotland	
—414	Southwestern Scotland	
—415	Ireland	
—416	Ulster	Northern Ireland
—417	Republic of Ireland (Eire)	
—418	Leinster	
—419	Munster	

—411 Scotland

For northeastern Scotland, see —412; southeastern Scotland, —413; southwestern Scotland, —414

—411 1 Northern Scotland

For divisions of northern Scotland, see —4112–4119

▶ ## —411 2–411 9 Divisions of northern Scotland

Class comprehensive works in —4111

—411 2 Islands authorities

For Orkney and Shetland, see —4113; Western Isles, —4114

Table 2. Areas

—*411 3*   Orkney and Shetland

—411 32   Orkney

—411 35   Shetland

—*411 4*   Western Isles (Outer Hebrides)

> Barra, Benbecula, Lewis with Harris, North and South Uist, neighboring islands
>
> Class here comprehensive works on Hebrides
>
> *For Inner Hebrides, see —4118*

—*411 5*   Highland region

> Class here *Scottish Highlands
>
> *For districts of Highland, see —4116–4119*

▶   —411 6–411 9 Districts of Highland

> Class comprehensive works in —4115

—*411 6*   Northern districts of Highland

—411 62   Caithness district

> Including Thurso, Tongue and Farr, Wick; former Caithness county

—411 65   Sutherland district

> Including Dornoch, Kincardine; Loch Shin
>
> Class here former Sutherland county
>
> Class a specific part of former Sutherland county not provided for here with the subject, e.g., Tongue and Farr —41162

—*411 7*   Central districts of Highland

—411 72   Ross and Cromarty district

> Including Dingwall, Fortrose, Invergordon, Tain; Black Isle
>
> Class here former Ross and Cromarty county
>
> Class a specific part of former Ross and Cromarty county not provided for here with the subject, e.g., Kincardine —41165

*Class parts of this physiographic region or feature as instructed under —4–9

—411 75	Inverness district

Including Aird; Loch Ness

Class here former Inverness-shire; *Great Glen

Class a specific part of former Inverness-shire not provided for here with the subject, e.g., Kingussie —41192

—411 8	Western districts of Highland

Class here Inner Hebrides

Class a specific part of Inner Hebrides not provided for here with the subject, e.g., Mull —41423

—411 82	Skye and Lochalsh district
—411 85	Lochaber district

Including Ballachulish, Fort William, Kinlochleven; Ardnamurchan, Eigg, Rhum

—411 9	Eastern districts of Highland
—411 92	Badenoch and Strathspey district

Including Cromdale, Grantown-on-Spey, Kingussie

Class here *Spey River

—411 95	Nairn district

Former Nairnshire

—412	Northeastern Scotland
—412 1	Grampian region

Class here *Grampian Mountains

For districts of Grampian, see —4122–4124

▶   **—412 2–412 4 Districts of Grampian**

Class comprehensive works in —4121

—412 2	Northern districts of Grampian

*Class parts of this physiographic region or feature as instructed under —4–9

Table 2. Areas

—412 23   Moray district

> Including Aberlour, Buckie, Burghead, Cullen, Dufftown, Elgin, Findochty, Forres, Keith, Lossiemouth, Portknockie, Rothes, Tomintoul
>
> Class here former Morayshire
>
> Class a specific part of former Morayshire not provided for here with the subject, e.g., Grantown-on-Spey —41192

—412 25   Banff and Buchan district

> Including Aberchirder, Fraserburgh, Macduff, Peterhead, Portsoy, Rosehearty, Turriff
>
> Class here former Banffshire; *Deveron River
>
> Class a specific part of former Banffshire not provided for here with the subject, e.g., Aberlour —41223

—*412 3*   Central districts of Grampian

—412 32   Gordon district

> Including Ellon, Huntly, Inverurie, Kintore, Oldmeldrum
>
> Class here former Aberdeenshire; *Don River
>
> Class a specific part of former Aberdeenshire not provided for here with the subject, e.g., Fraserburgh —41225

—412 35   City of Aberdeen district

> Including Dyce, Nigg, Peterculter

—*412 4*   Kincardine and Deeside district

> Including Ballater, Banchory, Braemar, Inverbervie, Laurencekirk, Stonehaven
>
> Class here former Kincardineshire; *Cairngorm Mountains, *Dee River
>
> Class a specific part of former Kincardineshire not provided for here with the subject, e.g., Nigg —41235

—*412 5*   Tayside region

> Class here *Strathmore
>
> *For districts of Tayside, see —4126–4128*

*Class parts of this physiographic region or feature as instructed under —4–9

▶   —412 6–412 8 Districts of Tayside

             Class comprehensive works in —4125

—*412 6*   Angus district

            Including Arbroath, Brechin, Carnoustie, Forfar, Kirriemuir, Montrose

            Class here former Angus county

            Class a specific part of former Angus county not provided for here with the subject, e.g., Dundee —4127

—412 7   City of Dundee district

            Including Monifieth

—412 8   Perth and Kinross district

            Including Aberfeldy, Abernethy, Alyth, Auchterarder, Blairgowrie and Rattray, Coupar Angus, Crieff, Pitlochry; former Kinross-shire

            Class here former Perthshire; *Ochil Hills, *Tay River

            Class a specific part of former Perthshire not provided for here with the subject, e.g., Callander —41312

—412 9   Fife region

            Former Fifeshire

—412 92   North East Fife district

            Including Anstruther, Auchtermuchty, Crail, Cupar, Elie and Earlsferry, Falkland, Kilrenny, Ladybank, Newburgh, Newport-on-Tay, Pittenweem, Saint Andrews, Saint Monance, Tayport

—412 95   Kirkcaldy district

            Including Buckhaven and Methil, Burntisland, Kinghorn, Leslie, Leven, Markinch

—412 98   Dunfermline district

            Including Cowdenbeath, Culross, Inverkeithing, Lochgelly

*Class parts of this physiographic region or feature as instructed under —4–9

Table 2. Areas

—413   Southeastern Scotland

Class here *Central Lowlands

—413 1   Central region

Class here *Forth River

—413 12   Stirling district

Including Bridge of Allan, Callander, Doune, Dunblane

Class here *Lennox Hills; former Stirlingshire

Class a specific part of former Stirlingshire not provided
for here with the subject, e.g., Falkirk —41318

—413 15   Clackmannan district

Including Alloa, Alva, Dollar; former Clackmannanshire

—413 18   Falkirk district

Including Bo'ness, Denny and Dunipace, Grangemouth

—413 2   Lothian region

For districts of Lothian, see —4133–4136

▶   —413 3–413 6 Districts of Lothian

Class comprehensive works in —4132

—413 3   West Lothian district

Including Armadale, Bathgate, Linlithgow, Livingston, Whitburn

Class here former West Lothian county

Class a specific part of former West Lothian county not
provided for here with the subject, e.g., Bo'ness —41318

—413 4   City of Edinburgh district

Including Balerno, Currie, Queensferry

—413 5   Midlothian district

Including Bonnyrigg and Lasswade, Dalkeith, Loanhead, Penicuik

Class here former Midlothian county; *Pentland Hills

Class a specific part of former Midlothian county not provided
for here with the subject, e.g., Musselburgh —4136

*Class parts of this physiographic region or feature as instructed under —4–9

—413 6   East Lothian district

> Including Cockenzie and Port Seton, Dunbar, East Linton, Haddington, Musselburgh, North Berwick, Prestonpans, Tranent; former East Lothian county
>
> Class here *Lammermuir Hills

—413 7   Borders region

> Class here *Border Country, *Southern Uplands, *Tweed River
>
> *For districts of Borders, see —4138–4139*

▶   —413 8–413 9 Districts of Borders

Class comprehensive works in —4137 .

—413 8   Western districts of Borders

—413 82   Tweeddale district

> Former Peeblesshire

—413 85   Ettrick and Lauderdale district

> Including Galashiels, Lauder, Melrose; former Selkirkshire

—413 9   Eastern districts of Borders

—413 92   Roxburgh district

> Including Hawick, Jedburgh, Kelso; Teviotdale
>
> Class here former Roxburghshire
>
> Class a specific part of former Roxburghshire not provided for here with the subject, e.g., Melrose —41385

—413 95   Berwickshire district

> Including Coldstream, Duns, Eyemouth
>
> Class here former Berwickshire county
>
> Class a specific part of former Berwickshire county not provided for here with the subject, e.g., Lauder —41385

—414   Southwestern Scotland

*Class parts of this physiographic region or feature as instructed under —4–9

Table 2. Areas

SUMMARY

—414 1   Strathclyde region

Class here *Clyde River

For districts of Strathclyde, see —4142–4146

▶   **—414 2–414 6 Districts of Strathclyde**

Class comprehensive works in —4141

—414 2   Northwestern districts of Strathclyde

—414 23   Argyll and Bute district

Including Campbeltown, Duncan, Inveraray, Lochgilphead, Oban, Rothesay, Tobermory; islands of Bute, Coll, Colonsay, Islay, Jura, Mull, Tiree; Kintyre; Loch Awe

Class here former Argyllshire, former Buteshire

Class a specific part of former Argyllshire, of former Buteshire, not provided for here with the subject, e.g., Kinlochleven —41185

—414 25   Dumbarton district

Including Cove and Kilcreggan, Helensburgh

Class here former Dunbartonshire; *Loch Lomond

Class a specific part of former Dunbartonshire not provided for here with the subject, e.g., Clydebank —41432

—414 28   Inverclyde district

Including Gourock, Greenock, Port Glasgow

*Class parts of this physiographic region or feature as instructed under —4–9

43

—*414 3*	North central districts of Strathclyde
—414 32	Clydebank district
—414 34	Bearsden and Milngavie district
—414 36	Strathkelvin district
—414 38	Cumbernauld and Kilsyth district
—*414 4*	Central districts of Strathclyde
—414 41	Renfrew district

Including Barrhead, Johnstone, Paisley

Class here former Renfrewshire

Class a specific part of former Renfrewshire not provided for here with the subject, e.g., Greenock —41428

—414 43	City of Glasgow district

Including Cambuslang, Rutherglen

—414 46	Monklands district

Including Airdrie, Coatbridge

—414 49	Motherwell district

Including Wishaw

—*414 5*	South central districts of Strathclyde
—414 51	Eastwood district
—414 54	East Kilbride district
—414 57	Hamilton district
—*414 6*	Southern districts of Strathclyde Former Ayrshire
—414 61	Cunninghame district

Including Ardrossan, Irvine, Kilwinning, Largs, Millport, Saltcoats, Stevenston; islands of Arran, Cumbrae

—414 63	Kilmarnock and Loudoun district

Including Darvel, Galston, Newmilns and Greenholm, Stewarton

—414 64	Kyle and Carrick district

Including Ayr, Girvan, Maybole, Prestwick, Troon

—414 67	Cumnock and Doon Valley district

Including Holmhead

Table 2. Areas

—414 69	**Lanark district**
	Including Biggar
	Class here former Lanarkshire
	Class a specific part of former Lanarkshire not provided for here with the subject, e.g., Motherwell —41449
—414 7	**Dumfries and Galloway region**
	For districts of Dumfries and Galloway, see —4148–4149

▶	**—414 8–414 9 Districts of Dumfries and Galloway**
	Class comprehensive works in —4147
—414 8	**Eastern districts of Dumfries and Galloway** **Former Dumfriesshire**
—414 83	**Annandale and Eskdale district**
	Including Annan, Langholm, Lochmaben, Lockerbie, Moffat
—414 86	**Nithsdale district**
	Including Dumfries, New Abbey, Sanquhar, Thornhill
	Class here *Nith River
—414 9	**Western districts of Dumfries and Galloway**
	Class here former Galloway
	Class a specific part of former Galloway not provided for here with the subject, e.g., New Abbey —41486
—414 92	**Stewartry district**
	Including Castle Douglas, Dalbeattie, Gatehouse of Fleet, Kirkcudbright, New Galloway
	Class here former Kirkcudbrightshire
	Class a specific part of former Kirkcudbrightshire not provided for here with the subject, e.g., Creetown —41495
—414 95	**Wigtown district**
	Including Creetown, Glenluce, Newton Stewart, Portpatrick, Stranraer, Whithorn; former Wigtownshire

*Class parts of this physiographic region or feature as instructed under —4–9

—415   Ireland

For divisions of Ireland, see —416–419

▶   —416–419 Divisions of Ireland

Class comprehensive works in —415

—416   Ulster   Northern Ireland

Class here *Bann River, *Lough Neagh

SUMMARY

—416 1	**Northeast area**
—416 2	**Former Londonderry (Derry) county**
—416 3	**Fermanagh district**
—416 4	**Former Tyrone county**
—416 5	**Southeast area Former Down county**
—416 6	**Southern area**
—416 7	**Belfast district**
—416 9	**Counties of Republic of Ireland in Ulster**

▶   —416 1–416 7 Northern Ireland

Class comprehensive works in —416

—416 1   Northeast area

Class here former Antrim county

Class a specific part of former Antrim county not provided for here with the subject, e.g., Portrush —41627

—416 12   Antrim district

—416 13   Ballymena district

—416 14   Ballymoney district

—416 15   Moyle district

Including Ballycastle; Giant's Causeway, Rathlin Island

—416 16   Larne district

—416 17   Carrickfergus district

Including Whitehead

—416 18   Newtownabbey district

Including Ballyclare

—416 19   Lisburn district

*Class parts of this physiographic region or feature as instructed under —4–9

Table 2. Areas

▶   —416 2–416 4 Western area

         Class comprehensive works in —4162

—416 2   Former Londonderry (Derry) county

         Class here *Sperrin Mountains; comprehensive works on Western area

            For Fermanagh district, see —4163; former Tyrone county, —4164

—416 21   Londonderry district

            For Londonderry (Derry) city, see —41623

—416 23   Londonderry (Derry) city

—416 25   Limavady district

—416 27   Coleraine district

         Including Portrush, Portstewart

—416 29   Magherafelt district

—416 3   Fermanagh district

         Former Fermanagh county

—416 4   Former Tyrone county

—416 41   Strabane district

—416 43   Cookstown district

—416 45   Dungannon district

—416 47   Omagh district

—416 5   Southeast area   Former Down county

—416 51   Castlereagh district

—416 53   North Down district

         Including Bangor, Holywood

—416 54   Ards district

         Including Donaghadee, Newtownards

         Class here *Strangford Lough

—416 56   Down district

         Including Downpatrick, Newcastle

*Class parts of this physiographic region or feature as instructed under —4–9

—416 57	Banbridge district
	Including Dromore
—416 58	Newry and Mourne district
	Including Bessbrook, Kilkeel, Warrenpoint
	Class here *Mourne Mountains
—416 6	Southern area
	Class here former Armagh county
	Class a specific part of former Armagh county not provided for here with the subject, e.g., Bessbrook —41658
—416 61	Armagh district
	Including Keady, Tandragee
	For Armagh city, see —41662
—416 62	Armagh city
—416 64	Craigavon district
	Including Lurgan, Portadown
—416 7	Belfast district
	Class here Greater Belfast
	Class a specific part of Greater Belfast not provided for here with the subject, e.g., Newtownabbey —41618
—416 9	Counties of Republic of Ireland in Ulster
—416 93	Donegal county
—416 97	Monaghan county
—416 98	Cavan county
—417	Republic of Ireland (Eire)
	Class here *Shannon River
	For counties in Ulster, see —4169; Leinster, —418; Munster, —419
—417 1	Connacht
	For divisions of Connacht, see —4172–4176

*Class parts of this physiographic region or feature as instructed under —4–9

Table 2. Areas

▶ **—417 2–417 6 Divisions of Connacht**

　　　Class comprehensive works in —4171

—417 2	Sligo county
—417 25	Sligo city
—417 3	Mayo county
—417 4	Galway county
—417 45	Galway city
—417 48	Aran Islands
—417 5	Roscommon county
—417 6	Leitrim county
—418	Leinster

　　　Class here *Barrow River

—418 1	Northwest Leinster
—418 12	Longford county
—418 15	Westmeath county
—418 2	Northeast Leinster
—418 22	Meath county

　　　　　Class here *Boyne River

—418 25	Louth county
—418 256	Drogheda
—418 3	Dublin county

　　　Class here *Liffey River

—418 35	Dublin city
—418 38	Dun Laoghaire
—418 4	Wicklow county
—418 5	Kildare county

　　　Class here *Bog of Allen

—418 6	Offaly county
—418 7	Laois county

*Class parts of this physiographic region or feature as instructed under —4–9

—418 8	Southeast Leinster
—418 82	Carlow county
—418 85	Wexford county
—418 856	Wexford city
—418 9	Kilkenny county

Class here *Nore River

—419	Munster
—419 1	Waterford county

Class here *Suir River

—419 15	Waterford city
—419 2	Tipperary county
—419 25	Clonmel
—419 3	Clare county
—419 4	Limerick county
—419 45	Limerick city
—419 5	Cork county

Class here *Blackwater River

—419 56	Cork city
—419 6	Kerry county
—419 65	Killarney
—42	**England and Wales**

(It is optional to class here ancient southern Britain, ancient England; prefer —362)

SUMMARY

—421	**Greater London**
—422	**Southeastern England**
—423	**Southwestern England and Channel Islands**
—424	**Midlands of England**
—425	**East Midlands of England**
—426	**Eastern England East Anglia**
—427	**Northwestern England and Isle of Man**
—428	**Northeastern England**
—429	**Wales**

*Class parts of this physiographic region or feature as instructed under —4–9

Table 2. Areas

▶ **—421–428 England**

Class comprehensive works in —42

—421 **Greater London**

SUMMARY

—421 2 **City of London**
—421 3 **West London**
—421 4 **North London**
—421 5 **Tower Hamlets**
—421 6 **South London**
—421 7 **Outer London**
—421 8 **Former Middlesex**
—421 9 **Boroughs created from Surrey**

—421 2 **City of London**

—421 3 **West London**

—421 32 Westminster

Including Paddington, Saint Marylebone

—421 33 Hammersmith

Including Fulham

—421 34 Kensington and Chelsea

—421 4 **North London**

—421 42 Camden

Including Hampstead, Holborn, Saint Pancras

—421 43 Islington

Including Finsbury

—421 44 Hackney

Including Shoreditch, Stoke Newington

—421 5 **Tower Hamlets**

Including Bethnal Green, Poplar, Stepney

—421 6 **South London**

—421 62 Greenwich

Including Woolwich

—421 63 Lewisham

Including Deptford

—421 64 Southwark

Including Bermondsey, Camberwell

—421 65	Lambeth
—421 66	Wandsworth
	Including Battersea
—421 7	**Outer London**

For former Middlesex, see —4218; boroughs created from Surrey, —4219

▶ **—421 72–421 76 Boroughs created from Essex**

Class comprehensive works in —4217

—421 72	Waltham Forest
	Including Chingford, Leyton, Walthamstow
—421 73	Redbridge
	Including Ilford, Wanstead and Woodford
—421 74	Havering
	Including Hornchurch, Romford
—421 75	Barking
	Including Dagenham
—421 76	Newham
	Including East Ham, West Ham

▶ **—421 77–421 78 Boroughs created from Kent**

Class comprehensive works in —4217

—421 77	Bexley
	Including Crayford, Erith, Sidcup
—421 78	Bromley
	Including Beckenham, Chislehurst, Orpington, Penge
—421 8	**Former Middlesex**
—421 82	Hounslow
	Including Brentford and Chiswick, Feltham, Heston and Isleworth
—421 83	Hillingdon
	Including Hayes and Harlington, Ruislip-Northwood, Uxbridge, Yiewsley and West Drayton

Table 2. Areas

—421 84	Ealing
	Including Acton, Southall
—421 85	Brent
	Including Wembley, Willesden
—421 86	Harrow
—421 87	Barnet
	Including Finchley, Friern Barnet, Hendon
—421 88	Haringey
	Including Hornsey, Tottenham, Wood Green
—421 89	Enfield
	Including Edmonton, Southgate
—421 9	**Boroughs created from Surrey**
—421 91	Croydon
	Including Coulsdon and Purley
—421 92	Sutton
	Including Beddington and Wallington, Carshalton, Cheam
—421 93	Merton
	Including Mitcham, Morden, Wimbledon
—421 94	Kingston upon Thames
	Including Malden and Coombe, Surbiton
—421 95	Richmond upon Thames
	Including Barnes, Twickenham
—422	**Southeastern England**

Class here Home Counties; *Thames River

Class a specific Home County not provided for here with the subject, e.g., Hertfordshire —4258

For Greater London, see —421

*Class parts of this physiographic region or feature as instructed under —4–9

SUMMARY

—422 1	Surrey
—422 3	Kent
—422 5	East Sussex
—422 6	West Sussex
—422 7	Hampshire
—422 8	Isle of Wight
—422 9	Berkshire

—422 1	**Surrey**

Class London boroughs created from Surrey in —4219

—422 11	**Runnymede**

Including Chertsey, Egham

—422 12	**Spelthorne**

Including Staines, Sunbury-on-Thames

—422 13	**Surrey Heath**

Including Bagshot, Frimley and Camberley

—422 14	**Woking and Elmbridge**
—422 142	**Woking**
—422 145	**Elmbridge**

Including Esher, Walton and Weybridge

—422 15	**Epsom and Ewell**
—422 16	**Guildford and Mole Valley**
—422 162	**Guildford**
—422 165	**Mole Valley**

Including Dorking, Leatherhead

—422 17	**Reigate and Banstead**
—422 18	**Tandridge**
—422 19	**Waverley**

Including Farnham, Godalming, Haslemere

—422 3	**Kent**

Class here *North Downs

Class London boroughs created from Kent in —42177–42178

—422 31	**Dartford and Gravesham**
—422 312	**Dartford**

*Class parts of this physiographic region or feature as instructed under —4–9

Table 2. Areas

—422 315	Gravesham
	Including Gravesend, Northfleet
—422 32	Medway and Gillingham
—422 323	Medway
	Including Chatham, Rochester
—422 325	Gillingham
—422 33	Swale
	Including Faversham, Milton, Sittingbourne; Isle of Sheppey
—422 34	Canterbury
	Including Herne Bay, Whitstable
—422 35	Dover and Thanet
—422 352	Dover
	Including Deal, Sandwich
	Class here Cinque Ports
	Class a specific one of the Cinque Ports not provided for here with the subject, e.g., Hythe —422395
—422 357	Thanet
	Including Broadstairs, Margate, Ramsgate
—422 36	Sevenoaks
	Including Westerham
—422 37	Tonbridge and Malling, and Maidstone
—422 372	Tonbridge and Malling
—422 375	Maidstone
—422 38	Tunbridge Wells
—422 39	Ashford and Shepway
—422 392	Ashford
	Including Tenterden; Isle of Oxney
—422 395	Shepway
	Including Dungeness, Folkestone, Hythe, Lydd, New Romney, Romney Marsh

—422 5	East Sussex

Class here former Sussex; the *Weald

For West Sussex, see —4226

—422 51	Wealden

Including Hailsham, Uckfield; Ashdown Forest

—422 52	Rother

Including Battle, Bexhill, Rye, Winchelsea

—422 54	Hove

Including Portslade

—422 56	Brighton

—422 57	Lewes

Including Newhaven, Seaford

—422 58	Eastbourne

—422 59	Hastings

—422 6	West Sussex

Class here *South Downs

—422 61	Crawley

—422 62	Chichester

Including Midhurst, Petworth

—422 64	Horsham

—422 65	Mid Sussex

Including Burgess Hill, Cuckfield, East Grinstead

—422 67	Arun

Including Arundel, Bognor Regis, Littlehampton

—422 68	Worthing

—422 69	Adur

Including Shoreham-by-Sea, Southwick

*Class parts of this physiographic region or feature as instructed under —4–9

Table 2. Areas

—422 7	Hampshire
—422 71	Basingstoke
—422 72	Hart and Rushmoor
—422 723	Hart
	Including Fleet, Hartley Wintney
—422 725	Rushmoor
	Including Aldershot, Farnborough
—422 73	Test Valley and Winchester
—422 732	Test Valley
	Including Andover, Romsey, Stockbridge
	Class here *Test River
—422 735	Winchester
	Including Bishop's Waltham, Droxford
—422 74	East Hampshire
	Including Alton, Petersfield
—422 75	New Forest
	Including Fawley, Fordingbridge, Lymington, Lyndhurst, Ringwood
—422 76	Southampton
—422 77	Eastleigh and Fareham
—422 772	Eastleigh
—422 775	Fareham
—422 78	Gosport
—422 79	Portsmouth and Havant
—422 792	Portsmouth
	Including Southsea
—422 795	Havant
	Including Hayling Island

*Class parts of this physiographic region or feature as instructed under —4–9

—422 8	Isle of Wight
—422 82	Medina

Including Cowes, Newport, Ryde

—422 85	South Wight

Including Sandown, Shanklin, Ventnor, Yarmouth; Needles

—422 9	Berkshire
—422 91	Newbury
—422 93	Reading
—422 94	Wokingham
—422 96	Windsor and Maidenhead

Including Eton

—422 97	Slough
—422 98	Bracknell

Including Easthampstead

—423	Southwestern England and Channel Islands

SUMMARY

—423 1	Wiltshire
—423 3	Dorset
—423 4	Channel Islands
—423 5	Devon
—423 7	Cornwall and Scilly Isles
—423 8	Somerset
—423 9	Avon

—423 1	Wiltshire
—423 12	North Wiltshire

Including Calne, Chippenham, Malmesbury, Wootton Bassett

—423 13	Thamesdown

Including Swindon

—423 15	West Wiltshire

Including Bradford-on-Avon, Melksham, Trowbridge, Warminster, Westbury

—423 17	Kennet

Including Devizes, Marlborough; Vale of Pewsey

Table 2. Areas

—423 19	Salisbury	
	Including Amesbury, Wilton	
	Class here *East (Wiltshire and Hampshire) Avon River; *Salisbury Plain	
—423 3	Dorset	
	Class here *Stour River	
—423 31	West Dorset	
	Including Beaminster, Bridport, Dorchester, Lyme Regis, Sherborne; Chesil Beach	
—423 32	North Dorset	
	Including Blandford Forum, Shaftesbury, Sturminster Newton	
—423 34	Wimborne	
	Including Cranborne, Wimborne Minster	
—423 35	Weymouth and Portland	
—423 36	Purbeck	
	Including Lulworth, Swanage, Wareham; Isle of Purbeck	
—423 37	Poole	
—423 38	Bournemouth	
—423 39	Christchurch	
—423 4	Channel Islands	
—423 41	Jersey	
	For Minquiers, see —42348; Dirouilles, Ecrehous, Paternosters, —42349	
—423 42	Guernsey	
	For Jethou, see —42347; Lihou, Lihoumel, —42349	
—423 43	Alderney	
	For Burhou, see —42347; Casquets, —42348	
—423 45	Sark	
	For Brecqhou, see —42347	
—423 46	Herm	
—423 47	Burhou, Brecqhou, Jethou	

*Class parts of this physiographic region or feature as instructed under —4–9

—423 48	Casquets, Chausey Islands, Minquiers
—423 49	Other islands

Barnouic, Dirouilles, Ecrehous, Lihou, Lihoumel, Paternosters, Roches Douvres

—423 5   Devon

Class here *Exe River, *Tamar River

—423 51	Torridge

Including Bideford, Clovelly, Great Torrington, Hartland, Holsworthy; Lundy Island

—423 52	North Devon

Including Barnstaple, Ilfracombe, Lynton, South Molton

—423 53	West Devon

Including Okehampton, Princetown, Tavistock

Class here *Dartmoor

—423 54	Tiverton

Including Crediton

—423 55	Teignbridge

Including Ashburton, Bovey Tracey, Buckfastleigh, Dawlish, Newton Abbot, Teignmouth

—423 56	Exeter
—423 57	East Devon

Including Axminster, Budleigh Salterton, Exmouth, Honiton, Ottery Saint Mary, Seaton, Sidmouth

—423 58	Plymouth
—423 59	South Hams and Torbay
—423 592	South Hams

Including Dartmouth, Kingsbridge, Plympton, Salcombe, Totnes; Start Point

Class here *Dart River

—423 595	Torbay

Including Brixham, Paignton, Torquay

*Class parts of this physiographic region or feature as instructed under —4–9

Table 2. Areas

—423 7	Cornwall and Scilly Isles

▶ —423 71–423 78 Cornwall

Class comprehensive works in —4237

—423 71 North Cornwall

Including Bodmin, Boscastle, Bude-Stratton, Camelford, Launceston, Padstow, Tintagel, Wadebridge; Bodmin Moor

—423 72 Restormel

Including Fowey, Mevagissey, Newquay, Saint Austell

—423 74 Caradon

Including Liskeard, Looe, Polperro, Saint Germans, Saltash, Torpoint

—423 75 Penwith

Including Hayle, Penzance, Saint Ives, Saint Just; Land's End, Mount Saint Michael

—423 76 Kerrier

Including Camborne, Helston, Redruth; Lizard

—423 78 Carrick

Including Falmouth, Penryn, Perranporth, Truro

Class here *Fal River

—423 79 Scilly Isles

—423 8 Somerset

—423 81 Sedgemoor

Including Axbridge, Bridgwater, Burnham-on-Sea

—423 83 Mendip

Including Frome, Glastonbury, Shepton Mallet, Street, Wells

Class here *Mendip Hills

—423 85 West Somerset

Including Dulverton, Dunster, Minehead, Watchet

Class here *Exmoor, *Quantock Hills

*Class parts of this physiographic region or feature as instructed under —4–9

—423 87   Taunton Deane

           Including Taunton, Wellington

           Class here *Blackdown Hills

—423 89   Yeovil

           Including Chard, Crewkerne, Ilminster, Langport, Wincanton

—423 9   Avon

           Class here *Lower (Bristol) Avon River

—423 91   Northavon

           Including Chipping Sodbury, Thornbury

—423 93   Bristol

           Including Avonmouth

—423 94   Kingswood

           Including Mangotsfield

—423 96   Woodspring

           Including Clevedon, Portishead, Weston-super-Mare

—423 97   Wansdyke

           Including Clutton, Keynsham, Norton Radstock

—423 98   Bath

—424   Midlands of England

           Class here *Severn River, *Welsh Marches

           For East Midlands, see —425

SUMMARY

     —424 1   Gloucestershire
     —424 4   Hereford and Worcester   Former Herefordshire
     —424 5   Salop
     —424 6   Staffordshire
     —424 8   Warwickshire
     —424 9   West Midlands Metropolitan County   Black Country

—424 1   Gloucestershire

—424 12   Tewkesbury

—424 13   Forest of Dean

           Including Coleford, Lydney, Newent

—424 14   Gloucester

*Class parts of this physiographic region or feature as instructed under —4–9

Table 2. Areas

—424 16	Cheltenham
	Including Charlton Kings
—424 17	Cotswold
	Including Chipping Campden, Cirencester, Lechlade, Moreton-in-Marsh, Tetbury
	Class here *Cotswolds
—424 19	Stroud
	Including Berkeley, Dursley, Nailsworth

—424 4   Hereford and Worcester   Former Herefordshire

Class here former Worcestershire; *Upper (Warwickshire) Avon River

Class a specific part of former Worcestershire not provided for here with the subject, e.g., Stourbridge —42493

—424 41	Wyre Forest
	Including Bewdley, Kidderminster, Stourport-on-Severn
—424 42	Bromsgrove
—424 43	Redditch
—424 44	Leominster
	Including Kington
—424 45	South Herefordshire
	Including Ross-on-Wye
—424 46	Hereford
—424 47	Malvern Hills
	Including Bromyard, Ledbury, Malvern, Upton-upon-Severn
—424 48	Worcester
—424 49	Wychavon
	Including Droitwich, Evesham, Pershore; Vale of Evesham

*Class parts of this physiographic region or feature as instructed under —4–9

—424 5	Salop
	Former Shropshire
—424 51	Oswestry
—424 53	North Shropshire
	Including Ellesmere, Market Drayton, Wem, Whitchurch
—424 54	Shrewsbury and Atcham
—424 56	The Wrekin
	Including Dawley, Ironbridge, Newport, Oakengates, Telford, Wellington
—424 57	South Shropshire
	Including Bishop's Castle, Church Stretton, Cleobury Mortimer, Ludlow; Long Mynd
—424 59	Bridgnorth
	Including Much Wenlock, Shifnal
—424 6	Staffordshire
—424 61	Staffordshire Moorlands
	Including Biddulph, Cheadle, Leek
—424 62	Newcastle-under-Lyme
	Including Kidsgrove
—424 63	Stoke-on-Trent
	Including Potteries
—424 64	Stafford
	Including Eccleshall, Stone
—424 65	East Staffordshire
	Including Burton upon Trent, Uttoxeter
—424 66	South Staffordshire
—424 67	Cannock Chase
	Including Cannock, Rugeley
—424 68	Lichfield
—424 69	Tamworth

Table 2. Areas

—424 8	Warwickshire
—424 81	North Warwickshire
	Including Atherstone
—424 83	Nuneaton
	Including Bedworth
—424 85	Rugby
—424 87	Warwick
	Including Kenilworth, Leamington Spa
—424 89	Stratford-on-Avon
	Including Alcester, Henley-in-Arden, Shipston-on-Stour, Southam
—424 9	West Midlands Metropolitan County Black Country
—424 91	Wolverhampton
—424 92	Walsall
	Including Aldridge-Brownhills
—424 93	Dudley
	Including Halesowen, Stourbridge
—424 94	Sandwell
	Including Warley, West Bromwich
—424 96	Birmingham
	Including Sutton Coldfield
—424 97	Solihull
	Including Meriden
—424 98	Coventry
—425	East Midlands of England
	Class here *Chilterns, *Trent River

*Class parts of this physiographic region or feature as instructed under —4–9

SUMMARY

—425 1	Derbyshire
—425 2	Nottinghamshire
—425 3	Lincolnshire
—425 4	Leicestershire
—425 5	Northamptonshire
—425 6	Bedfordshire
—425 7	Oxfordshire
—425 8	Hertfordshire
—425 9	Buckinghamshire

—425 1   Derbyshire

Class here *Derwent River of Derbyshire

—425 11   High Peak

Including Buxton, Chapel-en-le-Frith, Glossop, New Mills, Tintwistle, Whaley Bridge

Class here *Peak District

—425 12   Chesterfield

Including Staveley

—425 13   West Derbyshire

Including Ashbourne, Bakewell, Matlock, Wirksworth

Class here *Dove River

—425 14   North East Derbyshire

Including Clay Cross, Dronfield

—425 15   Bolsover

—425 16   Amber Valley

Including Alfreton, Belper, Heanor, Ripley

—425 17   Derby

—425 18   Erewash

Including Ilkeston, Long Eaton

—425 19   South Derbyshire

Including Melbourne, Repton, Swadlincote

*Class parts of this physiographic region or feature as instructed under —4–9

Table 2. Areas

—425 2	Nottinghamshire
—425 21	Bassetlaw
	Including the Dukeries, East Retford, Worksop
—425 23	Mansfield
	Including Warsop
—425 24	Newark
	Including Southwell
	Class here *Sherwood Forest
—425 25	Ashfield
	Including Hucknall, Kirkby-in-Ashfield, Sutton-in-Ashfield
—425 26	Broxtowe
	Including Beeston, Eastwood, Stapleford
—425 27	Nottingham
—425 28	Gedling
	Including Arnold, Carlton
—425 29	Rushcliffe
	Including West Bridgford; Vale of Belvoir
—425 3	Lincolnshire
	Class here *Lincoln Heath, the *Wash, *Witham River
—425 31	West Lindsey
	Including Caistor, Gainsborough, Market Rasen
	Class here former Parts of Lindsey
	Class a specific part of former Parts of Lindsey not provided for here with the subject, e.g., Scunthorpe —42831
—425 32	East Lindsey
	Including Alford, Horncastle, Louth, Mablethorpe and Sutton, Skegness, Woodhall Spa; Lincoln Marsh
	Class here *Lincoln Wolds
—425 34	Lincoln

*Class parts of this physiographic region or feature as instructed under —4–9

—425 35	North Kesteven
	Including Sleaford
	Class here former Parts of Kesteven
	For South Kesteven, see —42538
—425 37	Boston
—*425 38*	South Kesteven
	Including Bourne, Grantham, Stamford
—*425 39*	South Holland
	Including Spalding
	Class here *Welland River; former Parts of Holland
	For Boston, see —42537
—425 4	Leicestershire
—425 41	Blaby
—425 42	Leicester
—425 43	Oadby and Wigston
—425 44	Harborough
	Including Lutterworth, Market Harborough
—425 45	Rutland
	Former county
	Including Oakham, Uppingham
—425 46	Melton
	Including Melton Mowbray
—425 47	Charnwood
	Including Loughborough, Shepshed
—425 48	North West Leicestershire
	Including Ashby-de-la-Zouch, Coalville
—425 49	Hinckley and Bosworth

*Class parts of this physiographic region or feature as instructed under —4–9

Table 2. Areas

—425 5	Northamptonshire
	Class here *Nene River
—425 51	Corby
—425 52	Kettering
	Including Burton Latimer, Desborough, Rothwell
—425 54	East Northamptonshire
	Including Higham Ferrars, Irthlingborough, Oundle, Raunds, Rushden
—425 56	Daventry
	Class here *Northampton Uplands
—425 57	Northampton
—425 58	Wellingborough
—425 59	South Northamptonshire
	Including Brackley, Towcester
—425 6	Bedfordshire
—425 61	North Bedfordshire
	Including Bedford, Kempston
—425 63	Mid Bedfordshire
	Including Ampthill, Biggleswade, Sandy
—425 65	South Bedfordshire
	Including Dunstable, Leighton-Linslade
—425 67	Luton
—425 7	Oxfordshire
—425 71	West Oxfordshire
	Including Chipping Norton, Witney, Woodstock
—425 73	Cherwell
	Including Banbury, Bicester
—425 74	Oxford
—425 76	Vale of White Horse
	Including Abingdon, Faringdon, Wantage

*Class parts of this physiographic region or feature as instructed under —4–9

—425 79	South Oxfordshire
	Including Henley-on-Thames, Thame, Wallingford

—425 8   Hertfordshire

—425 81	North Hertfordshire
	Including Baldock, Hitchin, Letchworth, Royston
—425 82	Stevenage
—425 83	East Hertfordshire
	Including Bishop's Stortford, Hertford, Sawbridgeworth, Ware
—425 84	Dacorum
	Including Berkhamsted, Hemel Hempstead, Tring
—425 85	Saint Albans
	Including Harpenden
—425 86	Welwyn Hatfield
—425 87	Broxbourne
	Including Cheshunt, Hoddesdon
—425 88	Three Rivers
	Including Chorleywood, Rickmansworth
—425 89	Watford and Hertsmere
—425 892	Watford
—425 895	Hertsmere
	Including Bushey, Elstree, Potters Bar

—*425 9*   Buckinghamshire

—425 91	Milton Keynes
	Including Bletchley, Newport Pagnell, Wolverton
—425 93	Aylesbury Vale
	Including Aylesbury, Buckingham
—425 95	Wycombe
	Including High Wycombe, Marlow
—425 97	Chiltern
	Including Amersham, Chesham
—425 98	Beaconsfield

Table 2. Areas

—426   Eastern England   East Anglia

Class here the *Fens, *Great Ouse River

▶   —426 1–426 5 East Anglia

Class comprehensive works in —426

—426 1   Norfolk

Class here *Yare River

—426 12   North Norfolk

Including Cromer, North Walsham, Sheringham, Walsingham, Wells-next-the-Sea

—426 13   West Norfolk

Including Downham Market, Hunstanton, King's Lynn

—426 14   Breckland

Including East Dereham, Swaffham, Thetford

—426 15   Norwich

—426 17   Broadland

Class here *Norfolk Broads

—426 18   Great Yarmouth

—426 19   South Norfolk

Including Diss, Loddon, Wymondham

Class here *Waveney River

—426 4   Suffolk

—426 41   Waveney

Including Beccles, Bungay, Halesworth, Lowestoft, Southwold

—426 43   Forest Heath

Including Mildenhall, Newmarket

—426 44   Saint Edmundsbury

Including Bury Saint Edmunds, Clare, Haverhill

Class here former West Suffolk

Class a specific part of West Suffolk not provided for here with the subject, e.g., Mildenhall —42643

*Class parts of this physiographic region or feature as instructed under —4–9

—426 45	Mid Suffolk

Including Eye, Stowmarket

—426 46	Suffolk Coastal

Including Aldeburgh, Felixstowe, Leiston-cum-Sizewell, Saxmundham, Woodbridge

Class here former East Suffolk

Class a specific part of East Suffolk not provided for here with the subject, e.g., Lowestoft —42641

—426 48	Babergh

Including Hadleigh, Lavenham, Sudbury

—426 49	Ipswich
—426 5	Cambridgeshire
—426 51	Peterborough

Including former Soke of Peterborough; Old Fletton

—426 53	Fenland

Including Chatteris, March, Whittlesey, Wisbech

Class here former Isle of Ely

Class city of Ely in —42656

—426 54	Huntingdon

Former Huntingdonshire

Including Godmanchester, Ramsey, Saint Ives, Saint Neots

—426 56	East Cambridgeshire

Including Ely

—426 57	South Cambridgeshire

Including Gog Magog Hills

—426 59	Cambridge
—426 7	Essex

Class London boroughs created from Essex in —42172–42176

—426 71	Uttlesford and Braintree
—426 712	Uttlesford

Including Great Dunmow, Saffron Walden, Thaxted

Table 2. Areas

—426 715   Braintree

                   Including Bocking, Coggeshall, Halstead, Witham

—426 72   Colchester and Tendring

—426 723   Colchester

                   Including West Mersea, Wivenhoe

—426 725   Tendring

                   Including Brightlingsea, Clacton, Frinton, Harwich, Manningtree, Walton-on-the-Naze

—426 73   Harlow

—426 74   Epping Forest

                   Including Chigwell, Epping, Waltham Holy Cross

—426 75   Chelmsford and Maldon

—426 752   Chelmsford

—426 756   Maldon

                   Including Burnham-on-Crouch

—426 76   Brentwood

—426 77   Basildon and Rochford

—426 772   Basildon

—426 775   Rochford

                   Including Rayleigh; Foulness Island

—426 78   Thurrock

                   Including Tilbury

—426 79   Castle Point and Southend-on-Sea

—426 792   Castle Point

                   Including Benfleet, Canvey Island

—426 795   Southend-on-Sea

                   Including Shoeburyness

—427   **Northwestern England and Isle of Man**

               Class here comprehensive works on northern England

               For northeastern England, see —428

SUMMARY

—427 1   Cheshire

—427 12   Crewe and Nantwich

—427 13   Congleton

Including Alsager, Middlewich, Sandbach

—427 14   Chester

—427 15   Vale Royal

Including Northwich, Winsford

—427 16   Macclesfield

Including Alderley Edge, Bollington, Knutsford, Wilmslow

—427 17   Ellesmere Port and Neston

—427 18   Halton

Including Runcorn, Widnes

—427 19   Warrington

Including Lymm

—427 3   Greater Manchester Metropolitan County

—427 31   Trafford

Including Altrincham, Bowdon, Hale, Sale, Stretford, Urmston

—427 32   Salford

Including Eccles, Irlam, Swinton and Pendlebury, Worsley

—427 33   Manchester

—427 34   Stockport

Including Bredbury and Romiley, Cheadle and Gatley, Hazel Grove and Bramhall, Marple

—427 35   Tameside

Including Ashton-under-Lyne, Audenshaw, Denton, Droylsden, Dukinfield, Hyde, Longdendale, Mossley, Stalybridge

Table 2. Areas

—427 36 | Wigan

Including Abram, Ashton-in-Makerfield, Aspull, Atherton, Golborne, Hindley, Ince-in-Makerfield, Leigh, Orrell, Standish-with-Langtree, Tyldesley

—427 37 | Bolton

Including Blackrod, Farnworth, Horwich, Kearsley, Little Lever, Westhoughton

—427 38 | Bury

Including Prestwich, Radcliffe, Tottington, Whitefield

—427 39 | Rochdale and Oldham

—427 392 | Rochdale

Including Heywood, Littleborough, Middleton, Milnrow, Wardle

—427 393 | Oldham

Including Chadderton, Crompton, Failsworth, Lees, Royton, Saddleworth

—427 5 | **Merseyside Metropolitan County**

Class here *Mersey River

—427 51 | Wirral

Including Bebington, Birkenhead, Hoylake, Wallasey

—427 53 | Liverpool

—427 54 | Knowsley

Including Huyton-with-Roby, Kirkby, Prescot

—427 57 | Saint Helens

Including Billinge-and-Winstanley, Haydock, Newton-le-Willows, Rainford

—427 59 | Sefton

Including Bootle, Crosby, Formby, Litherland, Southport

*Class parts of this physiographic region or feature as instructed under —4–9

—427.6	Lancashire

Class here former Lancashire

Class a specific part of former Lancashire not provided for here with the subject, e.g., Liverpool —42753

—427 61	West Lancashire and Chorley
—427 612	West Lancashire

Including Ormskirk, Skelmersdale and Holland

—427 615	Chorley

Including Adlington, Withnell

—427 62	Blackburn and Hyndburn
—427 623	Blackburn

Including Darwen

—427 625	Hyndburn

Including Accrington, Church, Clayton-le-Moors, Great Harwood, Oswaldtwistle, Rishton

—427 63	Rossendale

Including Bacup, Haslingden, Rawtenstall

—427 64	Burnley and Pendle
—427 642	Burnley

Including Padiham

—427 645	Pendle

Including Barnoldswick, Barrowford, Brierfield, Colne, Earby, Nelson, Trawden

—427 65	Blackpool
—427 66	Fylde and Preston
—427 662	Fylde

Including Kirkham, Lytham Saint Annes

—427 665	Preston

Including Fulwood

Table 2. Areas

—427 67	South Ribble
	Including Leyland, Walton-le-Dale
—427 68	Wyre and Ribble Valley
—427 682	Wyre
	Including Fleetwood, Garstang, Poulton-le-Fylde, Preesall, Thornton Cleveleys
—427 685	Ribble Valley
	Including Clitheroe, Longridge
	Class here *Forest of Bowland, *Ribble River
—427 69	Lancaster
	Including Carnforth, Heysham, Morecambe

—427 8   Cumbria (Lake District)   Former Cumberland and former Westmorland

Class here Cumbrian Mountains

—427 81	Barrow-in-Furness
	Including Dalton-in-Furness
—427 83	South Lakeland
	Including Ambleside, Grange, Kendal, Ulverston, Windermere; Coniston Water
—427 84	Copeland
	Including Ravenglass, Whitehaven; Scafell
—427 86	Eden
	Including Appleby, Penrith; Helvellyn, Inglewood, Shap Fell, Ullswater
	Class here *Eden River
—427 87	Allerdale
	Including Cockermouth, Keswick, Maryport, Workington; Bassenthwaite, Derwent Water, Skiddaw
—427 89	Carlisle

*Class parts of this physiographic region or feature as instructed under —4–9

—427 9	Isle of Man
—428	Northeastern England

Class here the *Pennines

SUMMARY

—428 1	West Yorkshire Metropolitan County
—428 2	South Yorkshire Metropolitan County
—428 3	Humberside
—428 4	North Yorkshire
—428 5	Cleveland
—428 6	Durham
—428 7	Tyne and Wear Metropolitan County
—428 8	Northumberland

—428 1   West Yorkshire Metropolitan County

Class here former Yorkshire, former West Riding of Yorkshire

Class a specific part of former Yorkshire, of former West Riding, not providedd for here with the subject, e.g., Sheffield —42821

—428 12   Calderdale

Including Brighouse, Elland, Halifax, Hebden Royd, Ripponden, Sowerby Bridge, Todmorden

—428 13   Kirklees

Including Batley, Colne Valley, Denby Dale, Dewsbury, Heckmondwike, Holmfirth, Huddersfield, Kirkburton, Meltham, Mirfield, Spenborough

—428 15   Wakefield

Including Castleford, Featherstone, Hemsworth, Horbury, Knottingley, Normanton, Ossett, Pontefract, Stanley

Class here *Aire River

—428 17   Bradford

Including Baildon, Bingley, Denholme, Ilkley, Keighley, Queensbury and Shelf, Shipley, Silsden

—428 19   Leeds

Including Aireborough, Garforth, Horsforth, Morley, Otley, Pudsey, Rothwell

*Class parts of this physiographic region or feature as instructed under —4–9

Table 2. Areas

—428 2	**South Yorkshire Metropolitan County**
—428 21	Sheffield
	Including Stocksbridge
—428 23	Rotherham
	Including Maltby, Rawmarsh, Swinton, Wath-upon-Dearne
—428 25	Barnsley
	Including Cudworth, Darfield, Darton, Dearne, Dodworth, Hoyland Nether, Penistone, Royston, Wombwell, Worsborough
—428 27	Doncaster
	Including Adwick-le-Street, Bentley with Arksey, Conisbrough, Mexborough, Tickhill
—428 3	**Humberside**
	Class here former East Riding of Yorkshire; *Humber River, *Yorkshire Wolds
	Class a specific part of former East Riding not provided for here with the subject, e.g., Norton —42846
—428 31	Scunthorpe
—428 32	Glanford
	Including Barton-upon-Humber, Brigg
—428 33	Cleethorpes
—428 34	Grimsby
—428 35	Boothferry
	Including Goole, Howden; Isle of Axholme
—428 36	Beverley
	Including Haltemprice
—428 37	Kingston upon Hull
—428 38	Holderness
	Including Hedon, Hornsea, Withernsea
—428 39	North Wolds
	Including Bridlington, Driffield, Pocklington

*Class parts of this physiographic region or feature as instructed under —4–9

—428 4   North Yorkshire

> Class here former North Riding of Yorkshire; *Derwent River of Yorkshire, *Ouse River, *Yorkshire Dales

> Class a specific part of former North Riding not provided for here with the subject, e.g., Middlesbrough —42853

—428 41   Craven

> Including Settle, Skipton, Wharfedale

—428 42   Harrogate

> Including Knaresborough, Masham, Ripon, Wetherby; Nidderdale

—428 43   York

—428 45   Selby

> Including Tadcaster

—428 46   Ryedale

> Including Helmsley, Kirkbymoorside, Malton, Norton, Pickering

> Class here *North Yorkshire Moors

—428 47   Scarborough

> Including Filey, Scalby, Whitby

—428 48   Richmondshire

> Including Askrigg, Leyburn, Reeth, Richmond; Swalesdale, Wensleydale

> Class here *Swale River, *Ure River

—428 49   Hambleton

> Including Bedale, Easingwold, Northallerton, Stokesley, Thirsk

> Class here *Cleveland Hills

—*428 5*   Cleveland

> Including former Teesside

> Class here *Tees River

—428 51   Stockton-on-Tees

> Including Billingham-on-Tees, Thornaby-on-Tees

*Class parts of this physiographic region or feature as instructed under —4–9

Table 2. Areas

—428 53	Middlesbrough
—428 54	Langbaurgh

Including Eston, Guisborough, Loftus, Redcar, Saltburn and Marske-by-the-Sea, Skelton and Brotton

—428 57	Hartlepool

—428 6   Durham

Class here *Wear River

—428 61	Teesdale

Including Barnard Castle

—428 62	Sedgefield

Including Shildon, Spennymoor

—428 63	Darlington
—428 64	Wear Valley

Including Bishop Auckland, Crook and Willington, Saint John's Chapel, Stanhope, Tow Law

—428 65	Durham

Including Brandon and Byshottles

—428 67	Easington

Including Seaham

—428 68	Derwentside

Including Consett, Stanley

—428 69	Chester-le-Street

—428 7   Tyne and Wear Metropolitan County

Class here *Tyne River

—428 71	Sunderland

Including Hetton, Houghton-le-Spring, Washington

—428 73	Gateshead

Including Blaydon, Felling, Ryton, Whickham

—428 75	South Tyneside

Including Boldon, Hebburn, Jarrow, South Shields

*Class parts of this physiographic region or feature as instructed under —4–9

—428 76	Newcastle upon Tyne
	Including Gosforth, Newburn
—428 79	North Tyneside
	Including Longbenton, Tynemouth, Wallsend, Whitley Bay
—428 8	Northumberland
	Class here *Cheviot Hills
—428 81	Tynedale
	Including Bellingham, Haltwhistle, Hexham, Prudhoe; Redesdale
	Class here Hadrian's Wall
	Class a specific part of Hadrian's Wall not provided for here with the subject, e.g., in Carlisle —42789
—428 83	Castle Morpeth
—428 84	Blyth Valley
—428 86	Wansbeck
	Including Ashington, Bedlington, Newbiggin-by-the-Sea
—428 87	Alnwick
	Including Amble, Rothbury
	Class here *Coquet River
—428 89	Berwick-upon-Tweed
	Including Belford, Wooler; Farne Islands, Holy Island
—429	Wales
	Class here *Cambrian Mountains

SUMMARY

—429 1	North Wales	
—429 2	Gwynedd	Former Caernarvonshire
—429 3	Clwyd	
—429 4	South Wales	
—429 5	Powys	
—429 6	Dyfed	
—429 7	Mid Glamorgan	
—429 8	West and South Glamorgan	
—429 9	Gwent	

*Class parts of this physiographic region or feature as instructed under —4–9

Table 2. Areas

—429 1	North Wales

For Gwynedd, see —4292; Clwyd, —4293; Montgomery, —42951

—429 2	Gwynedd Former Caernarvonshire
—429 21	Ynys Môn (Isle of Anglesey)

Former County of Anglesey

—429 23	Dwyfor

Including Criccieth, Porthmadog, Pwllheli

—429 25	Arfon

Including Bangor, Bethesda, Caernarvon

Class here *Snowdonia

—429 27	Aberconwy

Including Betws-y-Coed, Conway, Llandudno, Llanfairfechan, Llanrwst, Penmaenmawr

—429 29	Meironnydd

Including Bala, Barmouth, Dolgellau, Ffestiniog, Tywyn

Class here former Merioneth

Class a specific part of former Merioneth not provided for here with the subject, e.g., Edeyrnion —42937

—429 3	Clwyd

Class here former Denbighshire

Class a specific part of former Denbighshire not provided for here with the subject, e.g., Llanrwst —42927

—429 31	Colwyn

Including Abergele, Colwyn Bay

—429 32	Rhuddlan

Including Prestatyn, Rhyl

—429 33	Delyn

Including Holywell, Mold

Class here former Flintshire

Class a specific part of former Flintshire not provided for here with the subject, e.g., Buckley —42936

*Class parts of this physiographic region or feature as instructed under —4–9

—429 36	Alyn and Deeside
	Including Buckley, Connah's Quay
—429 37	Glyndŵr
	Including Denbigh, Edeyrnion, Llangollen, Ruthin
—429 39	Wrexham Maelor
	Including Wrexham

—429 4 South Wales

> *For Powys, see —4295; Dyfed, —4296; Mid Glamorgan, —4297; West and South Glamorgan, —4298; Gwent, —4299*

—429 5 Powys

Class here *Wye River, mid Wales

Class a specific part of mid Wales not provided for here with the subject, e.g., Aberystwyth —42961

—429 51	Montgomery

Former Montgomeryshire

Including Llanfyllin, Llanidloes, Machynlleth, Newtown and Llanllwchaiarn, Welshpool

Class here *Severn River in Wales

—429 54	Radnor

Former Radnorshire

Including Knighton, Llandrindod Wells, Presteigne, Rhayader

—429 56	Brecknock

Including Builth Wells, Hay, Llanwrtyd Wells

Class here former Breconshire

Class a specific part of former Breconshire not provided for here with the subject, e.g., Brynmawr —42995

—429 6 Dyfed

—429 61	Ceredigion

Former Cardiganshire

Including Aberaeron, Aberystwyth, Lampeter, New Quay

*Class parts of this physiographic region or feature as instructed under —4–9

Table 2. Areas

—429 62	Preseli

Including Fishguard, Haverfordwest, Milford Haven, Neyland

Class here former Pembrokeshire

Class a specific part of former Pembrokeshire not provided for here with the subject, e.g., Narberth —42963

—429 63	South Pembrokeshire

Including Narberth, Pembroke, Tenby

—429 65	Carmarthen

Including Newcastle Emlyn

Class here former Carmarthenshire

Class a specific part of former Carmarthenshire not provided for here with the subject, e.g., Burry Port —42967

—429 67	Llanelli

Including Burry Port, Kidwelly

—429 68	Dinefwr

Including Ammanford, Cwmamman, Llandeilo, Llandovery

—429 7	Mid Glamorgan

Class here former Glamorgan

For West and South Glamorgan, see —4298

—429 71	Ogwr

Including Bridgend, Maesteg, Ogmore and Garw, Penybont, Porthcawl

—429 72	Rhondda
—429 73	Cynon Valley

Including Aberdare, Moutain Ash

—429 75	Merthyr Tydfil
—429 76	Rhymney Valley

Including Bedwas and Machen, Caerphilly, Gelligaer, Rhymney

—429 78	Taff-Ely

Including Pontypridd

—*429 8*	West and South Glamorgan
—429 81	West Glamorgan

For Swansea, see —42982; Lliw Valley, —42983; Neath, —42984; Afan, —42985

—429 82	Swansea

District of West Glamorgan

Including Gower Peninsula

—429 83	Lliw Valley

District of West Glamorgan

Including Llwchwr

—429 84	Neath

District of West Glamorgan

—429 85	Afan

District of West Glamorgan

Including Glyncorrwg, Port Talbot

—429 86	South Glamorgan

For Cardiff, see —42987; Vale of Glamorgan, —42989

—429 87	Cardiff

District of South Glamorgan

—429 89	Vale of Glamorgan

District of South Glamorgan

Including Barry, Cowbridge, Penarth

—*429 9*	Gwent

Class here former Monmouthshire

Class a specific part of former Monmouthshire not provided for here with the subject, e.g., Rhymney —42976

—429 91	Newport

Including Caerleon

—429 93	Islwyn

Including Abercarn, Bedwellty, Mynyddislwyn, Risca

Table 2. Areas

—429 95	Blaenau Gwent

Including Abertillery, Brynmawr, Ebbw Vale, Nantyglo and Blaina, Tredegar

—429 97	Torfaen

Including Blaenavon, Cwmbran, Pontypool

—429 98	Monmouth

Including Abergavenny, Chepstow, Usk

—43	**Central Europe Germany**

Class here Federal Republic of Germany, Holy Roman Empire

(It is optional to class here ancient Germanic regions; prefer —363)

Class a specific part of Holy Roman Empire not provided for here with the subject, e.g., Lombardy —452

For Switzerland, see —494

SUMMARY

—431   **Northeastern Germany**
—432   **Saxony and Thuringia**
—433   **Bavaria**
—434   **Southwestern Germany**
—435   **Northwestern Germany**
—436   **Austria and Liechtenstein**
—437   **Czechoslovakia**
—438   **Poland**
—439   **Hungary**

▶   —431–435 Germany

Class comprehensive works in —43

▶   —431–432 East Germany (German Democratic Republic) and Berlin

Class comprehensive works in —431

—431	Northeastern Germany

Class here East Germany (German Democratic Republic)

For Saxony and Thuringia, see —432

—431 5	Brandenburg

Former state of German Democratic Republic

Districts of Potsdam, Frankfurt an der Oder, Cottbus

—431 55	Berlin

—431 552	East
—431 554	West
—431 7	Mecklenburg

       Former state of German Democratic Republic

       Districts of Rostock, Schwerin, Neubrandenburg

       Including German Pomerania

—431 8	Saxony-Anhalt

       Former state of German Democratic Republic

       Districts of Magdeburg, Halle

       Including Prussian Saxony

       For Anhalt, see —4319

—431 9	Anhalt
—432	Saxony and Thuringia
—432 1	Saxony

       Former state of German Democratic Republic

       Districts of Dresden, Leipzig, Karl-Marx-Stadt (Chemnitz)

—432 2	Thuringia

       Former state of German Democratic Republic

       Districts of Erfurt, Gera, Suhl

▶   **—433–435 West Germany (Federal Republic of Germany)**

       Class comprehensive works in —43

       For West Berlin, see —431554

—433	Bavaria

       State of Federal Republic of Germany

—433 1	Upper Franconia district
—433 2	Middle Franconia district
—433 3	Lower Franconia district
—433 4	Upper Palatinate district
—433 5	Lower Bavaria district
—433 6	Upper Bavaria district

       Including Munich

Table 2. Areas

—433 7	Swabia district
—434	Southwestern Germany

Class here *Rhine River, *Main River

—434 1	Hesse

State of Federal Republic of Germany

Including Frankfurt am Main

—434 2	Saarland

State of Federal Republic of Germany

Class here Rhine Province (Rhenish Prussia), *Saar River

> For Rhineland-Palatinate, see —4343; North
> Rhine-Westphalia, —4355

—434 3	Rhineland-Palatinate

State of Federal Republic of Germany

Class here Palatinate

> For Upper Palatinate, see —4334

—434 6	Baden-Württemberg

State of Federal Republic of Germany

Class here Lake *Constance

> For Württemberg, see —4347; Hohenzollern, —4349; Black
> Forest, —4348

—434 7	Württemberg

Including Stuttgart

—434 8	Black Forest

Class here *Danube River in Germany

—434 9	Hohenzollern
—435	Northwestern Germany
—435 1	Northernmost states
—435 12	Schleswig-Holstein

State of Federal Republic of Germany

—435 15	Hamburg

State of Federal Republic of Germany

*Class parts of this physiographic region or feature as instructed under —4–9

—435 2	Bremen
	State of Federal Republic of Germany
—435 5	North Rhine-Westphalia
	State of Federal Republic of Germany
	Including Bonn, Cologne, Ruhr district
	For Westphalia, see —4356
—435 6	Westphalia
—435 9	Lower Saxony
	State of Federal Republic of Germany
—436	Austria and Liechtenstein
	Class here Austrian Empire, Dual Monarchy of Austria-Hungary
	Class a specific part of Austrian Empire, of Dual Monarchy, not provided for here with the subject, e.g., Croatia —4972
—436 1	Northeastern provinces of Austria
—436 12	Lower Austria
—436 13	Vienna
—436 15	Burgenland
—436 2	Upper Austria province
—436 3	Salzburg province
—436 4	Western provinces of Austria, and Liechtenstein
—436 42	Tyrol
—436 45	Vorarlberg
—436 48	Liechtenstein
	Independent principality
—436 5	Styria province
—436 6	Carinthia province
—437	Czechoslovakia
—437 1	Bohemia
	Including Sudetenland
—437 12	Praha (Prague)

Table 2. Areas

—437 2	Moravia

Including Czech Silesia

—437 3	Slovakia
—438	Poland
—438 1	Northwestern provinces Polish Pomerania

Zielona Gora, Gorzow Wielkopolski, Szczecin, Koszalin, Slupsk

Class here Pomerania

For German Pomerania, see —4317

—438 2	North central provinces

Gdansk (Danzig), Bydgoszcz (Pomorze), Wloclawek, Torun, Elblag

Including West Prussia, Pomerelia

—438 3	Northeastern provinces

Olsztyn, Suwalki, Bialystok, Lomza

Including East Prussia

—438 4	Central provinces

Pila, Poznan, Leszno, Kalisz, Konin, Sieradz, Lodz, Piotrkow Trybunalski, Kielce, Radom, Warszawa, Skierniewice, Plock, Ciechanow, Ostroleka, Siedlce, Biala Podlaska, Lublin, Zamosc, Tarnobrzeg

—438 5	Southwestern provinces

Jelenia Gora, Legnica, Walbrzych, Wroclaw, Opole, Czestochowa, Katowice

Class here Silesia

For Czech Silesia, see —4372

—438 6	Southeastern provinces Polish Galicia

Bielsko-Biala, Krakow, Tarnow, Nowy Sacz, Rzeszow, Przemysl, Krosno

Class here Galicia

For East Galicia, see —47718

—439   Hungary

(It is optional to class here ancient Pannonia; prefer —398)

—439 1   Pest

Including Budapest

—439 7   Counties west of Danube

Györ-Sopron, Veszprem, Vas, Zala, Somogy, Baranya, Tolna, Fejer, Komarom

For Pest, see —4391

—439 8   Counties east of Danube

Nograd, Heves, Szolnok, Bacs-Kiskun, Csongrad

For Pest, see —4391; easternmost counties, —4399

—439 9   Easternmost counties

Bekes, Hajdu-Bihar, Borsod-Abauj-Zemplen, Szabolcs-Szatmar

—44   **France and Monaco**

(It is optional to class here ancient Celtic regions; prefer —364)

Class a specific overseas department of France with the subject, e.g., Martinique —72982

SUMMARY

—441	Northwestern France	Brittany (Bretagne) region
—442	Northern France	Normandy (Normandie) region
—443	Northeastern France	Champagne region
—444	Eastern France	Burgundy (Bourgogne) region
—445	Central France	Centre region
—446	Western France	Poitou region
—447	Southwestern France	Guienne (Aquitaine) region
—448	Southern France	Languedoc region
—449	Southeastern France and Monaco	Provence region

—441   Northwestern France   Brittany (Bretagne) region

▶   —441 1–441 5 Former region of Brittany   Modern region of Brittany

Class comprehensive works on former Brittany, on modern Brittany in —441

—441 1   Finistère department

—441 2   Côtes-du-Nord department

—441 3   Morbihan department

Table 2. Areas

—441 4   Loire-Atlantique department

> Formerly Loire-Inférieure

—441 5   Ille-et-Vilaine department

—441 6   Mayenne department

> Class here former region of Maine, modern region of Pays de la Loire
>
> Class each other specific department of Maine, of Pays de la Loire with the subject, e.g., Sarthe —4417

—441 7   Sarthe department

—441 8   Maine-et-Loire department

> Class here former region of Anjou
>
> Class each other specific department of Anjou with the subject, e.g., Sarthe —4417

—442   Northern France   Normandy (Normandie) region

▶   —442 1–442 5 Former region of Normandy   Modern region of Basse-Normandie

> Class comprehensive works on Normandy, on Basse-Normandie in —442

—442 1   Manche department

—442 2   Calvados department

—442 3   Orne department

—442 4   Eure department

> Class here modern region of Haute-Normandie
>
> *For Seine-Maritime department, see —4425*

—442 5   Seine-Maritime department

> Formerly Seine-Inférieure

—442 6   Somme department

> Class here former and modern regions of Picardy (Picardie)
>
> Class each other specific department of Picardy with the subject, e.g., Oise —4435

—442 7   Pas-de-Calais department

> Including former region of Artois
>
> Class here modern region of Nord-Pas de Calais
>
> *For Nord department, see —4428*

—442 8   Nord department (Former region of French Flanders)

—443   Northeastern France   Champagne region

> Class here *Marne River

SUMMARY

—443 1   Ardennes department
—443 2   Marne department
—443 3   Aube and Haute-Marne departments
—443 4   Former region of Île-de-France
—443 5   Oise department
—443 6   Paris metropolitan area
—443 7   Seine-et-Marne department
—443 8   Lorraine and Alsace regions
—443 9   Vosges department

▶   —443 1–443 3 Modern region of Champagne et Ardenne

> Class here former region of Champagne
>
> Class comprehensive works on Champagne, on Champagne et Ardenne in —443, each specific department of Champagne not provided for here with the subject, e.g., Yonne —4441

—443 1   Ardennes department

—443 2   Marne department

—443 3   Aube and Haute-Marne departments

—443 31   Aube department

—443 32   Haute-Marne department

—443 4   Former region of Île-de-France

> Class here *Seine River
>
> Class each specific department of Île-de-France not provided for here with the subject, e.g., Seine-et-Marne —4437

—443 45   Aisne department

*Class parts of this physiographic region or feature as instructed under —4–9

Table 2. Areas

—443 5	Oise department
—443 6	Paris metropolitan area

        Including former Seine department, former Seine-et-Oise department

        Class here modern Région Parisienne

        For Seine-et-Marne department, see —4437

—443 61	Paris department
—443 62	Seine-Saint-Denis department
—443 63	Val de Marne department
—443 64	Hauts-de-Seine department
—443 65	Essonne department
—443 66	Yvelines department
—443 67	Val d'Oise department
—443 7	Seine-et-Marne department
—443 8	Lorraine and Alsace regions

        Class here *Vosges Mountains, *Argonne

▶   —443 81–443 82 Former and modern regions of Lorraine

        Class comprehensive works in —4438, each specific department of Lorraine not provided for here with the subject, e.g., Vosges —4439

—443 81	Meuse department
—443 82	Meurthe-et-Moselle and Moselle departments
—443 823	Meurthe-et-Moselle department
—443 825	Moselle department
—443 83	Former and modern regions of Alsace

        For territory of Belfort, see —44455

—443 833	Haut-Rhin department
—443 835	Bas-Rhin department

*Class parts of this physiographic region or feature as instructed under —4–9

—443 9   Vosges department

—444   Eastern France   Burgundy (Bourgogne) region

Class here *Saône River

▶   —444 1–444 4 Former region of Burgundy   Modern
region of Burgundy

Class comprehensive works on former Burgundy, on modern Burgundy
in —444

Class each specific department of Burgundy not provided for here
with the subject, e.g., Nièvre —4456

—444 1   Yonne department

—444 2   Côte-d'Or department

—444 3   Saône-et-Loire department

—444 4   Ain department

Including former regions of Bugey and Dombes

—444 5   Former and modern regions of Franche-Comté, and
Territory of Belfort

Class here *Jura Mountains in France

Class each specific department of Franche-Comté not provided
for here with the subject, e.g., Doubs —4446

—444 53   Haute-Saône department

—444 55   Territory of Belfort

—444 6   Doubs department

—444 7   Jura department

—444 8   Savoie department

Class here former region of Savoy; *Alps in France

For Haute-Savoie department, see —4449

—444 9   Haute-Savoie department

—445   Central France   Centre region

Class here *Loire River

*Class parts of this physiographic region or feature as instructed under —4–9

Table 2. Areas

▶ —445 1–445 5 Modern region of Centre   Former region of Orléanais

> Class comprehensive works on modern Centre, on former Orléanais in —445
>
> Class a specific department of Orléanais not provided for here with the subject, e.g., Yonne —4441

—445 1   Eure-et-Loir department

—445 2   Loiret department

—445 3   Loir-et-Cher department

—445 4   Indre-et-Loire department

> Class here former region of Touraine
>
> *For Indre department, see —44551; Cher department, —44552*

—445 5   Former region of Berry

> *For Creuse department, see —4468*

—445 51   Indre department

—445 52   Cher department

—445 6   Nièvre department (Former region of Nivernais)

—445 7   Allier department

> Class here former region of Bourbonnais
>
> Class each other specific department of Bourbonnais with the subject, e.g., Cher —44552

—445 8   Former region of Lyonnais

> Class here *Rhone River [*formerly* —448], modern region of Rhône-Alpes
>
> Class each specific department of Rhône-Alpes not provided for here with the subject, e.g., Haute-Savoie —4449

—445 81   Loire department

*Class parts of this physiographic region or feature as instructed under —4–9

—445 82	Rhône department
—445 823	Lyon

—445 9 Former and modern regions of Auvergne

Class here *Massif Central

> *For Allier department, see —4457; Haute-Loire department, —44813*

—445 91	Puy-de-Dôme department
—445 92	Cantal department
—446	Western France Poitou region
—446 1	Vendée department

▶ **—446 2–446 5 Modern region of Poitou-Charentes**

Class here former region of Poitou

Class comprehensive works on modern Poitou-Charentes, on former Poitou in —446; Vendée department in —4461

—446 2	Deux-Sèvres department
—446 3	Vienne department
—446 4	Charente-Maritime department

Formerly Charente-Inférieure

Including former region of Aunis

Class here former region of Saintonge

Class each other specific department of Saintonge with the subject, e.g., Charente —4465

—446 5	Charente department

Class here former region of Angoumois, *Charente River

Class each other specific department of Angoumois with the subject, e.g., Deux-Sèvres —4462

—446 6	Haute-Vienne department

Class here former and modern regions of Limousin

Class each other specific department of Limousin with the subject, e.g., Corrèze —4467

—446 7	Corrèze department

*Class parts of this physiographic region or feature as instructed under —4–9

Table 2. Areas

—446 8   Creuse department

> Class here former region of Marche
>
> *For Haute-Vienne department, see —4466*

—447   Southwestern France   Guienne (Aquitaine) region

> Class here *Garonne River

▶   —447 1–447 6 Former region of Guienne (Aquitaine)

> Class here modern region of Aquitaine
>
> Class comprehensive works on former Guienne, on modern Aquitaine in —447; a specific province of modern Aquitaine not provided for here with the subject, e.g., Landes —44772

—447 1   Gironde department

—447 2   Dordogne department

—447 3   Lot department

—447 4   Aveyron department

> Including former region of Rouergue

—447 5   Tarn-et-Garonne department

—447 6   Lot-et-Garonne department

—447 7   Former region of Gascony (Gascogne)

> Class each specific department of Gascony not provided for here with the subject, e.g., Pyrénées-Atlantiques —4479

—447 71   Gers department

—447 72   Landes department

—447 8   Hautes-Pyrénées department

—447 9   Pyrénées-Atlantiques department

> Formerly Basses-Pyrénées
>
> Including former region of Béarn

—448   Southern France   Languedoc region

> Class here *Cévennes Mountains
>
> Class Rhone River [*formerly* —448] in —4458

*Class parts of this physiographic region or feature as instructed under —4–9

▶   —448 1–448 8 Former region of Languedoc

Class here modern region of Languedoc-Roussillon

Class comprehensive works on former Languedoc, on modern Languedoc-Roussillon in —448

For Tarn-et-Garonne department, see —4475; Pyrénées-Orientales department, —4489

—448 1   Haute-Loire and Lozère departments

—448 13   Haute-Loire department

—448 15   Lozère department

—448 2   Ardèche department

—448 3   Gard department

—448 4   Hérault department

—448 5   Tarn department

—448 6   Haute-Garonne department

Class here modern region of Midi-Pyrénées

Class each other specific department of Midi-Pyrénées with the subject, e.g., Aveyron —4474

—448 7   Aude department

—448 8   Ariège department

Including former region of Foix

—448 9   Pyrénées-Orientales department (Former region of Roussillon)

Class here *Pyrenees Mountains in France

—449   Southeastern France and Monaco   Provence region

Class here *Riviera

For Italian Riviera, see —4518

▶   —449 1–449 3 Former region of Provence

Class here modern region of Provence Côte-d'Azur

Class comprehensive works on Provence, on Provence-Côte d'Azur in —449; a specific department of Provence, of Provence-Côte d'Azur not provided for here with the subject, e.g., Alpes-de-Haute-Provence —4495

*Class parts of this physiographic region or feature as instructed under —4–9

Table 2. Areas

—449 1	Bouches-du-Rhône department
—449 12	Marseilles
—449 2	Vaucluse department
	Including Valréas enclave
—449 3	Var department
—449 4	Alpes-Maritimes, Corse, Monaco
—449 41	Alpes-Maritimes department
	Including former region of Nice
—449 45	Former and modern regions of Corse (Corsica [*formerly* —4595])
	(It is optional to class here ancient Corsica; prefer —379)
—449 452	Corse de Sud department
—449 456	Haute-Corse department
—449 49	Monaco
	Independent principality, enclave in Alpes-Maritimes
—449 5	Alpes-de-Haute-Provence department
	Formerly Basses-Alpes
—449 6	Former region of Dauphiné
	Class each specific department of Dauphiné with the subject, e.g., Isère —4499
—449 7	Hautes-Alpes department
—449 8	Drôme department
	For Valréas enclave of Vaucluse department, see —4492
—449 9	Isère department
—45	**Italy**

Class here *Apennines, *Alps in Italy

(It is optional to class here ancient Italian peninsula and adjacent territories, ancient Roman Empire; prefer —37)

*Class parts of this physiographic region or feature as instructed under —4–9

SUMMARY

—451	Northwestern Italy	Piedmont region
—452	Lombardy region	
—453	Northeastern Italy	Veneto region
—454	Emilia-Romagna region and San Marino	
—455	Tuscany region	
—456	Central Italy and Vatican City	
—457	Southern Italy	
—458	Sicily and adjacent islands	
—459	Sardinia	

—451   Northwestern Italy   Piedmont region

> (It is optional to class here ancient Gallia Cisalpina; prefer —372)

—451 1   Val d'Aosta region

▶   **—451 2–451 7 Piedmont region**

> Class comprehensive works in —451

—451 2   Torino province

—451 3   Cuneo province

—451 4   Alessandria province

—451 5   Asti province

—451 6   Novara province

> Class here *Lake Maggiore

—451 7   Vercelli province

—451 8   Liguria region

> Class here *Italian Riviera
>
> (It is optional to class here ancient Liguria; prefer —371)

—451 82   Genova province

—451 83   La Spezia province

—451 84   Savona province

—451 87   Imperia province

> Formerly Porto Maurizio

*Class parts of this physiographic region or feature as instructed under —4–9

Table 2. Areas

—452	Lombardy region
	Class here *Po River
—452 1	Milano province
—452 2	Varese province
—452 3	Como province
—452 4	Bergamo province
—452 5	Sondrio province
—452 6	Brescia province
	Class here *Lake Garda
—452 7	Cremona province
—452 8	Mantova province
—452 9	Pavia province
—453	Northeastern Italy Veneto region
	(It is optional to class here ancient Venetia; prefer —373)

► —453 1–453 7 Veneto region

Class comprehensive works in —453

—453 1	Venezia province
—453 2	Padova province
—453 3	Rovigo province (Polesine)
—453 4	Verona province
—453 5	Vicenza province
—453 6	Treviso province
—453 7	Belluno province
—453 8	Trentino-Alto Adige region
	Class here *Italian Tyrol
—453 83	Bolzano province (Alto Adige)
—453 85	Trento province (Trentino)

*Class parts of this physiographic region or feature as instructed under —4–9

—453 9	Friuli-Venezia Giulia region
—453 91	Udine province
—453 92	Gorizia province
—453 93	Trieste province
—454	Emilia-Romagna region and San Marino
—454 1	Bologna province
—454 2	Modena province
—454 3	Reggio nell'Emilia province
—454 4	Parma province
—454 5	Ferrara province
—454 6	Piacenza province
—454 7	Ravenna province
—454 8	Forlì province
—454 9	San Marino
	Independent state
—455	Tuscany region
	(It is optional to class here ancient Etruria; prefer —375)
—455 1	Firenze province
—455 2	Pistoia province
—455 3	Lucca province
—455 4	Massa e Carrara province
—455 5	Pisa province
—455 6	Livorno province
—455 7	Grosseto province
—455 8	Siena province
—455 9	Arezzo province
—456	Central Italy and Vatican City
	Class here former Papal States (States of the Church)
	Class a specific Papal State with the place where located, e.g., Marches —4567

Table 2. Areas

—456 2	Latium region

(It is optional to class here ancient Latium; prefer —376)

For Roma province, see —4563

—456 22	Frosinone province
—456 23	Latina province
—456 24	Rieti province
—456 25	Viterbo province
—456 3	Roma province
—456 32	City of Rome
—456 34	Vatican City

Independent papal state, enclave in Rome

—456 5	Umbria region

(It is optional to class here ancient Umbria; prefer —374)

—456 51	Perugia province
—456 52	Terni province
—456 7	Marches region

(It is optional to class here ancient Picenum; prefer —374)

—456 71	Ancona province
—456 73	Macerata province
—456 75	Ascoli Piceno province
—456 77	Pesaro e Urbino province
—457	Southern Italy

(It is optional to class here ancient southern Italy; prefer —377)

For Sicily, see —458

SUMMARY

—457 1	Abruzzi e Molise region
—457 2	Campania region
—457 3	Napoli province
—457 4	Salerno province
—457 5	Apulia region
—457 7	Basilicata (Lucania) region
—457 8	Calabria region

—457 1	Abruzzi e Molise region
	(It is optional to class here ancient Samnium; prefer —377)
—457 11	Aquila province
—457 13	Chieti province
—457 15	Teramo province
—457 17	Pescara province
—457 19	Campobasso province
—457 2	Campania region
	(It is optional to class here ancient Campania; prefer —377)
	For Napoli province, see —4573; Salerno province, —4574
—457 21	Avellino province
—457 23	Benevento province
—457 25	Caserta province
—457 3	Napoli province
—457 4	Salerno province
—457 5	Apulia region
	(It is optional to class here ancient Apulia, Calabria; prefer —377)
—457 51	Bari province
—457 53	Lecce province
—457 54	Brindisi province
—457 55	Taranto province
—457 57	Foggia province
—457 7	Basilicata (Lucania) region
	(It is optional to class here ancient Lucania; prefer —377)
—457 71	Potenza province
—457 72	Matera province
—457 8	Calabria region
	(It is optional to class here ancient Bruttium; prefer —377)
—457 81	Catanzaro province
—457 83	Reggio di Calabria province
—457 85	Cosenza province

Table 2. Areas

—458	Sicily and adjacent islands

(It is optional to class here ancient Sicily; prefer —378)

▶ **—458 1–458 2 Sicily region**

Class comprehensive works in —458

—458 1	Eastern Sicily
—458 11	Messina province
—458 12	Enna province
—458 13	Catania province
—458 14	Siracusa province
—458 15	Ragusa province
—458 2	Western Sicily
—458 21	Caltanissetta province
—458 22	Agrigento province
—458 23	Palermo province
—458 24	Trapani province
—458 5	Malta

Independent state

(It is optional to class here ancient Malta; prefer —378)

—459	Sardinia

(It is optional to class here ancient Sardinia; prefer —379)

—459 1	Cagliari province
—459 2	Nuoro province
—459 3	Sassari province
—[459 5]	Corsica

Class in —44945

—46	**Iberian Peninsula and adjacent islands**	**Spain**

(It is optional to class here ancient Iberian Peninsula and
adjacent islands; prefer —366)

SUMMARY

—461   Northwestern Spain   Galicia region
—462   Western Spain   Leon region
—463   Castile
—464   New Castile region
—465   Northeastern Spain
—466   Basque Provinces (Vascongadas)
—467   Eastern Spain and Andorra   Catalonia region
—468   Andalusia region and Gibraltar
—469   Portugal

▶   **—461–468 Spain**

Class comprehensive works in —46

For Canary Islands, see —649

—461   Northwestern Spain   Galicia region

▶   **—461 1–461 7 Galicia region**

Class comprehensive works in —461

—461 1   La Coruña province

—461 3   Lugo province

—461 5   Orense province

—461 7   Pontevedra province

—461 9   Asturias region (Oviedo province)

—462   Western Spain   Leon region

▶   **—462 1–462 5 Leon region**

Class comprehensive works in —462

—462 1   Leon province

—462 2   Palencia province

Sometimes considered part of Old Castile region

—462 3   Valladolid province

Sometimes considered part of Old Castile region

—462 4   Zamora province

—462 5   Salamanca province

—462 6   Estremadura region

For Badajoz province, see —4627; Cáceres province, —4628

—462 7   Badajoz province

Table 2. Areas

—462 8	Cáceres province

Class here *Tagus River in Spain

—463	Castile

For New Castile region, see —464

—463 5	Old Castile region

For Palencia province, see —4622; Valladolid province, —4623

—463 51	Santander province
—463 53	Burgos province

For Treviño, see —4667

—463 54	Logroño province
—463 55	Soria province
—463 57	Segovia province
—463 59	Ávila province
—464	New Castile region

Class here La Mancha

For Albacete province, see —46771

—464 1	Madrid province
—464 3	Toledo province
—464 5	Ciudad Real province
—464 7	Cuenca province
—464 9	Guadalajara province
—465	Northeastern Spain

Class here *Ebro River

For Catalonia region, see —467

—465 2	Navarre region (Navarra province)

Class here *Pyrenees Mountains

*Class parts of this physiographic region or feature as instructed under —4-9

—465 5	Aragon region
—465 51	Teruel province
—465 53	Zaragoza (Saragossa) province
—465 55	Huesca province
—466	Basque Provinces (Vascongadas)

Class here territory of the Basque people

For Navarra province, see —4652; Pyrénées-Atlantiques department of France, —4479

—466 1	Guipúzcoa
—466 3	Vizcaya (Biscay)

For Orduña, see —4669

—466 5	Álava
—466 7	Treviño

Enclave of Burgos province in Álava province

—466 9	Orduña

Enclave of Vizcaya province between Álava and Burgos provinces

—467	Eastern Spain and Andorra Catalonia region

► | —467 1–467 4 Catalonia region |

Class comprehensive works in —467

—467 1	Gerona province
—467 2	Barcelona province
—467 3	Tarragona province
—467 4	Lérida province
—467 5	Baleares province (Balearic Islands)
—467 6	Valencia region
—467 61	Castellón de la Plana province
—467 63	Valencia province
—467 65	Alicante province

Table 2. Areas

—467 7	Murcia region
—467 71	Albacete province
—467 73	Murcia province
—467 9	Andorra
	Independent state
—468	Andalusia region and Gibraltar
	Class here *Guadalquivir River

▶   —468 1–468 8 Andalusia region

Class comprehensive works in —468

—468 1	Almería province
—468 2	Granada province
—468 3	Jaén province
—468 4	Córdoba province
—468 5	Málaga province
	For Melilla, see —642
—468 6	Sevilla province
—468 7	Huelva province
—468 8	Cádiz province
	For Ceuta, see —642
—468 9	Gibraltar
	British crown colony
—469	Portugal
—469 1	Historic province of Entre Douro e Minho
—469 12	Modern province of Minho
	Braga and Viana do Castelo districts
—469 15	Modern province of Douro Litoral
	Including Pôrto district
	For Aveiro district, see —46935; Viseu district, —46931

*Class parts of this physiographic region or feature as instructed under —4–9

—469 2   Historic province of Trás-os-Montes   Modern province of Trás-os-Montes e Alto Douro

Including Bragança and Vila Real districts

For Viseu and Guarda districts, see —46931

—469 3   Historic province of Beira

For modern province of Douro Litoral, see —46915; modern province of Trás-os-Montes e Alto Douro, —4692

—469 31   Modern province of Beira Alta

Including Viseu and Guarda districts

For Coimbra district, see —46935

—469 33   Modern province of Beira Baixa

Including Castelo Branco district

For Coimbra district, see —46935; Santarém district, —46945

—469 35   Modern province of Beira Litoral

Including Aveiro and Coimbra districts

For Leiria district, see —46942; Santarém district, —46945

—469 4   Historic province of Estremadura

For modern province of Beira Litoral, see —46935; modern province of Baixo Alentejo, —46955

—469 42   Modern province of Estremadura

Including Lisboa (Lisbon), Leiria, Setúbal districts

—469 45   Modern province of Ribatejo

Including Santarém district

Class here *Tagus River

For Portalegre district, see —46952; Lisboa district, —46942

*Class parts of this physiographic region or feature as instructed under —4–9

Table 2. Areas

—469 5   Historic province of Alentejo

—469 52   Modern province of Alto Alentejo

          Evora and Portalegre districts

—469 55   Modern province of Baixo Alentejo

          Including Beja district

          For Setúbal district, see —46942

—469 6   Algarve province (Faro district)

—469 8   Funchal district (Madeira)

          Islands in Atlantic Ocean

—469 9   Azores

          Islands in Atlantic Ocean: Ponta Delgada, Angra do Heroísmo, Horta districts

—47   **Union of Soviet Socialist Republics (Soviet Union)**

          Russia (Russian Soviet Federated Socialist Republic), other Soviet Republics of Europe

          Class here eastern Europe

          For Balkan Peninsula, see —496; Finland, —4897; Soviet Union in Asia, —57

—[471]   Finland

          Class in —4897

SUMMARY

—472   **Northern area of Soviet Union**
—473   **West central area of Soviet Union**
—474   **Baltic Sea area of Soviet Union**
—475   **Lithuania (Lithuanian Soviet Socialist Republic)**
—476   **Western area of Soviet Union**
—477   **Black Sea area of Soviet Union**
—478   **Eastern area of European Soviet Union**
—479   **Caucasus area of Soviet Union**

—472   Northern area of Soviet Union

          Class here Lakes *Onega and *Ladoga

          For Komi Autonomous Soviet Socialist Republic, see —4787

—472 3   Arkhangelsk, Vologda, Murmansk Regions of Russia

          Including Nenets National Region

          For Franz Josef Land, see —985; Novaya Zemlya, —986

*Class parts of this physiographic region or feature as instructed under —4–9

—472 5	Karelia (Karelian Autonomous Soviet Socialist Republic of Russia)
—473	West central area of Soviet Union
—473 1	Industrial area

Moscow, Vladimir, Ivanovo, Yaroslavl, Kostroma, Ryazan, Tula Regions of Russia

—473 5	Black earth area

Orel, Kursk, Belgorod, Voronezh, Lipetsk, Tambov Regions of Russia

—474	Baltic Sea area of Soviet Union

For Lithuania, see —475

—474 1	Estonia (Estonian Soviet Socialist Republic)

Class here Livonia

For Latvia, see —4743

—474 3	Latvia (Latvian Soviet Socialist Republic)

Including Courland

—474 5	Leningrad, Novgorod, Pskov Regions of Russia
—474 7	Kaliningrad Region of Russia
—475	Lithuania (Lithuanian Soviet Socialist Republic)
—476	Western area of Soviet Union

For Baltic Sea area, see —474; Ukraine, —4771; Moldavia, —4775

—476 2	Bryansk, Kaluga, Smolensk, Kalinin Regions of Russia
—476 5	Belorussia (White Russia)

Belorussian Soviet Socialist Republic

Class here Pripet Marshes

—476 52	Western and central

Brest, Grodno, Minsk Regions

—476 56	Eastern

Vitebsk, Mogilev, Gomel Regions

Table 2. Areas

—477	**Black Sea area of Soviet Union**
	(It is optional to class here ancient Black Sea region; prefer —395)
—477 1	**Ukraine (Little Russia)**
	Ukrainian Soviet Socialist Republic
	Class here *Dnieper River
	(It is optional to class here ancient Sarmatia; prefer —395)
—477 14	**Regions west of Dnieper River**
	Kiev, Zhitomir, Khmelnitski, Vinnitsa, Kirovograd, Cherkassy
	For southern Ukraine, see —47717; western Ukraine, —47718
—477 15	**Regions east of Dnieper River**
	Chernigov, Sumy, Poltava, Kharkov Regions
	For Donets-Dnieper industrial basin, see —47716; southern Ukraine, —47717
—477 16	**Donets-Dnieper industrial basin**
	Lugansk (Voroshilovgrad), Donetsk, Dnepropetrovsk Regions
	Class here *Donets River
—477 17	**Southern Ukraine**
	Crimea, Zaporozhye, Kherson, Nikolayev, Odessa Regions
—477 18	**Western Ukraine**
	Rovno, Volyn, Lvov, Ternopol, Chernovtsy, Ivano-Frankov, Transcarpathian Regions
	Including East Galicia, North Bukovina
	Class here *Dniester River, *Carpathian Mountains
—477 5	**Soviet Moldavia (Moldavian Soviet Socialist Republic)**
	Class here Bessarabia
	Class each specific part of Bessarabia not in Soviet Moldavia with the subject, e.g., Odessa Region of Ukraine —47717; comprehensive works on Moldavia in —4981
—477 7	**Rostov Region of Russia**
	Class here *Don River

*Class parts of this physiographic region or feature as instructed under —4–9

—478   **Eastern area of European Soviet Union**

Class here *Volga River

—478 1   **Upper Volga**

Gorki and Kirov Regions, Mari and Udmurt Autonomous Soviet Socialist Republics of Russia

—478 3   **Middle Volga**

Ulyanovsk, Penza, Kuibyshev Regions; Chuvash, Mordovian, Tatar Autonomous Soviet Socialist Republics of Russia

—478 5   **Lower Volga**

Saratov, Volgograd, Astrakhan Regions; Kalmyk Autonomous Soviet Socialist Republic of Russia

—478 7   ***Ural Mountains**

Sverdlovsk, Perm, Chelyabinsk, Orenburg Regions; Bashkir and Komi Autonomous Soviet Socialist Republics of Russia

Including Komi-Permyak National Region

—479   **Caucasus area of Soviet Union**

Class here *Caspian Sea

(It is optional to class here ancient Caucasus; prefer —395)

—479 1   **Soviet Azerbaijan (Azerbaijan Soviet Socialist Republic)**

Including Nakhichevan Autonomous Soviet Socialist Republic, Nagorno-Karabakh Autonomous Region

(It is optional to class here ancient Albania; prefer —395)

Class comprehensive works on Azerbaijan in —553

—479 2   **Soviet Armenia (Armenian Soviet Socialist Republic)**

Class comprehensive works on Armenia in —5662

—479 5   **Georgia (Georgian Soviet Socialist Republic)**

Including Abkhaz and Adzhar Autonomous Soviet Socialist Republics, South Oset Autonomous Region

(It is optional to class here ancient Colchis, Iberia; prefer —395)

*Class parts of this physiographic region or feature as instructed under —4–9

Table 2. Areas

—479 7   **Russian areas**

       Krasnodar and Stavropol Territories; Kabardino-Balkar, North Oset, Chechen-Ingush, Dagestan Autonomous Soviet Socialist Republics

       Including Adyge and Karachai-Cherkess Autonomous Regions

—48   **Scandinavia**

       Class here northern Europe

       For northwestern islands, see —491

—481   **Norway**

       For divisions of Norway, see —482–484; Svalbard, —981; Jan Mayen Island, —983

▶   **—482–484 Divisions of Norway**

       Class comprehensive works in —481

—482   **Southeastern Norway**

       Vest-Agder, Aust-Agder, Telemark, Vestfold, Ostfold, Oslo, Akershus, Buskerud, Opland, Hedmark counties

—483   **Southwestern Norway**

       Rogaland, Hordaland, Bergen, Sogn og Fjordane, More og Romsdal counties

—484   **Central and northern Norway**

       Including Sor-Trondelag, Nord-Trondelag counties

—484 5   **Northern Norway**

       Nordland, Troms, Finnmark counties

—485   **Sweden**

       For divisions of Sweden, see —486–488

▶   **—486–488 Divisions of Sweden**

       Class comprehensive works in —485

—486   **Southern Sweden (Gotaland)**

       Malmohus, Kristianstad, Blekinge, Kalmar, Kronoberg, Halland, Jonkoping, Alvsborg, Goteborg och Bohus, Skaraborg, Ostergotland, Gotland counties

—487   Central Sweden (Svealand)

Sodermanland, Stockholm, Uppsala, Vastmanland, Orebro, Varmland, Kopparberg, Gavleborg counties; Stockholm city

—488   Northern Sweden (Norrland)

Jamtland, Vasternorrland, Vasterbotten, Norrbotten counties

—489   Denmark and Finland

▶   —489 1–489 5 Denmark

Class comprehensive works in —489

For Greenland, see —982

—489 1   Zealand island

Including Copenhagen

—489 2   Bornholm island

—489 3   Lolland and Falster islands

—489 4   Fyn and Langeland islands

—489 5   Jutland peninsula

—489 7   Finland [*formerly* —471]

—489 71   Southern departments

Uusimaa, Kymi

Including Helsinki

—489 73   Southwestern departments

Turku-Pori, Häme, Ahvenanmaa (Aland Islands), Vaasa, Keski-Suomi

—489 75   Southeastern departments

Mikkeli, Kuopio, Pohjois-Karjala

—489 76   Oulu department

—489 77   Lappi department

Class here Lapland

For northern Norway, see —4845; northern Sweden, —488; Murmansk Region of Russia, —4723

Table 2. Areas

—49   **Other parts of Europe**

SUMMARY

—491   **Northwestern islands**
—492   **Netherlands (Holland)**
—493   **Southern Low Countries   Belgium**
—494   **Switzerland**
—495   **Greece**
—496   **Balkan Peninsula**
—497   **Yugoslavia and Bulgaria**
—498   **Romania**
—499   **Aegean Sea islands**

—491   Northwestern islands

—491 2   Iceland

—491 5   Faeroes

—492   Netherlands (Holland)

Class here comprehensive works on Low Countries, on Benelux

For Surinam, see —883; Netherlands Antilles, —72986; southern Low Countries, —493

—492 1   Northeastern provinces

Groningen, Friesland, Drenthe, Overijssel, Gelderland

—492 3   Northwestern provinces

Utrecht, North Holland, South Holland

Including Amsterdam, The Hague

—492 4   Southern provinces

Zeeland, North Brabant, Limburg

—493   Southern Low Countries   Belgium

▶   —493 1–493 4 Belgium

Class comprehensive works in —493

—493 1   Northwestern provinces of Belgium

West Flanders, East Flanders

Class here Flanders

For French Flanders region, see —4428

—493 2   Northern provinces of Belgium

Antwerp, Limburg

—493 3   Brabant province

Including Brussels

—493 4   Southern provinces of Belgium

Hainaut, Namur, Liége, Luxembourg

Class here *Meuse River, *Ardennes

—493 5   Luxembourg

Grand duchy

—494   Switzerland

—494 3   *Jura region

Jura [*formerly* —4945], Vaud, Neuchâtel, Solothurn, Basel cantons

—494 5   Swiss Plateau (Mittelland)

Geneva, Fribourg, Bern, Lucerne, Aargau, Zurich, Schaffhausen, Thurgau cantons

Class Jura canton [*formerly* —4945 as part of Bern] in —4943

—494 7   Alpine region

Valais, Unterwalden (Nidwalden and Obwalden), Schwyz, Zug, Saint Gall, Appenzell, Glarus, Uri, Grisons, Ticino cantons

Class here *Alps

—495   Greece

(It is optional to class here ancient Greece; prefer —38)

For Aegean Sea islands, see —499

—495 1   Central Greece and Euboea

Euboea, Attica, Boeotia, Phocis, Phthietis, Aetolia and Acarnania, Eurytania nomes

(It is optional to class here ancient Euboea, Boeotia, Attica, Acarnania, Aetolia, Locris, Doris, Phocis; prefer —384 for Euboea, Boeotia; —385 for Attica; —383 for Acarnania, Aetolia, Locris, Doris, Phocis)

For Kythera island, see —4952

—495 12   Athens

*Class parts of this physiographic region or feature as instructed under —4–9

Table 2. Areas

—495 2	**Peloponnesus**

Achaea, Corinthia, Argolis, Elis, Arcadia, Messenia, Laconia nomes; Kythera island

(It is optional to class here ancient Peloponnesus and Megaris; prefer —386 and —384 respectively)

—495 3	**Epirus**

Arta, Preveza, Thesprotia, Ioannina nomes

Class here *Pindus, comprehensive works on Epirus

(It is optional to class here ancient Epirus; prefer —382)

Class Albanian Epirus in —4965

—495 4	**Thessaly**

Trikkala, Karditsa, Larissa, Magnesia nomes

(It is optional to class here ancient Thessaly; prefer —382)

—495 5	**Ionian Islands**

Zante, Cephalonia, Leukas, Corfu nomes

Including Ithaca

(It is optional to class here ancient Ionian islands; prefer —382 for northern islands, —383 for Ithaca, —386 for southern islands)

—495 6	**Macedonia**

Phlorina, Kastoria, Kozane, Grevena, Pella, Hematheia, Pieria, Thessaloniki, Kilkis, Chalcidice, Serrai, Drama, Kavalla nomes; Mount Athos

Class here comprehensive works on Macedonia

(It is optional to class here ancient Macedonia; prefer —381)

> *For Yugoslav Macedonia, see —4976; Bulgarian Macedonia, —49774*

—495 7	**Thrace**

Xanthe, Rhodope, Hevros nomes

Class here comprehensive works on Thrace

(It is optional to class here ancient Thracia; prefer —398)

> *For Bulgarian Thrace, see —49778; Turkish Thrace, —563*

*Class parts of this physiographic region or feature as instructed under —4–9

—496   **Balkan Peninsula**

Class here *Danube River

(It is optional to class here ancient southeastern Europe; prefer —398)

Class Ottoman Empire [*formerly* —496] in —56

Class each specific country of Balkan Peninsula not provided for here with the subject, e.g., Greece —495

—[496 1]   **Turkey in Europe (Turkish Thrace)**

Class in —563, except European part of Canakkale in —562

—496 5   **Albania**

—497   **Yugoslavia and Bulgaria**

(It is optional to class here ancient Illyria; prefer —398)

▶   **—497 1–497 6 Yugoslavia**

Class comprehensive works in —497

—497 1   **Serbia**

Including Vojvodina, Kosovo-Metohija; Yugoslav Banat, Belgrade

—497 2   **Croatia**

Including Slavonia, Dalmatia, Istria

(It is optional to class here ancient Istria; prefer —373)

—497 3   **Slovenia**

—497 4   **Central republics of Yugoslavia**

—497 42   Bosnia and Hercegovina

—497 45   Montenegro

—497 6   **Macedonia (Vardar Macedonia)**

—497 7   **Bulgaria**

Class here *Balkan Mountains

(It is optional to class here ancient Moesia; prefer —398)

—497 72   Northwestern region

Vidin, Mikhailovgrad, Vratsa provinces

*Class parts of this physiographic region or feature as instructed under —4–9

Table 2. Areas

—497 73	West central region
	Sofia, Pernik (Dimitrovo), Kyustendil provinces; Sofia city
—497 74	Southwestern region
	Blagoyevgrad, Pazardzhik provinces
	Including Bulgarian Macedonia
—497 75	South central region
	Smolyan, Kurdzhale, Khaskovo, Stara Zagora, Plovdiv provinces; Plovdiv city
	Class here *Rhodope Mountains
—497 76	North central region
	Pleven, Lovech, Gabrovo, Turnovo, Ruse provinces
—497 77	Northeastern region
	Razgrad, Silistra, Tolbukhin, Varna, Shumen (Kolarovgrad), Turgovishte provinces; Varna city
	Including South Dobruja
—497 78	Southeastern region
	Sliven, Burgas, Yambol provinces
	Including Bulgarian Thrace

—498   Romania

(It is optional to class here ancient Dacia; prefer —398)

—498 1   Northeast

Bacau, Botosani, Braila, Galati, Iasi, Neamt, Suceava, Vaslui, Vrancea districts

Class here Moldavia

For Moldavian Soviet Socialist Republic, see —4775

—498 2   Southeast (Walachia)

Arges, Bucuresti, Buzau, Dimbovita, Ialomita, Ilfov, Olt, Prahova, Teleorman, Vilcea districts

For Black Sea area, see —4983

*Class parts of this physiographic region or feature as instructed under —4–9

—498 3   Black Sea area

> Constanta, Dulcea districts
>
> Class here Dobruja
>
> (It is optional to class here ancient Scythia; prefer —3951)
>
> *For South Dobruja, see —49777*

—498 4   Central and west

> Alba, Arad, Bihor, Bistrita-Nasaud, Brasov, Caras-Severin, Cluj, Covasna, Dolj, Gorj, Harghita, Hunedoara, Maramures, Mehedinti, Mures, Satu Mare, Salaj, Sibiu, Timis districts
>
> Including Transylvania
>
> Class here Bukovina, comprehensive works on Banat
>
> *For North Bukovina, see —47718; Yugoslav Banat, —4971*

—499   Aegean Sea islands

> Including Lesbos, Chios, Samos, Cyclades nomes of Greece; Thasos, Samothrace, Northern Sporades islands of Greece
>
> (It is optional to class here ancient Aegean Sea islands; prefer —391)
>
> Class Imbros (Imroz) and Tenedos (Bozcaada) islands of Turkey [*formerly* —499] in —562
>
> *For Euboea, see —4951; Kythera, —4952*

—499 6   Dodecanese (Southern Sporades)

> Nome of Greece
>
> (It is optional to class here ancient Rhodes, Southern Sporades, Karpathos; prefer —3916 for Rhodes, Southern Sporades, —3917 for Karpathos)

—499 8   Crete

> Canea, Rethymne, Herakleion, Lasethi nomes of Greece
>
> (It is optional to class here ancient Crete; prefer —3918)

—5   Asia   Orient   Far East

> Class here Eurasia
>
> *For Europe, see —4*

—500 9   Regional treatment

> Add to base number —5009 the numbers following —1 in —11–18 of this table, e.g., Islamic Asia —50097671

Table 2. Areas

SUMMARY

—51	China and adjacent areas
—52	Japan and adjacent islands
—53	Arabian Peninsula and adjacent areas
—54	South Asia India
—55	Iran (Persia)
—56	Middle East (Near East)
—57	Siberia (Asiatic Russia)
—58	Central Asia
—59	Southeast Asia

—51   China and adjacent areas

(It is optional to class here ancient China; prefer —31)

SUMMARY

—511	Northeastern China
—512	Southeastern China and adjacent areas
—513	Southwestern China (South-Western Region)
—514	Northwestern China (North-Western Region)
—515	Tibet Autonomous Region
—516	Sinkiang-Uighur Autonomous Region
—517	Mongolia
—518	Manchuria
—519	Korea

—511   Northeastern China

Class here Northern Region, *Hwang Ho (Yellow River)

For Manchuria, see —518; Inner Mongolia Autonomous Region, —5177

—511 3   Kiangsu province

Including Nanking

—511 32   Shanghai municipality

—511 4   Shantung province

—511 5   Hopeh province

Including Tientsin

—511 56   Peking municipality

—511 7   Shansi province

—511 8   Honan province

*Class parts of this physiographic region or feature as instructed under —4–9

—512	Southeastern China and adjacent areas

Class here Eastern and Central-Southern Regions, *Yangtze River

For Honan, see —5118; Shantung, —5114; Kiangsu, —5113

—512 1	Hupeh and Hunan provinces
—512 12	Hupeh province
—512 15	Hunan province
—512 2	Kiangsi and Anhwei provinces
—512 22	Kiangsi province
—512 25	Anhwei province
—512 4	East China Sea area
—512 42	Chekiang province
—512 45	Fukien province
—512 49	Taiwan (Formosa) and adjacent islands

Republic of China (Nationalist China)

—512 5	Hong Kong

British crown colony

—512 6	Macao

Overseas territory of Portugal

—512 7	Kwangtung province
—512 8	Kwangsi-Chuang Autonomous Region
—513	Southwestern China (South-Western Region)

For Tibet, see —515

—513 4	Kweichow province
—513 5	Yunnan province
—513 8	Szechwan province

Including Chungking

*Class parts of this physiographic region or feature as instructed under —4–9

Table 2. Areas

—514	Northwestern China (North-Western Region)

          For Ningsia-Hui Autonomous Region, see —5175; Sinkiang-Uighur Autonomous Region, —516

—514 3	Shensi province
—514 5	Kansu province
—514 7	Tsinghai (Chinghai) province
—515	Tibet Autonomous Region
—516	Sinkiang-Uighur Autonomous Region

          Class here *Kunlun Mountains, *Tien Shan

—517	Mongolia

          Class here *Altai Mountains

—517 3	Outer Mongolia (Mongolian People's Republic)

          Independent state

          Class here *Gobi Desert

—517 5	Ningsia-Hui Autonomous Region
—517 7	Inner Mongolia Autonomous Region
—518	Manchuria

          Class here North-Eastern Region

—518 2	Liaoning province
—518 4	Heilungkiang province
—518 8	Kirin province
—519	Korea
—519 3	North Korea (People's Democratic Republic of Korea)
—519 5	South Korea (Republic of Korea)
—52	**Japan and adjacent islands**

▶	—521–524 Japan

          Class comprehensive works in —52

—521	Honshu (Hondo) island
—521 1	Northern Honshu prefectures

          Aomori, Iwate, Miyagi, Akita, Yamagata, Fukushima (Hukusima)

*Class parts of this physiographic region or feature as instructed under —4–9

—521 3   East central Honshu prefectures

> Including Ibaraki, Tochigi (Totigi), Gumma, Saitama, Chiba, Kanagawa

—521 35   Tokyo prefecture and city

—521 5   Northwest central Honshu prefectures

> Niigata, Toyama, Ishikawa (Isikawa), Fukui (Hukui)

—521 6   Southwest central Honshu prefectures

> Yamanashi (Yamanasi), Nagano, Gifu (Gihu), Shizuoka (Sizuoka), Aichi (Aiti)

—521 66   Fujiyama

—521 8   Southern Honshu prefectures

> Including Mie (Miye), Shiga (Siga), Nara, Wakayama

—521 83   Osaka prefecture and city

—521 9   Western Honshu prefectures

> Including Hyogo, Tottori, Shimane (Simane), Okayama, Hiroshima, Yamaguchi (Yamaguti)

—521 91   Kyoto prefecture and city

—522   Kyushu (Kyusyu) island

> Fukuoka (Hukuoka), Saga, Nagasaki, Kumamoto, Oita (Ooita), Miyazaki, Kagoshima (Kagosima) prefectures

—523   Shikoku (Sikoku) island

> Tokushima (Tokusima), Kagawa, Ehime, Kochi (Koti) prefectures

—524   Hokkaido (Yeso) island and prefecture

—528   Southern islands

—528 1   Ryukyu Islands (Luchu)

—528 5   Bonin Islands

—53   **Arabian Peninsula and adjacent areas**

> Class here *Rub' al Khali, *Dahana, *Syrian Desert
>
> (It is optional to class here ancient Arabia, Arabia Petraea; prefer —394 and —3948 respectively)

*Class parts of this physiographic region or feature as instructed under —4–9

Table 2. Areas

—531	**Sinai (Sinai Peninsula)**
	Governorate of Egypt
	Including Gaza Strip
	(It is optional to class here ancient Sinai Peninsula; prefer —3948)
—533	**Southwestern coast of Arabia**
—533 2	**Yemen (Yemen Arab Republic)**
—533 5	**Southern Yemen (People's Democratic Republic of Yemen)**
	Formerly Federation of South Arabia
	Including Socotra [*formerly* —6772], Aden
—535	**Oman and United Arab Emirates**
—535 3	**Oman**
—535 7	**United Arab Emirates**
	Former Trucial States: Abu Dhabi, Dubai, Sharjah, Ajman, Umm al Qaiwain, Ras al Khaimah, Fujairah
—536	**Persian Gulf states**
	For United Arab Emirates, see —5357
—536 3	**Qatar**
—536 5	**Bahrein**
—536 7	**Kuwait**
—538	**Saudi Arabia**
—54	**South Asia India**
	Class here *Himalayas, *Brahmaputra River
	(It is optional to class here ancient India; prefer —34)
	For southeast Asia, see —59

*Class parts of this physiographic region or feature as instructed under —4–9

SUMMARY

—541	Northeastern India
—542	Uttar Pradesh
—543	Madhya Pradesh
—544	Rajasthan
—545	Punjab region of India
—546	Jammu and Kashmir
—547	Western India
—548	Southern India
—549	Other jurisdictions

▶   —541–548 India

Class comprehensive works in —54

—541   Northeastern India

Class here *Ganges River

—541 2   Bihar

—541 3   Orissa

—541 4   West Bengal

Including Calcutta

Class here former province of Bengal

For former East Bengal, see —5492

—541 5   Tripura

—541 6   Far northeast

For Manipur, see —5417

—541 62   Assam

—541 63   Arunachal Pradesh

Formerly North East Frontier Agency

—541 64   Meghalaya

—541 65   Nagaland

—541 66   Mizoram

—541 67   Sikkim [*formerly* —5497]

*Class parts of this physiographic region or feature as instructed under —4–9

Table 2. Areas

—541 7	Manipur
—542	Uttar Pradesh
—543	Madhya Pradesh
—544	Rajasthan
	Class here *Thar (Indian) Desert
—545	Punjab region of India
	Class here former province of Punjab
	For Punjab of Pakistan, see —54914
—545 2	Himachal Pradesh
—545 5	Former Punjab state
—545 52	Punjab
	Including Chandigarh
—545 58	Haryana
—545 6	Delhi
—546	Jammu and Kashmir
	Kashmir is claimed by both India and Pakistan
	Class here *Karakoram Mountains
—547	Western India
—547 5	Gujarat
—547 9	Maharashtra and adjacent territories
—547 92	Maharashtra
	Including Bombay
—547 96	Dadra and Nagar Haveli
—547 99	Goa, Daman and Diu
—548	Southern India
—548 1	Laccadive, Minicoy and Amindivi Islands (Lakshadweep)
—548 2	Tamil Nadu
	Formerly Madras
—548 3	Kerala
—548 4	Andhra Pradesh

*Class parts of this physiographic region or feature as instructed under —4–9

—548 6	Pondicherry
—548 7	Karnataka
	Formerly Mysore
—548 8	Andaman and Nicobar Islands
—549	Other jurisdictions
	Class here Pakistan (West and East, 1947–1971)
—549 1	Pakistan
	Former West Pakistan
	Class here *Indus River
—549 12	North-West Frontier
—549 122	Districts and agencies north of Peshawar
	Including Swat, Dir, Kalam, Chitral
—549 123	Peshawar
—549 124	Dera Ismail Khan
—549 13	Kashmir
	Claimed by both Pakistan and India
—549 14	Punjab of Pakistan
—549 142	Rawalpindi
	Including Islamabad
—549 143	Lahore
—549 144	Sargodha
—549 145	Multan
—549 15	Eastern Baluchistan
	Class here comprehensive works on Baluchistan
	Class Iranian Baluchistan in —5583
—549 152	Quetta
—549 153	Kalat

*Class parts of this physiographic region or feature as instructed under —4–9

Table 2. Areas

—549 16	Bahawalpur
—549 17	Khairpur
—549 18	Sind
—549 182	Hyderabad
—549 183	Karachi
—549 2	Bangladesh

Former East Bengal, former East Pakistan

—549 22	Dacca
—549 23	Chittagong
—549 24	Rajshahi
—549 25	Khulna
—549 3	Sri Lanka (Ceylon)
—549 5	Maldives
—549 6	Nepal
—[549 7]	Sikkim

Class in —54167

—549 8	Bhutan
—55	**Iran (Persia)**

(It is optional to class here ancient Iranian Plateau; prefer —35)

—551	Gilan
—552	Mazanderan and Central
—552 3	Mazanderan

(It is optional to class here ancient Hyrçania; prefer —396)

—552 5	Central

Including Tehran

—553	East Azerbaijan

Class here Azerbaijan

For West Azerbaijan of Iran, see —554; Azerbaijan Soviet Socialist Republic, —4791

—554	West Azerbaijan

—555   Kermanshah and Kurdistan

—555 2   Kermanshah

           Including Hamadan

—555 4   Kurdistan

           Class comprehensive works on Kurdistan in —5667

—556   Khuzistan

—557   Fars and Sea of Oman-Persian Gulf

—557 2   Fars

—557 5   Sea of Oman-Persian Gulf (Ports and Islands of the Sea of Oman)

—558   Kerman, and Seistan and Baluchistan

—558 2   Kerman

—558 3   Seistan and Baluchistan

           Class comprehensive works on Baluchistan in —54915

—559   Khurasan and Isfahan

—559 2   Khurasan

—559 5   Isfahan

—56   **Middle East (Near East)**

           Class here Ottoman Empire [*formerly* —496]

           (It is optional to class here ancient Middle East; prefer —394)

           Class each specific country of Middle East, of Ottoman Empire, not provided for here with the subject, e.g., Saudi Arabia —538

SUMMARY

Table 2. Areas

—561   Turkey and Cyprus

Class here Asia Minor

(It is optional to class here ancient western Asia Minor, eastern Asia Minor; prefer —392 and —393 respectively)

For divisions of Turkey and Cyprus, see —562–566

▶   —562–566 Divisions of Turkey and Cyprus

Class comprehensive works in —561

—562   Western Turkey

Canakkale [*formerly also* —4961], Balikesir, Manisa, Kutahya, Usak, Afyon-Karahisar, Denizli, Burdur, Mugla, Aydin, Izmir (Smyrna) provinces

Including Imbros (Imroz) and Tenedos (Bozcaada) islands [*both formerly* —499]

(It is optional to class here ancient Mysia and Troas, Lydia, Ionia, Caria, Phrygia; prefer —3921, —3922, —3923, —3924, —3926 respectively)

—563   North central Turkey

Edirne (Adrianople), Kirklareli, Tekirdag, Istanbul, Bursa, Bilecik, Kocaeli, Sakarya, Bolu, Eskisehir, Ankara, Cankiri, Zonguldak, Kastamonu, Sinop, Samsun, Amasya, Corum, Yozgat provinces

Class here Turkey in Europe (Turkish Thrace) [*formerly* —4961]

(It is optional to class here ancient Bithynia, Paphlagonia, Galatia; prefer —3925, —3931, —3932 respectively)

—564   South central Turkey and Cyprus

Including Antalya, Isparta, Konya, Kirsehir, Kayseri, Nevsehir, Nigde, Icel, Seyhan (Adana), Hatay (Antakya), Gaziantep provinces of Turkey

(It is optional to class here ancient Pisidia, Lycia, Pamphylia, Cappadocia, Cilicia, Commagene; prefer —3927, —3928, —3929, —3934, —3935, —3936 respectively)

—564 5   Cyprus

Independent island state

(It is optional to class here ancient Cyprus; prefer —3937)

—565   **East central Turkey**

> Trabzon (Trebizond), Gumusane, Giresun, Ordu, Tokat, Sivas, Maras, Malatya, Adiyaman, Urfa provinces
>
> (It is optional to class here ancient Pontus; prefer —3933)

—566   **Eastern Turkey**

—566 2   **Northeastern Turkey**

> Including Rize, Coruh (Artvin), Erzurum, Kars, Agri, Van, Hakkari provinces
>
> Class here comprehensive works on Armenia
>
> (It is optional to class here ancient Armenia; prefer —3955)
>
> *For Armenian Soviet Socialist Republic, see —4792*

—566 7   **Southeast central Turkey**

> Erzincan, Tunceli, Elazig, Diyarbakir, Bingol, Mus, Bitlis, Sürt, Mardin provinces
>
> Class here comprehensive works on Kurdistan
>
> Class Iranian Kurdistan in —5554, Iraqi Kurdistan in —5672

—567   Iraq

—567 2   Kurdistan

> Sulaimaniya, Erbil (Arbil)
>
> Class comprehensive works on Kurdistan in —5667

—567 3   Desert

> Northern and Southern
>
> (It is optional to class here ancient Arabia Deserta; prefer —3947)
>
> *For Al-Jazira Desert, see —5674*

—567 4   Mesopotamia

> Including Al-Jazira Desert; Mosul, Kirkuk, Diyala, Baghdad, Ramadi (Dulaim)
>
> (It is optional to class here ancient Mesopotamia; prefer —35)
>
> *For lower Mesopotamia, see —5675*

Table 2. Areas

—567 5	**Lower Mesopotamia**

Karbala, Hilla, Kut, Diwaniya, Nasiriya (Muntafiq), Amara, Basra

—569	**Eastern Mediterranean**
—569 1	**Syria**

(It is optional to class here ancient Syria; prefer —394)

—569 12	**Desert**

Haseke, Raqqa (Rashid), Deir ez Zor (Der-Ezza), Homs

—569 13	**Northwest**

Aleppo, Idlib, Hama, Latakia, Tartous

—569 14	**Southwest**

Damascus, Dera, Jebel Druze (Es Suweida), Kunaitra (El Quneitra)

Class here *Anti-Lebanon

—569 2	**Lebanon**

(It is optional to class here ancient Phoenicia; prefer —3944)

—569 4	**Palestine Israel**

Class here *Jordan River, *Dead Sea

(It is optional to class here ancient Palestine; prefer —33)

For Jordan, see —5695; Gaza Strip, —531

—569 44	**Jerusalem district**

Class here comprehensive works on Jerusalem

For Jerusalem, Jordan, see —56952

—569 45	**Northern district**
—569 46	**Haifa district**
—569 47	**Central district**
—569 48	**Tel Aviv district**
—569 49	**Southern district**

(It is optional to class here ancient Edom; prefer —3946)

*Class parts of this physiographic region or feature as instructed under —4–9

—569 5   Jordan

—569 51   Hebron district

—569 52   Jerusalem district

—569 53   Noblus district (Samaria)

—569 54   Ajlun (Irbid) district

—569 55   Balqa district

—569 56   Karak district

> (It is optional to class here ancient Moab; prefer —3946)

—569 57   Maan district

—569 58   Amman district

—57   **Siberia (Asiatic Russia)**

> Class here Soviet Union in Asia
>
> *For Soviet Republics of central Asia, see —584*

—573   Western Siberia

> Altai Territory; Kurgan, Tyumen, Omsk, Novosibirsk, Tomsk, Kemerovo Regions
>
> Including Gorno-Altai Autonomous Region, Yamal-Nenets and Khanty-Mansi National Regions

—575   Eastern Siberia

> Krasnoyarsk Territory, Irkutsk and Chita Regions; Tuva, Buryat, Yakut Autonomous Soviet Socialist Republics
>
> Including Khakass Autonomous Region; Taimyr, Evenki, Ust-Orda Buryat, Agin Buryat National Regions
>
> Class here *Sayan Mountains
>
> *For Far Eastern Siberia, see —577; Severnaya Zemlya, —987; New Siberian Islands, —988*

—577   Far Eastern Siberia

> Khabarovsk and Primorski (Maritime) Territories; Amur, Magadan, Kamchatka, Sakhalin Regions
>
> Including Jewish Autonomous Region, Chukchi and Koryak National Regions; Kurile and Komandorski Islands, Wrangel Island
>
> Class here *Amur River

*Class parts of this physiographic region or feature as instructed under —4-9

Table 2. Areas

—58 **Central Asia**

(It is optional to class here ancient Central Asia; prefer —396)

—581 **Afghanistan**

Class here *Hindu Kush

(It is optional to class here ancient Bactria, Ariana; prefer —396)

—584 **Turkestan   Soviet Republics of central Asia**

Class Sinkiang in —516; Turkmen, Tadzhik, Uzbek Soviet Socialist Republics in —585–587

—584 3 **Kirghizistan (Kirghiz Soviet Socialist Republic)**

Class here *Tien Shan in Soviet Union

—584 5 **Kazakhstan (Kazakh Soviet Socialist Republic)**

—585 **Turkmenistan (Turkmen Soviet Socialist Republic)**

(It is optional to class here ancient Margiana; prefer —396)

—586 **Tadzhikistan (Tadzhik Soviet Socialist Republic)**

Including Gorno-Badakhshan Autonomous Region

Class here *Pamirs

—587 **Uzbekistan (Uzbek Soviet Socialist Republic)**

Including Kara-Kalpak Autonomous Soviet Socialist Republic

Class here *Aral Sea

(It is optional to class here ancient Sogdiana; prefer —396)

—59 **Southeast Asia**

SUMMARY

—591 **Burma**
—593 **Thailand (Siam)**
—594 **Laos**
—595 **Commonwealth of Nations territories   Malaysia**
—596 **Cambodia (Khmer Republic, Kampuchea)**
—597 **Vietnam**
—598 **Indonesia**
—599 **Philippines**

*Class parts of this physiographic region or feature as instructed under —4–9

—591	Burma
—593	Thailand (Siam)
—594	Laos
—595	Commonwealth of Nations territories Malaysia
—595 1	Peninsular Malaysia (Malaya, West Malaysia)

> States of Johore, Kedah, Kelantan, Malacca (Melaka), Negri (Negeri) Sembilan, Pahang, Penang (Pinang), Perak, Perlis, Selangor, Trengganu
>
> Class here Malay Peninsula
>
> *For Burma, see —591; Thailand, —593*

—[595 2]	Singapore

> Class in —5957

—595 3	Sabah

> State of Malaysia
>
> Class here northern Borneo, East Malaysia
>
> *For Sarawak, see —5954; Brunei, —5955*

—595 4	Sarawak

> State of Malaysia

—595 5	Brunei protectorate
—595 7	Singapore [*formerly* —5952]

> Independent republic

—596	Cambodia (Khmer Republic, Kampuchea)
—597	Vietnam

> Class here *Mekong River

—598	Indonesia

> Class here Malay Archipelago
>
> *For Philippines, see —599; Irian Jaya, —951*

—598 1	Sumatra
—598 2	Java and Madura

*Class parts of this physiographic region or feature as instructed under —4–9

Table 2. Areas

—598 3	Kalimantan

Class here Borneo

For northern Borneo, see —5953

—598 4	Celebes (Sulawesi)
—598 5	Moluccas (Maluku)
—598 6	Lesser Sunda Islands (Nusa Tenggara)

Bali, Lombok, Sumbawa, Sumba, Flores, Solor, Adonara, Lomblen, Alor, Wetar, Timor

Including former Portuguese Timor

—599	Philippines
—599 1	Luzon

Abra, Albay, Bataan, Batanes, Batangas, Benguet, Bulacan, Cagayan, Camarines Norte, Camarines Sur, Catanduanes, Cavite, Ifugao, Ilocos Norte, Ilocos Sur, Isabela, Kalinga-Apayao, Laguna, La Union, Marinduque, Mountain, Nueva Ecija, Nueva Vizcaya, Pampanga, Pangasinan, Quezon, Rizal, Sorsogon, Tarlac, Zambales provinces; Manila city

—599 3	Mindoro

Occidental Mindoro, Oriental Mindoro provinces

—599 4	Palawan (Palawan province)
—599 5	Visayan Islands

Bohol, Cebu, Masbate, Leyte, Negros, Panay, Samar

Aklan, Antique, Bohol, Capiz, Cebu, Eastern Samar, Iloilo, Leyte, Masbate, Negros Occidental, Negros Oriental, Northern Samar, Romblon, Southern Leyte, Western Samar provinces

—599 7	Mindanao

Agusan del Norte, Agusan del Sur, Bukidno, Camiguin, Cotabato, Cotabato del Sur, Davao del Norte, Davao del Sur, Davao Oriental, Lanao del Norte, Lanao del Sur, Misamis Occidental, Misamis Oriental, Surigao del Norte, Surigao del Sur, Zamboanga del Norte, Zamboanga del Sur provinces

—599 9	Sulu Archipelago (Sulu province)

—6 Africa

—600 9   Regional treatment

>   Add to base number —6009 the numbers following —1 in —11–18
>   of this table, e.g., Anglophone Africa —60097521

SUMMARY

—61	Tunisia and Libya
—62	Egypt and Sudan
—63	Ethiopia (Abyssinia)
—64	Northwest African coast and offshore islands Morocco
—65	Algeria
—66	West Africa and offshore islands
—67	Central Africa and offshore islands
—68	Southern Africa Republic of South Africa
—69	South Indian Ocean islands

—61   **Tunisia and Libya**

>   Class here Barbary States, comprehensive works on North Africa
>
>   (It is optional to class here ancient North Africa; prefer —397)
>
>   Class each specific part of North Africa, of Barbary States, not
>   provided for here with the subject, e.g., Algeria —65

—611   **Tunisia**

>   (It is optional to class here ancient Carthage; prefer —3973)

—612   **Libya**

>   Class here *Libyan Desert
>
>   (It is optional to class here ancient Tripolis, Cyrenaica,
>   Marmarica; prefer —3974, —3975, —3976 respectively)

—62   **Egypt and Sudan**

>   Class here Federation of Arab Republics, *Nile River
>
>   (It is optional to class here ancient Egypt; prefer —32)
>
>   *For Libya, see —612; Syria, —5691*

▶   **—621–623 Egypt**

>   Class comprehensive works in —62
>
>   *For Sinai, see —531*

*Class parts of this physiographic region or feature as instructed under —4–9

Table 2. Areas

—621	Lower Egypt

Including Alexandria, Damietta, Beheira, Gharbiya, Daqahliya, Sharqiya, Minufiya, Qalyubiya, Kafr el Sheikh, Matruh governorates; Nile Delta

—621 5	Isthmus of Suez

Suez, Port Said, Ismailia governorates

—621 6	Cairo governorate and city
—622	Middle Egypt

Giza, Beni Suef, Faiyum, Minya, Asyut, New Valley governorates

Class here *Western Desert, *Qattara Depression

—623	Upper Egypt

Sohag, Qena, Aswan, Red Sea governorates

Class here *Eastern (Arabian) Desert

—624	Sudan

For provinces of Sudan, see —625–629

▶	—625–629 Provinces of Sudan

Class comprehensive works in —624

—625	Northern Province of Sudan

Class here *Nubian Desert

(It is optional to class here ancient Ethiopia; prefer —3978)

—626	Central provinces of Sudan
—626 2	Khartoum Province
—626 4	Blue Nile Province

Class here *Blue Nile River

—627	Darfur Province
—628	Kordofan Province

*Class parts of this physiographic region or feature as instructed under —4–9

—629	Eastern and southern provinces of Sudan
—629 2	Kassala Province
—629 3	Upper Nile Province

Class here *White Nile River

—629 4	Bahr el Ghazal Province
—629 5	Equatoria Province
—63	**Ethiopia (Abyssinia)**
—632	Provinces east of Rift Valley

Harar, Arusi, Bale, Sidamo

—633	Provinces west of Rift Valley

Gamu-Gofa, Kaffa, Ilubabor, Wallaga, Shoa, Gojjam

Including Addis Ababa

—634	Northern provinces

Begemdir, Wallo, Tigre

For Eritrea, see —635

—635	Eritrea province
—64	**Northwest African coast and offshore islands Morocco**

(It is optional to class here ancient Mauretania; prefer —3971)

▶ —642–646 Morocco

Class comprehensive works in —64

—642	Mediterranean provinces of Morocco

Al-Homina, Nador, Tangier, Tetuan

Including former Spanish Morocco, Spanish cities of Ceuta and Melilla

Class here *Rif Mountains

—643	Northern provinces of Morocco

Meknes, Fez, Taza, Oujda, Kenitra, Khouribga, Settat, Al Jadida provinces; Casablanca, Rabat-Salé prefectures

For Mediterranean provinces, see —642

*Class parts of this physiographic region or feature as instructed under —4–9

Table 2. Areas

—644	Beni-Mellal province
	Class here *Atlas Mountains
—645	Ksar-es-Souk province
—646	Southwestern provinces of Morocco
	Marrakesh, Agadir, Ouarzazate, Safi, Tarfaya
	Including Ifni
—648	Sahara (Western Sahara)
	Formerly Spanish West Africa, Spanish Sahara (Saguia el Hamra, Rio de Oro)
—649	Canary Islands
	Santa Cruz de Tenerife and Las Palmas provinces of Spain
—65	**Algeria**
—651	Northwestern departments
	Oran, Tlemcen, Mostaganem, Tiaret, Saïda
—653	North central departments
	Algiers, Grand Kabylia, El Asnam (Orléansville), Titteri
—655	Northeastern departments
	Sétif, Constantine, Annaba (Bône), Aurès
	(It is optional to class here ancient Numidia; prefer —3972)
—657	Sahara departments
	Oasis, Saoura
	(It is optional to class here ancient Gaetulia; prefer —3977)
—66	**West Africa and offshore islands**
	Class here *Sahara Desert
—660 097 521	Anglophone West Africa
—660 097 541	Francophone West Africa

*Class parts of this physiographic region or feature as instructed under —4-9

SUMMARY

—661 Mauritania
—662 Mali, Upper Volta, Niger (Western Sudan)
—663 Senegal
—664 Sierra Leone
—665 Upper Guinea area
—666 Liberia and Ivory Coast
—667 Ghana
—668 Togo and Benin
—669 Nigeria and islands of Gulf of Guinea

—661 Mauritania

—662 Mali, Upper Volta, Niger (Western Sudan)

Class here *Niger River

—662 3 Mali

—662 5 Upper Volta

—662 6 Niger

—663 Senegal

Class here Senegambia

Class the Gambia in —6651

—664 Sierra Leone

—665 Upper Guinea area

Class each specific country of Upper Guinea not provided for here with the subject, e.g., Sierra Leone —664

—665 1 The Gambia

—665 2 Guinea republic

—665 7 Guinea-Bissau

—665 8 Cape Verde Islands (Cape Verde Republic)

—666 Liberia and Ivory Coast

—666 2 Liberia

—666 8 Ivory Coast

—667 Ghana

Class here *Volta River

*Class parts of this physiographic region or feature as instructed under —4-9

Table 2. Areas

—668	Togo and Benin
—668 1	Togo
—668 3	Benin (Dahomey)
—669	Nigeria and islands of Gulf of Guinea

▶   —669 1–669 5 Nigeria

Class comprehensive works in —669

—669 1	Lagos state
—669 2	Former Western state

Ogun, Ondo, Oyo states

—669 3	Bendel state

Formerly Mid-Western state

—669 4	Former Eastern Region

Anambra, Ino, Cross River, Rivers states

—669 5	Former Northern Region

Niger, Sokoto, Kaduna, Kano, Bauchi, Borno, Gongola, Benue, Plateau, Kwara states

Including former Northern Cameroons [*formerly* —67112]

—669 9	Islands of Gulf of Guinea
—669 91	Fernando Po

Province of Equatorial Guinea

For Annobón, see —66996

—669 93	Principe
—669 94	São Tomé
—669 96	Annobón
—67	**Central Africa and offshore islands**

Class here Negro Africa, Black Africa, Africa south of the Sahara

Class each specific country of Negro Africa, of Black Africa, of Africa south of the Sahara not provided for here with the subject, e.g., Nigeria —669

SUMMARY

—671	Lower Guinea area
—672	Gabon and Congo
—673	Angola
—674	Central African Republic and Chad
—675	Former Belgian territories
—676	Uganda and Kenya
—677	Somaliland
—678	Tanzania
—679	Mozambique

—671　Lower Guinea area

Class each specific country of Lower Guinea not provided for here with the subject, e.g., Gabon —6721

—671 1　Cameroon

—671 12　West Cameroon

Former Southern Cameroons

Class former Northern Cameroons [*formerly* —67112] in —6695

—671 13　East Cameroon

Former Cameroon

—671 8　Equatorial Guinea

Former Spanish Guinea

Including Rio Muni

For Fernando Po, see —66991

—672　Gabon and Congo

—672 1　Gabon

—672 4　Republic of the Congo

Former French Congo, Middle Congo

—673　Angola

—673 1　Cabinda district

Exclave of Angola

—673 2　Other northern districts

Zaïre, Uige, Luanda, Cuanza-Norte, Cuanza-Sul

—673 4　Central districts

Malange, Lunda, Moxico, Bié, Huambo, Benguela

Table 2. Areas

—673 5	Southern districts
	Moçâmedes, Huíla, Cuando Cubango
—674	**Central African Republic and Chad**
—674 1	Central African Republic (Empire)
	Former Ubangi-Shari
—674 3	Chad
—675	**Former Belgian territories**
—675 1	Zaïre
	Former Congo Republic, Belgian Congo
	Class here *Zaïre (Congo) River
—675 11	Kinshasa, Bas-Zaïre, Bandundu
—675 112	Kinshasa (Leopoldville)
—675 114	Bas-Zaïre
—675 116	Bandundu
—675 12	Former Kasai
—675 123	Kasai West
—675 126	Kasai East
—675 13	Equateur
—675 15	Haute-Zaïre
—675 17	Kivu
	Class here Lakes *Edward, *Kivu
—675 18	Shaba (Katanga)
	Class here *Lake Mweru
—675 7	**Rwanda and Burundi**
	Former Ruanda-Urundi
—675 71	Rwanda
—675 72	Burundi

*Class parts of this physiographic region or feature as instructed under —4–9

—676   **Uganda and Kenya**

 Class here East Africa, *Great Rift Valley

 Class a specific part of East Africa not provided for here with the subject, e.g., Tanzania —678

—676 1   **Uganda**

 Class here *Lake Albert

—676 2   **Kenya**

—676 22   North East province

—676 23   Coast province

—676 24   Eastern province

—676 25   Nairobi Area

—676 26   Central province

—676 27   Rift Valley province

 Class here *Lake Turkana (Rudolf)

—676 28   Western province

—676 29   Nyanza province

—677   Somaliland

—677 1   Djibouti

 Former French Somaliland, French Territory of the Afars and the Issas

—[677 2]   Socotra

 Class in —5335

—677 3   Somalia

—678   Tanzania

—678 1   **Zanzibar and adjacent islands**

—678 2   **Tanganyika**

—678 22   Tanga region

—678 23   Coast region

 Including Dar es Salaam, Mafia Island

—678 24   Mtwara region

*Class parts of this physiographic region or feature as instructed under —4–9

Table 2. Areas

—678 25	South central
	Ruvuma (Songea), Morogoro, Iringa regions
	Class here *Lake Nyasa
—678 26	North central
	Singida, Dodoma, Arusha, Kilimanjaro (Moshi) regions
	Class here *Kilimanjaro
—678 27	*Lake Victoria
	Mara (Musoma), Mwanza, West Lake (Bukoba) regions
—678 28	Shinyanga, Kigoma, Tabora, Mbeya regions
	Class here *Lake Tanganyika
—679	Mozambique
	Class here *Zambesi River
—679 1	Lourenço Marques (Maputo) district
—679 2	Gaza district
—679 3	Inhambane district
—679 4	Manica and Sofala district
—679 5	Tete district
—679 6	Zambézia district
—679 7	Moçambique district
—679 8	Cabo Delgado district
—679 9	Niassa district
—68	Southern Africa Republic of South Africa

SUMMARY

—681	Former high commissioner territories
—682	Transvaal
—684	Natal
—685	Orange Free State
—687	Cape of Good Hope
—688	Namibia (South-West Africa)
—689	Rhodesia, Zambia, Malawi

*Class parts of this physiographic region or feature as instructed under —4–9

—681	Former high commissioner territories
—681 1	Botswana

> Independent republic, formerly Bechuanaland Protectorate
> Class here *Kalahari Desert

—681 3	Swaziland [*formerly* —683]

> Independent kingdom

—681 6	Lesotho [*formerly* —686]

> Independent kingdom, formerly Basutoland, Basotho

—682	Transvaal

> Province of Republic of South Africa

—682 2	Witwatersrand
—682 21	Johannesburg
—682 9	Homelands (Bantustans)
—682 91	Venda
—682 92	Gazankulu
—682 93	Lebowa
—682 94	Bophuthatswana
—682 95	South Ndebele
—[683]	Swaziland

> Class in —6813

—684	Natal

> Province of Republic of South Africa

—684 9	Homelands (Bantustans)
—684 91	Kwa-Zulu (Zululand)
—685	Orange Free State

> Province of Republic of South Africa

—685 9	Homelands (Bantustans)
—685 91	Basotho-Qwaqwa

*Class parts of this physiographic region or feature as instructed under —4–9

Table 2. Areas

—[686]	Lesotho
	Class in —6816
—687	Cape of Good Hope
	Province of Republic of South Africa
	For Walvis Bay exclave, see —688
—687 9	Homelands (Bantustans)
—687 91	Transkei
—687 92	Ciskei
—688	Namibia (South-West Africa)
	Including Walvis Bay exclave of Cape of Good Hope
—689	Rhodesia, Zambia, Malawi
—689 1	Rhodesia (Zimbabwe)
	Formerly Southern Rhodesia
	Including Matabeleland, Mashonaland
	Class here *Victoria Falls
—689 4	Zambia
	Formerly Northern Rhodesia
—689 7	Malawi
	Formerly Nyasaland
—69	**South Indian Ocean islands**
—691	Madagascar (Malagasy Republic)
—694	Islands north of Madagascar
	Comoro, Aldabra, Cosmoledo, Glorioso, Providence, Farquhar, Agalega
—695	Amirantes
—696	Seychelles
—697	Chagos Islands

*Class parts of this physiographic region or feature as instructed under —4–9

—698	Mascarene Islands

Including Rodrigues; Cargados Carajos Shoals

For Agalega, see —694

—698 1	Réunion

Overseas department of France

—698 2	Mauritius

—699	Isolated islands

Cocos, Amsterdam, Saint Paul, Kerguelen, Crozet, Prince Edward

—7   North America

Class Western Hemisphere in —1812

—700 09	Regional treatment

Add to base number —70009 the numbers following —1 in —11–18 of this table, e.g., urban regions of North America —70009732

—[701]	North American native races in North America

(Use of this number is optional; prefer specific discipline or subject, using "Standard Subdivisions" notation —08997 from Table 1)

SUMMARY

—71	Canada
—72	Middle America Mexico
—73	United States
—74	Northeastern United States (New England and Middle Atlantic states)
—75	Southeastern United States (South Atlantic states)
—76	South central United States Gulf Coast states
—77	North central United States Lake states
—78	Western United States
—79	Great Basin and Pacific Slope region of United States Pacific Coast states

—71	Canada

SUMMARY

—711	British Columbia
—712	Prairie provinces
—713	Ontario
—714	Quebec
—715	New Brunswick
—716	Nova Scotia
—717	Prince Edward Island
—718	Newfoundland and adjacent territories
—719	Northern territories

Table 2. Areas

—711	**British Columbia**

Class here *Rocky Mountains in Canada

—711 1	**Northern region**

Area north of 55° N

—711 2	**Central interior region**

Area north of 55° N and 51° N, and east of Coast Mountains

Class here *Fraser River and Valley, *Bulkley and *Cariboo Mountains

—711 3	**Coastal region**

Area south of 55° N to international boundary, and west of Coast Mountains

Class here *Cascade and *Coast Ranges in Canada

—711 31	Queen Charlotte Islands
—711 32	Northwest coastal region

Area between 55° N and 51° N, and west of Coast Mountains

Including Prince Rupert, Kitimat, Ocean Falls

—711 33	Lower coastal mainland

Area south of 51° N to international boundary, and west of Coast Mountains

Including Vancouver, Port Moody, Port Coquitlam, New Westminster, Mission City, Chilliwack

—711 34	Vancouver and neighboring islands

Including Victoria

—711 4	**Southern interior region**

Area south of 51° N to international boundary, and east of Coast Mountains

—711 41	Valleys of lower Thompson, Nicola, Similkameen Rivers

Including Kamloops

—711 42	Okanagan Valley

Including Kelowna, Vernon, Penticton

—711 43	Selkirk Mountains region

*Class parts of this physiographic region or feature as instructed under —4–9

—711 44	Area between Monashee and Selkirk Mountains
	Including Trail, Nelson
—711 45	Kootenay-Upper Columbia Rivers Valley
	Rocky Mountain trench region
	Class here *Columbia River in British Columbia
—712	Prairie provinces
	Class here western Canada
	Class northern territories [*formerly* —712] in —719
	Class a specific part of western Canada not provided for here with the part, e.g., British Columbia —711
—712 3	Alberta
—712 31	Northwestern region
	Area north of 55° N, and west of 114° W
	Including Peace River, Grande Prairie
	Class here Peace River District
	Class Peace River District in British Columbia in —7111
—712 32	Northeastern region
	Area north of 55° N, and east of 114° W
	Class here *Athabaska River, Wood Buffalo National Park
	Class Wood Buffalo National Park west of 114° W in —71231, in Fort Smith region in —7193
—712 33	Central region
	Area between 55° N and 51° N
	Including Edmonton, Banff, Calgary, Drumheller, Lacombe
	Class here *North and *South Saskatchewan and *Red Deer Rivers
—712 34	Southern region
	Area south of 51° N to international boundary
	Including Blairmore, Coleman, Macleod, Lethbridge, Medicine Hat

*Class parts of this physiographic region or feature as instructed under —4–9

Table 2. Areas

—712 4   Saskatchewan

—712 41   Northern region (Forest region)

                              Area north of 55° N

                              Class here *Lake Athabaska

—712 42   Central region (Park lands region)

                              Area between 55° N and 51° N

                              Including Battleford, Biggar, Prince Albert, Saskatoon

                              Class here *Saskatchewan River

—712 43   Southwestern region

                              Area south of 51° N, and west of 106° W

                              Including Maple Creek, Shaunavon, Swift Current

—712 44   Southeastern region

                              Area south of 51° N, and east of 106° W

                              Including Regina, Fort Qu'Appelle, Indian Head, Melville, Moose Jaw, Weyburn

—712 7   Manitoba

—712 71   Northern region

                              Area north of 55° N

                              Including Churchill, Port Nelson

                              Class here *Hudson Bay Lowland

—712 72   Lake region

                              Area between 55° N and 50°30′N

                              Including Flin Flon, The Pas

                              Class here *Laurentian Plateau in Manitoba

—712 73   Southwestern region

                              Area south of 50°30′N, and west of 98° W

                              Including Brandon, Portage la Prairie, Minnedosa, Morden, Virden

                              Class here *Assiniboine River

*Class parts of this physiographic region or feature as instructed under —4–9

—712 74	Southeastern region

        Area south of 50°30′N, and east of 98° W

        Including Winnipeg, Saint Boniface, Transcona

        Class here *Red River of the North in Manitoba

—713	Ontario

        Class here *Great Lakes in Canada, eastern Canada

        Class a specific part of eastern Canada not provided for here with the subject, e.g., Nova Scotia —716

SUMMARY

—713 1	**Northern Ontario**
—713 2	**Lake Huron counties**
—713 3	**Lake Erie counties**
—713 4	**West central counties**
—713 5	**Lake Ontario counties**
—713 6	**East central counties**
—713 7	**Saint Lawrence River counties**
—713 8	**Ottawa River counties**

—713 1	Northern Ontario

        Including Patricia portion of Kenora District

        Class here Laurentian Plateau in Ontario [*formerly* —7134]

—713 11	Northwestern Ontario

        Class here *Lake of the Woods in Ontario

        For Thunder Bay District, see —71312

—713 112	Kenora District

        Class Patricia portion in —7131

—713 117	Rainy River District
—713 12	Thunder Bay District

        Class here *Lake Superior in Ontario

—713 13	Northeastern Ontario

        For clay belt, see —71314; *Parry Sound District,* —71315; *District Municipality of Muskoka,* —71316

—713 132	Algoma District

        Class here *North Channel

—713 133	Sudbury District

*Class parts of this physiographic region or feature as instructed under —4–9

Table 2. Areas

—713 135	Manitoulin District
—713 14	Clay belt
—713 142	Cochrane District

> Class here *Lake Abitibi

—713 144	Timiskaming District
—713 147	Nipissing District

> Including Algonquin Provincial Park
>
> Class here *Lake Nipissing

—713 15	Parry Sound District

> Class here *Georgian Bay

—713 16	District Municipality of Muskoka
—713 17	Simcoe County
—713 18	Grey County

▶   **—713 2–713 8 Southern Ontario**

Class comprehensive works in —713

For Simcoe County, see —71317; Grey County, —71318

—713 2	Lake Huron counties

> Class here *Lake Huron in Ontario, southwestern Ontario
>
> Class a specific part of southwestern Ontario not provided for here with the subject, e.g., Essex County —71331

—713 21	Bruce County
—713 22	Huron County
—713 23	Perth County
—713 25	Middlesex County

> *For London, see —71326*

—713 26	London
—713 27	Lambton County

> Class here *Saint Clair River in Ontario

*Class parts of this physiographic region or feature as instructed under —4–9

—713 3	**Lake Erie counties**
	Class here *Lake Erie in Canada
—713 31	Essex County
	Class here *Lake Saint Clair in Ontario
	For Windsor, see —71332
—713 32	Windsor
—713 33	Kent County
—713 34	Elgin County
	For Saint Thomas, see —71335
—713 35	Saint Thomas
—713 36	Regional Municipality of Haldimand-Norfolk
	Class here former Norfolk County
	For former Haldimand County, see —71337
—713 37	Former Haldimand County
—713 38	Regional Municipality of Niagara
	Class here former Welland County
	For Niagara Falls, see —71339; former Lincoln County, —71351
—713 39	*Niagara Falls
—713 4	**West central counties**
	Class Laurentian Plateau in Ontario [*formerly* —7134] in —7131
—713 41	Dufferin County
—713 42	Wellington County
	For Guelph, see —71343
—713 43	Guelph
—713 44	Regional Municipality of Waterloo
	Class here former Waterloo County
	For Kitchener, see —71345
—713 45	Kitchener
—713 46	Oxford County

*Class parts of this physiographic region or feature as instructed under —4–9

Table 2. Areas

—713 47	Brant County
	For Brantford, see —71348
—713 48	Brantford
—713 5	**Lake Ontario counties**
	Class here *Lake Ontario in Canada
—713 51	Former Lincoln County
—713 52	Regional Municipality of Hamilton-Wentworth
	Including city of Hamilton
	Class here former Wentworth County
—713 53	Halton and Peel Regional Municipalities
—713 533	Regional Municipality of Halton
	Class here former Halton County
—713 535	Regional Municipality of Peel
	Class here former Peel County
—713 54	Toronto and York (Former York County)
—713 541	Metropolitan Toronto
	Including boroughs of York, East York, North York, Etobicoke, Scarborough; city of Toronto
—713 547	Regional Municipality of York
—713 55	Former Ontario County
—713 56	Regional Municipality of Durham
	Class here former Durham County
	For former Ontario County, see —71355
—713 57	Northumberland County
	Class here *Rice Lake
—713 58	Hastings and Prince Edward Counties
—713 585	Hastings County
—713 587	Prince Edward County

*Class parts of this physiographic region or feature as instructed under —4–9

—713 59	Lennox and Addington County
—713 6	**East central counties**
—713 61	Haliburton County
—713 64	Victoria County
—713 67	Peterborough County
	For Peterborough city, see —71368
—713 68	Peterborough city
—713 7	**Saint Lawrence River counties**

Class here *Thousand Islands in Ontario, *Saint Lawrence River in Ontario, eastern Ontario

Class a specific part of eastern Ontario not provided for here with the subject, e.g., Lanark County —71382

—713 71	Frontenac County
	For Kingston, see —71372
—713 72	Kingston
—713 73	United Counties of Leeds and Grenville

Class here former Leeds County

For former Grenville County, see —71374

—713 74	Former Grenville County
—713 75	United Counties of Stormont, Dundas and Glengarry

Class here former Dundas County

For former Stormont County, see —71376; former Glengarry County, —71377

—713 76	Former Stormont County
—713 77	Former Glengarry County
—713 8	***Ottawa River counties**
—713 81	Renfrew County
—713 82	Lanark County
—713 83	Regional Municipality of Ottawa-Carleton (Former Carleton County)
	For Ottawa, see —71384
—713 84	Ottawa

*Class parts of this physiographic region or feature as instructed under —4–9

Table 2. Areas

—713 85	United Counties of Prescott and Russell

Class here former Russell County

For former Prescott County, see —71386

—713 86	Former Prescott County
—714	Quebec

Class here *Saint Lawrence River, *Laurentian Plateau

SUMMARY

—714 1	**Northern region**
—714 2	**Western counties (Ottawa Valley counties)**
—714 3	**Southwestern counties**
—714 4	**North central counties**
—714 5	**South central counties**
—714 6	**Southern counties**
—714 7	**Southeastern counties**

—714 1	Northern region
—714 11	Mistassini Territory
—714 12	Abitibi Territory
—714 13	Abitibi County
—714 14	Lake Saint John (Lac-Saint-Jean) County

Lake Saint John East and Lake Saint John West Counties

—714 16	Chicoutimi County

Class here *Saguenay River

—714 17	Saguenay County and New Quebec (Nouveau-Québec) Territory

Including *Anticosti Island

Class here Ungava

For Labrador, see —7182

—714 2	Western counties (Ottawa Valley counties)

Class here *Ottawa River in Quebec

—714 21	Timiscaming and Pontiac Counties
—714 212	Timiscaming (Témiscamingue) County
—714 215	Pontiac County

*Class parts of this physiographic region or feature as instructed under —4–9

—714 22	Hull, Labelle, Papineau Counties
—714 221	Hull County
	Including Gatineau County
—714 225	Labelle County
—714 227	Papineau County
—714 23	Argenteuil County
—714 24	Terrebonne County
—714 25	Two Mountains (Deux-Montagnes) County
—714 26	Vaudreuil and Soulanges Counties
—714 263	Vaudreuil County
—714 265	Soulanges County
—714 27	Montreal and Jesus Islands County
	For Montreal Island, see —71428
—714 271	Laval County (Jesus Island)
—714 28	Montreal Island
	Hochelaga, Jacques Cartier Counties
—714 281	Greater Montreal
	Including Verdun, Outremont, West Mount, Mount Royal
—714 3	Southwestern counties
	Area south of Saint Lawrence River, and west of Richelieu River
	Class here *Richelieu River
—714 31	Huntingdon County
—714 32	Beauharnois County
—714 33	Châteauguay County
—714 34	Laprairie County
—714 35	Napierville County
—714 36	Verchères County
—714 37	Chambly County
—714 38	Saint Johns (Saint-Jean) County

*Class parts of this physiographic region or feature as instructed under —4–9

Table 2. Areas

—714 4	North central counties

Area north of Saint Lawrence River from Montreal to Saguenay River

Class here Montagne Tremblante Provincial Park, Laurentides Provincial Park

Class a specific part of Montagne Tremblante, of Laurentides Provincial Parks not provided for here with the subject, e.g., Laurentides Park in Chicoutimi County —71416

—714 41	Montcalm and L'Assomption Counties
—714 415	Montcalm County
—714 416	L'Assomption County
—714 42	Joliette County
—714 43	Berthier County
—714 44	Maskinongé County
—714 45	Saint Maurice County
—714 46	Champlain and Portneuf Counties
—714 465	Champlain County
—714 466	Portneuf County
—714 47	Quebec County
—714 471	Quebec city
—714 48	Montmorency Counties no. 1 and no. 2
—714 49	Charlevoix County

Charlevoix East and Charlevoix West Counties

—714 5	South central counties

Area south of Saint Lawrence River, and east of Richelieu River to Quebec

For southern border area, see —7146

—714 51	Richelieu County

—714 52	Saint Hyacinthe and Bagot Counties
—714 523	Saint Hyacinthe County
—714 525	Bagot County
—714 53	Rouville County
—714 54	Yamaska County
—714 55	Nicolet County
—714 56	Drummond and Arthabaska Counties
—714 563	Drummond County
—714 565	Arthabaska County
—714 57	Wolfe and Megantic Counties
—714 573	Wolfe County
—714 575	Megantic County
—714 58	Lotbinière County
—714 59	Levis County

—714 6   Southern counties

Southern border area east of Richelieu River

—714 61	Iberville County
—714 62	Missisquoi County
—714 63	Shefford County
—714 64	Brome County
	Class here *Lake Memphremagog
—714 65	Richmond County
—714 66	Sherbrooke County
—714 67	Stanstead County
—714 68	Compton County
—714 69	Frontenac County

*Class parts of this physiographic region or feature as instructed under —4–9

Table 2. Areas

—714 7	Southeastern counties
	Area south of Saint Lawrence River from Quebec to Gulf of Saint Lawrence
	Class here *Notre Dame Mountains
—714 71	Beauce County
—714 72	Dorchester County
—714 73	Bellechasse and Montmagny Counties
—714 733	Bellechasse County
—714 735	Montmagny County
—714 74	L'Islet County
—714 75	Kamouraska County
—714 76	Temiscouata County
	Including Rivière du Loup County
—714 77	Gaspé Peninsula
	For Bonaventure County, see —71478; Gaspé County, —71479
—714 771	Rimouski County
—714 775	Matane County
	Including Matapédia County
—714 78	Bonaventure County
—714 79	Gaspé County
	Gaspé East and Gaspé West Counties
—714 797	Magdalen (Madeleine) Islands
—715	New Brunswick
	Class here Maritime Provinces, Atlantic Provinces
	For Nova Scotia, see —716; Prince Edward Island, —717
—715 1	Northern counties
—715 11	Restigouche County
—715 12	Gloucester County

*Class parts of this physiographic region or feature as instructed under —4–9

—715 2	Eastern counties
—715 21	Northumberland County
—715 22	Kent County
—715 23	Westmorland County
—715 3	Southern counties
—715 31	Albert County
—715 32	Saint John County
—715 33	Charlotte County

Class here *Saint Croix River in New Brunswick

—715 4	Central counties
—715 41	Kings County
—715 42	Queens County
—715 43	Sunbury County
—715 5	Western counties

Class here *Saint John River

—715 51	York County

Including Fredericton

—715 52	Carleton County
—715 53	Victoria County
—715 54	Madawaska County
—716	Nova Scotia
—716 1	Northern counties
—716 11	Cumberland County
—716 12	Colchester County
—716 13	Pictou County
—716 14	Antigonish County
—716 2	Southern counties
—716 21	Guysborough County
—716 22	Halifax County
—716 23	Lunenburg County
—716 24	Queens County

*Class parts of this physiographic region or feature as instructed under —4–9

Table 2. Areas

—716 25	Shelburne County
—716 3	Bay of Fundy counties
—716 31	Yarmouth County
—716 32	Digby County
—716 33	Annapolis County
—716 34	Kings County
—716 35	Hants County
—716 9	Cape Breton Island

Class here *Bras d'Or Lake

—716 91	Inverness County

Class here Cape Breton Highlands National Park

Class Cape Breton Highlands National Park in Victoria County in —71693

—716 93	Victoria County
—716 95	Cape Breton County

For Sydney, see —71696

—716 96	Sydney
—716 98	Richmond County
—717	Prince Edward Island
—717 1	Prince County
—717 4	Queens County

For Charlottetown, see —7175

—717 5	Charlottetown
—717 7	Kings County
—718	Newfoundland and adjacent territories
—718 2	Labrador [*formerly* —719]

District of province of Newfoundland

—718 8	Saint Pierre and Miquelon

French territory

*Class parts of this physiographic region or feature as instructed under —4–9

—719	Northern territories [*formerly* —712]

Class Labrador [*formerly* —719] in —7182

—719 1	Yukon Territory
—719 2	Northwest Territories

For Fort Smith region, see —7193; Keewatin region, —7194; Baffin region, —7195; Inuvik region, —7196

—719 3	Fort Smith region

Class here former Mackenzie district

—719 4	Keewatin region
—719 5	Baffin region

Class here former Franklin district

—719 6	Inuvik region
—719 9	*Canadian Arctic
—72	**Middle America Mexico**

SUMMARY

—721	Northern states of Mexico
—722	Lower California peninsula
—723	Central Pacific states of Mexico
—724	Central states of Mexico
—725	Valley of Mexico
—726	Southern Gulf region of Mexico
—727	Southern Pacific states of Mexico
—728	Central America
—729	West Indies (Antilles) and Bermuda

▶   —721–727 Mexico

Class comprehensive works in —72

—721	Northern states of Mexico
—721 2	Tamaulipas
—721 3	Nuevo León
—721 4	Coahuila
—721 5	Durango
—721 6	Chihuahua
—721 7	Sonora

*Class parts of this physiographic region or feature as instructed under —4–9

Table 2. Areas

—722	Lower California peninsula
—722 3	Baja California state
—722 4	Baja California Sur territory
—723	Central Pacific states of Mexico
—723 2	Sinaloa
—723 4	Nayarit
—723 5	Jalisco
—723 6	Colima
—723 7	Michoacán
—724	Central states of Mexico
	For Valley of Mexico, see —725
—724 1	Guanajuato
—724 2	Aguascalientes
—724 3	Zacatecas
—724 4	San Luis Potosí
—724 5	Querétaro
—724 6	Hidalgo
—724 7	Tlaxcala
—724 8	Puebla
—724 9	Morelos
—725	Valley of Mexico
—725 2	Mexico state
—725 3	Federal District
	Including Mexico City
—726	Southern Gulf region of Mexico
—726 2	Veracruz state
—726 3	Tabasco state
—726 4	Campeche state
—726 5	Yucatán state
—726 7	Quintana Roo territory

—727	Southern Pacific states of Mexico
—727 3	Guerrero
—727 4	Oaxaca
—727 5	Chiapas
—728	Central America

SUMMARY

—728 1	Guatemala
—728 2	Belize (British Honduras)
—728 3	Honduras
—728 4	El Salvador
—728 5	Nicaragua
—728 6	Costa Rica
—728 7	Panama

—728 1	Guatemala

SUMMARY

—728 11	Central District (Guatemala department)
—728 12	Petén province and department
—728 13	Izabal province
—728 14	Oriente province
—728 15	Verapaz province
—728 16	Atitlán province
—728 17	Quiché province
—728 18	Los Altos province

—728 11	Central District (Guatemala department)
	Including Guatemala City
—728 12	Petén province and department
—728 13	Izabal province
—728 131	Izabal department
—728 132	Zacapa department
—728 14	Oriente province
—728 141	Chiquimula department
—728 142	Jalapa department
—728 143	Jutiapa department
—728 144	Santa Rosa department

Table 2. Areas

—728 15	Verapaz province
—728 151	Alta Verapaz department
—728 152	Baja Verapaz department
—728 153	El Progreso department
—728 16	Atitlán province
—728 161	Chimaltenango department
—728 162	Sacatepéquez department
—728 163	Escuintla department
—728 164	Sololá department
—728 165	Suchitepéquez department
—728 17	Quiché province
—728 171	Huehuetenango department
—728 172	Quiché department
—728 18	Los Altos province
—728 181	Totonicapán department
—728 182	Quezaltenango department
—728 183	Retalhuleu department
—728 184	San Marcos department
—728 2	Belize (British Honduras)
—728 21	Corozal district
—728 22	Belize district
—728 23	Stann Creek district
—728 24	Toledo district
—728 25	Cayo district
—728 26	Orange Walk district
—728 3	Honduras
—728 31	Northern departments
—728 311	Cortés
—728 312	Atlántida
—728 313	Colón
—728 314	Yoro
—728 315	Islas de la Bahía

—728 32	Gracias a Dios department
—728 33	Olancho department
—728 34	El Paraíso department
—728 35	Southern departments
—728 351	Choluteca
—728 352	Valle
—728 36	La Paz department
—728 37	Central departments
—728 371	Francisco Morazán
	Including Tegucigalpa
—728 372	Comayagua
—728 38	Western departments
—728 381	Intibucá
—728 382	Lempira
—728 383	Ocotepeque
—728 384	Copán
—728 385	Santa Bárbara
—728 4	El Salvador
—728 41	Western departments
—728 411	Ahuachapán
—728 412	Santa Ana
—728 413	Sonsonate
—728 42	Central departments
—728 421	Chalatenango
—728 422	La Libertad
—728 423	San Salvador
—728 424	Cuscatlán
—728 425	La Paz
—728 426	Cabañas
—728 427	San Vicente

Table 2. Areas

—728 43	Eastern departments
—728 431	Usulután
—728 432	San Miguel
—728 433	Morazán
—728 434	La Unión
—728 5	Nicaragua
—728 51	Pacific departments
—728 511	Chinandega
—728 512	León
—728 513	Managua
—728 514	Masaya
—728 515	Granada
—728 516	Carazo
—728 517	Rivas
—728 52	Central departments
—728 521	Nueva Segovia
—728 522	Jinotega
—728 523	Madriz
—728 524	Estelí
—728 525	Matagalpa
—728 526	Boaco
—728 527	Chontales
—728 53	Atlantic region
—728 531	Río San Juan department
—728 532	Zelaya department
—728 533	Cabo Gracias a Dios territory
—728 6	Costa Rica
—728 61	Limón province
—728 62	Cartago province
—728 63	San José province
—728 64	Heredia province
—728 65	Alajuela province

—728 66	Guanacaste province
—728 67	Puntarenas province
—728 7	Panama [*formerly* —862]
—728 71	Western provinces
—728 711	Chiriquí
—728 712	Bocas del Toro
—728 72	Central provinces
—728 721	Coclé
—728 722	Veraguas
—728 723	Los Santos
—728 724	Herrera
—728 73	Metropolitan provinces
	Class Panama Canal Zone in —72875
—728 731	Panamá
—728 732	Colón
—728 74	Darién province
—728 75	Panama Canal Zone [*formerly* —863]
—729	West Indies (Antilles) and Bermuda

SUMMARY

—729 1	**Cuba**
—729 2	**Jamaica and Cayman Islands**
—729 3	**Dominican Republic**
—729 4	**Haiti**
—729 5	**Puerto Rico**
—729 6	**Bahama Islands**
—729 7	**Leeward Islands**
—729 8	**Windward and other southern islands**
—729 9	**Bermuda**

▶ —729 1–729 5 Greater Antilles

Class comprehensive works in —729

—729 1	Cuba
—729 11	Pinar del Rio province

Table 2. Areas

—729 12	Havana and Isle of Pines
—729 123	Havana city
—729 124	Havana province
—729 125	Isle of Pines
—729 13	Matanzas province
—729 14	Former Las Villas province
—729 142	Villa Clara province
—729 143	Cienfuegos province
—729 145	Sancti Spiritus province
—729 15	Ciego de Avila and Camaguey provinces
—729 153	Ciego de Avila province
—729 156	Camaguey province
—729 16	Former Oriente province
—729 162	Las Tunas province
—729 163	Granma province
—729 164	Holguin province
—729 165	Santiago de Cuba province
—729 167	Guantanamo province
—729 2	**Jamaica and Cayman Islands**
—729 21	Cayman Islands
—729 3	**Dominican Republic**

Class here comprehensive works on Hispaniola

For Haiti, see —7294

SUMMARY

—729 32	**Southwestern provinces**
—729 34	**Western provinces**
—729 35	**Northwestern provinces**
—729 36	**North central provinces**
—729 37	**South central provinces**
—729 38	**Eastern provinces**

—729 32	Southwestern provinces
—729 323	Pedernales
—729 324	Barahona
—729 325	Independencia
—729 326	Baoruco
—729 34	Western provinces
—729 342	San Juan
—729 343	La Estrelleta
—729 345	Dajabón
—729 35	Northwestern provinces
—729 352	Montecristi
—729 353	Santiago Rodríguez
—729 356	Santiago
—729 357	Valverde
—729 358	Puerto Plata
—729 36	North central provinces
—729 362	Espaillat
—729 363	Salcedo
—729 364	María Trinidad Sánchez
—729 365	Samaná
—729 367	Duarte
—729 368	Sánchez Ramírez
—729 369	La Vega
—729 37	South central provinces
—729 372	Azua
—729 373	Peravia
—729 374	San Cristóbal
—729 375	Distrito Nacional
	Including Santo Domingo

Table 2. Areas

—729 38	Eastern provinces
—729 382	San Pedro de Macorís
—729 383	La Romana
—729 384	El Seibo
—729 385	La Altagracia
—729 4	Haiti
—729 42	Nord-Ouest department
—729 43	Nord department
—729 44	Artibonite department
—729 45	Ouest department

Including Port-au-Prince

—729 46	Sud department
—729 5	Puerto Rico
—729 51	San Juan district
—729 52	Bayamón district
—729 53	Arecibo district
—729 54	Aguadilla district
—729 56	Mayagüez district
—729 57	Ponce district
—729 58	Guayama district
—729 59	Humacao district

Including Vieques, Culebra islands

—729 6	Bahama Islands
—729 61	Turks and Caicos Islands

▶   —729 7–729 8 Lesser Antilles (Caribbees)

Class comprehensive works in —729

—729 7	Leeward Islands

For Dominica, see —729841

—729 72	Virgin Islands
—729 722	Virgin Islands of the United States
—729 725	British Virgin Islands

—729 73	Saint Christopher, Nevis, Anguilla

Including Sombrero island

Class here West Indies Associated States

For Antigua, see —72974; Windward West Indies Associated States, —72984

—729 74	Antigua

Including Barbuda

—729 75	Montserrat
—729 76	Guadeloupe

Overseas department of France consisting of islands of Guadeloupe, Marie Galante, Les Saintes, Désirade, Saint Barthélemy, part of Saint Martin

Class here French West Indies, comprehensive works on Saint Martin

For Martinique, see —72982; Netherlands part of Saint Martin, —72977

—729 77	Netherlands islands

Saint Eustatius, Saba, part of Saint Martin

Class comprehensive works on Netherlands Antilles in —72986

—729 8	**Windward and other southern islands**

For Nueva Esparta, Venezuela, see —8754

—729 81	Barbados
—729 82	Martinique

Overseas department of France

—729 83	Trinidad and Tobago
—729 84	Windward West Indies Associated States

Class comprehensive works on Leeward and Windward West Indies Associated States in —72973

—729 841	Dominica
—729 843	Saint Lucia
—729 844	Saint Vincent and Grenadines

For Carriacou, see —729845

—729 845	Grenada and Carriacou

Table 2. Areas

—729 86	Netherlands islands

        Curaçao, Aruba, Bonaire

        Class here Netherlands Antilles

            For Leeward Netherlands islands, see —72977

—729 9   **Bermuda**

—73   **United States**

        For specific states, see —74–79

—[734–739]   **Specific states**

        (Use of these numbers is optional; prefer —74–79)

        Add to base number —73 the numbers following —7 in —74–79, e.g., Pennsylvania —7348

▶   **—74–79 Specific states of United States**

        If preferred, class in —734–739

        Class comprehensive works in —73

        For Hawaii, see —969

—74   **Northeastern United States (New England and Middle Atlantic states)**

        Class here *Appalachian Mountains, *Connecticut River, United States east of Allegheny Mountains, United States east of Mississippi River

        For southeastern United States, see —75; south central United States, —76; north central United States, —77

SUMMARY

—741	Maine
—742	New Hampshire
—743	Vermont
—744	Massachusetts
—745	Rhode Island
—746	Connecticut
—747	New York
—748	Pennsylvania
—749	New Jersey

*Class parts of this physiographic region or feature as instructed under —4–9

►   —741–746 New England

                 Class comprehensive works in —74

—741   Maine

—741 1   Aroostook County

—741 2   Northwestern counties

                 Including Moosehead Lake

—741 22   Somerset County

                 Class here *Kennebec River

—741 25   Piscataquis County

—741 3   Penobscot County

                 Including Bangor

                 Class here *Penobscot River

—741 4   Southeastern counties

—741 42   Washington County

                 Class here *Saint Croix River

—741 45   Hancock County

                 Including Mount Desert Island

                 Class here Acadia National Park

                 Class Acadia National Park in Knox County in —74153

—741 5   South central counties

—741 52   Waldo County

—741 53   Knox County

—741 57   Lincoln County

—741 6   Kennebec County

                 Including Augusta

*Class parts of this physiographic region or feature as instructed under —4–9

Table 2. Areas

—741 7	West central counties
	Class here *Rangeley Lakes
—741 72	Franklin County
—741 75	Oxford County
—741 8	Southwest central counties
	Class here *Androscoggin River
—741 82	Androscoggin County
—741 85	Sagadahoc County
—741 9	Southwestern counties
—741 91	Cumberland County
	Including Portland
—741 95	York County
—742	New Hampshire
—742 1	Coos County
	Class here *Umbagog Lake
—742 2	*White Mountains
—742 3	Grafton County
	Class here *Squam Lake
—742 4	Counties bordering *Lake Winnipesaukee
—742 42	Carroll County
—742 45	Belknap County
—742 5	Strafford County
—742 6	Rockingham County
—742 7	West central counties
—742 72	Merrimack County
	Including Concord
	Class here *Merrimack River
—742 75	Sullivan County

*Class parts of this physiographic region or feature as instructed under —4–9

—742 8	Hillsboro County
	Including Manchester
—742 9	Cheshire County
—743	Vermont
	Class here *Green Mountains
—743 1	Northwestern counties
	Class here *Lake Champlain in Vermont
—743 12	Grand Isle County
—743 13	Franklin County
—743 17	Chittenden County
	Including Burlington
	Class here *Winooski River
—743 2	Northeastern counties
—743 23	Orleans County
—743 25	Essex County
—743 3	North central counties
—743 34	Caledonia County
—743 35	Lamoille County
	Class here *Lamoille River
—743 4	Washington County
	Including Montpelier
—743 5	Addison County
—743 6	East central counties
—743 63	Orange County
—743 65	Windsor County
	Class here *White River
—743 7	Rutland County
—743 8	Bennington County
—743 9	Windham County

*Class parts of this physiographic region or feature as instructed under —4–9

Table 2. Areas

—744	Massachusetts
—744 1	Berkshire County
	Class here *Hoosic River
—744 2	Connecticut River counties
—744 22	Franklin County
—744 23	Hampshire County
—744 26	Hampden County
—744 3	Worcester County
—744 4	Middlesex County
	Class here *Charles River
—744 5	Essex County
—744 6	Suffolk County
—744 61	Boston
—744 7	Norfolk County
—744 8	Southeastern counties
	For counties bordering Nantucket Sound, see —7449
—744 82	Plymouth County
—744 85	Bristol County
—744 9	Counties bordering Nantucket Sound
—744 92	Barnstable County (Cape Cod)
—744 94	Dukes County
	Martha's Vineyard, Elizabeth Islands
—744 97	Nantucket County (Nantucket Island)
—745	Rhode Island
—745 1	Providence County
	For Providence city, see —7452; Pawtucket, —7453
—745 2	Providence city
—745 3	Pawtucket
—745 4	Kent County
—745 5	Bristol County

*Class parts of this physiographic region or feature as instructed under —4-9

—745 6	Newport County

For Newport city, see —7457

—745 7	Newport city
—745 8	Block Island
—745 9	Washington County

For Block Island, see —7458

—746	Connecticut
—746 1	Litchfield County
—746 2	Hartford County

For Hartford city, see —7463

—746 3	Hartford city
—746 4	Northeastern counties
—746 43	Tolland County
—746 45	Windham County
—746 5	New London County
—746 6	Middlesex County
—746 7	New Haven County

For New Haven city, see —7468

—746 8	New Haven city
—746 9	Fairfield County

►   —747–749 Middle Atlantic states

Class comprehensive works in —74

—747	New York

SUMMARY

—747 1	New York City Borough of Manhattan (Manhattan Island, New York County)
—747 2	Other parts of New York metropolitan area
—747 3	Other southeastern counties
—747 4	Middle eastern counties
—747 5	Northern counties
—747 6	North central counties
—747 7	South central counties
—747 8	West central counties
—747 9	Western counties

Table 2. Areas

—747 1	New York City Borough of Manhattan (Manhattan Island, New York County)

For borough of Brooklyn, see —74723; of Queens, —747243; of Richmond, —74726; of the Bronx, —747275

—747 2	Other parts of New York metropolitan area

For Fairfield County, Connecticut, see —7469; New Jersey counties of metropolitan area, —7493

—747 21	Long Island

For specific parts of Long Island, see —74723–74725

▶   —747 23–747 25 Specific parts of Long Island

Class comprehensive works in —74721

—747 23	Borough of Brooklyn (Kings County)
—747 24	Queens and Nassau Counties
—747 243	Borough of Queens (Queens County)
—747 245	Nassau County
—747 25	Suffolk County
—747 26	Staten Island (Borough of Richmond, Richmond County)
—747 27	Mainland east of Hudson River
—747 275	Borough of the Bronx (Bronx County)
—747 277	Westchester County
—747 28	Rockland County
—747 3	Other southeastern counties

Class here *Hudson River

—747 31	Orange County
—747 32	Putnam County
—747 33	Dutchess County
—747 34	Ulster County
—747 35	Sullivan County
—747 36	Delaware County
—747 37	Greene County
—747 38	*Catskill Mountains

*Class parts of this physiographic region or feature as instructed under —4–9

—747 39	Columbia County
—747 4	Middle eastern counties
—747 41	Rensselaer County
—747 42	Albany County

For Albany city, see —74743

—747 43	Albany city
—747 44	Schenectady County
—747 45	Schoharie County
—747 46	Montgomery County
—747 47	Fulton County
—747 48	Saratoga County
—747 49	Washington County
—747 5	Northern counties
—747 51	Warren County
—747 52	Hamilton County
—747 53	Essex County

Class here *Adirondack Mountains

—747 54	Clinton County

Class here *Lake Champlain

—747 55	Franklin County
—747 56	Saint Lawrence County
—747 57	Jefferson County
—747 58	*Thousand Islands
—747 59	Lewis County
—747 6	North central counties

Class here *Mohawk River and Valley

—747 61	Herkimer County
—747 62	Oneida County

Class here *Oneida Lake

For Utica, see —74763

—747 63	Utica

*Class parts of this physiographic region or feature as instructed under —4–9

Table 2. Areas

—747 64	Madison County
—747 65	Onondaga County
	Class here *Skaneatales Lake
	For Syracuse, see —74766
—747 66	Syracuse
—747 67	Oswego County
—747 68	Cayuga County
	Class here *Cayuga Lake
—747 69	Seneca County
	Class here *Seneca Lake
—747 7	South central counties
—747 71	Tompkins County
—747 72	Cortland County
—747 73	Chenango County
	Class here *Chenango River
—747 74	Otsego County
—747 75	Broome County
	For Binghamton, see —74776
—747 76	Binghamton
—747 77	Tioga County
—747 78	Chemung County
	For Elmira, see —74779
—747 79	Elmira
—747 8	West central counties
	Class here *Finger Lakes
—747 81	Schuyler County
—747 82	Yates County
	Class here *Keuka Lake
—747 83	Steuben County
—747 84	Allegany County
—747 85	Livingston County

*Class parts of this physiographic region or feature as instructed under —4–9

—747 86	Ontario County
	Class here *Canandaigua Lake
—747 87	Wayne County
—747 88	Monroe County
	Class here *Genesee River
	For Rochester, see —74789
—747 89	Rochester
—747 9	Western counties
	Class here *Lake Ontario
—747 91	Orleans County
—747 92	Genesee County
—747 93	Wyoming County
—747 94	Cattaraugus County
—747 95	Chautauqua County
—747 96	Erie County
	For Buffalo, see —74797
—747 97	Buffalo
—747 98	Niagara County
	For Niagara Falls, see —74799
—747 99	Niagara Falls in New York
—748	Pennsylvania
	Class here *Susquehanna River

SUMMARY

—748 1	Southeastern counties
—748 2	Eastern counties
—748 3	Northeastern counties
—748 4	Southeast central counties
—748 5	Northeast central counties
—748 6	Northwest central counties
—748 7	Southwest central counties
—748 8	Southwestern counties
—748 9	Northwestern counties

*Class parts of this physiographic region or feature as instructed under —4–9

Table 2. Areas

—748 1	Southeastern counties
	Class here *Schuylkill River
—748 11	Philadelphia (Philadelphia County)
—748 12	Montgomery County
—748 13	Chester County
—748 14	Delaware County
	Class here *Brandywine Creek
—748 15	Lancaster County
—748 16	Berks County
—748 17	Schuylkill County
—748 18	Dauphin County
	Including Harrisburg
—748 19	Lebanon County
—748 2	Eastern counties
	Class here *Pocono Mountains
—748 21	Bucks County
—748 22	Northampton County
—748 23	Wayne County
	Class here *Lake Wallenpaupack
—748 24	Pike County
—748 25	Monroe County
	Class here *Delaware Water Gap
—748 26	Carbon County
—748 27	Lehigh County
—748 3	Northeastern counties
	Class here *East Branch of Susquehanna River
—748 31	Northumberland County
—748 32	Luzerne County
	For Wilkes-Barre, see —74833
—748 33	Wilkes-Barre
—748 34	Susquehanna County

*Class parts of this physiographic region or feature as instructed under —4-9

—748 35	Wyoming County
—748 36	Lackawanna County
	For Scranton, see —74837
—748 37	Scranton
—748 38	Columbia County
—748 39	Montour County
—748 4	Southeast central counties
—748 41	York County
—748 42	Adams County
—748 43	Cumberland County
—748 44	Franklin County
	Class here *Tuscarora Mountains
—748 45	Perry County
	Class here *Juniata River
—748 46	Mifflin County
—748 47	Juniata County
—748 48	Union County
—748 49	Snyder County
—748 5	Northeast central counties
	Class here *West Branch of Susquehanna River
—748 51	Lycoming County
—748 53	Centre County
—748 54	Clinton County
—748 55	Potter County
—748 56	Tioga County
—748 57	Bradford County
—748 59	Sullivan County

*Class parts of this physiographic region or feature as instructed under —4–9

Table 2. Areas

—748 6	Northwest central counties
	Class here *Allegheny River
—748 61	Clearfield County
—748 62	Jefferson County
—748 63	McKean County
—748 65	Elk County
—748 66	Cameron County
—748 67	Warren County
—748 68	Forest County
—748 69	Clarion County
—748 7	Southwest central counties
	Class here *Allegheny Mountains
—748 71	Bedford County
—748 72	Fulton County
—748 73	Huntingdon County
—748 75	Blair County
	For Altoona, see —74876
—748 76	Altoona
—748 77	Cambria County
—748 79	Somerset County
—748 8	Southwestern counties
	Class here *Chestnut Ridge, *Laurel Hill, *Monongahela River
—748 81	Westmoreland County
—748 82	Washington County
—748 83	Greene County
—748 84	Fayette County
—748 85	Allegheny County
	For Pittsburgh, see —74886
—748 86	Pittsburgh
—748 88	Armstrong County
—748 89	Indiana County

*Class parts of this physiographic region or feature as instructed under —4–9

—748 9	Northwestern counties
—748 91	Butler County
—748 92	Beaver County
—748 93	Lawrence County
—748 95	Mercer County
—748 96	Venango County
—748 97	Crawford County
—748 99	Erie County
—749	New Jersey

Class here *Delaware River

SUMMARY

—749 2	Northeastern counties
—749 3	Counties of New York metropolitan area
—749 4	East central counties
—749 6	West central counties
—749 7	Northwestern counties
—749 8	South central counties
—749 9	Southern counties

—749 2	Northeastern counties
—749 21	Bergen County

Class here *Hackensack River

—749 23	Passaic County

For Paterson, see —74924

—749 24	Paterson
—749 26	Hudson County

For Jersey City, see —74927; Hoboken, —74928

—749 27	Jersey City
—749 28	Hoboken
—749 3	Counties of New York metropolitan area

Class here *Passaic River

Class each specific metropolitan county not provided for here with the subject, e.g., Hudson County —74926

—749 31	Essex County

For Newark, see —74932; the Oranges, —74933

*Class parts of this physiographic region or feature as instructed under —4–9

Table 2. Areas

—749 32	Newark
—749 33	The Oranges
—749 36	Union County
	For Elizabeth, see —74937; Rahway, —74938
—749 37	Elizabeth
—749 38	Rahway
—749 4	East central counties
—749 41	Middlesex County
	For New Brunswick, see —74942
—749 42	New Brunswick
—749 44	Somerset County
	Class here *Raritan River
—749 46	Monmouth County
—749 48	Ocean County
—749 6	West central counties
—749 61	Burlington County
	Class here *Mullica River
—749 65	Mercer County
	For Trenton, see —74966; Princeton, —74967
—749 66	Trenton
—749 67	Princeton
—749 7	Northwestern counties
—749 71	Hunterdon County
—749 74	Morris County
	Class here *Lake Hopatcong
—749 76	Sussex County
	Class here *Kittatinny Mountains
—749 78	Warren County

*Class parts of this physiographic region or feature as instructed under —4–9

—749 8	South central counties
—749 81	Gloucester County
—749 84	Atlantic County
	For Atlantic City, see —74985
—749 85	Atlantic City
—749 87	Camden County
	For Camden city, see —74988
—749 88	Camden city
—749 9	Southern counties
—749 91	Salem County
	For Salem city, see —74992
—749 92	Salem city
—749 94	Cumberland County
	For Bridgeton, see —74995
—749 95	Bridgeton
—749 98	Cape May County

—75   **Southeastern United States (South Atlantic states)**

Class here southern states, *Piedmont, *Atlantic Coastal Plain

For south central United States, see —76

SUMMARY

—751	Delaware
—752	Maryland
—753	District of Columbia (Washington)
—754	West Virginia
—755	Virginia
—756	North Carolina
—757	South Carolina
—758	Georgia
—759	Florida

—751	Delaware
—751 1	New Castle County
	For Wilmington, see —7512
—751 2	Wilmington
—751 4	Kent County
	For Dover, see —7515

*Class parts of this physiographic region or feature as instructed under —4–9

Table 2. Areas

—751 5	Dover
—751 7	Sussex County
—752	Maryland

Class here *Potomac River

SUMMARY

—752 1	Eastern Shore
—752 2	Southern counties of Eastern Shore
—752 3	Northern counties of Eastern Shore
—752 4	Southern counties
—752 5	South central counties
—752 6	Independent city of Baltimore
—752 7	North central counties
—752 8	West central counties
—752 9	Western counties

| —752 1 | Eastern Shore |

Class here *Delmarva Peninsula, *Tidewater Maryland

For southern counties of Eastern Shore, see —7522; northern counties, —7523

| —752 2 | Southern counties of Eastern Shore |
| —752 21 | Worcester County |

Class here *Assateague Island

—752 23	Somerset County
—752 25	Wicomico County
—752 27	Dorchester County
—752 3	Northern counties of Eastern Shore
—752 31	Caroline County

Class here *Choptank River

| —752 32 | Talbot County |
| —752 34 | Queen Annes County |

Class here *Chester River

| —752 36 | Kent County |
| —752 38 | Cecil County |

*Class parts of this physiographic region or feature as instructed under —4–9

▶   —752 4–752 9 Maryland west of Chesapeake Bay

Class comprehensive works in —752

—752 4	Southern counties
—752 41	Saint Marys County
	Class here *Patuxent River
—752 44	Calvert County
—752 47	Charles County
—752 5	South central counties
—752 51	Prince Georges County
—752 55	Anne Arundel County
	For Annapolis, see —75256
—752 56	Annapolis
—752 6	Independent city of Baltimore
—752 7	North central counties
	Class here *Piedmont in Maryland
—752 71	Baltimore County
—752 74	Harford County
	Class here *Susquehanna River in Maryland
—752 77	Carroll County
—752 8	West central counties
—752 81	Howard County
—752 84	Montgomery County
—752 87	Frederick County
	For Frederick city, see —75288
—752 88	Frederick city
—752 9	Western counties
—752 91	Washington County
	For Hagerstown, see —75292
—752 92	Hagerstown

*Class parts of this physiographic region or feature as instructed under —4–9

Table 2. Areas

—752 94	Allegany County
	For Cumberland, see —75295
—752 95	Cumberland
—752 97	Garrett County
—753	District of Columbia (Washington)
—754	West Virginia

SUMMARY

—754 1	**Northern Panhandle counties**
—754 2	**Little Kanawha Valley counties**
—754 3	**Kanawha Valley counties**
—754 4	**Southwestern border counties**
—754 5	**Monongahela Valley counties**
—754 6	**Central counties**
—754 7	**New River Valley counties**
—754 8	**Allegheny Crest counties**
—754 9	**Eastern Panhandle counties**

—754 1	Northern Panhandle counties
	Class here *Ohio River in West Virginia
—754 12	Hancock County
—754 13	Brooke County
—754 14	Ohio County
	For Wheeling, see —75415
—754 15	Wheeling
—754 16	Marshall County
—754 18	Wetzel County
—754 19	Tyler County
—754 2	Little Kanawha Valley counties
	Class here *Little Kanawha River
—754 21	Pleasants County
—754 22	Wood County
	For Parkersburg, see —75423
—754 23	Parkersburg
—754 24	Ritchie County
—754 26	Wirt County
—754 27	Gilmer County

*Class parts of this physiographic region or feature as instructed under —4–9

—754 29	Calhoun County
—754 3	Kanawha Valley counties
	Class here *Kanawha River
—754 31	Jackson County
—754 33	Mason County
—754 35	Putnam County
—754 36	Roane County
—754 37	Kanawha County
	For Charleston, see —75438
—754 38	Charleston
—754 39	Boone County
—754 4	Southwestern border counties
	Class here *Guyandot, *Big Sandy Rivers, *Tug Fork
—754 42	Cabell County
—754 43	Lincoln County
—754 44	Logan County
—754 45	Wyoming County
—754 47	Wayne County
—754 48	Mingo County
—754 49	McDowell County
—754 5	Monongahela Valley counties
	Class here *Monongahela River in West Virginia
—754 52	Monongalia County
	For Morgantown, see —75453
—754 53	Morgantown
—754 54	Marion County
—754 55	Taylor County
—754 56	Doddridge County
—754 57	Harrison County
	For Clarksburg, see —75458
—754 58	Clarksburg

*Class parts of this physiographic region or feature as instructed under —4-9

Table 2. Areas

—754 59	Barbour County
—754 6	Central counties
	Class here *Elk, *Gauley Rivers
—754 61	Lewis County
—754 62	Upshur County
—754 65	Webster County
—754 66	Braxton County
—754 67	Clay County
—754 69	Nicholas County
—754 7	*New River Valley counties
—754 71	Fayette County
—754 73	Raleigh County
—754 74	Mercer County
—754 76	Summers County
—754 78	Monroe County
—754 8	Allegheny Crest counties
	Class here *Cheat River, *Greenbrier River, *Allegheny Mountains in West Virginia
—754 82	Preston County
—754 83	Tucker County
—754 85	Randolph County
—754 87	Pocahontas County
—754 88	Greenbrier County
	For White Sulphur Springs, see —75489
—754 89	White Sulphur Springs
—754 9	Eastern Panhandle counties
	Class here *Potomac Valley of West Virginia
—754 91	Pendleton County
—754 92	Grant County
—754 93	Hardy County
—754 94	Mineral County

*Class parts of this physiographic region or feature as instructed under —4-9

—754 95	Hampshire County
—754 96	Morgan County
—754 97	Berkeley County
—754 99	Jefferson County
—755	Virginia

Class here *Blue Ridge

SUMMARY

—755 1	**Eastern Peninsula and Chesapeake Bay area**
—755 2	**Northern Neck**
—755 3	**Rappahannock-York region**
—755 4	**York-James region**
—755 5	**Southeastern region**
—755 6	**South central region**
—755 7	**Southwestern region**
—755 8	**Central western region**
—755 9	**Northwestern region**

—755 1	Eastern Peninsula and Chesapeake Bay area

Class here *Tidewater Virginia

—755 15	Northampton County
—755 16	Accomack County
—755 18	*Chesapeake Bay area
—755 2	Northern Neck

Class here *Rappahannock River

—755 21	Northumberland County
—755 22	Lancaster County
—755 23	Richmond County
—755 24	Westmoreland County
—755 25	King George County
—755 26	Stafford County
—755 27	Prince William and Fauquier Counties and environs
—755 273	Prince William County, Manassas, Manassas Park
—755 273 2	Prince William County
—755 273 4	Independent city of Manassas
—755 273 6	Independent city of Manassas Park

*Class parts of this physiographic region or feature as instructed under —4–9

Table 2. Areas

—755 275	Fauquier County
—755 28	Loudoun County
—755 29	Washington metropolitan area of Virginia
—755 291	Fairfax County
—755 292	Independent city of Fairfax
—755 293	Independent city of Falls Church
—755 295	Arlington County
—755 296	Independent city of Alexandria
—755 3	**Rappahannock-York region**
	Class here *York River
—755 31	Mathews County
—755 32	Gloucester County
—755 33	Middlesex County
—755 34	Essex County
—755 35	King and Queen and King William Counties
—755 352	King and Queen County
—755 355	King William County
—755 36	Caroline and Spotsylvania Counties and environs
—755 362	Caroline County
—755 365	Spotsylvania County
—755 366	Independent city of Fredericksburg
—755 37	Orange and Greene Counties
—755 372	Orange County
—755 375	Greene County
—755 38	Madison County
—755 39	Culpeper and Rappahannock Counties
—755 392	Culpeper County
—755 395	Rappahannock County

*Class parts of this physiographic region or feature as instructed under —4–9

—755 4	York-James region
	Class here *James River
—755 41	Southern end of peninsula
—755 412	Independent city of Hampton
	Including former Elizabeth City County
—755 416	Independent city of Newport News
	Including former Warwick County
—755 42	York and James City Counties and environs
—755 423	York County
—755 425	James City County and Williamsburg
—755 425 1	James City County
—755 425 2	Independent city of Williamsburg
—755 43	New Kent County
—755 44	Charles City County
—755 45	Henrico and Goochland Counties and environs
—755 451	Independent city of Richmond
—755 453	Henrico County
—755 455	Goochland County
—755 46	Hanover and Louisa Counties
—755 462	Hanover County
—755 465	Louisa County
—755 47	Fluvanna County
—755 48	Albermarle County and environs
—755 481	Independent city of Charlottesville
—755 482	Albemarle County
—755 49	Nelson and Amherst Counties
—755 493	Nelson County
—755 496	Amherst County

*Class parts of this physiographic region or feature as instructed under —4-9

Table 2. Areas

—755 5   Southeastern region

SUMMARY

—755 51	**Independent city of Virginia Beach**
—755 52	**Independent cities of Norfolk, Portsmouth, Chesapeake**
—755 53	**Independent city of Suffolk**
—755 54	**Isle of Wight County**
—755 55	**Southampton County and environs**
—755 56	**Surry and Sussex Counties**
—755 57	**Greensville and Brunswick Counties and environs**
—755 58	**Dinwiddie and Prince George Counties and environs**
—755 59	**Chesterfield County and environs**

—755 51   Independent city of Virginia Beach

Including former Princess Anne County

—755 52   Independent cities of Norfolk, Portsmouth, Chesapeake

—755 521   Independent city of Norfolk

—755 522   Independent city of Portsmouth

—755 523   Independent city of Chesapeake

Formerly Norfolk County and independent city of South Norfolk

Class here *Dismal Swamp

—755 53   Independent city of Suffolk

Including former Nansemond County

—755 54   Isle of Wight County

—755 55   Southampton County and environs

—755 552   Southampton County

—755 553   Independent city of Franklin

—755 56   Surry and Sussex Counties

—755 562   Surry County

—755 565   Sussex County

—755 57   Greensville and Brunswick Counties and environs

—755 572   Greensville County

—755 573   Independent city of Emporia

—755 575   Brunswick County

*Class parts of this physiographic region or feature as instructed under —4–9

—755 58	Dinwiddie and Prince George Counties and environs
—755 581	Independent city of Petersburg
—755 582	Dinwiddie County
—755 585	Prince George County
—755 586	Independent city of Hopewell
—755 59	Chesterfield County and environs
—755 594	Chesterfield County
—755 595	Independent city of Colonial Heights
—755 6	South central region

Class here *Piedmont in Virginia, *Roanoke River in Virginia

SUMMARY

—755 61	**Powhatan and Cumberland Counties**
—755 62	**Buckingham and Appomattox Counties**
—755 63	**Prince Edward, Amelia, Nottoway Counties**
—755 64	**Lunenburg and Mecklenburg Counties**
—755 65	**Charlotte County**
—755 66	**Halifax and Pittsylvania Counties and environs**
—755 67	**Campbell and Bedford Counties and environs**
—755 68	**Franklin County**
—755 69	**Henry and Patrick Counties and environs**

—755 61	Powhatan and Cumberland Counties
—755 612	Powhatan County
—755 615	Cumberland County
—755 62	Buckingham and Appomattox Counties
—755 623	Buckingham County
—755 625	Appomattox County
—755 63	Prince Edward, Amelia, Nottoway Counties
—755 632	Prince Edward County
—755 634	Amelia County
—755 637	Nottoway County
—755 64	Lunenburg and Mecklenburg Counties
—755 643	Lunenburg County
—755 645	Mecklenburg County

*Class parts of this physiographic region or feature as instructed under —4–9

Table 2. Areas

—755 65	Charlotte County
—755 66	Halifax and Pittsylvania Counties and environs
—755 661	Halifax County
—755 662	Independent city of South Boston
—755 665	Pittsylvania County
—755 666	Independent city of Danville
—755 67	Campbell and Bedford Counties and environs
—755 671	Independent city of Lynchburg
—755 672	Campbell County
—755 675	Bedford County
—755 676	Independent city of Bedford
—755 68	Franklin County
—755 69	Henry and Patrick Counties and environs
—755 692	Henry County
—755 693	Independent city of Martinsville
—755 695	Patrick County
—755 7	Southwestern region

SUMMARY

—755 71	Floyd, Carroll, Grayson Counties and environs
—755 72	Smyth and Washington Counties and environs
—755 73	Scott and Lee Counties
—755 74	Wise and Dickenson Counties and environs
—755 75	Buchanan and Russell Counties
—755 76	Tazewell and Bland Counties
—755 77	Wythe and Pulaski Counties
—755 78	Giles and Montgomery Counties and environs
—755 79	Roanoke and Craig Counties and environs

—755 71	Floyd, Carroll, Grayson Counties and environs
—755 712	Floyd County
—755 714	Carroll County
—755 715	Independent city of Galax
—755 717	Grayson County

—755 72	Smyth and Washington Counties and environs
—755 723	Smyth County
—755 725	Washington County
—755 726	Independent city of Bristol
—755 73	Scott and Lee Counties
—755 732	Scott County
—755 735	Lee County
—755 74	Wise and Dickenson Counties and environs
—755 743	Wise County
—755 744	Independent city of Norton
—755 745	Dickenson County
—755 75	Buchanan and Russell Counties
—755 752	Buchanan County
—755 755	Russell County
—755 76	Tazewell and Bland Counties
—755 763	Tazewell County
—755 765	Bland County
—755 77	Wythe and Pulaski Counties
—755 773	Wythe County
—755 775	Pulaski County
—755 78	Giles and Montgomery Counties and environs
—755 782	Giles County
—755 785	Montgomery County
—755 786	Independent city of Radford
—755 79	Roanoke and Craig Counties and environs
—755 791	Independent city of Roanoke
—755 792	Roanoke County
—755 793	Independent city of Salem
—755 795	Craig County

Table 2. Areas

—755 8	**Central western region**
—755 81	Alleghany County and environs
—755 811	Independent city of Clifton Forge
—755 812	Independent city of Covington
—755 816	Alleghany County
—755 83	Botetourt County
—755 85	Rockbridge County and environs
—755 851	Independent city of Buena Vista
—755 852	Rockbridge County
—755 853	Independent city of Lexington
—755 87	Bath County
—755 89	Highland County
—755 9	**Northwestern region**

Class here *Shenandoah Valley, Shenandoah National Park

Class a specific part of Shenandoah National Park not provided for here with the subject, e.g., in Madison County —75538

—755 91	Augusta County and environs
—755 911	Independent city of Staunton
—755 912	Independent city of Waynesboro
—755 916	Augusta County
—755 92	Rockingham County and environs
—755 921	Independent city of Harrisonburg
—755 922	Rockingham County
—755 94	Page County
—755 95	Shenandoah County
—755 97	Warren County
—755 98	Clarke County

*Class parts of this physiographic region or feature as instructed under —4–9

—755 99	Frederick County and environs
—755 991	Independent city of Winchester
—755 992	Frederick County
—756	North Carolina

SUMMARY

—756 1	Northeast Coastal Plain counties
—756 2	Southeast Coastal Plain counties
—756 3	Southwest Coastal Plain counties
—756 4	Northwest Coastal Plain counties
—756 5	Northeast Piedmont counties
—756 6	Northwest Piedmont counties
—756 7	Southern Piedmont counties
—756 8	Northern Appalachian region counties
—756 9	Southern Appalachian region counties

—756 1	Northeast Coastal Plain counties

Class here *Roanoke River, *Chowan River, *Coastal Plain in North Carolina

—756 13	Currituck and Camden Counties
—756 132	Currituck County
—756 135	Camden County

Class here *Dismal Swamp in North Carolina

—756 14	Pasquotank, Perquimans, Chowan Counties
—756 142	Pasquotank County
—756 144	Perquimans County
—756 147	Chowan County
—756 15	Gates and Hertford Counties
—756 153	Gates County
—756 155	Hertford County
—756 16	Bertie and Washington Counties
—756 163	Bertie County
—756 165	Washington County

*Class parts of this physiographic region or feature as instructed under —4-9

Table 2. Areas

—756 17	Tyrrell and Dare Counties
—756 172	Tyrrell County
—756 175	Dare County
—756 18	Hyde and Beaufort Counties
—756 184	Hyde County
—756 186	Beaufort County
—756 19	Craven, Pamlico, Carteret Counties
	Class here *Neuse River
—756 192	Craven County
—756 194	Pamlico County
—756 197	Carteret County
—756 2	Southeast Coastal Plain counties
	Class here *Cape Fear River
—756 21	Jones County
—756 23	Onslow County
—756 25	Pender County
—756 27	New Hanover County
—756 29	Brunswick County
—756 3	Southwest Coastal Plain counties
—756 31	Columbus County
—756 32	Bladen County
—756 33	Robeson and Scotland Counties
—756 332	Robeson County
—756 335	Scotland County
—756 34	Richmond County
—756 35	Moore and Lee Counties
—756 352	Moore County
—756 355	Lee County

*Class parts of this physiographic region or feature as instructed under —4–9

—756 36	Harnett and Hoke Counties
—756 362	Harnett County
—756 365	Hoke County
—756 37	Cumberland and Sampson Counties
—756 373	Cumberland County
—756 375	Sampson County
—756 38	Duplin and Lenoir Counties
—756 382	Duplin County
—756 385	Lenoir County
	For Kinston, see —756386
—756 386	Kinston
—756 39	Greene and Wayne Counties
—756 393	Greene County
—756 395	Wayne County
	For Goldsboro, see —756396
—756 396	Goldsboro
—756 4	Northwest Coastal Plain counties
—756 41	Johnston County
—756 43	Wilson County
—756 44	Pitt County
—756 45	Martin County
—756 46	Edgecombe County
—756 47	Nash County
—756 48	Halifax County
—756 49	Northampton County
—756 5	Northeast Piedmont counties
	Class here *Piedmont in North Carolina
—756 52	Warren County

*Class parts of this physiographic region or feature as instructed under —4-9

Table 2. Areas

—756 53	Vance and Granville Counties
—756 532	Vance County
—756 535	Granville County
—756 54	Franklin County
—756 55	Wake County
	Including Raleigh
—756 56	Durham and Orange Counties
—756 563	Durham County
—756 565	Orange County
—756 57	Person and Caswell Counties
—756 573	Person County
—756 575	Caswell County
—756 58	Alamance County
—756 59	Chatham County
—756 6	**Northwest Piedmont counties**
—756 61	Randolph County
—756 62	Guilford County
—756 63	Rockingham County
—756 64	Stokes County
—756 65	Surry County
—756 66	Yadkin County
—756 67	Forsyth County
—756 68	Davidson County
	Class here *Yadkin River
—756 69	Davie County
—756 7	**Southern Piedmont counties**
—756 71	Rowan County
—756 72	Cabarrus County
—756 73	Stanly County
—756 74	Montgomery County

*Class parts of this physiographic region or feature as instructed under —4–9

—756 75	Anson and Union Counties
—756 753	Anson County
—756 755	Union County
—756 76	Mecklenburg County
	Including Charlotte
—756 77	Gaston and Cleveland Counties
—756 773	Gaston County
—756 775	Cleveland County
—756 78	Lincoln and Catawba Counties
—756 782	Lincoln County
—756 785	Catawba County
—756 79	Iredell and Alexander Counties
—756 793	Iredell County
—756 795	Alexander County
—756 8	Northern Appalachian region counties
	Class here *Blue Ridge in North Carolina, *Appalachian region in North Carolina
—756 82	Wilkes County
—756 83	Alleghany and Ashe Counties
—756 832	Alleghany County
—756 835	Ashe County
—756 84	Watauga and Caldwell Counties
—756 843	Watauga County
—756 845	Caldwell County
—756 85	Burke County
—756 86	Avery and Mitchell Counties
—756 862	Avery County
—756 865	Mitchell County

*Class parts of this physiographic region or feature as instructed under —4–9

Table 2. Areas

—756 87	Yancey and Madison Counties
—756 873	Yancey County
—756 875	Madison County
—756 88	Buncombe County
	Including Asheville
—756 89	McDowell County
—756 9	Southern Appalachian region counties
—756 91	Rutherford and Polk Counties
—756 913	Rutherford County
—756 915	Polk County
—756 92	Henderson County
—756 93	Transylvania County
—756 94	Haywood County
—756 95	Jackson County
—756 96	Swain County
	Class here *Great Smoky Mountains in North Carolina
—756 97	Graham County
—756 98	Macon and Clay Counties
—756 982	Macon County
—756 985	Clay County
—756 99	Cherokee County
—757	South Carolina

SUMMARY

—757 2	Mountain counties
—757 3	Southwest Piedmont counties
—757 4	Northeast Piedmont counties
—757 6	Northeast counties of sand hills and upper pine belt
—757 7	Southwest counties of sand hills and upper pine belt
—757 8	Northeast counties of lower pine belt
—757 9	Southwest counties of lower pine belt

*Class parts of this physiographic region or feature as instructed under —4–9

—757 2	Mountain counties
	Class here *Blue Ridge in South Carolina, *Saluda River
—757 21	Oconee County
—757 23	Pickens County
—757 25	Anderson County
—757 27	Greenville County
—757 29	Spartanburg County
—757 3	Southwest Piedmont counties
	Class here *Piedmont in South Carolina
—757 31	Laurens County
	Class here *Enoree River
—757 33	Greenwood County
—757 35	Abbeville County
—757 36	McCormick County
—757 37	Edgefield County
—757 38	Saluda County
—757 39	Newberry County
—757 4	Northeast Piedmont counties
—757 41	Union County
	Class here *Broad River
—757 42	Cherokee County
—757 43	York County
—757 45	Lancaster County
	Class here *Catawba River
—757 47	Chester County
—757 49	Fairfield County

*Class parts of this physiographic region or feature as instructed under —4–9

Table 2. Areas

—757 6	Northeast counties of sand hills and upper pine belt
	Class here *Pee Dee, *Lynches Rivers, *Coastal Plain in South Carolina
—757 61	Kershaw County
—757 63	Chesterfield County
—757 64	Marlboro County
—757 66	Darlington County
—757 67	Lee County
—757 69	Sumter County
	Class here *Wateree River
—757 7	Southwest counties of sand hills and upper pine belt
—757 71	Richland County
	Including Columbia
—757 72	Calhoun County
—757 73	Lexington County
—757 75	Aiken County
—757 76	Barnwell County
—757 77	Allendale County
—757 78	Bamberg County
—757 79	Orangeburg County
—757 8	Northeast counties of lower pine belt
	Class here *Santee River
—757 81	Clarendon County
	Class here *Lake Marion
—757 83	Williamsburg County
	Class here *Black River
—757 84	Florence County
—757 85	Dillon County
—757 86	Marion County
—757 87	Horry County

*Class parts of this physiographic region or feature as instructed under —4–9

—757 89	Georgetown County
—757 9	Southwest counties of lower pine belt
—757 91	Charleston County
—757 915	Charleston city
—757 93	Berkeley County
—757 94	Dorchester County
—757 95	Colleton County
—757 97	Hampton County
—757 98	Jasper County
—757 99	Beaufort County

Class here *Sea Islands

—758   Georgia

Class here *Chattahoochee River

SUMMARY

—758 1	Northeastern counties
—758 2	North central counties
—758 3	Northwestern counties
—758 4	West central counties
—758 5	Central counties
—758 6	East central counties
—758 7	Southeastern counties
—758 8	South central counties
—758 9	Southwestern counties

—758 1   Northeastern counties

Class here *Savannah River

—758 12	Rabun and Habersham Counties
—758 123	Rabun County
—758 125	Habersham County
—758 13	Stephens and Franklin Counties
—758 132	Stephens County
—758 135	Franklin County

*Class parts of this physiographic region or feature as instructed under —4–9

Table 2. Areas

—758 14	Banks and Jackson Counties
—758 143	Banks County
—758 145	Jackson County
—758 15	Madison and Hart Counties
—758 152	Madison County
—758 155	Hart County
—758 16	Elbert and Lincoln Counties
—758 163	Elbert County
—758 165	Lincoln County
—758 17	Wilkes and Oglethorpe Counties
—758 172	Wilkes County
—758 175	Oglethorpe County
—758 18	Clarke County
—758 19	Oconee and Barrow Counties
—758 193	Oconee County
—758 195	Barrow County
—758 2	North central counties

SUMMARY

—758 21	Walton and Rockdale Counties
—758 22	Gwinnett and De Kalb Counties
—758 23	Fulton County
—758 24	Douglas and Cobb Counties
—758 25	Cherokee and Pickens Counties
—758 26	Dawson and Forsyth Counties
—758 27	Hall, Lumpkin, White Counties
—758 28	Towns and Union Counties
—758 29	Fannin and Gilmer Counties

—758 21	Walton and Rockdale Counties
—758 212	Walton County
—758 215	Rockdale County
—758 22	Gwinnett and De Kalb Counties
—758 223	Gwinnett County
—758 225	De Kalb County

—758 23	Fulton County
	Including former Campbell County, Milton County
—758 231	Atlanta
—758 24	Douglas and Cobb Counties
—758 243	Douglas County
—758 245	Cobb County
—758 25	Cherokee and Pickens Counties
—758 253	Cherokee County
—758 255	Pickens County
—758 26	Dawson and Forsyth Counties
—758 263	Dawson County
—758 265	Forsyth County
—758 27	Hall, Lumpkin, White Counties
—758 272	Hall County
—758 273	Lumpkin County
	Class here *Blue Ridge in Georgia
—758 277	White County
—758 28	Towns and Union Counties
—758 282	Towns County
—758 285	Union County
—758 29	Fannin and Gilmer Counties
—758 293	Fannin County
—758 295	Gilmer County
—758 3	Northwestern counties
—758 31	Murray County
—758 32	Whitfield and Catoosa Counties
—758 324	Whitfield County
—758 326	Catoosa County

*Class parts of this physiographic region or feature as instructed under —4–9

Table 2. Areas

—758 33	Walker County
—758 34	Dade and Chattooga Counties
—758 342	Dade County

Class here *Lookout Mountain in Georgia

—758 344	Chattooga County
—758 35	Floyd County
—758 36	Gordon and Bartow Counties
—758 362	Gordon County
—758 365	Bartow County
—758 37	Paulding and Polk Counties
—758 373	Paulding County
—758 375	Polk County
—758 38	Haralson County
—758 39	Carroll County
—758 4	West central counties

Class here *Piedmont in Georgia

SUMMARY

—758 42	Heard, Coweta, Fayette Counties
—758 43	Clayton and Henry Counties
—758 44	Spalding and Lamar Counties
—758 45	Pike and Meriwether Counties
—758 46	Troup and Harris Counties
—758 47	Muscogee and Chattahoochee Counties
—758 48	Marion, Talbot, Upson Counties
—758 49	Taylor and Schley Counties

—758 42	Heard, Coweta, Fayette Counties
—758 422	Heard County
—758 423	Coweta County
—758 426	Fayette County
—758 43	Clayton and Henry Counties
—758 432	Clayton County
—758 435	Henry County

*Class parts of this physiographic region or feature as instructed under —4–9

—758 44	Spalding and Lamar Counties
—758 443	Spalding County
—758 446	Lamar County
—758 45	Pike and Meriwether Counties
—758 453	Pike County
—758 455	Meriwether County
—758 46	Troup and Harris Counties
—758 463	Troup County
—758 466	Harris County
—758 47	Muscogee and Chattahoochee Counties
—758 473	Muscogee County
—758 476	Chattahoochee County
—758 48	Marion, Talbot, Upson Counties
—758 482	Marion County
—758 483	Talbot County
—758 486	Upson County
—758 49	Taylor and Schley Counties
—758 493	Taylor County
—758 495	Schley County
—758 5	Central counties

Class here *Ocmulgee River

SUMMARY

—758 51	**Macon and Houston Counties**
—758 52	**Pulaski and Bleckley Counties**
—758 53	**Dodge and Laurens Counties**
—758 54	**Wilkinson and Twiggs Counties**
—758 55	**Bibb and Peach Counties**
—758 56	**Crawford, Monroe, Jones Counties**
—758 57	**Baldwin and Putnam Counties**
—758 58	**Jasper and Butts Counties**
—758 59	**Newton and Morgan Counties**

*Class parts of this physiographic region or feature as instructed under —4–9

Table 2. Areas

—758 51	Macon and Houston Counties
—758 513	Macon County
—758 515	Houston County
—758 52	Pulaski and Bleckley Counties
—758 523	Pulaski County
—758 525	Bleckley County
—758 53	Dodge and Laurens Counties
—758 532	Dodge County
—758 535	Laurens County
—758 54	Wilkinson and Twiggs Counties
—758 543	Wilkinson County
—758 545	Twiggs County
—758 55	Bibb and Peach Counties
—758 552	Bibb County
—758 556	Peach County
—758 56	Crawford, Monroe, Jones Counties
—758 562	Crawford County
—758 563	Monroe County
—758 567	Jones County
—758 57	Baldwin and Putnam Counties
—758 573	Baldwin County
—758 576	Putnam County
—758 58	Jasper and Butts Counties
—758 583	Jasper County
—758 585	Butts County
—758 59	Newton and Morgan Counties
—758 593	Newton County
—758 595	Morgan County

—758 6	East central counties
	Class here *Oconee River
—758 61	Greene and Taliaferro Counties
—758 612	Greene County
—758 616	Taliaferro County
—758 62	Hancock and Warren Counties
—758 623	Hancock County
—758 625	Warren County
—758 63	McDuffie and Columbia Counties
—758 632	McDuffie County
—758 635	Columbia County
—758 64	Richmond County
—758 65	Burke County
—758 66	Jefferson and Glascock Counties
	Class here *Ogeechee River
—758 663	Jefferson County
—758 666	Glascock County
—758 67	Washington and Johnson Counties
—758 672	Washington County
—758 676	Johnson County
—758 68	Treutlen and Emanuel Counties
—758 682	Treutlen County
—758 684	Emanuel County
—758 69	Jenkins and Screven Counties
—758 693	Jenkins County
—758 695	Screven County

*Class parts of this physiographic region or feature as instructed under —4–9

Table 2. Areas

—758 7	Southeastern counties

Class here *Sea Islands of Georgia

SUMMARY

—758 72	**Effingham and Chatham Counties**
—758 73	**Bryan, Liberty, McIntosh Counties**
—758 74	**Glynn and Camden Counties**
—758 75	**Charlton, Brantley, Wayne Counties**
—758 76	**Long, Evans, Bulloch Counties**
—758 77	**Candler and Tattnall Counties**
—758 78	**Toombs, Appling, Bacon Counties**
—758 79	**Pierce and Ware Counties**

—758 72	Effingham and Chatham Counties
—758 722	Effingham County
—758 724	Chatham County

Including Savannah

—758 73	Bryan, Liberty, McIntosh Counties
—758 732	Bryan County
—758 733	Liberty County
—758 737	McIntosh County
—758 74	Glynn and Camden Counties
—758 742	Glynn County
—758 746	Camden County
—758 75	Charlton, Brantley, Wayne Counties

Class here *Okefenokee Swamp

—758 752	Charlton County
—758 753	Brantley County
—758 756	Wayne County

Class here *Altamaha River

—758 76	Long, Evans, Bulloch Counties
—758 762	Long County
—758 763	Evans County
—758 766	Bulloch County

*Class parts of this physiographic region or feature as instructed under —4–9

—758 77	Candler and Tattnall Counties
—758 773	Candler County
—758 775	Tattnall County
—758 78	Toombs, Appling, Bacon Counties
—758 782	Toombs County
—758 784	Appling County
—758 787	Bacon County
—758 79	Pierce and Ware Counties
—758 792	Pierce County
—758 794	Ware County
	For Waycross, see —758795
—758 795	Waycross
—758 8	South central counties

SUMMARY

—758 81	**Clinch, Echols, Lanier Counties**
—758 82	**Atkinson, Coffee, Jeff Davis Counties**
—758 83	**Montgomery and Wheeler Counties**
—758 84	**Telfair and Wilcox Counties**
—758 85	**Ben Hill and Irwin Counties**
—758 86	**Berrien and Lowndes Counties**
—758 87	**Brooks and Cook Counties**
—758 88	**Tift and Turner Counties**
—758 89	**Crisp and Dooly Counties**

—758 81	Clinch, Echols, Lanier Counties
—758 812	Clinch County
—758 814	Echols County
—758 817	Lanier County
—758 82	Atkinson, Coffee, Jeff Davis Counties
—758 822	Atkinson County
—758 823	Coffee County
—758 827	Jeff Davis County
—758 83	Montgomery and Wheeler Counties
—758 832	Montgomery County
—758 835	Wheeler County

Table 2. Areas

—758 84	Telfair and Wilcox Counties
—758 843	Telfair County
—758 845	Wilcox County
—758 85	Ben Hill and Irwin Counties
—758 852	Ben Hill County
—758 855	Irwin County
—758 86	Berrien and Lowndes Counties
—758 862	Berrien County
—758 864	Lowndes County

For Valdosta, see —758865

—758 865	Valdosta
—758 87	Brooks and Cook Counties
—758 874	Brooks County
—758 876	Cook County
—758 88	Tift and Turner Counties
—758 882	Tift County
—758 885	Turner County
—758 89	Crisp and Dooly Counties
—758 893	Crisp County
—758 895	Dooly County
—758 9	Southwestern counties

Class here *Flint River

SUMMARY

—758 91	Sumter and Webster Counties
—758 92	Stewart, Quitman, Clay Counties
—758 93	Randolph and Terrell Counties
—758 94	Lee and Worth Counties
—758 95	Dougherty and Calhoun Counties
—758 96	Early, Miller, Baker Counties
—758 97	Mitchell and Colquitt Counties
—758 98	Thomas and Grady Counties
—758 99	Decatur and Seminole Counties

*Class parts of this physiographic region or feature as instructed under —4–9

—758 91	Sumter and Webster Counties
—758 913	Sumter County
—758 916	Webster County
—758 92	Stewart, Quitman, Clay Counties
—758 922	Stewart County
—758 924	Quitman County
—758 927	Clay County
—758 93	Randolph and Terrell Counties
—758 932	Randolph County
—758 935	Terrell County
—758 94	Lee and Worth Counties
—758 943	Lee County
—758 945	Worth County
—758 95	Dougherty and Calhoun Counties
—758 953	Dougherty County
—758 956	Calhoun County
—758 96	Early, Miller, Baker Counties
—758 962	Early County
—758 964	Miller County
—758 967	Baker County
—758 97	Mitchell and Colquitt Counties
—758 973	Mitchell County
—758 975	Colquitt County
—758 98	Thomas and Grady Counties
—758 984	Thomas County
—758 986	Grady County
—758 99	Decatur and Seminole Counties
—758 993	Decatur County
—758 996	Seminole County

Table 2. Areas

—759   Florida

SUMMARY

—759 1	Northeastern counties
—759 2	East central counties
—759 3	Southeastern counties
—759 4	Southwestern counties
—759 5	South central counties
—759 6	Southern west central counties
—759 7	Northern west central counties
—759 8	North central counties
—759 9	Northwestern counties (Panhandle)

—759 1	Northeastern counties
—759 11	Nassau County
	Class here *Saint Marys River
—759 12	Duval County
—759 121	Jacksonville
—759 13	Baker County
—759 14	Union County
—759 15	Bradford County
—759 16	Clay County
—759 17	Putnam County
—759 18	Saint Johns County
—759 19	Flagler County
—759 2	East central counties
—759 21	Volusia County
—759 22	Lake County
—759 23	Seminole County
—759 24	Orange County
—759 25	Osceola County
—759 27	Brevard County
—759 28	Indian River County
—759 29	Saint Lucie County

*Class parts of this physiographic region or feature as instructed under —4–9

—759 3	Southeastern counties
—759 31	Martin County
—759 32	Palm Beach County
—759 35	Broward County
—759 38	Dade County
—759 381	Miami and Miami Beach
—759 39	*The Everglades and *Lake Okeechobee
—759 4	Southwestern counties
—759 41	Monroe County
	Class here *Florida Keys
—759 44	Collier County
	Class here *Ten Thousand Islands, *Big Cypress Swamp
—759 46	Hendry County
	Class here *Okaloacoochee Slough
—759 48	Lee County
	Class here *Caloosahatchee River
—759 49	Charlotte County
—759 5	South central counties
—759 51	Glades County
—759 53	Okeechobee County
	Class here *Kissimmee River
—759 55	Highlands County
—759 57	Hardee County
	Class here *Peace River
—759 59	De Soto County
—759 6	Southern west central counties
—759 61	Sarasota County
—759 62	Manatee County
—759 63	Pinellas County
—759 65	Hillsborough County
—759 67	Polk County

*Class parts of this physiographic region or feature as instructed under —4–9

Table 2. Areas

—759 69	Pasco County
—759 7	**Northern west central counties**
—759 71	Hernando County
—759 72	Citrus County
	Class here *Withlacoochee River
—759 73	Sumter County
—759 75	Marion County
—759 77	Levy County
—759 78	Gilchrist County
—759 79	Alachua County
	Class here *Santa Fe River
—759 8	**North central counties**
	Class here *Suwannee River
—759 81	Dixie and Lafayette Counties
—759 812	Dixie County
—759 816	Lafayette County
—759 82	Suwannee County
—759 83	Columbia County
—759 84	Hamilton County
—759 85	Madison County
—759 86	Taylor County
—759 87	Jefferson County
—759 88	Leon County
	Including Tallahassee
—759 89	Wakulla County
—759 9	**Northwestern counties (Panhandle)**
—759 91	Franklin County

*Class parts of this physiographic region or feature as instructed under —4–9

—759 92	Liberty and Gadsden Counties
	Class here *Apalachicola River
—759 923	Liberty County
—759 925	Gadsden County
—759 93	Jackson County
—759 94	Calhoun and Gulf Counties
—759 943	Calhoun County
—759 947	Gulf County
—759 95	Bay County
—759 96	Washington and Holmes Counties
—759 963	Washington County
—759 965	Holmes County
—759 97	Walton County
—759 98	Okaloosa and Santa Rosa Counties
—759 982	Okaloosa County
—759 985	Santa Rosa County
—759 99	Escambia County
—76	**South central United States Gulf Coast states**

SUMMARY

—761	**Alabama**
—762	**Mississippi**
—763	**Louisiana**
—764	**Texas**
—766	**Oklahoma**
—767	**Arkansas**
—768	**Tennessee**
—769	**Kentucky**

▶   **—761–764 Gulf Coast states**

Class comprehensive works in —76

For Florida, see —759

—761	**Alabama**

*Class parts of this physiographic region or feature as instructed under —4–9

Table 2. Areas

SUMMARY

—761 2   Gulf and Lower Coastal Plain counties

Class here *Tombigbee River, *Alabama River

—761 21   Baldwin County

Class here *Perdido River

—761 22   Mobile County

Including Mobile city

Class here *Mobile River

—761 23   Lime Hills counties

Class specific counties in —76124–76127

—761 24   Washington and Clarke Counties

—761 243   Washington County

—761 245   Clarke County

—761 25   Monroe County

—761 26   Conecuh and Escambia Counties

—761 263   Conecuh County

—761 265   Escambia County

—761 27   Covington County

—761 29   Lime sink counties (Wire-grass region)

—761 292   Geneva County

—761 295   Houston County

—761 3   Southern red hills counties

—761 31   Henry County

—761 32   Barbour County

—761 33   Dale County

—761 34   Coffee County

*Class parts of this physiographic region or feature as instructed under —4–9

—761 35	Pike County
—761 36	Crenshaw County
—761 37	Butler County
—761 38	Wilcox County
—761 39	Marengo and Choctaw Counties
—761 392	Marengo County
—761 395	Choctaw County
—761 4	Black Belt counties
—761 41	Sumter County
—761 42	Greene County
—761 43	Hale County
—761 44	Perry County
—761 45	Dallas County
—761 46	Autauga and Lowndes Counties
—761 463	Autauga County
—761 465	Lowndes County
—761 47	Montgomery County
	Including Montgomery city
—761 48	Bullock and Russell Counties
—761 483	Bullock County
—761 485	Russell County
—761 49	Macon County
—761 5	Piedmont counties
—761 52	Elmore County
—761 53	Tallapoosa County
	Class here *Tallapoosa River, *Martin Lake
—761 55	Lee County
—761 56	Chambers County
—761 57	Randolph County
—761 58	Clay County
—761 59	Coosa County

*Class parts of this physiographic region or feature as instructed under —4-9

Table 2. Areas

—761 6	Coosa Valley region counties
	Class here *Lookout Mountain in Alabama, *Raccoon Mountains, *Coosa River
—761 61	Talladega County
—761 63	Calhoun County
—761 64	Cleburne County
—761 65	Cherokee County
—761 66	De Kalb County
—761 67	Etowah County
—761 69	Saint Clair County
—761 7	Central Plateau and Basin counties
—761 72	Blount County
—761 73	Cullman County
—761 74	Winston County
—761 76	Walker County
—761 78	Jefferson County
—761 781	Birmingham
—761 79	Shelby County
—761 8	Central pine belt counties
—761 81	Chilton County
—761 82	Bibb County
—761 84	Tuscaloosa County
—761 85	Pickens County
—761 86	Lamar County
—761 87	Fayette County
—761 89	Marion County
—761 9	Tennessee Valley counties
	Class here *Tennessee River in Alabama
—761 91	Franklin and Colbert Counties
—761 913	Franklin County
—761 915	Colbert County

*Class parts of this physiographic region or feature as instructed under —4–9

235

—761 92	Lawrence County
—761 93	Morgan County
—761 94	Marshall County .
	Class here *Guntersville Reservoir
—761 95	Jackson County
—761 97	Madison County
—761 98	Limestone County
	Class here *Wheeler Lake
—761 99	Lauderdale County
	Class here *Lake Wilson
—762	Mississippi

SUMMARY

—762 1	Southeastern counties
—762 2	Southwestern counties
—762 4	West central counties (Yazoo-Mississippi Delta)
—762 5	South central counties (Piney woods region)
—762 6	Central and east central counties (Plateau region)
—762 8	Northwestern counties (Northern Plateau region)
—762 9	Northeastern counties

—762 1	Southeastern counties
—762 12	Jackson County
	Class here *Pascagoula River
—762 13	Harrison County
—762 14	Hancock County
—762 15	Pearl River County
—762 16	Stone and George Counties
—762 162	Stone County
—762 165	George County
—762 17	Greene and Perry Counties
—762 173	Greene County
—762 175	Perry County

*Class parts of this physiographic region or feature as instructed under —4-9

Table 2. Areas

—762 18	Forrest County
—762 19	Lamar County
—762 2	**Southwestern counties**
—762 21	Marion County
—762 22	Walthall County
—762 23	Pike County
—762 24	Amite County
—762 25	Wilkinson County
—762 26	Adams County
—762 27	Franklin County
—762 28	Jefferson and Claiborne Counties
—762 283	Jefferson County
—762 285	Claiborne County
—762 29	Warren County
—762 4	**West central counties (Yazoo-Mississippi Delta)**
	Class here *Big Black, *Yazoo Rivers
—762 41	Issaquena and Sharkey Counties
—762 412	Issaquena County
—762 414	Sharkey County
—762 42	Washington County
—762 43	Bolivar County
—762 44	Coahoma County
—762 45	Quitman and Tallahatchie Counties
—762 453	Quitman County
—762 455	Tallahatchie County
—762 46	Leflore County
—762 47	Sunflower County
—762 48	Humphreys County
—762 49	Yazoo County

*Class parts of this physiographic region or feature as instructed under —4–9

—762 5	**South central counties (Piney woods region)**
	Class here *Pearl River, *Jackson Prairie
—762 51	Hinds County
	Including Jackson
—762 52	Copiah County
—762 53	Lincoln and Lawrence Counties
—762 534	Lincoln County
—762 536	Lawrence County
—762 54	Jefferson Davis and Covington Counties
—762 543	Jefferson Davis County
—762 545	Covington County
—762 55	Jones County
—762 57	Wayne and Jasper Counties
—762 573	Wayne County
—762 575	Jasper County
—762 58	Smith and Simpson Counties
—762 582	Smith County
—762 585	Simpson County
—762 59	Rankin County
—762 6	**Central and east central counties (Plateau region)**
	For Northern Plateau region, see —7628
—762 62	Madison and Holmes Counties
—762 623	Madison County
—762 625	Holmes County
—762 63	Carroll and Grenada Counties
—762 633	Carroll County
—762 635	Grenada County

*Class parts of this physiographic region or feature as instructed under —4–9

Table 2. Areas

—762 64	Montgomery and Attala Counties
—762 642	Montgomery County
—762 644	Attala County
—762 65	Leake and Scott Counties
—762 653	Leake County
—762 655	Scott County
—762 67	Newton, Clarke, Lauderdale Counties
—762 672	Newton County
—762 673	Clarke County
—762 676	Lauderdale County
	For Meridian, see —762677
—762 677	Meridian
—762 68	Kemper and Neshoba Counties
—762 683	Kemper County
—762 685	Neshoba County
—762 69	Winston, Choctaw, Webster Counties
—762 692	Winston County
—762 694	Choctaw County
—762 697	Webster County
—762 8	**Northwestern counties (Northern Plateau region)**
—762 81	Calhoun County
—762 82	Yalobusha County
—762 83	Lafayette County
	Class here *Sardis Reservoir
—762 84	Panola County
—762 85	Tate County
	Class here *Arkabutla Reservoir
—762 86	Tunica County
—762 87	De Soto County
—762 88	Marshall County
—762 89	Benton County

*Class parts of this physiographic region or feature as instructed under —4–9

—762 9	Northeastern counties
—762 92	Tippah and Union Counties
—762 923	Tippah County
—762 925	Union County
—762 93	Pontotoc and Lee Counties
—762 932	Pontotoc County
—762 935	Lee County
—762 94	Chickasaw and Clay Counties
—762 942	Chickasaw County
—762 945	Clay County
—762 95	Oktibbeha and Noxubee Counties
—762 953	Oktibbeha County
—762 955	Noxubee County
—762 97	Lowndes and Monroe Counties
—762 973	Lowndes County
—762 975	Monroe County
—762 98	Itawamba and Prentiss Counties
—762 982	Itawamba County
—762 985	Prentiss County
—762 99	Alcorn and Tishomingo Counties
—762 993	Alcorn County
—762 995	Tishomingo County
—763	Louisiana

SUMMARY

—763 1	Eastern parishes
—763 3	Southeastern parishes (Mississippi Delta)
—763 4	South central parishes
—763 5	Southwestern parishes
—763 6	West central parishes
—763 7	East central parishes
—763 8	Northeastern parishes
—763 9	Northwestern parishes

Table 2. Areas

—763 1	Eastern parishes
—763 11	Washington Parish
—763 12	Saint Tammany Parish
—763 13	Tangipahoa Parish
—763 14	Livingston Parish
—763 15	Saint Helena Parish
—763 16	East Feliciana Parish
—763 17	West Feliciana Parish
—763 18	East Baton Rouge Parish
	Including Baton Rouge city
—763 19	Ascension Parish
—763 3	Southeastern parishes (Mississippi Delta)
—763 31	Saint James Parish
—763 32	Saint John the Baptist Parish
	Class here *Lake Maurepas, *Lake Des Allemands
—763 33	Saint Charles Parish
	Class here *Lake Salvador
—763 34	*Lake Pontchartrain
—763 35	New Orleans (Orleans Parish)
—763 36	Saint Bernard Parish
—763 37	Plaquemines Parish
—763 38	Jefferson Parish
—763 39	Lafourche Parish
—763 4	South central parishes
—763 41	Terrebonne Parish
—763 42	Saint Mary Parish
—763 43	Assumption Parish
—763 44	Iberville Parish

*Class parts of this physiographic region or feature as instructed under —4–9

—763 45	West Baton Rouge and Pointe Coupee Parishes
—763 452	West Baton Rouge Parish
—763 454	Pointe Coupee Parish
—763 46	Saint Landry Parish
—763 47	Lafayette Parish
—763 48	Saint Martin Parish
—763 49	Iberia Parish
	Class here *Grand Lake
—763 5	Southwestern parishes
—763 51	Vermilion Parish
—763 52	Cameron Parish
	Class here *Sabine Lake
—763 54	Calcasieu Parish
—763 55	Jefferson Davis Parish
—763 56	Acadia Parish
—763 57	Evangeline Parish
—763 58	Allen Parish
—763 59	Beauregard Parish
—763 6	West central parishes
	Class here *Red River in Louisiana
—763 61	Vernon Parish
—763 62	Sabine Parish
—763 63	De Soto Parish
—763 64	Red River Parish
—763 65	Natchitoches Parish
—763 66	Winn Parish
	Class here *Saline Lake
—763 67	Grant Parish
—763 69	Rapides Parish

*Class parts of this physiographic region or feature as instructed under —4–9

Table 2. Areas

—763 7	East central parishes
	Class here *Ouachita River
—763 71	Avoyelles Parish
—763 73	Concordia Parish
—763 74	Catahoula Parish
—763 75	La Salle Parish
—763 76	Caldwell Parish
—763 77	Franklin Parish
—763 79	Tensas Parish
—763 8	Northeastern parishes
—763 81	Madison Parish
—763 82	East Carroll Parish
—763 83	West Carroll Parish
—763 84	Morehouse Parish
—763 86	Richland Parish
—763 87	Ouachita Parish
—763 89	Union Parish
—763 9	Northwestern parishes
—763 91	Lincoln Parish
—763 92	Jackson Parish
—763 93	Bienville Parish
—763 94	Claiborne Parish
—763 96	Webster Parish
—763 97	Bossier Parish
—763 99	Caddo Parish
	Class here *Caddo Lake
—764	Texas

*Class parts of this physiographic region or feature as instructed under —4–9

SUMMARY

—764 1	Coastal plains
—764 2	East Texas timber belt and blackland prairie
—764 3	Austin-San Antonio region
—764 4	Rio Grande Plain (Lower Rio Grande Valley)
—764 5	North central plains
—764 6	Burnet-Llano region
—764 7	Northwestern lowland
—764 8	Great Plains
—764 9	Western mountain and basin region

—764 1   Coastal plains

> Class here *Trinity, *Brazos, *Colorado, *Guadalupe, *San Antonio, *Nueces Rivers
>
> *For East Texas timber belt and blackland prairie, see —7642; Rio Grande Plain, —7644*

SUMMARY

—764 11	Nueces and neighboring counties
—764 12	Calhoun and neighboring counties
—764 13	Matagorda and neighboring counties
—764 14	Harris and neighboring counties
—764 15	Montgomery and neighboring counties
—764 16	Newton, Tyler, and neighboring counties
—764 17	Trinity and neighboring counties
—764 18	Nacogdoches and neighboring counties
—764 19	Harrison and neighboring counties

—764 11	Nueces and neighboring counties
—764 113	Nueces County
—764 115	San Patricio County
—764 117	Bee County
—764 119	Refugio County
—764 12	Calhoun and neighboring counties
—764 121	Calhoun County
—764 122	Aransas County
—764 123	Goliad County
—764 125	Victoria County
—764 127	Jackson County

*Class parts of this physiographic region or feature as instructed under —4–9

Table 2. Areas

—764 13	Matagorda and neighboring counties
—764 132	Matagorda County
—764 133	Wharton County
—764 135	Fort Bend County
—764 137	Brazoria County
—764 139	Galveston County
—764 14	Harris and neighboring counties
—764 141	Harris County
—764 141 1	Houston
—764 143	Chambers County
—764 145	Jefferson County
—764 147	Orange County
—764 15	Montgomery and neighboring counties
	Class here *Neches River, *pine woods region
—764 153	Montgomery County
—764 155	Liberty County
—764 157	Hardin County
—764 159	Jasper County
—764 16	Newton, Tyler, and neighboring counties
—764 162	Newton County
—764 163	Tyler County
—764 165	Polk County
—764 167	San Jacinto County
—764 169	Walker County
—764 17	Trinity and neighboring counties
—764 172	Trinity County
—764 173	Angelina County
—764 175	San Augustine County
—764 177	Sabine County
—764 179	Shelby County

*Class parts of this physiographic region or feature as instructed under —4–9

—764 18	Nacogdoches and neighboring counties
—764 182	Nacogdoches County
—764 183	Cherokee County
—764 185	Rusk County
—764 187	Panola County
—764 189	Gregg County
—764 19	Harrison and neighboring counties
—764 192	Harrison County
—764 193	Marion County
—764 195	Cass County
—764 197	Bowie County
—764 2	East Texas timber belt and blackland prairie

For Austin-San Antonio region, see —7643

SUMMARY

—764 21	Red River and neighboring counties
—764 22	Upshur and neighboring counties
—764 23	Freestone and neighboring counties
—764 24	Burleson and neighboring counties
—764 25	Fayette and neighboring counties
—764 26	Lamar and Fannin Counties
—764 27	Hunt and neighboring counties
—764 28	Dallas and neighboring counties

—764 21	Red River and neighboring counties
—764 212	Red River County
—764 213	Franklin County
—764 215	Titus County
—764 217	Morris County
—764 219	Camp County
—764 22	Upshur and neighboring counties
—764 222	Upshur County
—764 223	Wood County
—764 225	Smith County
—764 227	Henderson County
—764 229	Anderson County

Table 2. Areas

—764 23	Freestone and neighboring counties
—764 232	Freestone County
—764 233	Leon County
—764 235	Houston County
—764 237	Madison County
—764 239	Robertson County
—764 24	Burleson and neighboring counties
—764 241	Burleson County
—764 242	Brazos County
—764 243	Grimes County
—764 245	Washington County
—764 247	Lee County
—764 249	Waller County
—764 25	Fayette and neighboring counties
—764 251	Fayette County
—764 252	Austin County
—764 253	Colorado County
—764 255	Lavaca County
—764 257	Gonzales County
—764 259	De Witt County
—764 26	Lamar and Fannin Counties
	Class here *blackland prairie
—764 263	Lamar County
—764 265	Fannin County
—764 27	Hunt and neighboring counties
—764 272	Hunt County
—764 273	Delta County
—764 274	Hopkins County
—764 275	Rains county
—764 276	Van Zandt County
—764 277	Kaufman County

*Class parts of this physiographic region or feature as instructed under —4–9

—764 278	Rockwall County
—764 28	Dallas and neighboring counties
—764 281	Dallas and Ellis Counties
—764 281 1	Dallas County

                                 For Dallas city, see —7642812

—764 281 2	Dallas city

                                 Class here Dallas-Fort Worth metropolitan area

                                 For Fort Worth, see —7645315

—764 281 5	Ellis County
—764 282	Navarro County
—764 283	Hill County
—764 284	McLennan County
—764 285	Limestone County
—764 286	Falls County
—764 287	Bell County
—764 288	Milam County
—764 289	Williamson County
—764 3	Austin-San Antonio region

                                 For Hays County, see —764888; Comal County, —764887

—764 31	Travis County

                                 Including Austin

—764 32	Bastrop County
—764 33	Caldwell County
—764 34	Guadalupe County
—764 35	Bexar County
—764 351	San Antonio
—764 4	Rio Grande Plain (Lower Rio Grande Valley)

                                 Class here *Rio Grande

*Class parts of this physiographic region or feature as instructed under —4–9

Table 2. Areas

SUMMARY

—764 42   Medina County
—764 43   Uvalde and neighboring counties
—764 44   Frio and neighboring counties
—764 45   McMullen and neighboring counties
—764 46   Webb and neighboring counties
—764 47   Kleberg and neighboring counties
—764 48   Jim Hogg and neighboring counties
—764 49   Hidalgo and neighboring counties

—764 42   Medina County

—764 43   Uvalde and neighboring counties

—764 432   Uvalde County

—764 433   Kinney County

—764 435   Maverick County

—764 437   Zavala County

—764 44   Frio and neighboring counties

—764 442   Frio County

—764 443   Atascosa County

—764 444   Karnes County

—764 445   Wilson County

—764 447   Live Oak County

—764 45   McMullen and neighboring counties

—764 452   McMullen County

—764 453   La Salle County

—764 455   Dimmit County

—764 46   Webb and neighboring counties

—764 462   Webb County

—764 463   Duval County

—764 465   Jim Wells County

—764 47   Kleberg and neighboring counties
                 Class here *Padre Island

—764 472   Kleberg County

—764 473   Kenedy County

—764 475   Brooks County

*Class parts of this physiographic region or feature as instructed under —4–9

—764 48	Jim Hogg and neighboring counties
—764 482	Jim Hogg County
—764 483	Zapata County
—764 485	Starr County
—764 49	Hidalgo and neighboring counties
—764 492	Hidalgo County
—764 493	Willacy County
—764 495	Cameron County
—764 5	North central plains

For Burnet-Llano region, see —7646; Northwestern lowland, —7647

SUMMARY

—764 51	**Mills and neighboring counties**
—764 52	**Somervell and neighboring counties**
—764 53	**Tarrant and neighboring counties**
—764 54	**Montague and neighboring counties**
—764 55	**Erath and neighboring counties**

—764 51	Mills and neighboring counties

Class here *Grand Prairie

—764 512	Mills County
—764 513	Lampasas County
—764 515	Coryell County
—764 518	Bosque County
—764 52	Somervell and neighboring counties
—764 521	Somervell County
—764 522	Hood County
—764 524	Johnson County
—764 53	Tarrant and neighboring counties
—764 531	Tarrant County
—764 531 5	Fort Worth

Class comprehensive works on Dallas-Fort Worth metropolitan area in —7642812

*Class parts of this physiographic region or feature as instructed under —4–9

Table 2. Areas

—764 532	Wise County
—764 533	Cooke County
—764 54	Montague and neighboring counties
	Class here *cross timbers belt
—764 541	Montague County
—764 542	Clay County
—764 543	Archer County
—764 544	Jack County
—764 545	Young County
—764 546	Stephens County
—764 547	Eastland County
—764 548	Brown County
—764 549	Hamilton County
—764 55	Erath and neighboring counties
—764 551	Erath County
—764 552	Palo Pinto County
—764 553	Parker County
—764 554	Comanche County
—764 555	Denton County
—764 556	Collin County
—764 557	Grayson County
—764 6	**Burnet-Llano region**
—764 62	Llano County
—764 63	Burnet County
—764 64	Blanco County
—764 65	Gillespie County
—764 66	Mason County
—764 67	McCulloch County
—764 68	San Saba County

*Class parts of this physiographic region or feature as instructed under —4–9

—764 7   Northwestern lowland

SUMMARY

     —764 71   **Concho County**
     —764 72   **Tom Green and neighboring counties**
     —764 73   **Scurry and neighboring counties**
     —764 74   **Dickens and neighboring counties**
     —764 75   **Cottle and neighboring counties**

—764 71   Concho County

—764 72   Tom Green and neighboring counties

—764 721   Tom Green County

—764 723   Coke County

—764 724   Runnels County

—764 725   Coleman County

—764 726   Callahan County

—764 727   Taylor County

—764 728   Nolan County

—764 729   Mitchell County

—764 73   Scurry and neighboring counties

—764 731   Scurry County

—764 732   Fisher County

—764 733   Jones County

—764 734   Shackelford County

—764 735   Throckmorton County

—764 736   Haskell County

—764 737   Stonewall County

—764 738   Kent County

—764 74   Dickens and neighboring counties

—764 741   Dickens County

—764 742   King County

—764 743   Knox County

—764 744   Baylor County

—764 745   Wichita County

—764 746   Wilbarger County

—764 747   Hardeman County

Table 2. Areas

—764 748	Foard County
—764 75	Cottle and neighboring counties
—764 751	Cottle County
—764 752	Motley County
—764 753	Hall County
—764 754	Childress County
—764 8	Great Plains

Class here *Llano Estacado

SUMMARY

—764 81	Northern Panhandle counties
—764 82	Middle Panhandle counties
—764 83	Southern Panhandle counties
—764 84	Floyd and neighboring counties
—764 85	Lynn and neighboring counties
—764 86	Midland and neighboring counties
—764 87	Edwards Plateau counties
—764 88	Val Verde and neighboring counties

—764 81	Northern Panhandle counties
—764 812	Dallam County
—764 813	Sherman County
—764 814	Hansford County
—764 815	Ochiltree County
—764 816	Lipscomb County
—764 817	Hemphill County
—764 818	Roberts County
—764 82	Middle Panhandle counties
—764 821	Hutchinson County
—764 822	Moore County
—764 823	Hartley County
—764 824	Oldham County
—764 825	Potter County
—764 826	Carson County
—764 827	Gray County
—764 828	Wheeler County

*Class parts of this physiographic region or feature as instructed under —4–9

—764 83	Southern Panhandle counties
—764 831	Collingsworth County
—764 832	Donley County
—764 833	Armstrong County
—764 834	Randall County
—764 835	Deaf Smith County
—764 836	Parmer County
—764 837	Castro County
—764 838	Swisher County
—764 839	Briscoe County
—764 84	Floyd and neighboring counties
—764 841	Floyd County
—764 842	Hale County
—764 843	Lamb County
—764 844	Bailey County
—764 845	Cochran County
—764 846	Hockley County
—764 847	Lubbock County
—764 848	Crosby County
—764 849	Yoakum County
—764 85	Lynn and neighboring counties
—764 851	Lynn County
—764 852	Garza County
—764 853	Borden County
—764 854	Dawson County
—764 855	Gaines County
—764 856	Andrews County
—764 857	Martin County
—764 858	Howard County
—764 859	Terry County

Table 2. Areas

—764 86	Midland and neighboring counties
—764 861	Midland County
—764 862	Ector County
—764 863	Upton County
—764 87	*Edwards Plateau counties
	Class here *Balcones Escarpment
—764 871	Sterling County
—764 872	Glasscock County
—764 873	Reagan County
—764 874	Irion County
—764 875	Crockett County
—764 876	Schleicher County
—764 877	Menard County
—764 878	Kimble County
—764 879	Sutton County
—764 88	Val Verde and neighboring counties
—764 881	Val Verde County
—764 882	Edwards County
—764 883	Real County
—764 884	Kerr County
—764 885	Bandera County
—764 886	Kendall County
—764 887	Comal County
—764 888	Hays County
—764 9	Western mountain and basin region
	Class here *Pecos River
—764 91	Pecos Basin counties
—764 912	Loving County
—764 913	Winkler County
—764 914	Ward County
—764 915	Crane County

*Class parts of this physiographic region or feature as instructed under —4–9

—764 92	Stockton Plateau counties
—764 922	Terrell County
—764 923	Pecos County
—764 924	Reeves County
—764 93	Big Bend counties
—764 932	Brewster County
	Including Big Bend National Park
—764 933	Presidio County
—764 934	Jeff Davis County
—764 94	Culberson County
—764 95	Hudspeth County
—764 96	El Paso County
	Class here *upper Rio Grande of Texas
—766	Oklahoma

SUMMARY

—766 1	Northwestern counties
—766 2	North central counties
—766 3	Central counties
—766 4	Southwestern counties
—766 5	South central counties
—766 6	Southeastern counties
—766 7	Southeast central counties
—766 8	Northeast central counties
—766 9	Northeastern counties

—766 1	Northwestern counties

Class here *Canadian River, former Oklahoma Territory

Class a specific part of former Oklahoma Territory not provided for here with the subject, e.g., Beckham County —76643

—766 13	Panhandle counties

For Beaver County, see —76614

—766 132	Cimarron County
—766 135	Texas County

*Class parts of this physiographic region or feature as instructed under —4–9

Table 2. Areas

—766 14	Beaver County
—766 15	Harper and Ellis Counties
—766 153	Harper County
—766 155	Ellis County
—766 16	Roger Mills County
—766 17	Custer County
—766 18	Dewey County
—766 19	Woodward County
—766 2	North central counties
—766 21	Woods County
—766 22	Alfalfa County
—766 23	Grant County
—766 24	Kay County
—766 25	Osage County
—766 26	Pawnee County
—766 27	Noble County
—766 28	Garfield County
—766 29	Major County
—766 3	Central counties
	Class here *Cimarron River
—766 31	Blaine County
—766 32	Kingfisher County
—766 33	Logan County
—766 34	Payne County
—766 35	Lincoln County
—766 36	Pottawatomie County
—766 37	Cleveland County
—766 38	Oklahoma County
	Including Oklahoma City
—766 39	Canadian County

*Class parts of this physiographic region or feature as instructed under —4–9

—766 4	Southwestern counties
—766 41	Caddo County
—766 42	Washita County
—766 43	Beckham County
—766 44	Greer and Harmon Counties
—766 443	Greer County
—766 445	Harmon County
—766 45	Jackson County
—766 46	Tillman County
—766 47	Kiowa County
—766 48	Comanche County
—766 49	Cotton County
—766 5	South central counties

Class here *Washita River, *Arbuckle Mountains, former Indian Territory

Class a specific part of former Indian Territory not provided for here with the subject, e.g., Choctaw County —76663

—766 52	Jefferson County
—766 53	Stephens County
—766 54	Grady County
—766 55	McClain County
—766 56	Garvin County
—766 57	Murray County

Including Platt National Park

—766 58	Carter County
—766 59	Love County
—766 6	Southeastern counties

Class here *Red River, *Ouachita Mountains

—766 61	Marshall County

Class here *Lake Texoma

—766 62	Bryan County

*Class parts of this physiographic region or feature as instructed under —4–9

Table 2. Areas

—766 63	Choctaw County
—766 64	McCurtain County
—766 65	Pushmataha County
—766 66	Atoka County
—766 67	Coal County
—766 68	Johnston County
—766 69	Pontotoc County

—766 7   Southeast central counties

—766 71	Seminole County
—766 72	Hughes County
—766 73	Okfuskee County
—766 74	McIntosh County
—766 75	Pittsburg County
—766 76	Latimer County
—766 77	Haskell County
—766 79	Le Flore County

—766 8   Northeast central counties

     Class here *Arkansas River in Oklahoma, *Ozark Plateau in Oklahoma, *Boston Mountains in Oklahoma

—766 81	Sequoyah County
—766 82	Muskogee County
—766 83	Okmulgee County
—766 84	Creek County
—766 86	Tulsa County

     Including Tulsa city

—766 87	Wagoner County

     Class here *Fort Gibson Reservoir

—766 88	Cherokee County

     Class here *Tenkiller Ferry Reservoir

—766 89	Adair County

*Class parts of this physiographic region or feature as instructed under —4–9

—766 9	Northeastern counties
—766 91	Delaware County

Class here *Lake of the Cherokees

—766 93	Mayes County
—766 94	Rogers County
—766 96	Washington County
—766 97	Nowata County
—766 98	Craig County
—766 99	Ottawa County
—767	Arkansas

SUMMARY

—767 1   Northwestern counties
—767 2   North central counties
—767 3   Northwest central counties
—767 4   Southwest central counties
—767 5   Southwestern counties
—767 6   South central counties
—767 7   Central counties
—767 8   Southeastern counties
—767 9   Northeastern counties

—767 1	Northwestern counties

Class here *Ozark Plateau, *Boston Mountains

—767 13	Benton County
—767 14	Washington County
—767 15	Madison County
—767 16	Newton County
—767 17	Carroll County
—767 18	Boone County
—767 19	Marion and Searcy Counties
—767 193	Marion County

Class here *Bull Shoals Lake

—767 195	Searcy County

*Class parts of this physiographic region or feature as instructed under —4–9

Table 2. Areas

—767 2	North central counties
	Class here *Black, *White Rivers
—767 21	Baxter County
	Class here *Norfork Lake
—767 22	Fulton County
—767 23	Sharp County
—767 24	Randolph County
—767 25	Lawrence County
—767 26	Independence County
—767 27	Izard County
—767 28	Stone and Cleburne Counties
—767 283	Stone County
—767 285	Cleburne County
—767 29	Van Buren County
—767 3	Northwest central counties
	Class here *Arkansas River
—767 31	Conway County
—767 32	Pope County
—767 33	Johnson County
—767 34	Franklin County
—767 35	Crawford County
—767 36	Sebastian County
—767 37	Logan County
	Class here *Blue Mountain Reservoir
—767 38	Yell County
—767 39	Perry County
—767 4	Southwest central counties
	Class here *Ouachita Mountains in Arkansas
—767 41	Garland County
	Including Hot Springs National Park
—767 42	Hot Spring County

*Class parts of this physiographic region or feature as instructed under —4–9

—767 43	Montgomery County
—767 44	Scott County
—767 45	Polk County
—767 47	Sevier County
—767 48	Howard and Pike Counties
—767 483	Howard County
—767 485	Pike County
—767 49	Clark County
—767 5	**Southwestern counties**
—767 52	Nevada County
—767 54	Hempstead County
—767 55	Little River County
—767 56	Miller County
—767 57	Lafayette County
—767 59	Columbia County
—767 6	**South central counties**
—767 61	Union County
—767 63	Bradley County
—767 64	Calhoun County
—767 66	Ouachita County
—767 67	Dallas County
—767 69	Cleveland County
—767 7	**Central counties**
—767 71	Grant County
—767 72	Saline County
—767 73	Pulaski County
	Including Little Rock
—767 74	Faulkner County
—767 76	White County
—767 77	Prairie County
—767 78	Lonoke County
—767 79	Jefferson County

Table 2. Areas

—767 8	Southeastern counties

Class here *Mississippi River in Arkansas

—767 82	Lincoln and Drew Counties
—767 823	Lincoln County
—767 825	Drew County
—767 83	Ashley County
—767 84	Chicot County
—767 85	Desha County
—767 86	Arkansas County
—767 87	Monroe County
—767 88	Phillips County
—767 89	Lee County
—767 9	Northeastern counties

Class here *Saint Francis River

—767 91	Saint Francis County
—767 92	Woodruff County
—767 93	Cross County
—767 94	Crittenden County
—767 95	Mississippi County
—767 96	Poinsett County
—767 97	Jackson County
—767 98	Craighead County
—767 99	Greene and Clay Counties
—767 993	Greene County
—767 995	Clay County
—768	Tennessee

Class here *Tennessee River and Valley

*Class parts of this physiographic region or feature as instructed under —4–9

SUMMARY

—768 1	Mississippi Valley counties
—768 2	West Tennessee Plain counties
—768 3	Western Tennessee River Valley counties
—768 4	West Highland Rim counties
—768 5	Central Basin counties
—768 6	East Highland Rim counties
—768 7	Cumberland Plateau counties
—768 8	Southeastern counties
—768 9	Northeastern counties

—768 1	Mississippi Valley counties
—768 12	Lake County
	Class here *Reelfoot Lake
—768 13	Obion County
—768 15	Dyer County
—768 16	Lauderdale County
—768 17	Tipton County
—768 19	Shelby County
	Including Memphis
—768 2	West Tennessee Plain counties
—768 21	Fayette County
—768 22	Haywood and Crockett Counties
—768 223	Haywood County
—768 225	Crockett County
—768 23	Gibson County
—768 24	Weakley County
—768 25	Carroll County
—768 26	Henderson and Chester Counties
—768 263	Henderson County
—768 265	Chester County
—768 27	Madison County
—768 28	Hardeman County
—768 29	McNairy County

*Class parts of this physiographic region or feature as instructed under —4–9

Table 2. Areas

—768 3	Western Tennessee River Valley counties
—768 31	Hardin County
—768 32	Decatur County
—768 33	Benton County
—768 34	Henry County
—768 35	Stewart County
—768 36	Houston County
—768 37	Humphreys County
—768 38	Perry County
—768 39	Wayne County
—768 4	West Highland Rim counties

Class here comprehensive works on Highland Rim counties

For east Highland Rim counties, see —7686

—768 42	Lawrence County
—768 43	Lewis and Hickman Counties
—768 432	Lewis County
—768 434	Hickman County

Class here *Duck River

—768 44	Dickson County
—768 45	Montgomery County
—768 46	Cheatham and Robertson Counties
—768 462	Cheatham County
—768 464	Robertson County
—768 47	Sumner County
—768 48	Trousdale and Macon Counties
—768 482	Trousdale County
—768 484	Macon County

*Class parts of this physiographic region or feature as instructed under —4–9

—768 49	Clay County
	Class here *Dale Hollow Reservoir
—768 5	**Central Basin counties**
	Class here *Cumberland River
—768 51	Jackson County
—768 52	Smith County
—768 53	De Kalb and Cannon Counties
—768 532	De Kalb County
	Class here *Center Hill Reservoir
—768 535	Cannon County
—768 54	Wilson County
—768 55	Davidson County
	Including Nashville
—768 56	Williamson County
—768 57	Rutherford County
—768 58	Bedford and Marshall Counties
—768 583	Bedford County
—768 585	Marshall County
—768 59	Maury County
—768 6	**East Highland Rim counties**
—768 61	Giles County
—768 62	Lincoln and Moore Counties
—768 624	Lincoln County
—768 627	Moore County
—768 63	Franklin County
—768 64	Coffee County

*Class parts of this physiographic region or feature as instructed under —4–9

Table 2. Areas

—768 65	Warren and Van Buren Counties
—768 653	Warren County
—768 657	Van Buren County
—768 66	White County
—768 67	Putnam County
—768 68	Overton and Pickett Counties
—768 684	Overton County
—768 687	Pickett County
—768 69	Fentress County
—768 7	**Cumberland Plateau counties**
—768 71	Scott County
—768 72	Campbell County
—768 73	Anderson County
	Class here *Clinch River
—768 74	Morgan County
—768 75	Cumberland County
—768 76	Bledsoe County
—768 77	Sequatchie County
	Class here *Sequatchie River
—768 78	Grundy County
—768 79	Marion County
—768 8	**Southeastern counties**
—768 82	Hamilton County
	Including Chattanooga
	Class here *Lookout Mountain, *Lake Chickamauga
—768 83	Rhea and Meigs Counties
—768 834	Rhea County
—768 836	Meigs County

*Class parts of this physiographic region or feature as instructed under —4–9

—768 84	Roane County
—768 85	Knox County
	Including Knoxville
	Class here *Fort Loudoun Reservoir
—768 86	Loudon and McMinn Counties
—768 863	Loudon County
	Class here *Little Tennessee River
—768 865	McMinn County
—768 87	Bradley and Polk Counties
—768 873	Bradley County
—768 875	Polk County
—768 88	Monroe and Blount Counties
—768 883	Monroe County
—768 885	Blount County
—768 89	*Great Smoky Mountains area
—768 893	Sevier County
—768 895	Cocke County
	Class here *French Broad River
—768 9	Northeastern counties
	Class here *Holston River
—768 91	Greene County
	Class here *Bald Mountains
—768 92	Hamblen and Jefferson Counties
	Class here *Cherokee Reservoir
—768 923	Hamblen County
—768 924	Jefferson County
	Class here *Douglas Reservoir

*Class parts of this physiographic region or feature as instructed under —4–9

Table 2. Areas

—768 93	Grainger and Union Counties
—768 932	Grainger County
	Class here *Clinch Mountains
—768 935	Union County
	Class here *Norris Lake
—768 94	Claiborne and Hancock Counties
—768 944	Claiborne County
	Class here *Cumberland Mountains in Tennessee, *Cumberland Gap
—768 946	Hancock County
—768 95	Hawkins County
—768 96	Sullivan County
	Class here *Boone Reservoir
—768 97	Washington County
—768 98	Unicoi and Carter Counties
—768 982	Unicoi County
—768 984	Carter County
	Class here *Iron Mountains, *Watauga Reservoir
—768 99	Johnson County
	Class here *Roan and *Stone Mountains
—769	Kentucky
	Class here *Ohio River
	Class Ohio Valley in —77

SUMMARY

—769 1	Southern mountain region counties
—769 2	Northern mountain region counties
—769 3	Northern Bluegrass counties
—769 4	Southern Bluegrass counties
—769 5	The Knobs counties
—769 6	Eastern Pennyroyal counties
—769 7	Western Pennyroyal counties
—769 8	Western Basin counties
—769 9	Counties west of Tennessee River

*Class parts of this physiographic region or feature as instructed under —4–9

—769 1	Southern mountain region counties
	Class here *Cumberland Mountains
—769 12	Bell and Knox Counties
—769 123	Bell County
	Class here *Pine Mountain
—769 125	Knox County
—769 13	Whitley and McCreary Counties
—769 132	Whitley County
—769 135	McCreary County
—769 14	Laurel and Clay Counties
—769 143	Laurel County
—769 145	Clay County
—769 15	Leslie and Harlan Counties
—769 152	Leslie County
—769 154	Harlan County
	Class here *Big Black Mountains
—769 16	Letcher and Knott Counties
—769 163	Letcher County
—769 165	Knott County
—769 17	Perry and Owsley Counties
—769 173	Perry County
—769 176	Owsley County
—769 18	Jackson and Lee Counties
—769 183	Jackson County
—769 185	Lee County
—769 19	Breathitt County

*Class parts of this physiographic region or feature as instructed under —4–9

Table 2. Areas

—769 2	**Northern mountain region counties**
	Class here *Big Sandy River and *Tug Fork in Kentucky, *Levisa River
—769 21	Wolfe and Magoffin Counties
—769 213	Wolfe County
—769 215	Magoffin County
—769 22	Floyd County
—769 23	Pike County
—769 24	Martin and Johnson Counties
—769 243	Martin County
—769 245	Johnson County
—769 25	Morgan and Elliott Counties
—769 253	Morgan County
—769 255	Elliott County
—769 26	Lawrence County
—769 27	Boyd County
—769 28	Carter County
—769 29	Greenup and Lewis Counties
—769 293	Greenup County
—769 295	Lewis County
—769 3	**Northern Bluegrass counties**
	Class here *Licking, *Kentucky Rivers
—769 32	Mason and Bracken Counties
—769 323	Mason County
—769 325	Bracken County
—769 33	Pendleton County
—769 34	Campbell County
—769 35	Kenton County

*Class parts of this physiographic region or feature as instructed under —4–9

—769 36	Boone and Gallatin Counties
—769 363	Boone County
—769 365	Gallatin County
—769 37	Carroll and Trimble Counties
—769 373	Carroll County
—769 375	Trimble County
—769 38	Oldham and Henry Counties
—769 383	Oldham County
—769 385	Henry County
—769 39	Owen and Grant Counties
—769 393	Owen County
—769 395	Grant County
—769 4	Southern Bluegrass counties
—769 41	Harrison, Robertson, Nicholas Counties
—769 413	Harrison County
—769 415	Robertson County
—769 417	Nicholas County
—769 42	Bourbon and Scott Counties
—769 423	Bourbon County
—769 425	Scott County
—769 43	Franklin and Shelby Counties
—769 432	Franklin County
	Including Frankfort
—769 435	Shelby County
—769 44	Jefferson County
	Including Louisville

Table 2. Areas

—769 45	Bullitt and Spencer Counties
	Class here *Salt River
—769 453	Bullitt County
—769 455	Spencer County
—769 46	Anderson and Woodford Counties
—769 463	Anderson County
—769 465	Woodford County
—769 47	Fayette County
	Including Lexington
—769 48	Jessamine and Mercer Counties
—769 483	Jessamine County
—769 485	Mercer County
—769 49	Washington and Nelson Counties
—769 493	Washington County
—769 495	Nelson County
—769 5	The Knobs counties
—769 51	Marion County
—769 52	Boyle and Garrard Counties
—769 523	Boyle County
—769 525	Garrard County
—769 53	Madison County
—769 54	Clark County
—769 55	Montgomery and Bath Counties
—769 553	Montgomery County
—769 555	Bath County
—769 56	Fleming County
—769 57	Rowan County

*Class parts of this physiographic region or feature as instructed under —4–9

—769 58	Menifee and Powell Counties
—769 583	Menifee County
—769 585	Powell County
—769 59	Estill County
—769 6	Eastern Pennyroyal counties

Class here *Highland Rim in Kentucky, comprehensive works on Pennyroyal counties

For western Pennyroyal counties, see —7697

—769 62	Rockcastle and Lincoln Counties
—769 623	Rockcastle County
—769 625	Lincoln County
—769 63	Pulaski County

Class here *Lake Cumberland

—769 64	Wayne County
—769 65	Clinton and Russell Counties
—769 653	Clinton County
—769 655	Russell County
—769 66	Casey County
—769 67	Taylor and Adair Counties
—769 673	Taylor County
—769 675	Adair County
—769 68	Cumberland and Monroe Counties
—769 683	Cumberland County
—769 685	Monroe County
—769 69	Metcalfe and Green Counties
—769 693	Metcalfe County
—769 695	Green County

*Class parts of this physiographic region or feature as instructed under —4-9

Table 2. Areas

—769 7	Western Pennyroyal counties
—769 71	Larue and Hart Counties
—769 713	Larue County
—769 715	Hart County
—769 72	Barren County
—769 73	Allen and Simpson Counties
—769 732	Allen County
—769 735	Simpson County
—769 74	Warren County
—769 75	Edmonson and Butler Counties and environs
—769 752	Edmonson County
—769 754	*Mammoth Cave National Park
—769 755	Butler County
—769 76	Logan County
—769 77	Todd County
—769 78	Christian County
—769 79	Trigg County
—769 8	Western Basin counties

Class here *Green River

SUMMARY

—769 81	Lyon and Caldwell Counties
—769 82	Hopkins and McLean Counties
—769 83	Muhlenberg and Ohio Counties
—769 84	Grayson and Hardin Counties
—769 85	Meade and Breckinridge Counties
—769 86	Hancock and Daviess Counties
—769 87	Henderson County
—769 88	Webster and Union Counties
—769 89	Crittenden and Livingston Counties

—769 81	Lyon and Caldwell Counties
—769 813	Lyon County
—769 815	Caldwell County

*Class parts of this physiographic region or feature as instructed under —4–9

—769 82	Hopkins and McLean Counties
—769 823	Hopkins County
—769 826	McLean County
—769 83	Muhlenberg and Ohio Counties
—769 832	Muhlenberg County
—769 835	Ohio County
—769 84	Grayson and Hardin Counties
—769 842	Grayson County
—769 845	Hardin county
—769 85	Meade and Breckinridge Counties
—769 852	Meade County
—769 854	Breckinridge County
—769 86	Hancock and Daviess Counties
—769 862	Hancock County
—769 864	Daviess County

For Owensboro, see —769865

—769 865	Owensboro
—769 87	Henderson County
—769 88	Webster and Union Counties
—769 883	Webster County
—769 885	Union County
—769 89	Crittenden and Livingston Counties
—769 893	Crittenden County
—769 895	Livingston County

Class here *Kentucky Reservoir

—769 9	**Counties west of Tennessee River**
—769 91	Marshall County
—769 92	Calloway County
—769 93	Graves County
—769 95	McCracken County
—769 96	Ballard County

*Class parts of this physiographic region or feature as instructed under —4–9

Table 2. Areas

—769 97	Carlisle County
—769 98	Hickman County
—769 99	Fulton County
—77	**North central United States Lake states**

Class here Middle West, *Mississippi River and Valley, *Ohio Valley, *Great Lakes

Class Ohio River in —769, each specific state of Middle West not provided for here with the subject, e.g., Kansas —781

SUMMARY

—771	**Ohio**
—772	**Indiana**
—773	**Illinois**
—774	**Michigan**
—775	**Wisconsin**
—776	**Minnesota**
—777	**Iowa**
—778	**Missouri**

▶   **—771–776 Lake states**

Class comprehensive works in —77

For New York, see —747; Pennsylvania, —748

—771   Ohio

SUMMARY

—771 1	**Northwestern counties**
—771 2	**North central counties**
—771 3	**Northeastern counties**
—771 4	**West central counties**
—771 5	**Central counties**
—771 6	**East central counties**
—771 7	**Southwestern counties**
—771 8	**South central counties**
—771 9	**Southeastern counties**

—771 1	**Northwestern counties**

Class here *Maumee River

—771 11	Williams and Fulton Counties
—771 113	Williams County
—771 115	Fulton County

*Class parts of this physiographic region or feature as instructed under —4–9

—771 12	Lucas County
	For Toledo, see —77113
—771 13	Toledo
—771 14	Defiance County
—771 15	Henry County
—771 16	Wood County
—771 17	Paulding County
—771 18	Putnam County
—771 19	Hancock County
—771 2	North central counties
	Class here *Lake Erie, *Sandusky River
—771 21	Ottawa and Sandusky Counties
—771 212	Ottawa County
—771 214	Sandusky County
	Class here *Sandusky Bay
—771 22	Erie County
—771 23	Lorain County
—771 24	Seneca County
—771 25	Huron County
—771 26	Wyandot County
—771 27	Crawford County
—771 28	Richland County
—771 29	Ashland County
—771 3	Northeastern counties
—771 31	Cuyahoga County
	Class here *Cuyahoga River
	For Cleveland, see —77132
—771 32	Cleveland

*Class parts of this physiographic region or feature as instructed under —4–9

Table 2. Areas

—771 33	Lake and Geauga Counties
—771 334	Lake County
—771 336	Geauga County
—771 34	Ashtabula County
—771 35	Medina County
—771 36	Summit County
	Including Akron
—771 37	Portage County
	Class here *Berlin Reservoir
—771 38	Trumbull County
	Class here *Meander Reservoir
—771 39	Mahoning County
	Class here *Mahoning River
—771 4	West central counties
—771 41	Van Wert and Mercer Counties
—771 413	Van Wert County
—771 415	Mercer County
	Class here *Lake Saint Marys
—771 42	Allen County
—771 43	Auglaize County
—771 44	Hardin County
—771 45	Shelby County
—771 46	Logan and Champaign Counties
—771 463	Logan County
—771 465	Champaign County
—771 47	Darke County
—771 48	Miami County
—771 49	Clark County

*Class parts of this physiographic region or feature as instructed under —4–9

—771 5	Central counties
	Class here *Scioto River
—771 51	Marion and Morrow Counties
—771 514	Marion County
—771 516	Morrow County
—771 52	Knox County
—771 53	Union and Delaware Counties
—771 532	Union County
—771 535	Delaware County
—771 54	Licking County
—771 55	Madison County
—771 56	Franklin County
	For Columbus, see —77157
—771 57	Columbus
—771 58	Fairfield County
—771 59	Perry County
—771 6	East central counties
—771 61	Wayne County
—771 62	Stark County
—771 63	Columbiana County
—771 64	Holmes County
—771 65	Coshocton County
—771 66	Tuscarawas County
	Class here *Tuscarawas River
—771 67	Carroll County
—771 68	Harrison County
—771 69	Jefferson County

*Class parts of this physiographic region or feature as instructed under —4–9

Table 2. Areas

—771 7	Southwestern counties
	Class here *Miami River
—771 71	Preble County
—771 72	Montgomery County
	For Dayton, see —77173
—771 73	Dayton
—771 74	Greene County
—771 75	Butler County
—771 76	Warren and Clinton Counties
—771 763	Warren County
—771 765	Clinton County
—771 77	Hamilton County
	For Cincinnati, see —77178
—771 78	Cincinnati
—771 79	Clermont and Brown Counties
—771 794	Clermont County
—771 796	Brown County
—771 8	South central counties
—771 81	Fayette and Pickaway Counties
—771 813	Fayette County
—771 815	Pickaway County
—771 82	Ross County
—771 83	Hocking and Vinton Counties
—771 835	Hocking County
—771 837	Vinton County
—771 84	Highland and Pike Counties
—771 845	Highland County
—771 847	Pike County

*Class parts of this physiographic region or feature as instructed under —4–9

—771 85	Jackson County
—771 86	Adams County
—771 87	Scioto County
—771 88	Lawrence County
—771 89	Gallia County
—771 9	Southeastern counties
—771 91	Muskingum County
	Class here *Muskingum River
—771 92	Guernsey County
—771 93	Belmont County
—771 94	Morgan County
—771 95	Noble County
—771 96	Monroe County
—771 97	Athens County
	Class here *Hocking River
—771 98	Washington County
—771 99	Meigs County
—772	Indiana

SUMMARY

—772 1	Southeastern counties
—772 2	South central counties
—772 3	Southwestern counties
—772 4	West central counties
—772 5	Central counties
—772 6	East central counties
—772 7	Northeastern counties
—772 8	North central counties
—772 9	Northwestern counties

—772 1	Southeastern counties
—772 11	Dearborn County

*Class parts of this physiographic region or feature as instructed under —4–9

Table 2. Areas

—772 12	Ohio and Switzerland Counties
—772 123	Ohio County
—772 125	Switzerland County
—772 13	Jefferson County
—772 14	Ripley County
—772 15	Franklin County
—772 16	Decatur County
—772 17	Jennings county
—772 18	Scott and Clark Counties
—772 183	Scott County
—772 185	Clark County
—772 19	Floyd County
—772 2	South central counties
—772 21	Harrison County
—772 22	Washington County
—772 23	Jackson County
—772 24	Bartholomew County
—772 25	Brown and Monroe Counties
—772 253	Brown County
—772 255	Monroe County
—772 26	Lawrence County
—772 27	Orange County
—772 28	Crawford County
—772 29	Perry County
—772 3	Southwestern counties
	Class here *White River
—772 31	Spencer County
—772 32	Warrick County
—772 33	Vanderburgh County
—772 34	Posey County
—772 35	Gibson County

*Class parts of this physiographic region or feature as instructed under —4–9

—772 36	Pike County
—772 37	Dubois County
—772 38	Martin and Daviess Counties
—772 382	Martin County
—772 385	Daviess County
—772 39	Knox County
—772 4	West central counties
	Class here *Wabash River
—772 41	Sullivan County
—772 42	Greene County
—772 43	Owen County
—772 44	Clay County
—772 45	Vigo County
—772 46	Vermillion and Parke Counties
—772 462	Vermillion County
—772 465	Parke County
—772 47	Fountain County
—772 48	Montgomery County
—772 49	Putnam County
—772 5	Central counties
—772 51	Morgan and Johnson Counties
—772 513	Morgan County
—772 515	Johnson County
—772 52	Marion County
	Including Indianapolis
—772 53	Hendricks County
—772 54	Boone County

*Class parts of this physiographic region or feature as instructed under —4–9

Table 2. Areas

—772 55	Clinton and Tipton Counties
—772 553	Clinton County
—772 555	Tipton County
—772 56	Hamilton County
—772 57	Madison County
—772 58	Hancock County
—772 59	Shelby County
—772 6	East central counties
—772 61	Rush County
—772 62	Fayette and Union Counties
—772 623	Fayette County
—772 625	Union County
—772 63	Wayne County
—772 64	Henry County
—772 65	Delaware County
	Including Muncie
—772 66	Randolph county
—772 67	Jay County
—772 68	Blackford County
—772 69	Grant County
—772 7	Northeastern counties
—772 71	Huntington County
—772 72	Wells County
—772 73	Adams County
—772 74	Allen County
	Including Fort Wayne
—772 75	Whitley County
—772 76	Noble County
—772 77	De Kalb County
—772 78	Steuben County
—772 79	Lagrange County

—772 8	North central counties
—772 81	Elkhart County
—772 82	Kosciusko County
—772 83	Wabash County
—772 84	Miami County
—772 85	Howard County
—772 86	Cass County
—772 87	Fulton County
—772 88	Marshall County
—772 89	Saint Joseph County
	Including South Bend
—772 9	Northwestern counties
—772 91	La Porte County
—772 92	Starke and Pulaski Counties
—772 923	Starke County
—772 925	Pulaski County
—772 93	White County
—772 94	Carroll County
—772 95	Tippecanoe County
—772 96	Warren County
—772 97	Benton, Newton, Jasper Counties
—772 972	Benton County
—772 974	Newton County
—772 977	Jasper County
—772 98	Porter County
—772 99	Lake County
	Including Gary
—773	Illinois

Table 2. Areas

SUMMARY

—773 1	Cook County
—773 2	Northeastern counties
—773 3	Northwestern counties
—773 4	West central counties
—773 5	Central counties
—773 6	East central counties
—773 7	Southeastern counties
—773 8	Southwestern counties
—773 9	Southern counties

—773 1   Cook County

—773 11   Chicago

—773 2   Northeastern counties

Class here *Des Plaines River

For Cook County, see —7731

—773 21   Lake County

—773 22   McHenry County

—773 23   Kane County

—773 24   Du Page County

—773 25   Will County

—773 26   Kendall and Grundy Counties

—773 263   Kendall County

—773 265   Grundy County

—773 27   La Salle County

—773 28   De Kalb County

—773 29   Boone County

—773 3   Northwestern counties

Class here *Rock River

—773 31   Winnebago County

—773 32   Ogle County

—773 33   Stephenson County

*Class parts of this physiographic region or feature as instructed under —4–9

—773 34	Jo Daviess and Carroll Counties
—773 343	Jo Daviess County
—773 345	Carroll County
—773 35	Whiteside County
—773 36	Lee County
—773 37	Bureau and Putnam Counties
—773 372	Bureau County
—773 375	Putnam County
—773 38	Henry County
—773 39	Rock Island and Mercer Counties
—773 393	Rock Island County

> Class comprehensive works on Davenport-Rock Island-Moline tri-city area in —77769

—773 395	Mercer County
—773 4	West central counties
—773 41	Henderson and Warren Counties
—773 413	Henderson County
—773 415	Warren County
—773 42	McDonough County
—773 43	Hancock County
—773 44	Adams County
—773 45	Pike and Scott Counties
—773 453	Pike County
—773 455	Scott County
—773 46	Morgan and Cass Counties
—773 463	Morgan County
—773 465	Cass County
—773 47	Brown and Schuyler Counties
—773 473	Brown County
—773 475	Schuyler County

Table 2. Areas

—773 48	Fulton County	
—773 49	Knox County	
—773 5	**Central counties**	
	Class here *Illinois River	
—773 51	Stark and Marshall Counties	
—773 513	Stark County	
—773 515	Marshall County	
—773 52	Peoria County	
—773 53	Woodford County	
—773 54	Tazewell County	
—773 55	Mason and Menard Counties	
	Class here *Sangamon River	
—773 553	Mason County	
—773 555	Menard County	
—773 56	Sangamon County	
	Including Springfield	
—773 57	Logan County	
—773 58	Macon and De Witt Counties	
—773 582	Macon County	
—773 585	De Witt County	
—773 59	McLean County	
—773 6	**East central counties**	
—773 61	Livingston County	
—773 62	Ford County	
—773 63	Kankakee County	
—773 64	Iroquois County	
—773 65	Vermilion County	
—773 66	Champaign County	

*Class parts of this physiographic region or feature as instructed under —4–9

—773 67	Piatt and Moultrie Counties
—773 673	Piatt County
—773 675	Moultrie County
—773 68	Douglas County
—773 69	Edgar County
—773 7	Southeastern counties
—773 71	Clark County
—773 72	Coles County
—773 73	Cumberland County
—773 74	Jasper County
—773 75	Crawford County
—773 76	Lawrence County
—773 77	Richland County
—773 78	Wabash County
—773 79	Counties south of Decatur
—773 791	Edwards County
—773 792	Wayne County
—773 793	Jefferson County
—773 794	Marion County
—773 795	Clay County
—773 796	Effingham County
—773 797	Fayette County
—773 798	Shelby County
—773 8	Southwestern counties
—773 81	Christian County
—773 82	Montgomery County
—773 83	Macoupin County
—773 84	Greene County

Table 2. Areas

—773 85	Calhoun and Jersey Counties
—773 853	Calhoun County
—773 855	Jersey County
—773 86	Madison County
—773 87	Bond and Clinton Counties
—773 873	Bond County
—773 875	Clinton County
—773 88	Washington County
—773 89	Saint Clair County
—773 9	Southern counties
—773 91	Monroe County
—773 92	Randolph County
—773 93	Perry County
—773 94	Franklin County
—773 95	Hamilton County
—773 96	White County
—773 97	Gallatin County
—773 98	Hardin County
—773 99	Southernmost counties
—773 991	Pope County
—773 992	Saline County
—773 993	Williamson County
—773 994	Jackson County
—773 995	Union County
—773 996	Johnson County
—773 997	Massac County
—773 998	Pulaski County
—773 999	Alexander County

—774   Michigan

                Class here Lakes *Huron, *Michigan

SUMMARY

—774 1	Southwestern counties of Lower Peninsula
—774 2	South central counties of Lower Peninsula
—774 3	Southeastern counties of Lower Peninsula
—774 4	Southeast central counties of Lower Peninsula
—774 5	Southwest central counties of Lower Peninsula
—774 6	Northwest central counties of Lower Peninsula
—774 7	Northeast central counties of Lower Peninsula
—774 8	Northern counties of Lower Peninsula
—774 9	Upper Peninsula

▶   —774 1–774 8 Lower Peninsula

             Class comprehensive works in —774

—774 1   Southwestern counties of Lower Peninsula

                Class here *Kalamazoo River

—774 11   Berrien County

—774 12   Cass County

—774 13   Van Buren County

—774 14   Allegan County

—774 15   Ottawa County

—774 16   Barry County

—774 17   Kalamazoo County

                For Kalamazoo city, see —77418

—774 18   Kalamazoo city

—774 19   Saint Joseph County

—774 2   South central counties of Lower Peninsula

—774 21   Branch County

—774 22   Calhoun County

—774 23   Eaton County

—774 24   Clinton County

—774 25   Shiawassee County

—774 26   Ingham County

                For Lansing and East Lansing, see —77427

*Class parts of this physiographic region or feature as instructed under —4–9

Table 2. Areas

—774 27	Lansing and East Lansing
—774 28	Jackson County
—774 29	Hillsdale County
—774 3	**Southeastern counties of Lower Peninsula**
	Class here *Lake Saint Clair
—774 31	Lenawee County
—774 32	Monroe County
—774 33	Wayne County
	Class here *Detroit River
	For Detroit, see —77434
—774 34	Detroit
—774 35	Washtenaw County
—774 36	Livingston County
—774 37	Genesee County
	Including Flint
	Class here *Flint River
—774 38	Oakland County
—774 39	Macomb County
—774 4	**Southeast central counties of Lower Peninsula**
	Class here *Saginaw Bay
—774 41	Saint Clair County
	Class here *Saint Clair River
—774 42	Lapeer County
—774 43	Sanilac County
—774 44	Huron County
—774 45	Tuscola County
—774 46	Saginaw County
—774 47	Bay County
	Class here *Saginaw River
—774 48	Midland County
—774 49	Gratiot County

*Class parts of this physiographic region or feature as instructed under —4-9

—774 5	Southwest central counties of Lower Peninsula
	Class here *Muskegon River
—774 51	Isabella County
—774 52	Mecosta County
—774 53	Montcalm County
—774 54	Ionia County
—774 55	Kent County
	For Grand Rapids, see —77456
—774 56	Grand Rapids
—774 57	Muskegon County
—774 58	Newaygo County
—774 59	Oceana County
—774 6	Northwest central counties of Lower Peninsula
	Class here *Manistee River
—774 61	Mason County
	Class here *Pere Marquette River
—774 62	Manistee County
—774 63	Benzie and Leelanau Counties
—774 632	Benzie County
—774 635	Leelanau County
—774 64	Grand Traverse County
	Class here *Grand Traverse Bay
—774 65	Kalkaska County
—774 66	Missaukee County
—774 67	Wexford County
—774 68	Lake County
—774 69	Osceola County

*Class parts of this physiographic region or feature as instructed under —4-9

Table 2. Areas

—774 7	**Northeast central counties of Lower Peninsula**
	Class here *Au Sable River
—774 71	Clare County
—774 72	Gladwin County
—774 73	Arenac County
—774 74	Iosco County
—774 75	Ogemaw County
—774 76	Roscommon County
—774 77	Crawford County
—774 78	Oscoda County
—774 79	Alcona County
—774 8	**Northern counties of Lower Peninsula**
	Class here *Straits of Mackinac
—774 81	Alpena County
—774 82	Presque Isle County
—774 83	Montmorency County
—774 84	Otsego County
—774 85	Antrim County
—774 86	Charlevoix County
—774 87	Cheboygan County
—774 88	Emmet County
—774 9	**Upper Peninsula**
	Class here *Lake Superior
—774 91	Chippewa County
	Class here *Whitefish Bay, *Saint Marys River
—774 92	Mackinac and Luce Counties
—774 923	Mackinac County
—774 925	Luce County

*Class parts of this physiographic region or feature as instructed under —4–9

—774 93	Alger and Schoolcraft Counties
—774 932	Alger County
—774 935	Schoolcraft County
—774 94	Delta County
—774 95	Menominee and Dickinson Counties
	Class here *Menominee River
—774 953	Menominee County
—774 955	Dickinson County
—774 96	Marquette County
—774 97	Baraga and Iron Counties
—774 973	Baraga County
—774 975	Iron County
—774 98	Gogebic and Ontonagon Counties
—774 983	Gogebic County
—774 985	Ontonagon County
—774 99	Houghton and Keweenaw Counties
	Class here Keweenaw Peninsula
—774 993	Houghton County
—774 995	Keweenaw County
	For Isle Royale, see —774997
—774 997	Isle Royale
—775	Wisconsin
	Class here *Wisconsin River

SUMMARY

—775 1	Northwestern counties
—775 2	North central counties
—775 3	Northeastern counties
—775 4	West central counties
—775 5	Central counties
—775 6	East central counties
—775 7	Southwestern counties
—775 8	South central counties
—775 9	Southeastern counties

*Class parts of this physiographic region or feature as instructed under —4–9

Table 2. Areas

—775 1	Northwestern counties
	Class here *Saint Croix River
—775 11	Douglas County
	For Superior, see —77512
—775 12	Superior
	Class comprehensive works on Duluth, Minnesota, and Superior in —776771
—775 13	Bayfield County
—775 14	Burnett County
—775 15	Washburn County
—775 16	Sawyer County
—775 17	Polk County
—775 18	Barron County
—775 19	Rusk County
—775 2	North central counties
—775 21	Ashland County
—775 22	Iron County
—775 23	Vilas County
—775 24	Price County
—775 25	Oneida County
—775 26	Taylor County
—775 27	Lincoln County
—775 28	Clark County
—775 29	Marathon County
—775 3	Northeastern counties
	Class here *Green Bay
—775 31	Forest County
—775 32	Florence County
—775 33	Marinette County
	For Marinette city, see —77534
—775 34	Marinette city

*Class parts of this physiographic region or feature as instructed under —4–9

—775 35	Langlade and Menominee Counties
—775 354	Langlade County
—775 356	Menominee County
—775 36	Shawano County
—775 37	Oconto County
—775 38	Waupaca County
—775 39	Outagamie County
—775 4	West central counties
	Class here *Chippewa River
—775 41	Saint Croix County
—775 42	Pierce County
—775 43	Dunn County
—775 44	Chippewa County
—775 45	Eau Claire County
	For Eau Claire city, see —77546
—775 46	Eau Claire city
—775 47	Pepin County
—775 48	Buffalo County
—775 49	Trempealeau County
—775 5	Central counties
—775 51	Jackson County
—775 52	Wood County
—775 53	Portage County
—775 54	Monroe County
—775 55	Juneau County
—775 56	Adams County
—775 57	Waushara County
—775 58	Marquette County
—775 59	Green Lake County

*Class parts of this physiographic region or feature as instructed under —4–9

Table 2. Areas

—775 6	**East central counties**
	Class here *Fox River
—775 61	Brown County
—775 62	Kewaunee County
—775 63	Door County
—775 64	Winnebago County
	Class here *Lake Winnebago
	For Oshkosh, see —77565
—775 65	Oshkosh
—775 66	Calumet County
—775 67	Manitowoc County
—775 68	Fond du Lac County
—775 69	Sheboygan County
—775 7	**Southwestern counties**
—775 71	La Crosse County
	For La Crosse city, see —77572
—775 72	La Crosse city
—775 73	Vernon County
—775 74	Crawford County
—775 75	Richland County
—775 76	Sauk County
—775 77	Grant County
—775 78	Iowa County
—775 79	Lafayette County
—775 8	**South central counties**
—775 81	Columbia County
—775 82	Dodge County
—775 83	Dane County
	For Madison, see —77584
—775 84	Madison
—775 85	Jefferson County

*Class parts of this physiographic region or feature as instructed under —4–9

—775 86	Green County
—775 87	Rock County
	For Beloit, see —77588
—775 88	Beloit
—775 89	Walworth County
—775 9	Southeastern counties
—775 91	Washington County
—775 92	Ozaukee County
—775 93	Waukesha County
—775 94	Milwaukee County
	For Milwaukee city, see —77595
—775 95	Milwaukee city
—775 96	Racine County
	For Racine city, see —77597
—775 97	Racine city
—775 98	Kenosha County
	For Kenosha city, see —77599
—775 99	Kenosha city
—776	Minnesota

SUMMARY

—776 1	Southeastern counties
—776 2	Southwestern counties
—776 3	Southwest central counties
—776 4	West central counties
—776 5	Southeast central counties
—776 6	East central counties
—776 7	Northeastern counties
—776 8	North central counties
—776 9	Northwestern counties

—776 1	Southeastern counties
—776 11	Houston County
—776 12	Winona County
—776 13	Wabasha County
	Class here *Lake Pepin
—776 14	Goodhue County

*Class parts of this physiographic region or feature as instructed under —4–9

Table 2. Areas

—776 15	Dodge and Olmsted Counties
—776 153	Dodge County
—776 155	Olmsted County
—776 16	Fillmore County
—776 17	Mower County
—776 18	Freeborn County
—776 19	Steele and Waseca Counties
—776 193	Steele County
—776 195	Waseca County
—776 2	Southwestern counties
—776 21	Blue Earth County
—776 22	Faribault County
—776 23	Martin and Jackson Counties
—776 232	Martin County
—776 235	Jackson County
—776 24	Nobles County
—776 25	Rock County
—776 26	Pipestone County
—776 27	Murray County
—776 28	Cottonwood County
—776 29	Watonwan County
—776 3	Southwest central counties
	Class here *Minnesota River
—776 31	Brown County
—776 32	Nicollet County
—776 33	Sibley County
—776 34	Renville County
—776 35	Redwood County

*Class parts of this physiographic region or feature as instructed under —4-9

—776 36	Lyon and Lincoln Counties
—776 363	Lyon County
—776 365	Lincoln County
—776 37	Yellow Medicine County
—776 38	Lac Qui Parle County
—776 39	Chippewa County
—776 4	West central counties
—776 41	Swift County
—776 42	Stevens County
—776 43	Big Stone and Traverse Counties
—776 432	Big Stone County
—776 435	Traverse County
—776 44	Grant County
—776 45	Douglas County
—776 46	Pope County
—776 47	Stearns County
—776 48	Kandiyohi County
—776 49	Meeker County
—776 5	Southeast central counties
—776 51	Wright County
—776 52	McLeod County
—776 53	Carver County
—776 54	Scott County
—776 55	Le Sueur and Rice Counties
—776 553	Le Sueur County
—776 555	Rice County
—776 56	Dakota County

Table 2. Areas

—776 57	Hennepin County
—776 579	Minneapolis

> Class here Twin Cities
>
> *For Saint Paul, see —776581*

—776 58	Ramsey County
—776 581	Saint Paul

> Class Twin Cities in —776579

—776 59	Washington County
—776 6	East central counties
—776 61	Chisago County
—776 62	Pine County
—776 63	Kanabec County
—776 64	Isanti County
—776 65	Anoka County
—776 66	Sherburne County
—776 67	Benton County
—776 68	Mille Lacs County

> Class here *Mille Lacs Lake

—776 69	Morrison County
—776 7	Northeastern counties
—776 71	Crow Wing County
—776 72	Aitkin County
—776 73	Carlton County
—776 75	Cook County
—776 76	Lake County
—776 77	Saint Louis County

> Class here *Mesabi Range, *La Croix Lake

—776 771	Duluth

> Class here comprehensive works on Duluth and Superior, Wisconsin
>
> *For Superior, see —77512*

*Class parts of this physiographic region or feature as instructed under —4–9

—776 78	Itasca County
	Class here *Winnibigoshish Lake
—776 79	Koochiching County
	Class here *Rainy River and *Lake
—776 8	North central counties
—776 81	Lake of the Woods County
	Class here *Lake of the Woods
—776 82	Beltrami County
—776 83	Clearwater County
—776 84	Becker County
—776 85	Hubbard County
—776 86	Cass County
—776 87	Wadena County
—776 88	Todd County
—776 89	Otter Tail County
—776 9	Northwestern counties
	Class here *Red River of the North in Minnesota
—776 91	Wilkin County
—776 92	Clay County
—776 93	Norman County
—776 94	Mahnomen County
—776 95	Polk County
—776 96	Red Lake and Pennington Counties
—776 963	Red Lake County
—776 965	Pennington County
—776 97	Marshall County
—776 98	Roseau County
—776 99	Kittson County

*Class parts of this physiographic region or feature as instructed under —4–9

Table 2. Areas

—777   Iowa

Class here *Des Moines River

SUMMARY

—777 1	Northwestern counties
—777 2	North central counties
—777 3	Northeastern counties
—777 4	West central counties
—777 5	Central counties
—777 6	East central counties
—777 7	Southwestern counties
—777 8	South central counties
—777 9	Southeastern counties

—777 1   Northwestern counties

Class here *Big Sioux River in Iowa, *Little Sioux River

—777 11   Lyon and Osceola Counties

—777 114   Lyon County

—777 116   Osceola County

—777 12   Dickinson and Emmet Counties

—777 123   Dickinson County

—777 125   Emmet County

—777 13   Sioux County

—777 14   O'Brien County

—777 15   Clay and Palo Alto Counties

—777 153   Clay County

—777 155   Palo Alto County

—777 16   Plymouth County

—777 17   Cherokee County

—777 18   Buena Vista County

—777 19   Pocahontas County

—777 2   North central counties

—777 21   Kossuth County

—777 22   Winnebago County

*Class parts of this physiographic region or feature as instructed under —4–9

—777 23	Worth and Mitchell Counties
—777 232	Worth County
—777 234	Mitchell County
—777 24	Hancock County
—777 25	Cerro Gordo County
—777 26	Floyd County
—777 27	Humboldt and Wright Counties
—777 272	Humboldt County
—777 274	Wright County
—777 28	Franklin County
—777 29	Butler County
—777 3	Northeastern counties
—777 31	Howard and Chickasaw Counties
—777 312	Howard County
—777 315	Chickasaw County
—777 32	Winneshiek County
—777 33	Allamakee County
—777 34	Bremer County
—777 35	Fayette County
—777 36	Clayton County
—777 37	Black Hawk County
—777 38	Buchanan and Delaware Counties
—777 382	Buchanan County
—777 385	Delaware County
—777 39	Dubuque County
—777 4	West central counties
	Class here *Boyer, *Raccoon Rivers
—777 41	Woodbury County
	Including Sioux City

*Class parts of this physiographic region or feature as instructed under —4–9

Table 2. Areas

—777 42	Ida and Sac Counties
—777 422	Ida County
—777 424	Sac County
—777 43	Calhoun County
—777 44	Monona County
—777 45	Crawford County
—777 46	Carroll and Greene Counties
—777 465	Carroll County
—777 466	Greene County
—777 47	Harrison County
—777 48	Shelby and Audobon Counties
—777 484	Shelby County
—777 486	Audubon County
—777 49	Guthrie County
—777 5	Central counties
—777 51	Webster County
—777 52	Hamilton County
—777 53	Hardin and Grundy Counties
—777 535	Hardin County
—777 537	Grundy County
—777 54	Boone and Story Counties
—777 544	Boone County
—777 546	Story County
—777 55	Marshall County
—777 56	Tama County
—777 57	Dallas County
—777 58	Polk County
	Including Des Moines

—777 59	Jasper and Poweshiek Counties
—777 594	Jasper County
—777 596	Poweshiek County
—777 6	East central counties

Class here *Wapsipinicon, *Cedar, *Iowa Rivers

—777 61	Benton County
—777 62	Linn County
—777 63	Jones County
—777 64	Jackson County
—777 65	Iowa and Johnson Counties
—777 653	Iowa County
—777 655	Johnson County
—777 66	Cedar County
—777 67	Clinton County
—777 68	Muscatine County
—777 69	Scott County

Class here Davenport-Rock Island-Moline tri-city area

For Rock Island County, Illinois, see —773393

—777 7	Southwestern counties

Class here *Nishnabotna River

—777 71	Pottawattamie County
—777 72	Cass County
—777 73	Adair County
—777 74	Mills County
—777 75	Montgomery County
—777 76	Adams County
—777 77	Fremont County
—777 78	Page County
—777 79	Taylor County

*Class parts of this physiographic region or feature as instructed under —4–9

Table 2. Areas

—777 8	South central counties
—777 81	Madison County
—777 82	Warren County
—777 83	Marion County
—777 84	Mahaska County
—777 85	Union and Clarke Counties
—777 853	Union County
—777 856	Clarke County
—777 86	Lucas and Monroe Counties
—777 863	Lucas County
—777 865	Monroe County
—777 87	Ringgold and Decatur Counties
—777 873	Ringgold County
—777 875	Decatur County
—777 88	Wayne County
—777 89	Appanoose County
—777 9	Southeastern counties
	Class here *Skunk River
—777 91	Keokuk County
—777 92	Washington and Louisa Counties
—777 923	Washington County
—777 926	Louisa County
—777 93	Wapello County
—777 94	Jefferson County
—777 95	Henry County
—777 96	Des Moines County
—777 97	Davis County
—777 98	Van Buren County
—777 99	Lee County

*Class parts of this physiographic region or feature as instructed under —4–9

—778   Missouri

Class here *Missouri River in Missouri

SUMMARY

—778 1 Northwestern counties
—778 2 North central counties
—778 3 Northeastern counties
—778 4 West central counties
—778 5 Central counties
—778 6 East central counties
—778 7 Southwestern counties
—778 8 South central counties
—778 9 Southeastern counties

—778 1   Northwestern counties

—778 11   Atchison and Holt Counties

—778 113   Atchison County

—778 115   Holt County

—778 12   Nodaway and Andrew Counties

—778 124   Nodaway County

—778 126   Andrew County

—778 13   Buchanan and Platte Counties

—778 132   Buchanan County

—778 135   Platte County

—778 14   Worth and Gentry Counties

—778 143   Worth County

—778 145   Gentry County

—778 15   De Kalb and Clinton Counties

—778 153   De Kalb County

—778 155   Clinton County

—778 16   Clay County

—778 17   Harrison County

*Class parts of this physiographic region or feature as instructed under —4–9

Table 2. Areas

—778 18	Daviess and Caldwell Counties
—778 183	Daviess County
—778 185	Caldwell County
—778 19	Ray County
—778 2	North central counties
	Class here *Chariton River
—778 21	Mercer and Grundy Counties
—778 213	Mercer County
—778 215	Grundy County
—778 22	Livingston and Carroll Counties
—778 223	Livingston County
—778 225	Carroll County
—778 23	Putnam and Sullivan Counties
—778 232	Putnam County
—778 235	Sullivan County
—778 24	Linn County
—778 25	Chariton County
—778 26	Schuyler and Adair Counties
—778 262	Schuyler County
—778 264	Adair County
—778 27	Macon County
—778 28	Randolph and Howard Counties
—778 283	Randolph County
—778 285	Howard County
—778 29	Boone County
—778 3	Northeastern counties
—778 31	Scotland and Knox Counties
—778 312	Scotland County
—778 315	Knox County

*Class parts of this physiographic region or feature as instructed under —4–9

—778 32	Shelby and Monroe Counties
—778 323	Shelby County
—778 325	Monroe County
—778 33	Audrain and Callaway Counties
—778 332	Audrain County
—778 335	Callaway County
—778 34	Clark and Lewis Counties
—778 343	Clark County
—778 345	Lewis County
—778 35	Marion and Ralls Counties
—778 353	Marion County
—778 355	Ralls County
—778 36	Pike County
—778 37	Lincoln County
—778 38	Montgomery and Warren Counties
—778 382	Montgomery County
—778 386	Warren County
—778 39	Saint Charles County
—778 4	West central counties
—778 41	Jackson County
—778 411	Kansas City

Class here Greater Kansas City

For Wyandotte County, Kansas, see —78139

—778 42	Cass County
—778 43	Bates County
—778 44	Vernon County
—778 45	Lafayette and Johnson Counties
—778 453	Lafayette County
—778 455	Johnson County

Table 2. Areas

—778 46	Henry and Saint Clair Counties
—778 462	Henry County
—778 466	Saint Clair County
—778 47	Saline County
—778 48	Pettis County
—778 49	Benton and Hickory Counties
—778 493	Benton County
	Class here *Lake of the Ozarks
—778 496	Hickory County
—778 5	Central counties
—778 51	Cooper County
—778 52	Moniteau County
—778 53	Morgan County
—778 54	Camden County
—778 55	Cole County
	Including Jefferson City
—778 56	Miller County
—778 57	Pulaski County
—778 58	Osage County
—778 59	Maries and Phelps Counties
—778 592	Maries County
—778 594	Phelps County
—778 6	East central counties
—778 61	Gasconade County
—778 62	Crawford County
—778 63	Franklin County
—778 64	Washington County
—778 65	Saint Louis County
—778 66	Independent city of Saint Louis
—778 67	Jefferson County
—778 68	Saint Francois County

*Class parts of this physiographic region or feature as instructed under —4–9

—778 69	Sainte Genevieve and Perry Counties
—778 692	Sainte Genevieve County
—778 694	Perry County
—778 7	Southwestern counties
—778 71	Barton County
—778 72	Jasper County
—778 73	Newton and McDonald Counties
—778 732	Newton County
—778 736	McDonald County
—778 74	Cedar and Dade Counties
—778 743	Cedar County
—778 745	Dade County
—778 75	Lawrence County
—778 76	Barry County
—778 77	Polk County
—778 78	Greene County
—778 79	Christian, Stone, Taney Counties
—778 792	Christian County
—778 794	Stone County
—778 797	Taney County
—778 8	South central counties
	Class here *Ozark Plateau in Missouri
—778 81	Dallas and Laclede Counties
—778 813	Dallas County
—778 815	Laclede County
—778 82	Webster and Wright Counties
—778 823	Webster County
—778 825	Wright County

*Class parts of this physiographic region or feature as instructed under —4–9

Table 2. Areas

—778 83	Douglas and Ozark Counties
—778 832	Douglas County
—778 835	Ozark County
—778 84	Texas County
—778 85	Howell County
—778 86	Dent County
—778 87	Shannon and Oregon Counties
—778 873	Shannon County
—778 875	Oregon County
—778 88	Iron and Reynolds Counties
—778 883	Iron County
—778 885	Reynolds County
—778 89	Carter and Ripley Counties
—778 892	Carter County
—778 894	Ripley County
—778 9	Southeastern counties
—778 91	Madison County
—778 92	Wayne County
—778 93	Butler County
—778 94	Bollinger County
—778 95	Stoddard County
—778 96	Cape Girardeau County
—778 97	Scott County
—778 98	Mississippi and New Madrid Counties
—778 983	Mississippi County
—778 985	New Madrid County
—778 99	Dunklin and Pemiscot Counties
—778 993	Dunklin County
—778 996	Pemiscot County

—78   **Western United States**

Class here the West, *Missouri River, *Rocky Mountains, *Great
Plains

For Great Basin and Pacific Slope region, see —79

SUMMARY

—781	Kansas
—782	Nebraska
—783	South Dakota
—784	North Dakota
—786	Montana
—787	Wyoming
—788	Colorado
—789	New Mexico

—781   Kansas

Class here *Kansas (Kaw) River

SUMMARY

—781 1	Northwestern counties
—781 2	North central counties
—781 3	Northeastern counties
—781 4	West central counties
—781 5	Central counties
—781 6	East central counties
—781 7	Southwestern counties
—781 8	South central counties
—781 9	Southeastern counties

—781 1   Northwestern counties

—781 11   Cheyenne and Sherman Counties

—781 112   Cheyenne County

—781 115   Sherman County

—781 12   Wallace and Rawlins Counties

—781 123   Wallace County

—781 125   Rawlins County

—781 13   Thomas and Logan Counties

—781 132   Thomas County

—781 135   Logan County

*Class parts of this physiographic region or feature as instructed under —4–9

Table 2. Areas

—781 14	Decatur and Sheridan Counties
—781 143	Decatur County
—781 145	Sheridan County
—781 15	Gove and Norton Counties
—781 152	Gove County
—781 155	Norton County
—781 16	Graham and Trego Counties
—781 163	Graham County
—781 165	Trego County
—781 17	Phillips County
—781 18	Rooks County
—781 19	Ellis County
—781 2	**North central counties**
	Class here *Solomon, *Republican, *Big Blue Rivers
—781 21	Smith and Osborne Counties
—781 213	Smith County
—781 215	Osborne County
—781 22	Jewell County
—781 23	Mitchell County
—781 24	Republic County
—781 25	Cloud County
—781 26	Ottawa County
—781 27	Washington and Clay Counties
—781 273	Washington County
—781 275	Clay County
—781 28	Riley County
—781 29	Geary County

*Class parts of this physiographic region or feature as instructed under —4–9

—781 3	Northeastern counties
—781 31	Marshall County
—781 32	Pottawatomie County
—781 33	Nemaha and Jackson Counties
—781 332	Nemaha County
—781 335	Jackson County
—781 34	Brown County
—781 35	Doniphan County
—781 36	Atchison County
—781 37	Jefferson County
—781 38	Leavenworth County
—781 39	Wyandotte County

Class comprehensive works on Greater Kansas City in —778411

—781 4	West central counties

Class here *Arkansas River in Kansas

—781 41	Greeley and Hamilton Counties
—781 413	Greeley County
—781 415	Hamilton County
—781 42	Wichita and Kearny Counties
—781 423	Wichita County
—781 425	Kearny County
—781 43	Scott County
—781 44	Finney County
—781 45	Lane County
—781 46	Ness County
—781 47	Hodgeman County
—781 48	Rush County
—781 49	Pawnee County

*Class parts of this physiographic region or feature as instructed under —4–9

Table 2. Areas

—781 5	Central counties
—781 51	Russell County
—781 52	Barton County
—781 53	Lincoln and Ellsworth Counties
—781 532	Lincoln County
—781 535	Ellsworth County
—781 54	Rice and Saline Counties
—781 543	Rice County
—781 545	Saline County
—781 55	McPherson County
—781 56	Dickinson County
—781 57	Marion County
—781 58	Morris County
—781 59	Chase County
—781 6	East central counties
—781 61	Wabaunsee County
—781 62	Lyon County
—781 63	Shawnee County
	Including Topeka
—781 64	Osage and Coffey Counties
—781 643	Osage County
—781 645	Coffey County
—781 65	Douglas County
—781 66	Franklin County
—781 67	Anderson and Johnson Counties
—781 672	Anderson County
—781 675	Johnson County
—781 68	Miami County
—781 69	Linn County

—781 7	Southwestern counties
—781 71	Stanton and Morton Counties
—781 712	Stanton County
—781 715	Morton County
—781 72	Grant and Stevens Counties
—781 723	Grant County
—781 725	Stevens County
—781 73	Haskell and Seward Counties
—781 732	Haskell County
—781 735	Seward County
—781 74	Gray County
—781 75	Meade County
—781 76	Ford County
—781 77	Clark County
—781 78	Edwards and Kiowa Counties
—781 782	Edwards County
—781 785	Kiowa County
—781 79	Comanche County
—781 8	South central counties
—781 81	Stafford and Pratt Counties
—781 813	Stafford County
—781 815	Pratt County
—781 82	Barber County
—781 83	Reno County
—781 84	Kingman and Harper Counties
—781 843	Kingman County
—781 845	Harper County
—781 85	Harvey County
—781 86	Sedgwick County
	Including Wichita
—781 87	Sumner County
—781 88	Butler County

Table 2. Areas

—781 89	Cowley County
—781 9	Southeastern counties
—781 91	Greenwood, Elk, Chautauqua Counties
—781 913	Greenwood County
—781 915	Elk County
—781 918	Chautauqua County
—781 92	Woodson and Wilson Counties
—781 923	Woodson County
—781 925	Wilson County
—781 93	Montgomery County
—781 94	Allen County
—781 95	Neosho County
—781 96	Labette County
—781 97	Bourbon County
—781 98	Crawford County
—781 99	Cherokee County
—782	Nebraska

Class here *Platte River

SUMMARY

—782 2	Missouri River lowland counties
—782 3	South central counties
—782 4	Central counties
—782 5	Northeast central counties
—782 7	North central counties
—782 8	Southwestern counties
—782 9	Northwestern counties (Panhandle)

—782 2	Missouri River lowland counties

SUMMARY

—782 22	Dixon, Dakota, Thurston Counties
—782 23	Cuming and Dodge Counties
—782 24	Burt and Washington Counties
—782 25	Douglas and Sarpy Counties
—782 27	Cass and neighboring counties
—782 28	Richardson, Pawnee, Gage Counties
—782 29	Lancaster and Saunders Counties

*Class parts of this physiographic region or feature as instructed under —4–9

—782 22	Dixon, Dakota, Thurston Counties
—782 223	Dixon County
—782 224	Dakota County
—782 227	Thurston County
—782 23	Cuming and Dodge Counties
—782 232	Cuming County
—782 235	Dodge County
—782 24	Burt and Washington Counties
—782 243	Burt County
—782 245	Washington County
—782 25	Douglas and Sarpy Counties
—782 254	Douglas County
	Including Omaha
—782 256	Sarpy County
—782 27	Cass and neighboring counties
—782 272	Cass County
—782 273	Otoe County
—782 276	Johnson County
—782 278	Nemaha County
—782 28	Richardson, Pawnee, Gage Counties
—782 282	Richardson County
—782 284	Pawnee County
—782 286	Gage County
	For Beatrice, see —782287
—782 287	Beatrice
—782 29	Lancaster and Saunders Counties
—782 293	Lancaster County
	Including Lincoln
—782 296	Saunders County

Table 2. Areas

—782 3   South central counties

Class here *Republican River in Nebraska

SUMMARY

—782 32	Butler, Seward, Saline Counties
—782 33	Jefferson and Thayer Counties
—782 34	Fillmore and York Counties
—782 35	Polk, Hamilton, Clay Counties
—782 37	Nuckolls, Webster, Franklin Counties
—782 38	Harlan, Furnas, Gosper Counties
—782 39	Phelps, Kearney, Adams Counties

—782 32   Butler, Seward, Saline Counties

—782 322   Butler County

—782 324   Seward County

—782 327   Saline County

—782 33   Jefferson and Thayer Counties

—782 332   Jefferson County

—782 335   Thayer County

—782 34   Fillmore and York Counties

—782 342   Fillmore County

—782 345   York County

—782 35   Polk, Hamilton, Clay Counties

—782 352   Polk County

—782 354   Hamilton County

—782 357   Clay County

—782 37   Nuckolls, Webster, Franklin Counties

—782 372   Nuckolls County

—782 374   Webster County

—782 377   Franklin County

—782 38   Harlan, Furnas, Gosper Counties

—782 382   Harlan County

—782 384   Furnas County

—782 387   Gosper County

*Class parts of this physiographic region or feature as instructed under —4–9

—782 39	Phelps, Kearney, Adams Counties
—782 392	Phelps County
—782 394	Kearney County
—782 397	Adams County

For Hastings, see —782398

—782 398	Hastings
—782 4	**Central counties**

Class here *Loup River

—782 41	Hall County
—782 42	Merrick and Nance Counties
—782 423	Merrick County
—782 425	Nance County
—782 43	Howard County
—782 44	Sherman County
—782 45	Buffalo County
—782 46	Dawson County
—782 47	Custer County
—782 48	Valley County
—782 49	Greeley County
—782 5	**Northeast central counties**

Class here *Elkhorn River

—782 51	Boone County
—782 52	Platte County
—782 53	Colfax and Stanton Counties
—782 532	Colfax County
—782 535	Stanton County
—782 54	Madison County
—782 55	Antelope County
—782 56	Pierce County
—782 57	Wayne County
—782 58	Cedar County

*Class parts of this physiographic region or feature as instructed under —4-9

Table 2. Areas

—782 59	Knox County
—782 7	North central counties
	Class here *Niobrara River
—782 72	Boyd and Keya Paha Counties
—782 723	Boyd County
—782 725	Keya Paha County
—782 73	Cherry and Brown Counties
—782 732	Cherry County
—782 736	Brown County
—782 74	Rock and Holt Counties
—782 743	Rock County
—782 745	Holt County
—782 76	Wheeler, Garfield, Loup Counties
—782 762	Wheeler County
—782 764	Garfield County
—782 767	Loup County
—782 77	Blaine, Thomas, Hooker Counties
—782 772	Blaine County
—782 774	Thomas County
—782 777	Hooker County
—782 78	Grant and Arthur Counties
—782 783	Grant County
—782 785	Arthur County
—782 79	McPherson and Logan Counties
—782 793	McPherson County
—782 795	Logan County
—782 8	Southwestern counties
—782 82	Lincoln County

*Class parts of this physiographic region or feature as instructed under —4–9

—782 83	Hayes and Frontier Counties
—782 832	Hayes County
—782 835	Frontier County
—782 84	Redwillow and Hitchcock Counties
—782 843	Redwillow County
—782 845	Hitchcock County
—782 86	Dundy County
—782 87	Chase County
—782 88	Perkins County
—782 89	Keith County
	Class here *McConaughy Lake
—782 9	Northwestern counties (Panhandle)
—782 91	Deuel and Garden Counties
—782 913	Deuel County
—782 915	Garden County
—782 92	Sheridan County
—782 93	Dawes County
—782 94	Box Butte County
—782 95	Morrill County
—782 96	Cheyenne County
—782 97	Kimball and Banner Counties
—782 973	Kimball County
—782 975	Banner County
—782 98	Scotts Bluff County
—782 99	Sioux County
—783	South Dakota

SUMMARY

—783 1	Northeastern counties
—783 2	East central counties
—783 3	Southeastern counties
—783 4	Northwestern counties
—783 5	Central counties
—783 6	South central counties
—783 9	Black Hills counties

*Class parts of this physiographic region or feature as instructed under —4–9

Table 2. Areas

—783 1	Northeastern counties
—783 12	Roberts County
—783 13	Marshall County
—783 14	Day and Brown Counties
—783 142	Day County
—783 144	Brown County
—783 15	Edmunds County
—783 16	McPherson County
—783 17	Campbell County
—783 18	Walworth County
—783 19	Potter County
—783 2	East central counties
—783 21	Faulk and Spink Counties
—783 213	Faulk County
—783 217	Spink County
—783 22	Clark County
—783 23	Codington County
—783 24	Grant County
—783 25	Deuel County
—783 26	Hamlin County
—783 27	Brookings, Kingsbury, Beadle Counties
—783 272	Brookings County
—783 273	Kingsbury County
—783 274	Beadle county
—783 28	Hand, Hyde, Sully Counties
—783 282	Hand County
—783 283	Hyde County
—783 284	Sully County

—783 29	Hughes County
	Including Pierre
—783 3	**Southeastern counties**
	Class here *James, *Big Sioux Rivers, *Missouri River in South Dakota
—783 31	Buffalo County
—783 32	Jerauld County
—783 33	Sanborn County
—783 34	Miner County
—783 35	Lake County
—783 36	Moody County
—783 37	Minnehaha and neighboring counties
—783 371	Minnehaha County
	Including Sioux Falls
—783 372	McCook County
—783 373	Hanson County
—783 374	Davison County
—783 375	Aurora County
—783 38	Brule and neighboring counties
—783 381	Brule County
—783 382	Charles Mix County
—783 383	Douglas County
—783 384	Hutchinson County
—783 385	Turner County
—783 39	Lincoln and neighboring counties
—783 391	Lincoln County
—783 392	Union County
—783 393	Clay County
—783 394	Yankton County
—783 395	Bon Homme County

*Class parts of this physiographic region or feature as instructed under —4–9

Table 2. Areas

—783 4	Northwestern counties
—783 42	Harding County
—783 43	Butte County
—783 44	Meade County
—783 45	Perkins County
—783 5	Central counties

Class here *Grand, *Moreau, *Cheyenne Rivers

—783 52	Corson County
—783 53	Ziebach County
—783 54	Dewey County
—783 55	Stanley County
—783 56	Haakon County
—783 57	Jackson and Jones Counties
—783 572	Jackson County
—783 577	Jones County
—783 58	Lyman County
—783 59	Gregory County
—783 6	South central counties

Class here *White River

—783 61	Tripp County
—783 62	Todd County
—783 63	Mellette County
—783 64	Washabaugh County
—783 65	Bennett County
—783 66	Shannon County
—783 9	Black Hills counties
—783 91	Lawrence County
—783 93	Pennington County

Class here *Badlands

—783 95	Custer County

Including Wind Cave National Park

*Class parts of this physiographic region or feature as instructed under —4–9

—783 97   Fall River County

—784   North Dakota

SUMMARY

—784 1   Red River Valley counties
—784 3   Sheyenne River Valley and adjacent counties
—784 5   James River Valley and adajacent counties
—784 6   Souris River Valley counties
—784 7   Counties north and east of Missouri River
—784 8   Counties south and west of Missouri River
—784 9   Badlands counties

—784 1   Red River Valley counties

Class here *Red River of the North

—784 12   Richland County

—784 13   Cass County

Including Fargo

—784 14   Traill County

—784 16   Grand Forks County

—784 18   Walsh County

—784 19   Pembina County

—784 3   *Sheyenne River Valley and adjacent counties

—784 31   Sargent and Ransom Counties

—784 314   Sargent County

—784 315   Ransom County

—784 32   Barnes County

—784 33   Steele County

—784 34   Griggs County

—784 35   Nelson County

—784 36   Ramsey County

Class here *Devils Lake

—784 37   Cavalier County

—784 38   Towner County

—784 39   Benson County

*Class parts of this physiographic region or feature as instructed under —4-9

Table 2. Areas

—784 5	James River Valley and adajacent counties
	Class here *James River in North Dakota
—784 51	Eddy and Foster Counties
—784 512	Eddy County
—784 516	Foster County
—784 52	Stutsman County
—784 53	La Moure County
—784 54	Dickey County
—784 55	McIntosh County
—784 56	Logan County
—784 57	Kidder County
—784 58	Wells County
—784 59	Pierce and Rolette Counties
—784 591	Pierce County
—784 592	Rolette County
—784 6	*Souris River Valley counties
	Class here *Turtle Mountians
—784 61	Bottineau County
—784 62	McHenry County
—784 63	Ward County
—784 64	Renville County
—784 7	Counties north and east of Missouri River
	Class here *Missouri River in North Dakota
—784 71	Divide County
—784 72	Burke County
—784 73	Williams County
—784 74	Mountrail County
—784 75	McLean County
	Class here *Garrison Reservoir
—784 76	Sheridan County

*Class parts of this physiographic region or feature as instructed under —4–9

—784 77	Burleigh County
	Including Bismarck
—784 78	Emmons County
—784 8	Counties south and west of Missouri River
	Class here *Little Missouri River
	For Badlands counties, see —7849
—784 81	McKenzie County
—784 82	Dunn County
—784 83	Mercer County
—784 84	Oliver and Stark Counties
—784 843	Oliver County
—784 844	Stark County
—784 85	Morton County
—784 86	Hettinger County
—784 87	Grant County
—784 88	Sioux County
—784 89	Adams County
—784 9	Badlands counties
—784 92	Bowman County
—784 93	Slope County
—784 94	Billings County
—784 95	Golden Valley County

▶ —786–789 Rocky Mountains states

Class comprehensive works in —78

For Idaho, see —796

—786 Montana

SUMMARY

—786 1	North central counties
—786 2	Northeastern and central plains counties
—786 3	Southeastern counties
—786 5	Northwest central counties
—786 6	Southwestern and central mountain counties
—786 8	Northwestern counties

*Class parts of this physiographic region or feature as instructed under —4-9

Table 2. Areas

—786 1	North central counties
	Class here *Milk River, *Missouri River in Montana, *Great Plains in Montana
—786 12	Toole County
—786 13	Liberty County
—786 14	Hill County
—786 15	Blaine County
—786 16	Phillips County
—786 17	Valley County
	Class here *Fort Peck Reservoir
—786 2	Northeastern and central plains counties
—786 21	Daniels and Sheridan Counties
—786 213	Daniels County
—786 218	Sheridan County
—786 22	Roosevelt County
—786 23	Richland County
—786 24	Dawson County
—786 25	Prairie County
—786 26	McCone County
—786 27	Garfield County
—786 28	Petroleum County
—786 29	Fergus and Chouteau Counties
—786 292	Fergus County
—786 293	Chouteau County
—786 3	Southeastern counties
	Class here *Yellowstone River
—786 31	Golden Valley, Musselshell, Treasure Counties
—786 311	Golden Valley County
—786 312	Musselshell County
—786 313	Treasure County

*Class parts of this physiographic region or feature as instructed under —4–9

—786 32	Rosebud County
—786 33	Custer County
—786 34	Wibaux County
—786 35	Fallon County
—786 36	Carter County
—786 37	Powder River County
—786 38	Big Horn County
—786 39	Yellowstone County

—786 5   Northwest central counties

Class here *Rocky Mountains in Montana

—786 52   Glacier County

> Class here Glacier National Park, Waterton-Glacier International Peace Park
>
> Class each specific part of Glacier National Park, of Waterton-Glacier International Peace Park, not provided for here with the subject, e.g., in Flathead County —78682

—786 53	Pondera County
—786 55	Teton County

—786 6   Southwestern and central mountain counties

—786 61	Cascade, Meagher, Lewis and Clark Counties
—786 611	Cascade County
—786 612	Meagher County
—786 615	Lewis and Clark County

Including Helena

—786 62	Judith Basin County
—786 63	Wheatland County
—786 64	Sweet Grass County

*Class parts of this physiographic region or feature as instructed under —4–9

Table 2. Areas

—786 65	Stillwater and Carbon Counties
—786 651	Stillwater County
—786 652	Carbon County
—786 66	Park and neighboring counties
—786 661	Park County
—786 662	Gallatin County
—786 663	Madison County
—786 664	Broadwater County
—786 67	Jefferson County
—786 68	Silver Bow County
	Including Butte
—786 69	Beaverhead County
—786 8	**Northwestern counties**
	Class here *Bitterroot Range
—786 81	Lincoln County
—786 82	Flathead County
—786 83	Lake and Sanders Counties
—786 832	Lake County
	Class here *Flathead Lake
—786 833	Sanders County
—786 84	Mineral County
—786 85	Missoula County
—786 86	Powell County
—786 87	Deer Lodge County
	Including Anaconda
—786 88	Granite County
—786 89	Ravalli County

*Class parts of this physiographic region or feature as instructed under —4–9

—787   Wyoming

SUMMARY

—787 1   **Eastern counties (High Plains region)**
—787 2   **Rocky Mountains in Wyoming**
—787 3   **Big Horn Mountains counties**
—787 4   **Absaroka Range counties**
—787 5   **Teton Range area**
—787 6   **Wind River Range counties**
—787 8   **Southwestern counties**
—787 9   **Laramie Range counties**

—787 1   Eastern counties (High Plains region)

—787 12   Campbell County

—787 13   Crook County

Class here *Belle Fourche River

—787 14   Weston County

—787 15   Niobrara County

—787 16   Converse County

Class here *North Platte River

—787 17   Platte County

—787 18   Goshen County

—787 19   Laramie County

Including Cheyenne

—787 2   *Rocky Mountains in Wyoming

—787 3   *Big Horn Mountains counties

—787 32   Sheridan County

—787 33   Big Horn County

—787 34   Washakie County

—787 35   Johnson County

—787 4   *Absaroka Range counties

—787 42   Park County

—787 43   Hot Springs County

Class here *Owl Creek Mountains

*Class parts of this physiographic region or feature as instructed under —4–9

Table 2. Areas

—787 5	*Teton Range area
—787 52	Yellowstone National Park

Class each specific part with the subject, e.g., in Teton
County, Wyoming —78755

—787 55	Teton County

Including Grand Teton National Park

Class here *Snake River Range, *Gros Ventre Range, *Snake
River in Wyoming

—787 6	*Wind River Range counties
—787 63	Fremont County
—787 65	Sublette County
—787 8	Southwestern counties
—787 82	Lincoln County
—787 84	Uinta County

Class here *Bear River Divide

—787 85	Sweetwater County

Class here *Green River in Wyoming

—787 86	Carbon County

Class here *Medicine Bow Range, *Pathfinder Reservoir

—787 9	*Laramie Range counties
—787 93	Natrona County
—787 95	Albany County
—788	Colorado

SUMMARY

—788 1	Northern counties of Colorado Plateau
—788 2	Southern counties of Colorado Plateau
—788 3	Southern counties of Rocky Mountains
—788 4	West central counties of Rocky Mountains
—788 5	East central counties of Rocky Mountains
—788 6	Northern counties of Rocky Mountains
—788 7	Northern counties of Great Plains
—788 8	Central counties of Great Plains
—788 9	Southern counties of Great Plains

*Class parts of this physiographic region or feature as instructed under —4–9

—788 1	Northern counties of *Colorado Plateau

Class here *Colorado River in Colorado

—788 12	Moffat County

Class here Dinosaur National Monument

Class Dinosaur National Monument in Uintah County, Utah in —79221

—788 14	Routt County
—788 15	Rio Blanco County
—788 16	Garfield County
—788 17	Mesa County
—788 18	Delta County
—788 19	Montrose County
—788 2	Southern counties of Colorado Plateau
—788 22	Ouray County
—788 23	San Miguel County
—788 25	San Juan County
—788 26	Dolores County
—788 27	Montezuma County

Including Mesa Verde National Park

—788 29	La Plata County

Class here *La Plata Mountains

—788 3	Southern counties of Rocky Mountains

Class here *Rocky Mountains in Colorado

—788 32	Archuleta County
—788 33	Conejos County

Class here *San Luis Valley, *Rio Grande in Colorado

—788 35	Costilla County
—788 36	Alamosa County
—788 37	Rio Grande County
—788 38	Mineral County

Class here *San Juan Mountains

*Class parts of this physiographic region or feature as instructed under —4–9

Table 2. Areas

—788 39	Hinsdale County
—788 4	**West central counties of Rocky Mountains**
	Class here *Sawatch Range
—788 41	Gunnison County
	Class here *Elk Mountains
—788 43	Pitkin County
—788 44	Eagle County
—788 45	Summit County
	Class here *Gore Range
—788 46	Lake County
—788 47	Chaffee County
—788 49	Saguache County
	Class here *Sangre de Cristo Range, Great Sand Dunes National Monument
	Class Great Sand Dunes National Monument in Alamosa County in —78836
—788 5	**East central counties of Rocky Mountains**
—788 51	Huerfano County
—788 52	Custer County
—788 53	Fremont County
	Class here *Arkansas River in Colorado
—788 55	Pueblo County
—788 56	El Paso County
	Including Colorado Springs
—788 58	Teller County
—788 59	Park County
	Class here *Mosquito Range

*Class parts of this physiographic region or feature as instructed under —4–9

—788 6	Northern counties of Rocky Mountains
—788 61	Clear Creek County
—788 62	Gilpin County
—788 63	Boulder County
—788 65	Grand County

Class here *Rabbit Ears Range

—788 66	Jackson County

Class here *Park Range

—788 68	Larimer County
—788 69	Rocky Mountain National Park

Class each specific part with the subject, e.g., in Larimer County —78868

—788 7	Northern counties of Great Plains

Class here *South Platte River, *Great Plains in Colorado

—788 72	Weld County
—788 74	Morgan County
—788 75	Logan County
—788 76	Sedgwick County
—788 77	Phillips County
—788 78	Yuma County
—788 79	Washington County
—788 8	Central counties of Great Plains
—788 81	Adams County
—788 82	Arapahoe County
—788 83	Denver (Denver County)
—788 84	Jefferson County
—788 86	Douglas County
—788 87	Elbert County
—788 89	Lincoln County

*Class parts of this physiographic region or feature as instructed under —4–9

Table 2. Areas

—788 9	Southern counties of Great Plains
—788 91	Kit Carson County
—788 92	Cheyenne County
—788 93	Kiowa County
—788 94	Crowley County
—788 95	Otero County
—788 96	Las Animas County
—788 97	Bent County
—788 98	Prowers County
—788 99	Baca County
—789	New Mexico

SUMMARY

—789 2	Northeastern counties
—789 3	Llano Estacado counties
—789 4	Pecos Valley counties
—789 5	Rocky Mountains region counties
—789 6	Basin and Range region counties
—789 8	Northwestern counties
—789 9	West central counties

—789 2	Northeastern counties
—789 22	Colfax County
—789 23	Union County
—789 24	Harding County
—789 25	Guadalupe County
—789 26	Quay County
—789 27	Curry County
—789 3	Llano Estacado counties
—789 32	Roosevelt County
—789 33	Lea County
—789 4	Pecos Valley counties
—789 42	Eddy County
	Including Carlsbad Caverns National Park
—789 43	Chaves County
—789 44	De Baca County

—789 5	Rocky Mountains region counties
—789 52	Rio Arriba County
—789 53	Taos County
—789 54	Mora County
—789 55	San Miguel County
—789 56	Santa Fe County
	Including Santa Fe city
—789 57	Sandoval County
—789 58	Los Alamos County
—789 6	Basin and Range region counties
	Class here *Rio Grande in New Mexico
—789 61	Bernalillo County
	Including Albuquerque
—789 62	Socorro County
	Class here *Elephant Butte Reservoir, *Jornada del Muerto, *San Andres Mountains
—789 63	Torrance County
—789 64	Lincoln County
—789 65	Otero County
	Class here *Tularosa Valley, White Sands National Monument, *Sacramento Mountains
	Class White Sands National Monument in Dona Ana County in —78966
—789 66	Dona Ana County
—789 67	Sierra County
—789 68	Luna County

*Class parts of this physiographic region or feature as instructed under —4–9

Table 2. Areas

—789 69	Grant and Hidalgo Counties
—789 692	Grant County
—789 693	Hidalgo County
	Class here *Peloncillo Mountains
—789 8	Northwestern counties
—789 82	San Juan County
—789 83	McKinley County
—789 9	West central counties
—789 92	Valencia County
—789 93	Catron County

—79   **Great Basin and Pacific Slope region of United States   Pacific Coast states**

SUMMARY

—791	**Arizona**
—792	**Utah**
—793	**Nevada**
—794	**California**
—795	**Oregon**
—796	**Idaho**
—797	**Washington**
—798	**Alaska**

—791	Arizona
—791 3	Colorado Plateau region
	Class here *Colorado River
—791 32	*Grand Canyon National Park and Monument
—791 33	Coconino County
	Class here *Painted Desert, *Little Colorado River
—791 35	Navajo County
—791 37	Apache County
	Class here Petrified Forest National Park
	Class Petrified Forest National Park in Navajo County in —79135

*Class parts of this physiographic region or feature as instructed under —4–9

—791 5	Mountain region
—791 51	Greenlee County
—791 53	Cochise County
—791 54	Graham County
	Class here *San Carlos Lake
—791 55	Gila County
—791 57	Yavapai County
—791 59	Mohave County
—791 7	Plains region
	Class here *Gila River
—791 71	Yuma County
—791 73	Maricopa County
	Including Phoenix
—791 75	Pinal County
—791 77	Pima County
	Including Tucson
—791 79	Santa Cruz County
—792	Utah
—792 1	Wyoming Basin region
—792 12	Cache County
—792 13	Rich County
—792 14	Summit County
	Class here *Uinta Mountains
—792 15	Daggett County
—792 2	Rocky Mountains region
	Class here *Wasatch Range
—792 21	Uintah County
	Class here *Green River
—792 22	Duchesne County
—792 23	Wasatch County
—792 24	Utah County

*Class parts of this physiographic region or feature as instructed under —4-9

Table 2. Areas

—792 25	Salt Lake County
	Including Salt Lake City
—792 26	Morgan County
—792 27	Davis County
—792 28	Weber County
—792 4	Great Basin region
—792 42	Box Elder County
	Class here *Great Salt Lake
—792 43	Tooele County
	Class here *Great Salt Lake Desert
—792 44	Juab County
—792 45	Millard County
—792 46	Beaver County
—792 47	Iron County
—792 48	Washington County
	Class here Zion National Park
	Class Zion National Park in Kane County in —79251, in Iron County in —79247
—792 5	Colorado Plateau region
	Class here *Colorado River in Utah
—792 51	Kane County
	Class Bryce Canyon National Park [*formerly* —79251] in —79252
—792 52	Garfield County
	Class here Bryce Canyon National Park [*formerly* —79251]
	Class Bryce Canyon National Park in Kane County in —79251
—792 53	Piute County
—792 54	Wayne County
—792 55	Sevier County

*Class parts of this physiographic region or feature as instructed under —4–9

—792 56	Sanpete and Carbon Counties
—792 563	Sanpete County
—792 566	Carbon County
—792 57	Emery County
—792 58	Grand County
—792 59	San Juan County

        Class here *San Juan River, Canyonlands National Park

        Class Canyonlands National Park in Wayne County in —79254

—793	Nevada
—793 1	Eastern region
—793 12	*Lake Mead National Recreation Area
—793 13	Clark County

        Including Las Vegas

—793 14	Lincoln County
—793 15	White Pine County
—793 16	Elko County

        Class here *Humboldt River

—793 3	Central region
—793 32	Eureka County
—793 33	Lander County
—793 34	Nye County

        Class here *Yucca Flats, *Frenchman Flat

—793 35	Esmeralda County
—793 5	Western region
—793 51	Mineral County
—793 52	Churchill County
—793 53	Pershing County
—793 54	Humboldt County

        Class here *Black Rock Desert

—793 55	Washoe County

        Including Reno

*Class parts of this physiographic region or feature as instructed under —4-9

Table 2. Areas

—793 56	Storey County
	Including Virginia City
—793 57	Ormsby County
	Including Carson City
	Class here *Lake Tahoe in Nevada
—793 58	Lyon County
—793 59	Douglas County
—794	California

SUMMARY

—794 1	Northwestern counties
—794 2	Northeastern counties
—794 3	North central counties
—794 4	East central counties
—794 5	Central counties
—794 6	West central counties
—794 7	Southern Coast Range counties
—794 8	South central counties
—794 9	Southern counties (Southern California)

—794 1	Northwestern counties
	Class here *Coast Ranges in California
—794 11	Del Norte County
—794 12	Humboldt County
—794 14	Trinity County
—794 15	Mendocino County
—794 17	Lake County
—794 18	Sonoma County
—794 19	Napa County
—794 2	Northeastern counties
	Class here *Cascade Range in California
—794 21	Siskiyou County
	Class here Lava Beds National Monument, *Klamath Mountains in California
	Class Lava Beds National Monument in Modoc County in —79423
—794 23	Modoc County

*Class parts of this physiographic region or feature as instructed under —4–9

—794 24	Shasta County
	Class here *Lassen Volcanic National Park
—794 26	Lassen County
—794 27	Tehama County
—794 29	Plumas County
—794 3	North central counties
—794 31	Glenn County
—794 32	Butte County
—794 33	Colusa County
—794 34	Sutter County
—794 35	Yuba County
—794 36	Sierra County
—794 37	Nevada County
—794 38	Placer County
	Class here *Lake Tahoe
—794 4	East central counties
	Class here *Sierra Nevada
—794 41	El Dorado County
—794 42	Amador County
—794 43	Alpine County
—794 44	Calaveras County
—794 45	Tuolumne County
—794 46	Mariposa County
—794 47	Yosemite National Park
	Class each specific part with the subject, e.g., in Mariposa County —79446
—794 48	Mono County

*Class parts of this physiographic region or feature as instructed under —4–9

Table 2. Areas

—794 5	Central counties

Class here *Sacramento River and Valley, *Great Valley (Central Valley)

—794 51	Yolo County
—794 52	Solano County
—794 53	Sacramento County

For Sacramento city, see —79454

—794 54	Sacramento city
—794 55	San Joaquin County

For Stockton, see —79456

—794 56	Stockton
—794 57	Stanislaus County
—794 58	Merced County
—794 6	West central counties

Class here *San Francisco Bay area

—794 61	San Francisco (San Francisco County)
—794 62	Marin County
—794 63	Contra Costa County
—794 65	Alameda County

For Oakland, see —79466; Berkeley, —79467

—794 66	Oakland
—794 67	Berkeley
—794 69	San Mateo County
—794 7	Southern Coast Range counties
—794 71	Santa Cruz County
—794 73	Santa Clara County

For San Jose, see —79474

—794 74	San Jose
—794 75	San Benito County
—794 76	Monterey County

Class here *Salinas River

*Class parts of this physiographic region or feature as instructed under —4–9

—794 78   San Luis Obispo County

Class here *Santa Lucia Range

—794 8   South central counties

Class here *San Joaquin River and Valley

—794 81   Madera County

—794 82   Fresno County

Class here Kings Canyon National Park

Class Kings Canyon National Park in Tulare County in —79486

For Fresno city, see —79483

—794 83   Fresno city

—794 85   Kings County

—794 86   Tulare County

Including Sequoia National Park

Class here *Mount Whitney

—794 87   Inyo County

Class here *Death Valley National Monument

—794 88   Kern County

—794 9   Southern counties (Southern California)

—794 91   Santa Barbara County

—794 92   Ventura County

—794 93   Los Angeles County

Class here *San Gabriel Mountains

For Los Angeles city, see —79494

—794 94   Los Angeles city

—794 95   San Bernardino County

Class here *Mojave Desert, *San Bernardino Mountains

—794 96   Orange County

Class here *Santa Ana Mountains

*Class parts of this physiographic region or feature as instructed under —4–9

Table 2. Areas

—794 97   Riverside County

>   Class here Joshua Tree National Monument
>
>   Class Joshua Tree National Monument in San Bernardino County in —79495

—794 98   San Diego County

—794 99   Imperial County

>   Class here *Salton Sea, *Imperial Valley, *Colorado Desert

—795   Oregon

>   Class here Pacific Northwest, *Cascade and *Coast Ranges
>
>   *For Idaho, see —796; Washington, —797; British Columbia, —711*

SUMMARY

—795 2	**Southwestern counties**
—795 3	**West cental counties**
—795 4	**Northwestern counties**
—795 6	**North central counties**
—795 7	**Northeastern counties**
—795 8	**Central counties**
—795 9	**Southeastern counties**

—795 2   Southwestern counties

>   Class here *Klamath Mountains

—795 21   Curry County

>   Class here *Rogue River

—795 23   Coos County

—795 25   Josephine County

>   Class here *Siskiyou Mountains

—795 27   Jackson County

—795 29   Douglas County

>   Class here *Umpqua River

—795 3   West cental counties

>   Class here *Willamette Valley

—795 31   Lane County

—795 33   Lincoln County

—795 34   Benton County

*Class parts of this physiographic region or feature as instructed under —4–9

—795 35	Linn County
—795 37	Marion County
	Including Salem
—795 38	Polk County
—795 39	Yamhill County
—795 4	**Northwestern counties**
	Class here *Columbia River and Valley in Oregon
—795 41	Clackamas County
—795 43	Washington County
—795 44	Tillamook County
—795 46	Clatsop County
—795 47	Columbia County
—795 49	Multnomah County
	Including Portland
—795 6	**North central counties**
	Class here *Deschutes River
—795 61	Hood River County
	Class here *Mount Hood
—795 62	Wasco County
—795 64	Sherman County
—795 65	Gilliam County
—795 67	Morrow County
—795 69	Umatilla County
—795 7	**Northeastern counties**
	Class here *Blue and *Wallowa Mountains, *Snake River in Oregon
—795 71	Union County
—795 73	Wallowa County
—795 75	Baker County
—795 78	Grant County

*Class parts of this physiographic region or feature as instructed under —4–9

Table 2. Areas

—795 8	Central counties
—795 81	Wheeler County
—795 83	Crook County
	Class here *Maury Mountains
—795 85	Jefferson County
—795 87	Deschutes County
—795 9	Southeastern counties
—795 91	Klamath County
—795 915	Crater Lake National Park
—795 93	Lake County
—795 95	Harney County
—795 97	Malheur County
—796	Idaho

SUMMARY

—796 1	Southern Idaho
—796 2	Southwestern counties
—796 3	South central counties
—796 4	Southeastern counties
—796 5	Northeastern counties of southern Idaho
—796 6	Central Idaho
—796 7	Southeast central counties
—796 8	North central counties
—796 9	Northern Idaho

—796 1	Southern Idaho
	Class here *Snake River
	Class specific counties in —7962–7965
—796 2	Southwestern counties
—796 21	Owyhee County
—796 23	Canyon County
—796 24	Payette County
—796 25	Washington County
—796 26	Adams County
	Class here *Seven Devils Mountains
—796 27	Gem County

*Class parts of this physiographic region or feature as instructed under —4–9

—796 28	Ada County
	Including Boise
—796 29	Elmore County
	Class here *Arrow Rock Reservoir, *Sawtooth Range
—796 3	**South central counties**
—796 31	Camas County
—796 32	Blaine County
	Class here *Pioneer Mountains
—796 33	Minidoka County
—796 34	Lincoln County
—796 35	Jerome County
—796 36	Gooding County
—796 37	Twin Falls County
—796 39	Cassia County
	Class here *Goose Creek Mountains, *Lake Walcott
—796 4	**Southeastern counties**
—796 41	Oneida County
—796 42	Franklin County
—796 44	Bear Lake County
	Class here *Wasatch Range in Idaho
—796 45	Caribou County
	Class here *Preuss Range, *Aspen Ridge
—796 47	Bannock County
	Class here *Bannock Range
—796 49	Power County
	Class here *American Falls Reservoir
—796 5	**Northeastern counties of southern Idaho**
—796 51	Bingham County
—796 53	Bonneville County
	Class here *Grays Lake
—796 54	Teton County

*Class parts of this physiographic region or feature as instructed under —4-9

Table 2. Areas

—796 55	Madison County
—796 56	Fremont County
—796 57	Clark County
—796 58	Jefferson County
—796 59	Butte County

> Class here Craters of the Moon National Monument
>
> Class Craters of the Moon National Monument in Blaine County in —79632

—796 6   Central Idaho

> Class here *Bitterroot Range in Idaho
>
> Class specific counties in —7967–7968

—796 7   Southeast central counties

> Class here *Sawtooth Mountains

—796 72	Custer County

> Class here *Lost River Range

—796 74	Boise County
—796 76	Valley County
—796 78	Lemhi County

> Class here *Salmon River Mountains, *Beaverhead Mountains

—796 8   North central counties

—796 82	Idaho County

> Class here *Salmon River, *Clearwater Mountains

—796 84	Lewis County
—796 85	Nez Perce County

> Class here *Clearwater River

—796 86	Latah County
—796 88	Clearwater County

*Class parts of this physiographic region or feature as instructed under —4–9

—796 9	Northern Idaho
—796 91	Shoshone County

Class here *Coeur d'Alene Mountains

—796 93	Benewah County
—796 94	Kootenai County
—796 96	Bonner County
—796 98	Boundary County
—797	Washington

Class here *Columbia River

SUMMARY

—797 2	**Northeastern counties**
—797 3	**East central counties**
—797 4	**Southeastern counties**
—797 5	**Central counties**
—797 7	**Puget Sound counties**
—797 8	**Southwest central counties**
—797 9	**Coastal counties**

—797 2	Northeastern counties
—797 21	Pend Oreille County
—797 23	Stevens County

Class here *Franklin D. Roosevelt Lake

—797 25	Ferry County

Class here *Kettle River Range

—797 28	Okanogan County

Class here *Sawtooth Ridge

—797 3	East central counties
—797 31	Douglas county

Class here *Grand Coulee

—797 32	Grant County
—797 33	Franklin County
—797 34	Adams County
—797 35	Lincoln County
—797 37	Spokane County

Including Spokane city

*Class parts of this physiographic region or feature as instructed under —4–9

Table 2. Areas

—797 39	Whitman County
	Class here *Palouse River
—797 4	**Southeastern counties**
	Class here *Snake River in Washington
—797 42	Asotin County
—797 44	Garfield County
—797 46	Columbia County
	Class here *Blue Mountains in Washington
—797 48	Walla Walla County
—797 5	**Central counties**
	Class here *Cascade Range in Washington
—797 51	Benton County
—797 53	Klickitat County
—797 55	Yakima County
	Class here *Yakima River and Valley
—797 57	Kittitas County
	Class here *Wenatchee Mountains
—797 59	Chelan County
	Class here *Entiat Range
—797 7	**Puget Sound counties**
—797 71	Snohomish County
—797 72	Skagit County
—797 73	Whatcom County
—797 74	San Juan County
—797 75	Island County
—797 76	Kitsap County
—797 77	King County
	Including Seattle
—797 78	Pierce County
	Including Tacoma
	Class here *Mount Rainier National Park

*Class parts of this physiographic region or feature as instructed under —4–9

—797 79	Thurston County
	Including Olympia
—797 8	**Southwest central counties**
—797 82	Lewis County
	Class here *Cowlitz River
—797 84	Skamania County
—797 86	Clark County
—797 88	Cowlitz County
—797 9	**Coastal counties**
	Class here *Coast Range in Washington
—797 91	Wahkiakum County
—797 92	Pacific County
—797 94	*Olympic Peninsula
	Class here *Olympic Mountains
—797 95	Grays Harbor County
—797 97	Mason County
—797 98	Jefferson County
	Class here Olympic National Park
	Class Olympic National Park in Mason County in —79797, in Clallam County in —79799
—797 99	Clallam County
—798	**Alaska**
—798 2	**Southeastern region (Panhandle)**
	Ketchikan, Outer Ketchikan, Prince of Wales, Wrangell-Petersburg, Angoon, Sitka, Juneau, Haines, Skagway-Yakutat election districts

*Class parts of this physiographic region or feature as instructed under —4–9

Table 2. Areas

—798 3   **South central region**

Pacific Coast area from Icy Bay to Cook Inlet, inland to Alaska Range

Cordova-McCarthy, Valdez-Chitina-Whittier, Matanuska-Susitna, Anchorage, Seward, Kenai-Cook Inlet election districts

Including Mount McKinley National Park, Willow (site of projected new capital)

Class here *Alaska Range

—798 4   **Southwestern region**

Area from Cook Inlet to Norton Sound

Kodiak, Aleutian Islands, Bristol Bay, Bethel, Kuskokwim election districts

—798 6   **Central Plateau region**

Area from Alaska Range to Brooks Range

Fairbanks Southeast, Fairbanks, Yukon-Koyokuk, Upper Yukon, Wade Hampton election districts

—798 7   **Arctic Slope (Polar) region**

Area between Brooks Range and Arctic Ocean

Barrow, Kobuk election districts

—8   **South America**

Class here Latin America, Spanish America, the *Andes

For Middle America, see —72

—800 09   **Regional treatment**

Add to base number —80009 the numbers following —1 in —11–18 of this table, e.g., forest areas of South America —8000952

—[801]   **South American native races in South America**

(Use of this number is optional; prefer specific discipline or subject, using "Standard Subdivisions" notation 08998 from Table 1)

*Class parts of this physiographic region or feature as instructed under —4–9

SUMMARY

—81   Brazil
—82   Argentina
—83   Chile
—84   Bolivia
—85   Peru
—86   Colombia and Ecuador
—87   Venezuela
—88   Guianas
—89   Paraguay and Uruguay

—81   **Brazil**

SUMMARY

—811   Northwestern region
—812   North central states
—813   Northeastern region
—814   East central states
—815   Southeastern states
—816   Southern states
—817   West central region

—811   Northwestern region

         Class here *Amazon River

—811 2   Acre state

—811 3   Amazonas state

—811 4   Roraima (Former Rio Branco) territory

—811 5   Pará state

—811 6   Amapá territory

—812   North central states

—812 1   Maranhão

—812 2   Piauí

—813   Northeastern region

—813 1   Ceará state

—813 2   Rio Grande do Norte state

—813 3   Paraíba state

—813 4   Pernambuco state

—813 5   Alagoas state

—813 6   Fernando de Noronha territory

*Class parts of this physiographic region or feature as instructed under —4–9

Table 2. Areas

—814	East central states
—814 1	Sergipe
—814 2	Bahia
—815	Southeastern states
—815 1	Minas Gerais
—815 2	Espírito Santo
—815 3	Rio de Janeiro

Including former Guanabara, Rio de Janeiro city

—816	Southern states

Class here *Paraná River in Brazil

—816 1	São Paulo
—816 2	Paraná
—816 4	Santa Catarina
—816 5	Rio Grande do Sul
—817	West central region
—817 2	Mato Grosso state
—817 3	Goiás state
—817 4	Federal District

Including Brasilia

—817 5	Rondônia territory
—82	**Argentina**

SUMMARY

—821	South central region
—822	Mesopotamian provinces
—823	Northeastern provinces
—824	Northwestern provinces
—825	North central provinces
—826	Central Highland provinces
—827	Patagonian region

—821	South central region
—821 1	Federal Capital

Including Buenos Aires city

—821 2	Buenos Aires province
—821 3	La Pampa province

*Class parts of this physiographic region or feature as instructed under —4–9

—822	Mesopotamian provinces
	Class here *Paraná, *Uruguay Rivers
—822 1	Entre Ríos
—822 2	Corrientes
—822 3	Misiones
—822 4	Santa Fe
—823	Northeastern provinces
	Class here *Gran Chaco
—823 4	Chaco
—823 5	Formosa
—824	Northwestern provinces
—824 1	Jujuy
—824 2	Salta
—824 3	Tucumán
—824 5	Catamarca
—824 6	La Rioja
—825	North central provinces
—825 2	Santiago del Estero
—825 4	Córdoba
—826	Central Highland provinces
—826 2	San Luis
—826 3	San Juan
—826 4	Mendoza
—827	Patagonian region
—827 2	Neuquén province
—827 3	Río Negro province
—827 4	Chubut province
—827 5	Santa Cruz province

*Class parts of this physiographic region or feature as instructed under —4–9

Table 2. Areas

—827 6	Tierra del Fuego territory

Class here comprehensive works on Tierra del Fuego island

Class south Atlantic Ocean islands claimed by Argentina in —9711

For Magallanes province of Chile, see —8364

—83	**Chile**

SUMMARY

—831	**Desert region provinces**
—832	**Northern region provinces**
—833	**Central region provinces**
—834	**Frontier region provinces**
—835	**Southern region provinces**
—836	**Austral region provinces**

—831	Desert region provinces
—831 2	Tarapacá
—831 3	Antofagasta
—831 4	Atacama
—832	Northern region provinces

For desert region provinces, see —831

—832 3	Coquimbo
—832 4	Aconcagua
—832 5	Valparaiso
—833	Central region provinces
—833 1	Santiago
—833 2	O'Higgins
—833 3	Colchagua
—833 4	Curicó
—833 5	Talca
—833 6	Maule
—833 7	Linares
—833 8	Ñuble
—833 9	Concepción

—834	Frontier region provinces
—834 2	Arauco
—834 3	Bío-Bío
—834 5	Malleco
—834 6	Cautín
—835	Southern region provinces

For austral region provinces, see —836

—835 2	Valdivia
—835 3	Osorno
—835 4	Llanquihue
—835 6	Chiloé
—836	Austral region provinces
—836 2	Aysén (Aisen)
—836 4	Magallanes

Class comprehensive works on Tierra del Fuego island in —8276

—84	**Bolivia**
—841	Mountain region departments
—841 2	La Paz

Class here *Lake Titicaca

—841 3	Oruro
—841 4	Potosí
—842	Valley region departments
—842 3	Cochabamba
—842 4	Chuquisaca

Including Sucre

—842 5	Tarija
—843	Plains region (Santa Cruz department)

*Class parts of this physiographic region or feature as instructed under —4–9

Table 2. Areas

—844	Amazon region departments
—844 2	Beni
—844 3	Pando
—85	**Peru**
—851	Northern departments
—851 2	Tumbes
—851 3	Piura
—851 4	Lambayeque
—851 5	Cajamarca
—851 6	La Libertad
—852	Central departments
—852 1	Ancash
—852 2	Huánuco
—852 3	Pasco
—852 4	Junín
—852 5	Lima
—852 6	Callao
—852 7	Ica
—852 8	Huancavelica
—852 9	Ayacucho and Apurimac
—852 92	Ayacucho
—852 94	Apurimac
—853	Southern departments
—853 2	Arequipa
—853 4	Moquegua
—853 5	Tacna
—853 6	Puno
	Including Lake Titicaca in Peru
—853 7	Cuzco

—854	Eastern departments
—854 2	Madre de Dios
—854 3	Loreto

Class here *Amazon River in Peru

—854 5	San Martín
—854 6	Amazonas
—86	**Colombia and Ecuador**
—861	Colombia

SUMMARY

—861 1	Caribbean Coast region
—861 2	Northwestern region
—861 3	North central region
—861 4	Cundinamarca
—861 5	South central region
—861 6	Southern region
—861 7	Amazonas
—861 8	San Andrés y Providencia

—861 1	Caribbean Coast region
—861 12	Córdoba
—861 13	Sucre
—861 14	Bolívar
—861 15	Atlántico
—861 16	Magdalena
—861 17	Guajira
—861 2	Northwestern region
—861 23	Cesar
—861 24	Norte de Santander
—861 25	Santander
—861 26	Antioquia
—861 27	Chocó

*Class parts of this physiographic region or feature as instructed under —4–9

Table 2. Areas

—861 3	**North central region**
	For Cundinamarca, see —8614
—861 32	Risaralda
—861 34	Quindio
—861 35	Caldas
—861 36	Tolima
—861 37	Boyacá
—861 38	Arauca
—861 39	Vichada
—861 4	**Cundinamarca**
	Including Bogotá
—861 5	**South central region**
—861 52	Valle del Cauca
—861 53	Cauca
—861 54	Huila
—861 56	Meta
—861 6	**Southern region**
	For Amazonas, see —8617
—861 62	Nariño
—861 63	Putumayo
—861 64	Caquetá
—861 65	Vaupés
—861 67	Guainía
—861 7	**Amazonas**
—861 8	**San Andrés y Providencia**
	Islands in Caribbean Sea
—[862]	**Panama**
	Class in —7287
—[863]	**Panama Canal Zone**
	Class in —72875

—866	Ecuador
—866 1	Northern interior provinces
—866 11	Carchi
—866 12	Imbabura
—866 13	Pichincha
	Including Quito
—866 14	Cotopaxi
—866 15	Tungurahua
—866 16	Bolívar
—866 17	Chimborazo
—866 2	Southern interior provinces
—866 23	Cañar
—866 24	Azuay
—866 25	Loja
—866 3	Coastal provinces
—866 31	El Oro
—866 32	Guayas
—866 33	Los Ríos
—866 34	Manabí
—866 35	Esmeraldas
—866 4	Eastern provinces
—866 41	Napo
—866 42	Pastaza
—866 43	Morona-Santiago
—866 44	Zamora-Chinchipe
—866 5	Galápagos Islands (Colón)
—87	**Venezuela**

Class here *Orinoco River

*Class parts of this physiographic region or feature as instructed under —4–9

Table 2. Areas

SUMMARY

—871	Southwestern states
—872	Northwestern states
—873	North central states
—874	Central states
—875	Northeastern states
—876	Southeastern region
—877	Federal District

—871	Southwestern states
—871 2	Táchira
—871 3	Mérida
—871 4	Trujillo
—872	Northwestern states
—872 3	Zulia

Class here *Lake Maracaibo

—872 4	Falcón
—872 5	Lara
—872 6	Yaracuy
—873	North central states

Including Federal Dependencies

For Federal District, see —877

—873 2	Carabobo
—873 4	Aragua
—873 5	Miranda
—874	Central states
—874 2	Apure
—874 3	Barinas
—874 5	Portuguesa
—874 6	Cojedes
—874 7	Guárico

*Class parts of this physiographic region or feature as instructed under —4–9

—875	Northeastern states
—875 2	Anzoátegui
—875 3	Sucre
—875 4	Nueva Esparta
—875 6	Monagas
—876	Southeastern region
—876 2	Delta Amacuro territory
—876 3	Bolívar state
—876 4	Amazonas territory
—877	Federal District
	Including Caracas
—88	**Guianas**
—881	Guyana
	Formerly British Guiana
—881 1	North West district
—881 2	Essequibo district
—881 3	Essequibo Islands district
—881 4	West Demerara district
—881 5	East Demerara district
	Including Georgetown
—881 6	West Berbice district
—881 7	East Berbice district
—881 8	Rupununi
—881 9	Mazaruni-Potaro district
—882	Guyane (French Guiana)
	Overseas department of France
—882 3	Cayenne district
—882 4	Inini district

Table 2. Areas

—883	Surinam
	Formerly Dutch Guiana
—883 1	Nickerie district
—883 2	Coronie district
—883 3	Saramacca district
—883 4	Para district
—883 5	Paramaribo district
—883 6	Suriname district
—883 7	Commewijne district
—883 8	Marowijne district
—883 9	Brokopondo district
—89	**Paraguay and Uruguay**
—892	Paraguay
—892 1	Departments east of Paraguay River
—892 12	South
—892 121	Capital District
	Including Asunción
—892 122	Central
—892 123	Paraguarí
—892 124	Ñeembucú
—892 125	Misiones
—892 126	Itapúa
—892 127	Caazapá
—892 128	Guairá
—892 13	North
—892 132	Alto Paraná
—892 133	Canendiyú
—892 134	Caaguazú
—892 135	La Cordillera
—892 136	San Pedro
—892 137	Amambay
—892 138	Concepción

—892 2	Departments west of Paraguay River
	Class here *Chaco Boreal
—892 23	Presidente Hayes
—892 24	Boquerón
—892 25	Nueva Asunción
—892 26	Chaco
—892 27	Alto Paraguay
—895	Uruguay
	Class here *Uruguay River in Uruguay
—895 1	Coastal departments
—895 11	Colonia
—895 12	San José
—895 13	Montevideo
—895 14	Canelones
—895 15	Maldonado
—895 16	Rocha
—895 2	Central departments
—895 21	Lavalleja
—895 22	Treinta y Tres
—895 23	Cerro Largo
—895 24	Durazno
—895 25	Florida
—895 26	Flores
—895 27	Soriano
—895 28	Río Negro
—895 3	Northern departments
—895 31	Paysandú
—895 32	Tacuarembó
—895 34	Rivera
—895 35	Salto
—895 36	Artigas

*Class parts of this physiographic region or feature as instructed under —4–9

Table 2. Areas

—9   **Other parts of world and extraterrestrial worlds*Pacific Ocean islands (Oceania)**

SUMMARY

—93   New Zealand and Melanesia
—94   Australia
—95   New Guinea (Papua)
—96   Other parts of Pacific   Polynesia
—97   Atlantic Ocean islands
—98   Arctic islands and Antarctica
—99   Extraterrestrial worlds

▶   **—93–96 Pacific Ocean islands (Oceania)**

Class comprehensive works in —9; each specific island or group of islands not provided for here with the subject, e.g., Japan —52

—93   **New Zealand and Melanesia**

—931   New Zealand

—931 1   Outlying islands

Chatham, Pitt, Auckland, Antipodes, Campbell

For Cook Islands, see —9623

—931 2   North Island

—931 22   Auckland provincial district

Northland, Central Auckland, South Auckland, East Coast

Including Hamilton

—931 23   Taranaki provincial district

—931 25   Hawke's Bay provincial district

—931 27   Wellington provincial district

—931 5   South Island and Stewart Island

—931 52   Marlborough provincial district

—931 53   Nelson provincial district

—931 54   Westland provincial district

—931 55   Canterbury provincial district

Including Christchurch

—931 57	Otago provincial district
	Otago, Southland
	Including Dunedin
—931 575	Stewart Island

▶   **—932–937 Melanesia**

Class comprehensive works in —93

For Louisiade Archipelago, D'Entrecasteaux Islands, see —953; Fiji, —9611

—932   New Caledonia territory

Island of New Caledonia, Isle of Pines, Huon Islands, Chesterfield Islands, Walpole Island, Belep Islands, Wallis and Futuna Islands

For Loyalty Islands, see —933

—933   Loyalty Islands

—934   New Hebrides

—935   Solomon Islands

—936   Bismarck Archipelago

For Admiralty Islands, see —937

—937   Admiralty Islands

—94   **Australia**

Class here *Great Dividing Range

SUMMARY

—941	**Western Australia**
—942	**Central Australia**
—943	**Queensland**
—944	**New South Wales**
—945	**Victoria**
—946	**Tasmania**
—947	**Australian Capital Territory**
—948	**Outlying islands**

*Class parts of this physiographic region or feature as instructed under —4–9

Table 2. Areas

—941	**Western Australia**
—941 1	**Perth metropolitan district**

Including Fremantle

—941 2	**Southwestern district**

Including Albany, Bunbury, Collie, Geraldton, Katanning, Manjimup, Merredin, Narrogin, Northam; Kalbarri, Nelson and Hay, Nornalup, Stirling Range National Parks; Blackwood, Greenough, Swan Rivers; Darling, Stirling Ranges

For Perth metropolitan district, see —9411

—941 3	**Northwestern district**

Including Carnarvon, Port Hedland; Barrow Island, Bernier and Dorre Islands, Cape Range National Parks; Ashburton, Gascoyne Rivers; Lake Austin; Hammersley Range; North West Cape; Dampier Archipelago; Dirk Hartogs Island

Class here *Murchison River

—941 4	**Kimberley district**

Including Broome, Derby, Wyndham; Fitzroy, Ord Rivers; King Leopold Ranges; Bonaparte Archipelago

—941 5	**North central district**

Including Lake Nabberu; Gibson, Great Sandy Deserts

Class here *Great Victoria Desert

—941 6	**South central district**

Including Coolgardie, Kalgoorlie, Wiluna; Lakes Barlee, Carey, Carnegie

—941 7	**Southern district**

Including Esperance, Norseman; Cape Le Grand, Esperance National Parks; Archipelago of the Recherche

—942	**Central Australia**
—942 3	**South Australia**
—942 31	Adelaide metropolitan district

*Class parts of this physiographic region or feature as instructed under —4–9

—942 32   Central district

Including Angaston, Clare, Gawler, Mannum, Murray Bridge, Port Noarlunga, Port Pirie, Salisbury, Strathalbyn, Victor Harbour; Chaunceys Line Reserve National Park; Mount Lofty Ranges

For Adelaide metropolitan district, see —94231

—942 33   Eastern district

Including Barmera, Berri, Loxton, Renmark, Tailem Bend; Billiatt, Mount Rescue National Parks; Lake Alexandrina

Class here the Coorong

—942 34   Southern district

Including Bordertown, Kingston, Mount Gambier, Naracoorte; Canunda, Messent National Parks

—942 35   West central district

Including Kadina, Maitland, Moonta, Wallaroo; Flinders Chase National Park; Yorke Peninsula; Kangaroo Island

—942 36   North central district

Including Peterborough, Quorn

—942 37   Northern district

Including Leigh Creek; Wilpena Pound National Park; Lakes Blanche, Callabonna, Frome; Sturts Stony Desert

Class here *Coopers Creek, the *Warburton, *Flinders Ranges

—942 38   Western district

Including Port Augusta, Port Lincoln, Whyalla; Hambridge, Hincks, Lincoln National Parks; the Alberga, the Neales; Lakes Eyre, Gairdner, Torrens; Musgrave Ranges; Eyre Peninsula

Class here *Nullarbor Plain

—942 9   Northern Territory

Class here northern Australia

For Western Australia, see —941; Queensland, —943

*Class parts of this physiographic region or feature as instructed under —4–9

Table 2. Areas

—942 91   Southern district

> Including Alice Springs; Ayers Rock-Mount Olga, Ormiston Gorge, Palm Valley National Parks; Tanami Desert Fauna Reserve; Todd River; Davenport, Harts, Macdonnell, Peterman Ranges; Ayers Rock; Mount Zeil
>
> Class here *Finke River, *Murchison Range, *Simpson Desert

—942 95   Northern district

> Including Daly Waters, Darwin, Katherine, Tennant Creek; Katherine Gorge National Park; Cobourg Peninsula, Daly River, Murganella, Woolwonga Fauna Reserves; Daly, Roper, Victoria Rivers; Newcastle Range; Arnhem Land; Bathurst, Elcho, Melville Islands; Sir Edward Pellew Group; Groote Eylandt
>
> Class here *Barkly Tableland

—943   Queensland

> Class here Great Barrier Reef

—943 1   Brisbane metropolitan district

—943 2   Southeastern district

> Including Beaudesert, Bundaberg, Gatton, Gympie, Ipswich, Kingaroy, Maryborough, Mundubberah, Nambour, Southport, Surfers Paradise, Wondai; Cooloolah Fauna Reserve; Bunya Mountains, Lamington, Mount Barney National Parks; Burnett River; Glasshouse Mountains; Fraser Island
>
> Class here *Brisbane River, *Bunya Mountains, * McPherson Range
>
> *For Brisbane metropolitan district, see —9431*

—943 3   Downs district

> Including Chinchilla, Dalby, Goondiwindi, Inglewood, Miles, Millmerran, Oakey, Pittsworth, Stanthorpe, Texas, Toowoomba, Warwick; Granite Belt National Park; Darling Downs

—943 4   Southwestern district

> Including Charleville, Cunnamulla, Mitchell, Roma, Saint George; Channel Country
>
> Class here *Moonie, *Paroo, *Warrego Rivers; *Grey Range

*Class parts of this physiographic region or feature as instructed under —4-9

—943 5   Central district

Including Barcaldine, Biloela, Blackall, Clermont, Emerald, Gladstone, Longreach, Monto, Mount Morgan, Rockhampton, Winton, Yeppoon; Carnarvon Range, Isla Gorge, Robinson Gorge, Salvator Rosa National Parks; Barcoo, Fitzroy Rivers; Northumberland Islands

Class here *Eyre Creek; *Diamantina, *Georgina, *Thomson Rivers; *Connors Range

—943 6   Northeastern district

Including Atherton, Ayr, Bowen, Cairns, Charters Towers, Ingham, Innisfail, Mackay, Mareeba, Townsville, Tully; Bellenden Ker, Conway Range, Eungella, Hinchinbrook Island, Mount Elliott, Mount Spec, Whitsunday Island, Windsor Tableland National Parks; Swans Lagoon Fauna Reserve; Burdekin River; Lake Barrine; Clarke, Leichhardt Ranges; Hinchinbrook, Whitsunday Islands

—943 7   Northwestern district

Including Cloncurry, Hughenden, Mary Kathleen, Mount Isa, Richmond; Simpson Desert National Park; Flinders, Gilbert, Leichhardt Rivers; Selwyn Range; Wellesley Islands

Class here *Mitchell River

—943 8   Peninsula and Torres Strait Islands

Including Archer, Normanby, Wenlock Rivers; Cape York Peninsula; Murray Islands; Thursday Island

—944   New South Wales

Class here *Murray River

—944 1   Sydney metropolitan district

Including Hornsby, Liverpool, Parramatta, Penrith; Ku-ring-gai Chase National Park

—944 2   Lower north coast district

Including Cessnock, Dungog, the Entrance, Forster, Gloucester, Gosford, Maitland, Muswellbrook, Newcastle, Port Macquarie, Scone, Singleton, Taree, Toronto, Woy Woy; Brisbane Waters National Park; Hawkesbury, Hunter Rivers

*Class parts of this physiographic region or feature as instructed under —4–9

Table 2. Areas

—944 3   **Upper north coast district**

Including Ballina, Casino, Coffs Harbour, Grafton, Kempsey, Kyogle, Lismore, Murwillumbah; Gibraltar Range National Park; Richmond River; Point Lookout

Class here *Clarence, *Macleay Rivers

—944 4   **North central district**

Including Armidale, Barraba, Boggabri, Coonabarabran, Glen Innes, Gunnedah, Inverell, Moree, Murrurundi, Narrabri, Quirindi, Tamworth, Tenterfield; Kaputar, New England National Parks; Nandewar, New England, Warrumbungle Ranges

Class here *Namoi, *Gwydir Rivers

—944 5   **Central district**

Including Bathurst, Cowra, Crookwell, Dubbo, Forbes, Gilgandra, Katoomba, Lithgow, Mudgee, Orange, Parkes, Wellington; Blue Mountains National Park; Curumbenya Fauna Reserve; Jenolan Caves

Class here *Blue Mountains

—944 6   **Upper south coast district**

Including Camden, Campbelltown, Mittlagong, Moss Vale, Narellan, Port Kembla, Wollongong; Morton, Royal National Parks; Nepean, Wollondilly Rivers; Lake Illawarra

—944 7   **Southeastern district**

Including Batemans Bay, Bega, Bomaderry, Bombala, Braidwood, Captains Flat, Cooma, Eden, Goulburn, Kiama, Moruya, Narooma, Nowra, Queanbeyan, Ulladulla, Yass; Kosciusko State, Shoalhaven National Parks; Nadgee Fauna Reserve; Shoalhaven River; Lake George; Yarrangobilly Caves

Class here *Snowy River, *Snowy Mountains, *Mount Kosciusko

Class Australian Capital Territory in —947

—944 8   **Southern district**

Including Albury, Balranald, Cootamundra, Corowa, Deniliquin, Grenfell, Griffith, Gundagai, Hay, Junee, Leeton, Murrumburrah, Temora, Tumut, Wagga Wagga, Wentworth, Young; Cocopara Fauna Reserve; Edward, Murrumbidgee, Tooma, Wakool Rivers; Lake Victoria

*Class parts of this physiographic region or feature as instructed under —4–9

—944 9   Western district

Including Bourke, Brewarrina, Broken Hill, Cobar, Condobolin, Coonamble, Nyngan, Walgett, Warren; Round Hill Fauna Reserve; Barwon River; Menindee Lakes; Main Barrier Range

Class here *Castlereagh, *Darling, *Lachlan, *Macquarie Rivers

—945   Victoria

—945 1   Melbourne metropolitan district

—945 2   Central district

Including Bacchus Marsh, Geelong, Healesville, Korumburra, Mornington, Pakenham, Queenscliff, Rosebud, Sorrento, Sunbury, Torquay, Werribee, Winchelsea, Wonthaggi; Kinglake National Park; French, Phillip Islands

Class here Yarra River

For Melbourne metropolitan district, see —9451

—945 3   North central district

Including Alexandra, Broadford, Castlemaine, Creswick, Daylesford, Heathcote, Kilmore, Kyneton, Maldon, Maryborough, Seymour, Woodend, Yea

—945 4   Northern district

Including Bendigo, Charlton, Echuca, Inglewood, Kerang, Kyabram, Nathalia, Numurkah, Rochester, Rushworth, Shepparton, Tatura, Yarrawonga

Class here *Campaspe, *Goulburn, *Loddon Rivers

—945 5   Northeastern district

Including Beechworth, Benalla, Corryong, Euroa, Mansfield, Mount Beauty, Myrtleford, Rutherglen, Tallangatta, Wangaratta, Wodonga; Mount Buffalo National Park; Mitta Mitta River; Mounts Bogong, Buffalo, Feathertop

Class here *Ovens River

*Class parts of this physiographic region or feature as instructed under —4-9

Table 2. Areas

—945 6	**Gippsland district**

Including Bairnsdale, Lakes Entrance, Leongatha, Maffra, Moe, Morwell, Orbost, Sale, Traralgon, Warragul, Yallourn, Yarram; Ewings Morass, Lake Reeve, Nooramunga, Rocky Range Fauna Reserves; Mallacoota Inlet, Wilsons Promontory National Parks; Mitchell, Tambo Rivers; Lake Wellington; Buchan Caves; Snake Island

Class here *La Trobe, *Macallister Rivers

—945 7	**Western district**

Including Ararat, Ballarat, Camperdown, Casterton, Colac, Coleraine, Hamilton, Mortlake, Port Fairy, Portland, Terang, Warrnambool; the Stones Fauna Reserve; Glenelg River; Lake Corangamite

—945 8	**Wimmera district**

Including Dimboola, Donald, Horsham, Kaniva, Murtoa, Nhill, Saint Arnaud, Stawell, Warracknabeal

Class here *Lake Hindmarsh, the *Grampians

—945 9	**Mallee district**

Including Birchip, Hopetoun, Irymple, Merbein, Mildura, Ouyen, Red Cliffs, Robinvale, Sea Lake, Swan Hill; Hattah Lakes, Wyperfeld National Parks; Wimmera River; Lakes Albacutya, Tyrell

—946	**Tasmania**
—946 1	**Hobart metropolitan district**
—946 2	**Southern district**

Including Cygnet, Huonville, Kingston, New Norfolk; Hartz Mountains, Lake Pedder, Mount Field National Parks; Huon River; Arthur, Frankland Ranges; Hartz Mountains; Hastings Caves; Port Davey; Bruny Island

Class here *Derwent River

For Hobart metropolitan district, see —9461

—946 3	**Central district**

Including Campbell Town, Deloraine, Longford, Oatlands, Perth, Poatina, Wayatinah, Westbury; Cradle Mountain-Lake Saint Clair, Lyell Highway National Parks; Great Lake; Lakes Crescent, King William, Saint Clair, Sorell; Cradle Mountain; Ducane Range; Great Western Mountains; Mole Creek Caves

*Class parts of this physiographic region or feature as instructed under —4–9

—946 4   **Eastern district**

         Including George Town, Port Arthur, Rossarden, Scottsdale; Ben Lomond, Freycinet Peninsula National Parks; Tooms Lake Fauna Reserve; Ben Lomond; Tasman Peninsula; Maria, Schouten Islands

         Class here *North Esk, *South Esk Rivers

—946 5   **Northwestern district**

         Including Beaconsfield, Burnie, Devonport, Latrobe, Launceston, Penguin, Railton, Smithton, Somerset, Stanley, Ulverstone, Wynyard

         Class here *Arthur, *Forth, *Mersey, *Tamar Rivers

—946 6   **Western district**

         Including Queenstown, Rosebery, Zeehan; Frenchmans Cap National Park; Norfolk Range

         Class here *Gordon River, *Eldon Range

—946 7   **Bass Strait Islands**

         Including Furneaux Group (Cape Barren, Clarke, Flinders Islands); Hunter, King, Robbins, Three Hummocks Islands

—947   **Australian Capital Territory**

         Including Tidbinbilla Fauna Reserve

—947 1   **Canberra**

—948   **Outlying islands**

         Including Ashmore, Cartier, Christmas Islands

         For Cocos Islands, see —699

—948 1   **Lord Howe Island**

—948 2   **Norfolk Island**

—95   **New Guinea (Papua)**

—951   **Irian Jaya (West Irian, West New Guinea) and offshore islands**

         Province of Indonesia

*Class parts of this physiographic region or feature as instructed under —4–9

Table 2. Areas

—953   Papua New Guinea

Including Louisiade Archipelago, D'Entrecasteaux Islands

Class Bismarck Archipelago in —936, Buka and Bougainville in —935

For former Territory of New Guinea, see —955

—955   Former Territory of New Guinea

—96   **Other parts of Pacific   Polynesia**

SUMMARY

—961	Southwest central Pacific, and isolated islands of southeast Pacific
—962	South central Pacific
—963	Southeast central Pacific
—964	Central Pacific (Line Islands)
—965	West central Pacific (Micronesia) Trust Territory of the Pacific Islands
—966	Caroline Islands
—967	Marianas (Ladrone) Islands
—968	Islands of eastern Micronesia
—969	North central Pacific Hawaii

—961   Southwest central Pacific, and isolated islands of southeast Pacific

—961 1   Fiji

—961 2   Tonga (Friendly Islands)

—961 3   American Samoa

Class here comprehensive works on Samoa

For Western Samoa, see —9614

—961 4   Western Samoa

—961 5   Tokelau (Union Islands)

—961 8   Isolated islands of southeast Pacific

Easter, Pitcairn, Henderson, Ducie, Oeno

—962   South central Pacific

Class here French Polynesia

For Marquesas Islands, see —9631; Tuamotu Islands, —9632

—962 1   Society Islands

—962 11   Tahiti

—962 2   Tubuai (Austral), Gambier, Rapa Islands

—962 3   Cook Islands

> Part of New Zealand
>
> *For Manihiki Islands, see —9624*

—962 4   Manihiki Islands

> Part of Cook Islands

—963   Southeast central Pacific

> *For isolated islands of southeast Pacific, see —9618*

—963 1   Marquesas Islands

> Part of French Polynesia

—963 2   Tuamotu Islands (Low Archipelago)

> Part of French Polynesia
>
> *For Gambier Islands, see —9622*

—964   Central Pacific (Line Islands)

> *For Palmyra, see —9699*

—965   West central Pacific (Micronesia)   Trust Territory of the Pacific Islands

> Class each specific island or group of islands with the subject, e.g., Marshall Islands —9683

—966   Caroline Islands

—967   Marianas (Ladrone) Islands

> Including Guam

—968   Islands of eastern Micronesia

—968 1   Gilbert, Ellice, Phoenix Islands

—968 3   Marshall Islands

—968 5   Nauru (Pleasant Island)

—969   North central Pacific   Hawaii

▶   —969 1–969 4 Hawaii

> State of the United States of America
>
> Class comprehensive works in —969

—969 1   Hawaii County (Hawaii Island)

Table 2. Areas

—969 2	Maui and Kalawao Counties
—969 21	Maui Island
—969 22	Kahoolawe Island
—969 23	Lanai Island
—969 24	Molokai Island

Including Kalawao County (leper settlement)

—969 3	Honolulu County (Oahu Island)
—969 31	Honolulu city
—969 4	Kauai County
—969 41	Kauai Island
—969 42	Niihau Island
—969 9	Outlying islands

Johnston, Baker, Howland Islands; Palmyra, Midway

—97   Atlantic Ocean islands

Class each specific island or group of islands not provided for
here with the subject, e.g., Azores —4699

—971	Falklands and Bouvet
—971 1	Falklands and dependent islands

Including South Georgia; South Orkney, South Sandwich, South
Shetland Islands

—971 3	Bouvet Island
—973	Saint Helena and dependencies

Including Ascension Island, Tristan da Cunha Island

—98   Arctic islands and Antarctica

▶   **—981–988 Arctic islands**

Class comprehensive works in —98; each Arctic island or group of
islands not provided for here with the subject, e.g., Baffin
region, Canada —7195

—981	Svalbard (Spitsbergen Archipelago)
—982	Greenland
—983	Jan Mayen Island

—985	Franz Josef Land
	Part of Arkhangelsk Region of Russia
—986	Novaya Zemlya (New Land)
	Part of Arkhangelsk Region of Russia
—987	Severnaya Zemlya (Northern Land)
	Part of Krasnoyarsk Territory of Russia
—988	New Siberian Islands
	Part of Yakut Autonomous Soviet Socialist Republic of Russia
—989	Antarctica
—99	**Extraterrestrial worlds**
	Worlds other than Earth
	Class space in —19

▶	—991–994 Solar system
	Class comprehensive works in —99
—991	Earth's moon
—992	Planets of solar system and their satellites
—992 1	Mercury
—992 2	Venus
—992 3	Mars and its two satellites
—992 4	Asteroids (Planetoids)
—992 5	Jupiter and its twelve satellites
—992 6	Saturn and its ten satellites
—992 7	Uranus and its five satellites
—992 8	Neptune and its two satellites
—992 9	Pluto and transplutonian planets
—993	Meteoroids and comets
—994	Sun

Table 3. Subdivisions of Individual Literatures

The following notations are never used alone, but may be used as required with the base numbers for individual literatures identified by * under 810–890. Full instructions are given below.

Table 3 is followed and supplemented by Table 3–A, which provides additional elements for building numbers within Table 3.

Procedures for building numbers in literatures of specific languages:

1. Find the base number that is designated by note or appears in the number column of the schedule 810–890, e.g., English-language literature 82, Dutch-language literature 839.31. If there is a specific literary form, proceed to step 2; if not, skip to step 7.

2. Turn to Table 3 to find the correct subdivision for the literary form, e.g., poetry 1. Add this to the base number, e.g., English poetry 821, Dutch poetry 839.311. (If the specific literary form is miscellaneous writings, follow the special instructions under 8 in Table 3.) If the work deals with or falls within a limited time period, proceed to step 3; if not, skip to step 6.

3. Turn back to the appropriate number in the schedule 810–890 and see if there is a period table. If there is a period table, proceed to step 4; if not, or if it cannot be used, the class number is completed by insertion of a decimal point between the third and fourth digits, e.g., 20th century drama in English by New Zealand authors 822, Cambodian poetry 895.9321. Note the optional use of letter prefixes or special numbers such as 828.99 to distinguish literatures of countries other than the "mother country," which makes the use of period tables feasible, e.g., 20th century drama in English by New Zealand authors NZ822.2 or 828.993322.

4. Select the appropriate period number, e.g., Elizabethan period in English literature of Great Britain 3. Add this number to the base language and form numbers already derived, e.g., English poetry of Elizabethan period 821.3; always insert a decimal point after the third digit. If the work deals with more than one author, proceed to step 5. If the work is description, critical appraisal, biography, single or collected works of an individual author, the class number is complete (except for William Shakespeare), e.g., Spenser's Faerie Queene 821.3.

(continued)

Table 3. Subdivisions of Individual Literatures (continued)

5.   Return to x1–x9 under the particular form in Table 3,
e.g., poetry 11–19, and for further extension of the correct
number follow the instructions given there, making use of Table
3–A when specified, e.g, critical appraisal of idealism in
English Elizabethan poetry 821.30913. If the work deals with a
specific kind of the literary form, the notation selected in
step 4 for the period is not used, e.g., English lyric poetry of
Elizabethan period 821.04; see final note under 11–19, 21–29,
31–39, 51–59.

6.   If the work has no time period limitation, consult
x001–x08 in Table 3 under the particular form, and follow the
appropriate instructions, making use of Table 3–A when
specified, e.g., collections of English poetry 821.008,
collections of English poetry by rural authors 821.008091734,
collections of English poetry about war 821.0080358.

7.   If the work is not limited to a specific literary form,
consult 01–09 in Table 3 and follow the appropriate
instructions, making use of Table 3–A when specified, e.g.,
collections of English literature in many forms on holidays
820.8033. If the work is not limited to a specific literary
form, and is limited to a time period from a period table that
cannot be used, do not use 001–009 following 08 or 09. The base
number from step 1, extended if necessary to three-digit length
by addition of a 0 is the complete class number, e.g.,
collections of later 20th century Australian writings in English
820. Note the optional use of letter prefixes or special numbers
such as 828.99 to distinguish literatures of countries other
than the "mother country," which makes the use of period tables
feasible, e.g., collections of later 20th century Australian
writings in English A820.8003 or 828.993408003.

The procedures described above require the use of schedule
810–890, Table 3, and Table 3–A in varying order. Sometimes also
other tables are used. Example:

English (810–890)	82
poetry (Table 3)	1
of later 20th century (810–890)	914
collections (Table 3)	080
by racial, ethnic, national groups (Table 3–A)	8
Africans (Table 5)	96

Thus, collections of contemporary English-language poetry by
African authors 821.914080896.

Note that literary form 8 Miscellaneous writings is arranged first
by period and then by specific miscellaneous forms.

Table 3. Subdivisions of Individual Literatures

—01–07	**Standard subdivisions**

Notations from Table 1

—08	**Collections**

In more than one form by more than one author

Class here works giving equal attention to collections of literary texts and to history, description, critical appraisal of the specific literature

Add to —080 notations 01–99 from Table 3-A, e.g., collections on holidays —08033

Class collections by individual authors in —1–8, history and description of the subject among groups of persons in —098–099

For history, description, critical appraisal, see —09

—09	**History, description, critical appraisal**

Of more than one form by more than one author

Class here biography

Class description, critical appraisal, biography of individual authors in —1–8

—090 01–090 09	Literature from specific periods

Add to —0900 the notation from the period table for the specific literature, e.g., earliest period —09001

—091–099	**Literature displaying specific features or emphasizing subject values, and for and by specific kinds of persons**

Add to —09 notations 1–9 from Table 3-A, e.g., history and description of literature on Faust —09351

► ## —1–8 Specific forms

Observe the following table of precedence for works combining two or more literary forms, e.g., poetic drama —2

Drama
Poetry
    Class epigrams in verse as epigrams
Fiction
Essays
Speeches
Letters
Miscellaneous writings
Satire and humor
    Class collections of satire and humor in two or more literary forms as satire and humor
    If preferred, give precedence to satire and humor over all other forms

Add to each subdivision identified by * as follows:

01–07	Standard subdivisions
	Notations from Table 1
08	Collections
	By more than one author regardless of period
	Class here works giving equal attention to collections of literary texts and to history, description, critical appraisal of the specific form
	Add to 08 notations 1–9 from Table 3–A, e.g., collections by Africans 08896, collections dealing with places 0832
	For history, description, critical appraisal, see 09
09	History, description, critical appraisal
	Of more than one author regardless of period
	Class here biography
	Add to 09 notations 1–9 from Table 3–A, e.g., critical appraisal of works by children 099282, of pornographic works 093538

Class description, critical appraisal, biography, collected works of an individual author with the form with which he is chiefly identified; or, if preferred, class description, critical appraisal, biography, single and collected works of all individual authors regardless of form in —8

Table 3. Subdivisions of Individual Literatures

SUMMARY

—1	Poetry
—2	Drama
—3	Fiction
—4	Essays
—5	Speeches
—6	Letters
—7	Satire and humor
—8	Miscellaneous writings

—1   Poetry

—100 1–100 7   Standard subdivisions

Notations from Table 1

—100 8   Collections of poetry by more than one author from more than one period

Add to —10080 notations 1–9 from Table 3–A, e.g., collections of poetry by rural authors —1008091734

—100 9   History, description, critical appraisal of poetry from more than one period

Class here biography of poets of more than one period

Add to —1009 notations 1–9 from Table 3–A, e.g., critical appraisal of poetry by Africans —1009896

▶   **—102–108 Specific kinds of poetry**

Class comprehensive works in —1; works by, description, critical appraisal, biography of individual authors in —11–19

—102   *Dramatic

—103   *Epic

—104   *Lyric and balladic

—104 2   *Sonnets

—104 3   *Odes

—104 4   *Ballads

—105   *Didactic

Class collections of poetry dealing with religious concepts in —10080382, history, description, critical appraisal in —1009382

—106   *Descriptive

Class lyric descriptive poetry in —104

*Add as instructed under —1–8

391

—107   *Satirical and humorous

>   Including limericks, clerihews [*both formerly* —108]
>
>   Within the restrictions provided in the table of precedence
>   under —1–8, class satire and humor in —7

—108   *Light and ephemeral verse

>   Including greeting card verse
>
>   Class limericks, clerihews [*both formerly* —108] in —107

—11–19   **Poetry of specific periods**

>   Add to —1 the notation from the period table for the specific
>   literature, e.g., earliest period —11; then to the result add the
>   numbers following —10 in —1001–1009, e.g., collections of poetry
>   by rural authors of earliest period —1108091734. If there is no
>   period table, use —1 without further subdivision for all periods
>
>   Class in each period without further subdivision description,
>   critical appraisal, biography, single and collected works of
>   individual authors regardless of kind of poetry
>
>   Class specific kinds of poetry by more than one author regardless
>   of period in —102–108

—2   **Drama**

—200 1–200 9   Standard subdivisions

>   Add to —200 the numbers following —100 in —1001–1009, e.g.,
>   collections of drama from more than one period by rural
>   authors —2008091734

▶   —202–205 Drama of specific media, scopes, kinds

>   Class comprehensive works in —2; works by, description, critical
>   appraisal, biography of individual authors in —21–29

▶   —202–203 Drama for mass media

>   Class comprehensive works in —2

—202   *For radio and television

—203   *For motion pictures

—204   Drama of restricted scope

>   Class drama of restricted scope for mass media in —202–203

—204 1   *One-act plays

—204 5   *Monologues

*Add as instructed under —1–8

Table 3. Subdivisions of Individual Literatures

—205	Specific kinds of drama

> Class specific kinds of drama for mass media in —202–203, specific kinds of drama of restricted scope in —204

—205 1	*Tragedy and serious drama
—205 12	*Tragedy
—205 14	*Historical drama
—205 16	*Religious and morality plays

> Including passion, miracle, mystery plays

> Class collections of plays dealing with religious concepts in —20080382; history, description, critical appraisal in —2009382

—205 2	*Comedy and melodrama
—205 23	*Comedy

> Within the restrictions provided in the table of precedence under —1–8, class satire and humor in —7

—205 27	*Melodrama

> Including modern mystery (suspense) drama

—205 7	*Variety and miscellaneous
—21–29	**Drama of specific periods**

> Add to —2 the notation from the period table for the specific literature, e.g., earliest period —21; then to the result add the numbers following —10 in —1001–1009, e.g., critical appraisal of drama of earliest period by African authors —2109896. If there is no period table, use —2 without further subdivision for all periods

> Class in each period without further subdivision description, critical appraisal, biography, single and collected works of individual authors regardless of medium, scope, or kind of drama

> Class drama of specific media, scopes, kinds by more than one author regardless of period in —202–205

—3	**Fiction**
—300 1–300 9	Standard subdivisions

> Add to —300 the numbers following —100 in —1001–1009, e.g., critical appraisal of fiction by Africans of more than one period —3009896

*Add as instructed under —1–8

▶ —301–308 Fiction of specific scopes and types

> Class comprehensive works in —3; works by, description, critical appraisal, biography of individual authors in —31–39

—301 *Short stories

> Class short stories of specific types in —308

—[302–303] Novelets and novels

> Numbers discontinued; class in —3

—306 *Cartoon fiction (Comics)

> Class cartoon fiction of specific types in —308

—308 Specific types of fiction

—308 1 *Historical and period

—308 3 *Sociological, psychological, realistic

—308 4 *Occupational

—308 5 *Love and romance

—308 7 *Adventure

—308 72 *Mystery and suspense

> Including gothics

—308 74 *Western

—308 76 *Science

—31–39 **Fiction of specific periods**

> Add to —3 the notation from the period table for the specific literature, e.g., earliest period —31; then to the result add the numbers following —10 in —1001–1009, e.g., collections of fiction by rural authors of earliest period —3108091734. If there is no period table, use —3 without further subdivision for all periods

> Class in each period without further subdivision description, critical appraisal, biography, single and collected works of individual authors regardless of scope or type of fiction

> Class specific scopes and types by more than one author regardless of period in —301–308

—4 **Essays**

—400 1–400 9 Standard subdivisions

> Add to —400 the numbers following —100 in —1001–1009, e.g., collections of essays from more than one period by rural authors —4008091734

*Add as instructed under —1–8

Table 3. Subdivisions of Individual Literatures

—41–49   Essays of specific periods

> Add to —4 the notation from the period table for the specific literature, e.g., earliest period —41; then to the result add the numbers following —10 in —1001–1009, e.g., collections of essays by rural authors of earliest period —4108091734. If there is no period table, use —4 without further subdivision for all periods

> Class in each period without further subdivision description, critical appraisal, biography, single and collected works of individual authors

—5   Speeches

—500 1–500 9   Standard subdivisions

> Add to —500 the numbers following —100 in —1001–1009, e.g., critical appraisal of speeches from more than one period —5009

▶   **—501–506 Specific kinds of speeches**

> Class comprehensive works in —5; works by, description, critical appraisal, biography of individual persons in —51–59

—501   *Public speeches (Oratory)

> Platform, radio, after-dinner speeches

> Including speeches and toasts for special occasions

> *For debates and public discussions, see —503*

—503   *Debates and public discussions

—504   *Recitations

—505   *Texts for choral speaking

—506   *Conversations

—51–59   Speeches of specific periods

> Add to —5 the notation from the period table for the specific literature, e.g., earliest period —51; then to the result add the numbers following —10 in —1001–1009, e.g., collections of speeches of earliest period —5108. If there is no period table, use —5 without further subdivision for all periods

> Class in each period without further subdivision description, critical appraisal, biography, single and collected works of individual persons regardless of kind of speeches

> Class specific kinds by more than one person regardless of period in —501–506

—6   Letters

*Add as instructed under —1–8

—600 1–600 9   Standard subdivisions

> Add to —600 the numbers following —100 in —1001–1009, e.g., collections of letters from more than one period by rural authors —6008091734

—61–69   Letters of specific periods

> Add to —6 the notation from the period table for the specific literature, e.g., earliest period —61; then to the result add the numbers following —10 in —1001–1009, e.g., collections of letters by rural authors of earliest period —6108091734. If there is no period table, use —6 without further subdivision for all periods

> Class in each period without further subdivision description, critical appraisal, biography, single and collected works of individual authors

—7   Satire and humor

> Class here parody

—700 1–700 9   Standard subdivisions

> Add to —700 the numbers following —100 in —1001–1009, e.g., critical appraisal of humor from more than one period —7009

—71–79   Satire and humor of specific periods

> Add to —7 the notation from the period table for the specific literature, e.g., earliest period —71; then to the result add the numbers following —10 in —1001–1009, e.g., critical appraisal of satire and humor of earliest period by African authors —7109896. If there is no period table, use —7 without further subdivision for all periods

> Class in each period without further subdivision description, critical appraisal, biography of individual authors

> Class a single work of satire or humor, or a collection by an individual author in one form, with the form, e.g., satirical fiction —31–39; humor without identifiable form in subdivision 07 under —81–89; a collection by an individual author in more than one form in subdivision 09 under —81–89

—8   Miscellaneous writings

> (It is optional to class here description, critical appraisal, biography, single and collected works of all individual authors regardless of form; prefer —1–8)

—800 1–800 9   Standard subdivisions

> Add to —800 the numbers following —100 in —1001–1009, e.g., critical appraisal of miscellaneous writings from more than one period —8009

Table 3. Subdivisions of Individual Literatures

▶ **—802–808 Specific kinds of miscellaneous writings**

Class in each number without further subdivision history, description, critical appraisal, biography, collections of works of authors from more than one period

Class comprehensive works in —8

—802 Quotations, epigrams, anecdotes

—803 Diaries, journals, reminiscences

—807 Experimental and nonformalized works

Works without identifiable form

Including jokes

Class anecdotal jokes in —802

—808 Prose literature

Class a specific form of prose literature with the form, e.g., essays —4; experimental prose without identifiable form in —807

—81–89 Miscellaneous writings of specific periods

Add to —8 the notation from the period table for the specific literature, e.g., earliest period —81; then add further as follows:

02   Quotations, epigrams, anecdotes
Class here without further subdivision description, critical appraisal, biography, single and collected works of individual authors

0201–0209   Standard subdivisions
Add to 020 the numbers following —100 in —1001–1009, e.g., collections by more than one author 0208

03   Diaries, journals, reminiscences
Class here without further subdivision description, critical appraisal, biography, single and collected works of individual authors

0301–0309   Standard subdivisions
Add to 030 the numbers following —100 in —1001–1009, e.g., collections by more than one author 0308

07   Experimental and nonformalized works
Works without identifiable form
Including jokes
Class here without further subdivision description, critical appraisal, biography, single and collected works of individual authors
Class anecdotal jokes in 02

(continued)

—81–89   Miscellaneous writings of specific periods (continued)

0701–0709	Standard subdivisions
	Add to 070 the numbers following —100 in —1001–1009, e.g., collections of stream of consciousness writings 0708025
08	Prose literature
	Class here without further subdivision description, critical appraisal, collected works of individual authors
	Class a specific form of prose literature with the form, e.g., essays —4; experimental prose without identifiable form in 07
0801–0809	Standard subdivisions
	Add to 080 the numbers following —100 in —1001–1009, e.g., collections by more than one author 0808
09	Individual authors not limited to or chiefly identified with one specific form
	Class here without further subdivision description, critical appraisal, biography, collected works of individual authors

If there is no period table, class quotations, epigrams, anecdotes of all periods in —802; diaries, journals, reminiscences of all periods in —803; experimental and nonformalized works of all periods in —807; prose literature of all periods in —808; individual authors of all periods not limited to or chiefly identified with one specific form in —8

Table 3–A

Notations to be added where instructed throughout Table 3

01–09	Specific periods
	Add to 0 the notation from the period table for the specific literature, e.g., earliest period 01
▶1–3	Literature displaying specific features
	Do not use if redundant, e.g., humor displaying comedy, descriptive poetry displaying description, science fiction about science
	Class comprehensive works in number in Table 3 to which notations from Table 3–A are being added
1	Literature displaying specific qualities
	Class literature displaying specific elements regardless of quality displayed in 2, literature dealing with specific themes and subjects regardless of quality displayed in 3
12	Realism and naturalism
13	Idealism

(continued)

Table 3. Subdivisions of Individual Literatures

Table 3–A (continued)

14	Classicism and romanticism
142	Classicism
145	Romanticism
15	Symbolism, allegory, fantasy
16	Tragedy and horror
17	Comedy

Within the restrictions provided in the table of precedence under —1-8 of Table 3, class satire and humor in —7

2	Literature displaying specific elements

Class literature dealing with specific themes and subjects regardless of element displayed in 3

22	Description
23	Narrative
24	Plot
25	Stream of consciousness
26	Dialogue
27	Characters
3	Literature dealing with specific themes and subjects
[31]	Major disciplines

Class with specific subject, e.g., literature on science 356

32	Places

Class here civilization of places

Add "Areas" notation 1–9 from Table 2 to 32

Class historical and political themes, historical events in specific places in 358

33	Times

Seasons, special days, holidays; parts of day, e.g., darkness, dawn

35	Humanity and human existence

(continued)

Table 3–A (continued)

351	Individual persons
	Real, fictional, legendary, mythological
	Examples: Abraham Lincoln, King Arthur, Faust, Odysseus, Pierrot
352	Specific kinds of persons
	Add "Persons" notation 03–99 from Table 7 to 352
	For individual persons, see 351
353	Human psychological and moral qualities and activities
	Former heading: Human qualities and attributes
	Examples: chivalry, friendship, insanity, pride, sex, success
	Class crime [*formerly* 353] in 355
	For love, see 354
3538	Erotica
	Including pornography
354	Life cycle
	Birth, love, marriage, death
355	Social themes
	Former heading: Everyday life
	Examples: crime [*formerly* 353], commerce, dwellings, economics, environment, food, law, occupations, recreation, violence
	Class historical and political themes in 358
356	Scientific and technical themes
	Former heading: Man-made things and materials
	Examples: engineering, flight, medicine, science, ships
	Class physical and natural phenomena in 36
357	Artistic and literary themes
	Examples: books, music, painting

(continued)

Table 3. Subdivisions of Individual Literatures

Table 3–A (continued)

358	Historical and political themes
	Examples: nationalism, war
	Class here historical events in specific places
36	Physical and natural phenomena
	Examples: animals, fire, gardens, plants, weather
37	The supernatural, mythological, legendary
	Class legendary and mythological persons in 351
372	Places
	Example: Atlantis
375	Beings
	Examples: fairies, ghosts, ogres, vampires
[376]	Things
	Number discontinued; class in 37
38	Philosophic and abstract concepts
382	Religious concepts
	Examples: Christianity, God
384	Philosophic concepts
	Example: humanism
4	Literature emphasizing subject values
	Works not basically belles-lettres
	Add 001–999 to 4, e.g., religious works as literature 42, biography as literature 492

(continued)

Table 3–A (continued)

▶8–9   Literature for and by specific kinds of persons

> Do not use if redundant, e.g., English-language poetry for and by Englishmen

> Observe the following table of precedence, e.g., literature for or by Roman Catholic girls 92827 (*not* 9222 or 9287)

Persons of specific age groups	9282–9285
Persons of specific sexes	9286–9287
Persons of specific occupational and nonoccupational characteristics	9204–9279, 929
Persons of specific racial, ethnic, national groups	8
Persons resident in specific continents, countries, localities	93–99
Persons resident in specific regions	91

> Class comprehensive works in number in Table 3 to which notations from Table 3–A are being added; literature displaying specific features for and by specific kinds of persons in 1–3

8   Literature for and by various specific racial, ethnic, national groups

> Add "Racial, Ethnic, National Groups" notation 03–99 from Table 5 to 8, e.g., literature by Africans and persons of African descent 896

9   Literature for and by other specific kinds of persons

91   For and by persons resident in specific regions

> Not limited by continent, country, locality

> Add "Areas" notation 1 from Table 2 to 9, e.g., literature by rural authors 91734

92   For and by persons of specific classes

9204–9279   Of specific occupational and nonoccupational characteristics

> Add "Persons" notation 04–79 from Table 7 to 92, e.g., literature by painters 9275; however, class persons of specific age groups and sexes in 928

> *For persons occupied with geography, history, related disciplines, see 929*

928   Of specific age groups and sexes

(continued)

Table 3. Subdivisions of Individual Literatures

Table 3–A (continued)

▶9282–9285	Age groups
	Class comprehensive works in 928
9282	Children
92826	Boys
92827	Girls
9283	Adolescents
92836	Young men
92837	Young women
9285	Adults aged 65 and over
▶9286–9287	Sexes
	Class comprehensive works in 928
9286	Men
9287	Women
929	Occupied with geography, history, related disciplines
	Add "Persons" notation 9 from Table 7 to 92, e.g., literature by archaeologists 9293
93–99	For and by persons resident in specific continents, countries, localities
	Do not use for literatures of specific countries if they are separately identified as suggested under 810, 820, 840, 860, 869
	Add "Areas" notation 3–9 from Table 2 to 9, e.g., literature (other than in Japanese language) by residents of Japan 952, Japanese-language literature by residents of Hokkaido 895.60809524

Table 4. Subdivisions of Individual Languages

The following notations are never used alone, but may be used as required with the base numbers for individual languages identified by * as explained under 420–490, e.g., English (base number 42) phonology (—15 in this table): 421.5. A decimal point is always inserted following the third digit of any number thus constructed.

—01–02 **Standard subdivisions**

> Notations from Table 1

—03 **Dictionaries, encyclopedias, concordances**

> Class dictionaries of the standard form of the language in —3, of nonstandard forms in —7

—05–09 **Standard subdivisions**

> Notations from Table 1

SUMMARY

- **—1** Written and spoken codes of the standard form of the language
- **—2** Etymology of the standard form of the language
- **—3** Dictionaries of the standard form of the language
- **—5** Structural system (Grammar) of the standard form of the language
- **—7** Nonstandard forms of the language
- **—8** Standard usage of the language (Applied (Prescriptive) linguistics)

▶ **—1–5 Description and analysis of the standard form of the language**

> Class comprehensive works in the base number for the language (adding 0 when required to make a three-figure number), standard usage in —8

—1 **Written and spoken codes of the standard form of the language**

> Class here abbreviations, acronyms, punctuation, capitalization
>
> *For etymology, see —2; dictionaries, —3; structural system, —5*

—11 **Notation**

> Alphabet and ideographs

—15 **Phonology**

> *For intonation, see —16*

—152 Spelling and pronunciation

Table 4. Subdivisions of Individual Languages

—16 **Intonation**

Pitch, stress, juncture (pauses)

—17 **Paleography**

Study of early writings

Class a specific element with the subject, e.g., notation —11

—2 **Etymology of the standard form of the language**

Phonetic, graphic, semantic development of words and morphemes

For notation, see —11; phonology, —15

—24 **Foreign elements**

Add "Languages" notation 1–9 from Table 6 to —24, e.g., French words in the language —2441 (in English 422.441)

—3 **Dictionaries of the standard form of the language**

—31 **Specialized**

Abbreviations, acronyms, synomyms, antonyms, homonyms

Class bilingual specialized dictionaries in —32–39, etymological dictionaries in —203

—32–39 **Bilingual**

Add "Languages" notation 2–9 from Table 6 to —3, e.g., dictionaries of the language and English —321 (French and English 443.21)

Class a bilingual dictionary with the language in which it will be the more useful, e.g., most libraries in English-speaking regions will find English-French dictionaries most useful classed with French in 443.21, Chinese-French dictionaries with Chinese in 495.1341. If classification with either language is equally useful, class with the language coming later in the sequence 420–490, e.g., French-German dictionaries 443.31

—5 **Structural system (Grammar) of the standard form of the language**

Historical and descriptive study of morphology and syntax

Class prescriptive grammar in —8

—[6] **Prosody of the standard form of the language**

Class in 808.1

—7   **Nonstandard forms of the language**

> Description, analysis, usage, dictionaries of dialects, slang, early forms
>
> Subdivisions are spelled out under individual languages where their use is recommended

—8   **Standard usage of the language (Applied (Prescriptive) linguistics)**

> General, formal, informal usage
>
> Use —8001–8009 for standard subdivisions
>
> *For dictionaries, see —3; rhetoric, 808.04*

—802   **Translation to and from other languages**

> Including mechanized translation [*formerly* 029.756], interpretation

—81   **Words**

> Spelling, pronunciation, meaning

—82   **Structural approach to expression**

> Formal (traditional) presentation of grammar, vocabulary, reading selections
>
> *For words, see —81; reading, —84*

—824   **For those whose native language is different**

> Add "Languages" notation 2–9 from Table 6 to —824, e.g., the language for Spanish-speaking people —82461 (English 428.2461)

—83   **Audio-lingual approach to expression**

> Informal presentation through practice in correct usage
>
> *For pronunciation, see —81*

—834   **For those whose native language is different**

> Add "Languages" notation 2–9 from Table 6 to —834, e.g., the language for Spanish-speaking people —83461 (English 428.3461)

—84   **Reading**

> *For readers, see —86*

—842   **Remedial reading**

> Correcting faulty habits and increasing proficiency of poor readers

—843   **Developmental reading**

> Including reading power and efficiency of good readers

Table 4. Subdivisions of Individual Languages

—86   **Readers**

Graded selections with emphasis on structure and vocabulary as needed

If preferred, class elementary readers in 372.412

—862   Remedial

—864   For those whose native language is different

Add "Languages" notation 2–9 from Table 6 to —864, e.g., readers for Spanish-speaking people —86461 (English 428.6461)

Table 5. Racial, Ethnic, National Groups

The following notations are never used alone, but may be used as required (either directly when so noted or through the interposition of "Standard Subdivisions" notation 089 from Table 1) with any number from the schedules, e.g., ethnopsychology (155.84) of Japanese (—956 in this table): 155.84956; ceramic arts (738) of Jews (—924 in this table): 738.089924. They may also be used when so noted with numbers from other tables, e.g., "Areas" notation 174 from Table 2.

Except where the schedules instruct otherwise, and unless it is redundant, add 0 to the number from this table and to the result add "Areas" notation 1–9 from Table 2, e.g., Germans in Brazil —31081, but Germans in Germany —31.

—01	**Indigenes**
—011	Aborigines
—012	Nonaborigines
—03	**Basic races**
—034	Caucasoids
—035	Mongoloids
—036	Negroids
—04	**Mixtures of basic races**
—042	Caucasoids and Mongoloids
—043	Mongoloids and Negroids
—044	Negroids and Caucasoids
—046	Caucasoids, Mongoloids, Negroids

▶ **—1–9 Specific racial, ethnic, national groups**

By origin or situation

Arrange as below; but, if it is desired to give local emphasis and a shorter number to a specific group, place it first by use of a letter or other symbol, e.g., Arabs —A (preceding —1)

Table 5. Racial, Ethnic, National Groups

SUMMARY

—1 North Americans
—2 Anglo-Saxons, British, English
—3 Nordics
—4 Modern Latins
—5 Italians, Romanians, related groups
—6 Spanish and Portuguese
—7 Other Italic peoples
—8 Greeks and related groups
—9 Other racial, ethnic, national groups

—1 North Americans

(If it is desired to give local emphasis and a shorter number to a specific group, e.g., Sinhalese, it is optional to class it in this number; in that case class North Americans in —2)

For Spanish Americans, see —68; North American native races, —97

—11 Canadians

—112 Of British origin

—114 Of French origin

—13 People of United States ("Americans")

—2 Anglo-Saxons, British, English

Class North Americans of British origin in —1, people of Celtic origin in —916, Anglo-Indians in —91411

—21 People of British Isles

—23 New Zealanders

For Polynesians, see —994

—24 Australians

For Australian native races, see —9915

—28 South African Anglo-Saxons

—3 Nordics

For Anglo-Saxons, see —2

—31 Germans

—35 Swiss

—36 Austrians

—39 Other

—392 Frisians

—393 Netherlandish persons

—393 1 Dutch

—393 2	Flemings

> Class here comprehensive works on Belgians
>
> *For Walloons, see —42*

—393 6	Afrikaners
—395	Scandinavians

> Class specific Scandinavian groups in —396–398

—396	West Scandinavians
—396 1	Icelanders
—396 9	Faeroese
—397	Swedes
—398	Danes and Norwegians
—398 1	Danes
—398 2	Norwegians

—4 Modern Latins

> *For Italians, Romanians, related groups, see —5; Spanish and Portuguese, —6*

—41	**French**

> Class Canadians of French origin in —114
>
> *For Basques, see —9992; Corsicans, —58*

—42	**Walloons**
—49	**Catalans**

—5 Italians, Romanians, related groups

—51	**Italians**
—56	**Sardinians**
—57	**Dalmatians**
—58	**Corsicans**
—59	**Romanians**

—6 Spanish and Portuguese

—61	**People of Spain (Spaniards)**

> *For Catalans, see —49; Basques, —9992*

—68	**Spanish Americans**

> Class here Latin Americans
>
> Class Latin Americans not provided for here with the subject. e.g., Brazilians —698

Table 5. Racial, Ethnic, National Groups

—687–688	National groups

Add "Areas" notation 7–8 from Table 2 to base number —68, e.g., Chileans —6883

—69	**Portuguese**
—691	People of Portugal
—698	Brazilians

—7   Other Italic peoples

—71	**Ancient Romans**
—79	**Other**

For Etruscans, see —9994

—799	Osco-Umbrians

—8   Greeks and related groups

For Macedonians, see —91819

—81	**Ancient Greeks**

Class here comprehensive works on ancient Greeks and Romans

For ancient Romans, see —71

—89	**Modern Greeks and related groups**
—893	Greek nationals
—895	Cypriots

Class Turkish Cypriots in —9435

—9   Other racial, ethnic, national groups

SUMMARY

—91	Other Indo-European peoples
—92	Semites
—93	North Africans
—94	Peoples of North and West Asian origin or situation, and Dravidians
—95	Peoples of East and Southeast Asia
—96	Africans and people of African descent
—97	North American native races
—98	South American native races
—99	Other peoples

—91	**Other Indo-European peoples**

SUMMARY

—914	South Asians
—915	Iranians
—916	Celts
—917	East Slavs
—918	Slavs
—919	Other East Indo-Europeans

—914   **South Asians**

Class here Indo-Aryans

For Dravidians and Scytho-Dravidians, see —948

—914 1   **National groups**

Class nationals of specific ethnolinguistic groups in —9142–9149, Trinidadians of South Asian origin in —96972983, Guyanans of South Asian origin in —969881, Fijians of South Asian origin in —995

—914 11   Indians

Including Anglo-Indians

—914 12   Pakistanis and people of Bangladesh

—914 13   Ceylonese (Sri Lankians)

—914 17   Sikkimese

—914 18   Bhutanese

—914 2   Punjabis

—914 3   Hindis

—914 4   Bengalis

—914 5   Assamese, Biharis, Oriyas

—914 7   Gujars

—914 8   Sinhalese

—914 9   Other Indo-Aryan peoples

—914 95   Nepalis

—914 96   Paharis

—914 97   Gypsies

—914 99   Dards

Including Kohistanis, Kashmiris, Kafirs

For Gypsies, see —91497

—915   **Iranians**

—915 5   Persians

Table 5. Racial, Ethnic, National Groups

—915 9	Others
	Kurds, Baluchis, Tajiks, Afghans, Ossets, Pamiris, Galchas
—916	Celts
	Including Gauls
—916 2	Irish
—916 3	Scots
—916 4	Manxmen
—916 6	Welsh (Cymry)
—916 7	Cornishmen
—916 8	Bretons
—917	East Slavs
	Class here people of Soviet Union
	Class a specific Soviet group with the subject, e.g., Uzbeks —943
—917 1	Russians
—917 14	Cossacks
—917 9	Other
—917 91	Ukrainians
—917 99	Belorussians
—918	Slavs
	For East Slavs, see —917
—918 1	Bulgarians and Macedonians
—918 11	Bulgarians
—918 19	Macedonians
—918 2	Yugoslavs
	For Slovenes, see —9184; Macedonians, —91819
—918 22	Serbs
—918 23	Croats
—918 4	Slovenes
—918 5	Poles and Kashubs
	For Cossacks, see —91714

—918 6	Czechs

Class here Czechoslovaks

For Slovaks and Moravians, see —9187

—918 7	Slovaks and Moravians
—918 8	Wends (Sorbs, Lusatians)
—919	Other East Indo-Europeans
—919 2	Lithuanians
—919 3	Latvians (Letts)
—919 9	Others
—919 91	Albanians
—919 92	Armenians
—92	**Semites**
—921	Assyrians, Babylonians, Chaldeans, Akkadians, Amorites
—922	Arameans
—924	Hebrews, Israelis, Jews
—926	Phoenicians and Canaanites

For Amorites, see —921

—927	Arabs and Maltese
—927 5–927 6	National groups of Arabs

Add "Areas" notation 5–6 from Table 2 to base number —927, e.g., Iraqis —927567, Sudanese —927624

—927 7	Maltese
—928	Ethiopians (Abyssinians)

Including Amharas, Hararis

—929	Mahris and Socotrans
—93	**North Africans**

For Arabs, see —927; Ethiopians, —928

—931	Ancient Egyptians
—932	Copts
—933	Berbers and Tuaregs
—935	Cushites

Including Somalis

—937	Hausas

Table 5. Racial, Ethnic, National Groups

—94	**Peoples of North and West Asian origin or situation, and Dravidians**
	Class Indo-Europeans of these regions in —91, Semites in —92
—941	Tungus, Lamuts, Manchus, Goldis
—942	Mongols
—943	Turkic peoples
	Including Azerbaijanis, Kazaks, Kirghizes, Turkomans, Uighurs, Uzbeks, Yakuts
	Class Chuvashes in —9456, Cossacks in —91714
—943 5	Turks
	Including Turkish Cypriots
—944	Samoyeds
—945	Finno-Ugrians
—945 1	Ugrians
	Including Ostyaks, Voguls
—945 11	Hungarians
—945 3	Permiaks, Votyaks, Zyrians (Komis)
—945 4	Finnic peoples
	Including Karelians, Livonians, Veps
	For Lapps, see —9455; Mordvins, Cheremises (Maris), Chuvashes, —9456
—945 41	Finns
—945 45	Estonians
—945 5	Lapps
—945 6	Mordvins, Cheremises (Maris), Chuvashes
—946	Paleo-Asiatics
	Including Ainus
—948	Dravidians and Scytho-Dravidians
	Including Marathas (Mahratta), Sindhis
—95	**Peoples of East and Southeast Asia**
—951	Chinese
—954	Tibetans
—956	Japanese and Ryukyuans
	For Ainus, see —946

—957	Koreans
—958	Burmese
—959	Others

For Malays, see —992

—959 1	Thais (Siamese), Laos, Shans, Khamtis, Ahoms, Karens
—959 2	Vietnamese (Annamese)
—959 3	Cambodians
—959 5	Mundas

—96   **Africans and people of African descent**

For North Africans, see —93

—960 73   United States blacks (Afro-Americans)

> Add "Areas" notation 1–9 from Table 2 to base number —960730, e.g., United States blacks in England —96073042

—961   Hottentots (Khoi-Khoin) and Bushmen (San)

—963   Bantus, Zulus, Ewes, Ibos (Igbos), Yorubas, Fulanis, Mandingoes

> Arrange alphabetically by name of tribe or other group

—966–968   National groups in Africa

> Add to base number —96 the numbers following 6 in "Areas" notation 66–68 from Table 2, e.g., Nigerians —9669, South Africans —968
>
> Class nationals of specific ethnolinguistic groups in —961–963
>
> *For South African Anglo-Saxons, see —28; Afrikaners, —3936*

—969   Other national populations of largely African descent

> Add "Areas" notation 4–9 from Table 2 to base number —969, e.g., Trinidadians —96972983
>
> Class nationals of specific ethnolinguistic groups in —961–963; minority groups of African descent in a specific population in —9604–9609

—97   **North American native races**

> Amerindians and Eskimos
>
> Class here comprehensive works on American native races
>
> Arrange alphabetically by name of tribe, nation, other group
>
> *For South American native races, see —98*

Table 5. Racial, Ethnic, National Groups

—98	**South American native races**
	Arrange alphabetically by name of tribe, nation, other group
—99	**Other peoples**
—991	Negritos, Papuans, Australian native races
—991 1	Negritos
—991 2	Papuans
—991 5	Australian native races
—992	Malays and related peoples
—992 1	Filipinos
—992 2	Indonesians
	For Taiwanese (Formosans), see —9925
—992 5	Taiwanese (Formosans)
—993	Malagasy
—994	Polynesians
	For Fijians, see —995
—995	Melanesians and Micronesians
	Examples: Fijians, Gilbertese
—999	Others
—999 2	Basques
—999 3	Elamites
—999 4	Etruscans
—999 5	Sumerians
—999 6	Georgians, Ingush, Chechens, Circassians

Table 6. Languages

The following notations are never used alone, but may be used with those numbers from the schedules and other tables to which the classifier is instructed to add "Languages" notation, e.g., translations of Bible (220.5) into Dutch (—3931 in this table): 220.53931; regions ("Areas" notation 175 from Table 2) where Spanish language (—61 in this table) predominates: "Areas" notation 17561. When adding to a number from the schedules, always insert a decimal point between the third and fourth digits of the complete number.

Arrange as below; but, if it is desired to give local emphasis and a shorter number to a specific language, place it first by use of a letter or other symbol, e.g., Arabic language —A (preceding —1).

Unless specifically provided for, class old and middle form of a specific modern language with the language, e.g., Old High German —31, but Old English —29.

The notations in this table do not necessarily correspond exactly to the numbers used for individual languages in 420–490 and in 810–890. Follow the notations from this table only when so instructed.

SUMMARY

—1	Indo-European (Indo-Germanic) languages
—2	English and Anglo-Saxon languages
—3	Germanic (Teutonic) languages
—4	Romance languages
—5	Italian, Romanian, Rhaeto-Romanic
—6	Spanish and Portuguese
—7	Italic languages
—8	Hellenic languages
—9	Other languages

—1 Indo-European (Indo-Germanic) languages

(If it is desired to give local emphasis and a shorter number to a specific language, e.g., Ukrainian, it is optional to class it in this number; in that case class Indo-European languages in —91)

For specific Indo-European languages, see —2–8

Table 6. Languages

▶ **—2–8 Specific Indo-European languages**

Class comprehensive works in —1

For East Indo-European and Celtic languages, see —91

—2 English and Anglo-Saxon languages

—21 English

—29 Anglo-Saxon (Old English)

—3 Germanic (Teutonic) languages

For English and Anglo-Saxon languages, see —2

—31 German

—32 Franconian

—33 Swabian

—34 Alsatian

—35 Swiss German

—37 Yiddish (Judeo-German)

—38 Pennsylvania Dutch (Pennsylvania German)

—39 Other

▶ **—391–394 West Germanic languages**

Class comprehensive works in —39

—391 Old Low Germanic languages

Old Saxon, Old Frisian, Old Low Franconian, Old Low German

▶ **—392–394 Modern Low Germanic languages**

Class comprehensive works in —39

—392 Frisian

—393 Netherlandish languages

—393 1 Dutch

—393 2 Flemish

—393 6 Afrikaans

—394 Low German (Plattdeutsch)

—395 Scandinavian (North Germanic) languages

For specific Scandinavian languages, see —396–398

▶ **—396–398 Specific Scandinavian languages**

Class comprehensive works in —395

—396	West Scandinavian languages
—396 1	Old Norse (Old Icelandic)
—396 9	Modern West Scandinavian languages
—396 91	Icelandic
—396 99	Faeroese

▶ **—397–398 East Scandinavian languages**

Class comprehensive works in —395

—397	Swedish
—398	Danish and Norwegian
—398 1	Danish

Class Dano-Norwegian [*formerly* —3981] in —3982

—398 2	Norwegian (Bokmal, Riksmal)

Dano-Norwegian [*formerly* —3981]

—398 3	New Norse (Landsmal, Nynorsk)
—399	East Germanic

Gothic, Vandalic, Burgundian

—4 Romance languages

For Italian, Romanian, Rhaeto-Romanic, see -5; Spanish and Portuguese, —6

—41	**French**
—49	**Provençal and Catalan**
—491	Provençal
—499	Catalan

—5 Italian, Romanian, Rhaeto-Romanic

—51	**Italian**
—56	**Sardinian**
—57	**Dalmatian (Vegliote)**
—59	**Romanian and Rhaeto-Romanic**
—591	Romanian
—599	Rhaeto-Romanic languages

Romansh, Ladin, Friulian

Table 6. Languages

—6	**Spanish and Portuguese**
—61	**Spanish**
—67	**Judeo-Spanish (Ladino)**
—68	**Papiamento**
—69	**Portuguese**

Including Galician (Gallegan)

—7	**Italic languages**

For Romance languages, see —4

—71	**Latin**
—79	**Other**
—794	Latinian languages other than Latin

Venetic, Lanuvian, Faliscan, Praenestian

—797	Sabellian languages

Aequian, Marrucinian, Marsian, Paelignian, Sabine, Vestinian, Volscian

—799	Osco-Umbrian languages

Oscan, Umbrian

—8	**Hellenic languages**

Class here comprehensive works on classical languages

For Latin, see —71

—81	**Classical Greek**
—87	**Postclassical (Hellenistic and Byzantine) Greek**

Including Biblical Greek (Koine)

—89	**Modern Greek**

Katharevusa and Demotic

—9	**Other languages**

SUMMARY

—91	**East Indo-European and Celtic languages**
—92	**Afro-Asiatic (Hamito-Semitic) languages**
—93	**Hamitic and Chad languages**
—94	**Ural-Altaic, Paleosiberian, Dravidian languages**
—95	**Sino-Tibetan and other languages of East and Southeast Asia**
—96	**African languages**
—97	**North American native languages**
—98	**South American native languages**
—99	**Other languages**

—91	**East Indo-European and Celtic languages**

SUMMARY

—911 **Indo-Iranian (Aryan) languages**
—912 **Sanskrit**
—913 **Middle Indic languages (Secondary Prakrits)**
—914 **Modern Indic languages (Tertiary Prakrits)**
—915 **Iranian languages**
—916 **Celtic languages**
—917 **East Slavic languages**
—918 **Slavic languages**
—919 **Baltic and other languages**

—911   Indo-Iranian (Aryan) languages

> *For Indic (Indo-Aryan) languages, see —912–914; Iranian languages, —915*

▶   —912–914 Indic (Indo-Aryan) languages

Class comprehensive works in —911

—912   Sanskrit

Vedic (Old Indic) and classical

—913   Middle Indic languages (Secondary Prakrits)

—913 7   Pali

—914   Modern Indic languages (Tertiary Prakrits)

—914 1   Sindhi and Lahnda

—914 11   Sindhi

—914 19   Lahnda

—914 2   Panjabi

—914 3   Western Hindi languages

—914 31   Standard Hindi

—914 39   Urdu

—914 4   Bengali

—914 5   Assamese, Bihari (Bhojpuri, Magahi, Maithili), Oriya

—914 6   Marathi

Including Konkani

—914 7   Gujarati and Rajasthani

—914 71   Gujarati

—914 79   Rajasthani

Including Jaipuri, Marwari

Table 6. Languages

—914 8	Sinhalese
	Including Mahl
—914 9	Other
	Including Nepali, Pahari, Eastern Hindi (Awadhi, Begheli, Chattisgarhi)
—914 99	Dard languages
	Shina, Khowar, Kafiri, Kohistani, Kashmiri, Romany (Gypsy)
—915	Iranian languages
—915 1	Old Persian (West Iranian)
—915 2	Avestan (East Iranian)
—915 3	Middle Iranian languages
	Pahlavi (Middle Persian), Sogdian, Khotanese (Saka)
—915 5	Modern Persian (Farsi)
—915 9	Other modern Iranian languages
	Kurdish, Baluchi, Tajiki, Pashto (Afghan), Ossetic, Pamir (Galcha), Yaghnobi
—916	Celtic languages
	Including Gaulish, Cornish
—916 2	Irish Gaelic
—916 3	Scottish Gaelic
—916 4	Manx
—916 6	Welsh (Cymric)
—916 7	Cornish
—916 8	Breton
—917	East Slavic languages
—917 1	Russian
—917 9	Other
—917 91	Ukrainian
—917 99	Belorussian
—918	Slavic languages
	Including Common Slavic
	Class here comprehensive works on Balto-Slavic languages
	For East Slavic languages, see —917; Baltic languages, —919

—918 1	South Slavic languages

For Serbo-Croatian, see —9182; Slovenian, —9184

—918 11	Bulgarian
—918 17	Old Bulgarian (Church Slavonic)
—918 19	Macedonian
—918 2	Serbo-Croatian
—918 4	Slovenian
—918 5	West Slavic languages

For Czech, see —9186; Slovak, —9187; Wendish, —9188; Polabian, —9189

—918 51	Polish

Including Kashubian

—918 6	Czech

For Moravian dialects, see —9187

—918 7	Slovak

Including Moravian dialects

—918 8	Wendish (Sorbian, Lusatian)
—918 9	Polabian
—919	Baltic and other languages

▶ —919 1–919 3 Baltic languages

Class comprehensive works in —919

—919 1	Old Prussian
—919 2	Lithuanian
—919 3	Latvian (Lettish)
—919 9	Other Indo-European languages
—919 91	Albanian
—919 92	Armenian
—919 93	Thraco-Phrygian and Illyrian languages

Ligurian, Messapian, Illyrian, Thracian, Phrygian

—919 94	Tocharian languages
—919 96	Agnean and Kuchean languages

Relationship to Indo-European family not clear

Table 6. Languages

—919 98	Anatolian languages
	Hittite, Luwian, Palaic, Lydian, Lycian
	Membership in Indo-European family not certain
—92	**Afro-Asiatic (Hamito-Semitic) languages**
	For Hamitic and Chad languages, see —93
—921	East Semitic (Akkadian) languages
	Examples: Assyrian, Babylonian, Chaldean

▶ **—922–929 West Semitic languages**

Class comprehensive works in —92

▶ **—922–926 Northwest Semitic languages**

Class comprehensive works in —92

—922	Aramaic languages
	For Eastern Aramaic languages, see —923
—922 9	**Biblical Aramaic (Chaldee) and Samaritan**
—923	Eastern Aramaic languages
	Example: Syriac
—924	Hebrew
	Including Ammonite, Moabite
—926	Canaanite-Phoenician languages
	Including Punic, Ugaritic
	Class here comprehensive works on Canaanitic languages
	For Hebrew, see —924

▶ **—927–929 Southwest Semitic languages**

Class comprehensive works in —92

—927	North Arabic languages
	Examples: classical and modern Arabic, Maltese
—928	Ethiopic languages
	Examples: Geez, Tigre, Tigrinya, Amharic, Argobba, Harari, Gurage
—929	South Arabic languages
	Examples: Mahri, Sokotri, Qarawi, Shkhauri
—93	**Hamitic and Chad languages**

▶ **—931–935 Hamitic languages**

Class comprehensive works in —93

—931 Egyptian languages

Including Old, Middle, New, Demotic Egyptian

For Coptic, see —932

—932 Coptic

—933 Berber languages

Examples: Tamashek (Tuareg), Rif, Siwi, Kabyle

—935 Cushitic languages

Examples: Beja, Galla, Somali

—937 Chad languages

Including Angas

—937 2 Hausa

—94 **Ural-Altaic, Paleosiberian, Dravidian languages**

SUMMARY

—941 **Tungusic languages**
—942 **Mongolic languages**
—943 **Turkic (Turko-Tatar) languages**
—944 **Samoyedic languages**
—945 **Finno-Ugric languages**
—946 **Paleosiberian languages**
—948 **Dravidian languages**

▶ **—941–943 Altaic languages**

Class comprehensive works in —94, Japanese in —956, Korean in —957

—941 Tungusic languages

Examples: Tungus, Lamut, Manchu, Goldi

—942 Mongolic languages

Examples: Mongolian, Buryat, Kalmuck

—943 Turkic (Turko-Tatar) languages

Including Azerbaijani, Chuvash, Kazak, Kirghiz, Turkoman, Uighur, Uzbek, Yakut

—943 5 Turkish

Table 6. Languages

▶ **—944–945 Uralic languages**

Class comprehensive works in —94

—944 **Samoyedic languages**

Examples: Yenisei, Yurak, Kamasin, Ostyak Samoyed

—945 **Finno-Ugric languages**

—945 1 **Ugric languages**

Including Ostyak, Vogul

—945 11 **Hungarian (Magyar)**

—945 3 **Permian languages**

Examples: Votyak (Udmurt), Zyrian

—945 4 **Finnic languages**

Including Karelian, Livonian, Veps

For Lapp, see —9455; Middle Volga languages, —9456

—945 41 **Finnish (Suomi)**

—945 45 **Estonian**

—945 5 **Lapp**

—945 6 **Middle Volga languages**

Examples: Mordvin, Cheremis

—946 **Paleosiberian languages**

Luorawetlin, Yukaghir, Gilyak, Yeniseian families; Ainu (relationship not clear)

—948 **Dravidian languages**

—948 1 **Dravida group**

Including Kurukh (Orâon), Malto, Kota, Toda

—948 11 **Tamil**

—948 12 **Malayalam**

—948 14 **Kanarese (Kannada)**

—948 2 **Andhra group**

—948 23 **Gondi**

—948 24 **Khond (Kandh)**

—948 27 **Telugu**

—948 3 **Brahui**

—95	**Sino-Tibetan and other languages of East and Southeast Asia**
—951	Chinese
—951 1	Mandarin
—951 7	Amoy, Cantonese, Foochow, Hakka, Pekingese, Swatow, Wu dialects
—954	Tibeto-Burman languages

> *For Burmese, see* —958

—954 1	Tibetan
—954 9	Himalayan dialects
—956	Japanese
—957	Korean
—958	Burmese
—959	Other languages of Southeast Asia

> *For Malayan languages, see* —992

—959 1	Thai languages
—959 11	Thai (Siamese)
—959 19	Other

> Including Lao, Shan, Khamti, Ahom, Karen
>
> *For Annam-Muong languages, see* —9592

—959 2	Annam-Muong languages

> Relationship to Thai and Austroasiatic languages not clear

—959 22	Vietnamese (Annamese)
—959 3	Mon-Khmer languages

> Including Mon, Khmer, Palaung, Wa, Khasi, Senoi, Semang (Negrito [*formerly* —9911])
>
> Class here Austroasiatic languages
>
> Class Jakun [*formerly* —9593] in —9928
>
> > *For Munda languages, see* —9595; *Annam-Muong languages,* —9592

—959 32	Cambodian
—959 5	Munda languages

> Relationship to Austroasiatic languages not certain
>
> Examples: Santali, Ho, Mundari, Gadaba

Table 6. Languages

—96	**African languages**
	For Afro-Asiatic languages, see —92
—961	Macro-Khoisan languages
	Examples: Hottentot (Khoi-Khoin), Bushman (San) languages
—963	Niger-Congo languages
—963 2	West-Atlantic languages
	Examples: Fulani, Wolof, Serer
—963 3	Kwa languages
	Including Ewe
—963 32	Ibo
—963 33	Yoruba
—963 4	Mande (Mandingo) languages
	Examples: Malinke, Bambara, Mende
—963 5	Gur (Voltaic) languages
	Examples: Dagomba, Senuf
—963 6	Benue-Niger languages
	Including Adamawa, Ubangi, Kordofanian languages
	For Bantu languages, see —9639
—963 9	Bantu languages
	Including Zulu
—963 92	Swahili
—965	Chari-Nile (Macrosudanic) languages
	Examples: Nubian, Nilotic languages
—969	Commercial languages
	Class a specific language with its family, e.g., Swahili —96392
—97	**North American native languages**
	Class here comprehensive works on American native languages
	For South American native languages, see —98
—971	Eskimo-Aleut languages
—972	Na-Dene languages
	Including Tlingit, Athapaskan (Chipewyan, Apachean, Navaho)
—973	Algonkian-Mosan languages
	Including Delaware, Ojibway, Cree, Nootka

—974	Macro-Penutian languages

Including Coos, Tsimshian, Mixe, Hopi, Ute, Aztec, Maya, Quiche, Chinook

—975   Hokan-Siouan languages

Including Yukian, Huron, Cherokee, Choctaw, Creek, Iroquois

—976   Macro-Otomanguean languages

Including Poploca, Manguean, Mixtec, Zapotec

—977   Tarascan languages

—978   Miskito-Matagalpan languages

—979   Other North and Middle American languages

Examples: Cuitlatec, Olmec

—98   South American native languages

—982   Macro-Chibchan languages

Chibchan, Paezan subfamilies

—983   Andean-Equatorial languages

Andean, Macro-Tucanoan, Equatorial subfamilies

Including Kechua (Quechua), Tupí, Guaraní, Jiraro, Esmeralda, Yaruro

—984   Gê–Pano-Carib languages

Macro-Gê, Macro-Panoan, Macro-Carib subfamilies

Including Nambicura, Huarpe, Taruma

—985   Hokan languages

—99   Other languages

—991   Nonaustronesian languages of Oceania

—[991 1]   Negrito languages

Class in —9593

—991 2   Papuan languages

—991 5   Australian languages

▶   —992–995 Austronesian (Oceanic, Malayo-Polynesian) languages

Class comprehensive works in —992

Table 6. Languages

—992	Malay languages

Class here comprehensive works on Austronesian languages

For Malagasy, see —993; Polynesian languages, —994; Melanesian and Micronesian languages, —995

—992 1	Philippine (Tagala) languages
—992 11	Tagalog (Filipino)
—992 2	Indonesian languages

Including Balinese, Madurese, Sundanese; Bornean languages

—992 21	Indonesian (Bahasa Indonesia)
—992 22	Javanese
—992 8	Malay (Bahasa Malaysia)

Including Melayu Asli (Proto-Malay) languages; Jakun [*formerly* —9593]

Class Senoi and Semang languages in —9593

—993	Malagasy
—994	Polynesian languages

Examples: Hawaiian, Samoan, Tahitian, Maori

—995	Melanesian and Micronesian languages
—999	Miscellaneous languages
—999 2	Basque
—999 3	Elamite
—999 4	Etruscan
—999 5	Sumerian
—999 6	Caucasic (Caucasian) languages

Examples: Georgian, Chechen, Circassian

—999 9	Artificial languages
—999 92	Esperanto
—999 93	Interlingua

Table 7. Persons

The following notations are never used alone, but may be used as required (either directly when so noted or through the interposition of "Standard Subdivisions" notation 088 from Table 1) with any appropriate number from the schedules, e.g., collections from more than one literature (808.8992) by Lutherans (—241 in this table): 808.8992241; ceramic arts (738) by the blind (—08161 in this table): 738.08808161. They may also be used when so noted with numbers from other tables, e.g., "Standard Subdivisions" notation 024 from Table 1. Do not add from this table if the resultant concept is redundant, e.g., medicine by physicians, Lutheran doctrine among Lutherans.

SUMMARY

—01	Individual persons
—02	Groups of persons
—03	Persons by racial, ethnic, national background
—04	Persons by sex and kinship characteristics
—05	Persons by age
—06	Persons by social and economic characteristics
—08	Persons by physical and mental characteristics
—09	Generalists and novices

—01   Individual persons

Class specific kinds of individuals in —03–99

—02   Groups of persons

Class groups of specific kinds of persons in —03–99

▶
—03–08 Persons by various nonoccupational characteristics

Unless other instructions are given, class complex subjects with aspects in two or more subdivisions of this table in the number coming last in the table, e.g., gifted upper middle-class Jewish male adolescents —0829 (*not* —0622, —055, —041, or —03924)

—03   Persons by racial, ethnic, national background

Add "Racial, Ethnic, National Groups" notation 01–99 from Table 5 to base number —03, e.g., North American persons —031

—04   Persons by sex and kinship characteristics

▶
—041–042 Persons by sex

Class comprehensive works in —04

Table 7. Persons

—041   Males

—042   Females

▶   —043–046 Persons by kinship characteristics

        Class comprehensive works in —04

—043   Direct ancestors and their surrogates

—043 1   Parents

        Natural, adoptive, foster parents; stepparents

—043 2   Grandparents

        Direct forebears other than parents

—044   Direct descendants and their counterparts

—044 1   Offspring (Sons and daughters)

        Natural, adopted, foster children; stepchildren

—044 2   Grandchildren

        Direct descendants other than first generation

—045   Siblings

        Brothers and sisters by blood, adoption, foster care, remarriage of parents

—046   Indirect ancestors and descendants, and collateral kinsmen

        Uncles, aunts, nephews, nieces, cousins, of all degrees

—05   **Persons by age**

—054   Children

—054 2   Infants

        From birth to age two

—054 3   Preschool children

        Ages three to five

—054 4   School children

        Ages six to eleven

—055   Adolescents (Young adults)

        Ages twelve to twenty

—056   Adults

—056 4   Middle-aged

—056 5   Aged 65 and over

—06   **Persons by social and economic characteristics**

—062   By social and economic levels

—062 1	Upper classes

    Royalty, nobility, elite, wealthy

        For reigning monarchs and their regents, see —3511

—062 2	Middle classes

    Well-to-do persons; professional, managerial middle classes

        For lower middle classes, see —0623

—062 3	Lower middle classes

    Moderate-income persons, working class in developed areas

—062 4	Low-income classes
—062 5	Slaves, serfs, peons
—063	By level of cultural development
—063 1	High
—063 2	Medium
—063 3	Low

    Including nonliterates

—065	By marriage status
—065 2	Single persons

        For separated and divorced persons, see —0653; widowed persons, —0654

—065 23	Engaged persons
—065 3	Separated and divorced persons
—065 4	Widowed persons
—065 5	Married persons

    Including persons married in common law

        For polygamous persons, see —0659

—065 9	Polygamous persons
—069	By special social status
—069 2	Asocial and antisocial persons

    Including vagrants, criminals and other offenders, convicts

—069 3	Socially exceptional persons

    Members of nondominant racial, ethnic, national, socioeconomic, religious groups

    Class socially exceptional persons of specific racial, ethnic, national groups in —03; of specific religious groups in —2

Table 7. Persons

—069 4   **Socially disadvantaged persons**

> Class here war victims, unemployed
>
> Class persons socially disadvantaged by reason of inclusion in nondominant racial, ethnic, national, socioeconomic, religious groups in —0693

—069 42   Poverty-stricken and destitute persons

—069 45   Illegitimate and abandoned children and orphans

—069 47   Unmarried mothers

—069 6   Retired persons

—069 7   War veterans

—08   **Persons by physical and mental characteristics**

—081   By physical condition

—081 2   Healthy persons

—081 4   Ill persons

—081 6   Persons with handicaps and disablements

—081 61   Blind and partially sighted persons

—081 62   Deaf and hard-of-hearing persons

—081 64   Persons with speech defects

—081 66   Crippled persons

—082   By mental condition

—082 2   Healthy persons

—082 4   Ill and emotionally disturbed persons

—082 6   Persons with handicaps and deficiencies (Mentally retarded)

—082 9   Gifted persons

> Including geniuses

▶   **—09–99 Persons by various occupational characteristics**

—09   **Generalists and novices**

> Generalists: persons occupied with several or many subjects and activities, or with specific subjects and activities of a general nature, as study, profession, vocation, hobby

—090 1   Scholars, academicians, research workers

—090 9   Novices and amateurs

> Laymen, dabblers, uninitiated, collectors

—091	Persons occupied with bibliography
—092	Persons occupied with library and information science

For persons occupied with bibliography, see —091

—093	Encyclopedists

Class lexicographers in —4

—096	Persons occupied with museology
—097	Persons occupied with publishing and journalism

▶ ## —1–9 Specialists

Persons occupied with specific disciplines, subjects, activities as study, profession, vocation, hobby, affiliation

Class persons occupied with specific subjects or activities of a general nature in —09

SUMMARY

—1	Persons occupied with philosophy and related disciplines
—2	Persons occupied with or adherent to religion
—3	Persons occupied with the social sciences and socioeconomic activities
—4	Persons occupied with linguistics and lexicography
—5	Persons occupied with pure sciences
—6	Persons occupied with applied sciences (Technologists)
—7	Persons occupied with the arts
—8	Persons occupied with creative writing and speaking
—9	Persons occupied with geography, history, related disciplines and activities

—1 Persons occupied with philosophy and related disciplines

—11	With philosophy
—13	With parapsychology and the occult
—15	With psychology

—2 Persons occupied with or adherent to religion

Founders, central and local administrative heads, clergy, missionaries, members of religious congregations and orders, saints, laymen

Class here persons occupied with or adherent to Christianity

Table 7. Persons

SUMMARY

—21   With primitive and Oriental churches
—22   With Roman Catholic Church
—23   With Anglican churches
—24   With Protestant churches of Continental origin
—25   With Presbyterian, American Reformed, Congregational churches
—26   With Baptist, Disciples of Christ, Adventist churches
—27   With Methodist churches
—28   With other churches
—29   With other religions

▶ **—21–28 Persons occupied with or adherent to Christianity and Christian church**

Class comprehensive works in —2

—21   **With primitive and Oriental churches**

—211   Apostolic

Including church fathers

—215   Eastern other than Orthodox

—219   Eastern Orthodox

—22   **With Roman Catholic Church**

—23   **With Anglican churches**

—24   **With Protestant churches of Continental origin**

—241   Lutheran

—242   Calvinistic and Reformed

—243   Hussite and Anabaptist

—244   Albigensian and Waldensian

—245   Huguenot

—246   Moravian

—248   Modern Catholic schismatic

—249   Arminian and Remonstrant

—25   **With Presbyterian, American Reformed, Congregational churches**

—251   Presbyterian

—257   American Reformed

—258   Congregational

—26   **With Baptist, Disciples of Christ, Adventist churches**

—261   Baptist

—266	Disciples of Christ
—267	Adventist
—27	**With Methodist churches**
	Including United Church of Canada
—28	**With other churches**
—281	Unitarian and Universalist
—283	Latter-Day Saint
—284	New Jerusalemite (Swedenborgian)
—285	Church of Christ, Scientist (Christian Science)
—286	Friends (Quaker)
—287	Mennonite
—288	Shaker
—289	Other
—29	**With other religions**

SUMMARY

—291	**Atheism, agnosticism, deism, theosophy**
—292	**Classical (Greek and Roman) religion**
—293	**Germanic religion**
—294	**Indic religions**
—295	**Zoroastrianism (Parsees)**
—296	**Judaism**
—297	**Islam and religions derived from it**
—299	**Other religions**

—291	Atheism, agnosticism, deism, theosophy
—292	Classical (Greek and Roman) religion
—293	Germanic religion
—294	Indic religions
—294 3	Buddhism
—294 4	Jainism
—294 5	Hinduism (Brahmanism)
—294 6	Sikhism
—295	Zoroastrianism (Parsees)
—296	Judaism
—297	Islam and religions derived from it
—297 1	Islam (Muslims)

Table 7. Persons

—297 7	Black Muslim religion
—297 8	Babism
—297 9	Bahai faith
—299	Other religions
—299 1	Druidism
—299 5	Religions of East and Southeast Asian origin
—299 51	Chinese
—299 512	Confucianism
—299 514	Taoism
—299 56	Shintoism
—299 6	Religions of black African and Negro origin

> *For persons occupied with or adherent to Black Muslim religion, see —2977*

—299 7	Religions of North American native origin
—299 8	Religions of South American native origin
—299 9	Religions of Austronesian, Oceanic, miscellaneous origin

—3 Persons occupied with the social sciences and socioeconomic activities

—301	Social scientists
—309	Sociologists

Including social ecologists, social anthropologists

SUMMARY

—31	Persons occupied with statistics
—32	Persons occupied with political science and politics
—33	Persons occupied with economics and related activities
—34	Persons occupied with law
—35	Persons occupied with public administration
—36	Persons occupied with welfare and public protection
—37	Persons occupied with education
—38	Persons occupied with commerce, communication, transportation
—39	Persons occupied with customs and folklore

—31 Persons occupied with statistics

—32 Persons occupied with political science and politics

> *For persons occupied with public administration, see —35; with law, —34*

—321	Political scientists and theorists
—323	Civil rights workers

—328	Legislators
—329	Politicians

Other than legislators, public administrators, judges, legal officers

—33	**Persons occupied with economics and related activities**
—331	Labor-oriented persons
—331 7	Workers
—331 8	Labor leaders
—332	Bankers and financiers
—333	Landowners and conservationists
—335	Communists, socialists, anarchists
—338	Entrepreneurs
—339	Economists
—34	**Persons occupied with law**
—341	Delegates to and employees of international organizations to promote peace and order
—342	Justices of supreme courts
—343	Other judges
—344	Lawyers
—349	Local and auxiliary legal officers

Justices of the peace, sheriffs, notaries public, bailiffs, coroners

—35	**Persons occupied with public administration**
—351	Heads of state and central governments
—351 1	Reigning monarchs and their regents
—351 2	Presidents and vice-presidents
—351 3	Prime ministers and premiers
—351 4	Dictators

Class dictators occupying a specific position with the subject, e.g., presidents —3512

—351 8	Governors
—352	Other state and central government personnel

For military personnel, see —355

—352 1	Cabinet members and councilors of state

440

Table 7. Persons

—352 2   Ambassadors and other envoys

For delegates to international organizations, see —341

—352 3   Administrators and commissioners

—352 7   Civil service personnel

Class civil service personnel occupied with a specific discipline, subject, activity with persons occupied with that discipline, subject, activity, e.g., economists —339

—354   Local government personnel

Elected and appointed

—355   Military personnel

For air and space forces personnel, see —358; naval personnel, —359

—358   Air and space forces personnel

—359   Naval personnel

—36   Persons occupied with welfare and public protection

—361   With philanthropy, humanitarianism, social reform

—362   Social workers

—363   With public protection

—363 2   Police

—363 3   Fire fighters

—363 6   Persons occupied with public utility services .

—364   With crime and delinquency

Including criminologists

For persons occupied with law, see —34; with public protection, —363; criminals and other offenders, —0692

—365   With prison administratiion

—366   Persons occupied with or belonging to esoteric associations and societies

—366 1   With Freemasonry

Including Orders of DeMolay, of the Eastern Star

—366 2   With Knights of Pythias

—366 3   With Independent Order of Odd Fellows and Daughters of Rebekah

—366 4   With Rosicrucianism

—366 5   With Benevolent and Protective Order of Elks

—367	Persons occupied with or belonging to general clubs
	Examples: social clubs, study clubs
—368	Persons occupied with insurance
—369	Persons occupied with or belonging to hereditary, military, patriotic, young people's societies; service clubs
—369 2	With hereditary, military, patriotic societies
—369 4	With young people's societies
—369 5	With service clubs
—37	**Persons occupied with education**

▶   —371–375 With specific educational activities

Class comprehensive works in —37, persons associated with specific educational institutions in —379

—371	With school and college administration
—372	With teaching
—375	Students
—379	Persons associated with various specific educational institutions
	Administrators, teachers, students, alumni
—38	**Persons occupied with commerce, communication, transportation**
—381	With domestic trade
—382	With foreign trade
—383	With postal communication services
—384	With telecommunication and other communication services
—385	With railroad transportation services
—386	With inland waterway transportation services
—387	With other transportation services
	For persons occupied with ground transportation services other than nonlocal rail, see —388
—387 5	Maritime transportation
—387 7	Air transportation
—387 8	Space transportation
—388	With ground transportation services other than nonlocal rail

Table 7. Persons

—39   Persons occupied with customs and folklore

—4   Persons occupied with linguistics and lexicography

—5   Persons occupied with pure sciences

SUMMARY

—51	With mathematics
—52	With astronomy and allied sciences
—53	With physics
—54	With chemistry and allied sciences
—55	With the earth sciences
—56	With paleontology
—57	With anthropological and biological sciences
—58	With botany
—59	With zoology

—51   **With mathematics**

—52   **With astronomy and allied sciences**

—521   Astronomy

—526   Geodesy, map making, surveying

—527   Celestial navigation

—529   Chronology

—53   **With physics**

—539   Nuclear physics

—54   **With chemistry and allied sciences**

—541   Chemistry

—548   Crystallography

—549   Mineralogy

—55   **With the earth sciences**

—551   Meteorology and climatology

—552   Petrology

—553   Geology

—56   **With paleontology**

—57   **With anthropological and biological sciences**

—572   Ethnology

—573   Physical anthropology

—574   Biology

For persons occupied with botany, see —58; with zoology, —59

—58	**With botany**
—581	General botany
—589	Bacteriology
—59	**With zoology**
—591	General zoology
—593	Protozoology
—595	Helminthology and entomology
—597	Ichthyology
—598	Herpetology and ornithology
—599	Mammalogy

—6 Persons occupied with applied sciences (Technologists)

—604	With technical drawing

SUMMARY

—61 Persons occupied with medical sciences
—62 Persons occupied with engineering and allied operations, and manufacturing
—63 Persons occupied with agriculture and related technologies
—64 Persons occupied with domestic arts and sciences
—65 Persons occupied with managerial services
—66 Persons occupied with chemical technology and related industries
—67 Persons occupied with manufacturing
—68 Persons occupied with manufacture of products for specific uses
—69 Persons occupied with building

—61 Persons occupied with medical sciences

—613	With nursing and hygiene
—614	With public health
—615	With pharmacology, pharmacy, toxicology
—616	With general medicine
—617	With surgical specialties
	Including anesthesiology
—617 1	Surgery
—617 6	Dentistry
—617 7	Ophthalmology
—617 8	Otology and audiology
—618	With other medical specialties
	Including geriatrics

Table 7. Persons

—618 1	Gynecology and obstetrics
—618 9	Pediatrics

—62 **Persons occupied with engineering and allied operations, and manufacturing**

> Class comprehensive works on persons occupied with manufacturing in —67

—620 1	With materials engineering and applied mechanics
—620 2	With acoustical engineering
—620 7	With systems engineering
—620 8	With biotechnology
—621	With applied physics

> Including mechanical, steam, hydraulic-power, pneumatic, cryogenic, tool engineering

—621 3	Electrical, electronic, electromagnetic engineering
—621 4	Heat engineering

> Including solar engineering

—621 48	Nuclear engineering
—622	With mining engineering and operations

> Including prospecting

—623	With military and nautical engineering
—623 1	Military engineering
—623 8	Nautical engineering and seamanship
—624	With civil engineering

> Structural, tunnel, bridge engineering
>
> Class persons associated with other specific kinds of civil engineering in —625–628

—625	With railroad and highway engineering
—627	With hydraulic engineering
—628	With sanitary and municipal engineering
—629	With other branches of engineering
—629 1	Aeronautical and aerospace engineering and operation

> Pilots, copilots, navigators, aircraft engineers, air controllers

> *For persons occupied with astronautical engineering and operation, see —6294*

—629 2	Motor vehicle engineering and operation

For persons occupied with motor vehicle racing, see —7967

—629 4	Astronautical engineering and operation

Astronauts and cosmonauts, vehicle engineers, ground-control personnel

—629 8	Automatic control engineering
—63	**Persons occupied with agriculture and related technologies**
—631	With farming

Class persons occupied with specific kinds of farming in —633–638

—633	With crop farming
—634	With fruitgrowing and forestry
—635	With horticulture and gardening
—636	With stock raising
—637	With dairying
—638	With insect culture
—639	With commercial hunting and fishing, conservation, related activities
—639 1	Hunting and trapping
—639 2	Fishing, whaling, sealing
—639 3	Culture of fish and other cold-blooded animals

Class persons occupied with insect culture in —638

—639 9	Conservation
—64	**Persons occupied with domestic arts and sciences**
—641	Cooks and nutritionists
—642	Restaurateurs and caterers
—646	Seamstresses, cosmetologists, related occupational personnel
—646 4	Seamstresses and tailors
—646 5	Milliners and hatters
—646 7	Cosmetologists, hairdressers, barbers
—647	Hotelkeepers
—648	Launderers
—649	Homemakers

Table 7. Persons

—65	**Persons occupied with managerial services**
—651	With office services

Examples: secretaries, office managers, stenographers, bookkeepers, filers, typists, clerks

—657	With accounting

For bookkeepers, see —651

—658	With management

Including salesmanship, merchandising

Class entrepreneurs in —338

—659	With advertising
—66	**Persons occupied with chemical technology and related industries**

Including chemical engineering

—661	With industrial chemistry
—662	With fuel and explosives technology
—663	With beverage technology
—664	With food technology
—665	With petroleum and gas technology
—666	With ceramic technology
—669	With metallurgy
—67	**Persons occupied with manufacturing**

Class here comprehensive works on persons occupied with manufacturing

Class persons occupied with manufactures not provided for here with the subject, e.g., automobile manufacturers —6292, furniture makers —684, millers —664

—672	With iron and steel manufacture
—673	With manufacture of nonferrous metals
—674	With lumbering and manufacture of wooden products

For persons occupied with furniture manufacture, see —684

—675	With leather and fur industries

Tanners and furriers

—676	With pulp and paper manufacture
—677	With textile manufacture
—678	With rubber manufacture

—679	With manufacture of other products
—679 7	Of tobacco products

—68 **Persons occupied with manufacture of products for specific uses**

Class comprehensive works on persons occupied with manufacturing in —67

—681	With manufacture of precision wares

Including calculating equipment

—681 1	Watch- and clockmaking
—681 4	Optical work
—681 8	Manufacture of musical istruments
—682	With blacksmithing
—683	With lock- and gunsmithing and manufacture of household appliances
—684	With furniture manufacture
—685	With manufacture of leather goods and their substitutes
—685 1	Saddlery and harness making
—685 3	Shoemaking and shoe repairing
—685 4	Glovemaking
—686	With printing and related activities
—686 2	Printing
—686 3	Bookbinding
—686 4	Photoduplication
—687	With garmentmaking

For persons occupied with shoemaking, see —6853; with glovemaking, —6854; seamstresses and tailors, —6464; milliners and hatters, —6465

—688	Other

Manufacture of models, costume jewelry, smokers' supplies, accessories for personal grooming, recreational equipment

—69 **Persons occupied with building**

Construction work and related occupations

—693	With construction work

Masonry, bricklaying, plastering, lathing, riveting

For persons occupied with carpentry, see —694

Table 7. Persons

—694	With carpentry
—695	With roofing
—696	With plumbing and pipe fitting
—697	With heating, ventilating, air conditioning
—698	With painting, glazing, paperhanging

—7   Persons occupied with the arts

For persons occupied with creative writing and speaking, see —8

SUMMARY

—71	With civic and landscape art
—72	With architecture
—73	With sculpture and other plastic arts
—74	With drawing and decorative arts
—75	With painting
—76	With graphic arts
—77	With photography
—78	With music
—79	With recreational and performing arts

—71	**With civic and landscape art**
—72	**With architecture**
—73	**With sculpture and other plastic arts**
—731	Sculpture
—736	Glyptics
—737	Numismatics
—738	Ceramic arts
—739	Art metalwork
—74	**With drawing and decorative arts**
—741	Commercial art
—743	Drawing
—745	Handicrafts

For persons occupied with textile handicrafts, see —746; with glass handicrafts, —748

—746	Textile handicrafts
—747	Interior decoration
—748	Glass handicrafts
—749	Furniture design
—75	**With painting**

—76	**With graphic arts**

Including print making

Class persons occupied with a specific graphic art with the subject, e.g., painting —75

—77	**With photography**
—78	**With music**
—781	Music theory
—782	Dramatic music
—783	Sacred music

▶   **—784–789 Individual mediums of musical expression**

Class comprehensive works in —78, persons occupied with dramatic or sacred music regardless of medium in —782–783

—784	Vocal music
—785	Instrumental ensembles and their music
—786	Keyboard instruments and their music
—787	String instruments and their music
—788	Wind instruments and their music
—789	Percussion, mechanical, electrical instruments
—79	**With recreational and performing arts**

For persons occupied with music, see —78

SUMMARY

—791	Public entertainment
—792	Theater (Stage presentations)
—793	Other forms of entertainment
—794	Games of skill
—795	Card playing and gambling
—796	Athletics and sports
—797	Aquatic and air sports
—798	Equestrian sports
—799	Fishing, hunting, related sports

—791	Public entertainment

For persons occupied with theater, see —792; with dancing, —7933; with magic, —7938

—791 3	Circus performance
—791 4	Motion-picture, radio, television performance
—791 5	Puppetry

Table 7. Persons

—792	Theater (Stage presentations)
—792 1	Drama
—792 8	Ballet
—793	Other forms of entertainment
	For persons occupied with athletics and sports, see —796
—793 3	Dancing
	For persons occupied with ballet, see —7928
—793 8	Magic
—794	Games of skill
	For persons occupied with card playing, see —795
—794 1	Chess
—794 6	Bowling
—794 7	Billiards and pool
—795	Card playing and gambling
—796	Athletics and sports
	For persons occupied with aquatic and air sports, see —797; with equestrian sports, —798; with fishing, hunting, related sports, —799
—796 3	Ball games
—796 32	Basketball and volleyball
—796 33	Football
—796 34	Tennis, rackets, squash, badminton, table tennis, lacrosse
—796 35	Golf, polo, field hockey, baseball, cricket
—796 4	Track and field athletics
—796 5	Hiking, mountaineering, spelunking
—796 6	Cycling
—796 7	Motor vehicle racing
—796 8	Wrestling, boxing, fencing
—796 9	Ice and snow sports
—797	Aquatic and air sports
—797 1	Boating
—797 2	Swimming and diving

—797 5	Air sports
	Stunt flying, gliding, soaring, skydiving
—798	Equestrian sports
—799	Fishing, hunting, related sports
—799 1	Fishing
—799 2	Hunting
—799 3	Trapshooting, skeet and target shooting, archery

—8   Persons occupied with creative writing and speaking

—81	With poetry
—82	With drama
—83	With fiction
—84	With essays
—85	With oratory, debate, conversation
—86	With letter writing
—87	With satire and humor

—9   Persons occupied with geography, history, related disciplines and activities

—91	With geography and travel
—92	With biography
—93	With archaeology
—97	With history
—99	With genealogy

Relocations and Schedule Reductions

Here for the convenience of classifiers wishing to survey the changes between the past and present editions are brought together in one list all the relocations between Editions 18 and 19, and all schedule (and table) reductions since Edition 18, except relocations and reductions in phoenix schedules.

In a relocation one or more topics are shifted to a new number differing from the old in respects other than length. If the relocation is partial, the original number remains, but if it is total the original number is vacated and, therefore, without use; in a few instances a vacated number has been immediately reused with a new meaning. A schedule reduction is the result of shifting one or more topics to a new number shorter than the old but otherwise not differing from it. If all topics in a given number are thus shifted, the number is "discontinued." These features are described and explained in the Editor's Introduction, sections 8.56 and 14.2.

In addition, several numbers have been dropped because their content in Edition 18 was meaningless within the context.

The column headed *Edition 18* indicates in numerical order each number in that edition from which a topic or group of topics has been shifted; the column headed *Edition 19* indicates each corresponding number in the present edition to which those topics or groups of topics have been shifted. If two or more topics have been shifted from one number to two or more numbers, each separate shift is shown.

Numbers in the *Edition 18* column printed in square brackets are no longer in use (or, if in use, have completely new meanings, and are therefore also listed among the reused numbers in section 2.4 of the introduction): if followed by an asterisk, they have been discontinued as a result of schedule reduction; otherwise, they have lost their content as a result of total relocation.

Numbers in the *Edition 18* column not printed in brackets have lost part of their meaning through relocation or reduction, but still retain some of their original meaning. An asterisk signifies loss through reduction, its lack a loss through relocation.

For example, part of what was in 001.552 has been relocated to 002; all that was in 010.28 has been relocated to 010.44; all that was in 016.05 has been relocated, some to 011.34 and some to 017–019. 021.1 and 021.4 have been discontinued and all their content moved up to the broader number 021, while only part of the content of 021.6 has been moved up to 021.

Only numbers appear in this list; for details of the topics concerned the classifier should consult the appropriate parts of the schedules and tables.

"Scatter" means that a topic has been split and relocated to so many numbers that it is not feasible to name them all; "s.s." means standard subdivisions from Table 1; "area" means area subdivisions from Table 2; "lit. sub." means individual literature subdivisions from Table 3, and "lit. sub. A" means special notations from subsidiary Table 3–A; "lang. sub." means individual language subdivisions from Table 4; "lang." means language subdivisions from Table 6.

Edition 18	Edition 19	Edition 18	Edition 19
[001.539 2–.539 4]*	001.539	[137.7]*	137
001.552	002	147	299.934
[001.640 42–.640 44]*	001.64	149.3	299.935
[010.28]	010.44	152.5	153.8
[016.05]	011.34	[154.78]*	154.7
[016.05]	017–019	[155.61]	153.35
[016.071–.079]	011.35	156	574.5
[016.091]	011.31	156.2–.7	591.51
[016.093]	011.42	156.9	581.5
[016.094–.099]	011.44	[157.1]	616.892–.898
[020.75]	002.075	[175.83]*	175.8
021	027	[179.36]*	179.3
[021.1]*	021	181.3	181.06
[021.4]*	021	[181.49]*	181.4
021.6*	021	[200.4]	291.13
[021.63]*	021.6	[200.901 1]	291.042
[021.84–.88]*	021.8	[201.1]	230
[022.5–.6]*	022	[212.2]	211.32
[023.5]*	023	[212.3]	211.33
023.7	023.2–.4	[212.4]	211.34
[024]	025.56	[212.5]	211.2
[024.6]	025.62	[212.5]	299.933
[025.25]	025.7	[212.52]	299.934
[025.33]	025.47	[212.53]	299.935
[025.37]	025.317	[212.8]	211
[025.49]	025.396	[213.5]*	213
[025.542–.544]*	025.54	[217]*	meaningless
[027.42]*	027.4	[220.14]	220.66
[028.52]	010	[220.2]	220.4–.5
[029]	025	220.3	220.4–.5
[029.4]	025.402 8	[220.63]	220.601
[029.4]	808.062	220.66*	220.6
[029.756]	418.02	220.67	220.663
[029.756]	lang. sub. 802	220.91	220.95
[070.53–.54]	686	221.91	221.95
070.573*	070.5	[229.95]*	229.9
[112]	001.012	231.2	232.3
[113.2]*	113	231.7	241.2
[113.6]*	113	[233.2]	241.3
[115.4]*	115	[241.677]	241.4
[125]	111.6	[242.1]*	242
[129.4]*	129	[242.741–.742]*	242.74
[129.6]*	129	248.25	267.16
[131.3]*	131	[248.27]	248.47
[131.3]	158	248.29	248.46
[131.35]	158.9	[248.42]*	248.4
[133.47]	229.67	[248.9]	248.48
[133.7]*	133	[255.979]*	255.97
137	158.1	[262.925]*	262.92

Edition 18	Edition 19	Edition 18	Edition 19
264	248.3	341.47	341.756 79
[265.3]	264.36	344.047	343.093
[266.025]	362.1–.4	346.03	347.077
[266.025]	610.695	[346.043 42]*	346.043 4
[266.09]*	266	346.044	343.025 6
273.1	299.932	347.02–.03	347.05–.08
273.2	299.932	347.03	347.01
287.97	287.5	347.08	347.01
291.22	291.5	347.732 2–.732 6	347.735–.738
291.3	291.43	347.734	347.735–.738
291.42	291.447	[351.002]	320.4
[294.1]	294.592 12–.592 15	351.003 12	351.003 13
295	299.15	[351.003 14–.003 15]*	351.003 1
[296.129]*	296.12	[351.003 8–.003 9]*	351.003
296.32	296.385	[351.005]	321.804 3
296.4	296.72	[351.005]	351.004
296.71	296.74	351.009 3	351.819
297.22	297.5	351.009 3	351.82
297.38	297.43	[351.123 22–.123 23]*	351.123 2
[301.21]	390	[351.123 3]*	351.123
[301.418]	613.96	[351.143–.145]*	351.14
[301.427 2]	646.78	[351.152–.154]*	351.15
[301.56]	370.19	[351.162]*	351.16
[309]	900	[351.181]*	351.18
[309.2]	361.6	[351.183]*	351.18
[309.26]	307	351.712	351.862
320.9	900	[351.721]	336.3
[327.01]	327.101	[351.724 01–.724 03]*	351.724
[329]	324	351.724 4	351.825 6
331.114*	331.11	[351.724 5]*	351.724
[331.114 4]	331.125	[351.724 711–.724 713]*	351.724 7
[331.121]*	331.12	351.724 711*	351.724 71
[331.259 23]*	331.259 2	[351.751–.753]*	351.75
[332.413]*	332.41	[351.756]*	351.75
[332.634]*	332.63	[351.762–.764]*	351.76
333.1	333.2	351.81	351.855 516 3
333.918	333.917	351.824 2	351.86
[335.438]	scatter	[351.866]*	351.86
336.243	336.207	[351.871 07–.871 08]*	351.871
[338.902–.903]*	338.9	[351.871 5]	351.823 25
338.91	337.3–.9	[351.871 6]*	351.871
339.41	339.43	[351.872 207–.872 208]*	351.872 2
340.09	349	[351.878 1]	351.864 2
340.57	346.004	[351.895]	355
341.33	341.22–.24	351.996	364.13
341.33	341.35	[352.002 2]	351.093
341.44	341.756 6	[352.002 9]*	352.002
341.448	341.45	352.008	352.007 2
341.46	341.756 7	352.009 2	351.877 1

Edition 18	Edition 19	Edition 18	Edition 19
352.009 3	352.62	371.22	371.206
[352.131–.133]*	352.13	371.22	379.13
[352.911]	352.61	[379.123]	379.13
[352.911 5]	352.942 325	382.1	337
[352.918 1]	352.74	[382.172]*	382.17
352.942 42	352.7	382.5	382.9
352.942 42	352.922	[382.74]	382.63
[352.95]	352.63	[382.74]*	382.7
[355.129 5]	365.48	[383.09]	383.49
[355.133 22]*	355.133	[383.185]	383.124
355.133 25	365.48	[387.01–.09]	387.501–.509
[355.135]	355.64	389.1	530.8
[355.212–.219]*	355.21	[389.152–.159]*	389.15
[355.229]*	355.22	[391.07]	391.1–.3
355.31	355.35	[398.18]	398.042
355.64	355.115 1	[416]	808.1
[355.65–.66]	355.81	[500.1]*	500
[361.5]	363.34	[500.9]*	500
[361.62–.63]*	361.6	[511.7]*	511
[361.73]*	361.7	513.93	332.802 12
362.104 22	614.4	523.01	523.02
[362.13]	362.16	527	623.89
362.6–.8	362.1–.4	[531.383]	531.32
[362.615]*	362.61	535.013*	535
[362.742–.745]*	362.74	[538.767 5]	538.766
[363.234]	363.232	[541.343]*	541.34
[363.242]*	363.24	[541.388 2]*	541.388
[363.244]	363.256	547.596	547.79
[363.351–.356]*	363.35	551.461–.469	551.460 8
363.5*	363	551.498	551.488
[364.12]	363.25	[551.523 2–.523 8]*	551.523
364.132	364.136	552.2	552.5
364.135	364.164	567.4	567.5
[364.157]	364.177	[567.9]	567.6
[364.242–.243]*	364.24	[568.1]	567.9
[364.255]*	364.25	568.23*	568
[364.26]*	364.2	[573.221]	611.018 16
[364.32]*	364.3	[574.191 33]*	meaningless
[364.35]	362.74	574.52	560.45
[364.363–.364]*	364.36	574.526 32	574.526 4
[364.42–.43]*	364.4	[574.876 6]*	574.87
364.44	363.23	574.92	574.93–.99
[364.61]	365	[575.21]	574.873 22
[365.2]*	365	[581.151]	581.873 22
365.45	355.129 6	581.52	561.1
365.45	355.71	[589.7]*	589
365.46*	365.4	[591.151]	591.873 22
[365.642]*	365.6	591.52	560.45
[366.4]	135.43	593.71*	593.7

Edition 18	Edition 19	Edition 18	Edition 19
594.56	594.58	[617.762 2]*	617.762
595.147	594.19	[617.950 7]	362.17
[597.092 01]*	597.092	618.178	616.692
[597.092 03–.092 09]	597.093–.099	[618.920 05]	613.043 2
597.4	597.5	[618.920 06]	615.542
[597.9]	597.65	[618.970 5]	613.043 8
[598.1]	597.6	[618.970 6]	615.547
[598.1]	597.9	[620.22]	690
598.2*	598	621.312 13*	621.312 1
[598.292 3]	598.33	[621.312 137–.312 139]	621.312 4
599.31	599.75	[621.312 14]*	621.312 1
599.323 4	599.323 3	[621.35]	621.312 42
599.884	599.82	[621.385 3–.385 6]*	621.385
[604.26]	s.s. 022 1	[621.385 8]*	621.385
611.35	611.96	[621.387 3–.387 7]*	621.387
612.844*	612.84	[621.392]	621.312 43
[613.043 7]	613.043 4	[621.475]	621.312 44
[613.31–.38]*	613.3	621.481	621.312 5
[614.11–.12]	351.816	[621.7]	670.42
[614.14–.15]*	614	[621.757]	688.8
[614.17]	351.774	622.32	622.2
[614.19]*	614.1	[623.271–.277]*	623.27
[614.3]	363.19	[623.36]*	623.3
[614.432 9]*	614.432	623.37*	623.3
[614.439]*	614.43	[623.371–.377]*	623.3
[614.58]	362.2	[623.419 3]*	meaningless
614.6	363.75	623.441	623.442
[614.61–.68]*	614.6	[623.444]	623.441
[614.7]	363.7	[624.157 1–.157 6]*	624.157
[614.8]	363.1	[624.372–.378]*	624.37
[614.88]	616.025 2	624.7	624.55
[615.650 7]	362.17	624.7	624.6
[615.837]	614.851 54	[625.101–.102]*	625.1
[616.026]*	616	628.142	628.15
[616.126]*	616.12	[628.172–.177]*	628.17
[616.155]	616.994 19	629.132 524	629.132 521
616.21	617.51	[629.288]	629.287
[616.246]	616.995 24	[631.587 2–.587 5]*	631.587
[616.339]*	616.33	[633.59]*	633.5
616.42	616.994 46	636.76	636.72
[616.749]*	616.74	636.76	636.755
[616.858 82]*	616.858 8	[637.34]*	637.3
[616.926]	616.047	641.3	641.26
[616.933]	616.33	[641.502 4]	641.51
617.1	617.4–.5	641.592	641.591 3
617.471	616.71	[642.41–.47]*	642.4
617.539*	617.53	[642.56–.59]*	642.5
[617.539 5]*	617.539	[646.15–.16]*	646.1
[617.719 07]	362.17	646.2	646.6

Edition 18	Edition 19	Edition 18	Edition 19
646.21	646.204	731.47	738.82
[646.212–.216]*	646.21	[731.52]	732–735
[646.62–.63]*	646.6	[731.722–.724]*	731.72
[646.724 3]	646.724 2	[735.29]	735.23
[646.74]	646.724	736.4	730.97
[648.52–.53]*	648.5	736.4	731.462
651.2	658.72	736.4	745.51
[651.32]*	651.3	[741.61]*	741.6
[651.371]*	651.3	747.88*	747
[651.374 2]*	651.37	[751.48]	738.5
651.374 3	651.374 1	[759.941]	759.29
[651.4]*	651	778.37	778.72
652.302*	653.3	780.8*	780
[652.302 2]*	653.3	782.08*	782
658	s.s. 068	784.756	783.67
658.151*	658.15	[796.815 01]	616.025 2
[658.151 3–.151 4]*	658.151	799.12–.14	799.11
[658.152 7]*	658.152	799.12–.14	799.16
[658.155 5–.155 6]*	658.155	[808.023]	001.4
[658.159 04]*	658.159	[879.99]*	879.9
[658.159 04]	658.159 2	[901.9]	909
[658.159 04]	658.159 9	910	909
658.18	658.049	910	930–990
658.312 45	658.407 124 5	910.09	909.09
658.403	658.46	[910.8]	910.4
[658.451]*	658.45	913–919	930–990
658.51	658.53	914–919	940–990
[658.516]*	658.51	[940.11]	940.12
658.53*	658.5	949.120 4	949.120 5
[658.534]*	658.5	959.704 3	959.704 4
[663.29]*	663.2	961.03	961.04
671.2	671.32–.34	968.204	968.048
[677.635]	687.4	972.082	972.083
[687.102–.105]	687.04	973.1	970.01
[687.32]*	687.3	[s.s. 018 2]	s.s. 028
[687.38]	687.146	[s.s. 018 2]	s.s. 072
690.15	697.8	[s.s. 018 3]	s.s. 028 5
[694.22–.29]*	694.2	[s.s. 018 3]	s.s. 072
[694.61–.69]*	694.6	[s.s. 018 4]	s.s. 072
[695.1–.9]*	695	s.s. 06	350
[695.96]	690.15	[s.s. 062]	s.s. 060 1–060 9
[701.184]*	701.1	[s.s. 063]	s.s. 060 1–060 9
[704.92]*	700	[s.s. 065]	338.7–.8
704.947	704.948	[s.s. 08]*	main number
[708.941]	708.29	area 362	area 361
711.552	711.7	area 448	area 445 8
711.59*	711.5	[area 459 5]	area 449 45
728.1	728.3–.7	[area 471]	area 489 7
[728.64]	728.373	area 494 5	area 494 3

Edition 18	Edition 19	Edition 18	Edition 19
area 496	area 56	[area 719]	area 718 2
[area 496 1]	area 562	area 792 51	area 792 52
[area 496 1]	area 563	[area 862]	area 728 7
area 499	area 562	[area 863]	area 728 75
[area 549 7]	area 541 67	lit. sub. 108	lit. sub. 107
[area 595 2]	area 595 7	[lit. sub. 302–303]*	lit. sub. 3
area 671 12	area 669 5	lit. sub. A 353	lit. sub. A 355
[area 677 2]	area 533 5	[lit. sub. A 376]*	lit. sub. A 37
[area 683]	area 681 3	[lang. sub. 6]	808.1
[area 686]	area 681 6	lang. 398 1	lang. 398 2
area 712	area 719	lang. 959 3	lang. 992 8
area 713 4	area 713 1	[lang. 991 1]	lang. 959 3

Lists of Changed Numbers

As noted at their respective points in the schedules, the developments for 301–307 Sociology and 324 The political process, as well as many of those for "Areas" notation 41–42 from Table 2 British Isles, are new, though mostly built on the same base numbers as in the past. As is pointed out in section 14.24 of the Editor's Introduction, users will benefit from the adoption of these new schedules. So that this task may be somewhat simplified, the following lists show the number changes from Edition 18 to Edition 19 for a substantial list of topics. Not included are topics that have been relocated to a different schedule, e.g., educational sociology relocated from 301.56 to 370.19 and so shown under both the old and the new numbers.

Sociology

	Edition 18	Edition 19
Acculturation	301.241	303.482
Adolescents	301.431 5	305.23
Adultery	301.415 3	306.73
Adults	301.434	305.24
Age levels	301.43	305.2
Aged adults	301.435	305.26
Agricultural		
classes	301.444 3	305.56
sociology	301.35	307.72
villages	301.352	307.72
Alienated classes	301.449 4	305.56
Alienation	301.62	302.5
Anthropology	301.2	301
Audiences	301.181	302.33
mass communication	301.162	302.23
Authority	301.155 2	303.36
Automation *see* Technology		
Beliefs	301.21	306
Birth control	301.321	304.66
Births	301.321	304.63
Books	301.161	302.23
Bureaucracies	301.183 2	302.35
Change	301.24	303.4

	Edition 18	Edition 19
Children	301.431 4	305.23
Choice of mate	301.414 3	306.82
Cities	301.363	307.76
Class conflict	301.637	305.5
Cliques	301.185	302.34
Coercion	301.152	303.36
Committees	301.185	302.34
Communication	301.14	302.2
Communities	301.34	307
Community structure	301.361	307.3
Conflict	301.63	303.6
Conurbations	301.364	307.76
Courtship	301.414	306.7
Crowds	301.182	302.33
Cultural		
anthropology	301.2	306
processes	301.2	306
Culture	301.2	306
Dating	301.414 2	306.7
Deaths	301.322	304.64
Demography	301.32	304.6
Desertion	301.428	306.88
Deviation	301.62	302.5
Divorce	301.428 4	306.89
Ecology	301.31	304.2
Economic institutions	301.51	306.3
Elites	301.449 2	305.52
Emigration	301.325	304.8
Entrepreneurial classes	301.444 7	305.55
Ethnic groups	301.451	305.8
Excluded classes	301.449 4	305.56
Extended family	301.421 3	306.85
Extramarital relations	301.415 2–.415 4	306.73
Families	301.42	306.8
Family		
dissolution	301.428	306.88
planning	301.426	304.66
relationships	301.427	306.87
Fertility	301.321	304.63
Films	301.161	302.23
Gangs	301.185	302.34
Gentry	301.441	305.52
Governing classes	301.449 2	305.5
Group decision making	301.155 4	302.3
Groups	301.18	302.3
Hippies	301.449 4	305.56
Hobos	301.449 4	305.56
Homosexuality	301.415 7	306.76
Human ecology	301.31	304.2

	Edition 18	*Edition 19*
Husband-wife relations	301.427	306.87
Immigration	301.324	304.8
In groups	301.114	302.4
Individualism	301.113	302.5
Indoctrination	301.154	303.32
Industrial conflict	301.634	306.3
Institutions	301.5	306
Intellectuals	301.445	305.55
Intelligentsia	301.445	305.55
Internal migration	301.326	304.82
International assistance	301.241	303.482
Intrafamily relations	301.427	306.87
Invention *see* Technology		
Isolation	301.113	302.5
Laboring classes	301.444 2	305.56
Language	301.21	306
		302.22
Leadership	301.155 3	303.34
Managerial classes	301.444 7	305.55
Marriage	301.42	306.8
Mass		
communication	301.16	302.23
media	301.161	302.23
Men	301.411	305.3
Metropolitan areas	301.364	307.76
Middle classes	301.441	305.55
Migration	301.324–.328	304.8
Military institutions	301.593	306.2
Minorities	301.45	305
Minors	301.431	305.23
Mobs	301.182	302.33
Monogamy	301.422 2	306.84
Mores	301.21	306
Mortality	301.322	304.64
Moving pictures	301.161	302.23
National groups	301.451	305.8
Newspapers	301.161	302.23
Nobility	301.442	305.52
Nondominant aggregates	301.45	305
Nonviolence	301.632	303.6
Nuclear family	301.421 2	306.85
Official classes	301.449 2	305.5
Opinion measurement	301.154 2	303.38
Out groups	301.114	302.4
Parent-child relations	301.427	306.87
Peasants	301.444 3	305.56
Periodicals	301.161	302.23
Plantations	301.35	307.72
Play groups	301.185	302.34

	Edition 18	Edition 19
Political institutions	301.592	306.2
Polygamy	301.422 3	306.84
Poor classes	301.441	305.56
Population	301.32	304.6
characteristics	301.323	304.6
decrease	301.32	304.62
density	301.32	304.6
increase	301.32	304.62
movement	301.324–.328	304.8
Premarital relations	301.415 2	306.7
Primary groups	301.185	302.34
Professional classes	301.444 6	305.55
Prostitution	301.415 4	306.74
Public opinion	301.154	303.38
Publics	301.181	302.33
Racial conflict	301.636	305.8
Racial, ethnic, national groups	301.451	305.8
Racism	301.636	305.8
Radio	301.161	302.23
Recreational institutions	301.57	306.4
Reform	301.242	303.484
Religious		
conflict	301.635	305.6
groups	301.452	305.6
institutions	301.58	306.6
Revolutions	301.633 3	303.64
Riots	301.633 2	303.62
Role theory	301.113	302
Royalty	301.449 2	305.52
Rural		
communities	301.35	307.72
sociology	301.35	307.72
Science	301.21	306.4
in social change	301.243	303.483
Secondary groups	301.183	302.35
Separation	301.428	306.89
Serfs	301.449 3	305.56
Sex groups	301.41	305.3–.4
Sex relations	301.41	306.7
Sexism	301.6	305.3–.4
Sharecroppers	301.444 3	305.56
Slaves	301.449 3	305.56
Small groups	301.185	302.34
Social		
anthropology	301.2	306
classes	301.44	305.5
conflict	301.63	303.6
control	301.152–.155	303.3
innovation	301.242	303.484

	Edition 18	Edition 19
institutions	301.5	306
interaction	301.11	302
mobility	301.440 44	305.5
psychology	301.1	302
structure	301.4	305
Socialization	301.157	303.32
Sociometry	301.180 28	302
Subcultures	301.22	306.1
Suburbs	301.362	307.74
Technology	301.21	306.4
in social change	301.243	303.483
Television	301.161	302.23
Terrorism	301.633	303.62
Towns	301.36	307.76
Tramps	301.449 4	305.56
Untouchables	301.449 4	305.56
Unwed parenthood	301.415 2	306.7
Urban		
communities	301.36	307.76
sociology	301.36	307.76
Villages	301.35	307.72
Violence	301.633	303.6
Voluntary associations	301.183 1	302.3
War	301.633 4	303.66
Wealthy classes	301.441	305.52
White-collar classes	301.444 5	305.55
Women	301.412	305.4

The political process

	Edition 18	Edition 19
Absentee voting	324.242 4	324.65
American ("Know-Nothing") Party, U.S.	329.5	324.273 2
American Nazi Party, U.S.	329.86	324.273 38
Antifederalist Party, U.S.	329.2	324.273 26
Ballots	324.25	324.65
"Bull Moose" Party, U.S.	329.892	324.273 2
Campaign		
finance	329.025	324.78
literature	329.01	324.23
Campaigns	329.01	324.7
for nomination	329.022	324.5
history	329.023	324.9
strategy	329.01	324.72
Caucuses	329.021 4	324.21
nominations by	329.022 2	324.52
Certification of votes	324.242 3	324.65

	Edition 18	Edition 19
Communist		
front organizations	329.073	324.3
internationals	329.072	324.1
parties *see political parties of spec. jur.*		
Party, U.S.	329.82	324.273 75
political organizations	329.07	324
youth organizations	329.074	324.3
Conservative Party, New York	329.893	324.274 703
Contested elections	324.277	324.6
Conventions	329.022 1	324.56
Cooption, nomination by	329.022	324.52
Counting votes	324.242 3	324.65
Democratic Republican Party, U.S.	329.2	324.273 6
Democratic Party, U.S.	329.3	324.273 6
Dixiecrat Party, U.S.	329.892	324.273 3
Election		
officials	324.242 2	324.65
returns	324.202 1	324.9
Elections	324.2	324.6
frauds	324.271	324.66
history	329.023	324.9
Electoral		
colleges	324.21	324.63
systems	324.21	324.63
Enumeration of voters	324.241	324.64
Federalist Party, U.S.	329.1	324.273 22
Free Soil Party, U.S.	329.87	324.273 2
International communism	329.07	324.1
Irregular contributions and expenditures	324.273	324.78
Jeffersonian Republican Party	329.2	324.273 26
Liberal Party, New York	329.893	324.274 707
Literacy tests	324.14	324.62
Marxist political organizations	329.07	324
National Republican Party, U.S.	329.4	324.273 23
Nominating conventions and meetings	329.022 1	324.56
Nomination of candidates	329.022	324.5
Party		
finance	329.025	324.21
leadership	329.021 2	324.22
organization	329.021	324.21
Patronage	329.024	324.204
Platforms	329.021 3	324.23
Political		
machines	329.021 1	324.21
parties	329.02	324.2
and state	329.06	324.204
finance	329.025	324.21
leadership	329.021 2	324.22
membership	329.021	324.21

	Edition 18	Edition 19
of specific jurisdictions	329.02	
	329.1–.9	324.24–.29
of United States	329.02	
	329.1–.8	324.273–.279
organization	329.021	324.21
programs and platforms	329.021 3	324.23
slogans	329.021 3	324.23
Politicians	329.02	324.22
Poll tax	324.1	324.62
Polling	324.242	324.65
Populist Party, U.S.	329.88	324.273 27
Practical politics	329	324.7
Pressure groups	329.03	324.4
Primary elections	329.022 3	324.54
Prohibition Party, U.S.	329.894	324.273
Proportional representation	324.22	324.63
Provincial party organizations	329.021 1	324.21
		324.24–.29
Recall	324.29	324.68
Registration of voters	324.241	324.64
Representation	324.22	324.63
Republican Party, U.S.	329.6	324.273 4
Slogans	329.021 3	324.23
Socialist Labor Party, U.S.	329.81	324.273 7
Socialist Party, U.S.	329.81	324.273 7
Special-interest groups	329.03	324.4
State party organizations	329.021 1	324.21
		324.24–.29
Suffrage	324.1	324.62
Vote counting	324.242 3	324.65
Voting	324.242	324.65
machines	324.242	324.65
procedures	324.242	324.65
qualifications for	324.1	324.62
Whig Party, U.S.	329.4	324.273 23
Woman suffrage	324.3	324.623

British Isles

Only those places are listed that were named in Edition 18 and have different numbers in Edition 19.

	Edition 18	Edition 19
Aberdeenshire Scot.	*area*—412 5	*area*—412 32
city	—412 5	—412 35
Anglesey Co. Wales	—429 1	—429 21

	Edition 18	Edition 19
Angus Co. Scot.	area—413 1	area—412 6
Argyllshire Scot.	—413 8	—414 23
Ayrshire Scot.	—414 2	—414 6
Banffshire Scot.	—412 4	—412 25
Bedfordshire Eng.	—425 65	—425 6
Berwickshire Scot.	—414 55	—413 95
Birmingham Eng.	—424 8	—424 96
Breconshire Wales	—429 65	—429 56
British Isles	—42	—41
Buckinghamshire Eng.	—425 75	—425 9
Buteshire Scot.	—413 9	—414 23
Caernarvonshire Wales	—429 23	—429 2
Caithness Co. Scot.	—411 3	—411 62
Cambridgeshire Eng.	—425 9	—426 5
Canterbury Eng.	—422 3	—422 34
Cardiganshire Wales	—429 5	—429 61
Carmarthenshire Wales	—429 8	—429 65
Cheviot Hills Eng.-Scot.	—428 2	—428 8
Clackmannanshire Scot.	—413 5	—413 15
Clyde River Scot.	—414	—414 1
Connacht Ire.	—417	—417 1
Croydon London	—421 791	—421 91
Cumberland Eng.	—428 5	—427 8
Denbighshire Wales	—429 32	—429 3
Dunbartonshire Scot.	—413 7	—414 25
Durham Co. Eng.	—428 1	—428 6
East Lothian Co. Scot.	—414 52	—413 6
East Suffolk Eng.	—426 42	—426 46
East Sussex Eng.	—422 52	—422 5
Edinburgh Scot.	—414 45	—413 4
Eire	—415	—417
Ely Isle Eng.	—425 94	—426 53
Fens Eng.	—425	—426
Fermanagh Co. N. Ire.	—416 8	—416 3
Fifeshire Scot.	—413 3	—412 9
Flintshire Wales	—429 35	—429 33
Forth River Scot.	—413	—413 1
Glasgow Scot.	—414 35	—414 43
Grampian Mts. Scot.	—412	—412 1
Great Britain	—42	—41
Hebrides Scot.	—411 7	—411 4
Inner	—411 7	—411 8
Holland Parts Lincoln Eng.	—425 38	—425 39
Huntingdonshire Eng.	—425 62	—426 54
Inverness-shire Scot.	—412 1	—411 75
Irish Republic	—415	—417
Isle of Man	—428 9	—427 9
Kesteven Parts Lincoln Eng.	—425 39	—425 35

	Edition 18	Edition 19
Kincardineshire Scot.	*area—*412 6	*area—*412 4
Kingston upon Thames London	—421 794	—421 94
Kinross-shire Scot.	—413 4	—412 8
Lake District Eng.	—428	—427 8
Lanarkshire Scot.	—414 3	—414 69
Lancashire Eng.	—427 2	—427 6
Leicestershire Eng.	—425 42	—425 4
Leitrim Co. Ire.	—417 1	—417 6
Lewis with Harris Isl. Scot.	—411 6	—411 4
Lindsey Parts Lincoln Eng.	—425 32	—425 31
Liverpool Eng.	—427 2	—427 53
Lothian Scot.	—414 4	—413 2
Manchester Eng.	—427 2	—427 33
Merioneth Wales	—429 25	—429 29
Merton London	—421 793	—421 93
Midlothian Co. Scot.	—414 45	—413 5
Monmouthshire Wales	—424 3	—429 9
Montgomeryshire Wales	—429 4	—429 51
Morayshire Scot.	—412 3	—412 23
Nairnshire Scot.	—412 2	—411 95
Northern Scotland	—411	—411 1
Northumberland Eng.	—428 2	—428 8
Orkney Isls. Scot.	—411 2	—411 32
Oxfordshire Eng.	—425 72	—425 7
Peeblesshire Scot.	—414 62	—413 82
Pembrokeshire Wales	—429 9	—429 62
Perthshire Scot.	—413 2	—412 8
Peterborough Eng.	—425 62	—426 51
Radnorshire Wales	—429 62	—429 54
Renfrewshire Scot.	—414 1	—414 41
Richmond upon Thames London	—421 795	—421 95
Ross & Cromarty Co. Scot.	—411 6	—411 72
Roxburghshire Scot.	—414 7	—413 92
Scotland	—41	—411
Scottish Highlands	—411	—411 5
Selkirkshire Scot.	—414 65	—413 85
Shetland Isls. Scot.	—411 1	—411 35
Southampton Eng.	—422 7	—422 76
Stirlingshire Scot.	—413 6	—413 12
Strathmore Scot.	—413	—412 5
Sutherland Co. Scot.	—411 4	—411 65
Sutton London	—421 792	—421 92
Tweeddale Scot.	—414 62	—413 82
United Kingdom	—42	—41
West Lothian Co. Scot.	—414 42	—413 3
West Suffolk Eng.	—426 47	—426 44
West Sussex Eng.	—422 55	—422 6
Western Isles Scot.	—411 7	—411 4

	Edition 18	Edition 19
Westmorland	*area*—428 8	*area*—427 8
Worcestershire Eng.	—424 7	—424 4
Yorkshire Eng.	—427 4	—428 1
East Riding	—427 47	—428 3
North Riding	—427 48	—428 4
West Riding	—427 46	—428 1

Summaries

First Summary *
The 10 Main Classes

000   Generalities

100   Philosophy & related disciplines

200   Religion

300   Social sciences

400   Language

500   Pure sciences

600   Technology (Applied sciences)

700   The arts

800   Literature (Belles-lettres)

900   General geography & history

* Consult schedules for complete and exact headings

Second Summary *
The 100 Divisions

000	**Generalities**	**500**	**Pure sciences**
010	Bibliography	510	Mathematics
020	Library & information sciences	520	Astronomy & allied sciences
030	General encyclopedic works	530	Physics
040		540	Chemistry & allied sciences
050	General serial publications	550	Sciences of earth & other worlds
060	General organizations & museology	560	Paleontology
070	Journalism, publishing, newspapers	570	Life sciences
080	General collections	580	Botanical sciences
090	Manuscripts & book rarities	590	Zoological sciences
100	**Philosophy & related disciplines**	**600**	**Technology (Applied sciences)**
110	Metaphysics	610	Medical sciences
120	Epistemology, causation, humankind	620	Engineering & allied operations
130	Paranormal phenomena & arts	630	Agriculture & related technologies
140	Specific philosophical viewpoints	640	Home economics & family living
150	Psychology	650	Management & auxiliary services
160	Logic	660	Chemical & related technologies
170	Ethics (Moral philosophy)	670	Manufactures
180	Ancient, medieval, Oriental	680	Manufacture for specific uses
190	Modern Western philosophy	690	Buildings
200	**Religion**	**700**	**The arts**
210	Natural religion	710	Civic & landscape art
220	Bible	720	Architecture
230	Christian theology	730	Plastic arts Sculpture
240	Christian moral & devotional	740	Drawing, decorative & minor arts
250	Local church & religious orders	750	Painting & paintings
260	Social & ecclesiastical theology	760	Graphic arts Prints
270	History & geography of church	770	Photography & photographs
280	Christian denominations & sects	780	Music
290	Other & comparative religions	790	Recreational & performing arts
300	**Social sciences**	**800**	**Literature (Belles-lettres)**
310	Statistics	810	American literature in English
320	Political science	820	English & Anglo-Saxon literatures
330	Economics	830	Literatures of Germanic languages
340	Law	840	Literatures of Romance languages
350	Public administration	850	Italian, Romanian, Rhaeto-Romanic
360	Social problems & services	860	Spanish & Portuguese literatures
370	Education	870	Italic literatures Latin
380	Commerce (Trade)	880	Hellenic literatures Greek
390	Customs, etiquette, folklore	890	Literatures of other languages
400	**Language**	**900**	**General geography & history**
410	Linguistics	910	General geography Travel
420	English & Anglo-Saxon languages	920	General biography & genealogy
430	Germanic languages German	930	General history of ancient world
440	Romance languages French	940	General history of Europe
450	Italian, Romanian, Rhaeto-Romanic	950	General history of Asia
460	Spanish & Portuguese languages	960	General history of Africa
470	Italic languages Latin	970	General history of North America
480	Hellenic Classical Greek	980	General history of South America
490	Other languages	990	General history of other areas

* Consult schedules for complete and exact headings

Third Summary *
The 1000 Sections
Generalities

000	**Generalities**	050	**General serial publications**
001	Knowledge	051	American
002	The book	052	Others in English
003	Systems	053	In other Germanic languages
004		054	In French, Provençal, Catalan
005		055	In Italian, Romanian, Rhaeto-Romanic
006		056	In Spanish & Portuguese
007		057	In Slavic languages
008		058	In Scandinavian languages
009		059	In other languages
010	**Bibliography**	060	**General organizations & museology**
011	Bibliographies	061	In North America
012	Of individuals	062	In British Isles
013	Of works by specific classes of writers	063	In central Europe
014	Of anonymous & pseudonymous works	064	In France & Monaco
015	Of works from specific places	065	In Italy & adjacent territories
016	Subject bibliographies & catalogs	066	In Iberian Peninsula & adjacent islands
017	General subject catalogs	067	In eastern Europe
018	Author & date catalogs	068	In other areas
019	Dictionary catalogs	069	Museology (Museum science)
020	**Library & information sciences**	070	**Journalism, publishing, newspapers**
021	Library relationships	071	In North America
022	Physical plant	072	In British Isles
023	Personnel & positions	073	In central Europe
024		074	In France & Monaco
025	Library operations	075	In Italy & adjacent territories
026	Libraries for specific subjects	076	In Iberian Peninsula & adjacent islands
027	General libraries	077	In eastern Europe
028	Reading & use of information media	078	In Scandinavia
029		079	In other areas
030	**General encyclopedic works**	080	**General collections**
031	American	081	American
032	Others in English	082	Others in English
033	In other Germanic languages	083	In other Germanic languages
034	In French, Provençal, Catalan	084	In French, Provençal, Catalan
035	In Italian, Romanian, Rhaeto-Romanic	085	In Italian, Romanian, Rhaeto-Romanic
036	In Spanish & Portuguese	086	In Spanish & Portuguese
037	In Slavic languages	087	In Slavic languages
038	In Scandinavian languages	088	In Scandinavian languages
039	In other languages	089	In other languages
040		090	**Manuscripts & book rarities**
041		091	Manuscripts
042		092	Block books
043		093	Incunabula
044		094	Printed books
045		095	Books notable for bindings
046		096	Notable illustrations & materials
047		097	Notable ownership or origin
048		098	Works notable for content
049		099	Books notable for format

* Consult schedules for complete and exact headings

Philosophy and related disciplines

100	**Philosophy & related disciplines**	150	**Psychology**
101	Theory of philosophy	151	
102	Miscellany of philosophy	152	Physiological psychology
103	Dictionaries of philosophy	153	Intelligence & intellect
104		154	Subconscious states & processes
105	Serials on philosophy	155	Differential & genetic psychology
106	Organizations of philosophy	156	Comparative psychology
107	Study & teaching of philosophy	157	Abnormal & clinical psychologies
108	Treatment among groups of persons	158	Applied psychology
109	Historical treatment of philosophy	159	Other aspects
110	**Metaphysics**	160	**Logic**
111	Ontology	161	Induction
112		162	Deduction
113	Cosmology	163	
114	Space	164	
115	Time	165	Fallacies & sources of error
116	Evolution	166	Syllogisms
117	Structure	167	Hypotheses
118	Force & energy	168	Argument & persuasion
119	Number & quantity	169	Analogy
120	**Epistemology, causation, humankind**	170	**Ethics (Moral philosophy)**
121	Epistemology	171	Systems & doctrines
122	Causation	172	Political ethics
123	Determinism & indeterminism	173	Ethics of family relationships
124	Teleology	174	Professional & occupational ethics
125		175	Ethics of recreation & leisure
126	The self	176	Ethics of sex & reproduction
127	The unconscious & the subconscious	177	Ethics of social relations
128	Humankind	178	Ethics of consumption
129	Origin & destiny of individual souls	179	Other ethical norms
130	**Paranormal phenomena & arts**	180	**Ancient, medieval, Oriental philosophy**
131	Well-being, happiness, success	181	Oriental
132		182	Pre-Socratic Greek
133	Parapsychology & occultism	183	Sophistic, Socratic & related Greek
134		184	Platonic
135	Dreams & mysteries	185	Aristotelian
136		186	Skeptic & Neoplatonic
137	Analytic & divinatory graphology	187	Epicurean
138	Physiognomy	188	Stoic
139	Phrenology	189	Medieval Western
140	**Specific philosophical viewpoints**	190	**Modern Western philosophy**
141	Idealism & related systems & doctrines	191	United States & Canada
142	Critical philosophy	192	British Isles
143	Intuitionism & Bergsonism	193	Germany & Austria
144	Humanism & related systems	194	France
145	Sensationalism & ideology	195	Italy
146	Naturalism & related systems	196	Spain & Portugal
147	Pantheism & related systems	197	Russia & Finland
148	Liberalism & other systems	198	Scandinavia
149	Other systems & doctrines	199	Other geographical areas

Religion

Social sciences

300	**Social sciences**	350	**Public administration**
301	Sociology	351	Central governments
302	Social interaction	352	Local governments
303	Social processes	353	U.S. federal & state governments
304	Relation of natural factors	354	Other central governments
305	Social stratification	355	Military art & science
306	Culture and institutions	356	Foot forces & warfare
307	Communities	357	Mounted forces & warfare
308		358	Armored, technical, air, space forces
309		359	Sea (Naval) forces & warfare
310	**Statistics**	360	**Social problems & services**
311		361	Social problems & welfare
312	Statistics of populations *Census*	362	Social welfare problems & services
313		363	Other social problems & services
314	General statistics of Europe	364	Criminology
315	General statistics of Asia	365	Penal institutions
316	General statistics of Africa	366	Association
317	General statistics of North America	367	General clubs
318	General statistics of South America	368	Insurance
319	General statistics of other areas	369	Miscellaneous kinds of associations
320	**Political science**	370	**Education**
321	Kinds of governments and states	371	Generalities of education
322	Relation of state to social groups	372	Elementary education
323	Relation of state to its residents	373	Secondary education
324	The political process	374	Adult education
325	International migration	375	Curriculums
326	Slavery & emancipation	376	Education of women
327	International relations	377	Schools & religion
328	Legislation	378	Higher education
329		379	Education & the state
330	**Economics**	380	**Commerce (Trade)**
331	Labor economics	381	Internal commerce
332	Financial economics	382	International commerce
333	Land economics	383	Postal communication
334	Cooperatives	384	Other systems of communication
335	Socialism & related systems	385	Railroad transportation
336	Public finance	386	Inland waterway & ferry transportation
337	International economics	387	Water, air, space transportation
338	Production	388	Ground transportation
339	Macroeconomics & related topics	389	Metrology & standardization
340	**Law**	390	**Customs, etiquette, folklore**
341	International law	391	Costume & personal appearance
342	Constitutional & administrative law	392	Customs of life cycle & domestic life
343	Miscellaneous public law	393	Death customs
344	Social law	394	General customs
345	Criminal law	395	Etiquette (Manners)
346	Private law	396	
347	Civil procedure & courts	397	
348	Statutes, regulations, cases	398	Folklore
349	Law of individual states & nations	399	Customs of war & diplomacy

Language

400	**Language**	450	**Italian, Romanian, Rhaeto-Romanic**
401	Philosophy & theory	451	Written & spoken Italian
402	Miscellany	452	Italian etymology
403	Dictionaries & encyclopedias	453	Italian dictionaries
404	Special topics of general applicability	454	
405	Serial publications	455	Italian structural system
406	Organizations	456	
407	Study & teaching	457	Nonstandard Italian
408	Treatment among groups of persons	458	Standard Italian usage
409	Historical & geographical treatment	459	Romanian & Rhaeto-Romanic
410	**Linguistics**	460	**Spanish & Portuguese languages**
411	Notations	461	Written & spoken Spanish
412	Etymology	462	Spanish etymology
413	Polyglot dictionaries	463	Spanish dictionaries
414	Phonology	464	
415	Structural systems (Grammar)	465	Spanish structural system
416		466	
417	Dialectology & paleography	467	Nonstandard Spanish
418	Usage (Applied linguistics)	468	Standard Spanish usage
419	Verbal language not spoken or written	469	Portuguese
420	**English & Anglo-Saxon languages**	470	**Italic languages Latin**
421	Written & spoken English	471	Written & spoken classical Latin
422	English etymology	472	Classical Latin etymology
423	English dictionaries	473	Classical Latin dictionaries
424		474	
425	English structural system	475	Classical Latin structural system
426		476	
427	Nonstandard English	477	Old, Postclassical, Vulgar Latin
428	Standard English usage	478	Classical Latin usage
429	Anglo-Saxon (Old English)	479	Other Italic languages
430	**Germanic languages German**	480	**Hellenic languages Classical Greek**
431	Written & spoken German	481	Written & spoken classical Greek
432	German etymology	482	Classical Greek etymology
433	German dictionaries	483	Classical Greek dictionaries
434		484	
435	German structural system	485	Classical Greek structural system
436		486	
437	Nonstandard German	487	Postclassical Greek
438	Standard German usage	488	Classical Greek usage
439	Other Germanic languages	489	Other Hellenic languages
440	**Romance languages French**	490	**Other languages**
441	Written & spoken French	491	East Indo-European & Celtic
442	French etymology	492	Afro-Asiatic (Hamito-Semitic)
443	French dictionaries	493	Hamitic & Chad languages
444		494	Ural-Altaic, Paleosiberian, Dravidian
445	French structural system	495	Sino-Tibetan & other
446		496	African languages
447	Nonstandard French	497	North American native languages
448	Standard French usage	498	South American native languages
449	Provençal & Catalan	499	Other languages

Pure sciences

500	**Pure sciences**		550	**Sciences of earth & other worlds**
501	Philosophy & theory		551	Geology, meteorology, hydrology
502	Miscellany		552	Petrology (Rocks)
503	Dictionaries & encyclopedias		553	Economic geology
504			554	Treatment in Europe
505	Serial publications		555	Treatment in Asia
506	Organizations		556	Treatment in Africa
507	Study & teaching		557	Treatment in North America
508	Travel & surveys		558	Treatment in South America
509	Historical & geographical treatment		559	Treatment in other areas & worlds
510	**Mathematics**		560	**Paleontology**
511	Generalities		561	Paleobotany
512	Algebra		562	Fossil invertebrates
513	Arithmetic		563	Fossil Protozoa & other simple animals
514	Topology		564	Fossil Mollusca & molluscoidea
515	Analysis		565	Other fossil invertebrates
516	Geometry		566	Fossil Chordata
517			567	Fossil cold-blooded vertebrates
518			568	Fossil Aves (Fossil birds)
519	Probabilities & applied mathematics		569	Fossil Mammalia
520	**Astronomy & allied sciences**		570	**Life sciences**
521	Theoretical astronomy		571	
522	Practical & spherical astronomy		572	Human races
523	Descriptive astronomy		573	Physical anthropology
524			574	Biology
525	Earth (Astronomical geography)		575	Organic evolution & genetics
526	Mathematical geography		576	Microbes
527	Celestial navigation		577	General nature of life
528	Ephemerides (Nautical almanacs)		578	Microscopy in biology
529	Chronology (Time)		579	Collection & preservation of specimens
530	**Physics**		580	**Botanical sciences**
531	Mechanics		581	Botany
532	Mechanics of fluids		582	Spermatophyta
533	Mechanics of gases		583	Dicotyledones
534	Sound & related vibrations		584	Monocotyledones
535	Light & paraphotic phenomena		585	Gymnospermae
536	Heat		586	Cryptogamia
537	Electricity & electronics		587	Pteridophyta
538	Magnetism		588	Bryophyta
539	Modern physics		589	Thallophyta
540	**Chemistry & allied sciences**		590	**Zoological sciences**
541	Physical & theoretical chemistry		591	Zoology
542	Laboratories, apparatus, equipment		592	Invertebrates
543	Analytical chemistry		593	Protozoa & other simple animals
544	Qualitative chemistry		594	Mollusca & molluscoidea
545	Quantitative chemistry		595	Other invertebrates
546	Inorganic chemistry		596	Chordata
547	Organic chemistry		597	Cold-blooded vertebrates
548	Crystallography		598	Aves (Birds)
549	Mineralogy		599	Mammalia (Mammals)

Technology (Applied sciences)

600 **Technology (Applied sciences)**	650 **Management & auxiliary services**
601 Philosophy & theory	651 Office services
602 Miscellany	652 Written communication processes
603 Dictionaries & encyclopedias	653 Shorthand
604 General technologies	654
605 Serial publications	655
606 Organizations & management	656
607 Study & teaching	657 Accounting
608 Inventions & patents	658 General management
609 Historical & geographical treatment	659 Advertising & public relations
610 **Medical sciences Medicine**	660 **Chemical & related technologies**
611 Human anatomy, cytology, tissues	661 Industrial chemicals
612 Human physiology	662 Explosives, fuels, related products
613 General & personal hygiene	663 Beverage technology
614 Public health & related topics	664 Food technology
615 Pharmacology & therapeutics	665 Industrial oils, fats, waxes, gases
616 Diseases	666 Ceramic & allied technologies
617 Surgery & related topics	667 Cleaning, color, other technologies
618 Other branches of medicine	668 Other organic products
619 Experimental medicine	669 Metallurgy
620 **Engineering & allied operations**	670 **Manufactures**
621 Applied physics	671 Metal manufactures
622 Mining & related operations	672 Ferrous metals manufactures
623 Military & nautical engineering	673 Nonferrous metals manufactures
624 Civil engineering	674 Lumber, cork, wood technologies
625 Railroads, roads, highways	675 Leather & fur technologies
626	676 Pulp & paper technology
627 Hydraulic engineering	677 Textiles
628 Sanitary & municipal engineering	678 Elastomers & their products
629 Other branches of engineering	679 Other products of specific materials
630 **Agriculture & related technologies**	680 **Manufacture for specific uses**
631 Crops & their production	681 Precision & other instruments
632 Plant injuries, diseases, pests	682 Small forge work
633 Field crops	683 Hardware & household appliances
634 Orchards, fruits, forestry	684 Furnishings & home workshops
635 Garden crops Vegetables	685 Leather & fur goods
636 Animal husbandry	686 Printing & related activities
637 Dairy & related technologies	687 Clothing
638 Insect culture	688 Other final products & packaging
639 Nondomestic animals & plants	689
640 **Home economics & family living**	690 **Buildings**
641 Food & drink	691 Building materials
642 Meal & table service	692 Auxiliary construction practices
643 Housing & household equipment	693 Construction in specific materials
644 Household utilities	694 Wood construction Carpentry
645 Furnishing & decorating home	695 Roofing
646 Sewing, clothing, personal living	696 Utilities
647 Public households	697 Heating, ventilating, air conditioning
648 Housekeeping	698 Detail finishing
649 Child rearing & care of sick	699

The arts

700	**The arts**	750	**Painting & paintings**
701	Philosophy & theory	751	Processes & forms
702	Miscellany	752	Color
703	Dictionaries & encyclopedias	753	Abstractions, symbolism, legend
704	Special topics of general applicability	754	Subjects of everyday life
705	Serial publications	755	Religion & religious symbolism
706	Organizations & management	756	Historical events
707	Study & teaching	757	Human figures & their parts
708	Galleries, museums, art collections	758	Other subjects
709	Historical & geographical treatment	759	Historical & geographical treatment
710	**Civic & landscape art**	760	**Graphic arts Prints**
711	Area planning (Civic art)	761	Relief processes
712	Landscape design	762	
713	Landscape design of trafficways	763	Lithographic processes
714	Water features	764	Chromolithography & serigraphy
715	Woody plants	765	Metal engraving
716	Herbaceous plants	766	Mezzotinting & aquatinting processes
717	Structures	767	Etching & drypoint
718	Landscape design of cemeteries	768	
719	Natural landscapes	769	Prints
720	**Architecture**	770	**Photography & photographs**
721	Architectural construction	771	Apparatus, equipment, materials
722	Ancient & Oriental architecture	772	Metallic salt processes
723	Medieval architecture	773	Pigment processes of printing
724	Modern architecture	774	Holography
725	Public structures	775	
726	Buildings for religious purposes	776	
727	Buildings for education & research	777	
728	Residential buildings	778	Specific fields of photography
729	Design & decoration	779	Photographs
730	**Plastic arts Sculpture**	780	**Music**
731	Processes & representations	781	General principles
732	Nonliterate, ancient, Oriental	782	Dramatic music
733	Greek, Etruscan, Roman	783	Sacred music
734	Medieval sculpture	784	Voice & vocal music
735	Modern sculpture	785	Instrumental ensembles & their music
736	Carving & carvings	786	Keyboard instruments & their music
737	Numismatics & sigillography	787	String instruments & their music
738	Ceramic arts	788	Wind instruments & their music
739	Art metalwork	789	Percussion, mechanical, electrical
740	**Drawing, decorative & minor arts**	790	**Recreational & performing arts**
741	Drawing & drawings	791	Public performances
742	Perspective	792	Theater (Stage presentations)
743	Drawing & drawings by subject	793	Indoor games & amusements
744		794	Indoor games of skill
745	Decorative & minor arts	795	Games of chance
746	Textile arts & handicrafts	796	Athletic & outdoor sports & games
747	Interior decoration	797	Aquatic & air sports
748	Glass	798	Equestrian sports & animal racing
749	Furniture & accessories	799	Fishing, hunting, shooting

Literature (Belles-lettres)

800	**Literature (Belles-lettres)**	850	**Italian, Romanian, Rhaeto-Romanic**
801	Philosophy & theory	851	Italian poetry
802	Miscellany about literature	852	Italian drama
803	Dictionaries & encyclopedias	853	Italian fiction
804		854	Italian essays
805	Serial publications	855	Italian speeches
806	Organizations	856	Italian letters
807	Study & teaching	857	Italian satire & humor
808	Rhetoric & collections	858	Italian miscellaneous writings
809	History, description, critical appraisal	859	Romanian & Rhaeto-Romanic
810	**American literature in English**	860	**Spanish & Portuguese literatures**
811	Poetry	861	Spanish poetry
812	Drama	862	Spanish drama
813	Fiction	863	Spanish fiction
814	Essays	864	Spanish essays
815	Speeches	865	Spanish speeches
816	Letters	866	Spanish letters
817	Satire & humor	867	Spanish satire & humor
818	Miscellaneous writings	868	Spanish miscellaneous writings
819		869	Portuguese
820	**English & Anglo-Saxon literatures**	870	**Italic literatures Latin**
821	English poetry	871	Latin poetry
822	English drama	872	Latin dramatic poetry & drama
823	English fiction	873	Latin epic poetry & fiction
824	English essays	874	Latin lyric poetry
825	English speeches	875	Latin speeches
826	English letters	876	Latin letters
827	English satire & humor	877	Latin satire & humor
828	English miscellaneous writings	878	Latin miscellaneous writings
829	Anglo-Saxon (Old English)	879	Other Italic languages
830	**Literatures of Germanic languages**	880	**Hellenic literatures Greek**
831	German poetry	881	Classical Greek poetry
832	German drama	882	Classical Greek drama
833	German fiction	883	Classical Greek epic poetry
834	German essays	884	Classical Greek lyric poetry
835	German speeches	885	Classical Greek speeches
836	German letters	886	Classical Greek letters
837	German satire & humor	887	Classical Greek satire & humor
838	German miscellaneous writings	888	Classical Greek miscellaneous writings
839	Other Germanic literatures	889	Modern Greek
840	**Literatures of Romance languages**	890	**Literatures of other languages**
841	French poetry	891	East Indo-European & Celtic
842	French drama	892	Afro-Asiatic (Hamito-Semitic)
843	French fiction	893	Hamitic & Chad literatures
844	French essays	894	Ural-Altaic, Paleosiberian, Dravidian
845	French speeches	895	Sino-Tibetan & other Asian
846	French letters	896	African literatures
847	French satire & humor	897	North American native literatures
848	French miscellaneous writings	898	South American native literatures
849	Provençal & Catalan	899	Other literatures

General geography and history and their auxiliaries

900	**General geography & history**	950	**General history of Asia**
901	Philosophy of general history	951	China & adjacent areas
902	Miscellany of general history	952	Japan & adjacent islands
903	Dictionaries of general history	953	Arabian Peninsula & adjacent areas
904	Collected accounts of events	954	South Asia India
905	Serials on general history	955	Iran (Persia)
906	Organizations of general history	956	Middle East (Near East)
907	Study & teaching of general history	957	Siberia (Asiatic Russia)
908		958	Central Asia
909	General world history	959	Southeast Asia
910	**General geography Travel**	960	**General history of Africa**
911	Historical geography	961	North Africa
912	Graphic representations of earth	962	Egypt & Sudan
913	Geography of ancient world	963	Ethiopia (Abyssinia)
914	Europe	964	Northwest coast & offshore islands
915	Asia	965	Algeria
916	Africa	966	West Africa & offshore islands
917	North America	967	Central Africa & offshore islands
918	South America	968	Southern Africa
919	Other areas & worlds	969	South Indian Ocean islands
920	**General biography & genealogy**	970	**General history of North America**
921		971	Canada
922		972	Middle America Mexico
923		973	United States
924		974	Northeastern United States
925		975	Southeastern United States
926		976	South central United States
927		977	North central United States
928		978	Western United States
929	Genealogy, names, insignia	979	Great Basin & Pacific Slope
930	**General history of ancient world**	980	**General history of South America**
931	China	981	Brazil
932	Egypt	982	Argentina
933	Palestine	983	Chile
934	India	984	Bolivia
935	Mesopotamia & Iranian Plateau	985	Peru
936	Northern & western Europe	986	Colombia & Ecuador
937	Italian peninsula & adjacent areas	987	Venezuela
938	Greece	988	Guianas
939	Other parts of ancient world	989	Paraguay & Uruguay
940	**General history of Europe**	990	**General history of other areas**
941	British Isles	991	
942	England & Wales	992	
943	Central Europe Germany	993	New Zealand & Melanesia
944	France	994	Australia
945	Italy	995	New Guinea (Papua)
946	Iberian Peninsula Spain	996	Other parts of Pacific Polynesia
947	Eastern Europe Soviet Union	997	Atlantic Ocean islands
948	Northern Europe Scandinavia	998	Arctic islands & Antarctica
949	Other parts of Europe	999	Extraterrestrial worlds